Ebb Books
The Foundations of Zionism
2025

Sabri Jiryis is a Palestinian scholar, lawyer and writer. An Israeli citizen who lived through the Nakba as a child, he graduated from the Hebrew University in Jerusalem and dedicated his life to the study of the Palestinian cause and Zionism. He served in the Palestine Liberation Organization as director of its Research Center, member of the Palestine National Council and Fatah Advisory Council, and advisor to Yasser Arafat on Israeli affairs. He is the author of the seminal *The Arabs in Israel* (1966 in Hebrew). In 2025, Jiryis received the Arab Historian Award from the Union of Arab Historians, Baghdad, in recognition of his contributions to Arab historical research and writing.

Fida Jiryis is a writer and editor. She is the author of *Stranger in My Own Land* (2022) and three Arabic collections of short stories on life in Israel and the West Bank. She contributed to *Kingdom of Olives and Ash* (2017), a *Washington Post* bestseller on fifty years of Israeli occupation, and *Amputated Tongue* (2019), a Hebrew-language anthology of Palestinian literature. Fida is the author's daughter and has translated and edited this book from its original Arabic.

Liberated Texts series

> Books differ from all other propaganda media, primarily because one book can significantly change the reader's attitude and action to an extent unmatched by the impact of any other single medium... this is, of course, not true of all books at all times and with all readers – but it is true significantly often enough to make books the most important weapon of strategic (long-range) propaganda.
>
> Head of Covert Action, CIA, 1961

This series, a collaboration between *Liberated Texts* and Ebb Books, is dedicated to re-publishing, or publishing in English for the first time, works of ongoing relevance that have been forgotten, underappreciated, suppressed or misinterpreted in the cultural mainstream since their release.

We do so in the belief that despite the dramatic shift in the educational and media landscape that has taken place in the six decades since the statement quoted above was made, books remain powerful tools with the ability to fundamentally transform people's view of the world and spur them into action to change it for the better.

Series Editor, Louis Allday

The Foundations of Zionism

Sabri Jiryis

Translated by Fida Jiryis

Ebb

First published in two volumes in Arabic, 1977 and 1986
© Sabri Jiryis

The right of Sabri Jiryis to be identified as the author of this Work has been asserted in accordance with sections 77 and 78 of the Copyright, Designs and Patents Act 1988.

First published in English, 2025
Translation © Fida Jiryis

All rights reserved. No part of this book may be reproduced, stored in a retrieval system, or transmitted by any means, electronic, mechanical, photocopying, recording, or otherwise, without prior permission of the publisher.

Ebb Books, 54 The Oval, Rose Hill, Oxford, OX4 4SE

PB ISBN: 9781738468744
EB ISBN: 9781738468751

British Library Cataloguing-in-Publication Data
A catalogue record for this book is available from the British library.

Typeset in Dante

ebb-books.com
liberatedtexts.com

Front cover artwork: The Great Arab Revolt of 1936-1939. "A fire in the Armenian Quarter" (1936), Matson (G. Eric and Edith) Photograph Collection

Contents

Translator's Note	*i*
Preface	*iii*
Introduction	1
1. Pioneers of Zionism: Early Thinkers (1862-1884)	66
2. Lovers of Zion: Early Practitioners (1882-1904)	101
3. Herzl and the Zionist Organization: The Jewish State Project and its Agencies (1897-1904)	152
4. The Second Aliyah: Foundations of the Zionist Entity (1904-1914)	217
5. The First World War and the Balfour Declaration: The Alliance of Colonialism and Zionism (1914-1917)	307
6. British Mandate over Palestine, Part I: The Mandate System and its Frameworks (1918-1923)	337
7. British Mandate over Palestine, Part II: Foundations of the "Jewish National Home" (1918-1923)	421
Conclusion: Zionism in the Service of Colonialism	522
Bibliography	*551*
Index	*586*

To the memory of my wife, the martyr

Hanneh Shaheen (17.5.1946-5.2.1983)

who eagerly urged me to complete this book,

helped translate some of its material and check its sources,

but was not destined to see it

Translator's Note

This book, in its English translation, is a compilation of two Arabic volumes: *A History of Zionism, Volume I: Zionist Infiltration into Palestine (1862-1917)* and the first two chapters of *Volume II: The "Jewish National Home" in Palestine (1918-1939)*. The translation covers the period from 1862-1923. These volumes were published by the Palestine Research Center of the PLO, in Beirut, 1977, and Nicosia, 1986, respectively.

In addition, this book adds a newly written conclusion that summarizes the ensuing developments until the present.

I read these Arabic volumes during my research for my book, *Stranger in My Own Land* (Hurst, 2022). This account chronicled my family's story, including the circumstances in which *A History of Zionism* was written. The idea was born to translate it into English, which had not been done to date.

It has been particularly touching that I have been able to do this, half a century after my father wrote these volumes, through a shared effort with him, as he proofread the translation and composed the new conclusion. My mother, who lost her life in an attack by pro-Israel agents on the Palestine Research Center in Beirut, in 1983, would have been proud to see this family effort, which she had also contributed to during her lifetime.

I would like to extend my sincere thanks to the Germanacos Foundation, Open Society Foundations, and the Rockefeller Brothers Fund for their generous funding of this translation; to Louis Allday, Lewis Hodder and Ebb Books for publishing it; and to Jonathan Gribetz for making the connection and for his support.

This book was completed during the turbulent months after the Hamas attack of October 7, 2023 and the ensuing 2023-2025 Israeli genocide on Gaza. The book will hopefully serve to illuminate the founding ideology behind this enduring conflict, which has cost so many lives and brought so much suffering and turmoil to this region.

Fida Jiryis
Fassouta, the Galilee
August, 2025

Preface

This book examines the history of Zionism, from its inception in the mid-19th century until the early period of the British mandate over Palestine in 1923. An examination of this theoretical and practical history is of great benefit for scholars of the Arab-Israeli conflict, and an indispensable introduction to understand the nature of the Israeli regime and its strengths and weaknesses, thus contemplating its future. In addition, this history is part of the history of the Palestinian cause.

The history of Zionism is wide and complex, entwined in the history of many peoples and states, and extends over a relatively long period. This book is essentially the inner story of Zionism, starting from the reasons for its emergence and spread; through its proponents and ideology in its various stages; its organizations, parties and institutions; and ending with its efforts to control Palestine and the region, which culminated, in their first and primary phase, in the establishment of Israel. Of course, it was also necessary, to complete the picture, to follow international and Arab conditions that enabled or allowed Zionism to achieve a large part of its goals.

My encounter with Zionism began at a young age. As a child in my village of Fassouta, in the Galilee, I witnessed the Nakba of 1948 when I was 10 years old, and saw people from nearby villages fleeing to Lebanon. I was among the 160,000 Palestinians who remained on our land, and I grew up under Israeli military rule and discrimination. Early in my life, the question plagued me: "Who are these people? Why did they come here?"

I graduated from the Terra Sancta College in Nazareth and enrolled at the Hebrew University in Jerusalem to study law. There was a very small number of Palestinian students at the time, and my political activism began then. I was involved in al-Ard, a Palestinian national movement that emerged in the late 1950s and demanded the return of Palestinian refugees and plundered lands, and the establishment of a Palestinian state in accordance with the 1947 United Nations Partition Plan. The Israeli authorities hounded al-Ard and prevented it from legal avenues of work, then finally banned it. Meanwhile, I graduated and began to work with a Palestinian lawyer, Hanna Naqqara, in Haifa. Naqqara was known as "the land lawyer" for his work in helping Palestinians resist the seizure of their lands by the Israeli state. Our circle included young, revolutionary writers and poets such as Mahmoud Darwish, Samih al-Qasem and Fouzi el-Asmar, all of whom were engaged in the Palestinian struggle.

After the banning of al-Ard, a group of us who had led the movement attempted to run in the 1965 Knesset (Israeli parliament) elections, in the hope of gaining a seat and being able to influence policy from there. Before the elections took place, the authorities expelled each of us internally, to locations in Palestine that had been ethnically cleansed of all their Palestinian inhabitants, and placed us under administrative house arrest to prevent us from organizing and taking part. I was expelled to Safad, in the Galilee, where I was forbidden to leave the town for three months, or to leave my apartment after sunset each day. In Safad, I chanced upon a bookstore that sold the works of the founding fathers of Zionism, and I began to read about the movement.

At the time, I had written my first book, *The Arabs in Israel*, an expansion of my Master's thesis that sought to inform the Jews on the plight of the Palestinians in the newly established Zionist state. I wrote it in Hebrew and had to self-publish it, as no publisher would accept it in Israel. The book went on to become a reference on the subject and was later translated into several languages. After this, I decided to write on Zionism – this time in Arabic, for fellow Palestinians. After my expulsion ended, I began work and amassed Hebrew and English sources. Two years later, in the wake of the 1967 war, I secretly joined Fatah,

Preface

while continuing my legal work in Haifa. In 1970, after several more months in administrative detention, I was exiled with my late wife, Hanneh Shaheen, to Lebanon. This was a difficult step, for we left our families behind and knew that we could not return in the foreseeable future. As we were packing, I took the notes that I had made on Zionism with me.

In Beirut, I joined the Institute of Palestine Studies, moved to the Palestine Research Center of the PLO and eventually came to direct it. I held this position for 26 years, during which I also served as an advisor to the late chairman, Yasser Arafat, on Israeli affairs.

When I began working in Lebanon, I became even more aware of the serious gap in Palestinian knowledge about Zionism – or, in fact, about Israel. The blow of the Nakba and its dispossession of the Palestinians had left little room for accessing first-hand material on the Zionist movement, and Palestinian refugees had no knowledge of Hebrew. A few people like myself, who had grown up in Israel and acquired the language, had left to join the PLO in Lebanon, and we attempted to fill this gap. The Research Center translated Hebrew news and published studies on Israeli politics, economy, society and other aspects. My wife worked alongside me at the center as a researcher and analyst of Israeli affairs. In addition to my writing in this domain, I completed the first volume of *A History of Zionism*, in Arabic, in 1977. It was published by the Research Center in Beirut.

On February 5, 1983, eight months after the 1982 Israeli invasion of Lebanon, the center was targeted with a car bomb that killed a number of its employees, including my wife, Hanneh. Most of the remaining employees left Lebanon. In June, I moved with my two children, Fida and Mousa, to Cyprus. The Research Center was reopened, on a smaller scale. Hanneh had been helping me with my work on the second volume of *A History of Zionism* before her untimely death, urging me to complete it. In 1986, I finished this book and published it in Nicosia.

After the 1993 Oslo Accords, and through a particular stipulation in them, I managed to return, with my two children, to my native village of Fassouta in the Galilee. I continued to work with Yasser Arafat, in Gaza and then in Ramallah, before retiring in Fassouta.

Today, about half a century after this book was written, I am proud to present this English translation by my daughter, Fida, and I thank her for her efforts.

The translation comes at a critical juncture for Israel and the Palestinians. Since October 7, 2023, Israel has been engaged in a genocide on Gaza that has propelled the Palestinian cause to center-stage in the world. As Palestinians struggle towards a resolution of their tragedy, this book will hopefully provide an in-depth look at the roots of the movement that caused it.

Note: The phrase "Land of Israel", which is the name given by the Zionists to Palestine and its region, as well as the phrases "Jewish nation", "the Jewish people", "the Jewish question", and "Jewish national home" appear often in the book. This does not, of course, constitute an agreement with the meaning of these phrases or the concepts that the Zionists attribute to them, but I chose to keep the phrases, which appear especially in quotations from Hebrew sources, to reflect the text and spirit of those quotations.

Sabri Jiryis
Fassouta, the Galilee
August, 2025

Introduction

1

Zionism, a Jewish political-ideological movement, emerged in the second half of the 19th century among the Jews of Russia, Poland, and elsewhere in eastern Europe, where most Jewish people lived at the time. The movement was spurred by political, economic, social, cultural and religious factors. Some related to the conditions of the Jews and Judaism in that period, following developments in the previous centuries. Other factors were the general conditions in the countries that they inhabited, and changes that occurred in Europe and Russia in the 18th and 19th centuries. Zionism, in its causes and period of emergence, was only a derivative of the "Jewish question" created by the rulers and peoples of some of these countries. These, together with some Jewish groups, helped keep this "question" alive and support it.

The first era of the Jewish question, at least in its prelude to the emergence of Zionism, began with the expulsion of the Jews from Spain in 1492. This was mainly due to religious reasons. The conflict between Judaism and Christianity had raged for generations. This era ended with the outbreak of the French Revolution, in 1789.

Before their expulsion from Spain, its number of Jews had risen significantly and their living conditions had improved. The country had become a refuge for them, due to the spirit of religious tolerance under Arab rule. The history of the Jews in Europe, during this period, was generally marked by their expulsion from one country to another,[1] then on to others. They would then be allowed to return to their country of origin under various restrictions or, conversely, with some privileges granted to them. Christian Europe, especially in the Middle Ages, did not treat the Jews well. This ongoing movement was also spurred by the Jews pursuing their livelihoods and relocating to the main commercial hubs of the world.

These expulsions led to the establishment of new Jewish centers in a number of countries. The Jews who were expelled from Spain came to be known as Sephardic Jews, or "Sephardim", in Hebrew, in reference to "Sepharad", the Hebrew name for Spain. They are generally known as "Oriental Jews". These Jews moved to areas that were subject to Ottoman rule in Asia and Europe, and some went to Palestine (especially Safad, in the north) and North Africa. Another part headed to Italy and later spread to France, Holland, England and America.

The Jews of Austria and Germany were known as Ashkenazi Jews, or "Ashkenazim", in Hebrew, in reference to "Ashkenaz", the old Hebrew name for Germany. They are also known as "Western Jews". They were forced, due to the pressures against them, to leave their countries and move to Poland, whose Jewish population became, by the mid-17th century, larger than that in all other European countries. These developments were accompanied by a transition of the power center within Judaism from Sephardic to Ashkenazi Jews.[2]

The conditions of the Jews and the treatment they received in this period differed from one country to another. In Italy, for example, their situation was largely dependent on the papal attitudes towards them. These attitudes changed from one pope to another and ranged from preserving the Jews' rights and preventing harm to them, to imposing censorship on the printing of their religious books and forcing them to convert to

---

1   Shmuel Ettinger, *Toldot Am Yisrael ba'Et ha-Hadasha (History of the Jews in Modern Times)*, Vol. 3 (Haim Hillel Ben-Sasson, ed.), p. 13.

2   Simon Dubnow, *Divrei Yemei Am Olam (History of the Jews)*, pp. 389-390.

Introduction

Christianity.³ Venice, one of the cities that were not then subject to papal authority, was the first to introduce the ghetto system where, in 1516, the city council issued an order forcing its Jews to live in a closed neighborhood of their own.⁴ This system later spread to more European countries and was expanded, with new restrictions imposed on the employment of Jews, as well as limiting their population growth by restricting the number of marriages permitted among them. The creators of this system believed that it "served Christianity" and "avoided the harm of the Jews". Ultimately, however, they unknowingly helped Judaism to retain its essence throughout the upheavals of the Middle Ages, and prevented the integration of the Jews with the peoples amongst whom they lived.⁵ As a result, Zionism, in its attempt to harness Jewish religious sentiment to serve its purposes, found fertile ground among the secluded Orthodox Jews of the ghettos.

In the German and Austrian regions, although the number of Jews grew,⁶ their conditions did not generally differ from those in Italy, with many expulsions from one region to another. In 1616, following tensions against the Jews in Frankfurt, a Jewish Code of Residence was imposed on them, which restricted their residence, marriage and business rights. In 1624, the ghetto system was also imposed in Vienna, this time at the request of the Jews, themselves.⁷ These conditions persisted in the German regions until 1782, when Emperor Joseph II abolished most of the restrictions on the Jews and allowed them to engage in any form of work that they desired, as well as, in some areas, to own

---

3 Haim Hillel Ben-Sasson, *Toldot Am Yisrael be-Yemei ha-Binayim (History of the Jews in the Middle Ages)*, pp. 243-245, 267-269; Dubnow, *Divrei Yemei Am Olam (History of the Jews)*, pp. 405-407, 516-517.

4 Dubnow, *Divrei Yemei Am Olam (History of the Jews)*, p. 401.

5 Ben Halpern, *The Idea of the Jewish State*, p. 145.

6 Ben-Sasson, *Toldot Am Yisrael be-Yemei ha-Binayim (History of the Jews in the Middle Ages)*, p. 255.

7 Dubnow, *Divrei Yemei Am Olam (History of the Jews)*, pp. 420, 422, 497-498.

or lease land.⁸

The worst treatment that the Jews received in this period, however, was in Spain and Portugal. Although most of the Jews had been expelled from these countries, some remained, the Marranos ("Anosim", in Hebrew), who had converted to Christianity. Their conversion had been forced, and they did so outwardly to escape persecution, but they continued to practice Judaism, secretly, and to pass it to their children. The Inquisition, which was set up by the Catholic Church (and was not officially abolished until 1820), was active in pursuing these "infidels". They were usually sentenced to be burnt, or, in the best case, expelled from the country after their property had been seized.⁹

Other countries, however, behaved differently. Britain, which had a parliamentary life and semi-democratic rule from an early era, allowed the Jews to return to it in 1656, after they had been expelled in 1290.¹⁰ France, too, continued to receive the Jews who came to it, especially converts to Christianity, who then openly returned to Judaism. With time, an active Sephardic community grew in the country.¹¹ In Holland, the Jews were treated very well in comparison with elsewhere. The country, especially after the emergence of Protestantism, became a refuge for the Jews fleeing the persecution of Catholicism from all over Europe. They were granted most of the rights enjoyed by the native citizens, as well as autonomy of their Jewish communities. In that period, the Jews were active in Dutch commerce and some joined the pioneers of Dutch colonies in North and South America. A group of these Jews settled in New York, in 1654,¹² laying the basis for what became, about three centuries later, one of the largest Jewish communities in the world.

---

8   Ibid, p. 505.

9   Ibid, pp. 440-444, 518-519.

10 Ben-Sasson, *Toldot Am Yisrael be-Yemei ha-Binayim (History of the Jews in the Middle Ages)*, pp. 86, 256.

11 Dubnow, *Divrei Yemei Am Olam (History of the Jews)*, pp. 444-446, 508-510.

12 Ibid, pp. 446-451, 519-521; Ettinger, *Toldot Am Yisrael ba'Et ha-Hadasha (History of the Jews in Modern Times)*, Vol. 3, p. 24.

Introduction

The chief development in the history of the Jews during this period, before the French Revolution, was the emergence of the Ashkenazi Jewish center in Poland and later Russia. By the mid-17th century, Poland comprised more than half of all the Jews in Europe and played an important role in modern Jewish history – culturally and theologically – until the First World War. The Ashkenazi Jewish center did not come about by chance. Rather, it was encouraged by Polish rulers. In the early 16th century, when Ashkenazi Jews began to settle in Poland, they found kings who welcomed them and allowed them to live in most parts of the country and to engage in most forms of work that they chose, including agriculture as landowners or tenants. Not long after the arrival of the Jews, the authorities recognized them in 1551 as an independent sect and allowed them to exercise autonomy in their affairs. This helped the rabbis, the Jewish religious leaders and their followers, to impose their control over the Jewish communities. Private institutions ("ha-Kahal") were established and recognized by the authorities to supervise Jewish affairs in Poland, from tax collection on behalf of the authorities, to execution of judgments issued by the rabbis according to Jewish law. The authority of the Rabbinate rose in a manner unparalleled, then, in any European country,[13] and had an impact on the social and cultural life of Polish Jews. The powers granted to the Jewish community leaders were finally abolished in 1765, when there was no longer a need for the kings to facilitate tax collection from the Jews through their leaders. These powers had worked, however, for more than 200 years, to impart a clear, rabbinic, religious character on Jewish life in Poland which was not easy to change.[14] This was one of the factors that helped to spread Zionism among Polish Jews and led to their responding, with relative ease, to calls for immigration to Palestine.

In this period, the Jews also took some steps to enter Russia that had been prohibited to them until that time. The first step was taken by Jewish merchants in western Poland, who were

---

13   Dubnow, *Divrei Yemei Am Olam (History of the Jews)*, pp. 426-434.

14   Ibid, pp. 436-439, 472, 475-477.

secretly heading to Russia – especially to the Moscow region – for business. Then, in 1728, they were allowed to attend Russian trade fairs. This was followed by allowing some of them, especially the wealthy, to permanently reside in Russia.[15]

2

In the 16th and 17th centuries, significant developments took place within Judaism that had a clear impact on the social, cultural and political movements – religious or secular – including Zionism. The most significant change was in the religious concepts of traditional Judaism, as manifested in the jurisprudence issued by the rabbis of the time. Before presenting these developments, however, it is worth reviewing the preceding events, in order to assess the extent of the changes that occurred in this period and their impact.

From the time of the Torah, the holy book of Judaism, Jewish sages followed a practice of religious jurisprudence to interpret this book and fit it to the spirit of each age. The outcome of this effort was later known as the Oral Torah ("Torah Shebe'al-Peh", in Hebrew). It was not assembled in writing, for fear of affecting the sanctity of the original Torah, until the end of the second century. Judah ha-Nasi (135-220 AD) then compiled it into a book known as the *Mishnah*,[16] which was considered the binding book of Judaism after the Torah.

The jurisprudence of Jewish sages did not stop after the *Mishnah*, but continued at a greater pace – not only to interpret and expand the *Mishnah* itself, but to express views on other religious or worldly matters. Again, this jurisprudence was collected and named the *Talmud*. It was divided into two parts: the *Babylonian Talmud* (in reference to Iraq, where it was compiled in the fifth century),[17] and the *Jerusalem Talmud* (*Talmud Yerushalmi*,

---

15 Ibid, pp. 432, 488-489.

16 Shmuel Safrai, "Period of the Mishnah and the Talmud", in Haim Hillel Ben-Sasson, ed., *Toldot Am Yisrael be-Yemei Kedem (History of the Jews in the Old Ages)*, pp. 327-329.

17 Ibid, pp. 364-365.

in Hebrew, in reference to "Yerushalayim", or Jerusalem, as most of its content was compiled by Jewish sages in Palestine, in the second half of the fourth century).[18] The *Babylonian Talmud* is the larger and deeper of the two, in size and quality.

For centuries after the *Talmud* was compiled, rabbis and Jewish sages continued to study, interpret and comment on it. This produced an abundant literature in which Jewish teachings were scattered, almost to the point of being lost within it. This situation persisted until the end of the 12th century, when Maimonides (Moses ben Maimon, also known as Rambam; 1135-1204) collected and classified those teachings from the Torah and its subsequent literature based on a rational-logical view rooted in Aristotelian philosophy. He compiled them in his book, *Mishneh Torah (The Second Torah)*, in Egypt, in 1180. *Mishneh Torah* became an essential book of Jewish law and held a prominent position among the Jews of the Middle Ages.[19]

Maimonides' work remained central to Jewish teachings until the mid-16th century, and thereafter Joseph Karo (1488-1575) carried out a similar endeavor. Like Maimonides, Karo was of Sephardic origin; he had studied at the religious school of Safad, which had been established by Jewish immigrants after their expulsion from Spain,[20] and it was this school that had begun reviving the mystical practices of the Kabbalah. Karo proceeded to compile the code of Jewish law and reclassify it, working for almost 20 years. His compilation was so large that it was difficult to use, so he issued a short version of it, *Shulchan Aruch (Set Table)*, which was first printed in 1564. It became the ultimate, sometimes unique, reference for deciding on issues of Jewish law. However, this book, in which rabbinical law reached its peak, came after a "prolonged spiritual reactionary period", such that

---

18   Ibid, pp. 342-343.

19   Ibid, pp. 306-310. The *Mishneh Torah* still enjoys this standing (and is the only book that Maimonides originally wrote in Hebrew, as most of his books, including *Moreh Nevukhim – The Guide for the Perplexed*, were written in Arabic).

20   Ben-Sasson, *Toldot Am Yisrael be-Yemei ha-Binayim (History of the Jews in the Middle Ages)*, pp. 262, 266.

it was but a "summary of religious law in its rigid form".[21] Unlike Maimonides, Karo tended to be strict in religious and worldly matters. This view had its effect on the positions of Judaism during and after the Renaissance, when Orthodox Jews tended to confront modern situations and their ensuing problems by turning their backs and distancing themselves rather than trying to solve them. This led to the "fossilization of Judaism",[22] and was one of the main factors that spurred the emergence of reform movements, both religious and secular, within it.

With the difficulties of life for the Jews and their expulsion from one place to another, on the one hand, and the domination of reactionary religion over their public and private lives, on the other, movements began to emerge that opposed the traditional Judaism of the rabbis. These movements served as preludes to Zionism.

The first movement was known as Messianism ("Mashichiot", in Hebrew), which reappeared among the Jews in this period. This movement dated back, in Jewish tradition, to the Second Kingdom, and usually manifested when the Jews found themselves in distress.[23] Messianism had assumed different forms from one era to another, but it centered on a belief in the coming of the Savior-Messiah ("ha-Mashiach"), a living being of flesh and blood, whose mission was to save the Jews and help them to overcome their enemies, then unite them and create their own national entity.[24] The movement resurfaced in later eras after the Jews' expulsion from Spain, as they searched for an answer to the cause of their difficulties, concluding that it was necessary to be redeemed by way of a miracle. To bring this about, in their view, souls had to be readied for redemption and purified with prayer and reflection on the wisdom and teachings of God, to benefit

---

21   Dubnow, *Divrei Yemei Am Olam (History of the Jews)*, p. 396.

22   Halpern, B., *The Idea of the Jewish State*, p. 133.

23   Aaron Zeev Aescoly, *Ha-Tnu'ot ha-Mashiachot be-Yisrael (Jewish Messianic Movements in Israel)*, Vol. 1, pp. 15-17, 79-83, 93-103; Yehezkel Kaufmann, *Toldot ha-Imuna ha-Yisraelit (History of the Israelite Faith)*, Vol. 3, pp. 690-691.

24   Kaufmann, *Toldot ha-Imuna ha-Yisraelit (History of the Israelite Faith)*, Vol. 3, pp. 626-656.

Introduction 9

from His grace. The coming of the Savior-Messiah could only be hastened through prayer, repentance and self-denial.[25] The rabbis who came to Safad, in northern Palestine, after their expulsion from Spain, laid the groundwork for these views and developed them. They revived ancient practices of Judaism (Kabbalah), this time in a style based on the occult and mysticism, contradicting traditional Jewish teachings and explaining various natural phenomena to indicate the coming of the Savior-Messiah. The philosophical view of religious creed was replaced by the notion of a "holy spirit" that accompanies select individuals, as well as a pessimistic view of worldly developments.[26]

The Kabbalah theories led to the emergence of one of the major messianic movements in Europe, in the 17th century: the Shabtai Zvi movement, which began among the Jews of Izmir, in Turkey. Zvi (1626-1676) declared himself the Savior-Messiah who had come to save the Jews. He spread his call among them in Europe and the Levant, announcing that the time of redemption had neared, and that he was the chosen one to lead the return of the Jews to Palestine. Zvi's call found reception in many Jewish groups, which led the sultan of Turkey to arrest Zvi upon his arrival in Istanbul where he was given a choice between converting to Islam or death. Zvi took the first option and was sentenced to exile.[27]

The Shabtai Zvi movement did not end there, however. It spread among Jewish masses, especially in Europe, despite fierce resistance by the traditional Rabbinate. Over time, the movement led to the emergence of other, secondary messianic ones. In the long run, it resulted in profound reactions from the Rabbinate and Orthodox Jews and led most of them to be skeptical of Zionism at its outset, fearing that it was just another fake messianic movement. Ultimately, large groups of Orthodox Jews embraced Zionism, but only after religious "decrees" were

---

25 Dubnow, *Divrei Yemei Am Olam (History of the Jews)*, p. 397.

26 Ibid, pp. 398-399.

27 Ben-Sasson, *Toldot Am Yisrael be-Yemei ha-Binayim (History of the Jews in the Middle Ages)*, pp. 297-303.

issued on the matter. These, in turn, helped perpetuate the divisions between the various Jewish religious currents.

The Kabbalah was also one of the reasons that led to the emergence of another current, Hasidism or Hasidic Judaism,[28] whose founder, Israel ben Eliezer (also known as Baal Shem Tov; 1698-1760), was profoundly affected by Kabbalah theories.[29] Hasidism appeared among Ukrainian Jews in the mid-18th century and advocated principles contrary to traditional Jewish teachings, primarily that every person, provided he was a good "tzadik" (a righteous man, in Hebrew), could identify with God, who was everywhere, and could communicate with Him and know His mysteries. This tzadik, who led the faithful, played an important role among Hasidic Jews, which harmed the position of the rabbis among them. The second principle was that the goal of religion was nothing but adherence to God, which could only be achieved after focusing the entirety of the mind on the Creator – making efforts to identify all His characteristics without the need to delve into the study of religious teachings. Study could then be substituted by prayer and rituals.[30] This movement clearly angered the Rabbinate, which launched a fierce attack on it. However, Hasidism – more than the Shabtai Zvi movement – began to gain strength and spread among the Jews of eastern Europe, and from this movement came the first Ashkenazi Jews who settled in Palestine (especially in Jerusalem) in the late 18th century.

At the end of this era, during the Renaissance, the vanguards of another movement appeared among the Jews, the Haskalah.[31] Its pioneer was Moses Mendelssohn (1729-1786). Unlike the Rabbinate and Hasidism, the Haskalah was a secular liberation movement. Mendelssohn had received a traditional Talmudic

---

28 "Hasidut" in Hebrew. Singular member: "hasid", plural: "hasidim".

29 Ben-Zion Katz, *Rabanut, Hasidut, Haskalah (Rabbinate, Hasidism, and Haskalah)*, Vol. 2, pp. 82-84.

30 Dubnow, *Divrei Yemei Am Olam (History of the Jews)*, pp. 482-484.

31 Haskalah: A Hebrew word meaning "wisdom" or "enlightenment". Singular member: "maskil", plural: "maskilim".

upbringing but had later studied German, Latin and the philosophy of his time. He moved to Berlin, where he met the German writer Gotthold Ephraim Lessing who helped him to find his way into the world of German literature. In his search for means to improve the conditions of the Jews, Mendelssohn concluded that they had to be liberated from their spiritual isolation, and that cracks had to be made in the walls of their ghettos and teachings of their rabbis in order to view the European civilization of their time. He called for granting the Jews civil and economic freedoms, and appealed to the Jews themselves – and to their rabbis – to stop opposing freedom of thought and to reject the religious intolerance that had dominated their thinking since the Middle Ages.[32] In another vein, Mendelssohn decided to introduce foreigners to Judaism and began to translate the Torah into German,[33] excluding all Talmudic abstracts. This raised the ire of the rabbis, who debarred him and issued an order to boycott him and refrain from reading his books. Yet he translated the Psalms into German, as well. He went on to publish more writings on his views, and persisted in discussions with his compatriots and with the rabbis.[34]

The seed of Haskalah planted by Mendelssohn continued to grow after his death, albeit on a small scale, despite the cultural disputes that it spurred among German Jews. His students began to apply his theories. In 1778, they founded a free Jewish school in Berlin where, in addition to the Torah and Hebrew language, the studies included the foundations of modern science at the time.[35] This school introduced a very important change in the methods of education among the Jews, which had been essentially restricted to religious teachings. Again, this incurred the wrath of the traditional Rabbinate that added Mendelssohn's students to its enemies. The Rabbinate considered the study

---

32   Ibid, pp. 502-504.

33   Katz, *Rabanut, Hasidut, Haskalah (Rabbinate, Hasidism, and Haskalah)*, Vol. 1, pp. 217-220.

34   Ibid, pp. 220-229.

35   Dubnow, *Divrei Yemei Am Olam (History of the Jews)*, p. 506.

of subjects other than the Torah and religion an unforgivable crime, paving the way for blasphemy. About 500 Jewish students graduated from this school in its first decade, entering German society with new concepts outside the confines of the religious sphere.[36] They were the vanguards of those Jews who began to integrate into the European societies in which they lived and to progress in various social and cultural fields. This led to the establishment of similar secular schools in several German cities and, later, among Jewish communities in western Europe. It is noteworthy that, even during the Middle Ages, literacy was widespread among the Jews,[37] especially men, because of their need to impart the roots of their religion to their children, more so than the other peoples that they lived with. Italian Jews were the first to use printing, in 1475, to print their religious books. By 1500, about 100 books of this type had been printed in Hebrew. When this activity ceased in Italy, it moved to Poland where the first Hebrew book was printed in 1530.[38]

At the same time, Mendelssohn's students began to "renew" Hebrew literature and return Hebrew to its biblical origins, after the rabbis of that era and the preceding ones had – in the students' view – "defaced" the language. In 1784, the students began to issue *ha-Me'assef* (*The Collector*), a Hebrew periodical of poetry, natural science, history, studies on grammar and the Torah, and translations from German and French literature.[39] The periodical was the first of its kind in Hebrew and was issued intermittently until 1821. With this step, Mendelssohn's students paved a path no less important than their achievement in modernizing teaching methods among the Jews. They laid the foundations of a modern Hebrew literary movement, shattering the rabbis' monopoly on the language, which had been limited

---

36 Ibid.

37 Yehiel Halpern, *Ha-Mahpicha ha-Yehudit (The Jewish Revolution)*, Vol. 1, p. 131.

38 Dubnow, *Divrei Yemei Am Olam (History of the Jews)*, pp. 408, 438.

39 See presentation of the collection in Katz, *Rabanut, Hasidut, Haskalah (Rabbinate, Hasidism, and Haskalah)*, Vol. 1, pp. 248-266.

to publications of religious teachings and interpretations. At the time, most Ashkenazi Jews spoke Yiddish, which is – in essence – German mixed with Hebrew and some Aramaic, written in Hebrew letters. (Yiddish emerged in the 10th century when the Jews began to move to Germany and chose this method to write their documents, in order to preserve their "secrets".) Thus, for more than a century, the publications of Mendelssohn's students, which were the first of similar works, did not enjoy wide circulation, given the small number of Hebrew readers. However, it later became evident that they were very important. When Zionism emerged and began to revive Hebrew in order to use it as a national language in daily life, it found in Haskalah a path forward – making the task easier to achieve.

The work of Mendelssohn and his students, in the field of Haskalah, began at an early stage among the Jews of Germany in comparison with the remainder of western Europe. This work was one of the main reasons for the full integration of German Jews into their country and their contribution to all aspects of its political, scientific, cultural and social life. This situation persisted until the rise of Nazism in Germany, which uprooted those Jews before and during the Second World War. Nazism thus did a great service to Zionism, by supporting its position that opposed the integration of Jews in the countries in which they lived.

The early spread of Haskalah among German Jews was also a direct reason for the emergence of another movement in Judaism, in the first half of the 19th century. Reform Judaism appeared to be another branch of the Haskalah, but its followers were distinguished by the changes they made to their religious practices. They replaced Hebrew with German as the language of prayer, and excluded all that linked the Jews with their return to Palestine. The message of the Jews, as they saw it, was to spread among the peoples of the world and convey the ideals of Judaism to them. Their view was that Judaism was a religion, not a nation, and that it had to break out of patterns and traditions that had taken shape hundreds of years prior.[40] This call was the basis of Reform Judaism, which later spread among American Jews.

These three main currents – the Rabbinate, Hasidism, and Haskalah – were in conflict within Judaism during the second half of the 18th century, dominating Jewish lives on the threshold of historical developments in Europe.

3

In the late 18th century, about a century before the emergence of Zionism, two important events occurred in Europe that had a far-reaching impact on Judaism – affecting it throughout the 19th century and until at least the end of the First World War. The first event was the outbreak of the French Revolution in 1789, and the measures it took to liberate the Jews and grant them full political and social rights. The second was the partition of Poland among its neighboring countries, for the third time, in 1795, bringing the majority of Polish Jews under Russian tsarist rule.

In its revolution, France was the first European country to grant its Jews their civil rights in 1791, after abolishing the feudal system and prohibiting religious discrimination.[41] (The United States had preceded it in doing this, in its Declaration of Independence.) In 1830, France established equality between religions and granted Judaism the same position as Christianity.[42] It also worked to achieve this in other European countries that fell under its rule after the rise of Napoleon. The ruler had taken some measures to "reform" the conditions of the Jews and Judaism in France,[43] while trying to win their favor by working to recreate the Grand Sanhedrin, the supreme Jewish

---

40 Dubnow, *Divrei Yemei Am Olam (History of the Jews)*, pp. 579-584.

41 Dubnow, *Divrei Yemei Am Olam (History of the Jews)*, pp. 538-540.

42 Ettinger, *Toldot Am Yisrael ba'Et ha-Hadasha (History of the Jews in Modern Times)*, Vol. 3, p. 86.

43 For details, see Dubnow, *Divrei Yemei Am Olam (History of the Jews)*, pp. 542-546.

religious council, and turning its focus towards Palestine to serve his ambitions in the Levant. When the French armies entered Holland, Italy and Switzerland, Napoleon forced the rulers of these countries to grant their Jews the same rights as France had done. Yet this did not last long. After the French pulled out of these countries, the previous situation of the Jews resumed.[44]

The wave of reform spurred by the French Revolution, however, spread to various countries in western Europe despite the reactionary backlash that prevailed on the continent after containing the revolution. The Congress of Vienna, in 1815, had adopted various restrictions and counter-measures against the reforms, yet the demands for them continued. This turmoil peaked with the revolutions of 1848 and led most European countries to grant broader rights to their citizens, including the Jews.

In Italy, the rights that the French had granted the Jews were abolished in 1814. The situation only changed after the Italian liberation and unity movement grew in strength, and began to grant civil rights to the Jews in every region under its rule. This process began in 1859 and continued until the unification of Italy in 1870, when full rights were granted to the Jews in all the country.[45]

Switzerland, in turn, abolished the restrictions imposed on non-Christians, including the Jews, in 1874. (These restrictions had caused it many problems with other countries, including France, Holland and the United States, which had refused to have commercial dealings with Switzerland because of them.)

The Scandinavian countries had concluded their steps, in this regard, in 1849.[46]

In the 19th century, too, the last, minor restrictions on the Jews in Britain and Holland were lifted. They were the only countries in Europe that had not, since the Middle Ages, imposed restrictions on the rights of the Jews, such as their freedom of

---

44 Ibid, p. 548.

45 Ibid, pp. 550, 614, 642.

46 Ibid, pp. 645-646.

movement, place of residence or type of work.[47] In 1657, Holland had declared that it considered the Jews to be its citizens. Britain, after allowing the Jews to return to it in 1656, then passed a law in 1753 exempting them from taking the legal oath per Christian doctrine to obtain British citizenship. The parliament was forced to repeal this law due to public opposition, but it passed it – again – in 1826.[48] The conflict remained over canceling the obligation to take that oath until 1858, when it was abolished for Jewish members of the House of Commons. Lionel de Rothschild then took his seat in the Commons, after being elected for the third time, when he had previously been unable to participate in the sessions for refusing to take that oath. In 1866, a similar amendment was approved for members of the House of Lords,[49] thus lifting the last restrictions on Jews in Britain.

In 1808, Germany had granted its Jews the right to vote in municipal elections while part of it was still occupied by the French. In 1812, it passed a law granting the Jews equality with other citizens. The situation of the German Jews, however, periodically changed with the political tremors in the country. Finally, when Germany was united in 1871, it granted its Jews their full civil rights.[50]

In Austria, Emperor Joseph II had issued, in 1782, a law imposing military service on the Jews and limiting the number of marriages among them so as to prevent their population growth. This law was abolished in 1790, after the emperor's death, but the conditions of the Jews in Austria (which, at the time, was second to Russia in its number of Jews) persisted despite all the changes introduced in other European countries. Finally, the Austrian Jews were liberated in 1849 under the new constitution.

Efforts to liberate the Jews in western European countries and grant them full civil rights, like those of other citizens, were

---

47   Ettinger, *Toldot Am Yisrael ba'Et ha-Hadasha (History of the Jews in Modern Times)*, Vol. 3, p. 46.

48   Ibid, p. 47.

49   Dubnow, *Divrei Yemei Am Olam (History of the Jews)*, pp. 615-617, 644.

50   Ibid, pp. 552, 575-576, 621-622.

complete by 1871. The exceptions were Portugal, which granted Jewish people their rights in 1910, and Spain, which granted them civil rights in 1919.[51]

These changes had a clear impact on the social, cultural and economic conditions on the Jews in western Europe and, thus, on their political positions and the attitudes of other peoples towards them. The Jews responded to the rights that they were given and sought to integrate in the societies in which they lived. Some Jews were successfully assimilated, after the religious-sectarian ties that bound them together gradually waned[52] and were replaced by the new values that prevailed in their era.[53] Many Jews came to prominence in scientific, cultural and political arenas, and the number of mixed marriages between Jews and others rose, while many educated Jews – especially in Germany – converted to Christianity.[54] British Jews were, to some extent, an exception to this rule. Two currents, Orthodox and Maskilim, took shape among them,[55] seemingly as a result of the tranquil development that they had experienced. At the same time, like other peoples, Jews began to move from the villages to the cities, and their jobs and livelihoods changed accordingly. Many turned to work in trade, rising numbers took free professions, and still others came to prominence in literature and journalism.[56] With this trend, the Haskalah current calling for revival of the Hebrew heritage faded (moving to Russia and eastern Europe). In western Europe, the Jews began to study the languages and literature of the peoples with which they lived.

These trends manifested most clearly in Germany, the cradle

---

51   Ibid, pp. 532, 558-561, 590-594, 625-627.

52   Halpern, B., *The Idea of the Jewish State*, pp. 150, 164.

53   Ettinger, *Toldot Am Yisrael ba'Et ha-Hadasha (History of the Jews in Modern Times)*, Vol. 3, p. 115.

54   Dubnow, *Divrei Yemei Am Olam (History of the Jews)*, pp. 554-556; see also Walter Laqueur, *A History of Zionism*, pp. 3-39.

55   Dubnow, *Divrei Yemei Am Olam (History of the Jews)*, p. 614.

56   Ettinger, *Toldot Am Yisrael ba'Et ha-Hadasha (History of the Jews in Modern Times)*, Vol. 3, pp. 76-85; Halpern, B.,*The Idea of the Jewish State*, pp. 145-153.

of Haskalah, where the rulers also encouraged a class of Jewish financiers to emerge. The rulers entrusted them with managing their financial affairs, especially the provision of weapons and equipment to their armies.[57] The Jews had begun to deal in money and interest since the ninth century, when the church banned Christians from engaging with these dealings but turned a blind eye to the Jews.[58] The power of this class of Jewish financiers grew, with time, after similar classes emerged in France and England. They came to lead the Jewish communities in their countries. At the same time, they drew close to the rulers and intellectuals and mingled with them. Through this, they set an example in their communities that sought to emulate them.

With the Industrial Revolution in Europe, the power of Jewish capital rose as it turned to the establishment of banks. These soon held a prominent position in developing the economy of western Europe. They contributed to founding and financing various industries, as well as the construction of railways, which spurred a revolution in transport during that era.

By the last quarter of the 19th century, the Jews in western Europe – especially in France, Germany and Britain – had been granted civil rights and had reached an advanced level of integration with the people that they lived with, considering themselves part of them. Many Jews immersed themselves in the political lives of their countries, and it is evident from the activity of Jewish leaders and wealthy Jews that they felt their conditions were comfortable and their future secure, such that they saw fit to help the Jews in other regions. In France, some Jewish notables – including Adolphe Crémieux, member of the Chamber of Deputies and minister in the French government – founded the Alliance Israélite Universelle ("Kol Yisrael Haverim", in Hebrew). This was an international union that aimed to provide political and cultural assistance to the Jews, wherever they lived, through a call for a united Jewish people. At

---

57 Ettinger, *Toldot Am Yisrael ba'Et ha-Hadasha (History of the Jews in Modern Times)*, Vol. 3, pp. 25-27.

58 Haim Hillel Ben-Sasson, *Prakim be-Toldot Am Yisrael be-Yemei ha-Binayim (Chapters of the History of the Jews in the Middle Ages)*, pp. 65-73.

the outset, the Alliance worked to defend the political rights of the Jews in various European countries (including Switzerland and Romania). After the death of Crémieux, in 1880, the political action of the organization dwindled. It turned to cultural activity, especially the establishment of schools among the Jews in Turkey, the Middle East and North Africa. In 1870, the Alliance had founded Mikveh Israel, the first Jewish agricultural school in Palestine, near Jaffa. The school was supervised by one of its founders, Charles Netter.[59] It later helped support Zionist settlement in Palestine. In 1871, the branch of the Alliance in England broke off to form the Anglo-Jewish Association. (Some Jewish communities in Britain also established an association to manage their affairs, which they called the Board of Deputies.[60])

Likewise, in 1891, a Jewish settlement company – the Jewish Colonization Association (JCA or ICA) – was established in Britain by Baron Maurice de Hirsch, a German Jew. Its goal was to solve the oppression of Russian Jews by facilitating their immigration to Argentina.[61] From 1900, this company became active in Palestine. It pledged responsibility for supporting the Jewish settlements established by the Lovers of Zion movement in the country, after Baron Rothschild had ceased his assistance to them (details in Chapter 2).

In 1901, a similar association was founded to help in Germany, the Hilfsverein der Deutschen Juden (Aid Association of German Jews, "Ezra" in Hebrew).[62] This association worked in the cultural field in Palestine, founding many Jewish schools and later establishing the Technion, the Institute of Applied Engineering in Haifa, in 1912.

These comfortable conditions in which the Jews of western Europe found themselves were among the reasons that later prevented the substantial spread of Zionism among them. It

---

59   Dubnow, *Divrei Yemei Am Olam (History of the Jews)*, pp. 612-614, 641-642.

60   Ibid, p. 642.

61   Ettinger, *Toldot Am Yisrael ba'Et ha-Hadasha (History of the Jews in Modern Times)*, Vol. 3, p. 214.

62   Ibid, p. 212.

remained confined to small circles within their ranks, although a number of Zionist leaders and thinkers emerged from them.

4

In the same period, the conditions of the Jews in eastern Europe differed markedly from those in its west. They were particularly difficult in tsarist Russia, which then had the highest number of Jews worldwide. The number of Jewish people in the world was estimated at 2.25 million in 1800, of whom 2 million lived in Europe. More than half, or 1.4 million,[63] lived in Russia and the region of Poland that was annexed to it. That total number had risen five-fold during the 19th century, with a higher rate of population growth than that of other peoples amongst whom they lived – rising from 2.25 million in 1800 to 3.3 million in 1825; then to 4.7 million in 1850; 7.5 million in 1880; and 10.5 million in 1900; reaching about 13 million in 1914, at the outbreak of the First World War,[64] and 17 million in 1939 on the eve of the Second.

After the third partition of Poland in 1795, which took place between Russia, Germany and Austria, large areas of Poland, which were densely inhabited by Jewish people, were annexed by Russia. The tsarist authorities, which found hundreds of thousands of Jews under their rule, devised ways of dealing with them that differed from those in western Europe. Firstly, the Jews who lived on Polish lands annexed by Russia were prohibited to leave their areas and move to live elsewhere in the country. Those areas came to be known as the Pale of Settlement ("T'hum ha-Moshav", in Hebrew). The borders of this region were drawn in 1795 and remained in place for 122 years, until the outbreak of the Russian Revolution in 1917[65] (see *Map 1 Jewish Pale of*

---

63 Jacob Lestschinsky, *Ha-Tfutsa ha-Yehudit (Jewish Scattering)*, p. 89.

64 Yehuda Wallach, *Atlas Carta le-Toldot Eretz Yisrael (Carta's Atlas of History of the Land of Israel)*, p. 12, Map 3 and sources mentioned; see also Lestschinsky, *Ha-Tfutsa ha-Yehudit (Jewish Scattering)*, pp. 146, 148, 151, 158, 160; Ettinger, *Toldot Am Yisrael ba'Et ha-Hadasha (History of the Jews in Modern Times)*, Vol. 3, pp. 76, 78-79, 147-148, 150-151.

65 Dubnow, *Divrei Yemei Am Olam (History of the Jews)*, p. 565.

Settlement in Russia and Poland, 1795-1917, below). The Pale of Settlement soon turned into a large ghetto, in which tsarist rule imposed numerous restrictions and repressive measures against the Jews. Their economic and social conditions deteriorated, due to their high rate of population growth, the limited means of livelihood and the entrenched poverty among them. These conditions in the Pale of Settlement left a unique stamp on the lives of its Jews, which gave Zionism, upon its inception, fertile ground in this region.

Map 1 Jewish Pale of Settlement in Russia and Poland, 1795-1917[66]

The policy followed by tsarist Russia towards its Jewish subjects, which lasted throughout the 19th century and until 1917, differed from one tsar to another. It was generally marked,

---

66 *Encyclopaedia Judaica*, Vol. 13, p. 26.

however, by attempts to improve the conditions of the Jews, followed by measures against them, before the cycle would begin anew.

The first attempt by the Russian government to improve the conditions of the Jews was to issue a reform law in 1804, mainly to encourage them to work in crafts and agriculture (some Jewish communities had made this demand).[67] This was done by granting some facilities to those who did so, while blocking their work in renting and operating bars, especially in the villages – although the authorities were collecting sizeable taxes from them. With this law, the areas in which the Jews were permitted to live were expanded to include some parts of Ukraine and the southern region of Russia, along the Black Sea (the number of Jews there rose over time, especially in Odessa, and they had a later role in the formation of Zionism). When the Jews were reluctant to respond to the government's plans and move to the areas that were opened to them, the authorities expelled a number of them to those areas in order to raise the population and accelerate their development. These expulsions did not last long, however. The authorities were forced to stop them and temporarily abandon their reforms in 1812, after Napoleon's invasion of Russia.[68] The expulsions were then renewed after the Congress of Vienna in 1815, when Russia expanded its borders again and acquired additional Polish lands. This process included expulsions of the Jews from the villages to the cities as well, to prevent them from "exploiting Russian farmers" by operating bars and gambling establishments and engaging in moneylending.

This policy remained in effect during the last period of rule of Tsar Alexander I (1815-1825), until the arrival of Tsar Nicholas I (1825-1855). This latter tsar modified the policy and added a new one in 1827, imposing military service on Jewish young men of 12-25 years of age for a period of 25 years. The tsar forced

---

67 Lestschinsky, *Ha-Tfutsa ha-Yehudit (Jewish Scattering)*, p. 90.

68 Ettinger, *Toldot Am Yisrael ba'Et ha-Hadasha (History of the Jews in Modern Times)*, Vol. 3, pp. 45-46.

the Jewish leaders to implement this policy and made them responsible for providing the army with the prescribed number of Jewish conscripts. This situation persisted until the law was amended in 1874 to reduce the period of military service. The tsar had introduced an amendment to this policy in 1840, such that the government moved to implement its reforms through cultural means as well. It opened schools for Jews, encouraged them to study there, and allowed certain groups, such as intellectuals and artisans, to live and work outside the Jewish settlement areas. At the same time, the government clamped down on the powers of the heads of Jewish sects and imposed restrictions on traditional Orthodox schools (such as Heder, Yeshiva and others). The Russian government then abandoned this policy of cultural reform in 1873, but, in the meantime, a class of Jewish intellectuals had come into being that began to integrate in Russian society.[69]

The government's policy towards the Jews continued to ebb and flow until 1881, when Tsar Alexander II (reigned 1855-1881) was assassinated. This led to a violent reactionary backlash in Russia that resulted in dozens of attacks and pogroms against the Jews, due to the presence of a Jewish girl in the group that had assassinated the tsar. The attacks were among the main reasons that sparked a large-scale Jewish emigration from Russia and Poland, particularly to the United States. A tiny part of this migration went to Palestine and laid the foundations of Zionist settlement there, as will be discussed later.

In Romania, the conditions of the Jews did not differ much and were arguably worse than those in Russia. Romanian rulers attempted to imitate the Russian measures against the Jews, while adding another harsh stamp. Most Romanian Jews had come from Russia in the second quarter of the 19th century after their conditions had deteriorated there. For a long period, the Romanian authorities did not grant them rights as citizens and forbade them to work in trade, medical professions, the stock

---

69 Dubnow, *Divrei Yemei Am Olam (History of the Jews)*, pp. 597-602, 630-635; Ettinger, *Toldot Am Yisrael ba'Et ha-Hadasha (History of the Jews in Modern Times)*, Vol. 3, pp. 100-108.

exchange and even as street vendors. Romania insisted on not granting citizenship rights to its Jews even after the pledges it made in the Congress of Berlin (1878), which recognized Romania's independence and demanded that Romanian Jews be granted their rights.[70] As a result, they were among the first European Jews to immigrate to Palestine, where they established Zionist settlements (such as Rosh Pina and Zichron Ya'acov).

Evidently, the Russian policy of persecution against the Jews led to different cultural and intellectual developments from their counterparts in western Europe. Yet it was not easy to introduce radical changes to the situation of the Jews in Russia and Poland, as had happened in western Europe – even if the authorities had treated them in a better way. This was due to their unique religious and social characteristics that differed from those of western European Jews.

In Poland, the Jews formed a majority in most of the areas they inhabited despite being a minority among the population overall. They lived in cities and villages in close proximity to each other. This overcrowding led to the seclusion of the Jewish community, at a time when its surrounding conditions did not allow it to fully integrate with the remaining population. Thus, the community advanced very slowly due to the difficulty of infiltrating new ideas and values into it. The Haskalah, for example, appeared there nearly a century after it did in western Europe. A strict religious character marked the Jewish community in Poland and the thinking of most of its members, preventing much progress.

Also, in this period, the battle between the Rabbinate and Hasidism intensified.[71] The latter was the instigator, after it had come to dominate most of the Jewish communities in eastern Europe.[72] Hasidism had plunged into a state of self-seclusion as the status of the tzadikim (plural of tzadik, a righteous man), whom it considered the link between human beings and their Creator, had strengthened within it. It had turned more towards

---

70 Dubnow, *Divrei Yemei Am Olam (History of the Jews)*, pp. 646-648, 687-689.

71 Ibid, pp. 571-574; Halpern, B., *The Idea of the Jewish State*, p. 182.

72 Halpern, B., *The Idea of the Jewish State*, p. 161.

the occult, and its rituals were practiced with the consumption of alcohol.[73] With time, the Hasidic way became a kind of ideological justification for reluctance to engage in productive labor, moving away from the reality of life and towards a general contempt for work.[74] Clearly, advocates of progress within this society had to express their views very slowly and cautiously. Isaac Baer Levinsohn, the "father" of Haskalah in Russia,[75] published a book in 1828 in which he proved several controversial points based on the teachings of Jewish sages. He wrote that there was no objection for Jews to study foreign languages in addition to Hebrew, no danger to Judaism from studying general sciences, and that the Jews should also be taught crafts and tradesmanship to improve their conditions, rather than relying on brokerage and trade.[76] In response, he was labeled with heresy and blasphemy. The rabbis and tzadikim joined in fierce opposition to the entry of Jewish youth into modern schools and universities, lest they "spoil" their morals, preferring their study in religious institutions.[77] However, the Haskalah, despite the persecution it faced among Russian Jews, continued its call to reform their conditions by converting them to lives of productive work, especially in crafts and hired labor.[78] This call had a later effect at the end of the 19th and early 20th centuries, with the establishment of the General Jewish Labor Bund in Lithuania, Poland and Russia. It was also adopted by the Lovers of Zion movement, through which it passed to the Zionist labor wing with its socialist character.[79]

The 19th century witnessed changes in the conditions of

73　Dubnow, *Divrei Yemei Am Olam (History of the Jews)*, p. 610.

74　Halpern, B., *The Idea of the Jewish State*, p. 162.

75　Lestschinsky, *Ha-Tfutsa ha-Yehudit (Jewish Scattering)*, p. 127.

76　Dubnow, *Divrei Yemei Am Olam (History of the Jews)*, p. 610; Katz, *Rabanut, Hasidut, Haskalah (Rabbinate, Hasidism, and Haskalah)*, Vol. 2, pp. 208-213.

77　Yehuda Slutsky, *Ha-Itonout ha-Yehudit-Rusit ba-Meah ha-Tsha'esrei (Russian Jewish Press in the 19th Century)*, p. 26.

78　Lestschinsky, *Ha-Tfutsa ha-Yehudit (Jewish Scattering)*, p. 126.

79　Yehuda Slutsky, *Mevoa le-Toldot Tnu'at ha-Avoda ha-Yisraelit (Introduction to the History of the Israeli Labor Movement)*, pp. 33-42.

Russian and Polish Jews that were beyond their will as well as that of the authorities. During this century, in attempting to keep pace with western Europe, Russia embarked on the path of industrial development for which its government needed local Jewish capital to support its development of the country. These Jewish capitalists, in turn, sought the help of their wealthy brethren in France and Germany.[80] Jewish financiers established most of the large banks in Russia and were among its first railway builders.[81] They also founded many of its industries. The number and power of these financiers grew, such that, in 1825, for example, there were 12 Jewish millionaires in Warsaw alone.[82] They became an independent, albeit small, class. In Russia, they began to slowly integrate in society and acquire its culture, as other Jews of this class had done in western Europe. Some members of this class enjoyed wide influence with the ruling circles in Russia and won high titles. Meanwhile, restrictions remained in place on the Jewish masses that lived, generally, in a state of extreme poverty and destitution.

It is worth noting that the growth of Jewish capital in this way, and the activity of Jewish financiers, affected Karl Marx when he laid out his solutions to the Jewish question. Yet Marxism had no effect on the course of Zionism and the positions towards it until the early 20th century, after Zionism had carried out a good deal of practical activity, as will be discussed later.

In another vein, the Russian government sought to attract qualified individuals, including Jews, to support the capitalist progress of the country. It granted them good facilities and opened up many fields of work to them. In 1859, a law was passed allowing rich Jewish merchants to live and work anywhere in Russia (outside the Pale of Settlement). In 1865, this law was amended to include Jewish artisans and any Jew who had completed high school. Another amendment extended this right to all workers in the medical profession, including nurses

---

80 Lestschinsky, *Ha-Tfutsa ha-Yehudit (Jewish Scattering)*, p. 102.

81 Ibid, p. 101.

82 Ibid, p. 109.

and midwives. In 1864, Jews were allowed to work in the legal profession. These facilities peaked in 1874, when the laws of service in the Russian army were amended to reduce the period of conscription for high school graduates from four years to one.[83]

The privileges granted to qualified workers in general, and to the Jews in particular, had a clear effect on improving education among the latter, causing a near revolution in this regard. With the facilities granted to holders of academic degrees, the doubts and reservations of a certain class of Jews on giving their children a secular education, instead of a traditional religious one, dissipated. The government's attempts at opening special Jewish schools had failed to attract significant numbers of students, although the study of religion was among their subjects. Success was now achieved by Russian public schools, through the aforementioned facilities that were granted to their graduates – despite the absence of any Jewish religious teaching in them. These facilities led to an increase of Jewish students in secondary schools from 159 in 1853 to 9,225 in 1886, about 58 times as many. The number of Jewish students in Russian universities also rose from 129 in 1864 to 1,858 students in 1886, a 14-fold increase.[84] These students, and those who followed, became the pillar of the Jewish middle class in Russia. The Haskalah, and, later, Zionism, found many members within their ranks.

These developments, however, only affected the lives of a small segment of the Jews, not exceeding a quarter at most,[85] while the conditions of the majority changed differently. The first half of the 19th century saw a relative increase in the number of Jewish agricultural laborers, due to the facilities granted by the government, as well as its forcing certain groups of them into this profession. In 1859, about 65,000 Jews in Russia and

---

83   Slutsky, *Ha-Itonout ha-Yehudit-Rusit ba-Meah ha-Tsha'esrei (Russian Jewish Press in the 19th Century)*, pp. 23-25.

84   Ibid, p. 27; Lestchinsky, *Ha-Tfutsa ha-Yehudit (Jewish Scattering)*, p. 119.

85   Lestchinsky, *Ha-Tfutsa ha-Yehudit (Jewish Scattering)*, p. 124.

Poland lived from agriculture in 120 localities.[86] This number of laborers rose to 179,000 in 1897, according to a survey conducted by the JCA, but it only constituted about 3.5 percent of the Jewish population.[87] The desire to move to agricultural work had waned by the late 1850s, when the government stopped granting aid and facilities for it. Yet this experience later had a profound effect, as we shall see, on the thinking of the Zionist labor wing. This wing's demand to convert the Jews to a life of agricultural work was a major pillar of its ideology.

Another change in the conditions of the Jews began in the early 1860s and was caused by several factors. The Russian authorities expelled large numbers of Jews from the villages to the cities, and in 1863 they were expelled from all regions where the Polish uprising had erupted, again to the cities. The cities in which the Jews were allowed to live were already congested. Most of these Jews went to work in factories and workshops, which were established on a wide scale with the progress of Russia's industrialization. In time, this led to the growth of a relatively large Jewish working class, as well as an increase in the number of artisans among the Jews, the emergence of a class of factory workers and a significant rise in the number of hired laborers among them.[88] A survey in 1897 showed the number of Jewish workers in Russia and Poland to be about 1.53 million (out of a total of 5 million Jews). About a third of these workers, or 555,000, were laborers. They included approximately 280,000 artisans and 100,000 hired laborers.[89]

These social and economic changes that took place in the lives of significant numbers of Jews in Russia – from the emergence of hundreds of rich Jews, their closeness to Russian society and integration in it, to the thousands of students who received an education in Russian schools, then the growth of a working class of tens of thousands who mingled within society

---

86   Ibid, p. 129.

87   Ibid, p. 130.

88   Ibid, p. 131.

89   Ibid, p. 146.

– all led to the development of the Haskalah and its penetration into large sectors of the Jewish population. This was also aided by the authorities' embrace of Jewish Maskilim, who worked on fostering a Russian character in the life of the Jews.[90] In 1863, the Society for the Promotion of Culture among the Jews of Russia was established. It aimed to spread science and the Russian language among the Jews in Russia and Poland, viewing this as necessary for equality between them and the Russians. This Haskalah current, however, which arose out of conflict in a society where traditional religious values had their weight, was not the only one to take shape among Russian Jews in this period. Another Haskalah current appeared that preferred Hebrew heritage and its revival, instead of the Russian. Both currents faced resistance from the Rabbinate and Hasidism, which were losing successive battles in their war with the Haskalah.

Both these Haskalah currents, the Russian and Hebrew, were active among the Jews. While some Jewish intellectuals were working to publish their newspapers in Russian in the early 1860s,[91] and issuing literary and other works in Russian, their compatriots were doing the same in Hebrew. The results were relatively voluminous. In 1860, the first Russian weekly newspaper in the Hebrew language, *ha-Melitz* (*The Recommender*), was published in Odessa. In 1871, it moved to St. Petersburg and was issued daily until 1903. In 1860, as well, the weekly newspaper *ha-Carmel* (*The Carmel*) was published in Vilna, Lithuania, then it became a monthly and was issued until 1879. A weekly newspaper, *ha-Tsfira* (*The Whistle;* 1862-1931), was launched in Warsaw and later moved to Berlin (it was issued as a daily between 1886-1917). The monthly magazine *ha-Shahar* (*The Dawn*) was published in Vienna (1868-1884). Another weekly Hebrew-language newspaper, *ha-Magid* (*The Narrator;* 1856-1903), appeared in Leck, Germany, then moved to Berlin and later to Kraków. These newspapers were the most

---

90 Dubnow, *Divrei Yemei Am Olam (History of the Jews)*, pp. 636-637.

91 Slutsky, *Ha-Itonout ha-Yehudit-Rusit ba-Meah ha-Tsha'esrei (Russian Jewish Press in the 19th Century)*, pp. 37-55.

prominent and had contributions from the great Jewish writers of that era, such as Peretz Smolenskin, Judah Leib Gordon, Moshe Leib Lilienblum and Nahum Sokolow. The newspapers had a later impact on Lovers of Zion and the Zionist movement, due to the important role they played in disseminating views and shaping positions – both in favor of Zionism and against it.[92]

The political, social and economic conditions of the Jews in Russia and Poland had a crucial effect on the growth of the Zionist movement and the molding of its ideology. The largest Zionist wings, in size and quality, were formed among these Jews. Several bases of the Zionist movement, including those that are still current, were forms of response to the stage of development achieved by the Russian and Polish Jews. These Jews controlled the Zionist movement for a considerable period, the effects of which were long tangible in Israel.

Finally, the measures taken by tsarist Russia in the 19th century to reform the conditions of its Jews – and the subsequent progress among some Jewish groups in various fields, with the push of the country towards capitalist development – did not lead to a solution of the Jewish question in Russia. On the contrary, they complicated it. In the second half of the 19th century, most Jews in Russia still lived from trade, crafts and renting and operating farms, bars, restaurants and hotels. These formed a link between the Russian or Polish feudal lords and the peasants.[93] The new conditions then arose and destroyed the foundations of Jewish economic life; the capitalist development led to the emergence of a non-Jewish middle class that began to compete with the Jewish merchants, as well as to erode the livelihoods of their artisans who could not rival machinery. Large numbers of Jewish laborers were forced to move to the cities for work, while the authorities prohibited the Jews from operating farms, bars and hotels and expelled many of them to the cities. Thus the

---

92   See also Dubnow, *Divrei Yemei Am Olam (History of the Jews)*, pp. 638-640; Ettinger, *Toldot Am Yisrael ba'Et ha-Hadasha (History of the Jews in Modern Times)*, Vol. 3, pp. 133-134.

93   For details, see Ezra Mendelsohn, *Class Struggle in the Pale: The Formative Years of the Jewish Workers' Movement in Tsarist Russia*, pp. 1-26; Abram Leon, *The Jewish Question: A Marxist Interpretation*, pp. 159-224.

Russian Jews experienced a large internal migration from their villages, but the cities could not absorb all of these laborers who had moved to work in industries that were soon taken over by machinery.[94] In 1881, after the pogroms and attacks against the Jews in the wake of the tsar's assassination, they began to emigrate from Russia. This trend continued until the outbreak of the First World War, in 1914.

The emigration from Russia and Poland, from 1881-1914, led to a new distribution of the Jewish population. At the beginning of this period, the total number of Jews was estimated, as indicated previously, at 7.5 million, 4.25 million of whom lived in Russia and Poland, 1.5 million in the Austro-Hungarian Empire, 1 million in the remaining European countries, 0.25 million in the United States, and 0.5 million in Asia and Africa (see *Table 1 Number of Jews in the world, emigration, and distribution, 1880-1914 (estimates)*, below).

At the end of this period, in 1914, the number of Jews was estimated at 13 million, 5.5 million of whom lived in Russia and Poland, 2.5 million in the Austro-Hungarian Empire, 2.5 million in the United States, 1.7 million in Europe, and 800,000 in Asia and Africa (most of them in the Ottoman Empire).[95] It can be seen that the number of Jews rose, in particular, in the United States (from 0.25 million in 1881 to 2.5 million in 1914), at a rate higher than that of their general increase. The rate also rose in western Europe, while it dropped in Russia and Poland, although their Jewish communities remained the largest in the world due to the high growth in population. These changes were due to the large-scale emigration from Russia, Poland and elsewhere in eastern Europe to the United States and western Europe. From 1881-1914, about 2.65 million Jews emigrated from those areas; 2 million went to the United States, 350,000 to western Europe, and 300,000 to the rest of the world. Of the latter, about 50,000 went to Palestine, but a third of them left it again in the First

---

94   Ibid; see also Ettinger, *Toldot Am Yisrael ba'Et ha-Hadasha (History of the Jews in Modern Times)*, Vol. 3, p. 32.

95   Ettinger, *Toldot Am Yisrael ba'Et ha-Hadasha (History of the Jews in Modern Times)*, Vol. 3, pp. 76, 78-79, 147-148, 150-151.

World War.

Of particular note in the Jewish migration movement, during this period, is that the percentage of immigrants to Palestine did not exceed 2% (about 50,000 out of more than 2.5 million). That is, it was a tiny minority that had to immigrate mainly due to political pressures and poor economic conditions. Zionist political motives were only a secondary factor, at this stage – although these immigrants laid the foundations of the Zionist project in Palestine.

Table 1 Number of Jews in the world, emigration, and distribution, 1880-1914 (estimates)[96]

Region	1880		Emigration in this period		1914	
	Number	%	From	To	Number	%
Russia and Poland	4,250,000	56.7	2,650,000		5,500,000	42.3
Austria and Hungary	1,500,000	20.0			2,500,000	19.2
Other European countries	1,000,000	13.3		350,000	1,700,000	13.1
United States	250,000	3.3		2,000,000	2,500,000	19.2
Asia and Africa	478,000	6.4		250,000	715,000	5.5
Palestine	22,000	0.01		50,000	85,000	0.1
Total	7,500,000	100.0			13,000,000	100.0

---

96   Wallach, *Atlas Carta le-Toldot Eretz Yisrael (Carta's Atlas of History of the Land of Israel)*, p. 12; Lestschinsky, *Ha-Tfutsa ha-Yehudit (Jewish Scattering)*, pp. 146, 148, 151, 160; Ettinger, *Toldot Am Yisrael ba'Et ha-Hadasha (History of the Jews in Modern Times)*, Vol. 3, pp. 76, 78-79, 147-148, 150-151; *Encyclopaedia Judaica*, Vol. 5, pp. 1493-1502.

Further, the motives for the successive waves of immigration to Palestine, since that time, were similar to those that had prompted the first ones. Most immigrants moved due to poor living conditions or the disasters that befell them, which Zionism would exploit to achieve its goals.

5

If the conditions of the Jews in Russia, eastern or western Europe in the 19th century were among the constituent elements of Zionism, there were also factors related to developments in Europe itself during that time. Chief among these were the emergence of the national idea and the establishment of many nation states, the rising influence of European colonialism, and the emergence of anti-Semitism.[97]

In the 19th century, Europe witnessed the spread of the national idea and the outbreak of many revolutions such that a number of its peoples gained their independence or unification and established their own states. Although many of these revolutions, including the Polish insurrections against the Russians in 1830 and 1863, as well as other upheavals in France, Germany, Austria and Italy in 1848 – the "year of revolutions" and "spring of peoples" – failed to make any immediate achievements, several other European peoples were able, during that century, to achieve their goals of independence and unity. In 1829, for example, Greece became independent of Turkey. The following year, Serbia gained autonomy and its independence was recognized in 1878 after the Treaty of Berlin. In 1830, Belgium gained independence from the Netherlands. Similarly, in 1858-1859, the Romanian provinces obtained autonomy from Turkey and their independence was recognized in 1878. Italy completed its unification in 1870 after a series of wars since 1848. In 1871, the unification of Germany was declared. The Austro-Hungarian Empire was also founded in 1867, on a federal basis, after Hungary was granted autonomy. In addition, the early 19th century saw the independence of many South American peoples

---

97   Arieh Tartakower, *Am ve Olamo (A People and its World)*, pp. 142-147.

from Spain and Portugal, which, due to their involvement in the Napoleonic wars (1803-1815), lost control over these regions.

In another vein, European colonialism grew in an unprecedented manner in the 19th century, spreading over many regions of Asia and Africa. New colonial powers emerged, after Britain had almost been the exclusive one during the century before. The sweep of the Industrial Revolution in several European states was accompanied by their eager efforts to extend their power over new areas outside their borders, both to create markets for their goods and to secure raw materials for their factories. This led to the outbreak of many colonial wars and conflicts, or the conclusion of agreements to "share the spoils". The outcome of colonial activity was substantial, in this century, in terms of the area of land that came to be controlled. From 1800-1875, the area of colonial states and the territories they had colonized rose from 35% to 67% of the total land mass of the world, after these states had been able to colonize an average of 77,000 square miles (200,000 square kilometers) per year. This percentage rose to 85% in 1900, when the annual rate of colonization increased threefold with the division of most of the African continent among the European states. The number of colonial states rose to include most of western Europe: Britain, France, Germany, Spain, Italy, Portugal and Belgium, as well as an Asian state, Japan. Many Arab regions in Asia and Africa were colonized. In 1830, France occupied Algeria and, in 1839, Britain occupied Aden. Britain and France then spread their control over most of the Arab lands in Africa: Tunisia in 1881, Egypt in 1882, Sudan in 1899 and Marrakesh in 1912. By the end of the 19th century, the colonial states had tightened their control over most of Africa, vast areas of Asia, some areas of America and a good number of strategic islands around the world.

These developments, which created new national entities for many European peoples, had a great effect on Jewish intellectuals in Europe. Most, if not all, of the fathers of Zionism, including Theodor Herzl, proposed their solutions to the Jewish question based on the methods followed by Europe.[98] Their thinking was comparative: if the European peoples – including those who were considered by the Zionists to not have attained that level of progress which the Jews had – possessed the right to establish nation states of their own, why would this right be denied to the Jews? Further, if many European states were establishing colonies in Asia and Africa – tightening their control over their peoples, and creating various formations and quasi-political entities – then why did the Jews also not have the right to create an entity of their own in order to solve their own problems, as well as to avoid crises in their relations with European peoples? More than one Zionist leader or thinker was ready, in the early stages of Zionism, to establish a Jewish state or to settle the Jews anywhere in the world, not just in Palestine. The Zionists did not fix their position in terms of the location of their intended state until the Zionist Organization (later, the World Zionist Organization) was founded, and the First Zionist Congress, in 1897, decided that the Jewish state should be established in Palestine alone. Yet, even after this was announced, more than one Zionist group was willing to discuss the establishment of a Jewish state in any other suitable place, just as the European states were ready to colonize any region of the world if it brought about strategic or economic benefit. These comparisons were key to the emergence of Zionist ideology. They then acquired greater urgency in light of the rise in persecution of the Jews in some European countries – especially in tsarist Russia.

Anti-Semitism began to manifest noticeably in parts of Europe during the second half of the 19th century. It had appeared in Christian Europe since the Middle Ages, when the Jews were subjected to hatred and campaigns of persecution as they were blamed for the death of Christ,[99] as well as for their continued belief in Judaism and their refusal to convert to Christianity. Gradually, however, the reasons for anti-Semitism

---

98 Ben-Zion Dinur (Dinaburg), ed., *Shivat Tzion (Return to Zion)*, Vol. 1, p. 20.

99 Ettinger, *Toldot Am Yisrael ba'Et ha-Hadasha (History of the Jews in Modern Times)*, Vol. 3, p. 158.

changed, becoming primarily confined to the economic sphere. The Industrial Revolution and capitalist growth uprooted the Jews in eastern Europe but helped to assimilate them in its west.[100] Conversely to the situation in Russia, a Jewish middle class arose in western Europe that began to compete with the developing middle classes there. These classes were exploited by the rulers and financiers. They were also threatened by the advocates of socialism, who aimed to eliminate them and establish a working-class dictatorship in their place. Thus these classes found in their hatred of the Jews, who were in economic competition with them, an outlet for the exploitation and threats that they faced, as well as an expression of their identity.[101] This feeling was compounded by the continued immigration of Jews from Russia and eastern Europe to western Europe, with many being en route to the United States. The immigration aroused anti-Jewish sentiment such that wealthy Jews in western Europe, especially the barons Hirsch and Rothschild, devised ways of dealing with that immigration. They established special organizations to send immigrant Jews who arrived in western Europe to other countries (Argentina or Palestine, for example), lest their continued stay further rouse anti-Jewish sentiment in western Europe and affect the rights that the Jews had attained there.[102]

Further, as had happened in Russia, the growth of capitalism after the Industrial Revolution in western Europe raised the power of a number of Jews in the world of finance. Most founders of major European banks were Jews. This caused a wave of hatred and envy among the downtrodden masses, which held them responsible for the deterioration of their economic conditions – despite the fact that most of these Jews (except for Rothschild) later converted to Christianity.[103] Meanwhile, some

---

100   Ibid.

101   Jacob Talmon, *Be-Idan ha-Alimut (The Age of Violence)*, pp. 237-239.

102   Ahmad El Kodsy and Eli Lobel, *The Arab World and Israel*, p. 100.

103   Ettinger, *Toldot Am Yisrael ba'Et ha-Hadasha (History of the Jews in Modern Times)*, Vol. 3, pp. 82-84.

early advocates of socialism declared that Judaism – on the whole – was only a manifestation of capitalism.[104] This hatred of Jewish financiers, who wielded significant power despite their small number, soon spread to engulf all of the Jews, even though the majority of them, especially in eastern Europe, were from the poor classes whose conditions were no different than those of similar classes. Yet, those "theories", which were based on the behavior of Jewish financiers, were wrongly expanded to include the Jews as a whole, and led to harsh attitudes that Zionism later exploited to serve its ends.

Other reasons also led to the emergence of anti-Semitism. The Jews participated, in relatively large numbers, in the revolutionary movements of that period. In fact, there was hardly one such movement, regardless of its tint, that they did not take part in. This provoked fear and hatred of them by the conservative elements of society.[105] The era of emergence of anti-Semitism also saw greater numbers of Jewish intellectuals, especially those with free professions, rising in influence in the field of media and journalism. They founded some important, international news agencies – which created another excuse for hating them.

A factor in anti-Semitism was also the denunciation of Judaism, by some, as part of denouncing all of religion, including Christianity. The Jew was seen to be a unique element, incapable of integrating in society. This view prevailed especially in countries that had been established on a purely national basis. Anti-Semitic phenomena gradually spread among many groups in Europe, more so as various organizations exploited these phenomena for political gain.[106]

In Germany, organized anti-Semitic activity began in the last quarter of the 19th century. It was in tandem with the crisis sparked by the "cultural war" against Catholics, who were accused of

---

104   Ibid, pp. 92-93, 160.

105   For details, see Talmon, *Be-Idan ha-Alimut (The Age of Violence)*, pp. 183-264.

106   Ettinger, *Toldot Am Yisrael ba'Et ha-Hadasha (History of the Jews in Modern Times)*, Vol. 3, pp. 33-34, 158, 162.

double affiliation. In 1880, the League of Anti-Semites was established in Berlin. The founder, Wilhelm Marr (1819-1904), was the first to coin the term "anti-Semitism". He had published a book, the year before, titled *Semitism*, in which he warned of its "dangers". In the same year, a German university professor, Heinrich von Treitschke (1834-1896), tried to lay the scientific foundations of anti-Semitism after warning of increasing Jewish immigration to Germany from Russia. He declared that the Jews were a foreign element that did not wish to and could not integrate in German life. In this vein, he argued that the demand by some Jews for recognition of their national rights destroyed the legal foundations of the equality that was granted to them. The chief anti-Semite of that period, Eugen Duhring (1833-1921), declared in a book, published in 1886,[107] that the Jewish element was the worst of the Semitic race, whose goal was to dominate the world and exclude other peoples, and that Judaism had harmful, anti-social qualities, especially when active in politics or journalism.[108] German anti-Semites showed noticeable activity in this period and were able to attract many groups of university students. In 1880, an anti-Semitic league was formed in Dresden. In 1881, the anti-Semites submitted a petition to Otto von Bismarck, with 300,000 signatures, for the government to prohibit Jews from entering Germany and to stop them from taking influential positions in the country. The following year, a general conference of anti-Semites from Germany, Austria and Hungary was held with about 300 delegates.[109] Conversely, German societies were established to fight anti-Semitism. One of them, founded in 1890, gained 13,000 members in three years. A similar association was established in 1893. Then, in 1899, another "scientific" book was published, *Foundations of the Nineteenth Century*. Its author, Houston Stewart Chamberlain

---

107   Eugen Duhring, *Die Judenfrage als Frage der Rassenschadlichkeit fur Existenz, Sitte und Kultur der Volker, mit einer weltgeschichtlichen Antwort (The Jewish Question as a Question of Racial Harm to the Existence, Customs and Culture of the People, with a World-Historical Answer)*.

108   Dubnow, *Divrei Yemei Am Olam (History of the Jews)*, p. 651.

109   Ibid, p. 653.

(1855-1927), a Briton who lived in Germany, presented the history of civilization as a struggle between the good Aryans and evil Semites.[110] (These views later affected the intellectual foundations of Nazism.) At the same time, *The Protocols of the Elders of Zion* was published, in which the authors claimed the existence of a global Jewish leadership that worked secretly to dominate the world by spreading conflict between Christian peoples. It is alleged that the Russian tsar's secret police were behind the publication of this book. The book, which was based on a fabrication, became especially popular after the First World War.[111] Later, it gained wide circulation in the Arab world and contributed – perhaps more than any other publication – to misunderstanding Zionism and its schemes.

From Berlin, anti-Semitism spread to other cities in Germany and beyond. In 1886, anti-Semitic organizations were established in Budapest and Vienna. In the same year, an international conference of anti-Semites was held in Bucharest, and another in Kassel, Germany, which led to the unification of their organizations. In 1891, anti-Semites gained 13 seats in the municipality of Vienna. Their power grew in parliament, as well. In 1895, they elected their leader – Karl Lueger (1844-1910) – as mayor of Vienna. When the government refused to confirm him as mayor, Lueger was re-elected three consecutive times, but was refused each time. Finally, after his fifth election in 1897, he was able to assume the post. In response, organizations were also formed in Vienna against anti-Semitism.[112]

Anti-Semitism also appeared in France during this period, especially during the trial of Alfred Dreyfus and its accompanying anti-Jewish sentiment. Dreyfus, an officer of Jewish origin in the French army, was falsely accused of treason in 1894, and of giving French security information to Germany. In truth, one

---

110   Ibid, pp. 654-655.

111   Ettinger, *Toldot Am Yisrael ba'Et ha-Hadasha (History of the Jews in Modern Times)*, Vol. 3, pp. 264-265.

112   Ibid, pp. 163-165; Dubnow, *Divrei Yemei Am Olam (History of the Jews)*, pp. 658-660.

of his colleagues from a notable French family had done this. After a lengthy trial, Dreyfus was convicted and sentenced to expulsion from the army and exile from France. His trial was accompanied by an outpouring of anti-Semitism which found expression in French and other newspapers.[113] The Dreyfus case did not end with his conviction, however. Counter-pressures against the authorities led to his retrial and partial acquittal, then the issuance of a pardon for him. He was finally exonerated in 1906.

The trial of Dreyfus did a great service to Zionism. Herzl, who later founded the Zionist Organization, wrote in his memoirs that the cries of hostility against the Jews during this trial made him a Zionist. Herzl, who was following the Dreyfus case as a press reporter, published his book, *Der Judenstaat* (*The Jewish State*) in 1896, when the echoes of the Dreyfus affair were the strongest.

The phenomena of anti-Semitism made it clear to many Jews who wanted to integrate with the peoples that they lived with, and who felt that they had attained all their rights as citizens, that their Jewish origins were not forgotten. The writings of many Zionist leaders and thinkers revealed a great disappointment with anti-Semitism, which prompted them to fundamentally reconsider their positions. In doing so, affected by the very racism inherent in anti-Semitism, they adopted racist hypotheses of their own to counter it.[114] They searched for solutions to change their conditions, especially as the situation of Russian Jews worsened in the early 1880s, after the assassination of the tsar, and Jewish emigration increased from Russia. The conclusion of this review was with the call for the Jews to leave their countries and establish one of their own, like other peoples. The search for the location of this country continued for a significant period until it settled on Palestine – the so-called "historic Land of Israel".

---

113 Dubnow, *Divrei Yemei Am Olam (History of the Jews)*, pp. 683-685.

114 Morris R. Cohen, "Zionism: Tribalism or Liberalism?", in Gary V. Smith, ed., *Zionism: The Dream and the Reality; a Jewish Critique*, pp. 50-51.

6

Within Zionism, there is an indispensable religious element in its attempt to harness Judaism to serve its aims and to compel both the Jews and Christians to agree with its political goals. The key factor is the focus on the so-called "historic relationship" between Jews and the "Land of Israel".

The name "Land of Israel" ("Eretz Yisrael", in Hebrew),[115] according to Jewish teachings, refers to that part of the world in southwestern Asia which includes – in contemporary geography, before the establishment of Israel – Palestine, with its borders of the British Mandate, and parts of all its neighboring countries: Lebanon, Syria, Jordan and Egypt. Jews and Judaism consider this region to be the cradle of their birth. The name "Land of Israel" goes back to the Torah, although its contemporary use apparently began at the end of the Second Kingdom of Israel, in the 1st century.[116] The concept of the name expanded over the years, with the increasing dispersion of the Jews and jurisprudence of Jewish sages, to also mean a close and lasting relationship between the Jews and this Land of Israel, and a belief that they must return to it with the appearance of the Savior-Messiah. This was mainly an expression of latent political aspirations that ebbed and flowed with the conditions that the Jews found themselves in.

The essence of the relationship between the Jews and the Land of Israel, as well as the boundaries of this land, are not completely clear, and differ according to the Torah and other Jewish religious texts. This difference is mainly due to the changing historical context in which the Torah, or any parts of it, were written, as well as that of the succeeding eras in which the other texts were composed. There is, firstly, the relationship stipulated in the covenant that God made with Abraham, when He led him from Ur to Canaan, as stated in the Torah: "In that

---

115   The Hebrew word "Yisrael" (Israel) also means the Jews. It is the name of a people, place and state.

116   Joshua Prawer, "Ba-Shem Eretz Yisrael (In the Name of the Land of Israel)", in *Ha-Encyclopaedia ha-Ivrit (Encyclopaedia Hebraica)*, Vol. 6, p. 2.

day the Lord made a covenant with Abraham, saying: 'Unto thy seed have I given this land, from the river of Egypt unto the great river, the river Euphrates.'"[117] Likewise, He said to Isaac: "Sojourn in this land, and I will be with you and will bless you, for to you and to your offspring I will give all these lands, and I will establish the oath that I swore to Abraham your father."[118] The boundaries of the "Promised Land" ("T'hum ha-Avot", in Hebrew) are mentioned in other verses of the Torah: "And I will set your borders from the Sea of Reeds to the Sea of Philistia, and from the wilderness to the Euphrates; for I will deliver the inhabitants of the land into your hands; and you will drive them out before you."[119] Also: "Turn and take your journey, and go to the hill country of the Amorites and to all their neighbors in the Arabah, in the hill country and in the lowland and in the Negeb and by the seacoast, the land of the Canaanites, and Lebanon, as far as the great river, the river Euphrates."[120] Then: "Every place that the sole of your foot shall tread upon, that have I given unto you... Your border will be from the wilderness to Lebanon, and from the river, the river Euphrates, as far as the western sea."[121] Finally: "From the wilderness and this Lebanon even unto the great river, the river Euphrates, all the land of the Hittites, and unto the great sea toward the going down of the sun, shall be your coast."[122]

As can be seen, the boundaries are ambiguous and there is little consensus on them. The prevailing opinion, based on real or illusory interpretations and jurisprudence, is that this "Promised Land" includes that region which is bounded to the west by the Mediterranean Sea, and to the south by a line that begins from el-Arish in Sinai and turns, windingly, until it reaches Aqaba (Eilat), running north to the south of the Dead Sea, then

---

117 *Torah*, Genesis 15:18.

118 Ibid, 26:3.

119 *Torah*, Exodus 23:31.

120 *Torah*, Deuteronomy 1:7.

121 Ibid, 11:24.

122 *Torah*, Joshua 1:4.

continues north along the Jordan River (without including any area east of the river), until it reaches Mount Hermon. From there it continues north, passing west of Damascus and Homs until the boundary of Latakia, where it deviates eastward until it reaches the nearest point in the course of the Euphrates to the Mediterranean, before it turns west to the sea, passing south of Aleppo. In other words, the "Promised Land", by these borders, includes the entire area of Mandatory Palestine, with the parts of Syria and Lebanon that lie west of the Damascus-Homs-Hama line, while its northern border is a line that passes south of Aleppo. The area of the whole is about 62,000-66,000 square miles (160,000-170,000 square kilometers).[123]

However, these borders do not at all correspond to the boundaries of the areas in which the Jews supposedly lived or ruled for any period of time. Apart from the area extending from Dan (north of Tiberias) to Beersheba in Palestine, where the Jews were present or ruled partially during certain periods (but which they did not always control, in their entirety, nor were they the only peoples there), the "soles of their feet" – in the language of the Torah – did not tread the remaining areas, and the Jews did not, at any time, occupy these areas or live in them. The explanation for this contradiction is that the other areas were designated for future settlement, when the Jewish population grew.[124] Again, this interpretation is based on the Torah: "I will not drive them out before you in a single year, lest the land become desolate and wild animals multiply against you. Little by little I will drive them out ahead of you, until you become fruitful and possess the land."[125] Also:

> The Lord your God will drive out these nations before you,

---

123 Joshua Prawer, "Ha-Gvulot (The Borders)", in *Ha-Encyclopaedia ha-Ivrit (Encyclopaedia Hebraica)*, Vol. 6, pp. 27-31; Kaufmann, *Toldot ha-Imuna ha-Yisraelit (History of the Israelite Faith)*, Vol. 1, pp. 190-194; Nissan Aharon Tucazinsky, *Ha-Aretz le-Gvuluteiha, Yerushalayim be-Tmounot (The Borders of the Country – Jerusalem in Pictures)*, pp. 46-47.

124 Kaufmann, *Toldot ha-Imuna ha-Yisraelit (History of the Israelite Faith)*, Vol. 1, pp. 190-191.

125 *Torah*, Exodus 23:29,30.

little by little. You will not be enabled to eliminate them all at once, or the wild animals would multiply around you. But the Lord your God will deliver them over to you, throwing them into great confusion until they are destroyed. He will give their kings into your hand, and you will wipe out their names from under heaven. No one will be able to stand up against you; you will destroy them.[126]

There is, however, another "Promised Land", that which God promised Moses after the Jews left Egypt:

Then Moses climbed Mount Nebo from the plains of Moab to the top of Pisgah, across from Jericho. There the Lord showed him the whole land – from Gilead to Dan, all of Naphtali, the territory of Ephraim and Manasseh, all the land of Judah as far as the Mediterranean Sea, the Negev and the whole region from the Valley of Jericho, the City of Palms, as far as Zoar. Then the Lord said to him, "This is the land I promised on oath to Abraham, Isaac and Jacob when I said, 'I will give it to your descendants.'"[127]

According to the Torah, Moses divided this land among the Twelve Tribes of Israel: "Only allot the land to Israel for an inheritance, as I have commanded you. Now therefore divide this land for an inheritance to the nine tribes, and the half-tribe of Manasseh."[128] The remaining tribes had received their shares previously: "So at that time we took possession of this land. To the Reubenites and Gadites I gave the land ... To the half-tribe of Manasseh I gave the rest."[129] The boundaries of this land are spelled out at length in the Torah when laying out its division among the Twelve Tribes,[130] but these boundaries remain unclear. Again, based on many interpretations and jurisprudence, the

---

126 *Torah*, Deuteronomy 7:22-24.

127 Ibid, 34:1-4.

128 *Torah*, Joshua 13:6,7.

129 *Torah*, Deuteronomy 3:12,13.

130 *Torah*, Joshua, verses 15-24.

borders were drawn to include the area between the sea in the west and the desert in the east, with all of the inhabited part east of the Jordan River, while the southern borders extend in a line connecting el-Arish and Aqaba, and the northern borders are unclear, referring only to Mount Hermon.[131] The Land of Israel, per these boundaries, has an area of about 16,600 square miles (43,000 square kilometers). However, there are also the "natural borders" of the Land of Israel – as God must have implicitly permitted His people to amend the borders to be strategic. These natural borders are slightly larger than the original ones, reaching an area of about 23,000 square miles (59,000 square kilometers). About half of this lies west of the Jordan River ("western Land of Israel") and the other half east of the river ("eastern Land of Israel").[132]

The second definition of the "Land of Israel", with the boundaries promised by God to Moses, is more common than the first, and is based on the assertion that the Jews ruled parts of these lands and lived in them at one time.[133] The borders of the area requested by the Zionist Organization at the Paris Peace Conference, in 1919, to be recognized as a "national home" for the Jews, are consistent with this definition (see *Map 2 The "Land of Israel" and its division among the Twelve Tribes of Israel*, and *Map 3 Region of the "Jewish national home" demanded by the Zionist Organization at the Paris Peace Conference*, below).

As for the reason that God took it upon Himself to make covenants with Abraham, Isaac and Jacob, including granting the Land of Israel to the Jews, it is because He chose them to be His people to worship Him as the only God, and for this He would protect and defend them:

---

131 Prawer in *Ha-Encyclopaedia ha-Ivrit (Encyclopaedia Hebraica)*, Vol. 6, p. 30; Tucazinsky, *Ha-Aretz le-Gvuluteiha (The Borders of the Country)*, pp. 46-47.

132 Prawer in *Ha-Encyclopaedia ha-Ivrit (Encyclopaedia Hebraica)*, Vol. 6, p. 31.

133 For details, see, for example, maps in *Encyclopaedia Hebraica*, Vol. 6, pp. 270, 287, 302, 315, 364, 366, 423, 446, 458, 462.

46 The Foundations of Zionism

Map 2 The "Land of Israel" and its division among the Twelve Tribes of Israel[134]

---

134   Ibid, p. 270.

Map 3 Region of the "Jewish national home" demanded by the Zionist Organization at the Paris Peace Conference[135]

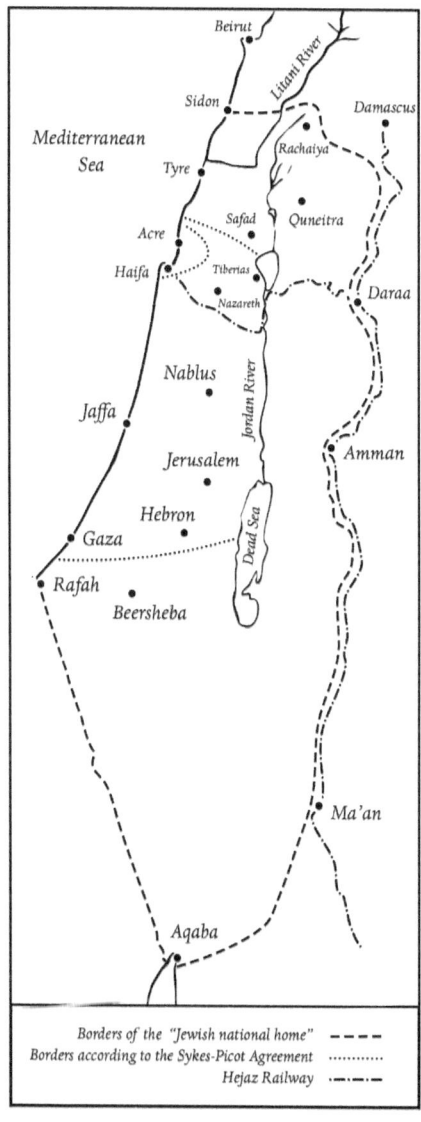

---
135 Ibid, p. 526.

> "I will remember my covenant with Jacob and my covenant with Isaac and my covenant with Abraham, and I will remember the land… I will remember the covenant with their ancestors whom I brought out of Egypt in the sight of the nations to be their God. I am the Lord." These are the decrees, the laws and the regulations that the Lord established at Mount Sinai between Himself and the Israelites through Moses.[136]

Then:

> Remember Your servants Abraham, Isaac, and Israel, to whom You swore by Your very self when You declared, "I will make your descendants as numerous as the stars in the sky, and I will give your descendants all this land that I have promised, and it shall be their inheritance forever."[137]

Also:

> I will establish my covenant as an everlasting covenant between Me and you and your descendants after you for the generations to come, to be your God and the God of your descendants after you, and I will give to you and your descendants after you the land of your pilgrimage, all of the land of Canaan as an everlasting possession, and I will be your God,[138]

and "You shall have no other gods before Me."[139]

According to the Torah, God did not choose the Jews to grant them these exceptional rights because of their benevolent virtues to him, but because they were a better people than others:

> It is not for your righteousness or for the uprightness of your heart that you are going to possess their land, but it is because of the wickedness of these nations that the Lord your God is

---

136 *Torah*, Leviticus 26:42,45,46.

137 *Torah*, Exodus 32:13.

138 *Torah*, Genesis 17:7,8.

139 *Torah*, Exodus 20:3 and Deuteronomy 5:7.

driving them out before you, in order to confirm the oath which the Lord swore to your fathers, to Abraham, Isaac and Jacob. Understand, then, that it is not because of your righteousness that the Lord your God is giving you this good land to possess, for you are a stiff-necked people.[140]

However, at the moment that God chose the Jews, He made them the "Chosen People", the "People of God", distinguished from others. "But the Lord took me from tending the flock and said to me, 'Go, prophesy to my people Israel... Behold, I will set a plumbline in the midst of my people Israel.'"[141] Likewise: "Then said the Lord to me, 'The end has come upon My people Israel,'" and "I will bring My people Israel back from exile. They will rebuild the ruined cities..."[142]

These texts and others from the Torah became, over time, the basis for endless interpretations and jurisprudence on the relationship between Jews and the Land of Israel and their duties towards it. Most prominent in this field was Nachmanides (Moses ben Nachman, also known as Ramban, 1194-1270), who left his country, Spain, and immigrated to Palestine in 1267. In his interpretation of the Torah, Ben Nachman added a character of sanctity to the Land of Israel and its standing in Judaism, making it difficult for devout Jews to forget this land. He believed that it was the center of the world, and that Jerusalem was the center of the Land of Israel[143] (the name, "Zionism", is relative to Mount Zion in Jerusalem). Ben Nachman asserted that the Land of Israel was the only suitable place to perform the religious commandments stipulated in the Torah,[144] and that, in it, both human and animal attained the

---

140 *Torah*, Deuteronomy 9:5.

141 *Torah*, Amos 7:15,8.

142 Ibid, 8:2 and 9:14.

143 Moses (Ramban) Ben Nachman, *Kitvei Ramban (Works of Ramban)*, Vol. 1, p. 252.

144 Ibid, p. 200.

peak of perfection.[145]

The novelty in Ben Nachman's interpretations, however, was his consideration of settlement in the Land of Israel as a religious duty, and classifying this duty, for the first time, as one of the 613 duties that Judaism binds its followers to fulfill.[146] He went further to assert that "settling the Land of Israel equals all the obligations of the Torah."[147] This duty was later explained as obliging the Jews, collectively and individually, to immigrate to the Land of Israel[148] in preparation for the coming of the Savior-Messiah. Based on subsequent jurisprudence, this obligation was expanded to the personal affairs of the Jews. A spouse's refusal, for example, to go and live in the Land of Israel was sufficient justification, in religious law, to seek a divorce. In the Land of Israel itself, the refusal to move from anywhere in the country to Jerusalem constituted a similar consequence – even if these moves led to a deterioration in the family's economic situation.[149]

This jurisprudence, with its sanctity for the Land of Israel, was deeply entrenched in Jewish mentality and spread to Christianity. It was one of the reasons that prompted some Jews, from time to time, to immigrate to Palestine. The significance of these beliefs, however, manifested in the mid-19th century, when the Zionist call to immigrate to Palestine (the "Land of Israel") found willing supporters in Orthodox Jewish societies in Russia and Poland. The call also found approval among many Christian and colonial circles that accepted the idea of a return of the Jews to Palestine, for various reasons. Some had a sincere desire to contribute to a solution of the Jewish question; others intended to get rid of the Jews by sending them elsewhere; and still others wanted to

---

145 Haim Rivlin, *Ma'alat ha-Aretz Eretz Yisrael be-Pirush ha-Ramban le-Torah (Greatness of the Country, the Land of Israel, in Ramban's Interpretation of the Torah)*, p. 61.

146 Ibid, p. 46; see also *Encyclopaedia Judaica*, Vol. 5, pp. 760-772.

147 Ben Nachman, *Kitvei Ramban (Works of Ramban)*, p. 204.

148 Rivlin, H., *Ma'alat ha-Aretz Eretz Yisrael be-Pirush ha-Ramban le-Torah (Greatness of the Country, the Land of Israel, in Ramban's Interpretation of the Torah)*, p. 46.

149 Ben-Zion Schereschewsky, *Dinei Mishpaha (Family Law)*, pp. 146-147.

exploit them to expand their own areas of control.

These beliefs and subsequent interpretations were integral to Zionism, and affected the thinking of its founders and leaders. The beliefs also underlay many of the exceptional rights and demands that Zionism claimed from other peoples and states – for a "chosen people" had to receive "chosen" treatment for its "chosen" demands. These opinions and beliefs are still prevalent, despite the revelations by Torah scholars – especially in light of the archaeological discoveries made in recent centuries – that the history of the Jews as stated in the Torah and other Jewish texts was largely a mythical tale, written hundreds of years after its "occurrence", and that its historical value is limited to being an element of the social, sometimes national, awareness of Jewish scholars.[150]

The explanation of the relationship between the Jews and the Land of Israel, as indicated, was the last element in the making of Zionism. When added to the other factors – a slight improvement in the conditions of the Jewish masses; the emergence of a class of Jewish intellectuals who were dissatisfied with their conditions, while they witnessed the liberation of a number of European peoples and the emergence of new states; the rising influence of colonialism; and the emergence of anti-Semitism – the foundations of Zionism were theoretically complete. All that remained was a motivating factor to drive it from theory to practice. This motivation was presented by the attacks that erupted against the Jews in Russia, after the tsar's assassination in 1881, prompting many of them to immigrate to Palestine.

7

At the end of the 19th century, when Zionist infiltration into Palestine began, the country was still under Ottoman rule. The country was administratively divided into three regions: the

---

150 See, for example, Halpern, Y., *Ha-Mahpicha ha-Yehudit (The Jewish Revolution)*, Vol. 1, pp. 13-34, and also Hayim Tadmor, "Days of the First Kingdom and the Return to Zion", in Ben-Sasson, ed., *Toldot Am Yisrael be-Yemei Kedem (History of the Jews in the Old Ages)*, pp. 111-114.

Mutasarrifate of Jerusalem, which was directly subordinate to the Ottoman administration in Istanbul, and the Sanjak of Nablus and Sanjak of Akka (Acre) which were part of the Vilayet (province) of Beirut (see *Map 4 Administrative divisions in Palestine and its region; Jewish population (approximate) and its places of residence*, below). According to the Ottoman divisions of 1908, those areas included 549 Arab villages: 126 in the vicinity of Jerusalem, 52 in Hebron, 75 in Gaza, 126 in Jaffa, 62 in Haifa, 78 in Safad, and 30 in Tiberias.[151] The Arab population of Palestine was estimated at half a million.

The Jews in Palestine, in the mid-19th century, before the arrival of the first Zionist immigrants from Russia and Romania, were a tiny minority among the Arab population, living in about ten regions in the country. The presence of Jews in Palestine, in modern times, dates back to the end of the 15th century. A number of Sephardic Jews, who were expelled from Spain in 1492, arrived and settled in Safad. They were later joined by some Jewish immigrants from the Balkans and Anatolia.

Most of these Jewish people remained in Safad until the majority were forced to leave due to multiple disasters, including an earthquake that led to heavy losses in 1837. These Jews moved to Jerusalem.[152] By the mid-1830s, Jerusalem had the largest Jewish community in Palestine. Ashkenazi Jews had also established a community in the city, which grew with the arrival of a few hundred Hasidic Jews from Poland in 1777.[153] Others followed later and settled in Jerusalem as well. There was also a community of French Jews in the city,[154] who arrived in 1808-1810. Most Jews in Palestine, until the mid-19th century, were Sephardic, before

---

151 Michael Assaf, *Ha-Yahasim bein Yehudim ve Aravim be-Eretz Yisrael, 1860-1948 (Jewish-Arab Relations in the Land of Israel, 1860-1948)*, pp. 340-341.

152 Ben-Zion Gat, *Ha-Yishuv ha-Yehudi be-Eretz Yisrael 1840-1881 (The Jewish Community in the Land of Israel in 1840-1881)*, pp. 22, 159-160.

153 Simon Federbusch, ed., *Ha-Hasidut ve Tzion (Hasidism and Zion)*, p. 16.

154 Gat, *Ha-Yishuv ha-Yehudi be-Eretz Yisrael 1840-1881 (The Jewish Community in the Land of Israel in 1840-1881)*, pp. 26-29; see also Eliezer Raphael Malachi, *Prakim be-Toldot ha-Yishuv ha-Yashan (Chapters in the History of the Old Yishuv)*, pp. 90-97.

the percentage of Ashkenazis began to rise with immigration to comprise half the Jewish population by 1875, then 60% by 1877.[155] With continued Zionist immigration from Russia and Poland, Sephardic Jews became a minority and remained so until 1948, the last year of the British mandate over Palestine. (The number of Sephardic Jews began to rise, again, after the establishment of Israel, as a result of the wide immigration to it from Asian and African countries, especially the Arab ones, in its first years. Sephardic Jews came to form more than half of its Jewish population.)

It is not known exactly how many Jews were living in Palestine prior to the onset of Zionist immigration in the early 1880s, despite numerous sources on the subject, and despite consensus on most of the places in which they lived. In an 1839 "census", their number was about 6,500,[156] while other sources indicate that, in the following year, this number was 10,500. The discrepancy diminishes, however, in 1860-1880. The number of Jews in Palestine was estimated at 14,400 in 1856-1860, rising to 22,350 in 1876-1881. More than half of them lived in Jerusalem, and the remainder were spread over seven towns: Safad, Tiberias, Acre, Haifa, Jaffa, Nablus and Hebron, and in two villages in the Galilee: Shafa'amr and al-Buqi'a (see *Map 4 Administrative divisions in Palestine and its region; Jewish population (approximate) and its places of residence*, below).

Palestine had been subject to Ottoman Muslim rule since 1517. The Jews in it, and elsewhere in the Ottoman Empire, enjoyed a degree of religious freedom that was not theirs anywhere in Europe. The Ottoman authorities took no significant measures against the Jews and did not discriminate between them and other residents,[157] as was the case in most, if not all, European countries. If the conditions of the Jews in the Ottoman Empire were generally unsatisfactory, they were not much different from

---

155   Gat, *Ha-Yishuv ha-Yehudi be-Eretz Yisrael 1840-1881 (The Jewish Community in the Land of Israel in 1840-1881)*, pp. 21-22.

156   Yitzhak Ben-Zvi, *Eretz Yisrael ve-Yishuvah be-Yemei ha-Shilton ha-Otomani (Land of Israel and its Settlers Under Ottoman Rule)*, pp. 361-362.

157   See, for example, Dubnow, *Divrei Yemei Am Olam (History of the Jews)*, pp. 525-527.

those of the remaining population. The status of Jews and other non-Muslim sects in the Ottoman Empire was also enhanced after the Crimean War. This led to a treaty, in 1856, with a pledge by the Ottoman authorities to safeguard the religious rights of Jews and Christians and grant them "autonomy" in this sphere.

At the same time, the privilege (Capitulations) system was expanded until many Jews and Christians, residents of the Ottoman Empire, were treated like citizens of foreign states that protected them via their consuls in the empire. The Ottoman administrative and legislative authorities lost their powers over them, which were turned to the consuls of those foreign states. This became, in itself, one of the means for those states to interfere in internal Ottoman affairs. The Ottoman authorities had granted Capitulations to France in 1735, then to Britain, Holland, Austria, Russia, Germany and the United States in 1830. This situation had two significant consequences. Firstly, thousands of Jews in Palestine sought protection from foreign states,[158] especially Britain and Germany, which strengthened Jewish people's position when dealing with the Ottoman authorities and the remaining population. Secondly, the Ottoman government recognized the chief Sephardic rabbi, Bashi, as the head of the Jewish sects in the empire, and granted him the authority to approve the election of a greater Sephardic rabbi of the Jews in Palestine ("ha-Rishon le-Zion", in Hebrew, The First in Zion). This rabbi was to be the head of all the Jews in the country and to oversee their religious and worldly affairs, such that the Ottoman authorities would implement his decisions.[159]

In 1838, a British consulate was opened in Jerusalem, whose mission included "providing protection to the Jews [there], in general". This became a significant task of the consulate for a considerable period.[160] It is clear from the consulate's archival documents that this was an excuse so that Britain could interfere

---

158 Ben-Zvi, *Eretz Yisrael ve-Yishuvah be-Yemei ha-Shilton ha-Otomani (Land of Israel and its Settlers Under Ottoman Rule)*, pp. 335-336; Dubnow, *Divrei Yemei Am Olam (History of the Jews)*, pp. 648-649.

159 Gat, *Ha-Yishuv ha-Yehudi be-Eretz Yisrael 1840-1881 (The Jewish Community in the Land of Israel in 1840-1881)*, p. 23.

160 Ibid, p. XXXIV.

in the country's affairs and strengthen its position – as France did, for example, in its stated capacity as protector of the Catholics. The British consul even proposed to the Ottoman government that the Jews present their grievances through his consulate, but his request was denied.[161] Yet, the consulate was able to find British subjects in Palestine by agreeing to requests for protection which were made by some Jews, especially those who had, for various reasons, lost the protection of their original countries.

The German consulate in Jerusalem, which opened in 1842, acted in the same way. It granted German protection to anyone who requested it, "ignoring the authenticity of documents" that were submitted to support the application. Protection was thus granted to many Jewish people who were "not really of German origin".[162] Other European states followed suit. By the mid-1850s, about 5,000 Jews in Palestine enjoyed foreign protection. Of those, Austria granted its protection to about 3,000, and the United States to 1,000.[163]

Over time, the consulates established branches in various parts of Palestine. They gave valuable services to the Jews, even preventing the Ottoman authorities, at times, from implementing the laws in force against them. About half the Jews in Palestine came under this protection, such that it was difficult to imagine the existence of any Jewish entity in the country without it.[164] The consuls were particularly active in helping the Jews to purchase land and settle in it.

---

161 Ibid, pp. 35-39.

162 Mordechai Eliav, "The German Consulate in Jerusalem and the Jewish Yishuv in the 19th Century", in Daniel Carpi, ed., *Ha-Tzionout, Me'asef le-Toldot ha-Tnu'ah ha-Tzionit ve ha-Yishuv ha-Yehudi be-Eretz Yisrael (Zionism: Studies in the History of the Zionist Movement and of the Jewish Community in the Land of Israel)*, Vol. 1, p. 59.

163 Gat, *Ha-Yishuv ha-Yehudi be-Eretz Yisrael 1840-1881 (The Jewish Community in the Land of Israel in 1840-1881)*, p. 87.

164 Ibid, pp. 86-92; Ben-Zvi, *Eretz Yisrael ve-Yishuvah be-Yemei ha-Shilton ha-Otomani (Land of Israel and its Settlers Under Ottoman Rule)*, pp. 363-365.

Map 4 Administrative divisions in Palestine and its region; Jewish population (approximate) and its places of residence[165]

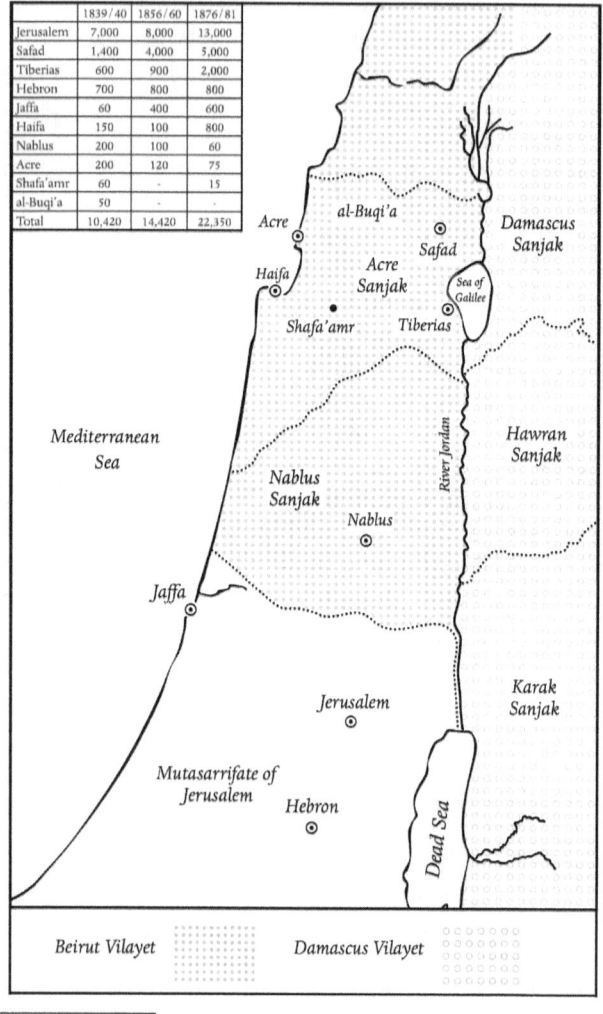

	1839/40	1856/60	1876/81
Jerusalem	7,000	8,000	13,000
Safad	1,400	4,000	5,000
Tiberias	600	900	2,000
Hebron	700	800	800
Jaffa	60	400	600
Haifa	150	100	800
Nablus	200	100	60
Acre	200	120	75
Shafa'amr	60	-	15
al-Buqi'a	50	-	-
Total	10,420	14,420	22,350

165 *Ha-Encyclopaedia ha-Ivrit (Encyclopaedia Hebraica)*, Vol. 6, p. 551; Gat, *Ha-Yishuv ha-Yehudi be-Eretz Yisrael 1840-1881 (The Jewish Community in the Land of Israel in 1840-1881)*, pp. 19-20, 160, 169, 174, 181, 185-186, 188-190 and sources mentioned; Ben-Zvi, *Eretz Yisrael ve-Yishuvah be-Yemei ha-Shilton ha-Otomani (Land of Israel and its Settlers Under Ottoman Rule)*, pp. 361-362, 365-366, 369-400.

Introduction 57

This comfortable legal situation of the Jews in Palestine in the second half of the 19th century did not apply to their personal conditions, which were marked by extreme poverty and torpor. Most Jewish people had come to Palestine with purely religious motives, in order to live near the Jewish holy sites and the tombs of the prophets and tzadiks, and to perform prayers and rituals to hasten the coming of the Savior-Messiah. These Jews had no work to make a living, but were completely occupied in prayer and religious study. They lived on alms from abroad. Venice was the first city in which the Jewish community self-imposed a tax to help the rabbi of the city and his companions who had immigrated to Palestine.[166] This custom later spread so that the Jews of Palestine sent emissaries each year to their countries of origin to collect donations. These were brought to Palestine and divided (hence the name of this system: "halukah", division, in Hebrew) among their community. At the start of the 19th century, the roles changed again and the Jews abroad collected donations through special institutions[167] and sent them to Palestine. There, the funds were divided according to lists of Jewish community members and their family status.[168]

The foundations of the halukah system were not as simple as they first appeared. However, they soon found religious justification. Payment towards the halukah was presented as a form of charity that the Jews had to undertake, particularly towards their brethren in Palestine and their difficult conditions, as they had gone to live there according to the teachings of the Torah.[169] In addition, participation in financing the halukah was a form of fulfillment of the obligation to settle the Land of Israel. If most Jews could not fulfill this obligation themselves and move

---

166 Gat, *Ha-Yishuv ha-Yehudi be-Eretz Yisrael 1840-1881 (The Jewish Community in the Land of Israel in 1840-1881)*, p. 93.

167 Meir Menachem Rothschild, *Ha-Halukah (The Charity Division)*, pp. 16-18; see also Gat, *Ha-Yishuv ha-Yehudi be-Eretz Yisrael 1840-1881 (The Jewish Community in the Land of Israel in 1840-1881)*, pp. 93-100.

168 Malachi, *Prakim be-Toldot ha-Yishuv ha-Yashan (Chapters in the History of the Old Yishuv)*, pp. 98-104.

169 Rothschild, *Ha-Halukah (The Charity Division)*, pp. 30-33, 37.

there, there was no harm, at least, in helping their brethren who did. This assistance was also necessary for other reasons. In the religious view, the prayers of the Jewish people in the diaspora could only reach God if they were accompanied by the prayers of those in Palestine (the "Land of Israel"). Further, the religious view held that the presence and prayers of the Jews in the country preserved its sanctity, and that an increase in the number of Jews there was necessary to hasten the hour of redemption.[170] Those beliefs clearly strengthened this system, which determined the economic conditions of the Jews in Palestine at the time. About 85% of them lived on these donations.[171]

Expectedly, the halukah system had a negative social impact on its beneficiaries. The donations were distributed in such a way that the head of the family, who studied the Torah (a student rabbi), received a greater share than the others. This prompted fathers to marry off their sons at a very young age and urge them to engage in this study, which deepened their lethargy and kept them from doing any productive work. It even pushed them to confront others, at times, who tried to do so. This also provoked, to some extent, the reaction of the first Zionist immigrants to Palestine who distanced themselves from the "old Yishuv",[172] the Jews of the halukah, as the Zionists tended to engage in manual labor, interpreting their concept of "work" in an exaggerated manner. The halukah system also led to the division of the Jewish community. After the Ashkenazis separated from the Sephardic Jews, who remained in one community ("kollel"), the Ashkenazis split within themselves into 19 kollels,[173] according to their countries of origin. Each kollel controlled the donations received from its respective country. Competition and hatred rose among these kollels, even eclipsing the unfriendly relations

---

170   Ibid, pp. 44, 48, 53-55, 57.

171   Gat, *Ha-Yishuv ha-Yehudi be-Eretz Yisrael 1840-1881 (The Jewish Community in the Land of Israel in 1840-1881)*, p. 93.

172   "Yishuv" is a Hebrew word meaning "a settlement" or "settlement (v.)". It was figuratively applied to all the Zionist settlers in Palestine before the establishment of Israel, with their institutions and organizations.

173   Ibid, pp. 112-125.

that generally existed between Ashkenazi and Sephardic Jews.[174]

These deteriorating social conditions prompted some Jews in and outside the country to find alternative solutions, such as encouraging work in agriculture or crafts. Moses Montefiore, a wealthy Jewish man from a notable family in Britain, was the first to show interest in the situation of Jews in Palestine and work on improving it. He had done the same for the Jewish population in Russia, where he met the tsars twice to achieve this end, and in Marrakesh and Romania.[175] In 1840, some Jews in Damascus were accused of kidnapping and killing a monk to use his blood in Jewish religious rituals. (This "blood libel" claim, by which the Jews were accused of killing followers of other religions, especially Christians, was especially prevalent in Europe during the Middle Ages. It was used as justification for the persecution of Jews and inflicting harm on them.) After the "Damascus affair", Montefiore was able to meet the Ottoman sultan and obtain an edict to guarantee the protection of the Jews and the freedom to practice their religious beliefs[176] throughout the Ottoman Empire. This was achieved, according to the edict, after "examining" Jewish religious books and finding them free of any justification for that libel, and after it became clear that the accusation against the Jews in Damascus was a plot by French Christian missionaries in the city.[177]

Montefiore showed a marked interest in the conditions of the Jews in Palestine and visited it seven times between 1827-1875 to assess their situation and help them. (On his second visit, in 1839, he funded a census of the Jewish population there.[178]) In addition to granting financial aid and establishing schools, clinics and workshops for the Jewish population, Montefiore tried, in various ways, to transfer them to a productive work life,

---

174 Ibid, p. 32.

175 Shlomo Umberto Nahon, *Moshe Montefiori (Moses Montefiori)*, pp. 36-41, 45-55.

176 Ibid, see text of edict on pp. 32-34.

177 Ibid.

178 Ibid, pp. 66, 69.

especially in agriculture – a suggestion that the Jews themselves had made. This prompted him to think about leasing 200 villages in Palestine, with their land, from Muhammad Ali, the ruler of the country. Montefiore intended to settle the Jews on this land, then establish a company that would bring other Jews from Europe and settle them there as well. His attempts failed, however.[179]

Although Montefiore's activities did not greatly improve the conditions of the Jews in Palestine, some of his projects succeeded. On his fourth visit to the country, in 1855, he passed by Istanbul where he met the sultan for the second time and obtained another edict to purchase an area of land in Jerusalem, outside the city walls, to build a hospital.[180] However, Montefiore then amended his plans based on the advice of prominent members of the Jewish community in Jerusalem. They proposed the establishment of popular housing on that land, instead of a hospital, due to the overcrowding in the Jewish neighborhood inside the city walls. The construction of those dwellings began in 1859. The Ottoman authorities tried to stop the work, which contravened the instructions of the edict granted by the sultan to Montefiore. The British consul in Jerusalem then intervened and sought the help of their government, which instructed its ambassador in Istanbul to address the issue. Finally, an order was issued to allow construction to continue.[181] Through this act, Montefiore unknowingly laid the foundations of the first Jewish residential neighborhood in Palestine – in Jerusalem, in particular. This neighborhood came to be known as Yemin Moshe and formed the nucleus of the Jewish part of the city that was built outside its walls. The intervention of the British consul was a prelude to many more, and a harbinger of the role that Britain, during its mandate in Palestine, would play in supporting

---

179   Gat, *Ha-Yishuv ha-Yehudi be-Eretz Yisrael 1840-1881 (The Jewish Community in the Land of Israel in 1840-1881)*, pp. 64-66; Nahon, *Moshe Montefiori (Moses Montefiori)*, p. 66.

180   Nahon, *Moshe Montefiori (Moses Montefiori)*, p. 72.

181   Hyamson, *The British Consulate in Jerusalem, 1838-1914*, Vol. 1, pp. 261-267.

and protecting Zionism. By 1892, the Jews of Jerusalem had built eight other residential neighborhoods in the same part of the city,[182] partly with the help of the "Mazkeret Moshe" (Moses Montefiore Testimonial Fund). This was established in Montefiore's memory and headed by Yechiel Michel Pines.[183]

The French association, Alliance Israélite Universelle, was also active in this field. In 1868, it sent one of its founders, Charles Netter, to Palestine to study the situation of the Jewish population. In his report, Netter declared that "all those who have visited Palestine, before me, have reached the unanimous conclusion that only by working the land can our Jewish brothers be helped." He proposed the establishment of a "new institution, in which the new generation would be trained to work the land".[184] The Alliance decided to establish a school in Palestine to teach Jewish youth the foundations of modern agriculture, announcing that it would also work to settle its graduates on land that it would purchase for this purpose.[185] The association made contact with the Ottoman government and obtained an edict from the sultan, leasing it 2,600 dunums[186] of land that were cultivated by the Arab village of Yazur,[187] southeast of Jaffa. The land was to be used as long as the school was in existence, with no rental fees for the first ten years.[188] In 1870, the first Jewish agricultural school in Palestine, "Mikveh Israel" (Hope of Israel), was inaugurated on that land. The name was chosen from the Torah ("O Lord, the hope of Israel, all who forsake you shall be put to shame"[189]). The school worked tirelessly, although it could

---

182   Gat, *Ha-Yishuv ha-Yehudi be-Eretz Yisrael 1840-1881 (The Jewish Community in the Land of Israel in 1840-1881)*, pp. 286-300.

183   Ibid, pp. 300-302.

184   Yosef Shapira, *Meah Shana Mikveh Yisrael (Mikveh Israel: 100 Years)*, p. 65.

185   Ibid, pp. 67-68.

186   A dunum is an Ottoman unit of area. 1 dunum = 1,000 square meters or 1,200 square yards.

187   Ibid, p. 76.

188   Ibid, see text of edict on pp. 443-444.

189   *Torah*, Jeremiah 17:13.

not fulfill its promises to settle its graduates on land purchased for them. Generations of specialized agricultural workers graduated from the school, who were of immense help to the Zionist movement in implementing its settlement projects in Palestine. (In 1956, in appreciation of the services provided by Mikveh Israel, the Israeli government made an agreement with the Alliance, pledging to provide the school with land and other services in return for symbolic compensation. The agreement was for 99 years, renewable for another 99.[190])

Meanwhile, the Jews in Palestine did not stand idly by – especially since the call to improve their conditions and remove the dangers of the halukah system, by transferring them to a life of agricultural production, had initially come from their ranks. This call grew stronger after the spread of Hebrew newspapers, which were mainly used to air the disputes between supporters and opponents of the halukah.[191]

Hebrew printing had been introduced to Jerusalem in 1841. In 1863, a Hebrew newspaper was launched in the city.[192] It was edited by Yoel Moshe Solomon, a major opponent of the halukah system. Hebrew newspapers then began to appear in succession, such that, from 1863 to 1904, 25 newspapers and periodicals were issued in Jerusalem, though most of them only had a short duration.[193] The largest one, *Havatzelet (Lily;* 1870-1911), which was edited by Solomon, waged a long, bitter war on the halukah.[194] In his war with the old Yishuv and the halukah system, Solomon did not suffice with words. With two of his colleagues, he founded an association of a number of Jews in Jerusalem. The association aimed to purchase land, anywhere in Palestine, and establish an agricultural settlement. In 1878,

---

190   Ibid, see text of agreement on pp. 444-446.

191   Gat, *Ha-Yishuv ha-Yehudi be-Eretz Yisrael 1840-1881 (The Jewish Community in the Land of Israel in 1840-1881)*, p. 258.

192   Galia Yardeni, *Ha-Itonout ha-Ivrit be-Eretz Yisrael (Hebrew Press in the Land of Israel)*, pp. 17-19.

193   Ibid, pp. 420-424.

194   See also Gat, *Ha-Yishuv ha-Yehudi be-Eretz Yisrael 1840-1881 (The Jewish Community in the Land of Israel in 1840-1881)*, pp. 259-266.

Solomon was able to purchase 3,375 dunums from Mlabes village, about six miles (10 kilometers) east of Jaffa, from an Arab merchant named Salim Qassar. The purchase contract was signed in the presence of the Austrian consul in Jerusalem, as Solomon and his colleague, David Gutmann, were Austrian citizens. The following year, they purchased an additional 10,000 dunums near the first plot of land from another Jaffa merchant named Anton Bishara Tayan.[195] Some of the landowners then proceeded to construct buildings on part of the land and founded a settlement, "Petah Tikva", Door of Hope ("I will give her back her vineyards from there and make the valley of Achor a door of hope"[196]). However, most of the settlers were forced to leave Petah Tikva in 1881, about three years after its founding, due to disease that spread among them and losses that they suffered because of their lack of agricultural experience. The lands were then handed over to Arab farmers to cultivate. The settlement was only renewed after the arrival of the first Zionist immigrants from Russia,[197] some of whom bought parts of the land and settled there. The Ottoman authorities tried to stop the new construction works, due to the restrictions imposed on the entry of Jews into Palestine and their settlement in it. However, the Austrian consul intervened and managed to compel the authorities to retreat after he threatened to involve Bismarck himself.[198] Petah Tikva – "mother of the settlements", as it was later known – played an important role in shaping many Zionist concepts. It became a transit hub for the Jews of the Second Aliyah ("aliyah" is "immigration", in Hebrew) of 1904-1914, who came from Russia and Poland to various parts of Palestine. Based on the nature of relations between the settlement's residents and the Arab laborers that they employed, as well as the Jewish immigrants

---

[195] Shmuel Yavnieli, *Tkufat Hibbat Zion (Period of Lovers of Zion)*, Vol. 1, pp. 184-187; Gat, *Ha-Yishuv ha-Yehudi be-Eretz Yisrael 1840-1881 (The Jewish Community in the Land of Israel in 1840-1881)*, pp. 334-342.

[196] *Torah*, Hosea 2:17.

[197] Yavnieli, *Tkufat Hibbat Zion (Period of Lovers of Zion)*, Vol. 2, pp. 32-34.

[198] Eliav in Carpi, ed., *Ha-Tzionout (Zionism)*, Vol. 1, p. 71.

who arrived in it, the leaders of the Zionist labor wing developed many of their theories on building a Zionist entity in Palestine. One of these was "Hebrew labor", some concepts of which are still alive today (see Chapter 4, sections 4-6).

Solomon and his colleagues were not the only Jews in Jerusalem who were purchasing land before the start of Zionist immigration to the country. In 1860, 18 years before they had established Petah Tikva, a resident of Jerusalem, Shlomo Ezekiel Yehuda, took possession of part of the lands of the village of Qalunya, near Jerusalem. He had the help of James Finn, the British consul.[199] Yehuda seized those lands by circumventing the law, which did not allow foreign citizens to own land in Palestine. He paid the price of the land to its owners, then registered a mortgage on it with the British consul, with a value of about twice the price of the land, while he deposited statements with the sellers that he would not ask them to pay the mortgage,[200] so that he could use the land for an indefinite period of time. (The Zionist organizations resorted to similar methods to purchase land in Palestine after Britain issued its White Paper in 1939, which imposed restrictions on the sale of land to Jews.) In 1894, the settlement of Motsa was established on the land that Yehuda had seized (its name was later changed to Motsa Tah'tit, Lower Motsa).

The Jews of Safad followed suit. When the Jewish population in Jerusalem acquired the lands of Petah Tikva, the Safad Jews bought half the lands (about 4,000 dunums) of al-Ja'una village, near Safad, to cultivate them.[201]

In late 1881, some Jews in Jerusalem, at the initiative of Yechiel Michel Pines – head of the Moses Montefiore Testimonial Fund – and Eliezer Ben-Yehuda – "reviver" of the Hebrew language – established a secret company to purchase land in Palestine. They

---

199 Gat, *Ha-Yishuv ha-Yehudi be-Eretz Yisrael 1840-1881 (The Jewish Community in the Land of Israel in 1840-1881)*, pp. 49-50, 90, 335.

200 Hyamson, *The British Consulate in Jerusalem, 1838-1914*, Vol. 2, pp. 312-313.

201 Yavnieli, *Tkufat Hibbat Zion (Period of Lovers of Zion)*, Vol. 1, pp. 7-9, 96-98; Gat, *Ha-Yishuv ha-Yehudi be-Eretz Yisrael 1840-1881 (The Jewish Community in the Land of Israel in 1840-1881)*, pp. 342-343.

called this company "T'hiyat Yisrael" (Renaissance of Israel),

> because there will be no redemption for the Land [of Israel] unless one, secret company is established whose nature and objectives the Arabs do not know, which can purchase land at any time, in any place where it finds it, regardless of whether the land is good or bad, or of benefit, now or later. Only in this way shall we be the masters of the country, when most of its lands are in our hands.[202]

Despite this statement, however, the company failed to carry out any activity in this regard.

The purchase of land in Palestine did not lead to tangible progress in the economic and social conditions of the old Yishuv. The initial achievements of the Yishuv, however, became a cornerstone to build on for the vanguards of Zionist settlers, who began to arrive in Palestine in the early 1880s.

---

202   Malachi, *Prakim be-Toldot ha-Yishuv ha-Yashan (Chapters in the History of the Old Yishuv)*, p. 195.

1. Pioneers of Zionism: Early Thinkers (1862-1884)

1

The Zionist idea of returning the Jews to Palestine and establishing an internationally recognized state was not born in the 19th century, although it developed rapidly then. The history of Zionism dates back nearly two centuries prior. In the 17th and 18th centuries, many Jewish and other figures took up this idea, for various reasons, and called for its realization.[1] Some attempted to propagate early Zionist thought in the 1830s. Others issued their call publicly in the early 1860s. However, they all met with failure,[2] mainly due to the lack of objective conditions in the Jewish and international arenas for the realization of such an idea. Zionism found no means of implementation until the 1880s, when the idea took hold among the Jews of Russia, Poland and Romania.

Prior to this period, during the Middle Ages and even before, religious movements had appeared among the Jews from time to time, in various countries, calling for their immigration to Palestine (the "Land of Israel"), and some of their religious leaders had immigrated there. This led some historians of Zionism to claim that their movement was an ancient one, almost as old as Judaism itself. A closer look, however, reveals no clear, objective relationship between the Zionist idea – with

---

1   For details, see Nahum Sokolow, *History of Zionism, 1600-1918*, Vol. 1, pp. 40-46, 55-59, 91-94, 133-139, 176-183, 202-212 and 241-247; Moshe Medzini, *Ha-Mediniut ha-Tzionit (Zionist Policy)*, pp. 21-48.

2   Jacob Katz, "An Explanation of the Missionary Concept of Zionism", in Ben-Zion Dinur (Dinaburg), ed., *Shivat Tzion (Return to Zion)*, Vol. 1, pp. 91-105.

1. Pioneers of Zionism

its concept of establishing a Jewish state in Palestine – and the attempts made by some Jewish groups or individuals to return to Palestine and to live near its Jewish holy sites. There is also no relationship between the Zionist idea and the calls made by some enterprising non-Jews to establish a Jewish state in the Levant. Thus, the history of Zionism, which gave birth to the State of Israel, in its political and social concept, began – in theory, at least – in the late 1830s.

The first Jewish figure to call for the establishment of a Jewish state in Palestine was Judah al-Kalai (1798-1878). Of Sephardic origin, he was the rabbi of Semlin (today's Zemun), near Belgrade.[3] In the late 1830s, al-Kalai called for the settlement of Jews in Palestine and published a book in 1839 explaining his views.[4] From the outset, he was mired in the mysteries of the Kabbalah, where, based on his calculations, he concluded that 1840 was the year of redemption of the Jews. When this did not transpire, he changed his mind – declaring that redemption could not happen in one instance, but that hard work had to be done to attain it.[5]

> God, in His blessed name, has commanded that our repentance be fulfilled through our awakening, in order to raise our value to Him. When God sees ... our desire to repent in glory of His name, even if as much as a needle's eye, He will send us His help and open the door wide, and then send the Messiah-King... We cannot wait until the Messiah appears ... and returns us to Jerusalem ... where we shall hear the trumpet blowing in the Galilee, and our feet shall stand on the Mount of Olives, and then repent... These are thoughts

---

[3] For a review of Rabbi al-Kalai's views and activities, see Jacob Katz, "Messianism and Nationalism in the Teachings of Rabbi Judah al-Kalai", in Dinur, ed., *Shivat Tzion (Return to Zion)*, Vol. 4, pp. 9-41, and Vols. 2-3, pp. 42-62.

[4] Zvi Zahavi, *Mi ha-Hatam Sofer ad Herzl (From the Hatam Sofer to Herzl)*, p. 150.

[5] Katz in Dinur, ed., *Shivat Tzion (Return to Zion)*, Vol. 4, p. 14.

planted in our hearts by Satan in order to deny us this grace."[6]

With this stance, al-Kalai openly called on the Jews to undertake special efforts to reassemble themselves in Palestine, attacking the prevailing religious jurisprudence that was contrary to his views.[7]

According to al-Kalai, the Jews were to be redeemed in practice by their notables, who "have no limits to their abilities ... whether in external influence or internal decisiveness. There are no limits preventing these notables from asking the leaders of countries to allow us to return to our country and to the land of our ancestors."[8] Al-Kalai did not doubt the fulfillment of these requests by the leaders of the major powers, for they all "love truth and integrity, and would all agree that it is fair to restore what is right to its path".[9] Al-Kalai also urged the Jews to accept his jurisprudence by drawing their attention to the activity of the national movement that he witnessed in Europe: "The spirit of the age obliges all peoples to attain their independence and revive their language, and it demands from us that we establish our entity ... and revive our sacred language."[10] He thus stressed the need to renew the Hebrew language and standardize its use, for "the nation, gathered in the country, would not succeed without a common language."[11] To this end, he wrote a book to teach the Hebrew language and its grammar.[12] In addition to spreading his views theoretically, through the books and pamphlets that he published from time to time, al-Kalai also took action, making several visits to Britain and to western European countries to spread his call among Jewish communities and to elicit the views

---

6   Zahavi, *Mi ha-Hatam Sofer ad Herzl (From the Hatam Sofer to Herzl)*, pp. 157-158.

7   Ibid, pp. 166, 169.

8   Katz in Dinur, ed., *Shivat Tzion (Return to Zion)*, Vol. 4, p. 16.

9   Ibid.

10 Ibid, p. 37.

11 Ibid, p. 34.

12 Zahavi, *Mi ha-Hatam Sofer ad Herzl (From the Hatam Sofer to Herzl)*, pp. 135, 169.

1. Pioneers of Zionism

of the rulers on his project, with the possibility of providing him with assistance.[13] He also tried to establish settlements in Palestine, alone and with the help of others, but did not succeed. In his last days, he immigrated there and died in Jerusalem. Al-Kalai is said to have had a good relationship with the family of Theodor Herzl, founder of the Zionist Organization.[14] Al-Kalai's teachings may have planted the seeds of Zionism in the young Herzl's heart, during the former's stay with Herzl's family in Hungary.[15]

Based on his writings, al-Kalai is considered to be one of the pioneers of Zionist thought. He influenced one of his compatriots, Zvi Hirsch Kalischer (1795-1874), who published a Hebrew book, in 1862, titled *Drishat Zion* (*Seeking Zion*), which expanded on al-Kalai's views. In the same year, another book, *Rome and Jerusalem*, was published by Moses Hess and promoted similar views. The two authors represented the twin main cultural, environmental and thought currents that prevailed among the Jews at the time: Kalischer was a traditional Orthodox Jew while Hess belonged to the "intellectual" Jewish class (Maskilim). The two books are considered among the basic literature of Zionism. They became, each in its environment, the forerunners of Zionist intellectual currents that quickly found recipients to adopt, develop, and implement them.

In the last 50 years of his life, Zvi Hirsch Kalischer, rabbi of the Jewish community in Thorn, in then Prussia, was one of the first Orthodox Zionist thinkers to publicly express their views and try to implement them. Kalischer began his activity in the early 1830s, when he visited a member of the wealthy Jewish Rothschild family in Paris and suggested that they purchase Palestine from its ruler, Muhammad Ali, to establish settlements for Jewish immigrants from eastern Europe.[16] About half a

---

13 Ibid, pp. 158-164.

14 This was founded in Basel in 1897. Since 1960, it has been known as the World Zionist Organization.

15 Ibid, p. 178.

16 Abraham Yitzchak Bromberg, "Miholelei ha-Tzionit ha-Datit be-Tk-

century later, Herzl undertook a similar mission. Kalischer, like Herzl afterwards, found no response to his request, but this did not deter him. He went to Montefiore and proposed the same project.[17] Later, Kalischer cooperated with the Alliance Israélite Universelle, the Jewish French organization that established an agricultural school, Mikveh Israel, near Jaffa in Palestine (see Introduction, sections 3 and 7). He also cooperated with other Jewish associations, formed in Frankfurt and Berlin, that aimed to settle Jews in Palestine.[18] He published a book in 1862, *Seeking Zion*, in which he called for a general conference of Jewish notables to establish "an association for settlement of the Land of Israel", whose primary mission would be to finance the settlement of Jews in Palestine[19] and to establish a state for them there. In his address, Kalischer stressed the need for the Jews to follow in the footsteps of other peoples,

> whose blood and possessions are freely given for the love of their country ... like the inhabitants of Italy and the people of Poland ... and Hungary... We should be ashamed of ourselves, for we do not work to commemorate our forefathers and glorify our God, who chose Zion as His abode.[20]

The views of Kalischer, in which he proposed a solution to the Jewish question by settling the Jews in Palestine and creating their own state there, did not differ much from the views held by the rabbis of his time or their religious jurisprudence regarding the relationship of the Jews to the "Land of Israel". Like the other rabbis, Kalischer viewed "the relationship between the Jews and the Land of Israel [and the Torah]" as an eternal, divine

---

ufat Shivat Tsion (Initiators of Religious Zionism during the Return of Zion)", in Simon Federbusch, ed., *Hazon Torah ve Tzion (The Vision of Torah and Zion)*, pp. 35-37.

17 Ibid, pp. 37-38, 55.

18 Ibid, pp. 57, 63.

19 Zvi Hirsch Kalischer, *Drishat Zion (Seeking Zion)*, pp. 88, 115, 119, 175-176.

20 Ibid, pp. 79, 179.

1. Pioneers of Zionism

one that could not be severed.[21] Like the other rabbis, too, he believed that immigration to the Land of Israel and settlement in it, before any other country, was a duty that faithful Jewish people had to fulfill.[22] He then added to these views the idea of calling on Jews to take matters into their own hands and to work to fulfill this duty through human effort. Until the emergence of Kalischer, Jewish religious jurisprudence and traditions had stipulated that a state gathering the Jewish diaspora would come into being with the appearance of the Savior-Messiah, who would save the Jews and unite them in the Land of Israel when the world neared its end, before the Apocalypse. Those who yearned for the hour of redemption and hoped to contribute to it had to offer their prayers and supplications to God, asking Him to hasten the sending of His Messiah. Efforts to establish a Jewish state through human effort, however, were initially viewed as blasphemy, for the establishment of such a state was considered a kind of "pressure" on the Savior-Messiah, forcing him to appear before he was due, and, thus, "pushing for the end of the world" ("d'hikat ha-ketz", in Hebrew) ahead of the predicted time.

The renewal of these views by Kalischer was thus no easy feat, especially in an Orthodox Jewish society that was suspicious of any call for the establishment of a Jewish state for fear of becoming a fake messianic movement. Thus he did not dare to put forth his own jurisprudence in *Seeking Zion* until he had presented dozens of pages of quotes from the Talmud and the writings of Jewish sages who had preceded him, which, in his opinion, supported his point of view. Upon reaching the crux of his argument, he explicitly declared that "reason and religious law oblige every Jew to work with courage, determination and strength ... to settle in the Land of Israel,"[23] and that the process of gathering the Jews, settling them there, and building the country should be considered the beginning of redemption

---

21 Ibid, p. 181.

22 Ibid, pp. 77, 83-84.

23 Ibid, p. 86.

("atchalta de'geula", in Hebrew).[24] According to Kalischer, it was wrong to believe that the Savior-Messiah would automatically appear to save the Jews, and it was not sufficient to pray to hasten his arrival. Rather, they had to help him by starting to gather themselves in the Land of Israel.[25]

This jurisprudence of Kalischer and al-Kalai was the first stage of a current of thought within Judaism that drew its strength from traditional religious teachings and combined them with the necessary political means to fulfill its obligations. This current grew in strength and later came to be known as religious Zionism.[26] Its advocates continued to issue occasional religious decrees to ease the way for Orthodox Jews to work with secular Zionists in their endeavors to establish a Jewish state in Palestine, and even to compel the Orthodox Jews to keep pace with the secular Zionists in all aspects of this activity.[27]

Although the views of Kalischer and al-Kalai did not receive the full support of Zionist rabbis who succeeded them, they were sufficient to compel those rabbis to present their own views, which helped strengthen the intellectual foundations of religious Zionism.[28] Kalischer and al-Kalai's views pushed many Orthodox Jewish masses in Russia to implement this jurisprudence practically, through their own means.[29] The rising pressure and campaigns of persecution against the Jews in tsarist Russia in the early 1880s, after the assassination of the tsar, led many Jews to believe that the only solution was to leave the country, and the jurisprudence of Kalischer and al-Kalai – which considered immigration to Palestine and settlement in it to be a fulfillment of religious duty – tempted many to make their way there. From these Orthodox masses came most of the Jewish

---

24 Ibid, p. 114.

25 Ibid, pp. 90, 117.

26 See also Jacob Katz, "Rabbi Zvi Hirsch Kalischer's Historical Character", in Dinur, ed., *Shivat Tzion (Return to Zion)*, Vols. 2-3, pp. 26-41.

27 Arieh Tartakower, *Am ve Olamo (A People and its World)*, pp. 160-162.

28 Katz in Dinur, ed., *Shivat Tzion (Return to Zion)*, Vol. 4, p. 41.

29 Ibid.

immigrants to Palestine in 1880-1900. They laid the foundations of Zionist settlement and paved the way for the later activity of the Zionist Organization.

As Kalischer's book was published, Moses Hess was writing the final chapters of his book, *Rome and Jerusalem*. Influenced by the triumph of the liberation and unity movement in Italy, Hess examined the conditions of the Jews in light of this triumph (hence the title of the book). In his hometown of Bonn, Germany, Hess had received a Talmudic education, like Kalischer and al-Kalai. However, as a young man he had distanced himself from that environment and assimilated into German, then European, society. By the early 1840s, Hess was working hard to organize labor movements in Germany and to spread socialist ideas (he was thus dubbed "the Red Rabbi"). In this sphere, he occasionally cooperated with Karl Marx and Friedrich Engels, but then fell into dispute with them and wandered from one European country to another.[30]

As evident in his writings, and despite his activity in labor movements and his sympathy with the liberation movements that he witnessed, Hess did not forget the Talmudic education of his youth. This education returned to a prominent position in his mind with his rising feeling of hatred towards the German society in which he had grown up, especially due to its anti-Semitic tendencies. At the same time, his admiration grew for France in its positions and policies, a feeling he expressed more than once in *Rome and Jerusalem*, heaping praise on France in an exaggerated manner.[31] Hess declared that "springtime in the life of nations began with the French Revolution… There began the regeneration of those nations which had acquired their national historical religion only through the influence of Judaism,"[32] while "fortified by its racial instinct and by its cultural and historical

---

30   Yehiel Halpern, *Ha-Mahpicha ha-Yehudit (The Jewish Revolution)*, Vol. 1, pp. 226-247.

31   Moses Hess, *Rome and Jerusalem*, pp. 49-51, 65, 68, 79-80, 107, 130, 138 and 141.

32   Ibid, pp. 35, 123.

mission to unite all humanity in the name of the Eternal Creator, this [Jewish] people has conserved its nationality in the form of its religion and united both inseparably with the memories of its ancestral land."[33]

Hess continued to present his ideas, attacking both "the nihilism of the Reformers, which never learned anything, and the staunch conservatism of the Orthodox, which never forgot anything".[34] In his writing, he intensified his attacks on the Reformists and Maskilim followers of Mendelssohn, "those modern Jews", who measured a person's degree of culture and enlightenment by the extent of his abandonment of Jewish values, and who finally joined the state services, in Hess's view, by showing a certificate of baptism [conversion to Christianity] as their diploma, believing their Judaism to be "more of a misfortune than a religion".[35] At the same time, Hess praised Judaism in terms not very different from those used by the traditional rabbis, declaring that he recognized a single religious fellowship, to "the old Synagogue, which is fortunately still in existence and will, I hope, exist until the national regeneration of world Jewry is accomplished".[36] When presenting his solutions to the Jewish question, Hess declared that European peoples had always considered the existence of Jews amongst them an anomaly and, thus, their hatred of the Jews would remain, no matter to what extent the Jews tried to change. He argued that "if it were true that Jewish emancipation in exile is incompatible with Jewish nationality, then it were the duty of the Jews to sacrifice the former for the sake of the latter."[37]

Based on these assumptions, Hess believed that the practical way to attain a solution to the Jewish question was to establish a Jewish state,

---

33 Ibid, p. 35.
34 Ibid, p. 38.
35 Ibid, pp. 97, 145.
36 Ibid, pp. 88, 121.
37 Ibid, pp. 55, 66-67.

1. Pioneers of Zionism

first, to keep alive the hope of the political rebirth of our people, and next, to reawaken that hope where it slumbers. When political conditions in the Orient shape themselves so as to permit the organization of a beginning of the restoration of a Jewish State, this beginning will express itself in the founding of Jewish colonies in the land of their ancestors.[38]

This project, according to Hess, would undoubtedly gain the support of France, because it would be in its interest to implement it. He also believed that other European countries would not oppose the project, which would rid them of their Jewish residents.[39] Hess clarified that the proposed state would not include, in any case, all the Jews of the world, because, even in the past, they had not all gathered in one state when it was established, despite the fact that the borders of this state would "extend from Suez to Jerusalem, and from the banks of the Jordan to the coast of the Mediterranean … [where] all Jewish classes will meet, Orthodox and progressive, rich and poor".[40] At the end of his address, Hess declared that

the hour has struck for the [Jewish] resettlement of the banks of the Jordan… You should be the bearers of civilization to the primitive people of Asia … the mediators between Europe and far Asia, open the roads that lead to India and China – those unknown regions which must ultimately be thrown open to civilization.

He then advised the Jews to "become, then, the educators of the wild Arabian hordes and the African peoples… Let the … Quran and the Gospels group themselves around your Bible."[41] At the end of his book, Hess did not neglect to praise Kalischer and his

---

38   Ibid, p. 129.

39   Ibid, pp. 129, 132, 142, 147-150.

40   Ibid, pp. 103, 133, 153.

41   Ibid, pp. 139-140.

views, after someone had drawn his attention to them.[42]

Hess, however, made no practical effort to realize his vision, alone or with others. After publishing *Rome and Jerusalem*, he promptly returned to his old work in organizing labor movements and spreading socialist teachings. His book did not receive much attention at the outset, although the Zionists would later classify it as one of their classic writings and consider him to be among the first to coin what they termed "Jewish nationalism".[43] It is worth mentioning that there are many similarities between the views and beliefs cited by Hess in *Rome and Jerusalem* and Herzl's statements in his book, *The Jewish State*, which was published 34 years later – although Herzl read Hess's book four years after publishing his own.

At any rate, the teachings of Kalischer, al-Kalai and their followers, as well as the views of Hess, remained in a state of stagnation for nearly two decades. They were then revived with the beginning of Jewish emigration from Russia in the early 1880s.

2

As mentioned in the previous chapter (see Introduction, section 4), in 1881-1882, important events transpired in Russia that significantly impacted its Jewish population, which then formed the largest Jewish community worldwide. On March 1, 1881, a group of Russians, including a Jewish woman, assassinated Tsar Alexander II, despite his "liberal" policy towards the Jews and others. This led to a reactionary sweep in Russia, whose tsarist authorities persecuted those in opposition with extreme cruelty. Tsar Alexander III, who succeeded Alexander II, was of a puritanical mindset, subject to the influence of reactionaries within the Russian clergy around him. The Jews in Russia strongly felt that reaction, especially as many of their intellectuals were active members of the revolutionary organizations that opposed

---

42   Ibid, pp. 153-155.

43   See also Jacob Leib Talmon, *Israel Among the Nations*, pp. 94-103.

tsarist rule.[44] After the tsar's assassination, in the period between April 1881 and June 1882, they suffered a wave of pogroms and organized attacks by the Russian population,[45] including murder, robbery, expulsion from their places of residence and burning their homes. The scale of attacks intensified, hitting more than 100 Jewish communities in Russian cities and villages, and spreading to Poland as well.[46] The tsarist authorities took no significant measures to stop or limit the attacks, possibly even abetting them and covering up for their perpetrators.

The pogroms had a great – perhaps decisive – effect on strengthening the Zionist idea and pushing it from thought into action. In fact, it seems that the Zionist movement would not have gained prominence and developed such momentum had these events not occurred.[47] The widening scope of these pogroms, and the harsh, primitive methods with which they were perpetrated, over more than a year, provoked deep reactions among Russian Jews of all classes.[48] One result was the start of a widespread debate on the feasibility of remaining in Russia, then the emergence of ideas calling for emigration from the country to the United States or to Palestine.[49] Practical steps were then taken in this regard, and numerous associations established to work on the emigration of their members. The result was the beginning of a large wave of Jewish emigration from Russia, most of which headed to the United States, while a small portion immigrated to Palestine, establishing the first Jewish settlements in the country. Meanwhile, other Jews in Russia, waiting for

---

44 See also Simon Dubnow, *Divrei Yemei Am Olam (History of the Jews)*, p. 665.

45 Shmuel Yavnieli, *Tkufat Hibbat Zion (Period of Lovers of Zion)*, Vol. 1, pp. 14-15.

46 Dubnow, *Divrei Yemei Am Olam (History of the Jews)*, p. 667; see also Moshe Shmueli, *Toldot ha-Tzionout ve Tnu'at ha-Avoda (History of Zionism and the Labor Movement)*, Vol. 1, p. 61.

47 Israel Klausner, *Ha-Tnu'ah le-Tzion be-Rusia (Zionist Movement in Russia)*, Vol. 1: *Be-Hit'orer Am (When a People Awakens)*, pp. 91-93.

48 Yavnieli, *Tkufat Hibbat Zion (Period of Lovers of Zion)*, Vol. 1, pp. 19-20, 35.

49 Ibid, pp. 40-41.

conditions to allow them to immigrate to Palestine as well, were uniting to form what became known as the Hovevei Zion (Lovers of Zion) movement.[50]

Lovers of Zion would also not have grown, and Jewish emigration from Russia would not have continued, had the tsarist authorities not continued their measures against the Jews, which made it clear that the pogroms of 1881-1882 were not incidental or transient events. In January 1882, before the pogroms had ended, the Russian interior minister told a delegation of Russian Jewish notables, who had come to meet him to elucidate the government's position and request additional protection for vulnerable Jews, that "Russia's western borders are open to the Jews"[51] to immigrate to Europe and the United States, and that the restrictions imposed on their Pale of Settlement would remain in effect. The minister stated that the Russian government would agree to any request for the establishment of a body to oversee the emigration of Jews from Russia, and would not allow those emigres to return.[52] This announcement of intention of the Russian government was only a prelude to a new era of oppressive policy against its Jewish population. In early May of the same year, the Russian authorities issued a set of "temporary laws" (which remained in effect for 35 years, until their abolishment in 1917, after the Russian Revolution) which prohibited Jewish people from living outside cities, and canceled any mortgage bonds and real estate rentals they had outside the cities[53] in order to prevent the "exploitation" of Russian villagers. The laws also prohibited Jews from engaging in commerce on Sundays and Christian holidays.

The tsarist authorities did not stop at these measures, which raised the population density among the Jews in places that were already overcrowded, and worsened their economic

---

50 Klausner, *Ha-Tnu'ah le-Tzion be-Rusia (Zionist Movement in Russia)*, Vol. 1, pp. 91-93.

51 See ibid, p. 133 and sources mentioned.

52 Ibid.

53 Dubnow, *Divrei Yemei Am Olam (History of the Jews)*, p. 671.

1. Pioneers of Zionism

conditions. Further measures were intermittently taken against them. In July 1887, the authorities limited the number of Jews who were allowed to enroll in Russian universities to 3-10% of the total number of students in those universities.[54] The law was even implemented in areas where the Jews were a majority. These measures prompted large numbers of Jewish students to seek education in western European countries, where they contributed to the establishment of Zionist organizations, from which – in time – a number of the major Zionist leaders emerged. In February 1891, Jewish people began to be expelled from Moscow and, later, their merchants were banned from moving to the city.[55] In 1892, a municipalities law was issued that prohibited Jews from voting or nominating themselves for the councils of municipalities where they lived.[56] At the same time, the attacks and pogroms against them continued, intermittently, in various parts of Russia, especially in 1884, 1891-1892, 1897, 1899, 1902 and 1906.

The result of these measures was continued Jewish emigration from Russia. During 1881-1904, about 1.5 million Jews left Russia and other eastern European countries, especially Romania. Most went to the United States, while a small part, estimated at 25,000-30,000, arrived in Palestine[57] – though some of them left it later. This wave of Jewish immigration to Palestine, known as the First Aliyah, would intensify when the conditions of the Jews in Russia worsened. Thus, the number of immigrants rose during 1881-1882, 1886 and 1891-1892, when political and economic pressures mounted against them.[58] After 1906, the number of immigrants dropped.

---

54   Ibid, p. 672.

55   Ibid, pp. 674-675, 678.

56   Ibid, p. 677.

57   Dinur, ed., *Shivat Tzion (Return to Zion)*, Vol. 1, p. 29; see also Moshe Braslavski, *Tnu'at ha-Poalim ha-Eretz Yisraelit (Labor Movement in the Land of Israel)*, Vol. 1, pp. 17-18.

58   Klausner, *Ha-Tnu'ah le-Tzion be-Rusia (Zionist Movement in Russia)*, Vol. 2-3: *Me-Katowice ad Basel (From Katowice to Basel)*, Vol. 2, pp. 140-142; Vol. 3, pp. 13-16.

As waves of Jewish emigres were pouring out of Russia, some Russian Jewish intellectuals, the Maskilim, affected by the official anti-Jewish policy, began to reconsider their previous position in which they had called for a solution to the Jewish question by integrating the Jews in Russian society and pushing for them to become ordinary Russian citizens. Those intellectuals gradually began to adopt the stance of their opponents, the rabbis who were calling for the immigration of Jews to Palestine instead of remaining in Russia.[59] In the early 1880s, before the attacks and pogroms against the Jews, the Jewish Maskilim in Russia had formed a distinct group that was particularly active in literature and journalism in Russian and Hebrew. Most, if not all, of those Maskilim believed that the effective means to reform the conditions of the Jews in Russia and to raise their standard of living was to work on spreading knowledge, or "haskalah", among them, and to teach them the Russian language to bring them closer to Russian culture and integrate them in society, as well as transforming Jewish life from unemployment and poverty to work and productivity.[60] Further, some Maskilim called for reforming the Jewish religion as a preliminary step towards improving the conditions of the Jews in general. They opposed both the "Orthodox, puritanical in their religion", who, in order to preserve this state, "had no qualms about keeping the situation of the Jews as it was in the Middle Ages", and the assimilated intellectuals, who "turned away from their people and neglected them", refusing to help solve their problems. Many Jewish intellectuals, on the other hand, had joined the revolutionary movements of that time in Russia, through their belief in the need to reform the conditions of governance in the country, overall, as a precondition to reforming the conditions of its Jews.

Despite these views of the Maskilim community, however, the idea of a solution to the Jewish question by establishing a

---

59 Klausner, *Ha-Tnu'ah le-Tzion be-Rusia (Zionist Movement in Russia)*, Vol. 1, pp. 94-100, 104-118, 135-155.

60 Ibid, p. 65.

1. Pioneers of Zionism

Jewish state persisted among them. In 1863, for example, David Gordon, influenced by Kalischer and Hess, wrote a series of articles in his newspaper, *ha-Magid*,[61] putting forth his view that the Jews were strangers in the diaspora, and that their denial of their religious and national values would not help them.[62] After reviewing the measures taken by some Jewish organizations in France, Britain and Russia for the settlement of Jews in Palestine, Gordon declared that, as a first step, the Jews must purchase land in Palestine to establish Jewish villages there, and that they must work together to achieve this goal.[63] In the late 1860s, notably in 1867-1869, when a wave of Jewish emigration began from the Pale of Settlement to inner Russia, especially to the Jewish areas in the south of the country and elsewhere, due to the poor economic conditions of the Jews, Gordon was among the first advocates for them not to immigrate inwardly in Russia, nor to the United States, but specifically to Palestine.[64]

Meanwhile, efforts continued to strengthen the Jewish presence in Palestine and support the Jewish minority that lived there. In 1874, as mentioned in the previous chapter (see Introduction, section 7), the Moses Montefiore Testimonial Fund was established in Britain on the occasion of Montefiore's 90th birthday. The fund aimed to improve the living conditions of the Jews in Palestine by encouraging them to engage in agricultural work, crafts and trade, and building homes for them. The fund, however, was unable to fulfill its promise, as there was little response to appeals to Jewish populations in the west for donations. In addition, the fund managers were slow to carry out concrete activities in Palestine. It took them nearly two years to elect their representative, the Russian rabbi Yechiel Michel Pines,

---

61 Shmueli, *Toldot ha-Tzionout ve Tnu'at ha-Avoda (History of Zionism and the Labor Movement)*, Vol. 1, p. 47.

62 Klausner, *Ha-Tnu'ah le-Tzion be-Rusia (Zionist Movement in Russia)*, Vol. 1, p. 39.

63 Ibid, p. 40.

64 Ibid, pp. 42, 77-79.

and send him to the country, only to arrive two years later in 1878.[65] Despite this, the establishment of this fund helped to keep alive the idea of settling the Jews in Palestine. At the same time, there was widespread discussion in Jewish newspapers – especially *ha-Magid* and *ha-Tsfira* in Russia, *ha-Levanon* in Palestine, and *The Jewish Chronicle* in Britain – of a project presented by Haim Guedalla, nephew of Moses Montefiore, to purchase land in Palestine for the settlement of Jews. Guedalla had proposed that this be done in exchange for the payment of Turkish government debts to foreign financiers. A similar discussion also ensued in the novel *Daniel Deronda*, published by the English writer Mary Ann Evans under the pen name of George Eliot in 1876, calling for the return of the Jews to Palestine and the establishment of a state for them there.[66] This discussion lasted for more than a year, generating great interest among Jewish circles in Russia.[67] In 1878, a pamphlet was issued in Vienna – allegedly by the Russian Jewish poet, Judah Leib Gordon – calling for a solution to the Jewish question "by returning the Jews to the Land of Israel, so that they may reestablish the Jewish state there, and, in this way, the Jewish question would be solved, naturally, like any common national problem".[68] This pamphlet was issued in an attempt to influence the Congress of Berlin, which was held during that year and recognized the independence of Romania, Serbia and Bulgaria, and to oblige these countries to work on solving the Jewish question within them as a condition for achieving their independence. This attempt failed, however. In 1880, an enterprising British journalist named Laurence Oliphant published *The Land of Gilead*, in which he called for the establishment of a Jewish state east of the Jordan River.

---

65   Ibid, pp. 45-47; see also Shmueli, *Toldot ha-Tzionout ve Tnu'at ha-Avoda (History of Zionism and the Labor Movement)*, Vol. 1, pp. 51-52.

66   Editor's note: *Daniel Deronda* and the Zionism of George Eliot are discussed in detail by Ghassan Kanafani, notably on pages 35-40, in *On Zionist Literature*, the first book published in this Liberated Texts series (Ebb, 2022).

67   Klausner, *Ha-Tnu'ah le-Tzion be-Rusia (Zionist Movement in Russia)*, Vol. 1, pp. 51-59.

68   Ibid, p. 61.

1. Pioneers of Zionism

These activities only caught the attention of a small group of Maskilim, however. Most of them retained their previous positions, calling for a solution to the Jewish problem in Russia to be found inside Russia itself, until the first wave of attacks and pogroms took place against the Jews in 1881-1882, forcing them to reconsider. Initially, they were stunned by what had happened, especially as large numbers of Russians had taken part in these attacks. Then, the Maskilim were disappointed by the tolerant attitude of the authorities towards the perpetrators.[69] Hence, it was not long before those Maskilim abandoned their positions, which sought to improve the conditions of the Jews in Russia, and moved to adopt the call for immigration to Palestine or elsewhere. They then worked to promote this idea, organize its operations and take leadership of the Lovers of Zion movement that emerged from it. This was accompanied by attempts to justify this immigration process and by new theories to solve the Jewish question, which were later considered to be foundational to Zionist thought. Four Russian Jewish Maskilim were prominent in this regard: Peretz Smolenskin, Moshe Leib Lilienblum, Judah Leib (Leon) Pinsker, and Eliezer Ben-Yehuda.

3

Peretz Smolenskin (1842-1885) was a Russian Jewish Maskil writer. From the outset, he joined the Haskalah camp despite his traditional Talmudic upbringing. At an early age, he moved to Odessa where he wrote articles and short stories for *ha-Meletz* newspaper. He immigrated to Vienna in 1868 where he became editor-in-chief of *ha-Shahar* magazine, a post he held until his death. The magazine criticized both the old-fashioned, Orthodox Jewish way of life and the Maskilim who called for assimilation and attempted to repudiate their brethren.[70] Smolenskin published novels and stories around the conditions

---

[69] See also Shmueli, *Toldot ha-Tzionout ve Tnu'at ha-Avoda (History of Zionism and the Labor Movement)*, Vol. 1, pp. 62-66.

[70] See his article, "Crimes of the Haskalah", in Peretz Smolenskin, *Peretz Smolenskin – Mivhar Ma'amarav (Peretz Smolenskin, Selected Articles)*, pp. 37-43.

and problems of the Jews, through his view of them as a distinct nationality. Some came to call him "the father of the idea of Jewish nationality".[71]

Smolenskin defined his position on the Jewish question by stating: "The Jewish people are a four-thousand-year-old riddle ... walking amongst other peoples who view them ... as a large, frightening animal..."[72] Thus, "all peoples despise the Jewish people, in their hearts, because their religion and beliefs are different from their counterparts, with respect to any other people."[73] Smolenskin believed that anti-Semitism was eternal and implanted in the hearts of all peoples, because the Jews were strangers in the countries in which they lived, with no homeland, and aroused the hatred of others for religious and economic reasons. He argued that, were religious hatred to diminish, then ethnic hatred would take its place, for even the opponents of anti-Semitism wanted to eliminate the Jews, in their own way, by "reforming" them.[74] In his view, the Jews would also not have benefited from the progress of humanity, nor from the spread of socialism, for the socialists also hated them.[75]

Smolenskin addressed internal Jewish affairs and stressed that many of the problems faced by the Jews in Russia were the result of their lack of education.[76] While he criticized them for not responding to the reforms that the Russian government had tried to install, he also blamed the government which had failed to treat them properly and had considered them citizens only by duties, not by rights.[77] Smolenskin added that the basis of the Jews' affliction was the existence of two conflicting currents

---

71 Israel Klausner, *Hibbat Tzion be-Romania (Lovers of Zion in Romania)*, p. 9.

72 Smolenskin, *Peretz Smolenskin – Mivhar Ma'amarav (Peretz Smolenskin, Selected Articles)*, p. 28.

73 Ibid, p. 30.

74 See S. Breiman, "The Change in Jewish Public Thinking in the Early 80s", in Dinur, ed., *Shivat Tzion (Return to Zion)*, Vols. 2-3, pp. 138-142.

75 Ibid, pp. 142, 156-157.

76 Klausner, *Hibbat Tzion be-Romania (Lovers of Zion in Romania)*, p. 10.

77 Breiman in Dinur, ed., *Shivat Tzion (Return to Zion)*, Vols. 2-3, pp. 144-145.

among them: the Orthodox and the assimilated intellectuals, albeit united by national feeling. Although they lacked most of the constituents of a nation, Smolenskin felt that they had the "distinguished Jewish spirit", and a unique message to humanity, which was "to spread the teachings of the prophets on the oneness of God, equality, brotherhood of nations and world peace".[78] It was a duty that the Jews had not fulfilled, and could not be considered to have fulfilled, except when total congruence was achieved between "Jewish values" and "human values".[79] At the same time, Smolenskin expressed his dissatisfaction with the state of weakness in which the Jews lived, for "if the Jews were a mighty people, [other peoples] would fear and respect them. But who would love or respect them after they had lost their dignity in being expelled from their country to others?"[80]

Smolenskin's writings also revealed that he was affected by the liberation and independence movements that had sprung up among the European peoples of his time, and his hope that the Jews would follow in the same path.

> We see, today, many new governments and new peoples, as if resurrected from the dead, joining the family of nations: Greece, Romania ... Serbia, Bulgaria, and who knows how many other peoples will rise, dust themselves off, and prove their existence? Even at this time, the time of resurrection of the dead, it does not occur to the Jews to open their mouths or to think: "Perhaps the day of our redemption has come, too; perhaps we, too, can rise and not remain humiliated and despised by other peoples."[81]

Until that day would come, he continued – the day of revival of the Jews – it was imperative to preserve Jewish spiritual nationalism in the diaspora by expanding Jewish culture,

---

78   Ibid, p. 149.

79   Ibid.

80   Smolenskin, *Peretz Smolenskin – Mivhar Ma'amarav (Peretz Smolenskin, Selected Articles)*, p. 32.

81   Ibid, p. 68.

establishing an international Jewish organization and keeping the hope of redemption alive among the Jews.[82]

Given such opinions, it was no surprise that Smolenskin joined those calling for the emigration of Jews from Russia after the first wave of attacks took place against them, especially since "the persecution of the Jews, which has now begun in practice, had theoretically begun many years ago."[83] In his view, this was caused by the "satanic" writings published against the Jews in the preceding 20 years. Thus, the Jews had to leave Russia in no small numbers and immigrate to other countries, both for the conditions of the emigres to improve, and the pressure on those remaining to drop as their antagonists saw them decreasing in number.[84] "Our rich brethren in Russia should request permission to establish an association to help emigres leaving the country,"[85] Smolenskin stated. He had no doubt that those emigres should go to Palestine, for "talk had begun, more than 20 years ago, on settling the Land of Israel."[86] Moreover, "there is no place in the world that we can hope will serve as a refuge for all the lost and dispersed, thwarted from their abodes, except the Land of Israel ... as almost all countries will try to apply laws that are unfavorable ... under which we cannot live."[87] Likewise, "if we do not forestall problems, and do not settle thousands of families in one place, where their remaining brethren can seek refuge with them, then the fate of those brethren will be annihilation, with no help or hope."[88] When the wave of Jewish emigration from Russia intensified, mostly to the United States, Smolenskin was one of the opponents of this trend, for immigration there did not serve the interests of the Jews, in his view – given that

---

82   Breiman in Dinur, ed., *Shivat Tzion (Return to Zion)*, Vols. 2-3, pp. 150-152.

83   Yavnieli, *Tkufat Hibbat Zion (Period of Lovers of Zion)*, Vol. 1, p. 118.

84   Ibid, p. 121.

85   Ibid.

86   Smolenskin, *Peretz Smolenskin – Mivhar Ma'amarav (Peretz Smolenskin, Selected Articles)*, p. 74.

87   Ibid, p. 75.

88   Ibid, p. 76.

there was no guarantee that conditions in the United States would not change, 100 years later, for example, and force the Jews to leave it. However, "if our brethren now settle in the Land of Israel, there is no fear that they would be expelled from it ... and when the number of [Jewish] settlers rises in the country, its rule shall pass into their hands."[89] Since "the idea of our unity, and all of our being, is linked to the idea of the Land of Israel ... the advice that we present now is to call for a conference of Jewish sages and writers, somewhere, to consult on this matter in good faith and with a merciful heart".[90]

Smolenskin was also a proponent of reviving the Hebrew language, on condition that "love of the language should not replace love of the homeland, but, rather, we can use the language to instill the love of the homeland in the hearts of our brethren." Thus, he called for "forming associations that can undertake the study and teaching of the Hebrew language".[91]

Smolenskin did not, at any rate, undertake significant activity to implement his views, despite his passionate support for the emigration of Jews from Russia to Palestine, and his joining the Lovers of Zion movement.

4

Moshe Leib Lilienblum (1843-1910), like his colleague, Smolenskin, received a Talmudic upbringing. He joined the Haskalah in older age, under the influence of the reform movement started by Tsar Alexander II. Lilienblum began his activity as a Maskil through a call for religious reforms, in order to ensure the survival of the Jews as a national unit. He soon left this sphere, however, and began calling for improving the conditions of the Jews in Russia by shifting them to a life of work and production.[92] He mocked those who called for teaching "our

---

89 Yavnieli, *Tkufat Hibbat Zion (Period of Lovers of Zion)*, Vol. 1, p. 141.

90 Ibid.

91 Ibid, Vol. 2, p. 108.

92 Breiman in Dinur, ed., *Shivat Tzion (Return to Zion)*, Vols. 2-3, pp. 83-85, 89-90; see also Klausner, *Hibbat Tzion be-Romania (Lovers of Zion in Romania)*,

sacred language, the language in which the prophets and poets wrote",[93] for he was convinced that Russia would follow in the steps of western European countries and grant its Jews their civil rights.[94]

With the intensifying persecution campaigns against the Jews in Russia, however, and the rising waves of Jewish emigration from the country, Lilienblum began to reconsider his positions. He gradually announced that the Jews were alien in Russia, although they had lived there for about 1,000 years, and that their existence was the source of their distress,[95] as civilization and human values did not form a barrier against their oppression, on the one hand, and their assimilation with other peoples was neither possible, nor necessary, on the other.[96] Based on this position, Lilienblum called to exploit the pressures that the Jews were under in Russia to direct their emigres to Palestine, in particular, and to establish their settlements there as a first step to establishing a Jewish state in the country. He continued to shape his views on solving the Jewish question in articles that he published in the Jewish press, in Russian or translated into Hebrew. These articles were republished, in 1884, in a pamphlet, *On the Revival of the Jewish People in the Land of Our Fathers*.[97]

Lilienblum began his pamphlet by stating that the attacks against the Jews in Russia had proven that there was no solution to their problem except by moving to live elsewhere, "an organized, normal and national life, like the rest of humanity".[98] He added that this had to be done in spite of the existence of two Jewish factions that opposed it: first, the majority of wealthy Jews and, second, the intellectual Maskilim who considered

---

p. 92.

93 Breiman in Dinur, ed., *Shivat Tzion (Return to Zion)*, Vols. 2-3, p. 94.

94 Halpern, Y., *Ha-Mahpicha ha-Yehudit (The Jewish Revolution)*, Vol. 1, p. 211.

95 Breiman in Dinur, ed., *Shivat Tzion (Return to Zion)*, Vols. 2-3, pp. 99-100.

96 Ibid, pp. 103-104.

97 See text in Yavnieli, *Tkufat Hibbat Zion (Period of Lovers of Zion)*, Vol. 2, pp. 116-133.

98 Ibid, p. 117.

themselves Russians, Poles, Germans, etc. and not Jews, who saw "every idea related to the revival of our people, including the establishment of settlements in the Land of Israel, as a kind of fantasy".[99] Lilienblum supported his view by stating that the Jews had been subject to persecution by different peoples for more than 2,000 years, and that they continued to behave as lowly slaves and savages, even in those countries that had granted them equal rights. He mocked the Jewish Maskilim, "who still look to that spike, known as 'civilization' ... which can rid us of the problems that we encounter".[100] He also mocked those who believed, instead, in miracles for solving the Jewish question, as the Orthodox did.

> The hatred of other peoples for us has persisted for almost 2,000 years, and the source of this hatred is an inner feeling that cannot be remedied... It is because we are strangers, everywhere... There will never be, nor can there be, complete equality between strangers and family, for this contradicts human nature, and no civilization will change it...[101]

Lilienblum continued to voice his views, summarizing civilization – until the beginning of the second quarter of the 19th century – as

> dealing with kingdoms and creeds, without any relation to nationalities and their rights. However, since that time, history has taken a new path, the nationalist path. That is, the latent civilization in the nationalist teachings of Moses has triumphed. Since then, Greece has gained independence, Hungary has been revitalized, Italy has been revived, Germany has been united, and the Balkan peoples have marched towards a new life.[102]

Moreover, "it is clear that the national movement, in general, is

---

99   Ibid, p. 118.
100 Ibid, p. 125.
101 Ibid.
102 Ibid, p. 127.

not a step backwards ... but, rather, is progress... But this real civilization ... is the same soil that sprouts anti-Semitism... Thus, our situation now is more precarious than it has ever been."[103] Based on this view, Jews had to change their life of diaspora and move to live

> an independent, national life like other peoples. The national idea, the source of our distress, can, and should be, for us, a kind of salvation... I do not speak of a Jewish government, for such thinking, on our part, is very insolent... We need refuge in our historical country ... like other peoples.[104]

He added that

> a people that possesses true national characteristics ... can realize the artificial qualities inherent in nationalism, so to speak, such as a country, a language, and the like... Or do you think that the right to control a particular country goes only to those who own the country ... those peoples who live on their lands and have no need, whatsoever, to own a new country?[105]

Again, Lilienblum opposed the immigration of the Jews to the United States for they would gain nothing there, and even if they succeeded in establishing a state in North America, it would never have the character of an independent Jewish state. Thus, he maintained, the solution lay in "settling the Land of Israel, and this is our only remedy, if we refuse to be annihilated"!

As for the means to achieve this,

> the leaders of our people in Europe should mediate with the leaders of all countries to help us reach our sacred goal, while the 8 million Jews, including their wealthiest, should collect 10 million rubles to begin our activity ... to purchase large swaths of land from the government of Turkey, in order to

---

103 Ibid.

104 Ibid, p. 128.

105 Ibid.

settle Jews on them ... and to attempt to obtain a license to establish an association for the settlement of the Land of Israel and Syria...[106]

Lilienblum concluded his pamphlet by stating that the Jews had three options:

A. Remain in our current situation, persecuted forever... B. Assimilate with the peoples we live amongst ... and in a complete manner: give up our religion and convert to the religions of those peoples... C. Begin our activity to revive the Jews on the land of their forefathers, where our future generations will live a normal and national life, in every sense of the word. The choice is yours![107]

Lilienblum, himself, made his own choice. He joined the Lovers of Zion movement, was elected to its executive committee, and worked to support the settlements established by the movement in Palestine. Later, he joined the Zionist movement, as well, and had a dispute with Herzl over his concept of Zionism. Lilienblum called for the merging of the two currents, the political and the practical, that dominated Zionism at the time.

5

Judah Leib (Leon) Pinsker (1821-1891), a Russian Jewish physician, differed in upbringing from his two colleagues above. He was an established Maskil, educated in secular schools, becoming a teacher, then studying law and medicine. At an early age, Pinsker was active in the field of Haskalah. By the early 1860s, he was the leader of the Maskilim in his hometown, Odessa,[108] and one of the supervisors of its branch of the Society for the Promotion of Culture among the Jews of Russia. The branch's action plan, which Pinsker had helped to draft, called for "helping the

---

106   Ibid, p. 131.

107   Ibid, p. 133.

108   See also Klausner, *Hibbat Tzion be-Romania (Lovers of Zion in Romania)*, pp. 54-56.

Jews to acquire the Russian language as a popular language", through "attention to the religious sphere of Jewish life", for "it is known and accepted by everyone, as historical fact supported by evidence, that the Jews must integrate with the inhabitants of the countries in which they live, and preserve their religion, only."[109] As Yiddish, rather than Russian, was the main language of the Jews in Russia, the branch of the society worked on issuing books to teach Judaism to Jewish children in Russian, with plans to translate the Psalms, then the Torah, into Russian, as well.[110] This incurred the wrath of the Orthodox Jews on the society and on Pinsker.

Thereafter, Pinsker was affected by the pogroms of 1881-1882 – more than any other Jewish leader of his time. His first action was to withdraw from the Society for the Promotion of Culture,[111] announcing his disappointment in the path that he had taken, until then, to solve the Jewish question by educating Jews and integrating them in Russian society. Pinsker then toured the countries of western Europe to become acquainted with the views and positions of Jewish leaders there, in an attempt to get them to combine efforts and provide aid to the Jews in Russia. When this attempt failed, he published his views in a German booklet, *Auto-Emancipation*, printed in Berlin, in 1882.

Auto-Emancipation was the first publication of its kind to put forth radical solutions to the Jewish question. It soon came to occupy center-stage among classic Zionist writings, and received wide reactions in the Russian Jewish press.[112] Ahad Ha'am, a renowned Jewish writer, translated it into Hebrew.[113] Herzl wrote in his diary, after reading the pamphlet, that had he read it

---

109 Ibid, p. 58; see also Yavnieli, *Tkufat Hibbat Zion (Period of Lovers of Zion)*, Vol. 2, pp. 9-13.

110 See also Breiman in Dinur, ed., *Shivat Tzion (Return to Zion)*, Vols. 2-3, pp. 213-214.

111 Klausner, *Hibbat Tzion be-Romania (Lovers of Zion in Romania)*, pp. 62-65.

112 Ibid, pp. 66-67.

113 See text in Yavnieli, *Tkufat Hibbat Zion (Period of Lovers of Zion)*, Vol. 2, pp. 3-21.

before, he would not have written *The Jewish State*.[114]

Pinsker began *Auto-Emancipation* by defining the problem:

> The Jews comprise a distinctive element among the nations under which they dwell, and as such can neither assimilate nor be readily digested by any nation. Hence, the solution lies in finding a means of so readjusting this exclusive element to the family of nations, that the basis of the Jewish question will be permanently removed.[115]

Only "when the equality of Jews with other nations becomes a fact, can the Jewish problem be considered solved".[116]

The reasons for this situation lay, according to Pinsker, in the absence of a state for the Jews, or a government or agency of their own. Other peoples had never dealt with a Jewish nation, but only with Jews, although the Jewish nation had ostensibly always existed as a spiritual one. As a result, in Pinsker's view, fear of the Jewish spirit dominated the entire human race and was the cause of Judeophobia. "Judeophobia is a psychic aberration. As [such] it is hereditary, and as a disease transmitted for two thousand years it is incurable."[117] Likewise, the emancipation of Jewish people and granting them civil rights in many countries was a legal emancipation, not a social one. If it was granted due to psychological development among the peoples who approved it, or through an official attitude, it was only "a rich gift, a splendid alms, willingly or unwillingly flung to the poor, humble beggars".[118] Pinsker concluded his presentation of the conditions of Jews in his time: "To the living the Jew is a corpse, to the native a foreigner, to the homesteader a vagrant, to the proprietary a

---

114   Theodor Herzl, *Kitvei Herzl (Works of Herzl)*, Vols. 2, 3, 4: *Ha-Yoman (Diaries)*, p. 222.

115   Leon Pinsker, *Auto-emancipatsia (Auto-Emancipation)*, translated to Hebrew by Ahad Ha'am, as quoted in Yavnieli, *Tkufat Hibbat Zion (Period of Lovers of Zion)*, Vol. 2, p. 3.

116   Ibid, p. 4.

117   Ibid, p. 5.

118   Ibid, p. 7.

beggar, to the poor an exploiter and a millionaire, to the patriot a man without a country, for all a hated rival."[119]

When presenting his solutions to the Jewish question, Pinsker declared:

> We are no more justified in leaving our national fortune in the hands of the other peoples than we are in making them responsible for our national misfortune... If other national movements which have risen before our eyes were their own justification, can it still be questioned whether the Jews have a similar right? ... The struggle of the Jews for national unity and independence ... must become an irresistible factor of contemporary international politics and destined for future greatness.[120]

The solution proposed by Pinsker, congruent with those offered by many Jewish Maskilim and in opposition to the stance of religious Zionists, was to find "a land of our own" in any region of the world – not in Palestine in particular – where Jewish people could live freely.

> We must, above all, not dream of restoring ancient Judea. We must not attach ourselves to the place where our political life was once violently interrupted and destroyed... In order to find a solution to our problems, we must not ask for a great deal, because the matter is difficult enough... The goal of our present endeavors must not be the "Holy Land", but a land of our own [quotes in original]... We need nothing but a large tract of land for our poor brethren, which shall remain our property and from which no foreign power can expel us. There we shall take with us the most sacred possessions which we have saved from the shipwreck of our former country, the God-idea and the Bible. It is these alone which have made our old fatherland the Holy Land, and not Jerusalem or the Jordan. Perhaps the Holy Land will again become ours. If

---

119   Ibid, p. 8.

120   Ibid, p. 13.

so, all the better, but first of all, we must determine – and this is the crucial point – what country is accessible to us, and at the same time adapted to offer the Jews of all lands who must leave their homes a secure and indisputed refuge, capable of productivization.[121]

Pinsker then clarified that "the territory to be acquired must be fertile, well-situated and sufficiently extensive to allow the settlement of several millions. The land, as national property, must be inalienable ... meeting all requirements ... This tract might form a small territory in North America, or a sovereign Pashalik in Asiatic Turkey."[122]

Pinsker went on, in presenting his solutions, to suggest that the Jewish emigration movements from Russia after the pogroms of 1881-1882 may have been the first step to solving the Jewish question. He called on the leaders of these movements to join ranks and begin implementing the Zionist project.[123]

After publishing *Auto-Emancipation*, Pinsker returned to Russia where he found himself leading the Lovers of Zion movement – secretly and then openly after it was licensed by the Russian authorities. He was elected chairman of its central committee (see Chapter 2, section 4) and remained in this post, except for a brief spell, working in the service of this movement until his death.

6

Among the early Zionist thinkers was also Eliezer Ben-Yehuda (1858-1922), who grew up in a conservative religious environment and was trained to become a rabbi. He left this path, however, and joined the Maskilim where he was especially influenced by the views of his older colleague, Smolenskin.[124]

---

121   Ibid, p. 15.

122   Ibid, p. 18.

123   Ibid, pp. 16-17.

124   Klausner, *Ha-Tnu'ah le-Tzion be-Rusia (Zionist Movement in Russia)*, Vol. 1, pp. 68-69.

Before the age of 21, Ben-Yehuda went to Paris to study and was affected by the popular views on the national idea and the rights of peoples. He announced his position on the Jewish question,[125] that the Jews were a distinct national unit that had been able to preserve its character through its religion and through others' hatred towards it. However, in Ben-Yehuda's view, these factors had begun to fade. Religious feeling had weakened among the Jews, and others' hatred of them had diminished, leading to their possible assimilation with other peoples. Thus he felt that it was necessary to establish a Jewish national center to ensure the preservation of Jewish existence in the only suitable place, the Land of Israel, especially since the area, in his view, lacked manpower, and Russian Jews could settle it. Ben-Yehuda called for the establishment of an association to purchase land in Palestine for Jewish settlement.[126]

Ben-Yehuda did not settle on this concept of nationalism for long, however, and quickly developed it, adding other features that distinguished him from all his compatriots.

> There are three things engraved in letters of fire on the national flag: a country, a national language, and a national culture. Whoever denies any of these foundations denies nationalism itself... The time is now ripe in Europe [to revive nationalism]. Every people, large or small, is rising from its slumber, affected by the spirit of its nationalism, so why should we delay? ... Our people's attention must be drawn to settlement of the Land of Israel... Let us transfer the surplus of our people in many countries to the Land of Israel.[127]

Ben-Yehuda added: "The Hebrew language is our national language... Our forefathers made a mistake by replacing our language with others... The revival of the language will be a sign

---

[125] See his article in Yavnieli, *Tkufat Hibbat Zion (Period of Lovers of Zion),* Vol. 2, pp. 159-160.

[126] Klausner, *Ha-Tnu'ah le-Tzion be-Rusia (Zionist Movement in Russia),* Vol. 1, p. 69; Vol. 2, p. 160.

[127] In Yavnieli, *Tkufat Hibbat Zion (Period of Lovers of Zion),* Vol. 1, p. 82.

1. Pioneers of Zionism

that the revival of the nation ... is near."[128]

Not merely an advocate for his views, Ben-Yehuda proceeded to implement them – making every effort to spread the Hebrew language among the Jews and encourage them to converse in it, even though it was considered a dead language by the Jews themselves and was only used in writing.

> The Jews cannot be considered a truly living people except when they return to the language of their forefathers and use it, not only in books or sacred rituals... Rather, it should be used as a language of speech by young and old, women and children, young men and women, in all aspects of life, at all hours of day and night, like other peoples: each people and its language.[129]

Ben-Yehuda worked to make this a reality. As a student in Paris, he began trying to speak to his colleagues in Hebrew. In 1881, he immigrated to Palestine and lived in Jerusalem where he was one of the first Zionist thinkers to take this step, in contrast to Smolenskin, Lilienblum and Pinsker, who were content with encouraging or supervising Jewish immigration to Palestine but did not immigrate there themselves.

In Palestine, Ben-Yehuda first worked for the Hebrew newspapers. He then published his own, for he had decided to address others exclusively in the Hebrew language – at a time when Ahad Ha'am, for example, one of the great Jewish writers in Hebrew, believed that this behavior was "childish", while Haim Nahman Bialik, a renowned Jewish poet, considered it a kind of "sport".[130] Ben-Yehuda, however, soon discovered that Hebrew, in its condition at the time, lacked crucial vocabulary and was not rich enough to allow for easy expression. He decided to work on modernizing and enriching the language, and developed a comprehensive dictionary of Hebrew as a reference.[131] He

---

128   Ibid, pp. 84-85.

129   Ibid.

130   Klausner, *Hibbat Tzion be-Romania (Lovers of Zion in Romania)*, p. 44.

131   From Eliezer Ben-Yehuda, "Introduction", *Hebrew Language Dictionary*,

spent most of his life, about 40 years, composing this dictionary, through studying the Talmud, Hebrew books and manuscripts, searching for terms and their derivatives, and using the Arabic language as well. This dictionary was published in five volumes, prior to his death.[132] Work continued on it thereafter, until it was completed in 1959 and published in 17 volumes.

Through this act, Ben-Yehuda did a great service to Zionism. His research actually led to the revival and modernization of the Hebrew language, such that it became suitable for daily use by Jewish immigrants to Palestine, with their different countries of origin and languages, and was one of the main tools to unify them. Ben-Yehuda had founded, in 1889, the "Hebrew Language Committee", with the aim of developing and enriching the language, and he served as its president until his death. (In 1953, this committee became the Academy of the Hebrew Language.)

7

The secular Jewish Maskilim did not work alone for long in consolidating the foundations of intellectual Zionism. Soon after, some religious Jews joined them – influenced by the teachings of al-Kalai and Kalischer. Among the most prominent religious Zionist leaders was Samuel Mohilever (1824-1898), a leader of the Lovers of Zion movement and a rabbi who coordinated the First Zionist Congress in 1897. Mohilever was a great believer in the theories of Kalischer, although he did not express this position openly lest he alienate his religious followers.[133] Finally, he immigrated with a group of them to Palestine where he helped to establish the settlement of Rehovot, in the center of the country. Mohilever was of the opinion that

> redemption ... will come in a natural way ... that is, when we

---

in Yavnieli, *Tkufat Hibbat Zion (Period of Lovers of Zion)*, Vol. 2, pp. 159-163.

132 Klausner, *Hibbat Tzion be-Romania (Lovers of Zion in Romania)*, p. 48.

133 Israel Schepansky, "Hogei ha-Re'ayon be-Tkufat Hibbat Zion (The Ideologists of the Return to Zion)", in Federbusch, ed., *Hazon Torah ve Tzion (The Vision of Torah and Zion)*, p. 13.

deserve it, and when we persuade all the kings of the world and princes of states to agree to do a favor to our people, in exchange for the distress and pain that their forefathers have caused our children. And God, blessed be His name, will help us to obtain our country and gather our diaspora.[134]

This position led Mohilever to call on his followers to immigrate to Palestine in natural ways, rather than waiting for the divine. Likewise, Mordechai Eliashberg, a rabbi and prominent scholar in Lovers of Zion, who worked hard to propagate its views among the most orthodox Jews, believed in this jurisprudence, for

when the number of settlers rises in the Land of Israel, and a large group is formed of Jews who love the country, work in it and defend it, only then will God bless us with His favors and send His angel to us... Prophet Eliyahu, to preach the coming of the Messiah...[135]

The same was true of Naftali Berlin – a rabbi and the father of Meir Berlin (Bar-Ilan), one of the founders of the religious Mizrahi movement (see Chapter 3, section 7) – who also believed that the Jews must settle in Palestine before the hour of their redemption would come. However, Berlin added a tone of his own by declaring that it was not enough for Jewish settlers in Palestine to be qualified to work in agriculture, but that they also had to observe the teachings of the Torah and religious traditions, "without quips ... for the Jews are not like other peoples. We exist in the world not as a people, but because we have the Torah of Israel. Religion and nationality are twins, for us, and one does not exist without the other."[136] Among those who also believed in this jurisprudence was Azriel Hildesheimer, rabbi of Berlin, who helped to spread the call among religious Jews in

---

134 Ibid.

135 Ibid, p. 123.

136 Ibid, p. 127.

Germany.[137] The jurisprudence and views presented by these rabbis, and others, helped support the intellectual foundations of the religious wing that took shape within the Zionist movement after the establishment of the Zionist Organization.

The early advocates of Zionism mentioned above, both secular and religious, were not the only ones who called for the emigration of Jews from Russia to Palestine and their resettlement there. Many Russian Jewish intellectuals, including poets, writers and journalists, joined them across various parts of Russia to promote this call,[138] and it received significant attention in the Russian Jewish press, published in Russian and Hebrew. The call was echoed in the Jewish press outside Russia as well, and spread to the Jews in some eastern European countries, especially Romania. As a result, segments of the Jewish masses turned their attention to immigrating to Palestine.

Most of these Zionist theorists did not, however, apply their theories to themselves and immigrate, like the emigres who responded to their calls. This was possibly because most of the theorists were of old age, and could not easily change their lifestyle; or because they believed that remaining in Russia and urging its Jews to immigrate to Palestine was, at that stage, better than actually going there themselves; or because, in their own hearts, they did not believe in the validity and feasibility of their theories. Despite this, however, these theories were the ideological foundations that drove the first waves of Jewish emigration from Russia to Palestine. The theories were the engine of Jewish settlement activity in the country until the early 20th century, and later became the forerunners of other Zionist theories.

---

137   Ibid, pp. 146-149.

138   For details, see Klausner, *Ha-Tnu'ah le-Tzion be-Rusia (Zionist Movement in Russia)*, Vol. 1, pp. 135-155.

2. Lovers of Zion: Early Practitioners (1882-1904)

1

Lovers of Zion ("Hovevei Zion", in Hebrew) was the name given to the movement of Jewish immigrants from Russia, Poland and Romania to Palestine, where they established the first Jewish settlements, and to their political strategy from 1882-1904. In the history of Zionism, this period is known as the First Aliyah.

Jewish immigration from Russia began in the summer of 1881, immediately after the first waves of attacks on Jews. As mentioned earlier, most of these immigrants headed to the United States except for a small number who went to Palestine. Initially, this immigration was spontaneous and unorganized but it soon assumed a stable framework in the form of immigration associations. These came in response to the calls of Zionist leaders and writers,[1] and aimed to oversee emigration operations from Russia and to secure the livelihood of the Jews who arrived in Palestine. The associations pooled together donations to help people immigrate to the country, in the hope that others would follow. Those in a hurry tended to sell their properties and leave Russia at the first opportunity. Later, a different type of association was formed that did not aim to help its members to emigrate but instead collected donations to help those who had already gone to Palestine, especially if they were from the towns or regions of the associations' members.[2] Some of these

---

[1] Israel Klausner, *Ha-Tnu'ah le-Tzion be-Rusia (Zionist Movement in Russia)*, Vol. 1: *Be-Hit'orer Am (When a People Awakens)*, pp. 93-100, 118-122, 155-164.

[2] For details, see ibid, pp. 155-164, 364-385; and Shmuel Yavnieli, *Tkufat*

associations laid the first foundations of Zionist settlement activity in Palestine. Two of them, in particular, which worked in the cities of Kremenchuk and Kharkov in Russia, sent an envoy to the country, Zalman David Levontin,[3] to purchase a piece of land and establish a settlement for their members. This was done after consulting with Yechiel Michel Pines in Jerusalem, representative of the Moses Montefiore Testimonial Fund, who advised them to send the envoy and confirmed the possibility of purchasing the required land.[4]

Levontin arrived in Palestine in early 1882. Quickly, he noticed the lack of organization and coordination among the new Russian Jewish immigrants, as well as the efforts of multiple Jewish entities to purchase land in the country, which generated competition and potentially hindered the Zionist scheme. He worked to bring these entities together and was able to establish the Committee of Yesud ha-Ma'ala Pioneers ("Va'ad Halutzei Yesud ha-Ma'ala"; in Hebrew, "Yesud ha-Ma'ala" means "Basis of the Ascent", after a phrase in Ezra, 7:9).[5] The committee aimed to coordinate Zionist settlement operations in Palestine and provide advice and assistance to new immigrants[6] – although it did not include representatives of all the settlement entities working in the country. After its establishment, the committee searched various parts of Palestine for a suitable piece of land to purchase, until it heard that the Ottoman government intended

---

Hibbat Zion (Period of Lovers of Zion), Vol. 1, pp. 51-55.

3 See his diary in Yavnieli, *Tkufat Hibbat Zion (Period of Lovers of Zion)*, Vol. 1, pp. 188-197.

4 Klausner, *Ha-Tnu'ah le-Tzion be-Rusia (Zionist Movement in Russia)*, Vol. 1, pp. 123-124.

5 Yesud ha-Ma'ala: literally "Basis of the Ascent" in honor of the return of the Jews from the captivity of Babylon to Palestine during the days of the Second Kingdom, "On the first day of the first month the journey up from Babylon was begun, and on the first day of the fifth month he came to Jerusalem, for the gracious hand of his God was upon him." (*Torah*, Ezra 7:9)

6 See minutes of committee's establishment and its regulations in Yavnieli, *Tkufat Hibbat Zion (Period of Lovers of Zion)*, Vol. 1, pp. 191-197, 261-263.

2. Lovers of Zion

to sell an area of land[7] belonging to the village of Uyun al-Qura, 7 miles (12 kilometers) south of Jaffa. The authorities had offered this land for sale by public auction after its Arab owners were allegedly unable to pay its taxes. The committee approved the purchase of this land, as

> the most suitable places for the settlement of Jews are in the south of the country. Beside the Bedouins who dwell in tents, far from the main Jaffa-Jerusalem road, we can organize large-scale settlement without arousing the envy of peoples who aspire to the Holy Land. Also, the Bedouins have much land that they have owned for many years, and we can purchase it from them, cheaply.[8]

However, this sale did not receive the approval of the wali (governor) of Jerusalem, who opposed selling the land and registering it to foreign citizens. The British vice-consul in Jaffa, Haim Amzaleg, then intervened and was able to purchase the entire land area, amounting to 3,340 dunums, for 15 francs per dunum, and register it to his name.[9] He then transferred it to the Jewish immigrants. On August 1, 1882, five immigrant families arrived on this land[10] and laid the foundations of a settlement named Rishon le-Zion (First in Zion), inspired by a verse in the Torah.[11]

As the Russian Lovers of Zion pioneers were establishing this settlement, Romanian Jews were undertaking similar activity due to a situation not very different from that in Russia. Anti-Jewish measures by the Romanian authorities, especially in the economic sphere, were harsher than those adopted by the

---

7   See Levontin's diary in Yavnieli, *Tkufat Hibbat Zion (Period of Lovers of Zion)*, Vol. 1, pp. 221-222.

8   Ibid, p. 60.

9   Moshe Smilansky, *Prakim be-Toldot ha-Yishuv (Chapters in the History of the Yishuv)*, Vol. 1, Book 1, p. 26.

10 Moshe Shmueli, *Toldot ha-Tzionout ve Tnu'at ha-Avoda (History of Zionism and the Labor Movement)*, Vol. 1, p. 114; see also Klausner, *Ha-Tnu'ah le-Tzion be-Rusia (Zionist Movement in Russia)*, Vol. 1, pp. 239-240.

11 *Torah*, Isaiah 41:27.

Russian tsarist ones. The conditions of the Jews in Romania worsened after it declared its independence in 1878, and refused to grant them citizenship, insisting that they were aliens.[12] Moreover, Romania – unlike Russia – openly encouraged its Jews to leave. When, in mid-January 1882, a central committee was formed of 32 active Jewish emigration associations in the country, the Romanian government announced its "recognition" of this central committee six days later, stressing that it would not only help the Jews to emigrate, but to establish a "kingdom in Palestine" as well.[13] Since 1872, a decade prior, the Romanian authorities had exempted Jews from paying fees for emigration procedures, in order to encourage them to leave.[14] Most Jewish emigrants from Romania, like those from Russia and eastern Europe, headed to the United States.

The organized activity of Lovers of Zion in Romania began at the initiative of sections of the Jewish population of Safad, in Palestine. These people bought half the lands of the village of al-Ja'una, near Safad, to establish an agricultural settlement (see Introduction, section 7). They faced many obstacles, including the opposition of the traditional Jewish leadership in Safad to their project. This forced them to abandon it and consider selling the land that they had bought, a decision compounded by their difficult financial situation. Yet, before doing so, they sent an envoy, Eliezer Rokeach, to Romania to collect donations.[15] Once there in 1880, Rokeach was able to establish the first association in Bucharest for the emigration of Jews.[16] This encouraged the establishment of similar associations in many Romanian cities. In 1882, these associations held a general conference to coordinate their activities, in preparation for organizing immigration to Palestine. They established a central committee to represent

---

12   Israel Klausner, *Hibbat Tzion be-Romania (Lovers of Zion in Romania)*, pp. 17-18, 44-45.

13   Ibid, pp. 60, 77, 85.

14   Ibid, p. 20.

15   Ibid, pp. 27-39.

16   Ibid, pp. 45, 63.

2. Lovers of Zion

them, based in Galatz, Romania. One of the associations, in the town of Moinesti, did not wait until the central committee began its settlement activity in Palestine, but sent an envoy to the country – Moshe David Shuv – to purchase land to settle the association's members.[17] In Palestine, Shuv purchased about 2,700 dunums, or two-thirds of the land that the Jews of Safad had bought from the village of al-Ja'una, while Russian Jews purchased the remaining third.[18] In September 1882, a month after the establishment of the settlement of Rishon le-Zion, a caravan of about 50 Jewish families from Moinesti, Romania, headed to Palestine, reaching Safad in late October. They proceeded to the lands of al-Ja'una,[19] laying the foundations of a second Jewish settlement[20] that was also given a name from the Torah, Rosh Pina (Cornerstone).[21]

Not long after the arrival of these new immigrants, however, a dispute erupted among them, leading some to leave the settlement and search for other land. This came at a time when a delegation of the central committee of Lovers of Zion, from Romania, was also searching for land in Palestine to purchase for the associations that it represented, after a first delegation – sent by the committee for the same purpose – had failed.[22] The two parties (the settlers and the delegation) came together and succeeded in purchasing 6,000 dunums from the village of Zamarin, about 12 miles (20 kilometers) south of Haifa.[23] The

---

17 Ibid, p. 68.

18 Smilansky, *Prakim be-Toldot ha-Yishuv (Chapters in the History of the Yishuv)*, Vol. 1, Book 1, pp. 32-36.

19 See Moshe David Shuv's diary in Yavnieli, *Tkufat Hibbat Zion (Period of Lovers of Zion)*, Vol. 1, pp. 227-229, 238-242.

20 See founding regulations of the settlement in ibid, Vol. 2, pp. 202-206.

21 "The stone the builders rejected has become the cornerstone." (*Torah*, Psalms 118:22)

22 Klausner, *Hibbat Tzion be-Romania (Lovers of Zion in Romania)*, pp. 89-94, 129-137.

23 Ibid, p. 129.

land was owned by a French citizen,[24] and the purchase was made with the assistance of Emile Franc. Franc worked in the Syrian ports as an agent for British shipping companies and was also the vice-consul of Germany and Austria in Alexandria.[25] In November 1882, another caravan of 142 Jewish immigrants from Romania headed to Palestine,[26] laying the foundations of the third Zionist settlement, in Zamarin. The settlement was later called Zikhron Ya'akov, in memory of the father of the French Baron Rothschild, after the baron pledged financial assistance to it.

While these three settlements were being established, the Jews of Jerusalem, who had founded the "mother of settlements", Petah Tikva, in 1878, were making similar efforts. In its early stages, the settlement process in Petah Tikva had failed. Disease had spread among the settlers, forcing them to leave the settlement and return to Jerusalem, after leasing their land to Arab peasants from the neighboring villages to cultivate (see Introduction, section 7).[27] In Jerusalem, the founders established the Yishuv Founders' Association in order to rebuild the settlement, after amending its bylaws to allow Jews from outside Palestine to join it.[28] They sent an envoy to Russia, who was able to convince some Jews who wished to immigrate to Palestine to purchase part of the settlement's lands.[29] The founders also purchased 130 dunums from the Arabs in Yehud village, close to the settlement, to establish homes at a distance from the lands of the original settlement, which appeared to be uninhabitable. They were able to build these homes with the help of the German consul in Jaffa, despite the opposition of the

---

24 Smilansky, *Prakim be-Toldot ha-Yishuv (Chapters in the History of the Yishuv)*, Vol. 1, Book 1, p. 37.

25 Klausner, *Hibbat Tzion be-Romania (Lovers of Zion in Romania)*, p. 38.

26 Ibid, p. 132.

27 Yavnieli, *Tkufat Hibbat Zion (Period of Lovers of Zion)*, Vol. 2, p. 32.

28 See regulations in Yavnieli, *Tkufat Hibbat Zion (Period of Lovers of Zion)*, Vol. 1, pp. 243-253.

29 Klausner, *Ha-Tnu'ah le-Tzion be-Rusia (Zionist Movement in Russia)*, Vol. 1, pp. 100-102, 213-214.

2. Lovers of Zion

Ottoman authorities.[30] In the spring of 1883, the first new settlers arrived at the settlement to rebuild it, while the founders were able to purchase another area of land adjacent to the settlement of about 2,600 dunums. The Ottoman government had offered this land for sale, as well, after its Arab peasants were unable to pay its taxes.[31]

In the next two years, 1883-1884, four more settlements were established. The first, in 1883, was Yesud ha-Ma'ala, near Lake Hula in northern Palestine. It was built on 2,500 dunums[32] acquired from a Jewish resident of Safad, Jacob Abu, who was the French consul in Acre and the agent of the French consulate's branch in Safad.[33] The settlement was inhabited by Polish Jews. The second settlement, established in the same year, was initially known as Wadi Hanin or Nahalat Reuben, and was later named Ness Ziona (Banner towards Zion).[34] It was 2.5 miles (4 kilometers) south of Rishon le-Zion. A Jewish immigrant had acquired the land of this settlement, about 2,000 dunums, from its German owner by exchanging a comparable area of land that the former owned in Odessa, Russia.[35] At the same time, Baron Rothschild, through Samuel Mohilever,[36] bought 3,750 dunums of land south of Ramla, in central Palestine, to establish a settlement for Russian Jewish immigrants who had been about to leave Palestine and return to Russia due to their inability to establish a settlement of their own. The baron laid

---

30 Smilansky, *Prakim be-Toldot ha-Yishuv (Chapters in the History of the Yishuv)*, Vol. 1, Book 1, pp. 66-68.

31 Klausner, *Ha-Tnu'ah le-Tzion be-Rusia (Zionist Movement in Russia)*, Vol. 1, pp. 284-285.

32 Smilansky, *Prakim be-Toldot ha-Yishuv (Chapters in the History of the Yishuv)*, Vol. 1, Book 1, p. 57.

33 Klausner, *Ha-Tnu'ah le-Tzion be-Rusia (Zionist Movement in Russia)*, Vol. 1, p. 305.

34 *Torah*, Jeremiah 4:6.

35 Smilansky, *Prakim be-Toldot ha-Yishuv (Chapters in the History of the Yishuv)*, Vol. 1, Book 1, pp. 77-78.

36 Ibid, pp. 62-63.

the foundations of a settlement known as Ekron[37] (later renamed Mazkeret Batya).

In the following year, 1884, Lovers of Zion in Russia, with the help of Yechiel Michel Pines, succeeded in purchasing another piece of land in Qatra, southwest of Ekron, owned by the son of the French vice-consul[38] in Jaffa. They established the Gedera settlement for Bilu'im immigrants (see section 3 of this chapter).

In total, there were eight settlements established in 1882-1884 by the pioneers of the First Aliyah.

Thus began the Zionist infiltration of Palestine.

2

As mentioned earlier, the objective conditions that existed in Russia, Poland and eastern Europe in the last quarter of the 19th century encouraged the emigration of Jews from these countries – an emigration that occasionally ebbed when the Russian authorities took temporary measures to stop the attacks on the Jews.[39] Meanwhile, the conditions and administrative situation that prevailed in Palestine in that period, under Ottoman rule, encouraged settlers' penetration of the country through purchasing land and establishing settlements and institutions.

On the arrival of the first Jewish immigrants in Palestine, its Turkish Ottoman administration was not known for its sound organization, effectiveness, or integrity, but, rather, the opposite. The central Ottoman authorities in Turkey were in a similar situation, especially as the empire's debts had risen, and, with them, the interference of foreign creditors in its internal affairs. The power of Western countries was then rising in the region, as was their influence on the Ottoman empire's foreign and domestic policies, and their ambitions to control various parts of

---

37   Klausner, *Ha-Tnu'ah le-Tzion be-Rusia (Zionist Movement in Russia)*, Vol. 1, p. 298.

38   Ibid, p. 435.

39   Klausner, *Ha-Tnu'ah le-Tzion be-Rusia (Zionist Movement in Russia)*, Vol. 1, p. 244; Yavnieli, *Tkufat Hibbat Zion (Period of Lovers of Zion)*, Vol. 1, p. 74.

the vast regions that were – theoretically or practically – under Ottoman rule. With the empire's weakening position and rising debts, the concessions granted to foreign citizens expanded during that period, as did the bases of the protection system that was approved to uphold them. Accordingly, the number and influence of foreign consuls rose in Palestine such that each of them, with the foreign citizens under their protection who enjoyed privileges and special rights, came to resemble a kind of independent state within the sprawling empire. These consuls, with growing concessions from the Ottomans, played a very important role in enabling early Zionist settlement in Palestine, whether through facilitating the entry of foreign Jews into the country or in helping them to acquire land and the necessary licenses to establish buildings, facilities and settlements.[40] The help that the Jewish settlers received by exploiting the privileges of this system of protection seemed so significant as to prompt a Haganah historian to state: "It is no exaggeration to say that, had it not been for the system of concessions, the new Yishuv could not have survived in the country, and even the old Yishuv would not have changed from being an Oriental sect, similar to [the Jews of] Iran and Afghanistan."[41] The problems that the system of concessions or the consuls could not solve could be solved through bribery, which was "a pillar of the Yishuv's security… Since we have no detailed information in this regard, we suffice in saying that no task, large or small, was carried out by the Yishuv that was not accompanied by offering bribery to employees, authoritarians, and notables, young and old."[42] It seems that reliance on bribery was so common in the dealings of the Zionist settlers with the authorities in that period, that, for example, when a new governor of Jerusalem was appointed (Rauf Pasha, who held the post from 1876-1888) who did not accept this behavior, people began to – in the words of Ben-

---

40   See also Ben-Zion Dinur (Dinaburg), ed., *Sefer Toldot ha-Haganah (History of the Haganah)*, Vol. 1, Part 1, pp. 114-116.

41   Ibid, p. 113.

42   Ibid.

Yehuda – "whisper among themselves about the great distress that has befallen us [the settlers], because the new wali has clean hands"[43] – that is, he did not accept bribes.

The first obstacle to the encroachment of Jewish immigrants on Palestine was, of course, the issue of their entry into the country. The authorities of their countries of origin did not usually place any obstacles in the way of their emigration – and mostly encouraged it, as noted earlier. The Ottoman authorities, in turn, had, up to that time, welcomed the arrival of Jews in the empire and allowed them to reside anywhere in it, a tradition that they had followed since the expulsion of the Jews from Spain at the end of the 15th century. This position changed, however, with the beginning of the waves of Zionist immigration to Palestine. The authorities feared that the rising number of these immigrants would lead to a new national problem within the Ottoman Empire, which had faced several such issues in various parts of it during the 19th century. The Ottoman authorities also feared the rising interference of European countries in their internal affairs, due to the increase in the number of citizens of those countries residing in the empire. Palestinian Arab protests against Jewish immigration also contributed to changing the authorities' stance towards it. In addition, most of the Jewish immigrants were citizens of Russia, Turkey's archenemy: four wars had been waged between the two countries in the 19th century alone. Thus the Ottoman authorities were vigilant, early on, of the waves of Jewish immigration to Palestine. After examining the issue, the authorities announced, at the end of 1881, a clear stance on the matter: they permitted the immigration of Jews to any part of the Ottoman Empire except to Palestine, on the condition that the immigrants agreed to exchange their original citizenship with an Ottoman one.[44] This policy remained in effect, generally, until the outbreak of the First World War in 1914. However, the

---

43 Ibid, p. 58.

44 Neville Mandel, "Ottoman Policy and Restrictions on Jewish Settlement in Palestine, 1881-1908", *Middle Eastern Studies*, Vol. 10, No. 3, pp. 312-314; see also Klausner, *Ha-Tnu'ah le-Tzion be-Rusia (Zionist Movement in Russia)*, Vol. 1, p. 198.

2. Lovers of Zion

policy did not satisfy the Jewish immigrants – most of whom were making their way to Palestine, specifically – and many of whom refused to give up their original citizenship so they could remain under the protection of the foreign consuls. Due to these conflicting positions, the Ottoman government occasionally forbade Jewish immigrants from entering Palestine, while the immigrants searched for circuitous routes to infiltrate the country – typically via the ports of Beirut or Alexandria. They also attempted to appease the Ottoman authorities and put pressure on them, via foreign countries, to cancel such measures. The rise in the number of immigrants would then force the authorities to readopt the measures. Thus, there appeared to be regular cycles of imposing and abolishing restrictions which continued until the end of Ottoman rule in Palestine.

The first measure taken by the Ottoman authorities to limit Jewish immigration to Palestine was to issue an order in 1882, when the number of immigrants rose significantly with the establishment of the first settlements. The order forbade Jewish immigrants from Russia, Romania, Serbia and Bulgaria from entering the country.[45] The immigrants tried to find a way to circumvent this, which "was not difficult in Turkey",[46] in those days. However, the governor of Jerusalem, Rauf Pasha, who was assigned with executing this order – and who used it not only to stop Jewish immigrants from entering Palestine, but also to obstruct the construction of new buildings in their settlements – was a "smart and knowledgeable man, who could not be bribed".[47] Hence, the struggle with him was very difficult, but Lovers of Zion did not neglect any effort to overcome these obstacles. Its leaders in Russia brought the situation to the attention of its authorities.[48] The Russian government, eager for Jewish emigration to continue, instructed its ambassador

---

45 Klausner, *Ha-Tnu'ah le-Tzion be-Rusia (Zionist Movement in Russia)*, Vol. 1, pp. 199, 339.

46 Ibid, p. 200.

47 Ibid, p. 339.

48 Yavnieli, *Tkufat Hibbat Zion (Period of Lovers of Zion)*, Vol. 2, p. 69.

to Turkey and its consuls in Palestine to lodge complaints.[49] The severity of these measures then eased, and immigration was allowed to resume until 1884.[50] This was after the disputes had been resolved between the new settlers and the old Yishuv, especially the residents of Jerusalem. The latter had been accused of inciting the authorities to prevent the new immigrants from entering Palestine, for fear that their rising number would affect the donations that were sent to the old Yishuv.[51]

However, it did not take long, after immigration was allowed to resume, for the restrictions to be re-imposed, especially when the authorities discovered that "employees at the port of Jaffa ... who were being bribed, used to send, each month, [false] statements to the governor, stating that all the Jews who had entered the country in the previous month had returned to where they had come from."[52] As a result, the measures preventing immigrants from entering Palestine increased in severity and effectiveness, especially in 1887 – when clashes had erupted between the Palestinian Arabs and the settlers of Petah Tikva the year before. The police force in the port of Jaffa was bolstered and the corrupt elements removed. The orders were expanded to prohibit immigrants from settling in the Galilee (the north of Palestine) and Jerusalem.[53] These measures led to an almost complete ban on the entry of Jewish immigrants to Palestine, which prompted Lovers of Zion to seek – once again – the intervention of foreign countries. The American, British and French ambassadors to Turkey put pressure on its government to abolish the measures, which was finally achieved

---

49   Klausner, *Ha-Tnu'ah le-Tzion be-Rusia (Zionist Movement in Russia)*, Vol. 1, p. 340.

50   Yavnieli, *Tkufat Hibbat Zion (Period of Lovers of Zion)*, Vol. 2, pp. 69-71.

51   See also ibid, pp. 71-73.

52   Klausner, *Ha-Tnu'ah le-Tzion be-Rusia (Zionist Movement in Russia)*, Vols. 2 - 3: *Me-Katowice ad Basel (From Katowice to Basel)*, Vol. 2, p. 302; see also Dinur, E., ed., *Sefer Toldot ha-Haganah (History of the Haganah)*, Vol. 1, Part 1, p. 113.

53   Klausner, *Ha-Tnu'ah le-Tzion be-Rusia (Zionist Movement in Russia)*, Vol. 2, pp. 300, 303-304.

in 1889. The American ambassador, Oscar Straus, himself Jewish, continued to pressure the Ottoman authorities until he succeeded in removing the governor of Jerusalem, Rauf Pasha, replacing him with another candidate who was less hostile to the Zionists.[54] Rauf Pasha had frozen Zionist settlement activity in the Mutasarrifate of Jerusalem during his tenure, such that the JCA company was forced to transfer its activities to the north of Palestine, which was administratively subordinate to the province of Beirut. In 1900, the JCA opened an office in Beirut and, the following year, it was able to purchase 31,500 dunums of land near Tiberias, in Palestine, from the Beirut-based Sursock family.[55] This deal had a far-reaching impact on Zionist settlement in Palestine, as a number of Jewish settlements were built on this land and became the nucleus of a second group, in the north of the country, in addition to the main group of settlements that existed in the Mutasarrifate of Jerusalem. This sale was a prelude to similar deals, in which the Sursock family sold large areas of land to the Zionists in various parts of Palestine.

The new situation regarding immigration procedures did not last long. Only two years after the abolishment of orders prohibiting Jewish immigrants from entering Palestine, the country witnessed a flood of new immigrants, in the spring of 1891, at a rate higher than any of the previous waves. An estimated 5,000 immigrants[56] entered Palestine within a few months. Again, the Ottoman authorities reverted to their old measures of prohibition, especially after the Palestinian Arabs – joined by representatives of some foreign states in the country – declared their opposition to this immigration.

> A meeting was held in Jerusalem of Muslims and Christians, in which it was decided to submit a request to the authorities to prohibit the Jews of Russia from entering the country and

---

54   For details, see ibid, pp. 306-314 and sources mentioned.

55   Neville Mandel, "Ottoman Practice as Regards Jewish Settlement in Palestine, 1881-1908", *Middle Eastern Studies*, Vol. 11, No. 1, p. 37.

56   Klausner, *Ha-Tnu'ah le-Tzion be-Rusia (Zionist Movement in Russia)*, Vol. 3, pp. 108-109.

settling in it, and to prohibit the sale of land to the Jews ... The representatives of the Catholic states: France, Austria, Spain and Italy, joined this request, outlining the danger posed by the increase in the number of Russian citizens, Jews or non-Jews [in Palestine]...[57]

Thus, very strict prevention measures were instituted in response. This led to the weakening of the immigration and settlement movement in Russia itself, and to the closing of many Lovers of Zion associations there, after it became clear to their members that the possibility of their entry into Palestine and settlement in it was almost non-existent. Yet Jewish immigration to Palestine did not cease completely with these measures, despite the fact that the Ottoman authorities stressed their implementation, again, in 1901, after the revival of the immigration movement. Among the measures adopted by the authorities that year was the "red card" system, by which Jewish immigrants had to surrender their passports to the Ottoman authorities upon arrival in Palestine, receiving red cards in their place that entitled them to reside in the country for three months. Despite these measures, however, and the number of Jewish immigrants dropping significantly, some of them continued to arrive in Palestine through circuitous routes.[58] The Ottoman authorities' failure to stop this entry, despite the official policy that opposed it, was due to several factors. Mismanagement characterized the work of the authorities, which sometimes issued contradictory instructions. Then, the representatives of foreign countries, as stated earlier, openly interfered in internal Ottoman affairs, based on the system of concessions. This prevented the authorities from fully implementing their decisions.[59]

---

57 Ibid, p. 112; Dinur, ed., *Sefer Toldot ha-Haganah (History of the Haganah)*, Vol. 1, Part 1, p. 66.

58 See also Klausner, *Ha-Tnu'ah le-Tzion be-Rusia (Zionist Movement in Russia)*, Vol. 3, pp. 113-126; Dinur, ed., *Sefer Toldot ha-Haganah (History of the Haganah)*, Vol. 1, Part 1, pp. 52-54.

59 For details, see Mandel, "Ottoman Policy and Restrictions on Jewish

In all, the conditions that prevailed in Russia under the tsars, combined with the administrative situation in Palestine under Ottoman rule, facilitated the entry of Jewish immigrants into the country. Meanwhile, the situation of the land ownership system in Palestine also helped the immigrants to purchase the land that they needed for settlement.

In the second half of the 19th century, the conditions of the Ottoman Empire deteriorated, particularly with its rise in government debts. The authorities resorted to numerous measures to augment the income of the state treasury. These included raising the taxes on agricultural lands and crops, especially the werko (land) tax and tithes,[60] despite the life of poverty and misery in which most peasants lived, while taxes imposed on urban residents remained relatively low.[61] In 1858, the authorities issued, as a prelude to these procedures, the temporary Ottoman Land Code – which, despite its "temporary" status, remained in effect, at least in Palestine, for more than a century, even after the end of the Ottoman era. The law contained many instructions to regulate the ownership of land and the resultant rights and obligations. These stipulated that the owner register the land to his name with the land registry department (Tabu) in order to guarantee his property rights. Another instruction stipulated that ownership of each piece of Miri land – agricultural land leased from the state, a definition that applied to most lands in Palestine – would be transferred back to the state if the owner did not cultivate the land for a period of three consecutive years.

The purpose of these instructions was clearly to determine the identity of landowners, on the one hand, and to urge them to exploit their lands, on the other, so that the state treasury could collect the highest possible tax revenue. However, the implementation of these instructions – in light of the conditions

---

Settlement in Palestine, 1881-1908", pp. 321-328.

60   Michael Assaf, *Ha-Yahasim bein Yehudim ve Aravim be-Eretz Yisrael, 1860-1948 (Jewish-Arab Relations in the Land of Israel, 1860-1948)*, pp. 349-353.

61   Ibid, p. 354.

in Palestine at the time – was fateful and extremely dangerous, as it directly harmed the right of Arab peasants to maintain ownership of their land. Many of them lost their property rights. The authorities' insistence on levying tithes on crops using exaggerated estimates, such that the peasants were unable to pay them, forced many peasants to give up cultivating parts of their land. The state then seized that land and sold it by public auction and usually at low prices to the effendis and wealthy urban dwellers, such that a small number of them took hold of large swaths of land.

> In this way, ownership of all the lands of Marj ibn Amer [Jezreel Valley or Valley of Megiddo, south of Nazareth] was transferred to the Sursock family ... in Beirut. Other wealthy individuals bought most of the lands near the towns of Safad, Jaffa, and Gaza. The new owners leased these lands to the villagers, although the number of tenants was low and their cultivation methods primitive, and they evaded paying the landowners' share. Thus, the landowners were always ready to sell the lands that came into their possession, at low prices. Even in the '80s and '90s [of the 19th century], the lands of Marj ibn Amer and the coastal plain between Haifa, Acre and Wadi al-Hawarith [south of Haifa] were offered for sale [by their new "owners"], without anyone buying them.[62]

Most of this land was subsequently sold to Jewish people who, in time, built dozens of settlements on it.

The authorities' instructions to register land in the name of its owners, at the land registry department (Tabu), also accelerated this process of concentration of land ownership in the hands of a few notables. Many peasants feared an increase in the burden of taxes imposed on them after completing this registration process, which would inform the authorities of all their properties. Thus, many turned to the effendis and notables and requested their consent to register the lands of the peasants

---

[62] Dinur, ed., *Sefer Toldot ha-Haganah (History of the Haganah)*, Vol. 1, Part 1, p. 63.

under the effendis' names, such that the effendis would pay the due taxes in exchange for a certain percentage of crops. Through this process, the ownership of large tracts of land was – officially, at least – transferred to these effendis, many of whom misused the trust and sold the land or transferred its ownership to their heirs. The Arab al-Zubayd tribe, for example, gave one third of its land, near Lake Hula in northern Palestine, to the Jewish French consul in Acre, Jacob Abu, in return for his protection. Subsequently, the consul sold this land to the settlers of Yesud ha-Ma'ala.[63]

In addition to raising taxes and requiring land to be registered to its owners, there was a third way to transfer land ownership to the effendis, through excessive moneylending. The peasants, whose economic conditions were poor, often borrowed money from the wealthy effendis. This was usually granted at high interest after mortgaging the peasants' lands as insurance. The interest often accumulated within a short period to several times the amount of the original loan, such that the peasants were unable to repay it. The effendi would then seize this mortgaged land.[64]

The result of these conditions, in sum, was to transfer and concentrate the ownership of large areas of fertile agricultural land, in various parts of Palestine, in the hands of a few effendis and notables. These elites were willing to sell large parts of the land to anyone who expressed a desire to purchase it. Thus, Lovers of Zion did not meet serious difficulties in their efforts to acquire the lands necessary for their settlements. They always found those who were willing to sell them land in various parts of the country for reasonable prices. However, this success in obtaining good amounts of land was the first and main reason for the clash between Zionist settlers and the Arabs of Palestine. The process of transferring land ownership from the peasants to the effendis and notables, and from them to the settlers, was limited to the land registry department; in practice, the peasants

---

63   Ibid, pp. 63-64.

64   Ibid, p. 64.

continued to live on these lands and use them until the Zionist settlers began proceedings to evict them in preparation for Jewish settlement, which erupted in conflict between the two sides.

3

The years 1882-1884, which saw the Lovers of Zion movement start its settlement activity, also saw the end of its independent work due to basic economic reasons. Lovers of Zion in Romania did not establish any further settlements in Palestine after Rishon le-Zion and Zichron Ya'acov. Thereafter, its activities were limited to providing financial support to these two settlements to help them survive. Russian Jews continued their settlement activity, but with the help of external parties.

The first Zionist settlers faced grave problems, especially economic ones, in their efforts to support their settlements and secure livelihoods for themselves and other Jewish immigrants who joined them. Most of these settlers were of the middle class, such as small property owners or artisans from Russia, and had families with many children. The settlers sold their properties before immigrating to Palestine, and spent the proceeds on purchasing land or constructing buildings and facilities.[65] It seems that these settlers did not fully appreciate the difficulties, for they quickly discovered that their financial means were insufficient to achieve their goals of establishing economically viable settlements. In addition, the immigrants found themselves in an alien environment, facing challenges in their attempts to move to agricultural work, and were inexperienced in exploiting the land that was handed to them. This, in turn, contributed to the deterioration of their economic conditions, and they were obliged to seek financial help from abroad.[66]

These first Russian Jewish immigrants, however, were not all of one class or environment. There was a minority among

---

65 Yavnieli, *Tkufat Hibbat Zion (Period of Lovers of Zion)*, Vol. 1, p. 70; Vol. 2, pp. 35-36.

66 Ibid.

them known as the Bilu'im.⁶⁷ They deviated from the general norm, at least in its social conditions or class affiliation, although their financial situation was as poor as the other immigrants. The Bilu'im were immigration associations, which were mostly composed of Jewish university students in Russia who had left their studies to immigrate to Palestine. Their views were that the

> settlement of the Land of Israel is the first step in the revival of our nation, and all good [elements] of our people are obliged, from this point, to sacrifice everything they have for its sake… This is a very difficult, but very great matter, so do not pin your hopes on the advancement of Europe and its civilization. If the Jews remain in Europe, they will have one of two options: the first … is to take the endless path of pain and suffering, and the second is to descend from the stage of life and disappear.⁶⁸

The Bilu'im established branches in various parts of Russia, with headquarters initially in Kharkov, then in Moscow, and later in Odessa on the Black Sea, in order to facilitate their immigration to Palestine through Turkey. They opened an office in Istanbul and worked to secure the approval of the Ottoman authorities to establish a settlement for them in Palestine.⁶⁹ The total number of Bilu'im did not, at any rate, exceed 500, about 50 of whom immigrated to Palestine, and only 20 remained in it.⁷⁰ However, they quickly became a revolutionary and inflammatory element to the other settlers due to their constant emphasis on the ideas of national revival, immigration and a "productive work life in the Land of Israel".⁷¹ This led to constant clashes with those

---

67   Plural of "bilu", the first letters of the Hebrew translation of the verse: "Come, descendants of Jacob, let us walk in the light of the Lord." (*Torah*, Isaiah 2:5)

68   From a statement by the Bilu'im, in Klausner, *Ha-Tnu'ah le-Tzion be-Rusia (Zionist Movement in Russia)*, Vol. 1, p. 167.

69   Ibid, pp. 164-170, 219-226.

70   Tzvi Ben-Shoshan, *Toldot Tnu'at ha-Poalim be-Eretz Yisrael (History of the Labor Movement in the Land of Israel)*, Vol. 1, p. 16.

71   See regulations of Bilu'im association in Moshe Braslavski, *Tnu'at*

responsible for organizing Zionist settlement operations in Palestine. The stance of the Bilu'im seems to have prompted some historians of Zionism to consider them the pioneers of Zionist settlement in the country. Yet, whatever the principles advocated by the Bilu'im, it is clear that they too were in need of economic assistance. In other words, all of the first Zionist settlers in Palestine – with their varying views and backgrounds – found themselves in financial hardship, which forced them to seek help from abroad shortly after their arrival in the country.

The settlers sought this help from the immigration associations that had been formed in their countries of origin and had worked to send them to Palestine. However, quite a few of these associations had dissolved themselves after the immigration movement had weakened in Russia, especially in 1883, with the temporary measures taken by the authorities to prevent the recurrence of attacks against the Jews after the pogroms of 1881-1882.[72] In place of these associations, which had worked on the emigration of their members, others were formed that focused on securing financial support for immigrants who had already gone to Palestine, and encouraging immigration generally without the members of these associations committing themselves to immigrate. These associations made noticeable efforts to strengthen their financial resources by collecting donations or starting projects and sending, from time to time, financial aid to various groups of settlers in Palestine.[73] However, these funds were sent intermittently and could only meet a small part of the settlers' needs. They had to seek assistance from other parties, especially from Jewish individuals and organizations in western Europe. One of the key figures was Baron Edmond de Rothschild (1845-1934) in Paris.

The baron Edmond James de Rothschild was one of the leaders

---

ha-Poalim ha-Eretz Yisraelit (Labor Movement in the Land of Israel), Vol. 1, pp. 293-296.

72 Klausner, Ha-Tnu'ah le-Tzion be-Rusia (Zionist Movement in Russia), Vol. 1, pp. 155-164, 261-262.

73 For details, see ibid, pp. 364-385, 398-405.

2. Lovers of Zion

of the French branch of the wealthy Jewish Rothschild family, which occupied a prominent position in banking and finance in several western European capitals, and enjoyed influence with the ruling circles in France. Unlike many aristocratic Rothschild leaders, the baron showed a marked interest in the conditions of the Jews in France and abroad, and made generous donations to Jewish institutions. When unrest broke out against the Jews in Russia in the early 1880s, Rothschild was one of the first to form a committee to help Jewish people leave the country. He donated substantial funds to the French Jewish association Alliance Israélite Universelle (also simply referred to as "the Alliance") to help it carry out its functions, even though he did not believe in all of its goals. Rothschild was religious and had a close relationship with Zadoc Kahn, the chief rabbi of Paris, who served as his alms consultant. The baron was also close to a group of wealthy British Jewish leaders affiliated with *The Jewish Chronicle*, the largest Jewish newspaper in Britain at the time. The newspaper attentively covered the news of the first Jewish settlers in Palestine.[74]

Rothschild's relationship with the Jewish settlers in Palestine began in the summer of 1882, after consultations with Karl Netter, an Alliance member and director of its agricultural school in Mikveh Israel. Netter informed the baron of the financial difficulties faced by the settlers who had arrived in Palestine and asked for assistance for them. Rothschild obliged, and delegated Netter to travel to Palestine to initiate the settlement of those immigrants and to disburse the necessary funds for that purpose. Netter, however, died shortly after his arrival in the country.[75] Not long after, Samuel Mohilever, a leader of Lovers of Zion in Russia, was also heading to Paris during a tour of western Europe to collect donations for his movement. With the help of Zadoc Kahn, he was able to meet Rothschild and persuade

---

74 See also Yavnieli, *Tkufat Hibbat Zion (Period of Lovers of Zion)*, Vol. 2, pp. 16-25 and sources mentioned.

75 Klausner, *Ha-Tnu'ah le-Tzion be-Rusia (Zionist Movement in Russia)*, Vol. 1, pp. 264-266; Yavnieli, *Tkufat Hibbat Zion (Period of Lovers of Zion)*, Vol. 2, pp. 19-20.

him to participate in the settlement of Jews in Palestine by establishing one settlement there, at least, as a trial.[76] In late 1882, Yosef Feinberg, a settler from Rishon le-Zion, also went to Paris to meet Rothschild and request assistance for the settlement. Rothschild pledged to provide initial financial aid of 25,000 francs on the following conditions: Hirsch, principal of the Mikveh Israel school, who had replaced Netter after his death, would supervise the distribution of the funds; another individual, appointed by Rothschild, would guide the settlers in their agricultural work; and the settlers would pledge not to seek financial aid from any other source.[77]

With Rishon le-Zion coming under the tutelage of Rothschild, and its settlers' consent to his adoption of them, other settlements in financial distress also sought his help. At the end of 1883, when his representative headed to Rishon le-Zion to assume management of the settlement and oversee the work of its settlers, the head of the central committee of Lovers of Zion in Romania was on his way to Paris to persuade the baron to adopt the two more settlements established by Romanian Jews in Palestine, Rosh Pina and Zamarin (Zichron Ya'acov).[78] Rothschild agreed to this request and sent one of his agents to Palestine to carry out this mission. Once there, the agent agreed with the settlers of Rosh Pina to register all their lands and properties to the baron in return for his pledge to pay off their debts and provide the necessary funds and tools for the settlement's growth.[79] A similar agreement was made with the settlers of Zamarin[80] (and the name of the settlement was changed to Zichron Ya'akov – "Memorial to Jacob" – after Rothschild's father). The baron did not stop there in his first

---

76   Klausner, *Ha-Tnu'ah le-Tzion be-Rusia (Zionist Movement in Russia)*, Vol. 1, pp. 269-271.

77   Ibid, pp. 273-274.

78   Klausner, *Hibbat Tzion be-Romania (Lovers of Zion in Romania)*, pp. 240-241.

79   Ibid, pp. 242-243; see also agreement in Yavnieli, *Tkufat Hibbat Zion (Period of Lovers of Zion)*, Vol. 2, p. 142.

80   Yavnieli, *Tkufat Hibbat Zion (Period of Lovers of Zion)*, Vol. 2, p. 69.

settlement steps in Palestine. In order to fulfill his pledge to Mohilever, he bought a piece of land in the country to establish a "model" settlement on it while Mohilever searched for suitable immigrants from Russia. By the end of 1883, the first immigrants arrived at this settlement which was named Ekron.[81] (Its name was then changed to Mazkeret Batya, "Memory of Batya", in memory of Rothschild's mother.) Thus, the outcome of Rothschild's settlement activity in 1882-1883 – and his first steps in Palestine – was to adopt and pledge to develop three settlements and to initiate the founding of a fourth.

With Rothschild's actions, he ushered in – perhaps unknowingly – a new era in the history of Zionist settlement in Palestine, which lasted for 18 years (1882-1900). During that period, he played the main role in overseeing most of the settlement operations, spending huge sums of money in the process. Given his activity, Rothschild was dubbed the "well-known benefactor" in the history of Zionism.

4

As Rothschild was extending his tutelage to some settlements established by Lovers of Zion in Palestine, the leaders of the movement in Russia were trying to revive it and end the lethargy that had almost paralyzed it after the halt of immigration to Palestine and the difficulties faced by the settlers who had emigrated. The first to work on this was Samuel Mohilever, who tried and failed, in 1883, to establish a central committee for the movement and coordinate its activities. A meeting held for this purpose in Katowice, near the Austrian-Polish border, in September 1883, also failed due to a poor turnout. In spite of this, the leaders of the movement continued their efforts to unify their ranks at the initiative of Leon Pinsker, and were able to hold a second conference in Katowice in November 1884, with delegates of 32 Lovers of Zion associations in Russia and Europe (22 from Russia, six from Germany, two from England

---

81 Klausner, *Ha-Tnu'ah le-Tzion be-Rusia (Zionist Movement in Russia)*, Vol. 1, p. 294; Vol. 2, pp. 184-185.

and one each from France and Romania). A central committee was formed of 19 members to oversee the work of Lovers of Zion in Palestine and abroad. Pinsker was elected chairman of this committee and Moshe Leib Lilienblum its secretary. The city of Odessa in southern Russia was chosen, due to its relative proximity to Palestine, as the headquarters of the central committee, while a sub-committee was formed in Warsaw to supervise the movement's work among the large Jewish community of Poland.[82]

The deliberations of the Katowice conference did not produce any novel ideas, in terms of the essence or goals of Zionist ideology. They were limited to searching for the most appropriate, practical methods to strengthen the Jewish settlements established in Palestine and to secure financial support for them. In addition, the conference discussed the means to unify the ranks of the movement in Palestine and abroad, and to establish sound relations with the Ottoman authorities.[83] This was done under the influence of Pinsker, who defined the work of Lovers of Zion in facilitating Jewish emigration from Russia to Palestine, and settlement there, as a mere transfer of the Jews from the life that they lived in Russia to a productive, working life in Palestine, with no intention of establishing any Jewish political entity in the country. It seems that this was an attempt to alleviate the suspicions that had formed among some Jewish groups in the West, regarding the goals of Lovers of Zion and their pursuit of establishing a Jewish state in Palestine, and thus to induce these groups to support the movement.[84] Many Jewish circles in Western countries, at the time, opposed the idea of establishing a Jewish state in Palestine, fearing that this would affect the acquired civil and political rights of the Jews in their countries. Regarding the work of Lovers of Zion in

---

82 For details, see Klausner, *Ha-Tnu'ah le-Tzion be-Rusia (Zionist Movement in Russia)*, Vol. 1, pp. 440-474.

83 Shmueli, *Toldot ha-Tzionout ve Tnu'at ha-Avoda (History of Zionism and the Labor Movement)*, Vol. 1, pp. 100-104.

84 Ibid.

2. Lovers of Zion

Palestine, the conference decided not to establish any new Jewish settlements until the process of establishing and strengthening the existing ones was complete, especially the settlements of Petah Tikva and Bat Shlomo[85] – which Rothschild had refused to assist, despite requests made by Lovers of Zion, declaring that he had spent about 4.5 million francs on the four settlements that he had adopted.[86] Thus the conference declared its commitment to provide financial support to these two settlements, in addition to Gedera, which the movement had begun establishing that year. The purpose of Gedera was to settle the Bilu'im, whom Rothschild had insisted on expelling from Rishon le-Zion, after they had incited its settlers to rebel against the director appointed by him to manage the settlement.[87] The decisions taken by the conference also included sending a delegation to Palestine to study the conditions of the settlements and identify ways to strengthen them, mediating with the Ottoman government to cancel the restrictions that it had imposed on the entry of Jewish immigrants to Palestine, and working to obtain recognition of the Lovers of Zion movement by the Russian government and permission to engage in public activity in Russia and Poland.[88]

After the Katowice conference, the central committee of Lovers of Zion set to work on implementing its decisions. It sent expedited financial aid to the three settlements that remained under its auspices – Petah Tikva, Yesud ha-Ma'ala and Gedera – and sought to secure permanent assistance for them from the membership fees paid by the associations of the Lovers of Zion movement.[89]

The committee also worked to unify the ranks of Lovers of Zion. By the first months of 1885, 55 associations had joined the

---

85   Klausner, *Ha-Tnu'ah le-Tzion be-Rusia (Zionist Movement in Russia)*, Vol. 1, p. 464.

86   Ibid, p. 456.

87   For details, see ibid, pp. 409-439.

88   Shmueli, *Toldot ha-Tzionout ve Tnu'at ha-Avoda (History of Zionism and the Labor Movement)*, Vol. 1, p. 102.

89   Klausner, *Ha-Tnu'ah le-Tzion be-Rusia (Zionist Movement in Russia)*, Vol. 2, pp. 23, 51, 77.

movement, including 51 within Russia, with an estimated 8,500 members, and four associations abroad.[90] By the end of that year – that is, a year after the Katowice conference – the members of these associations had risen to about 14,000.[91] The committee also dispatched an envoy to Palestine to study the conditions of the settlements and to establish a branch for the movement there. Due to the disputes that prevailed among the settlers, however, the envoy was unable to fulfill its mission, and only managed to appoint an agent of the committee in the country.[92] The central committee of Lovers of Zion was then unable to make any significant achievements in Palestine or Russia. The main reason for this was the opposition of the religious groups in the movement, spurred by Mohilever, to its leadership by liberal, non-religious Maskilim Jews headed by Pinsker.[93] The religious Jews did not see him as a "good Jew" who kept the traditions of his faith, and they could not forgive his call in his book, *Auto-Emancipation* (see Chapter 1, section 5) to establish a Jewish state wherever possible, such as in Argentina, for example, and not in the "Land of Israel, only". It is clear that the goal of opposition by the religious Jews was their attempt to take control of Lovers of Zion and its work.[94] These disputes reflected the emergence of two currents within the movement, secular and religious, each with its own view of Zionism and its own ideology, goals, and methods of implementation. The two currents were subsequently reflected within the Zionist movement and, later, in Israel.

The disagreements between the religious and secular

---

90 Ibid, p. 26.

91 Shmueli, *Toldot ha-Tzionout ve Tnu'at ha-Avoda (History of Zionism and the Labor Movement)*, Vol. 1, p. 134.

92 Klausner, *Ha-Tnu'ah le-Tzion be-Rusia (Zionist Movement in Russia)*, Vol. 2, pp. 51, 71, 89, 94-95; see also Shmueli, *Toldot ha-Tzionout ve Tnu'at ha-Avoda (History of Zionism and the Labor Movement)*, Vol. 2, p. 140.

93 Klausner, *Ha-Tnu'ah le-Tzion be-Rusia (Zionist Movement in Russia)*, Vol. 2, p. 106.

94 Shmueli, *Toldot ha-Tzionout ve Tnu'at ha-Avoda (History of Zionism and the Labor Movement)*, Vol. 1, pp. 143-144.

elements almost paralyzed the Lovers of Zion movement and threatened its demise. Voices called for a second conference to address this situation. This conference was held in Druskininkai, in June 1887, with delegates of only 30 Russian associations of Lovers of Zion. The attempts of the religious group to remove Pinsker from the movement's leadership failed, but they succeeded in electing three rabbis, including Mohilever, as members of the central committee. The decisions taken by the conference did not differ much from those of the first, in Katowice. It was decided, again, not to initiate any new settlements in Palestine until the process of establishing the existing ones and securing the livelihood of their residents was complete. A recommendation was made to set up an office in the country to purchase land and guide the immigrants and settlers.[95] The conference, though, was distinguished by the participation of a number of young Zionist leaders, including Menachem Ussishkin, who was destined to play an important role in organizing Jewish settlers in Palestine, and Meir Dizengoff, who would later become the first mayor of Tel Aviv. Yet, despite this conference and the convergence of Lovers of Zion associations around the elected leadership, the movement's situation did not improve much, especially financially. In the two and a half years after the Katowice conference, Lovers of Zion had sent the settlers in Palestine about 180,000 francs in assistance. Within the next three years, however, this sum dropped to 100,000 francs.[96] As a result, the movement only pledged financial assistance to the Gedera settlement – after Rothschild refused to provide assistance to it because most of its residents were Bilu'im – and to some families in Petah Tikva,[97] out of a total of eight Jewish settlements in Palestine. The movement was further weakened when Pinsker temporarily resigned its leadership. A

---

95   Ibid, pp. 144-146; see also Klausner, *Ha-Tnu'ah le-Tzion be-Rusia (Zionist Movement in Russia)*, Vol. 2, pp. 130-140.

96   Klausner, *Ha-Tnu'ah le-Tzion be-Rusia (Zionist Movement in Russia)*, Vol. 2, p. 363.

97   Ibid, pp. 358, 366-367.

third conference was held, in Vilna, in August 1889, and elected new leaders, including Mohilever.[98] The only achievement of Lovers of Zion in this period was in late February 1890, when it obtained official recognition from the Russian government to enable it to work publicly. This was the start of a new era in the history of the movement (as will be discussed, later).

On the other hand, the weakness of the Lovers of Zion movement and its lack of financial resources – and, thus, its inability to support the settlements that it had established in Palestine – significantly increased Rothschild's influence on settlement activity in the country. It did not take long after the baron's tutelage of these settlements for him to become, by the mid-1880s, the main force behind their growth and progress, and to have them under his control. Rothschild provided great services to these settlements at the start of their existence, paying off their settlers' debts, acquiring sizeable areas of land and placing them at their disposal, and providing them with the tools and livestock necessary to cultivate the land, in addition to his pledge to provide them with monthly financial assistance until their economic conditions stabilized.[99] However, this way of managing the settlements, which later became known as the "tutelage" method ("apotropsot", in Hebrew), was, in itself, the long-term reason for the deterioration in their conditions, especially socially. This led to a near failure of this initial experiment, had there not appeared some individuals who eventually corrected these mistakes and tried to mitigate their damage.

The main reason for the failure of Rothschild's settlement experiment, and his eventual abandonment of it, was his perception that the settlements and settlers who agreed to receive assistance from him somehow "belonged" to him. This led him to impose strict controls on the settlements and to interfere in the settlers' style of work, way of life, and most of their affairs, large or small. One of the settlers likened Rothschild's method to

---

98   Ibid, pp. 380-391.

99   Ibid, Vol. 1, pp. 294, 298; Vol. 2, pp. 176-177, 185, 210-211.

2. Lovers of Zion

"a mother who raises her children by feeling great pity for them, hindering their natural growth and making them ... disabled, unable to fight the battle for their existence".[100] Rothschild would not agree to extend his tutelage to a settlement unless its settlers pledged to transfer ownership of all their lands, homes, agricultural tools and public institutions to him. In return, they received monthly financial aid, according to their number of family members, in addition to the necessary funds for the functioning of the settlement, such as land cultivation expenses, employees' salaries, maintenance of institutions, construction of homes, and purchase of work tools. These expenses were considered loans, which the settlers had to repay once their settlement reached a situation in which it could support its residents.[101] To implement his plans, Rothschild appointed a number of employees and agricultural guides, usually chosen from among the French Jews around him or from the teachers at the Mikveh Israel agricultural school. They were tasked with managing the settlements, guiding the farmers and working on their advancement to lead them to economic independence. Rothschild personally followed the settlements' affairs in all their minute details.[102]

Despite Rothschild's attention, however, his employees and agricultural guides quickly took charge and began to run the settlements on their own whims, controlling the work and behavior of the settlers and enjoying the privileges of an authoritarian ruling class, which the settlers dared not oppose.[103] The first action of these guides was to force the settlers to switch

---

100 Smilansky, *Prakim be-Toldot ha-Yishuv (Chapters in the History of the Yishuv)*, Vol. 1, Book 2, p. 131.

101 Shmueli, *Toldot ha-Tzionout ve Tnu'at ha-Avoda (History of Zionism and the Labor Movement)*, Vol. 1, p. 207.

102 Klausner, *Ha-Tnu'ah le-Tzion be-Rusia (Zionist Movement in Russia)*, Vol. 2, pp. 177-180; for details, see also Rothschild's letters in Shmueli, *Toldot ha-Tzionout ve Tnu'at ha-Avoda (History of Zionism and the Labor Movement)*, Vol. 2, pp. 68-92.

103 Shmueli, *Toldot ha-Tzionout ve Tnu'at ha-Avoda (History of Zionism and the Labor Movement)*, Vol. 1, p. 209.

to cultivating vineyards in order to produce wine, with a view to exporting it to France, after Rothschild built two wine processing facilities in Rishon le-Zion and Zichron Ya'acov. This led to large financial losses that Rothschild bore, because the grapevines used were based on the experience in France, without considering the difficulties that its cultivation could face in Palestine.[104] This, in turn, raised the settlers' subservience to Rothschild's employees, as they were the only party that bought these grape crops.[105] Over time, the number of these employees rose, and, with it, their expenses – amounting to many times more than those allotted to the settlers themselves. In the settlement of Rishon le-Zion, for example, out of 46 resident families, 17 received assistance from Rothschild, amounting to 18,000 francs per year, while there were 40 families of permanent employees supervising the settlement with salaries of 100,000 francs and expenses of 130,000 francs per year. The salaries of their colleagues in Petah Tikva reached 140,000 francs per year, while annual assistance amounted to no more than 10,000 francs to support the 28 families who lived in the settlement.[106]

Unsurprisingly, disputes erupted between the settlers and the employees managing their settlements. In 1884, some residents of Rishon le-Zion rebelled against the manager of their settlement, leading to his temporary replacement. This rebellion was renewed, on a larger scale, two years later, led by members of a small organization that called itself the "Workers' League" ("Agudat Po'alim", in Hebrew). This was established in the settlement in 1885 and was the first known labor association in the history of Zionist settlement in Palestine. The rebellion angered Rothschild, who came to Palestine to visit his settlements and review their conditions. He decided to treat the rebels with an iron fist and ordered their expulsion from the settlement.[107]

---

[104] Ibid, p. 211.

[105] Smilansky, *Prakim be-Toldot ha-Yishuv (Chapters in the History of the Yishuv)*, Vol. 1, Book 1, pp. 98-99.

[106] Ibid, pp. 99, 101.

[107] Klausner, *Ha-Tnu'ah le-Tzion be-Rusia (Zionist Movement in Russia)*,

2. Lovers of Zion

This measure, however, did not prevent another rebellion, this time in Zichron Ya'acov which ended with the expulsion of a number of settlers and the withholding of financial assistance from the others.[108] In parallel, a series of acts of rebellion and disobedience took place in Ekron over a period of four years and almost led to the destruction of the settlement.[109]

Despite these acts carried out by the "ungrateful" settlers against the Rothschild administration and its employees, the baron did not stop helping these settlements. On the contrary, he worked to expand his activities in Palestine – taking on additional obligations to finance various projects that could benefit the settlers. He also purchased other areas of land to expand the existing settlements and establish new ones. In 1886, Rothschild purchased about 6,500 dunums belonging to the Arab village of Qastina in the Gaza region, south of the Gedera settlement, and laid the foundations of a new settlement which he called Be'er Tuvia.[110] Three years later, he agreed to convert two suburbs of the Zichron Ya'acov settlement – Bat Shlomo and Meir Shaveh – to two independent settlements and imposed his tutelage over them.[111] In 1890, he also agreed to extend his tutelage to the settlement of Yesud ha-Ma'ala, freeing Lovers of Zion from the economic burden of supporting it. The movement remained responsible for only one settlement, Gedera, and some families in Petah Tikva,[112] out of the 11 Jewish settlements in Palestine at the time.

Vol. 2, pp. 185-208; Shmueli, *Toldot ha-Tzionout ve Tnu'at ha-Avoda (History of Zionism and the Labor Movement)*, Vol. 1, p. 214.

108   Klausner, *Ha-Tnu'ah le-Tzion be-Rusia (Zionist Movement in Russia)*, Vol 2, pp. 318-322.

109   Shmueli, *Toldot ha-Tzionout ve Tnu'at ha-Avoda (History of Zionism and the Labor Movement)*, Vol. 1, p. 218.

110   Klausner, *Ha-Tnu'ah le-Tzion be-Rusia (Zionist Movement in Russia)*, Vol. 2, pp. 348-350; see also Smilansky, *Prakim be-Toldot ha-Yishuv (Chapters in the History of the Yishuv)*, Vol. 1, Book 1, pp. 82-85.

111   Smilansky, *Prakim be-Toldot ha-Yishuv (Chapters in the History of the Yishuv)*, Vol. 1, Book 2, pp. 72-75.

112   Klausner, *Ha-Tnu'ah le-Tzion be-Rusia (Zionist Movement in Russia)*, Vol. 2, p. 357.

Yet, despite expanding his activities in Palestine, and despite the rebellions in some of his settlements, Rothschild did not change his management style. He changed some of his employees, replacing those who were deemed to be the cause of the rebellions. This incurred additional expenses and financial assistance to the settlements, which, again, increased the power of their managers and employees over the settlers – who, for their part, became accustomed to a life of subservience and laziness.

> The settler farmers who were supported financially [by Rothschild] did no work in the vineyards, which were cultivated by hired labor [mostly Arab]. Every 20 laborers were overseen by a supervisor; general supervisors were subject to chief supervisors, the "horse riders"; all were subject to the gardeners, who were themselves subject to a master gardener … in each settlement. The chief gardener was in Paris, sending his instructions from there.[113]

Given this reality, the settlers' morale sank and they fell into despair. They turned into mercenaries, prompting Yechiel Pines to describe them by saying:

> The settlers are all tired and increasingly desperate, so that their lands are now considered their property against their will. They work to carry out the tasks entrusted to them just to receive their allocations… They are concerned with how to exploit the baron, and their thoughts are directed to collecting money in cash, to emigrate to America.[114]

The first Zionist settlement experiment in Palestine was thus unsuccessful in its initial stages. It did not meet the goal, declared by some Lovers of Zion leaders, of creating a new Jewish community in Palestine that lived a life of work and productivity and differed from the Jewish community in the diaspora, or even

---

113 Smilansky, *Prakim be-Toldot ha-Yishuv (Chapters in the History of the Yishuv)*, Vol. 1, Book 1, p. 99.

114 In Klausner, *Ha-Tnu'ah le-Tzion be-Rusia (Zionist Movement in Russia)*, Vol. 2, p. 355.

from the old Yishuv that had existed in Palestine before the start of Zionist settlement. Only a few years after the establishment of the first Jewish settlements in Palestine, their settlers were living on the alms of Rothschild's finances, just as the old Yishuv had lived on the alms of the halukah system, and the settlers were controlled by the same negative phenomena that had characterized the old Yishuv.

5

The deteriorating conditions of the Jewish settlements, especially socially, and the various problems that befell them, were clear to some of the leaders and thinkers of the Lovers of Zion movement who tried to rectify them and even radically reconsidered their activity. Among the pioneers in this respect was Asher Zvi Ginsberg (1856-1927), known as Ahad Ha'am (in Hebrew, a "commoner" or "ordinary person", the name he used to sign his articles). One of the most prominent and credible Jewish Zionist philosophers, he was considered by some to be the father of so-called "cultural Zionism". Like most leaders and thinkers of Lovers of Zion, Ahad Ha'am had received a traditional Talmudic education in his youth before joining the Haskalah in adulthood. He studied European languages and literature, and, in 1886, moved to Odessa where he worked in commerce and joined Lovers of Zion. He became acquainted with the editor of the newspaper *ha-Meletz*, who asked him to write for it. In early 1889 his first article was published, entitled *The Wrong Way*.[115] In the article, Ahad Ha'am criticized Lovers of Zion, whose concern was only to see "the few poor colonies" in Palestine prosper, and, when this did not transpire, the movement blamed the halukah regime and its rabbis or Rothschild and his staff. Ahad Ha'am accused the Lovers of Zion leaders, who,

> not satisfied with working among the people to train up those who would ultimately work in the land, they wanted

---

115   Ahad Ha'am, *Kol Kitvei Ahad Ha'am – Al Parshat Drachim (Complete Works of Ahad Ha'am – At the Crossroads)*, pp. 11-14.

> to see with their own eyes the actual work in the land and its results... Lacking the resources necessary to do things well, we should have been too prudent to do things badly.

Thus, in his view, it was necessary "to make of the devotion and the desire which are felt for its ideal an instrument for the strengthening of faith and the sharpening of resolution". Lovers of Zion had to use "all means by which men's hearts can be won", though this work was "very difficult and [took] a long time, not one year or one decade... If we had chosen this method we should not yet have had time to produce concrete results in Palestine." Ahad Ha'am stressed that "the heart of the people – that is the foundation on which the land will be regenerated. And the people is broken into fragments." He went on, criticizing the politics of Lovers of Zion and their excessive interest in "pettiness", and added that "all the blessings and curses of the Law of Moses have but one unvarying object: the well-being of the nation as a whole in the land of its inheritance – the happiness of the individual is not regarded." Moreover, "a national building founded on the expectation of profit and self-interest falls to ruins when it becomes generally known that the expectation has not been realized, and self-interest bids men keep away."[116] Following criticism he faced because of this article, Ahad Ha'am wrote another, with the same title, in which he confirmed his previous views, declaring that "it is not the quantity of our work [in Palestine], but rather the quality, which is the basis now."[117]

Those articles by Ahad Ha'am, with their opposition to the foundations of the theories of Lovers of Zion, provoked widespread reaction. There followed a sharp and prolonged debate between Ahad Ha'am and Simon Dubnow (1860-1941), the great Jewish historian, as well as with Moshe Leib Lilienblum.[118] This debate lasted about 20 years, until Lilienblum's death, with

---

116 Ibid.

117 Ibid, p. 14.

118 See S. Breiman, "Discussion between Ahad Ha'am, Lilienblum and Dubnow", in Ben-Zion Dinur (Dinaburg), ed., *Shivat Tzion (Return to Zion)*, Vol. 1, pp. 138-168.

each of the three men shaping his views on Zionism and the Jewish question. While Lilienblum stressed, time and again, that his concept of Zionism was based on the negative factor of anti-Semitism – that is, the existence of a common, external enemy that could unite the Jews[119] – Dubnow shaped his theory on secular Jewish nationalism in the diaspora. He concluded that the Jews, after losing their state and being dispersed, had been able to adapt, socially and ideologically, to life in the diaspora. From time to time, he added, the Jewish communities in various countries had assumed leadership and become a center for the world's Jews. The last of these developments was the transformation of most Jews in the world into European peoples; thus, they could live in the nation states of Europe, provided that they did not assimilate with those peoples but kept their national identity and were granted national minority rights in these countries. (This theory eventually became one of the ideological foundations of the Jewish labor organization, the Bund, which was established in Russia, in 1897.) According to Dubnow, Zionism was no more than a "modern messianic movement". As for Ahad Ha'am, despite his belief that anti-Semitism was not a transient phenomenon and could not be eliminated by the progress of mankind, he refused to consider it a driving force in the revival of Jewish nationalism. His belief lay in the "message of the Jews" among the peoples, put forth by the Haskalah, and he emphasized the need to "reform the Jews" in the diaspora as a precondition for their redemption.[120] Ahad Ha'am left no doubt that his intention was to solve the question of Judaism as a religion, message and culture, and not the problems of individual Jewish people. He declared that the goal of Zionism should be to establish a "national spiritual center" in Palestine, working to ensure the survival and development of Judaism.

> Material settlement [of Palestine] was only established, in the first place – regardless of whether the settlement build-

---

119 Ibid, pp. 145-146 and sources mentioned.

120 Ibid, p. 164.

ers, themselves, felt this, or not – to become the basis for the national spiritual center that should be created in the land of our forefathers, due to a living, inner need in the soul of the people that strongly demands fulfillment. The material distress of our people will not fade from the world even after the establishment of the safe haven... Not twenty, nor even a hundred agricultural settlements, even in their best possible conditions, would automatically realize our spiritual redemption in terms of gathering the scattered forces and concentrating them in the work of national culture... The establishment in Palestine of a single great school of learning or art, or of a single academy of language and literature, would, in my opinion, prove to be a national achievement of the very first order of importance, and would contribute more to the attainment of our aims than a hundred agricultural settlements... A great cultural institution in Palestine, which might attract a large number of gifted Jewish scholars and provide them with the opportunity of carrying on their work in a Jewish atmosphere, where they would be free from repression and relatively protected from extraneous influences – such an institution could even now become a source of new inspiration to the Jewish people as a whole, and bring about a true revival of both Judaism and Jewish culture.[121]

Ahad Ha'am moved from words to deeds.[122] His first act was to agree to serve as the head of a secret society, which some of his colleagues in Lovers of Zion – who had, like him, despaired of its settlement activity in Palestine – had established in order to rectify the conditions of the movement. In March 1889, the Bnei Moshe (Sons of Moses) society was formed with the proclaimed goal of correcting what others had spoiled, strengthening the

---

121 Ahad Ha'am, *Kol Kitvei Ahad Ha'am (Complete Works of Ahad Ha'am)*, p. 181.

122 For the views of Ahad Ha'am on Zionism and Judaism, and his overall activity, see also Yitzhak Gruenbaum, *Ha-Tnu'ah ha-Tzionit (The Zionist Movement)*, Vol. 1, pp. 53-64; Joseph Klausner, *Menehei ha-Yesod shel Medinat Yisrael (Founders of the State of Israel)*, pp. 95-103; and Yehiel Halpern, *Ha-Mahpicha ha-Yehudit (The Jewish Revolution)*, Vol. 1, pp. 216-235.

2. Lovers of Zion

national spirit of the Jews and considering nationalism "a moral idea that means the love of Jews and all things good".[123] In one of his articles, Ahad Ha'am explained his concept of the Bnei Moshe society:

> Every new idea, be it religious, moral or social, would not arise or be proven without a group of "priests"[124] who devote their lives to it and work towards it with all their will and vigor... This group of "priests" – call it "Lovers of Zion" or any name you choose – is also necessary for Lovers of Zion in the Land of Israel and outside it. Those who can immigrate to the country should do so and live there, and become guides for other immigrants and angels of mercy... Those whose conditions do not allow them to immigrate to the Land of Israel have a wide remit abroad, too: to gain supporters for the idea (not just members of the society) and purify hearts and deeds... Most importantly: to educate and nurture the new generation in the correct spirit, so that they may be more qualified than we are to do great work.[125]

The Bnei Moshe society held its first general conference in Warsaw, about a year after its establishment. It became clear that the members who had joined, despite being rigorously chosen, held differing views, but they all agreed that they must first act "for the sake of the people's desire for a national life".[126] Three years after its establishment, when it had about 170 members, the society decided to move its headquarters to Palestine and to establish three regional offices in Warsaw, Vilna and Odessa. However, Bnei Moshe, despite the hopes of its founders and many intellectuals of Lovers of Zion who joined it, did not do

---

123 Klausner, *Ha-Tnu'ah le-Tzion be-Rusia (Zionist Movement in Russia)*, Vol. 2, p. 386.

124 In quotes in the original.

125 Ahad Ha'am, *Kol Kitvei Ahad Ha'am (Complete Works of Ahad Ha'am)*, p. 19.

126 Klausner, *Ha-Tnu'ah le-Tzion be-Rusia (Zionist Movement in Russia)*, Vol. 3, p. 226.

much to achieve its goals beyond its endeavor to revive Hebrew literature and culture. In 1893, the society founded the Ahiasaf publishing house in Warsaw, which published several Hebrew literary works and issued a Hebrew magazine titled *ha-Shiloah (The Messenger)*, in 1896-1914, with contributions by great Jewish writers and poets. At a later stage, Ahiasaf itself moved to Palestine.

In mid-1897, about eight years after Bnei Moshe's establishment, and when preparations for the First Zionist Congress intensified, the society was breathing its last.[127] However, the ideas of Ahad Ha'am persisted and subsequently affected multiple Jewish and Zionist parties and leaders.

6

In the first ten years of its existence (1881-1890), the Lovers of Zion movement worked illegally in Russia. The tsarist authorities were, of course, aware of its existence, but they generally turned a blind eye to its activity as long as it was directed at the emigration of Jews from Russia and their resettlement in Palestine. Likewise, "the government knew full well that Lovers of Zion were not among the conspirators against the regime, and mediation and bribery also played their part, so that the authorities stopped working against the movement."[128] Lovers of Zion, however, did not cease its attempts to gain legitimacy, until it eventually succeeded in late March 1890 when the Russian ministry of interior approved a request to recognize the movement and allow it to work publicly. It was officially called "The Society for the Support of Jewish Farmers and Artisans in Syria and Eretz Israel". Popularly, it was known as the "Odessa Committee", in reference to the location of its headquarters. A Russian Jewish baron and well-known tea merchant, Kalonimus

---

127 Ibid, pp. 227-236, 325-326; Ahad Ha'am, *Kol Kitvei Ahad Ha'am (Complete Works of Ahad Ha'am)*, p. 437; for details, see also Eliezer Raphael Malachi, *Prakim be-Toldot ha-Yishuv ha-Yashan (Chapters in the History of the Old Yishuv)*, pp. 346-384.

128 Klausner, *Ha-Tnu'ah le-Tzion be-Rusia (Zionist Movement in Russia)*, Vol. 2, p. 393.

2. Lovers of Zion

Wolf Wissotzky, had helped Lovers of Zion to gain this legal recognition. Shortly afterwards, the movement held its first general conference with delegates of 26 of its associations. A new executive committee was elected, and Pinsker was re-elected head of the movement.[129] The rabbis did not attend this conference due to their anger at the settlers in Palestine, who did not all adhere to Jewish law and had not refrained from farming their land in the Jewish year 5649 (1889-1890) – which was a year of "Shmita".[130] (This year falls every seven years, and observant Jews must refrain from farming their lands or using their crops except by jurisprudence granted by accredited rabbis in compelling circumstances.)

After the legal recognition of Lovers of Zion, the first step taken by its new executive committee was to carry out widespread activity in Russia, collecting a good amount of fees and donations to support the settlers in Palestine. The committee also decided to establish a parallel, executive committee in Jaffa to supervise settlers' affairs. It sent one of its members, Ze'ev Tiomkin, to Palestine for this task. He arrived in Jaffa at the end of 1890 and worked to encourage the settlers and solve as many of their problems as possible.[131] Tiomkin was particularly active in coordinating land purchases, in order to eliminate competition among Jewish buyers and prevent prices from being raised. He was able to limit these purchases to the executive committee of Lovers of Zion alone, but Rothschild opposed this trend – insisting that this arena be left solely to him – and his wish was granted.[132]

In the same year, 1890, three new Jewish settlements were established in Palestine. The first was Rehovot, south of Jaffa. It was started by an offshoot of the Bnei Moshe society, founded

---

129 Ibid, pp. 394-407.

130 See also ibid, pp. 324-347.

131 Smilansky, *Prakim be-Toldot ha-Yishuv (Chapters in the History of the Yishuv)*, Vol. 1, Book 1, pp. 143-154; Klausner, *Ha-Tnu'ah le-Tzion be-Rusia (Zionist Movement in Russia)*, Vol. 3, pp. 31-47.

132 Klausner, *Ha-Tnu'ah le-Tzion be-Rusia (Zionist Movement in Russia)*, Vol. 3, pp. 69-72.

on the first anniversary of the society's establishment. Rehovot aimed to be a model settlement in Palestine, outside Rothschild's tutelage. However, its settlers eventually had to request limited financial assistance from him.[133] Lovers of Zion also established the settlement of Hadera (al-Khadeira) on the coastal plain, halfway between Jaffa and Haifa. In addition, they agreed to support the settlement of Mishmar ha-Yarden, which was established by some settlers from Rosh Pina near Banat Yaqoub (Daughters of Jacob) bridge on the Jordan River, south of Lake Hula.[134]

Despite this renewed settlement activity, however, and the attempts of Lovers of Zion to reform the conditions of the settlers in Palestine, the settlers' general situation did not significantly improve. Tiomkin had to leave the country shortly after his arrival, due to the refusal of the settler leaders to cooperate with him.[135] At the same time, the Ottoman authorities tightened their measures preventing Jewish immigration to Palestine, especially as the wave grew in 1890-1891 – when opposition emerged in the United States and Britain to the entry of large numbers of Jewish immigrants. The consuls of foreign countries in Palestine tried to intervene, as usual, to cancel the Ottoman measures, but the authorities disagreed and kept some restrictions in place. In return, however, and seemingly to demonstrate goodwill, the Ottoman authorities recognized the settlements that were present in Palestine and gave Baron Rothschild permission to register the lands that he had bought to his name. They also allowed Jews to purchase land all over Greater Syria, including land near the towns of Safad and Tiberias, in Palestine, and to build homes anywhere.[136] In the meantime, Pinsker, leader of Lovers of Zion, died in 1891. Ahad Ha'am made two visits to

---

133   Shmueli, *Toldot ha-Tzionout ve Tnu'at ha-Avoda (History of Zionism and the Labor Movement)*, Vol. 1, pp. 178-185.

134   Ibid, pp. 185-197, 200-202.

135   Klausner, *Ha-Tnu'ah le-Tzion be-Rusia (Zionist Movement in Russia)*, Vol. 3, pp. 81-84.

136   Ibid, pp. 84-94, 168-182.

2. Lovers of Zion 141

Palestine in 1891 and 1893, and wrote an article after each visit, entitled *The Truth from the Land of Israel*.[137] He painted a dark picture of the situation of the settlers and heaped sharp criticism on both Lovers of Zion and Rothschild, blaming them for these deteriorating conditions.

Collectively, these reasons led to the beginning of a wave of Jewish emigration from Palestine. Despite this, however, some settlers – with the help of the executive committee of Lovers of Zion in Jaffa – were able to purchase part of the land of Qalunya village, near Jerusalem, which had been purchased in 1860 by a Jewish resident of the city (see Introduction, section 7). In 1894, they established the settlement of Motza on this land.[138] Two years later, some religious settlers established a small settlement north of Hadera which they called Gan Shmuel, in honor of their leader, Samuel (Shmuel) Mohilever, on the occasion of his 70th birthday.[139] In the same year, 1896, Rothschild's agents took advantage of a rebellion in the Druze village of Metula against the Ottoman authorities and bought the lands of the village in northern Palestine, on the present-day Israeli-Lebanese border. The agents paid compensation to the villagers (tenants of the land), then expelled them with the help of the authorities and settled Jews in their place.[140]

With Metula, there were 17 Jewish settlements in Palestine in 1897 on the eve of the First Zionist Congress – nine in the Galilee region and eight in the center. A report on the conditions of these settlements presented to the congress[141] showed a population of 1,562 in the nine settlements of the Galilee and

---

137   Ahad Ha'am, *Kol Kitvei Ahad Ha'am (Complete Works of Ahad Ha'am)*, pp. 23-40.

138   Klausner, *Ha-Tnu'ah le-Tzion be-Rusia (Zionist Movement in Russia)*, Vol. 3, pp. 40, 75, 163.

139   Ibid, pp. 246-247.

140   Yitzhak Epstein, "The Hidden Question", in *ha-Shiloah* magazine, 1907, pp. 193-202, as referenced in Yosef Gorny, *Prakim Nivharim be-Tkufat ha-Aliya ha-Shnia (Selected Chapters from the Second Aliyah Period)*, pp. 52 d-f.

141   *Ha-Protocol shel ha-Congress ha-Tzioni ha-Rishon (Protocols of First Zionist Congress)*, p. 148.

an area of 91,100 dunums (Zichron Ya'acov, Bat Shlomo, and Meir Shaveh: population of 650 and area of 16,000 dunums; Hadera: 170, 29,000; Rosh Pina: 350, 6,000; Yesud ha-Ma'ala: 100, 22,500; Mishmar ha-Yarden: 87, 2,600; Gan Shmuel: 25, 3,000; and Metula: 180, 12,000). The population of the eight settlements in central Palestine was 2,305 and their land area was 48,130 dunums (Rishon le-Zion: population of 400 and area of 6,600 dunums; Petah Tikva: 670, 13,850; Ness Ziona: 670, 4,090; Gedera: 100, 3,000; Ekron/Mazkeret Batya: 160, 4,090; Rehovot: 170, 10,500; Be'er Tuvia: 120, 5,600; and Motza: 15, 400). In sum, there were 3,867 residents and 139,230 dunums of land – a tiny presence in Palestine.

The establishment of the Zionist Organization at the First Zionist Congress, in 1897, did not significantly impact the conditions of the Jewish settlers in Palestine. The organization refused, until the end of the Herzl era, to undertake any practical settlement activity in the country, for reasons that will be presented in the next chapter. Nevertheless, the winds of change were blowing on the Jewish settlers in Palestine as it was announced that Baron Rothschild was thinking of ending his settlement activity in the country. The establishment of the Zionist Organization, and its public talk of the need to establish a Jewish state in Palestine, were the two main reasons that prompted Rothschild to withdraw from the country, due to his conservative position on the establishment of such a state that he thought may affect the rights acquired by Jewish people in other states. Rothschild's stance provoked fear in the settlers. However, fortunately for them, the board of the Jewish Colonization Association (JCA) – which Baron Hirsch had established in 1891 to settle Russian Jews in Argentina (see Introduction, section 3) – had decided in October 1896, about half a year after Baron Hirsch's death, to expand the company's activities to include Algeria, Tunisia, Asia Minor and Palestine. This raised the hopes of the Zionist settlers.[142] (At the time of the JCA's establishment,

---

142 Hillel Yaffe, *Dor Ma'afilim (A Generation of Immigrants)*, pp. 154-155; see also Anne Ussishkin, "The Jewish Colonisation Association and a Rothschild in Palestine", *Middle Eastern Studies*, Vol. 9, No. 3, pp. 347-348.

2. Lovers of Zion

Baron Hirsch had refused a request, submitted by a delegation of the executive committee of Lovers of Zion that went to see him in Paris, to work on settling Jews in Palestine.[143]) After the new decision of the JCA, Baron Rothschild concluded a five-year agreement with the company, by which a six-party committee was formed – headed by him and with two members chosen by him and three by the JCA – to care for his settlements in Palestine. Rothschild paid this six-party administration 15 million francs, equivalent to 600,000 pounds sterling, to complete the construction of those settlements.[144] This agreement was renewed four times, with some amendments, in 1905, 1908, 1913 and 1919.[145] A delegation of the executive committee of Lovers of Zion had gone to Paris to meet Rothschild after this agreement was announced, and tried to compel him to change his decision. The committee asked Rothschild to hand over the management of the settlements to their own residents and provide them directly with financial aid, but he refused.[146] However, Rothschild maintained his habit of donating generously to various Zionist projects in Palestine – a tradition he bequeathed to his successors.

In January 1900, under supervision of the six-party committee, the JCA took over the administration of Rothschild's settlements. Its first action was to replace most of the baron's administrative staff, holding them responsible for the mismanagement and deterioration. The JCA used a new method to manage the settlements, which it also applied to the future ones it established. It worked to gradually transfer the ownership of their land, agricultural administration and properties to the

---

143   Klausner, *Ha-Tnu'ah le-Tzion be-Rusia (Zionist Movement in Russia)*, Vol. 3, pp. 126-135; see also Smilansky, *Prakim be-Toldot ha-Yishuv (Chapters in the History of the Yishuv)*, Vol. 1, Book 2, pp. 139-141.

144   Dinur, ed., *Sefer Toldot ha-Haganah (History of the Haganah)*, Vol. 1, Part 1, p. 37; Shmueli, *Toldot ha-Tzionout ve Tnu'at ha-Avoda (History of Zionism and the Labor Movement)*, Vol. 1, p. 224; Ussishkin, "The Jewish Colonisation Association and a Rothschild in Palestine", pp. 348-349.

145   Ussishkin, "The Jewish Colonisation Association and a Rothschild in Palestine", pp. 350-353.

146   Ahad Ha'am, *Kol Kitvei Ahad Ha'am (Complete Works of Ahad Ha'am)*, pp. 305-308.

settlers themselves, with loans granted by the company such that, ultimately, the settlers became independent farmers capable of managing their own affairs. The company also established new settlements in Palestine, and was able, by the end of the First Aliyah in 1904 (which was also the end of Herzl's era, as he died in the same year), to establish or help in the establishment of eight new settlements: Mahanayim (1899), Yavne'el (1900), Kfar Tavor (1901), Ilania (al-Shajarah), where a model farm was established to train Jewish farmers, and Menahemia (1902), Giv'at Ada and Kfar Saba (1903), and Atlit (1904) (see *Map 5 Jewish settlements in Palestine, 1882-1916* in section 7 of this chapter). Thus, by 1905, when the Zionist Organization took a decision to begin practical settlement activity in Palestine (and began implementing it in 1908), there were 25 Jewish settlements, with a population of 6,500.[147] The settlement experiment failed in five of them: Gan Shmuel, Meir Shaveh, Be'er Tuvia, Mahanayim, and Mishmar ha-Yarden, and they were abandoned and then resettled in 1913, 1923, 1930, 1939, and 1949, respectively.

The settlement activity of the JCA and Rothschild in Palestine did not stop there, however. After the approval of the British mandate over the country, the two parties reorganized their relationship and established a new company, the "Palestine Jewish Colonization Association" (PICA). However, the JCA returned to work in Palestine after the strikes of 1929. In 1933, it founded, in partnership with the Emergency Fund for Palestine, the EMICA association. PICA and EMICA worked, during the British Mandate, to encourage industry, agriculture and culture among the Jews in the country, in addition to establishing some new settlements. In the 1950s, the two companies transferred most of their rights to the State of Israel.[148]

---

147 Dinur, ed., *Sefer Toldot ha-Haganah (History of the Haganah)*, Vol. 1, Part 1, p. 41.

148 Ussishkin, "The Jewish Colonisation Association and a Rothschild in Palestine", p. 353.

2. Lovers of Zion 145

7

As noted above, the first Zionist settlement experiment in Palestine, initiated by Lovers of Zion and completed by Rothschild and then the JCA, was not met with great success. After 20 years of work to establish Jewish settlements in the country, during which Rothschild spent about 40 million francs (1.6 million pounds sterling) and the Lovers of Zion associations spent about 2 million francs (87,000 pounds sterling) to support the settlements,[149] their economic and social conditions were dismal, and they did not make any achievements commensurate with the funds spent or efforts made on them. It is clear from a report prepared by Ahad Ha'am – who was sent in 1900 by the executive committee of Lovers of Zion in Russia to investigate the conditions of Jewish settlements in Palestine, and was authorized by Rothschild and the JCA to study their settlements as well[150] – that the tutelage system followed by Lovers of Zion and Rothschild in managing the settlements was the direct reason for the deterioration of their conditions in all respects.[151]

The tutelage system was not the source of all the settlers' problems, however. New issues arose immediately after the settlers' entry into Palestine, the most important of which was adapting to the new environment and creating some form of relations with the overwhelming majority of the Arab population. Despite the great importance of relations with the Palestinian Arabs, since the settlers had to live among them, there is no objective evidence that the Zionist settlers, or their leaders, paid serious attention to this aspect. The international circumstances that facilitated the entry of the settlers into Palestine, through foreign pressure on

---

149 Ahad Ha'am, *Kol Kitvei Ahad Ha'am (Complete Works of Ahad Ha'am)*, pp. 230, 239; Dinur, ed., *Sefer Toldot ha-Haganah (History of the Haganah)*, Vol. 1, Part 1, p. 32.

150 Shmueli, *Toldot ha-Tzionout ve Tnu'at ha-Avoda (History of Zionism and the Labor Movement)*, Vol. 1, p. 213.

151 See his article, "The Yishuv and its Guardians", in Ahad Ha'am, *Kol Kitvei Ahad Ha'am (Complete Works of Ahad Ha'am)*, pp. 211-245.

146   The Foundations of Zionism

Map 5 Jewish settlements in Palestine, 1882-1916

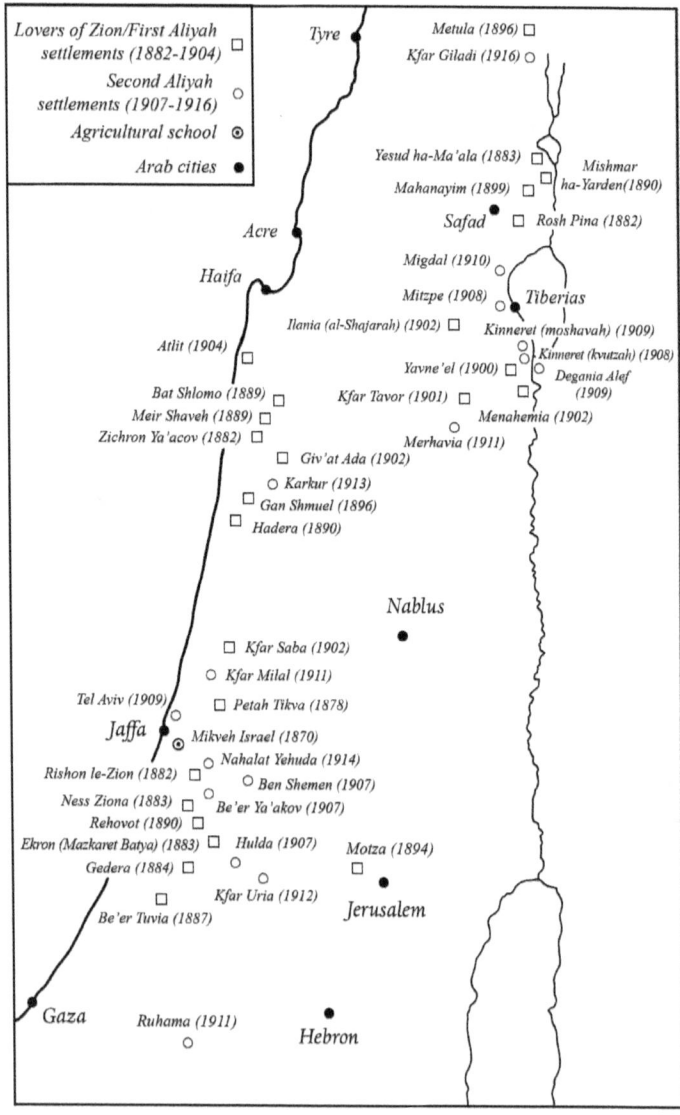

the Ottoman government as well as the use of mediation and bribery, without the need for consent of Palestine's Arab inhabitants – who, at any rate, took a hostile stance towards the settlers – further encouraged the Zionists towards this position. They were also encouraged by their relatively easy access to the lands that they needed, in the early stages of their settlement in Palestine, most of which they purchased from foreign feudal lords or owners.

Further, it appears that these conditions not only pushed the Zionist settlers to ignore the presence of the Arabs in Palestine, but also to treat them condescendingly and to despise and exploit them. On his first visit to Palestine in 1891, Ahad Ha'am noted that "the settlers treat the Arabs with hostility and cruelty, attack them without justification, beat them shamelessly for no reason," and that "there is not even one reliable person among us, so far, who can, at least, read Arabic properly."[152] Ahad Ha'am warned:

> Those of us outside the country are used to thinking that all Arabs are primitive men of the desert, a donkey-like nation that neither sees nor understands what is going on around it. But this is a great error, because Arabs, especially urban residents, see and understand our activity and goals in the country. They are silent and feign ignorance, because, as yet, they do not see our business as a threat to their future... But if there comes a time when the activity of our people in the Land of Israel will develop to the point of pulling the rug, a little or much, from under their feet, then these people will not easily step aside...[153]

Fourteen years after Ahad Ha'am's statements – that is, at the end of the First Aliyah – the practices of the Zionist settlers in Palestine had crystallized further and their stance towards the Arabs had become clearer. Yitzhak Epstein, a teacher in the Jewish settlements in Palestine, who later worked as an inspector in the Zionist administration's schools, gave a lecture to a group

---

152 Ibid, pp. 18-19.

153 Ibid, p. 14.

of delegates of the Seventh Zionist Congress (1905). The lecture was published in *ha-Shiloah* magazine, in 1907.[154] In it, Epstein described the settlement activity and position of the Zionists, in Palestine and abroad, towards the Arabs, in a manner no less alarming than that of Ahad Ha'am:

> [The issue of] our relations with the Arabs ... upon whose correct resolution hinges the revival of our national hope, has not been forgotten by the Zionists but has gone completely unnoticed by them and, in its true form, is barely mentioned in the literature of our movement... The sad fact that it is possible to ignore a fundamental issue like this, and after 30 years of settlement activity to speak about it as if it were new, virtually proves the irresponsibility of our movement, which deals with issues superficially and does not delve into their core. Since the emergence of the national movement, Zionist leaders have continuously studied the arrangements and laws of the land, but the question of people who are settled there, its workers and its true owners, has not arisen, not in practice and not in theory.[155]

Epstein continued:

> The time has come to dispel the misconceptions among the Zionists that land in Palestine lies uncultivated for lack of working hands or laziness of the local residents. There are no deserted fields. Indeed, every Arab peasant tries to add to his plot from the adjoining land... When we buy such a plot of land, we remove its previous peasants completely ... robbing destitute people of their meager possessions and taking away their livelihood... I can still hear the dirge of the Arab women on the day their families left their village of Ja'una, today Rosh Pina, to settle in Hawran, east of the Jordan. The men rode asses and the women walked behind them, bit-

---

154 See text in Gorny, *Prakim Nivharim be-Tkufat ha-Aliya ha-Shnia (Selected Chapters from the Second Aliyah Period)*, pp. 52 a-d.

155 Ibid, p. 52 a.

terly weeping, and the valley was filled with their keening. From time to time they would stop to kiss the stones and the earth... [Buying the land in this way] leaves [the peasant] with a festering wound that reminds him of the cursed day that his land fell into the hands of strangers... If there are farmers who water their fields with their sweat, these are the Arabs... In the end, they will wake up and return to us in blows what we have looted from them with our gold! ... The people ... are zealous of the nation and especially have not yet weakened; they are after all but a fraction of a large nation which controls all the surrounding lands: Syria, Iraq, Arabia and Egypt... It would be folly not to consider with whom we are dealing and the extent of our power and the power against us... One can definitely say, that at the present time, there is no Arab national or political movement in Palestine. But this people has no real need of a movement: it is large and numerous and does not require a revival because it never ceased to exist for even a moment. In its physical growth, it exceeds all the nations of Europe... Let us not make light of its rights, and especially let us not, Heaven forbid, take advantage of the evil exaltation of their own brothers. Let us not tease a sleeping lion! Let us not depend upon the ash that covers the embers: one spark escapes, and soon it will be a conflagration out of control.[156]

Finally, Epstein proposed to the settlers to carry out their settlement activity through agreement with the Peasants' Party, which had been formed in Palestine, as the Arab peasants were the majority of the country's population.

The Peasants' Party, at any rate, was not silent about the plundering of its lands from the moment the settlers laid their hands on the lands that were sold to them, and began trying to expel the peasants. The party entered into endless disputes with the new settlers. These disputes often developed into blatant attacks by the peasants against some settlements, in which the

---

156   Ibid, pp. 52 b-d.

Jewish settlers usually sought protection from the authorities.[157] During the First Aliyah, more than one attack took place against the Zionist settlements in Palestine – the most prominent of which was the attack on Rosh Pina in 1883. Other attacks followed: in late March 1886 on Petah Tikva, in October 1888 on Gedera, in March 1893 on Rehovot, in December 1896 on Be'er Tuvia, and in September 1901 on Hadera. Meanwhile, quarrels continued for a considerable time between the settlers of Metula and its original inhabitants who had been expelled.[158]

The new settlers did not lack the means to repel these attacks, or at least to mitigate their damage. Apparently on the advice of Epstein, the settlers concluded an alliance with the Peasants' Party – but in their own way. The new settlers arriving from Russia, who had moved to work in agriculture in an unfamiliar environment, needed the locals to guide them on how to do this work. The tutelage funds distributed to the settlers enabled them to hire laborers, most of whom were Palestinian Arabs from villages adjacent to the settlements. It is noteworthy that the disputes between the settlers and their Arab neighbors did not end, usually, until large numbers of Arab laborers had moved to work, and then to live, in the settlements. The laborers did not move by themselves but with their families, such that the men worked in the settlers' fields and the women in the service of their households. The number of Arab laborers in Jewish settlements rose, with time, to be greater than that of the settlers themselves, and some Arabs built their own homes close to these settlements. In this way, the early settlers resolved the issue of relations with their surrounding Arab environment while also learning about agriculture.[159] With time, the settlers' reliance

---

157 For details, see Dinur, ed., *Sefer Toldot ha-Haganah (History of the Haganah)*, Vol. 1, Part 1, pp. 75-78.

158 For details, see ibid, pp. 93-111.

159 Klausner, *Ha-Tnu'ah le-Tzion be-Rusia (Zionist Movement in Russia)*, Vol. 2, pp. 142, 152, 156, 163-164, 181; Ahad Ha'am, *Kol Kitvei Ahad Ha'am (Complete Works of Ahad Ha'am)*, pp. 223, 325; Smilansky, *Prakim be-Toldot ha-Yishuv (Chapters in the History of the Yishuv)*, Vol. 1, Book 2, p. 83; Assaf, *Ha-Yahasim bein Yehudim ve Aravim be-Eretz Yisrael, 1860-1948 (Jewish-Arab*

on the Arab laborers increased and they refused to replace them with Jewish ones – especially as the Arabs worked better and were paid less for doing the same work. However, these conditions in and of themselves later became a springboard for anti-Arab theories and practices, as we shall see, promulgated by Zionist labor organizations when the Second Aliyah began in 1904.

Relations in the Land of Israel, 1860-1948), pp. 15-16, note 35, and pp. 27-29.

3. Herzl and the Zionist Organization: The Jewish State Project and its Agencies (1897-1904)

1

Theodor (Benjamin Ze'ev) Herzl (1860-1904), founder of the Zionist Organization, was one of the most prominent Zionist leaders, who worked enthusiastically for Zionism and rendered it great services.

Herzl was born in Budapest, where he attended a Jewish elementary school, a scientific high school, and an Evangelical college at 15 years of age, completing his studies in 1878. In that year, his only sister died and the family decided to move to Vienna,[1] where Herzl enrolled at university and graduated in 1884 with a doctorate in law.[2] He briefly worked in the courts but soon left this and turned to writing stories and plays. In 1885, one of his plays was performed in New York. Two years later, he was appointed editor of the literary section of an Austrian newspaper. In 1891, he joined *Neue Freie Presse*, the leading Austrian newspaper, which was owned by two liberal Jews and published in Vienna. He was sent to Paris to work as a correspondent, where he lived for four years before returning to Vienna in 1895.[3] He was then appointed editor-in-chief of the literary section of the newspaper, a position he held until his death.

In terms of his background, culture and aspirations, Herzl did not show any signs that he might, one day, become a Zionist

---

[1] Zvi Zahavi, *Mi ha-Hatam Sofer ad Herzl (From the Hatam Sofer to Herzl)*, pp. 267, 272-273, 275.

[2] Alex Bein, *Theodor Herzl, Biographia (Theodor Herzl, A Biography)*, p. 15.

[3] Ibid, pp. 30, 31, 33, 37, 49.

3. Herzl and the Zionist Organization

or be interested in the Zionist movement. On the contrary, he came from a Jewish family that kept "few religious traditions".[4] His father had a tenuous relationship with the Lovers of Zion movement,[5] and later occasionally helped his son in his Zionist activities,[6] while his grandfather was an Orthodox Jew.[7] Herzl, however, like many young Jews of his generation who had grown up in Western countries that had granted Jewish people their civil rights, had distanced himself from traditional Judaism until he was obliged – in deference to the rabbis of Basel – to pray in the city's synagogue on the eve of the First Zionist Congress. To do this, he had to learn the Hebrew words of the prayer. In his diary, Herzl commented that those few words "caused [him] more anxiety than [his] welcoming and closing address [of the congress] and the whole direction of the proceedings".[8] In one of his novels, *Das neue Ghetto (The New Ghetto)*, his protagonist announced his desire to leave "the invisible [Jewish] ghetto" to the wide world.[9] Herzl also adhered to his German culture. In one of the sessions of the Third Zionist Congress (1899), when a debate raged on the position of the Zionist Organization on "Jewish culture", he openly asked, in a tone filled with irony: "What is Jewish culture?"[10] It was noted that Herzl's writing and speeches had no mention of Jewish culture, nor, for example, of Maimonides or Judah Halevi, two leading sages of Judaism, "nor even Josephus (Yosef ben Matityahu), known to Christians".[11] In

---

4   Ben-Zion Dinur (Dinaburg), *Binyamin Ze'ev Herzl (Benjamin Ze'ev Herzl)*, p. 14.

5   Zahavi, *Mi ha-Hatam Sofer ad Herzl (From the Hatam Sofer to Herzl)*, pp. 264-265.

6   Raphael Patai, ed., *The Complete Diaries of Theodor Herzl*, Vol. 1, p. 300; Vol. 2, p. 490.

7   Zahavi, *Mi ha-Hatam Sofer ad Herzl (From the Hatam Sofer to Herzl)*, pp. 268-296.

8   Patai, ed., *The Complete Diaries of Theodor Herzl*, Vol. 2, p. 589.

9   Bein, *Theodor Herzl, Biographia (Theodor Herzl, A Biography)*, pp. 17-18.

10   Theodor (Benjamin Ze'ev) Herzl, *Kitvei Herzl (Works of Herzl)*, Vols. 7, 8: *Bifnei Am ve-Olam (Before the Nation and the World)*, pp. 12-13.

11   Joseph Klausner, *Menehei ha-Yesod shel Medinat Yisrael (Founders of the State of Israel)*, pp. 159-178.

addition, Herzl, at the start of his Zionist work, was not well-informed on Zionist settlement activity in Palestine and had not even read the Zionist classics written by that time.[12] He had heard of Pinsker, for example, in a conversation with Narcisse Leven, the JCA president, who sent him the booklet, *Auto-Emancipation* – which Herzl did not finish reading until after the publication of his own book, *The Jewish State*.[13] He began reading Moses Hess's book, *Rome and Jerusalem*, only on his visit to Palestine in 1898 and finished the book in May 1901.[14]

Despite this background, which made it unlikely that Herzl would engage in Zionist work or even concern himself with the Jewish question, he began Zionist activity in 1895 at the age of 35, with unrivaled determination, and remained in it until his death in 1904. Herzl described the reason for this change by noting his transformation in 1881 or 1882, upon reading Eugen Duhring's anti-Semitic book.[15] This led Herzl to conclude that the solution to the Jews' problems lay in pushing them to convert to Christianity, provided that this was done "with festive processions and amidst the pealing of bells. Not in shame..."[16] Herzl had moved to Paris to work as a press correspondent, where he "gained a freer attitude toward anti-Semitism which [he] now began to understand historically and make allowances for".[17] However, this understanding of anti-Semitism and its causes ended with the end of the first stage of the Dreyfus trial (see Introduction, section 5). This trial made Herzl a Zionist – as he wrote in one of his articles[18] – due to the anti-Jewish calls that accompanied it.[19] It was clear that the basis of his Zionism

---

12 Bein, *Theodor Herzl, Biographia (Theodor Herzl, A Biography)*, pp. 143-144.

13 Patai, ed., *The Complete Diaries of Theodor Herzl*, Vol. 1, p. 143; Vol. 2, p. 584.

14 Ibid, Vol. 3, p. 1090.

15 Ibid, Vol. 1, p. 4.

16 Ibid, p. 6.

17 Ibid, p. 7.

18 Herzl, *Kitvei Herzl (Works of Herzl)*, Vol. 8, p. 44.

19 The French officer, Dreyfus, who was falsely accused of treason, was of Jewish origin.

3. Herzl and the Zionist Organization

was a reaction against anti-Semitism. Herzl insisted on the need to establish a Jewish state only because of the existence of anti-Semitism and the distress that it caused Jews, a view that he held during the entire course of his Zionist activity despite the harsh criticism he faced in several Zionist circles. His diary reveals extreme sensitivity towards anti-Semitism that he encountered:

> Anti-Semitism has grown and continues to grow – and so do I... Actually, anti-Semitism is a consequence of the emancipation of the Jews. However, the peoples who lack historical understanding – that is, all of them – do not see us as an historical product, as the victims of earlier, crueler, and still more narrow-minded times. They do not realize that we are what we are because they have made us that way amidst tortures, because the Church made usury dishonorable for Christians, and because the rulers forced us to deal in money. We cling to money because they flung us onto money. Moreover, we always had to be prepared to flee or to conceal our possessions from plunderers. This is how our relationship to money arose. Then, too, as Kammerknechte of the Emperor we constituted a kind of indirect taxation. We extracted money from the people which later was stolen or confiscated from us. All these sufferings rendered us ugly... But if the Jews turn from money to professions that were previously barred to them, they cause a terrible pressure on the area in which the middle classes earn their living, a pressure under which the Jews actually suffer most of all.[20]

Having reached these conclusions, Herzl set to work. His first steps were to seek a meeting with Baron Hirsch, a wealthy French Jew and founder of the JCA. Herzl explained his scheme to solve the Jewish question in Europe by purchasing land and establishing a state for the Jews there. The baron, however, was not in favour of the plan and ended the interview before Herzl could finish speaking.[21]

---

20 Patai, ed., *The Complete Diaries of Theodor Herzl*, Vol. 1, pp. 7, 9-10.

21 Ibid, pp. 18-24.

It appears that Herzl's views, which he presented in broad outline to Baron Hirsch, affected Herzl more than they did the latter. Immediately after leaving the baron, Herzl began writing them down in an organized, logical manner, which he could present to others in the form of a speech. This was to address a representative of the Rothschilds, the other notably wealthy Jewish family in France, whom Herzl had decided to meet.[22] At the same time, he attempted to gather supporters for his idea from among Jews and others. One of the most prominent was Max Nordau (1849-1923). In their first meeting, Herzl felt that "each took the words right out of the other's mouth," after they agreed that "only anti-Semitism had made Jews of [them both]."[23] Like Herzl, Nordau was a Jewish man of Hungarian origin. Son of a rabbi, "he had known Judaism in his youth, but forgotten it with age,"[24] when he went to Paris to practice medicine. He had also turned to writing. When Herzl met him, Nordau was a prominent writer whose books had been translated into several European languages. Thus, his support of Herzl at the outset of his path was crucial, and helped to propagate the Zionist idea and gain supporters for it. Nordau remained at Herzl's side as one of his greatest allies, as well as one of the most prominent theorists both during and after Herzl's era (see section 8 of this chapter). Herzl also became acquainted, at the beginning of his career, with David Wolffsohn (1856-1914), a timber merchant in Cologne, who became one of his top aides and president of the Zionist Organization after Herzl's death. In spite of this, however, Herzl did not gain a large following, especially among the Jews, because, he wrote, "old prisoners don't like to leave prison."[25] The head of the Rothschild family also refused to meet him at this stage, despite repeated requests. Thus, Herzl saw fit to write a book of his views. In February 1896, he published, in

---

22 See speech in ibid, pp. 129-183.

23 Ibid, p. 148.

24 Klausner, J., *Menehei ha-Yesod shel Medinat Yisrael (Founders of the State of Israel)*, p. 192.

25 Patai, ed., *The Complete Diaries of Theodor Herzl*, Vol. 1, p. 208.

3. Herzl and the Zionist Organization

Vienna, a German book titled *Der Judenstaat* (*The Jewish State*).

2

The Jewish State was published with the subtitle: *Proposal of a Modern Solution for the Jewish Question*. When presenting this solution, Herzl proceeded from certain assumptions[26] that "[t]he Jewish question exists wherever Jews live in perceptible numbers. Where it does not exist, it is carried by Jews in the course of their migrations. We naturally move to those places where we are not persecuted, and there our presence produces persecution."[27] The reasons for this persecution were many, in his view, but

> modern anti-Semitism is not to be confounded with the religious persecution of the Jews of former times. It does occasionally take a religious bias in some countries, but the main current of the aggressive movement has now changed. In the principal countries where anti-Semitism prevails, it does so as a result of the emancipation of the Jews. When civilized nations awoke to the inhumanity of discriminatory legislation and enfranchised us, our enfranchisement came too late. It was no longer possible to remove our disabilities in our old homes. For we had, curiously enough, developed while in the ghetto into a bourgeois people, and we stepped out of it only to enter into fierce competition with the middle classes [of other peoples]. Hence, our emancipation set us suddenly within this middle-class circle, where we have a double pressure to sustain, from within and from without. The Christian bourgeoisie would not be unwilling to cast us as a sacrifice to socialism, though that would not greatly improve matters. At the same time, the equal rights of Jews before the law cannot be withdrawn ... because it would immediately drive all Jews ... into the ranks of subversive parties.[28]

---

26   Theodor Herzl, *The Jewish State, Proposal of a Modern Solution for the Jewish Question*, p. 14.

27   Ibid, p. 15.

28   Ibid, pp. 25-26.

Thus, "the nations in whose midst Jews live, are all either covertly or openly anti-Semitic."[29]

Herzl declared that "I think the Jewish question is no more a social than a religious one, notwithstanding that it sometimes takes these and other forms. It is a national question, which can only be solved by making it a political world-question to be discussed and settled by the civilized nations of the world in council."[30] He added that the Jews are one people, for "our enemies have made us one in our despite, as repeatedly happens in history. Distress binds us together, and, thus united, we suddenly discover our strength. Yes, we are strong enough to form a state, and, indeed, a model state. We possess all ... resources necessary for the purpose."[31]

As for the means to form a state, Herzl's suggestion was to "let the sovereignty be granted us over a portion of the globe large enough to satisfy the rightful requirements of a nation; the rest we shall manage for ourselves."[32] He touched on the discussion that prevailed, among various Zionist circles, on Jewish settlement in Argentina or Palestine. Herzl declared that he had no preference for one country over the other, and that the Jews were ready to "take" whatever country was given to them. However,

> supposing His Majesty the Sultan were to give us Palestine, we could in return undertake to regulate the whole finances of Turkey. We should there form a portion of a rampart of Europe against Asia, an outpost of civilization as opposed to barbarism. We should as a neutral state remain in contact with all Europe, which would have to guarantee our existence. The sanctuaries of Christendom would be safeguarded by assigning to them an extra-territorial status such as is

---

29 Ibid, p. 23.
30 Ibid, p. 15.
31 Ibid, p. 27.
32 Ibid, p. 28.

3. Herzl and the Zionist Organization

well-known to the law of nations.[33]

In order to establish the Jewish state, Herzl called for the founding of two organizations: the "Society of Jews" and the "Jewish Company".[34] Each organization had its tasks: "The Society of Jews will do the preparatory work in the domains of science and politics, which the Jewish Company will afterwards apply practically."[35] The Society of Jews would be the "organ of the national movement ... [with] scientific and political tasks ... the gestor of the Jews..." and should gain acknowledgement from the largest number of Jewish people and from independent countries as a "state-forming power". It would then conduct general political affairs with the aim of forming that state, and setting up its main agencies prior to its formation.[36] The first goal of the Society of Jews would be, in Herzl's view, to obtain sovereignty over the country in which the Jewish state would be formed. Representatives of the society and the Jewish Company, as well as local companies, would then be sent to study the country's natural and economic potential, in order to plan methods to exploit them and settle there. The Jewish Company, on the other hand, should be "modeled on the lines of a great land-acquisition company. It might be called a Jewish Chartered Company."[37] Herzl admired the East India Company, which was a British company of this type, and called for drawing from the experience of its colonial settlements in India as a guideline to establish the Jewish state. He also admired Cecil Rhodes, founder of Rhodesia (now Zambia and Zimbabwe), and asked to meet him for consultation, but Rhodes died before this could take place.[38] However, this company "cannot exercise sovereign

---

33 Ibid, p. 30.

34 These English designations were given by Herzl within the German text of his book.

35 Ibid, p. 28.

36 Ibid, pp. 66-67.

37 Ibid, p. 33.

38 Patai, ed., *The Complete Diaries of Theodor Herzl*, Vol. 2, pp. 765-766, 793; Vol. 3, pp. 1169, 1193-1195, 1265.

power, and has other than purely colonial tasks. [It] will be founded as a joint stock company subject to English jurisdiction, framed according to English laws, and under the protection of England... It is strictly a business undertaking, and must be carefully distinguished from the Society of Jews."[39] The Jewish Company would establish branches in every place where it was permitted to do so, according to its capacities. It would work to liquidate the properties of Jews and their financial rights in the countries in which they lived, either by selling those assets or by purchasing them, at the company's expense, and selling them later, when economic conditions allowed. After the liquidation of their properties, the company would transfer the Jews from their countries of origin to the region in which their new state would be formed, and would help them start a new life there. The company would obtain its capital by offering its shares on financial markets to Jews and others, as it could not rely on major banks and Jewish financiers. Herzl considered himself to be at war with the Jewish financiers[40] since his early steps, especially after the barons Hirsch and Rothschild refused to adopt his schemes or support him in their implementation.

Herzl believed that Jewish laborers and the poor would be the first to immigrate to the new state, and would lay the foundations for its establishment and the formation of a new society. At the completion of this stage, the Jewish Company would target middle-class Jews and work to relocate them to the state. It would attempt to transfer every group of residents of a particular city or neighborhood together, and to resettle them in one neighborhood or settlement such that they would feel less alienated in their new country. The features of a new society would then begin to emerge in a modern state.

In his book, Herzl also called for drafting a constitution for the Jewish state, and suggested that this state should take the form of an aristocratic republic. "I am against democracy," he

---

39 Herzl, *The Jewish State, Proposal of a Modern Solution for the Jewish Question*, p. 33.

40 Patai, ed., *The Complete Diaries of Theodor Herzl*, Vol. 1, p. 252.

3. Herzl and the Zionist Organization 161

wrote in his diary.

> One can only govern aristocratically... The French Academy [for example] constitutes an elective aristocracy... If there is one thing I should like to be, it is a member of the old Prussian nobility... Care must be taken that the aristocracy does not degenerate into tyranny... Among us any great person can become an aristocrat.[41]

As for language, each person could speak the language of his country of origin, because "we cannot converse in Hebrew."

Laws would be uniform for everyone in the state, Herzl declared, and the establishment of a modern army would have a mission of defense only, since "the Jewish state will be neutral." He proposed a white flag, a symbol of pure, modern life, decorated with seven gilded stars, symbolizing the seven-hour workday of the state.

The Jewish State had nothing new in terms of its principal ideas. As mentioned earlier, several organizations and individuals had preceded him in this regard, including Kalischer, Hess and Pinsker (see Chapter 1, section 1 and section 5), who had all proposed the establishment of a Jewish state as a solution to the Jewish question. Ahad Ha'am commented on the book by saying: "Herzl's pamphlet gives us the impression of being a translation of Pinsker's teachings from the language of the old prophets to that of contemporary journalism."[42] In the end, however, Herzl's perseverance and insistence on implementing his plans led him to surpass all these thinkers and assume leadership of the Zionist movement.

In addition to *The Jewish State*, Herzl published a novel in 1902, *Altneuland* (*The Old New Land*), in which he explained his vision of the state to be formed in Palestine, and the imagined situation in it during the first quarter of the 20th century. In this novel, Herzl presented a picture of very close economic ties between

---

41 Ibid, pp. 191, 196, 213.

42 Ahad Ha'am, *Kol Kitvei Ahad Ha'am – Al Parshat Drachim (Complete Works of Ahad Ha'am – At the Crossroads)*, p. 171.

the Jewish state, Europe and the United States. Although the novel did not outline any of his practical Zionist views, it came to be considered, in Zionist tradition, as a complement to *The Jewish State*, such that, together, they summarized his views on Zionism. The reason for this classification may have been that, in his novel, Herzl explicitly named Palestine – after finding "the right path" and joining the group of Zionists who were claiming Palestine, specifically – when this had not been his exact position in his first book. Nahum Sokolow (1859-1936), a renowned Jewish writer and later president of the Zionist Organization, translated this novel into Hebrew,[43] with the title *Tel Aviv (Spring Hill)*. This name was later given to the first Jewish city established in Palestine, near the Arab city of Jaffa.

3

The Jewish State did not garner much attention in Jewish and other circles upon its publication, nor provoke much discussion. Herzl expressed his fear that public opinion was ignoring his book but, after a while, he recorded in his diary, with pleasure, that there were attacks on it in the press, and praise as well.[44] The book, however, gathered around Herzl a group of believers in the Zionist idea, both Jews and others, including a German clergyman, William Hechler, who worked at the British embassy in Vienna. Hechler had interpreted certain prophecies, which he published, in 1882, in a pamphlet titled *The Restoration of the Jews to Palestine*. He had reached the conclusion that Palestine would return to the Jews in the late 19th century. As soon as he heard of Herzl and his book, he rushed to meet him – seeing him as the one who would fulfill these prophecies.[45] The first thing this reverend did was to arrange a meeting for Herzl, at his request,

---

43   A Hebrew translation of this novel was published in Herzl, *Kitvei Herzl (Works of Herzl)*, Vol. 1: *Medinat ha-Yehudim, Altneuland (The Jewish State, the Old New Land)*, pp. 85-288; there is also an English translation titled "The Old New Land".

44   Patai, ed., *The Complete Diaries of Theodor Herzl*, Vol. 1, pp. 299-309.

45   Ibid, p. 310.

3. Herzl and the Zionist Organization 163

with Frederick I, the Grand Duke of Baden in Germany, whose children Hechler taught, so that Herzl could present his idea to the duke. The duke had the Kaiser's respect, having crowned the Kaiser after the unification of Germany. In Herzl's meeting with the duke, in late April 1896, the former described the benefits that both the West and the East would accrue from his scheme to establish a Jewish state in Palestine. He tried to convince the duke by assuring him that the emigration of Jews from Germany would weaken its revolutionary parties, which opposed the monarchy. Herzl hoped that these words would reach the Kaiser, and the duke promised to present the matter to the Kaiser at the earliest opportunity.[46] Herzl was able to gain the duke's confidence and subsequently turned to him, on more than one occasion, for help.

Herzl continued his efforts to meet the kings and leaders of his time and gain their support for his idea. Not long after this meeting, he went, in May 1896, to meet the pope's representative in Vienna. He entered his office cautiously, "looking around furtively, like a man entering a house of ill repute".[47] He gained nothing from this meeting, however, as the representative refused to support his scheme. In mid-June, Herzl traveled to Istanbul, accompanied by Philipp Newlinski, a Pole who had worked as an attaché at the Austrian embassy in Turkey and was well-informed about the country and its rulers. Herzl tried to meet the sultan, but was denied the opportunity and had to hold talks with a few ministers instead. Again, this was without benefit, after he had paid large sums to them in bribery.[48] From Istanbul, Herzl went to London, where he was finally able to meet Lord Rothschild, in mid-July, and give him the speech that he had prepared. They had a dispute, however, when Rothschild refused to support him. Herzl threatened to "set the masses in motion".[49]

---

46 Ibid, pp. 331-340.

47 Ibid, p. 352.

48 Ibid, pp. 366-399.

49 Ibid, pp. 426-431.

In another vein, Herzl had begun to publish a weekly newspaper, *Die Welt* (*The World*), with financial assistance from his father. Herzl used this publication to promote his views,[50] especially as the other newspaper he was working for flatly refused to refer to his schemes or activities, or even to print the word "Zionism". (Later, Herzl transferred ownership of *Die Welt* to the Zionist Organization.)

At this stage, Herzl saw that he could not continue his work in this way – trying to "solve the Jewish question" on his own. His individual negotiations with various parties had yielded no result. Rothschild's refusal to stand by him also seemed to convince him, finally, that he could not rely on wealthy Jews and their notables to support his plans. He thus had to follow through on his "threat" to Rothschild, to "set the masses in motion", and establish the "Society of Jews", as he had termed it in his book, in the form of a Zionist congress. The idea of holding a general congress to discuss the conditions of the Zionist "movement" – which, until that time, consisted of various associations among the Jews in eastern or western Europe, characterized mostly by internal conflict, organizational rivalries and, sometimes, the occult – was not the brainchild of Herzl, but had come into discussion several years earlier. One of the first to call for a Zionist congress was the "Kadimah" (Onward) association of Jewish university students in Vienna, headed by Nathan Birnbaum[51] (1864-1937). (He was the first to coin the word "Zionism", referring to Mount Zion, in Jerusalem, to define the movement calling for the return of the Jews to Palestine, although he abandoned this idea in his final days.) Birnbaum was one of the first to contact Herzl after the publication of *The Jewish State*, but they soon fell out.[52] Other Zionists also contacted Herzl for the same purpose,[53]

---

50 Ibid, p. 225; and Vol. 2, pp. 546, 557.

51 For details, see Bein, *Theodor Herzl, Biographia* (*Theodor Herzl, A Biography*), p. 147.

52 Patai, ed., *The Complete Diaries of Theodor Herzl*, Vol. 1, pp. 306-308, 314; Vol. 2, p. 589.

53 Moshe Medzini, *Ha-Mediniut ha-Tzionit* (*Zionist Policy*), p. 1020.

3. Herzl and the Zionist Organization 165

and more than one preparatory meeting was held, in the first half of 1896,[54] to deliberate on holding the congress. Herzl was quick to catch the wave of interest, and he called Jewish and Zionist leaders in several countries, seeking their support.[55] He also sent envoys to promote the idea[56] and appointed others to coordinate preparations for the congress.[57] He had resounding success in Romania, where Lovers of Zion decided unanimously to join him.[58] Lovers of Zion in Russia also agreed to attend the congress after he promised to hold it publicly and with the approval of the authorities.[59] Part of Lovers of Zion in Germany and all their associations in Britain, on the other hand, opposed holding the congress,[60] but Herzl and his supporters paid little heed and decided to hold it in Munich. They had to move it, however, after opposition from the rabbis in the city[61] – whom Herzl dubbed the "protest rabbis".

4

The First Zionist Congress was held in Basel, Switzerland, on August 29-31, 1897, with 204 delegates, part of whom represented 117 Zionist associations. About 70 delegates came from Russia alone, and delegates from the United States, Scandinavia and

---

54 For details, see Bein, *Theodor Herzl, Biographia (Theodor Herzl, A Biography)*, pp. 171-176; and Leib Yaffe, ed., *Sefer ha-Congress (Book of the [First Zionist] Congress)*, pp. 403-405.

55 Letters in Yaffe, L., ed., *Sefer ha-Congress (Book of the [First Zionist] Congress)*, pp. 407-414.

56 Israel Klausner, *Ha-Tnu'ah le-Tzion be-Rusia (Zionist Movement in Russia)*, Vols. 2-3: *Me-Katowice ad Basel (From Katowice to Basel)*, Vol. 3, pp. 358-359.

57 Ibid, p. 356.

58 Israel Klausner, *Hibbat Tzion be Romania (Lovers of Zion in Romania)*, pp. 301-323.

59 Klausner, I., *Ha-Tnu'ah le-Tzion be-Rusia (Zionist Movement in Russia)*, Vol. 3, p. 366.

60 Ibid, p. 360.

61 Yaffe, L., ed., *Sefer ha-Congress (Book of the [First Zionist] Congress)*, pp. 405-406.

even Algeria were also present.[62]

Herzl inaugurated the congress with a short speech, in which he emphasized that the aim was "to lay the cornerstone of the edifice which is one day to house the Jewish nation", declaring that "Zionism is a homecoming to the Jewish fold even before it becomes a homecoming to the Jewish land."[63] Max Nordau then gave a lecture in which he painted a dark picture of the conditions of Jews across the world[64] – he then repeated this lecture, with amendments, in a number of Zionist congresses afterwards.[65] Several speakers presented reports on their conditions in Galicia, Britain, Algeria, Romania, Austria, Germany, Bulgaria, Hungary and the United States.[66] Nathan Birnbaum also gave a lecture on "Jewish national life", in which he declared that the words "nationality", "race", and "people" were one and the same to Zionism. He added that "the Jewish people is currently divided into two parts ... the Jews of western countries and the Jews of eastern Europe and all of the Orient,"[67] and that the goal of Zionism should be "to return the Jews of the Orient to progress" and "revive [the Jews] of the West from their deadly Europeanism".[68] Finally, David Farbstein gave a lecture on "Jewish economic life",[69] concluding the first day of the congress.

The second day was that of Nordau, who presented a draft resolution defining the aims of the Zionist movement for

---

62 See list of delegates to First Zionist Congress in *Ha-Protocol shel ha-Congress ha-Tzioni ha-Rishon (Protocols of First Zionist Congress)*, pp. 164-166; see also Yaffe, L., ed., *Sefer ha-Congress (Book of the [First Zionist] Congress)*, pp. 443-447.

63 *Ha-Protocol shel ha-Congress ha-Tzioni ha-Rishon (Protocols of First Zionist Congress)*, pp. 11-12.

64 Ibid, pp. 15-24.

65 See Nordau's speeches in the Second - Sixth Zionist congresses in Max Nordau, *Kitvei Nordau (Works of Nordau)*, Vol. 1, pp. 108-119, 152-161, 199-210; Vol. 2, pp. 57-74, 149-157.

66 Reports in *Ha-Protocol shel ha-Congress ha-Tzioni ha-Rishon (Protocols of First Zionist Congress)*, pp. 25-70.

67 Ibid, p. 72.

68 Ibid, p. 74.

69 Lecture in ibid, pp. 80-91.

3. Herzl and the Zionist Organization

adoption by the congress. After a short discussion, the congress approved the aims of Zionism (henceforth known as the "Basel Program"), as follows:

> Zionism seeks to secure for the Jewish people a publicly recognized, legally assured homeland in Palestine.
>
> For the attainment of this purpose, the Congress considers the following means serviceable:
>
> The promotion of the settlement of Jewish agriculturists, artisans, and tradesmen in Palestine.
>
> The federation of all Jews into local or general groups, according to the laws of the various countries.
>
> The strengthening of the Jewish feeling and consciousness.
>
> Preparatory steps for the attainment of those governmental grants which are necessary to the achievement of the Zionist purpose.[70]

This program remained in effect for more than half a century, until it was amended by the 23rd Zionist Congress, held in Jerusalem in 1951 after the establishment of Israel, and amended again by the 27th Zionist Congress in 1968.

After adopting the Zionist program, the congress proceeded to lay down the organizational framework of the Zionist movement. Max Bodenheimer (1865-1940), a lawyer and member of the leading committee of the congress, gave a lecture that included his suggestions on the organizational bases of the movement. He declared that the dispersal of Jewish people across the world was what prevented them from developing in a national mold; thus it was necessary to form an organization that could overcome these barriers, provided it was a "comprehensive, general organization that brings Zionists of all countries into one framework, with a special program for each country in which there is a Zionist group". This "goal

---

70   Ibid, pp. 97, 102.

can be achieved without interfering in the internal political situations of the countries involved", for "the main goal of the organization, in each country, is to spread our principles among the Jewish masses and gain new members ... which would enable the implementation of our program."[71] Bodenheimer expressed his reservations on a proposal made by Hermann Schapira, professor of mathematics at Heidelberg University and member of the congress, calling for the establishment of a fund to purchase land in Palestine[72] (though the Second Zionist Congress later adopted this proposal). After discussing Bodenheimer's proposals, a preparatory committee was formed of 10 members (two representatives of the Zionists for each of Russia, Austria and Germany, and one representative for each of Romania, Bulgaria, the United States and Britain).[73] The next day, the committee submitted the results of its deliberations on the establishment of the "Zionist Organization" (from 1960, the World Zionist Organization) and its draft regulations, which were approved by the congress as follows:

A. The Congress is the main organization of the Zionists.

B. Paragraph A. Every Zionist who wishes to have voting rights to the Congress must willingly pay, every year, an amount of at least one shekel[74] towards Zionist goals...

Paragraph B. Every 100 shekel-payers elect one delegate, and

---

71 Ibid, pp. 105-106.

72 For details of this proposal and the general aims of the Zionist movement, see the correspondence between Bodenheimer and Schapira prior to the First Zionist Congress, in Henrietta Bodenheimer, *Toldot Tochnit Basel (History of the Basel Program)*, pp. 46-85.

73 *Ha-Protocol shel ha-Congress ha-Tzioni ha-Rishon (Protocols of First Zionist Congress)*, p. 117.

74 The shekel is an old Jewish currency. When the Zionist Congress adopted it as a unit to pay membership fees in the Zionist Organization, it considered it to be of little value, equal to one franc, two shillings, half a dollar, half a gulden, 40 klubeck, or one mark. Judah al-Kalai had been the first to present this suggestion, at an earlier time. In 1952, four years after the establishment of Israel, it changed the name of its currency from the Palestine pound to the Israeli pound, then, in 1980, to the shekel.

3. Herzl and the Zionist Organization

each delegate can represent several groups, to a maximum number of 10.

C. The Congress elects, by means of ballot cards (that is, by secret voting), a Zionist executive to implement decisions, manage affairs [of the organization], and designate the location of the next congress.

D. The Executive has its headquarters in Vienna and is composed of 15 members (Greater Actions Committee), of whom five must be based in Vienna (Inner Actions Committee).[75] The remaining members are distributed among the Zionist groups according to their countries... Members of the Zionist Executive outside Vienna are elected by the Congress, after nomination by the Zionist groups in the countries concerned, while the five permanent members are elected and appointed by the entire Congress.

E. Every member of the Zionist Executive who does not reside in Vienna has the right, per prior agreement with the Executive in Vienna, to appoint a Zionist representative of his to the Executive.

F. Members of the Executive represent the committee (as a whole) before the regional committees in their countries.

G. The Executive has the right to appoint a secretary, based in Vienna.

H. The Executive appoints committees, when necessary [for various tasks].

I. The affairs of Zionist organization and propaganda are organized, in each country, per need and according to the laws of that country, and the Executive must be notified of the manner in which this is done.[76]

---

75 The latter was, in practice, the real executive.

76 *Ha-Protocol shel ha-Congress ha-Tzioni ha-Rishon (Protocols of First Zionist Congress)*, pp. 128-129.

After approving these regulations, the congress heard reports on the conditions of Jewish settlers in Palestine, elected Herzl chairman of the Zionist Executive and president of the Zionist Organization, and adjourned.

The First Zionist Congress was a turning point in the history of the Zionist movement. The founders of the movement were able to gather most Zionists within the framework of the Zionist Organization, which then assumed supervision of the Zionist agencies. This gave it strength and flexibility when dealing with other parties, including states and rulers, in the pursuit of its goals. The establishment of the Zionist Organization ushered in a new era of activity, putting the movement on a path it had not taken before, and opened new horizons for it to work on implementing its schemes. The founders considered their accomplishment at Basel to be a very important and successful one. Upon his return to Vienna, Herzl wrote, in his diary: "At Basel I founded the Jewish State. If I said this out loud today I would be greeted by universal laughter. In five years perhaps, and certainly in 50 years, everyone will perceive it."[77]

In fact, this did come about exactly 50 years later, with the United Nations Partition Plan for Palestine, in 1947.

5

After the First Zionist Congress, Herzl set to work with great force and determination – especially after he had become the head of an international Zionist organization, which, albeit small, frail and just starting out, was sufficient in its presence to get more than one leader to meet and listen to its president. Herzl's standing also grew, after his election to this position, when dealing with various Jewish or Zionist groups. He focused his activity, from that time until his death (in 1904), on two axes. The first was strengthening the Zionist Organization by means of the successive Zionist congresses that he held, and establishing and supporting its complementary agencies. The second was going from one country to another to meet the

---

77   Patai, ed., *The Complete Diaries of Theodor Herzl*, Vol. 2, p. 581.

3. Herzl and the Zionist Organization 171

leaders and rulers of his time: kings, princes and others, to gain their support of his endeavors to obtain a region in the world and establish a Jewish state – in Palestine or elsewhere. The Zionists, however, also added a third axis that Herzl was forced to work in: his effort to face their opposition or criticism, or their push for him to change his path, and sometimes their conspiracies against him. The Zionist congresses were a focal point to work in these three axes such that, in Herzl's lifetime, five other congresses were held (the second, in Basel, on August 28-31, 1898, with 349 delegates, representing 913 Zionist groups;[78] the third, in Basel, on August 15-18, 1899, with 153 delegates, representing 114,370 shekel-paying Zionists; the fourth, in London, on August 13-16, 1900, with 498 delegates, representing 96,434 Zionists; the fifth, in Basel, on December 26-30, 1901, with 358 delegates, representing 96,626 Zionists; and the sixth, in Basel, on August 23-28, 1903, with 592 delegates, representing 232,645 Zionists.)[79]

In the first axis, which aimed to strengthen the Zionist Organization and establish its comprehensive agencies, Herzl considered that "the Basel Congress meant the creation of the Society of Jews." Thus, "the work of the coming year will be the establishment of the Jewish Company, provisionally named the Jewish Colonial Bank [Jewish Colonial Trust]."[80] This is what Herzl did at the Second Zionist Congress.[81] In his opening speech, he declared that the Zionist Executive had taken the necessary steps to establish a Zionist bank and that he expected the bank to begin operations within a year.[82] He then submitted the bank's incorporation contract to the congress for approval – and here the first disputes emerged between Herzl and his opponents.

---

78   Medzini, *Ha-Mediniut ha-Tzionit (Zionist Policy)*, p. 121.

79   See also *Ha-Protocol shel ha-Congress ha-Tzioni ha-Yud Tet (Protocols of 19th Zionist Congress)*, p. 11; and Moshe Shmueli, *Toldot ha-Tzionout ve Tnu'at ha-Avoda (History of Zionism and the Labor Movement)*, Vol. 1, p. 284.

80   Patai, ed., *The Complete Diaries of Theodor Herzl*, Vol. 2, pp. 593-594.

81   Yitzhak Gruenbaum, *Ha-Tnu'ah ha-Tzionit (The Zionist Movement)*, Vol. 2, p. 20.

82   See Herzl's speech at the Second Zionist Congress, in Herzl, *Kitvei Herzl (Works of Herzl)*, Vol. 7, p. 236.

Those disputes continued thereafter between Herzl's supporters, headed by Nordau, and their opponents, especially the Russian Zionists, who focused on a very important aspect related to the method of Zionist work itself. Herzl and his supporters believed that the Zionist movement had to seek political guarantees and public recognition by states, establishing the sovereignty of the Zionist Organization over a certain region, and only afterwards would Jewish people begin to emigrate and be resettled in that state – this line was known as "political Zionism". Conversely, its opponents demanded the encouragement of practical settlement in Palestine, regardless of circumstance, while seeking, at the same time, to obtain international guarantees for the establishment of a Jewish state in the country – a line that was known as "practical Zionism". Conflict raged between the two sides, with Herzl leaving no doubt about his position in favor of the "politicians", as he had referred to in *The Jewish State*. In his opening speech to the First Zionist Congress, he announced that

> There will be no question of intrigues, secret interventions, and devious methods in our ranks, but only of unhampered utterances under the constant and complete supervision of public opinion... Zionism cannot gain its ends otherwise than through an unreserved understanding with the political units involved... The results of [Jewish] colonization [in Palestine] as it has been carried on hitherto were as satisfactory as its scope permitted... But colonization in its present form is not, and cannot be the solution of the Jewish question.[83]

On another occasion, addressing Nordau, Herzl wrote that he was "opposed to infiltration [of Jews into Palestine], which has no future and is at the mercy of every pasha, subject to every immigration prohibition".[84] In his opening speech to the Fifth Zionist Congress, Herzl also launched a fierce attack on Lovers

---

83 *Ha-Protocol shel ha-Congress ha-Tzioni ha-Rishon (Protocols of First Zionist Congress)*, pp. 12-13.

84 Patai, ed., *The Complete Diaries of Theodor Herzl*, Vol. 2, p. 629.

3. Herzl and the Zionist Organization

of Zion and practical Zionists, declaring that "our position to the earlier Zionists is simply that of people who make modern improvements on an unserviceable old machine. Doubtless the old machine deserves veneration, but it belongs to a museum... Philanthropic colonization is a failure. National colonization will succeed."[85]

Nordau was fiercer than Herzl in his attack on practical Zionists and Lovers of Zion: "I protest vehemently, with all force," he wrote, in one of his articles,

> against any attempt to link Zionism with [Jewish] settlements that exist in the Land of Israel and to consider them related to each other... Zionism bears no responsibility for the settlements in the Land of Israel; if these settlements grow and flourish, this will not be recorded in its favor, and, if they disappear, it will not be its fault... A few settlements in the Land of Israel will not save the Jewish people, will not improve their conditions and will have no effect on their fate.[86]

Moreover, he saw the method of Lovers of Zion and practical Zionists in solving the Jewish question as akin to "wanting to pump the ocean by means of a pail".[87] They, according to Nordau, were trying to solve the problems of small numbers of Jews in a few settlements, while Zionism sought to solve the Jewish question as a whole. At a later stage, Nordau described the Lovers of Zion movement as "nothing but a title for a book of blank pages, and political Zionism has written the book for this blank title".[88] It is clear that Nordau's stance gained him the enmity of the practical Zionists, who took revenge on him after Herzl's death and removed him from the sphere of effective Zionist work.

The second point of dispute between the two parties was the opposition's suspicion that Herzl was willing to take any

---

85   Herzl, *Kitvei Herzl (Works of Herzl)*, Vol. 8, p. 115.

86   Nordau, *Kitvei Nordau (Works of Nordau)*, Vol. 1, pp. 167-168.

87   Ibid, Vol. 3, p. 148.

88   Ibid, Vol. 4, p. 166.

suitable region – not just Palestine – to establish a Jewish state in it. Those doubts were not out of place. When he presented the project to establish a bank to the congress, the practical Zionists saw that the bank's scope of operation – per the proposed incorporation contract – was the "Orient". They rose up and asked to replace this with the words "Palestine and Syria". This opposition was led by Menachem Ussishkin (1863-1941),[89] a prominent Russian Zionist leader, who would later render great services to Zionist settlement in Palestine after his election as president of Keren Kayemet le-Yisrael (Jewish National Fund) during the British Mandate.[90] Herzl, for his part, suspected that the opposition did not want to establish the bank at all. Thus he asked to form committees on the issue and "forced discussion so as to tire the people out. After [he] had let them scream on this point for four hours, [he] abandoned it,"[91] and the congress agreed to the original proposal. Herzl also insisted, prior to the establishment of the bank, to grant its founding shares to seven of his political Zionist friends, headed by Wolffsohn, to ensure that his political line would control the financial agency of the Zionist Organization. In the Third Zionist Congress, the opposition tried to prevent him but he threatened to "draw his conclusions"[92] and hinted at his resignation. Thus he attained his wish.

Herzl's troubles in establishing the bank did not end there, however. The major Jewish financiers refused to contribute to its establishment,[93] and even the JCA and the Alliance took the same position.[94] Thus the Zionist Organization had to offer the bank's shares for sale on the financial markets, but it could not find a

---

89   Patai, ed., *The Complete Diaries of Theodor Herzl*, Vol. 2, p. 797.

90   See his biography in *Sefer Ussishkin (Book of Ussishkin)*, pp. 11-28 (Introduction).

91   Patai, ed., *The Complete Diaries of Theodor Herzl*, Vol. 2, pp. 654-655.

92   Herzl, *Kitvei Herzl (Works of Herzl)*, Vol. 8, pp. 26, 28.

93   Patai, ed., *The Complete Diaries of Theodor Herzl*, Vol. 2, pp. 605, 620; Vol. 3, p. 1152.

94   Ibid, Vol. 4, pp. 1385-1386.

3. Herzl and the Zionist Organization 175

"proper bank" to handle the sale, because of a "first-class boycott on the part of Jewish high finance".[95] The sale of the bank's shares, after it was registered in London in late March 1899,[96] also did not go through as quickly as expected, and Herzl had to replace those charged with implementing it due to their inept work.[97] When the shares were offered for sale, Herzl was not confident that the process would succeed. He even announced, at one point, that he was ready to give "ten years of [his] life"[98] in return for its success. The bank's administrators could not amass 250,000 pounds sterling from the price of the shares that were offered for sale, out of a registered capital of 2 million pounds – the amount needed for the bank to begin operations – until 1901, two years after the bank's establishment. In the following year, the bank formed a subsidiary,[99] the "Anglo-Palestine Company", which opened a branch in Jaffa in 1903 and later changed its name to the "Anglo-Palestine Bank".[100]

It should be noted that the financial capabilities of the Zionist Organization, in Herzl's time, were very limited, and it found itself, more than once, in a state of financial deficit. It seems that this situation prompted Herzl to remain in his journalistic work and continue making a living from that, declining any salary from the organization.

At the Second Zionist Congress, Herzl announced another aim of the Zionist movement, "the conquest of the Jewish communities",[101] on the advice of Nordau.[102] This was in response

---

95 Ibid, Vol. 2, pp. 787, 827.

96 See the bank's articles of association and regulations in Hen-Melech Merchavia, *Am ou-Moledet (Nation and Homeland)*, pp. 210-218.

97 Patai, ed., *The Complete Diaries of Theodor Herzl*, Vol. 3, pp. 914, 948-949, 1083-1084.

98 Ibid, Vol. 2, pp. 786, 812.

99 Merchavia, *Am ou-Moledet (Nation and Homeland)*, pp. 218-219.

100 After the establishment of Israel, the name was changed to "Bank Leumi" – National Bank, in Hebrew.

101 Herzl's opening speech at the Second Zionist Congress, in Herzl, *Kitvei Herzl (Works of Herzl)*, Vol. 7, p. 237.

102 Nordau, *Kitvei Nordau (Works of Nordau)*, Vol. 4, p. 188.

to the opposition to Zionism among some Jewish groups. The congress also took measures to ensure the legitimacy of the Zionist associations in the countries in which they worked.

The third Zionist agency that was established during Herzl's era, after the Zionist Organization and its bank, was the Jewish National Fund. The purpose of this company was to acquire lands in Palestine for Jewish settlement. A proposal in this regard had been submitted to the First Zionist Congress by one of its delegates, Hermann Schapira, such that the company would be financed by donations from Jewish people.[103] At the first congress, the proposal was not discussed and the topic was not raised again due to differences between the political and practical Zionists. It was only brought up at the Fourth Zionist Congress in 1900, which took a decision, "in principle", to establish the company.[104] The Fifth Zionist Congress approved the project "provisionally".[105] However, Herzl was quick to put pressure on the delegates to amend their decision to a final one.[106] Upon setting up the regulations of this company and defining its powers to purchase land or act on it, the Zionist Executive decided that such land purchased by the company should be "the perpetual property of the Jewish people",[107] could not be sold, and could only "[be] cultivated or also [leased] (subleasing being prohibited) … to Jews" (a practice still adhered to in Israel).[108] The Sixth Zionist Congress ratified this decision. In 1905, the company began its work in Palestine and purchased the first plot of land, after Max Bodenheimer was appointed its chairman. In 1907, the Jewish National Fund was formally registered as a joint stock company in Britain, and declared, in the first article of its incorporation contract, that its goal was to work on acquiring

---

103 *Ha-Protocol shel ha-Congress ha-Tzioni ha-Rishon (Protocols of First Zionist Congress)*, pp. 142-144.

104 Merchavia, *Am ou-Moledet (Nation and Homeland)*, p. 178.

105 Ibid.

106 Herzl, *Kitvei Herzl (Works of Herzl)*, Vol. 8, pp. 135-142.

107 Merchavia, *Am ou-Moledet (Nation and Homeland)*, p. 178.

108 Ibid, p. 179.

3. Herzl and the Zionist Organization

land or any rights to it in the region that included "Palestine, Syria, any parts of Asiatic Turkey, and the Sinai Peninsula or any part thereof, in order to settle Jews on those lands".[109] (After the founding of Israel, this article was amended so that the region of the company's work included "the State of Israel, within any area that is subject to the laws of the government of Israel"[110]).

Upon its establishment, the Jewish National Fund became the main instrument of the Zionist Organization to purchase land in Palestine. The company adhered to the restrictions imposed on it, refrained from leasing its land to non-Jews (including Palestinian Arabs) and only leased it to Jews. This was usually for a period of 49 years (per Talmudic land laws), renewable for another 49 years. The company also obliged its tenants to only employ Jews on the land.[111]

6

The second axis of Herzl's activity was the pursuit of the establishment of a Jewish state, in almost any place in which it could be done. As mentioned earlier, he met with kings and leaders of his time to gain their support, always trying to convince them of the benefits that they themselves or their countries would gain as a result. In this activity, Herzl appeared to be trying to conclude a "commercial deal"[112] to establish a Jewish state with any party that would agree to it, and with the best conditions possible.

Germany was the first country that Herzl approached. This

---

109 *Report on the Legal Structure, Activities, Assets, Income and Liabilities of Keren Kayemet le-Yisrael*, p. 17; see also Henrietta Bodenheimer's article, "On the Crystallization of the Constitution of Keren Kayemet le-Yisrael", in Ben-Zion Dinur (Dinaburg), ed., *Shivat Tzion (Return to Zion)*, Vols. 2-3, pp. 495-505.

110 See Article 3(a) of the company's articles of incorporation in *Rishomot (Israeli Gazette)*, Bulletin Collection 354, 10/6/1954, p. 1196; see also ibid, *Book of Laws* 138, 3/12/1953, p. 264.

111 See the company's lease contract form in Merchavia, *Am ou-Moledet (Nation and Homeland)*, pp. 193-194.

112 Jacob Talmon, *Be-Idan ha-Alimut (The Age of Violence)*, p. 175.

was on the eve of the First Zionist Congress, when he heard that the German Kaiser intended to visit Palestine. Herzl estimated that "German policy has taken an eastern course"[113] and decided to link the Zionist movement with it, in the hope that its eastern course could reach Palestine. He contacted his old friend, the Grand Duke of Baden, then met with Philipp Eulenburg, the German ambassador to Austria; Bernhard von Bülow, the German foreign minister; and, finally, with the German chancellor himself, Hohenlohe (Chlodwig Karl Viktor).[114] During the meetings, Herzl persuaded the German officials to mediate with the Kaiser to extend his protection to the Zionist movement and adopt its demands, stressing that "with the Jews a German cultural element would come to the Orient,"[115] that the Zionist movement was "turning [the Jews] away from socialism",[116] and that it sought control over an area of land in and around Palestine, which would grow according to the number of immigrants.[117] Those talks raised great hopes in Herzl, for "to live under the protection of this strong, great, moral, splendidly governed, tightly organized Germany can only have the most salutary effect on the Jewish national character."[118] Herzl was then invited to meet the Kaiser, and decided to demand the lands "from the Brook of Egypt [in el-Arish] to the Euphrates" for his project.[119] He assured the Kaiser that Zionism was working to distance the Jews from the revolutionary parties that opposed his rule, and asked for German protection of the Zionist movement and mediation with the sultan of Turkey to encourage him to agree to a Jewish concession company settling Jews in Palestine and its vicinity.[120] The Germans then instructed Herzl to travel

---

113 Patai, ed., *The Complete Diaries of Theodor Herzl*, Vol. 2, p. 639.
114 Ibid, pp. 655, 662-664, 665-669, 701-705.
115 Ibid, p. 658.
116 Ibid, p. 688.
117 Ibid, pp. 701-702.
118 Ibid, p. 693.
119 Ibid, p. 711.
120 Ibid, p. 734.

3. Herzl and the Zionist Organization 179

to Palestine to meet the Kaiser there, at the end of his visit to the sultan. Herzl met the Kaiser in Jerusalem in November 1898, where he made a speech on the aims and demands of Zionism. The Kaiser's tepid response, however, convinced Herzl that the mediation with the sultan had not borne fruit.[121] Later, Herzl found out from his friend, the Grand Duke of Baden, that the sultan had heatedly replied to the Kaiser's remarks on Zionist requests, such that the latter did not see fit to revisit the subject,[122] especially since Germany was not prepared to put pressure on Turkey, fearing Britain and its fleet.[123]

Despite this failure, Herzl announced, in his opening speech to the Third Zionist Congress (1899), that the aim of his movement was to obtain a concession from the Turkish government to start implementing the Zionist scheme in Palestine under the protection of the sultan, and that Zionism preferred to wait and obtain a license rather than to send the Jews to the country illegally.[124] After the congress, Herzl spared no effort to reach the sultan. He called Nuri Pasha, director of the Turkish foreign ministry, and attempted to bribe him with a large sum of money in return for his help.[125] He also called a Jewish professor named Armin Vambery, at the University of Budapest, who, in Herzl's words, "doesn't know whether he is more Turk than Englishman, writes books in German, speaks twelve languages with equal mastery, and has professed five religions, in two of which he has served as a priest".[126] Vambery had a personal relationship with the sultan, so Herzl also promised him a sum of money if he could help. Those efforts bore fruit, and Herzl was called to Istanbul in May 1901 in his capacity as "Chief of the Jews and an

---

121 Ibid, pp. 756-757.

122 Ibid, Vol. 3, p. 1021.

123 Ibid, pp. 928-934.

124 Speech in Herzl, *Kitvei Herzl (Works of Herzl)*, Vol. 8, pp. 4-5.

125 For details, see Patai, ed., *The Complete Diaries of Theodor Herzl*, Vol. 3, pp. 847-924, 1090-1091.

126 Ibid, p. 961.

influential journalist", to meet the sultan.[127] He was forbidden to talk about Zionism, however. During the meeting, Herzl offered to help the Turkish government to consolidate its debts to foreign creditors, who were pressuring it and meddling in its internal affairs. He proposed a long-term loan to the Turkish government by some Jewish financiers. In return, he asked the sultan to issue a "pro-Jewish proclamation" to welcome the Jews coming to the Ottoman Empire and settling in it.[128] After this interview, Izzet Pasha, one of the sultan's advisers, summoned Herzl to negotiate his proposal and told him that the Jews could "come to us",[129] on condition that they agreed to accept Ottoman citizenship, and would not be permitted to settle collectively anywhere in the empire. In the negotiations that followed, Herzl was again summoned in February 1902 to Istanbul. Once more, he was informed that the Jews who came to the Ottoman Empire would not be allowed to settle, initially, in Palestine,[130] and that the government would periodically specify the places in which they could do so.[131] Herzl declined this offer. The position of the Turkish government, as well as Herzl's inability to find the funds to consolidate the debts, halted negotiations between the two sides. Herzl became convinced that he would not obtain a concession to settle the Jews in Palestine until after the partition of Turkey.[132]

Although Vambery stressed to Herzl, again, that the sultan refused to allow the Jews to settle in Palestine – and that he might allow this in Asia Minor or Iraq, on lands freely offered by the government[133] – Herzl tried to maintain some relationship with the Turkish authorities. He proposed, for example, the establishment of a university in Turkey staffed by Jewish

---

127 Ibid, p. 1092.

128 See minutes of Herzl's meeting with the sultan in ibid, pp. 1112-1118.

129 Ibid, p. 1134.

130 Ibid, pp. 1218-1219.

131 Ibid, pp. 1221-1224.

132 Ibid, p. 1225.

133 Ibid, p. 1251.

3. Herzl and the Zionist Organization 181

professors, which would prevent Turkish students from studying in Western universities and acquiring revolutionary principles that opposed the sultan's rule.[134] He received no answer to this proposal. In July 1902, Herzl was invited to Istanbul – for the last time – to discuss the issue of consolidating the empire's debts. Once there, however, he discovered that this call was only a form of pressure by the Turkish government on a group of French financiers, with whom it was negotiating the same issue. He returned with no success.[135]

From Turkey, Herzl moved to Britain after the Zionists had done some preparatory work there. The Fourth Zionist Congress (1900) had been held in London and had aroused interest in some British circles,[136] prompting Herzl to write, in his diary: "We have made a demonstration before the English world, and the demonstration has been noticed."[137] The Zionist Federation in Britain had also held a "referendum" among parliamentary candidates on their stance on Zionism, which showed that 60 of them supported it.[138] Further, Britain was somewhat eager to find a solution to the immigration of Jewish people from eastern Europe, which had aroused opposition among the British public to the extent that the government had had to form a committee to address the matter. Herzl himself was among those invited to testify before this committee.[139]

Before Herzl undertook any activity in Britain, he met with Mayer Rothschild, member of the House of Lords and a prominent Jewish leader. Herzl persuaded him to mediate with the British government to grant the Zionist Organization a concession to settle the Jews in the regions of el-Arish, the Sinai Peninsula, and Cyprus. In November 1902, Herzl was invited to

---

134   Ibid, Vol. 4, p. 1275.

135   Details of negotiations in ibid, pp. 1313-1348.

136   Yitzhak Mior, *Ha-Tnu'ah ha-Tzionit be-Rusia (Zionist Movement in Russia)*, p. 180.

137   Patai, ed., *The Complete Diaries of Theodor Herzl*, Vol. 3, p. 976.

138   Ibid, pp. 981-982.

139   See testimony in Herzl, *Kitvei Herzl (Works of Herzl)*, Vol. 8, pp. 164-204.

meet the British colonial secretary, Joseph Chamberlain. In the meeting, Herzl explained that it was possible to settle the Jews in Cyprus, after forcing its inhabitants to leave,[140] or in el-Arish and the Sinai Peninsula, but "we will not go to Egypt. We have been there."[141] Chamberlain, however, persuaded him to drop the idea of settlement in Cyprus and aim for el-Arish, an area in possession of the British foreign ministry, which he advised Herzl to contact. Herzl submitted a memorandum to the British foreign secretary, Lord Lansdowne, explaining his scheme and indicating that it would be favorable for Britain to gain the confidence of the Jews.[142] He then met with the secretary and they agreed that the Zionist Organization would send an envoy to Egypt to meet its ruler, Lord Cromer (Evelyn Baring), and seek his opinion. In Cairo, Herzl's envoy, Greenberg, agreed with Cromer that the Zionist Organization would send a commission to study the nature of the area that it proposed to allocate for Jewish settlement before deciding on the matter.[143] Meanwhile, Herzl drafted a concession project[144] that would be granted to the Zionist Organization in the area to be agreed upon. In early February 1903, the commission arrived in el-Arish and surveyed it until mid-April. During its work, it sent a discouraging preliminary report regarding the area's suitability for settlement due to its scarce water resources.[145] The final report was no more encouraging and confirmed that the area was completely unsuitable for settlers from European countries. It was a desert and had to be supplied with quantities of water that required huge sums to be drawn.[146] Herzl then traveled to Cairo, in March 1903, and met with Cromer twice to seek his position and that of the Egyptian government on the project, and noted that the

---

140   Patai, ed., *The Complete Diaries of Theodor Herzl*, Vol. 3, p. 1301.

141   Ibid.

142   Ibid, p. 1367.

143   Ibid, pp. 1381-1382.

144   Draft in Medzini, *Ha-Mediniut ha-Tzionit (Zionist Policy)*, pp. 320-321.

145   See also ibid, pp. 322-329.

146   Report in ibid, pp. 330-332.

reactions were "cooler".[147]

In April 1903, upon his return from Cairo, Herzl again met with the British colonial secretary, Chamberlain, to discuss the status of negotiations on the Jewish settlement scheme in el-Arish. Chamberlain informed him, after estimating that this project would not enjoy great success, that he had seen a "land for [him]" on his African tour, in Uganda, fit to establish a Jewish state. Herzl replied that he would first prefer a place for settlement near Palestine, from which, "later on, we could also settle in Uganda," and that he preferred to work on salvaging what he could of the settlement scheme in el-Arish. As for Uganda, he was ready to "take it" and settle the Jews there, but not at that time – for Palestine would not suffice to resettle all the Jews of the world, and Zionism may be forced to resettle part of them in Uganda later.[148]

The events that transpired after this, however, forced Herzl to reconsider his position. On April 6-8, 1903, which happened to be the end of the Jewish Passover and the beginning of Easter for Eastern Christians, a pogrom took place against the Jews in Kishinev, Russia, reminiscent of those in the early 1880s. The pogrom killed 47 Jews, injured hundreds, and left thousands homeless, due to the looting and destruction of about 1,500 Jewish residences and shops.[149] This violence sparked widespread international outrage and condemnation, for it was the first of its kind in the 20th century – but it was only a prelude to a wave of similar pogroms that lasted for about three years, until the suppression of the 1905 revolution in Russia. It was very clear that the tsarist authorities had orchestrated these pogroms, especially after the minister of the interior, Vyacheslav Konstantinovich von Plehve – "butcher" of the revolutionary movement and of the Jews – had decided to provoke hatred against them, seemingly to suppress dissent and divert the revolutionary outburst in

---

147 Patai, ed., *The Complete Diaries of Theodor Herzl*, Vol. 4, pp. 1446-1447.

148 See Herzl's discussion with Chamberlain in ibid, pp. 1473-1475.

149 Mior, *Ha-Tnu'ah ha-Tzionit be-Rusia (Zionist Movement in Russia)*, p. 209.

the country from the political sphere to racial hatred.[150] The Russian government did not bother to deny the accusations of its responsibility for these events. The pogroms ushered in a new wave of Jewish emigration from Russia to Palestine, starting in 1904. This wave became known as the Second Aliyah.

Barely a month after the Kishinev pogrom, Herzl learned that the expert commissioned by the British government to study the scheme of Jewish settlement in el-Arish had finally stated his opposition to it, because the amount of water needed to irrigate the area was more than twice that estimated by the Zionist Organization experts. Herzl also learned that Cromer had recommended the project be dropped. The Egyptian government finally announced its rejection,[151] explaining that it could not forgo the huge quantities of water that would be taken from the Nile to irrigate the lands of el-Arish for Jewish settlement.

Herzl, naturally, was not pleased with these results. The failure of this scheme, on the one hand, and the attacks on the Jews in Russia and their continued emigration from it, on the other, placed him in a critical dilemma that required an urgent solution. He began thinking of Uganda and Mozambique. The latter was then under the rule of Portugal, so Herzl called the Portuguese ambassador in Vienna and presented a project to settle the Jews in Mozambique, seeking the opinion of the Portuguese government.[152] Herzl also tried to meet the Russian tsar, but was invited to instead meet Plehve. In early August 1903, Herzl arrived in the Russian capital.

It was not difficult for the two men to understand each other. In fact, Herzl may not have had a better understanding with any of the non-Jewish officials whom he met than he did with the Russian minister of the interior. Plehve was an anti-Semite; he hated the Jews and had a long history of persecuting them,

---

150 See also ibid, p. 210.

151 Patai, ed., *The Complete Diaries of Theodor Herzl*, Vol. 4, pp. 1480-1481, 1486-1487.

152 Ibid, pp. 1487, 1491-1500.

because he saw them as the reason for the unrest caused to the tsar's government, due to the relatively large numbers of them participating in the revolutionary movements. Herzl saw, in Plehve's position, a vivid example of his Zionist theory based on anti-Semitism. Thus his only concern was that the exit of the Jews from Russia, if it had to happen, had to be done in the easiest way possible. He decided to reach an understanding with Plehve, especially as the bulk of the Zionist movement – in quantity and quality – was then among the Russian Jews, and it was better to reach an understanding with the authorities to prevent them from persecuting or banning the movement. The tsar's government was, of course, aware of Zionist activity in Russia, while Plehve himself – as was evident from his instructions to Russian interior ministry officials regarding such activity – was an expert on Zionist affairs. His government had not condoned the Zionist organizations in the country, yet had refrained from attacking them as long as their activity was focused on the emigration of Jews. This situation changed, however, after the establishment of the Zionist Organization, as Russian Zionists connected with their colleagues abroad and began to organize themselves in the country. They formed branches among the Jews in several regions, some of which were active in disseminating Hebrew culture in a manner that caught the attention of Plehve. In June 1903, he issued an order prohibiting any form of Zionist activity in Russia unless it was directed at the emigration of Jews from it.[153]

Herzl held long talks with Plehve in Russia, which he described as "most remarkable", and held talks with other officials as well. Plehve explained to Herzl the bases of Russian policy towards the Jews, stating that Russia was seeking to create a cohesive unit of its population. Thus it was working to assimilate part of the Jews into this population by means of higher education and economic progress, and to be rid of the other part by emigration. However, the situation among the Jews had worsened, and "there [was]

---

[153] For details, see Mior, *Ha-Tnu'ah ha-Tzionit be-Rusia (Zionist Movement in Russia)*, pp. 220-222.

less talk now of Palestinian Zionism than there [was] about culture, organization, and Jewish nationalism."[154] Herzl also met the Russian finance minister, Sergei Witte, to discuss lifting the ban on the sale of shares of the Jewish Colonial Trust in Russia. Witte informed him that the Jews made up about half of the members of revolutionary parties, even though the Jewish population was only about 7 million among 136 million in the country. Thus, "the Jews [were] being given encouragement to emigrate" in various ways, including "kicks".[155] At the end of these talks, Herzl reached an agreement with the officials that the Russian government would exert its good efforts with Turkey to facilitate the entry of Jews into Palestine; that the government would provide financial assistance to the emigrants, the funds of which would be collected from Jewish sources; and that it would facilitate the organization in Russia of Zionist associations committed to the Basel Program.[156] The Jewish Colonial Trust was also allowed to sell its shares in Russia, on condition that it would open a branch in the country so that the authorities could observe the sales transactions. Plehve provided Herzl with a signed letter after discussing its contents with the tsar, in which he declared that the Russian government was sympathetic to Zionism as long as its goal was to establish an independent state in Palestine, and that it was ready to assist. "This assistance may take the form of protection of Zionist representatives before the Ottoman government, facilitating the activities of immigration associations ... and granting them financial assistance ... from taxes levied from the Jews."[157] Herzl made use of this letter on more than one occasion.

In light of these events, Herzl inaugurated the Sixth Zionist Congress (1903) after the British government had officially informed the Zionist Organization of its willingness to permit

---

154   Patai, ed., *The Complete Diaries of Theodor Herzl*, Vol. 4, p. 1525.

155   Ibid, p. 1530.

156   Ibid, p. 1521.

157   Letter in Mior, *Ha-Tnu'ah ha-Tzionit be-Rusia (Zionist Movement in Russia)*, p. 228.

3. Herzl and the Zionist Organization

the resettlement of Jews in Uganda. A legal office in London, where David Lloyd George worked – who later became prime minister of the British government that would issue the Balfour Declaration in 1917 – drafted the settlement project and its concessions. In his opening speech to the congress, Herzl, in a rare instance when he publicly spoke of his political contacts, presented a summary of his activity, including his negotiations with the sultan and with the British government on el-Arish. He also praised the Russian government's position and then presented the Uganda project, before he had discussed the project with the Zionist Executive. In his presentation, Herzl noted that the proposal made by the British government "relates to an autonomous Jewish settlement in East Africa, with a Jewish administration, Jewish local government and a Jewish official at its head, under the suzerainty, I need not add, of Great Britain".[158] Herzl added that "Zion [Uganda] is not and can never be," but this proposal "must of necessity contribute to improving and alleviating the situation of the Jewish people, without our renouncing one iota of the great principles upon which our movement is based".[159] He asked the congress to elect a special committee to follow up on the matter. Nordau spoke afterwards, at Herzl's request, in eager defense of the proposal, asserting that the Uganda settlement project would be nothing but a "night shelter"[160] that would give its residents food and housing, become a political and social education tool, and make Jewish people, and the world, see an embodiment of the idea that the Jews are one people, even after 2,000 years of dispersion.[161]

The reactions to this proposal, however, were not as smooth as its presentation.[162] As soon as the request was made to the congress to form a committee to study the potential

---

158 Herzl, *Kitvei Herzl (Works of Herzl)*, Vol. 8, p. 224.

159 Ibid, pp. 224-225.

160 Nordau, *Kitvei Nordau (Works of Nordau)*, Vol. 4, p. 157.

161 Speech in ibid, pp. 149-157.

162 Due to this speech, a Jewish student later attempted to assassinate the "African Nordau" in Paris.

for settlement in Uganda, a fierce debate erupted among its members. Supporters of the idea saw no harm in accepting the proposal and establishing a Jewish state in Uganda, especially after a major power such as Britain had pledged to help, and they saw this as an opportunity not to be missed. Opponents, on the other hand, accused Herzl and the presidency of the Zionist Organization of "treason" and of violating the decisions of the First Zionist Congress and the Basel Program, which had called for the establishment of a Jewish state in Palestine alone. They saw Herzl's proposal of Uganda and his "giving up the Land of Israel" as an illegitimate act not permissible to the Zionist Organization. The chair of the congress had to take a public vote, in which 295 delegates agreed to the proposal – including those from the Orthodox Mizrahi organization (see section 7 of this chapter) – and 178 voted against it. Most of the opposition were Russian Jews, while the remainder (119) abstained. As soon as the result was announced, the opponents left the hall in protest, calling themselves the "Zionists of Zion" and threatening to split from the Zionist Organization. Herzl, however, managed to prevent this by repeating that his intention was only to form a committee to study the situation in Uganda. He pledged not to take any step obliging the Zionist Organization to carry out settlement activity there before obtaining the approval of a Zionist congress held especially for this purpose. The organization's presidency was also prohibited from using the funds of the Jewish Colonial Trust or the Jewish National Fund to finance a commission to Uganda,[163] and had to secure the necessary expenses from outside the organization's sources.

Despite these pledges, however, the adoption of the Uganda project by the Sixth Congress caused a violent storm in the Zionist camp, splitting it in two.[164] Protests were sent to the presidency of the Zionist Organization. These included a letter from Menachem Ussishkin who had been in Palestine while the

---

163   Mior, *Ha-Tnu'ah ha-Tzionit be-Rusia (Zionist Movement in Russia)*, pp. 249-253.

164   For details, see Medzini, *Ha-Mediniut ha-Tzionit (Zionist Policy)*, pp. 278-290.

3. Herzl and the Zionist Organization 189

congress was being held, working to organize the Zionist settlers. In his message, he stated that the decision of the congress to send a commission to Africa was not "binding" to him, because it meant "a renunciation of Palestine and a separation from it" – a letter that Herzl answered very cynically.[165] Soon after, it became evident that the disputes over the Uganda scheme were uncalled for. As soon as it was announced, the British settlers in Uganda staged a fierce opposition that forced the British government to withdraw the scheme immediately. This, however, did not stop the Russian Zionists from holding a meeting of their own in Kharkov in late October 1903, to protest the steps taken by Herzl. They decided to issue a warning to him to stop his attempts before the Zionist movement split. The meeting also established what it called a "Russian executive committee", which sent a few of its members to meet Herzl and present their protest, but he refused to see them.[166] Later, he held a reconciliation meeting of the Greater Actions Committee,[167] but the echoes of the Uganda project and its impact on the Zionist Organization did not end there.

After the Sixth Congress, Herzl returned to his old style of political work – instead trying to meet various leaders and enlist their help in implementing his schemes. In January 1904, he met the king of Italy, briefed him on Plehve's letter, and received his promise that Italy's ambassador to Turkey would join the Russian ambassador there in his efforts to persuade the Turkish government to facilitate the entry of Jews into Palestine.[168] In the same period, Herzl also met Pope Pius X, who refused to support his schemes – stressing that the Church could not recognize the Jews as a people and could not help them to acquire the holy sites, and that, if Herzl succeeded in his efforts to settle the Jews in Palestine, "we shall have churches and priests ready to baptize

---

165   Letters in Herzl, Vol. 8, pp. 270-275.

166   Mior, *Ha-Tnu'ah ha-Tzionit be-Rusia (Zionist Movement in Russia)*, pp. 260-265.

167   Ibid, pp. 265-267.

168   Patai, ed., *The Complete Diaries of Theodor Herzl*, Vol. 4, pp. 1585-1600.

all of you."[169]

After these two meetings, Herzl's activity lessened as he had grown gravely ill. On July 3, 1904, he died at the age of 44, with his efforts to establish a Jewish state bearing no fruit.

It is notable that Herzl did not refrain from contacting any government or party if he believed that it might benefit the Zionist movement, with the exception of France. This seems to have been due to Herzl's negative impression of the French regime when he had worked as a press correspondent in Paris, in 1891-1895. He had published a book on his experience there, titled *Das Palais Bourbon (Bourbon Palace)*.

It is also notable that Herzl's failure in his efforts to establish a Jewish state was due, primarily, to the lack of objective conditions to induce the Western countries to support this project at the time. Zionism had to wait for an opportune moment.

7

With the death of Herzl, the Zionist movement found itself in a situation quite different from that which had existed in his lifetime. This was not just due to Herzl's activity but also to the reactions of various Zionist groups to this activity or to the Herzl phenomenon itself. With the establishment of the Zionist Organization, an institution was practically formed that claimed the right to represent all Jews for the first time in their modern history. This was despite the fact that it never had the membership of more than 5% of Jewish people across the world. Western Jews were preoccupied with the means of confronting anti-Semitism or preventing the assimilation of Jews into their European communities, and Eastern Jews were largely mired in metaphysics – in search of the best way to hasten the coming of the Savior-Messiah to save them. When the Zionists discovered their underlying strength in their union within the framework of one, global organization, and the crystallization of the idea of establishing a Jewish state – followed by signs of hope as a result of Herzl's activity – they began to adapt themselves to this new

---

169 Ibid, p. 1604.

3. Herzl and the Zionist Organization 191

reality. They reorganized their agencies, set up alliances amongst themselves, and shifted from groups composed of immigration associations, political clubs, or individuals to a multi-party, political entity. Later, this shifted to a socioeconomic one as well, almost like that in any independent state, despite the Zionist dispersal in many countries.

The transformation in the Zionists' work, their organization, political positions, and finally their ideology, initially manifested in reaction to the Herzl phenomenon, which continued its force of development and interaction between the different Zionist groups. Despite the appreciation that Herzl received from the majority of Zionists, many found more than one fault in him. Chief among these was his view of anti-Semitism as the basis of Zionism, and his call for the establishment of a Jewish state as a response to anti-Semitism. He was also ignorant of Jewish heritage. Another grievance was his political line of Zionist work, by which he refused to begin any settlement activity in Palestine before receiving international guarantees; and, finally, his individualistic style in managing the policy and affairs of the Zionist Organization.

The first point of friction between the various groups, in and outside the Zionist Organization, was the position on Jewish culture. This was, essentially, an expression of the position on religion and the official Zionist policy on it. An ongoing conflict raged between the religious and secular groups on the matter. The differences mostly manifested among the Russian Zionists who, because of their high number, sent the largest number of delegates to the Zionist congresses. This number had risen from about a third of the members of the First Zionist Congress to more than half of the Sixth, after the Zionists had carried out extensive organizational activity in Russia. The number of Zionist associations there had risen from 23, on the eve of the First Zionist Congress, to 373, 825, 965, 1,146, and 1,572 associations during the next five congresses respectively.[170] The

---

170   Mior, *Ha-Tnu'ah ha-Tzionit be-Rusia (Zionist Movement in Russia)*, pp. 151, 189, 238-239.

Russian Zionists were divided, on the whole, into four main currents: Lovers of Zion, which gradually merged with the practical Zionists; political Zionists, followers of Herzl; spiritual (or cultural) Zionists, followers of Ahad Ha'am; and, finally, the Orthodox, who were appalled with talk of Jewish culture and saw it as nothing but a cover for blasphemy and making reforms in the religion. These latter differences also arose between Russian Zionists and the Zionists of western European countries, most of whom were secular.

In the First Zionist Congress, there was no broad discussion on cultural and religious affairs – especially since the Orthodox rabbis refused to attend. However, their position changed after the success of this congress. They attended the second one, seemingly after Herzl's appeal to the Orthodox and to the rabbis, in particular, to join the agencies of the Zionist Organization, where they became major supporters of political Zionism.[171] The Russian Zionists also held their first congress in Warsaw in August 1898, one week before the Second Zionist Congress was due to convene. In the Russian congress, which had 160 delegates, they discussed their position on cultural issues but did not reach an agreement.[172] Then, in the Second Zionist Congress, a discussion arose on the organization's position on culture – again without agreement. The Orthodox tried to push for a decision preventing the organization from working in cultural affairs, fearing that – if a decision was taken in this regard – it would be in favor of the secularists, unless the congress approved the establishment of a "rabbinical council", composed of leading sages of the Torah, to supervise Zionist cultural activity. The congress rejected this proposal and decided that "Zionism aims to revive the Jewish people, not just in their economic and political situation, but in their spiritual one, as well." However, the congress – taking into account the Orthodox sentiment and to avoid antagonizing them and pushing them towards a split – also added to its resolution that, "Zionism will not perform any act contrary to the

---

171   Ibid, p. 154.

172   Ibid, pp. 152-153.

3. Herzl and the Zionist Organization

teachings of the Jewish religion."[173] It was decided to establish an independent "cultural commission", whose work the Executive could not intervene in unless it exceeded the powers specified by the congress. A budget was allocated to the commission from the shekels paid in membership fees. It was tasked with following up cultural activity among the Jews in Palestine as well, and establishing Hebrew schools for them.[174]

The Orthodox Zionists were not, of course, happy with this decision, as the issue was one of principle to them. They were reluctantly silent. Their opponents, however, were also not satisfied, and each strengthened their forces such that another confrontation ensued at the Fourth Zionist Congress. Here, the debate on expanding the field of cultural activity of the Zionist Organization took a sizable part. The Orthodox took a rigid stance at this congress and demanded the appointment of three rabbis or Orthodox Jews as members of the Executive, but the attack came from their opponents and was directed at the individualism of Herzl, as well as the policy of both the Zionist Organization and the Orthodox rabbis. The attack was launched by congress member Chaim Weizmann (1874-1952; a later president of the Zionist Organization and the first president of Israel). He strongly stressed the need to expand Zionist cultural activity, but another prominent, Orthodox member of the congress, Isaac Reines (1839-1915) – rabbi of the city of Lida, in Russia, and a previous fellow of Samuel Mohilever in the Lovers of Zion movement – warned that such a measure may alienate thousands of Orthodox Jews from the organization. Herzl, at any rate, was not sympathetic to the Orthodox view but was aware that the rabbis represented large numbers of religious Jews who supported his movement, and he was not ready to waive this support. He then proposed removing the issue from the agenda, and the congress approved his proposal by a slim majority: 120 votes to 105.[175]

---

173 Medzini, *Ha-Mediniut ha-Tzionit (Zionist Policy)*, pp. 126-127.

174 Ibid, p. 127.

175 Ibid, pp. 181-182.

Again, neither side accepted this decision but the Orthodox Zionists were silent while the other side added Herzl's position to their list of grievances against him. Opposition to Herzl had sprung up among Zionist groups even before the First Zionist Congress,[176] and it grew after it was held – especially after it became clear, according to one view, that Herzl's Zionism was an "easy Zionism", which asked Jews to "pay the shekel fee, become Zionists, and be quiet".[177] The Zionists carried out the first two conditions, but did not keep quiet. With time, the opposition gained scope, accusing Herzl of treating the Zionist agencies – despite their continued growth and increasing strength – "like a father who refuses to acknowledge that his children have reached the age of maturity, and insists on treating them like children". They also saw Herzl's position towards Zionist activity as boiling down to

> the Zionist Organization working to sell the shekel and distribute the shares of the [Jewish] Colonial Trust, which was not working in colonization, and the congress turning into a beautiful demonstration, geared to the inside and outside, and no more – but the great work, solving the main problem, is to remain in the hands of [the leader].[178]

This description was not unfair to Herzl, who was individualistic in his actions and strangely conceited such that he wrote, in his diary, "I believe that if an acquaintance of mine were to invent a dirigible airship, I would box his ears. It would really be an awful insult to me. Why was it he and not I?"[179] Herzl was aware of the position of some Zionists towards him even before the First Zionist Congress was held: "Rivalries are beginning. I still haven't finished the preparations [for the congress] and they already want to depose me."[180] He also felt no great respect for

---

176 Patai, ed., *The Complete Diaries of Theodor Herzl*, Vol. 1, p. 358.

177 Medzini, *Ha-Mediniut ha-Tzionit (Zionist Policy)*, p. 302.

178 Ibid, pp. 302-303.

179 Patai, ed., *The Complete Diaries of Theodor Herzl*, Vol. 1, pp. 127-134.

180 Ibid, Vol. 2, p. 617.

3. Herzl and the Zionist Organization

these Zionist groups and responded to the criticism of one of them by saying:

> Dr. Kokesch[181] was deeply hurt because in the agenda (which I made) of the Congress (which I am making) of the Zionists (whom I am making) I did not include a change proposed by the 'Committee on Arrangements' (which doesn't do a thing).[182]

It seems that one reason for Herzl's dislike was the inability of the Zionist leaders and officials to keep up with his activity and dynamism, with most of them busy managing their own affairs, especially the members of the Zionist Executive – the "Inaction Committee", as Herzl once described it[183] – and their complaints about his behavior. Herzl expressed this by saying: "Difficulties in the Actions Committee. The gentlemen are complaining that I am giving them too little information. But if I issue a call to work, it falls flat."[184]

Herzl's style of political work and his insistence on control of all aspects of Zionist activity were among the main reasons for shaping another current within the Zionist movement, in opposition to both him and the Orthodox Zionists. This current was led by young Zionist intellectuals and Russian Jewish students in western Europe. Most of its members were Maskilim, who demanded democratic ways of managing Zionist work. Prominent among them were Chaim Weizmann; Leo Motzkin (1867 -1933), who participated in the formulation of the Basel Program and was among the first to have responded to Herzl's call to hold a Zionist congress; and Jacob Bernstein-Cohen. Weizmann, who had not attended the First Zionist Congress, had met Herzl at the second, but had not liked him

---

[181] Ozer Kokesch: Founder of the first Zionist association in Vienna, and later a member of the Zionist Executive.

[182] Ibid, pp. 573-574.

[183] Ibid, p. 628.

[184] Ibid, pp. 632-633.

much, because "his Zionism began as a sort of philanthropy,"[185] and because "*The Jewish State* contained not a single new idea for us."[186] Further, "to me Zionism was something organic, which had to grow like a plant, had to be watched, watered and nursed, if it was to reach maturity. I did not believe that things could be done in a hurry."[187] This view was the basis of what became known as "synthetic"[188] or "organic" Zionism, terms given to Weizmann's method of work, especially after he became head of the Zionist Organization during the British mandate over Palestine. Weizmann's group of young opponents to Herzl, to quote Weizmann himself, were not revolutionaries, but they were also not reactionaries: "We were a struggling group of young academicians, without power, and without outside support; but we had a definite outlook."[189] The youth had many criticisms, including the "extravagance" that characterized the Zionist congresses; Herzl's attention to religious elders rather than to the youth; his pursuit of kings and princes, hoping that they would "give" him Palestine; his failure to make any real political achievement, despite his "big talk"; and other issues.[190]

In April 1901, the opposition held a meeting in Munich which was attended by representatives of Zionist students from a number of western European universities, to consult on the appropriate ways to reform the conditions of the Zionist Organization. They decided to hold a general congress in mid-December of the same year, in Basel, just before the Fifth Zionist Congress was due to be held in the city. This opposition congress was inaugurated with about 40 delegates, whose number rose during the sessions when others joined them from Germany, Austria, France and Switzerland – most of them young academics. Several lectures were given in the congress, which

---

185   Chaim Weizmann, *Trial and Error*, p. 62.
186   Ibid, p. 61.
187   Ibid, p. 63.
188   Ibid, p. 158.
189   Ibid, p. 72.
190   Ibid, pp. 72-75.

3. Herzl and the Zionist Organization 197

lasted for several days, and new perspectives were put forth.[191] The congress ended by announcing the establishment of an independent entity within the Zionist Organization, the "Zionist Democratic Faction", to work towards achieving the goals that the delegates had agreed upon.

With the formation of the Democratic Faction, as it was later known, the first Zionist political party was established, which was largely a reaction to the Herzl phenomenon.

The Democratic Faction, in its program, seemed to consider itself an alternative to Herzl's Zionist Organization as a whole. In the first article, the faction put forth a new definition of Zionism that did not quite fit that of the Basel Program: "Zionism is the ambition to liberate the Jewish people from historical pressure, solving the problem of the Jewish individual, such that the economic problem of the Jewish people and the political problem of the Jews would be solved."[192] The faction also stated that

> the development of humanity is only possible through the development of people with the capacity to live... The capacity of the Jewish people to live, which gives them the right to aspire for national independence, is a result of the fact that the Jews form a national unit with a people's psyche, which emits vital signals, despite historical pressure.

Thus, the program declared,

> the liberation of the Jewish nation aims to revive the Jewish people and rebuild it as an organic unit, eligible, after reviving its youth, to develop its true, original talents and create worthy social and educational values... Zionism can be achieved ... by organizing Jewish masses within the Zionist concept ... creating main centers of power (bank, funds, etc.) and obtaining the approval of other concerned peoples and

---

[191] Mior, *Ha-Tnu'ah ha-Tzionit be-Rusia (Zionist Movement in Russia)*, pp. 182-185.

[192] Merchavia, *Am ou-Moledet (Nation and Homeland)*, p. 407.

their representatives.[193]

The Democratic Faction also demanded that the Zionist Organization recognize the right of its members to form independent parties, even those with differing views, provided that they worked in cooperation and solidarity with other parties under the umbrella of the organization. The faction stated that negative factors could not be the basis of Zionism, in response to Herzl's claim that anti-Semitism was this basis. The faction then demanded more democratic ways of managing the Zionist Organization, the adoption of elections to fill vacant positions in its agencies, and obliging the central Zionist newspaper to publish the manifestos of all Zionist factions. It stressed the need for settlement in Palestine to be on cooperative bases, and to keep the principle of nationalizing land in the country.[194] In a memorandum to Herzl about the goals of the faction, Weizmann wrote:

> The faction considers itself the link between the old generation and the new, and it, alone, can fight the revolutionaries, really fight them. It, alone, holds liberal, progressive views on social aspects. It derives from the masses their Jewish origins, refines them, and cloaks them in European forms. What is this Jewish element? This is what the Zionists in the West do not want to understand, and even the leaders have not yet properly understood.[195]

In the Fifth Zionist Congress, which convened days after the establishment of the Democratic Faction, conflict broke out again – this time between the Democratic Faction and the practical Zionists. The practical Zionists criticized its mere establishment and the manner in which it was done, claiming that it could cause harm to Zionism – especially in Russia. One of the practical Zionist leaders, Menachem Ussishkin, organized

---

193   Articles 2, 3, 4 and 27 of the program in ibid, pp. 407-409.
194   Ibid, p. 412.
195   Medzini, *Ha-Mediniut ha-Tzionit (Zionist Policy)*, p. 200.

3. Herzl and the Zionist Organization

a group of 35 delegates to confront the faction, which had 37. The faction's delegates, headed by Weizmann, spoke at the congress and demanded the deepening of Zionist ideology, more democratic bases for the administration of the organization, and greater care for the young generation. In particular, they insisted that the organization take a preliminary decision on the cultural issue, pointing out that the previous Zionist congresses had exhausted it in discussion and debate, leaving only the need to take a decision that clarified the official Zionist position on it.[196] The congress, however, urged by Herzl, rejected this proposal. The faction's members then left the hall in protest, but they were mollified and returned, and the congress adopted a resolution that "it sees the expression of culture as the national education of the Jews, considers this work an important tenet of the Zionist program and imposes it as a duty on each Zionist."[197]

This decision met with the approval of the Democratic Faction, but it provoked the anger of the Orthodox, especially as it became clear that the faction was seeking to secularize all areas of Zionist activity, based on its belief that "the Jews are like all peoples." This was one of the intellectual foundations of secular Zionism, but did not, of course, meet with the approval of the Orthodox.[198] They did not merely oppose this decision, nor were they satisfied with the announcement that the Zionist movement would not perform any act contrary to the teachings of the Jewish religion – rather, they demanded guarantees that the movement would not exceed the restrictions that it had imposed on itself, and would not weaken religious life, nor strengthen secular foundations at the expense of religion. In practice, however, the Zionist movement was moving further towards endorsing the concept of "secular nationalism". Meanwhile, a new religious concept of Zionism had taken shape among various Orthodox

---

196   Mior, *Ha-Tnu'ah ha-Tzionit be-Rusia (Zionist Movement in Russia)*, pp. 189-190.

197   Ibid, p. 191.

198   Yonah Cohen, *Prakim be-Toldot ha-Tnu'ah ha-Datit ha-Leumit (Chapters in the History of the National Religious Movement)*, p. 12.

groups, stating that "the goal of Zionism ... is to save the Jewish people and its religion, the two being an indivisible unit."[199] As soon as the Orthodox saw that the Democratic Faction was able, thanks to its organization, to secure a victory for the secularists at the Zionist congress – which seemed like a prelude to further victories towards more secularism – they decided to organize themselves into an independent, religious faction too. This aimed to attract the Orthodox, especially the rabbis, to Zionism, and to fight the integration of cultural activity into the official Zionist program. Barely a month and a half after the founding of the Democratic Faction, the Orthodox held a congress of their own, in Vilna, in February 1902. Chaired by Isaac Reines, the congress was attended by 72 representatives of religious Zionists, including 24 rabbis, from many Russian cities. At its conclusion, it was decided to inform the Zionist Organization of the formation of the "Mizrahi" (an abbreviation of the Hebrew words: "spiritual center"), an independent religious faction within the organization. Thus, the second Zionist political party was formed.

Upon its establishment, the Mizrahi issued a manifesto that

> in the countries of the diaspora, the Torah of Israel, which is the soul of the nation, can no longer rule with all its power, and it is not possible to perform all the duties of the Torah in all the force of their purity; thus, Jewish hearts must be turned to Zion and Jerusalem, to the place where our poor will also find desired comfort. The hope of return of Zion will give a secure base and a special character to our people, and a haven for its Torah and all its sanctuaries. Zion and the Torah are holy things, each of which complements the other and needs it.[200]

The Mizrahi launched its slogan at that congress: "The land of

---

199   Gruenbaum, *Ha-Tnu'ah ha-Tzionit (The Zionist Movement)*, Vol. 1, Part 2, p. 35.

200   Mior, *Ha-Tnu'ah ha-Tzionit be-Rusia (Zionist Movement in Russia)*, p. 196; see also Merchavia, *Am ou-Moledet (Nation and Homeland)*, pp. 415-416.

Israel for the people of Israel according to the Torah of Israel",[201] and approved its internal regulations, which stated that "our organization comprises religious or [religiously] moderate Zionists who approve the details of our platform."[202] At the first Mizrahi world congress, held in Pressburg, Hungary in August 1904, a constitution was approved for the organization, stating that

> (1) Mizrahi is an organization of Zionists who follow the Basel Program and desire to work for the perpetuation of Jewish national life. Mizrahi sees the perpetuation of the Jewish people in the observance of the Torah, Jewish tradition, and *mitzvot* [religious duties] and the return to the land of its forefathers. (2) Mizrahi will remain within the framework of the Zionist Organization, in which it will struggle for its opinions and views. However, it will create a special organization of its own for its religious and cultural activities. (3) Mizrahi will realize its goals by employing all legal means at its disposal to explain its ideas to all Orthodox circles, by creating and distributing national-religious literature, and by educating youth in the spirit of its ideals and programs.[203]

A few months after the Mizrahi's establishment, it had the opportunity to test its organizational strength. In September 1902, the second congress of Russian Zionists was held in Minsk (the only Zionist congress to be held legally in tsarist Russia). The Mizrahi, which had about 60 delegates out of 500 at the congress,[204] used the opportunity to urge it to support its position on cultural activity. The congress, however, took another position and agreed on a compromise: a joint draft resolution put forth by its presidency, in partnership with Isaac Reines and

---

201   Cohen, Y., *Prakim be-Toldot ha-Tnu'ah ha-Datit ha-Leumit (Chapters in the History of the National Religious Movement)*, p. 11.

202   Merchavia, *Am ou-Moledet (Nation and Homeland)*, p. 417.

203   Ibid, p. 418.

204   Mordechai Nurock, *Ve'idat Tzioni Rusia be-Minsk (Russian Zionist Congress in Minsk)*, pp. 31, 33.

Ahad Ha'am, in which it announced that it saw the two cultural currents, "traditional-national and progressive-national" as having equal rights, and thus decided to form two committees, one for religious cultural activity and the other for secular. The members of each committee would be chosen by the group concerned, and each committee would work independently of the other.[205] This was also the solution proposed at the Sixth Zionist Congress, when the semi-final confrontation took place between the Mizrahi (about 100 delegates) and the Democratic Faction (about 50) over the position of the Zionist Organization on cultural activity. Since that time, secular and religious bodies have coexisted within the Zionist Organization (a phenomenon that has also characterized political life in Israel since its establishment).

The Democratic Faction and the Mizrahi were not the only two organizations-parties formed within the Zionist Organization. The "children" of the Zionist movement – to the chagrin of Herzl and his supporters – grew and rebelled, and formed other parties as well, even though the organization's presidency did not look favorably on such developments. In its view, the Zionist Organization should have remained a cohesive unit, without parties or political currents, and maintained a moderate character acceptable to all the rulers of that era. The organization should have focused on resolving the Jewish question through the establishment of a Jewish state, and only after achieving this goal could a sense of security and prosperity be acted on, in terms of forming parties or such. Thus the presidency of the organization was ill at ease with the emergence of both the Democratic Faction and the Mizrahi, especially since the faction was issuing provocative slogans, with terms such as democratic, progressive and secular. The presidency reluctantly kept quiet, however.

The matter did not end there. Another current appeared within the organization, whose members called themselves the "socialist Zionists". This current resulted from key developments

---

205   Ibid, p. 75.

3. Herzl and the Zionist Organization

that had reached, by that time, a high level of intensity and contradiction, especially among Russian Jews (see Chapter 2). In 1897, less than one month after the First Zionist Congress and the establishment of the Zionist Organization, the first Jewish socialist party, the General Jewish Labor Bund in Poland and Russia (Lithuania was added later), was also founded in Vilna, in a secret meeting in September. The Bund and other Zionists then fought each other fiercely to win the support of Jewish masses in Russia and elsewhere. There were some who believed, however, that interest did not lie in conflict between the two currents, but in their unity – similar to the merger that Weizmann had brought about between political and practical Zionism, producing what he called "synthetic Zionism". A similar merger was thus carried out between Zionism and socialism, to produce "socialist/labor Zionism". Most prominent in this regard was Nachman Syrkin, who published an article titled "The Jewish Question and the Jewish Socialist State" in 1898, after he had decided "to be a socialist among Zionists, and a Zionist among socialists", although "each side vehemently rejected [him] and pushed [him] towards the other."[206]

The socialist Zionists appeared for the first time at the Second Zionist Congress. A group of them, led by Syrkin, showed noticeable activity that surprised and angered the remaining delegates, due to the proposals of the socialists, their manner of speaking and their adversarial tone. Syrkin announced that the class struggle also existed within the Zionist Organization. He proposed the appointment of representatives of the working class in all the committees formed by the congress. The response to this was a call for his expulsion from the congress, because "all our forces are presently directed to preserve our people from destruction and defeat... As for other matters, including the social aspect of the general system of the future, they are currently deferred to another time... They [the socialists] must not slip into our ranks."[207] At the Third Zionist Congress, Syrkin gave a

---

206 Mior, *Ha-Tnu'ah ha-Tzionit be-Rusia (Zionist Movement in Russia)*, p. 163.
207 Ibid, pp. 160-162.

lecture on the theme of socialist Zionism (the first instance that this term was used) after distributing invitations to the delegates at the congress to attend. Herzl was forced to publicly denounce this act, explaining that he did not want anyone to misunderstand that there was an analogy between Zionism and socialism.[208] At any rate, the socialist Zionists remained, in Herzl's era, a tiny, helpless minority in the Zionist congresses, and they remained so for quite a time – as the hour of their rising power and control of the Zionist movement had not yet arrived.

Nevertheless, the presidency of the Zionist Organization, despite its reservations on establishing political parties, hastened to make appropriate adjustments to the organization's structure so as to recognize the legitimacy of these independent parties and factions, and to deal with them. The Fifth Zionist Congress approved an amendment to the organization's bylaws, whereby every 50 Zionist associations that sold 5,000 shekels, at least, were permitted to establish an independent Zionist union with the right to directly contact the Executive. This was to augment the previous approach by which the organization recognized a single regional Zionist center in each country, representing all the Zionists in it. Another amendment was approved to hold the Zionist congress every two years, rather than annually as had been the case.[209]

The issue of the establishment of political parties was not the only one that the Zionists forced Herzl and his supporters to change their stance on. Another change came regarding the position of the organization on settlement activity in Palestine. Herzl's theory of political Zionist work stressed, as previously mentioned, the need to obtain international political recognition of the establishment of a Jewish state in Palestine. The theory opposed any initiation of Jewish settlements there before that took place, and ignored those existing settlements. Herzl's supporters were more extreme than he was in their support for

---

208 Herzl, *Kitvei Herzl (Works of Herzl)*, Vol. 8, p. 31.

209 Ibid, pp. 127-128; Mior, *Ha-Tnu'ah ha-Tzionit be-Rusia (Zionist Movement in Russia)*, p. 192.

3. Herzl and the Zionist Organization 205

this theory and it is clear that this situation raised, in particular, the ire of Jewish settlers in Palestine. Their representative, Hillel Yaffe, chairman of the executive committee of Lovers of Zion in the country – which was responsible for those settlements that Rothschild, or the JCA, had not pledged to support – launched an intense campaign against the "renewed Zionism" of Herzl, because it was "dangerous", and because those Zionists, "who have just hatched from the egg",[210] dared to belittle actual settlement activity in Palestine and even shunned the fate of Zionist settlements there.

However, those attitudes by both parties gradually changed and converged somewhat. Herzl and his supporters had to bend to pressure from the practical Zionists and express interest, at least, in the conditions of the settlements in Palestine. During preparations for the First Zionist Congress, Hillel Yaffe had sent Herzl, upon his request, a report on the conditions of these settlements,[211] and other reports were also submitted on the matter.[212] The congress decided to form a "Land of Israel Settlement Committee", and Leo Motzkin was sent to investigate the general conditions of Jewish settlement in Palestine. Upon his return, he submitted a report to the Second Zionist Congress in which he stated that the number of Jews in Palestine during his visit (1898) was 49,519, who owned 268,278 dunums of land. Of this population, 45,169 lived in the cities or towns (Jerusalem: 28,254 residents; Safad: 6,620; Jaffa: 3,000; Tiberias: 3,200; Hebron: 1,429; Haifa:1,375; and others) and the remainder (4,350 residents) in the settlements.[213] Motzkin demanded several measures to strengthen Jewish settlement in Palestine, but the congress decided that it only recognized the settlements that were based on prior authorization by the Turkish government and announced the readiness of the organization to provide

---

210 Hillel Yaffe, *Dor Ma'afilim (A Generation of Immigrants)*, pp. 181-183, 189.

211 Ibid, p. 178.

212 *Ha-Protocol shel ha-Congress ha-Tzioni ha-Rishon (Protocols of First Zionist Congress)*, pp. 145-156.

213 In Medzini, *Ha-Mediniut ha-Tzionit (Zionist Policy)*, p. 125, note 2.

assistance to such settlements, according to the programs of a committee elected by it, and under its supervision. The congress also decided that the Jewish people living in Turkey and the areas under its control would carry out the first settlement steps in Palestine, and a committee of 10 people was formed in London for settlement.[214] In other words, the congress adopted a compromise, but it remained, in effect, committed to the political Zionist line.

Pressure by the practical Zionists, however, persisted on Herzl and the presidency of the organization to take a clear stance and more effective procedures to support settlement in Palestine. In his opening address to the Fifth Zionist Congress, Herzl announced that it was decided to establish future Zionist settlements in the form of "cooperative agricultural-productive societies".[215] Franz Oppenheimer, a professor of economics and sociology at the universities of Berlin and Frankfurt, and author of this theory of settlement, was invited to give a lecture at the Sixth Zionist Congress.[216] (This method was later attempted with the establishment of Merhavia settlement, south of Nazareth in 1911, but did not enjoy great success.) In addition, Herzl improved his relationship with the leaders of the Zionist settlers in Palestine, so that Yaffe began periodically sending reports about the Zionist settlements in the country to "Mr. President",[217] and also agreed to participate in the commission sent by the Zionist Organization to survey el-Arish, even though "the place [was] not Zion."[218]

Despite this, the Zionist Organization did not, in fact, carry out any practical settlement activity in Palestine during Herzl's era, and only changed this position after his death, when the practical Zionists took over.

---

214 Mior, *Ha-Tnu'ah ha-Tzionit be-Rusia (Zionist Movement in Russia)*, p. 160.

215 Herzl, *Kitvei Herzl (Works of Herzl)*, Vol. 8, p. 116.

216 Gezel Kressel, *Franz Oppenheimer*, pp. 38-40.

217 Hillel Yaffe, *Dor Ma'afilim (A Generation of Immigrants)*, pp. 191, 200, 222-225.

218 Ibid, pp. 238-241.

3. Herzl and the Zionist Organization

8

One of the pillars of Zionism that Herzl left behind was Max Nordau, who lived 19 years after Herzl's death and died in Paris in 1923. Nordau was one of the first and most prominent Jews to gain the trust of Herzl (see section 1 of this chapter). From Herzl's early steps, he recruited Nordau to Zionism, stating that "Nordau will, I believe, go with me through thick and thin."[219] He was not disappointed. Nordau, however, refused to devote himself solely to Zionist activity and insisted on practicing his previous work as a writer as well,[220] and his name as an author was renowned across Europe. He did not show great interest in Zionist organizational activity, nor in working in Zionist agencies, such that Weizmann – one of his opponents – described him by saying: "He was an ardent Zionist only during the sessions of the Congresses. During the other three hundred and fifty odd days of the year we heard only occasionally of him within the movement; for then he attended to his business, which was that of writer [sic]."[221] Weizmann was not unfair to Nordau, who had even once decided not to attend the Third Zionist Congress – preferring to follow the trial of Dreyfus – until Herzl changed his mind.[222] However, through his work as a writer, Nordau rendered great services to Zionism. He not only defended Herzl and criticized his adversaries, but he worked hard to spread the Zionist idea, trying to deepen and embellish it in the eyes of the Jews and others, and launching numerous Zionist theories.

Nordau was a great believer in Herzl's theory of political Zionist work, and fervently defended this line and attacked its opponents – primarily the Lovers of Zion (see section 5 of this chapter). Other Zionist currents also did not escape his criticism. He mocked the Democratic Faction, its slogans and its activity.[223]

---

219 Patai, ed., *The Complete Diaries of Theodor Herzl*, Vol. 1, p. 272.

220 Ibid, Vol. 2, p. 673.

221 Weizmann, *Trial and Error*, p. 65.

222 Patai, ed., *The Complete Diaries of Theodor Herzl*, Vol. 3, p. 856.

223 Nordau, *Kitvei Nordau (Works of Nordau)*, Vol. 3, pp. 152-153.

He also attacked the theory of spiritual Zionism launched by Ahad Ha'am, even though it had gained some support – because this "tasteless" idea, in Nordau's words, even if it succeeded in establishing a Jewish "spiritual center" in Palestine, would not solve the problems of Jewish people in the diaspora.[224] Nordau also opposed religious Zionists, explaining that

> the new Zionism, which has been called the political one, differs from the old, religious Messianic one in that it disavows all mysticism, no longer identifies itself with Messianism, and does not expect the return to Palestine to be brought about by a miracle, but desires to pave the way through its own efforts.[225]

Nordau criticized socialist Zionists as well, because socialism "was achieved in Zionism, itself... Where can we find, among other peoples, something similar – even sparingly – to the social justice inherent in the teachings of Moses?"[226] Nordau also warned the Jews of disappointment in socialism, even if it was realized, just as they had been disappointed in religious reform or political emancipation movements in Europe, or within the Haskalah.[227] As for the Zionists of Zion, who had threatened to split from the Zionist Organization when the Sixth Zionist Congress approved the Uganda project, Nordau labeled them as only a "new, but unedited, version of Lovers of Zion".[228]

Nordau's long and bitter conflict was with the practical Zionists. It lasted about 27 years, from the time he joined the Zionist movement until his final days. Before his death, Herzl had recommended that his close associates elect Nordau in his place as president of the Zionist Organization. Nordau, however, rejected this offer, sensing that the practical Zionists would gradually overcome the politicians and control the organization.

---

224 Ibid, Vol. 4, pp. 168-170.

225 Ibid, Vol. 2, p. 92.

226 Ibid, Vol. 1, p. 143.

227 Ibid, p. 145.

228 Ibid, Vol. 4, p. 178.

3. Herzl and the Zionist Organization

The Tenth Zionist Congress (1911) did, in fact, bring this about. The congress adopted the practical Zionist line in its synthetic form put forth by Weizmann – who was, in Nordau's words, only a follower of those "amateurs" of Zionism, the Lovers of Zion.[229]. The congress also elected an executive composed mostly of practical Zionists. Nordau then declined to attend the next congress (the 11th, in 1913), and wrote a letter to its delegates, urging them to "set their sights on the Herzl idea, in all its comprehensiveness," and "not to take decisions that are difficult to implement".[230] In an article titled *Testament for the Zionist Movement*, written in his final days in 1920, Nordau explained his position: "The 11th Zionist Congress saw the victory of the 'young professionals' of Lovers of Zion in Russia and their allies in Berlin," who "ruined" Zionism, which Herzl had "taken out of the framework of the synagogue and religious jurisprudence" and formulated into a "political movement". They, however, converted it to a "private settlement enterprise, miserable and cowardly".[231] Nordau mocked the practical Zionists who had come to control the Zionist Executive yet were unable to make any noticeable achievements, so they returned to the Herzl way and, eventually, became "politicians".[232]

With his strong support for the political Zionist line and his ongoing struggle with all the other Zionist currents, Nordau formulated his own theories of Zionism which were destined to spread among large Zionist circles. He considered himself a "general Zionist", not inclined to the right, towards the Mizrahi, nor to the left, towards the socialists.[233] Based on this position, Nordau saw that

> the new Zionism has grown in part only out of the internal impulsions of Judaism itself, out of the enthusiasm of mod-

---

229   Ibid, p. 198.

230   Ibid, Vol. 3, p. 162.

231   Ibid, Vol. 4, pp. 159-160, 185.

232   Ibid, Vol. 2, p. 152.

233   See also Klausner, J., *Menehei ha-Yesod shel Medinat Yisrael (Founders of the State of Israel)*, p. 192.

ern educated Jews for their history and martyrology, out of the awakened consciousness of their racial qualities, out of their ambition to save the ancient blood, in view of the farthest possible future, and to add to the achievements of their forefathers the achievements of their posterity. On the other hand, Zionism is the effect of two impulses which came from without – first, the principle of nationality, which for half a century ruled thought and feeling in Europe, and governed the politics of the world; secondly, anti-Semitism, from which the Jews of all countries have more or less to suffer.[234]

Thus, Zionism had two main tasks, in Nordau's view, even though "they are in opposite directions: it must acquire the Land of Israel for the Jewish people, and prepare the Jewish people for the Land of Israel... The second task is far more important than the first..."[235] because, "if we reach the Land of Israel, we must be sure that we will appear, there, as a respectable nation."[236] Thus it was imperative to carry out extensive organizational and educational activity among the Jews, to prepare them.

Nordau believed that the main opposition to Zionism existed among Jewish people only, and that other peoples had no substantial relationship to it. While some rejected it, claiming that it posed a threat to Judaism or that it was unnecessary, he felt that Zionism was essential to save Judaism and that there was no truth to the counterclaims made by the opposition. The statement, for example, that the message of the Jews lay in their spreading their values among the peoples of the world, and that they should not think of establishing a state of their own, had no truth to it, in his view, and he cynically remarked that it was perhaps better to turn it over to the anti-Semites for an answer. He was convinced that anti-Semitism would not disappear in the near future, and that the danger lay in the Jews of western Europe having to completely negate themselves and

---

234 Nordau, *Kitvei Nordau (Works of Nordau)*, Vol. 2, pp. 92-93.

235 Ibid, Vol. 1, p. 103.

236 Ibid, p. 104.

3. Herzl and the Zionist Organization 211

wholly assimilate in their communities in order to avoid being targets. In eastern Europe, according to Nordau, the Jews could maintain their own identity as long as the people of the region were underdeveloped, but as soon as they reached the level of development of western Europe, the fate of the Eastern Jews would be similar to the Western ones. There was also a danger in the claim that the Jews would bear the persecution against them as they had in previous times, for there was no guarantee that the measures of persecution would not intensify and eventually lead to the genocide of the Jewish people. "It may be difficult to resettle six million Jews in the Land of Israel, Hawran and Syria ... but it is more difficult to influence the governments of Russia and Romania and compel them to abolish the laws of persecution of Jews in their countries."[237]

Nordau identified the Jewish segments opposed to Zionism: wealthy Jews, Orthodox rabbis, and the working class. He determined the positions to be taken towards each. In his view, Zionism could waive the services of wealthy Jews,

> and we will get our needed money, in spite of everything, partly from the middle and poor classes of our race, and partly, if there is a need, from the Christian world, which we should work to convince to find safe and profitable possibilities of financial investment for us; thus, without any sacrifice on its part, it would help to implement a perfect penance project.[238]

The Orthodox "protest rabbis" had no support, in Nordau's view, and "their value to Judaism is zero," for "they have ceased, for some time, to play the role of teachers and leaders of the people... They could not maintain a knowledge of the Hebrew language, Jewish history, and the habits and traits of Jews among the Jewish masses."[239]

---

237 From an article, "Zionism and its Opponents", in ibid, pp. 84-101.

238 From a lecture, "Zionism, Major Capitalists and the Working Class among the Jews", in ibid, p. 133.

239 Ibid, p. 140.

As for the Jewish working class, Zionism could not antagonize it.

> Our mission would end, for, in such a situation, we would have no choice but to bow our heads and admit defeat, and search, after our disappointment, for new ideals… We cannot forgo the Jewish working class, in any way, not even part of it, and, if they shun us, we should not play the game of haughty "anger" with them, but we should pursue them patiently, one step at a time, and try to convince them that only a lack of understanding separates us from them.[240]

Nordau also called for the creation of a new, "muscular" Jewish generation by encouraging Jews to engage in physical exercise.

Of greater importance, however, were Nordau's theories on the position of Zionism towards the Arabs and how to deal with them, especially the people of Palestine. Herzl, Nordau's teacher, had given no thought for the Arabs in Palestine or its vicinity, and had ignored their presence – not once mentioning the word "Arab" in *The Jewish State* nor in all of his diaries. Only on two occasions did Herzl declare what might be called his "attitude" to the Arabs: the first, when Eliezer Ben-Yehuda visited him and proposed the idea of issuing a Zionist newspaper in Arabic – in his diary, Herzl expressed his approval of this suggestion;[241] and the second, in his novel, *The Old New Land*, when he wrote about a character called Rashid, who lives peacefully in the future Zionist state.[242] Perhaps this stance was caused by the ignorance of Herzl and his companions, or ignoring – from the start – the presence of Arabs in Palestine. Martin Buber, the renowned Jewish Zionist philosopher, who was a member of the Democratic Faction in his youth, revealed that the first time he briefed Max Nordau with more details on the presence of Arabs

---

240   Ibid, pp. 141-142.

241   Patai, ed., *The Complete Diaries of Theodor Herzl*, Vol. 2, p. 804.

242   Theodor Herzl, *The Old New Land (Altneuland)*, pp. 115-126; see also Herzl's letter to Yousef Dia al-Khalidi in Walid Khalidi, ed., *From Haven to Conquest*, pp. 91-93.

3. Herzl and the Zionist Organization 213

in Palestine, Nordau rushed to Herzl, saying: "I did not know that – we are committing an injustice!"[243] More details of the Arabs then became known to the Zionists, and Herzl's lack of a position towards them was filled by Nordau.

Nordau ventured to talk about his position on the Arabs for the first time at the Seventh Zionist Congress, in 1905. He pointed out that the Arab nationalist movement could disrupt the authority of Turkey on Palestine and its neighboring countries, pushing Turkey to search for a factor to ensure calm in the region. Turkey could then be compelled, in Nordau's view – perhaps after coordination with the European states – to call on the Zionist movement and allow the settlement of Jews in Palestine, who would work to maintain the Turkish control of the country. Nordau urged the leaders of the Zionist movement to do everything in their power to benefit from this situation, so that it would not later be said that an opportunity was missed by an inept generation.[244]

After this speech, Nordau was silent on the "Arab question" for more than a decade until the Balfour Declaration was issued in 1917 – followed by Britain's occupation of Palestine and the imposition of its mandate over it in 1920 and the rise of Arab resistance. Nordau then launched his successive theories on the best ways for Zionism to defeat this resistance and secure control of Palestine (developments that will be examined later). Those theories later spread among many Zionist groups and became an ideological basis for a new Zionist current, characterized by its intransigent stance towards the Arabs.

9

With his death, Herzl did not leave many admirers behind nor a party committed to his political line and loyal to his views. During his lifetime, Zionism failed to make any practical political achievement. The Zionist agencies, however, which he

---

243 In Aharon Cohen, *Yisrael ve ha-Olam ha-Aravi (Israel and the Arab World)*, p. 74.

244 Nordau, *Kitvei Nordau (Works of Nordau)*, Vol. 3, pp. 32-33.

had established, and the emergence of other Zionist theories that quickly spawned independent organizations, created new conditions and spurred energies that, undoubtedly, would not have occurred to Herzl when he had launched his Zionist project. Those agencies, both administrative and partisan, grew, developed and played fundamental roles in Zionist activity after his death.

The World Zionist Organization still exists today, although with a secondary status after the establishment of Israel. In two instances, at least – at Britain's issuance of the Balfour Declaration in 1917 and the United Nations decision to partition Palestine in 1947 – the Zionist Organization (as it was named, until 1960) played a historic role, whether in preparation for these declarations or to address the subsequent challenges and exploit them for Zionist benefit.

The Jewish National Fund also still exists, although it has lost much of its prestige since the establishment of Israel. The company played a major role in supporting Zionist settlement in Palestine during the British mandate, especially in the realm of land purchase.

The Jewish Colonial Trust fared differently. It suffered heavy financial losses and, in 1934, terminated its banking activity and came under the subsidiary that it had established, the Anglo-Palestine Bank. After the founding of Israel, this changed its name to "Bank Leumi le-Israel" (National Bank of Israel), known simply as "Bank Leumi", and still exists as one of the largest banks in the country.

The same applied to the Zionist political factions that were formed within the Zionist Organization during Herzl's era. The Democratic Faction reduced its activity after the Sixth Zionist Congress, the last one that Herzl attended, and gradually disbanded, but its principles and some of its members reappeared in the General Zionists party, which dominated the Zionist movement in the 1920s.[245] After the establishment of

---

245 At the 14th Zionist Congress, in Vienna, in 1925, 57% of the delegates were affiliated to this party.

3. Herzl and the Zionist Organization

Israel, the General Zionists merged with the smaller Progressive Party to become the Liberal Party in 1961. Eventually, this was assimilated into the Likud Party.

The Mizrahi organization, since its founding, has been working in worldly affairs in the service of the afterlife – engaging in politics to uphold the word of religion. In 1922, it established a parallel organization, "ha-Po'el ha-Mizrahi" (the Mizrahi Laborer), to include the working classes among the religious. The two organizations came together in 1956 to establish the National Religious Party ("Mafdal", which later became the Religious Zionist Party). From the mid-1930s – except for short periods – the Mizrahi was a faithful partner to the Zionist labor wing in running the Zionist movement, then in ruling Israel from its establishment in 1948 until 1977. Later, the Mizrahi's successor parties changed course, joining the right-wing Likud Party in governing Israel.

As for the socialist/labor Zionists, whose representatives at the Second Zionist Congress faced the prospect of expulsion because they dared to associate Zionism with socialism, they had to work long and hard to assume leadership of the Zionist movement. They achieved this by the mid-1930s, then became the ruling party in Israel from its establishment until 1977, as noted above.

Even Nordau's theories did not subside for long. Only a few years after his death, they found multiple people willing to adopt and disseminate them. Most prominent in this regard was Ze'ev (Vladimir) Jabotinsky, who received those teachings and gave them a character of his own. He made Nordau's theories a foundation for the ideology of the Zionist right, fiercely hostile to the Arabs through belittling them and their abilities. During the 1930s, Jabotinsky brought these teachings to the new Zionist organization that he led, which influenced the National Military Organization (Irgun – "Etzel") in the early 1940s, which in turn influenced the "Herut" party after the establishment of Israel. From there, the theories were brought to the Movement for Greater Israel and other Zionist expansionist movements that appeared in Israel after the 1967 war. Other Zionist wings were also influenced by the underlying assumptions of Nordau's theories.

Herzl's views and teachings were almost eclipsed after his death, in the midst of these developments, which elevated the mystery that once shrouded him. There was no trace left of him, his ideas or even his family; his son and one of his two daughters converted to Christianity, and both committed suicide, while the third was killed at a Nazi concentration camp during the Second World War.

Among the first deeds carried out by the newly established Israel, after securing the foundations of its rule and signing armistice agreements with its neighboring Arab states, was to transfer Herzl's remains from Vienna in August 1949 and re-bury them in al-Hamama mountain, west of Jerusalem. The site was then re-named "Mount Herzl".

4. The Second Aliyah: Foundations of the Zionist Entity (1904-1914)

1

In early 1904, a few months before Herzl's death, a new wave of Jewish emigration began from Russia and continued until the outbreak of the First World War in 1914. Hundreds of thousands of Jewish people left the country, mostly emigrating to the United States. During this period, which later came to be known as the Second Aliyah, about 35,000-40,000 Jewish immigrants also made their way to Palestine – though most of them left shortly after their arrival or during the First World War, due to the hardships resulting from it.

The reasons for this new wave of emigration from Russia were similar to those that had triggered the first waves in the early 1880s, as well as developments during the period between the two. By the early 20th century, Russia had come a good way on the path of industrial development that it had begun some 50 years earlier. This led to an unprecedented deterioration in the economic and social conditions of the Jewish population, especially since most Russian Jews belonged to the middle class. In addition, the tsarist authorities – in planning their economic programs – strengthened the Russian middle class at the expense of the Jewish one. This situation was sufficient, in itself, to push large numbers of the Jewish population to emigrate to other countries in pursuit of better livelihoods. However, there were also certain groups that behaved differently. Many Jewish people in Russia, especially intellectuals, students and laborers, decided that the effective means to confront this policy was not to emigrate but to join Russian revolutionary movements, working with them to depose the tsarist regime and replace it with a progressive government that would better solve the country's problems. This trend, though, served as a pretext for the tsarist authorities to escalate their anti-Jewish measures, which led to further adverse reactions among the Jews. Larger numbers of them joined the revolutionary movements that the Russian authorities were doing their utmost to extinguish or, at least, mitigate.

In the last quarter of the 19th century, the tsarist authorities were working to divert public attention from the revolution, discredit Russian revolutionaries and facilitate their persecution and murder. There was repeated incitement against Jewish people, with claims that they sought to destroy Russia through their revolutionary movements. The authorities encouraged attacks on them and were often complicit in abetting pogroms or, at least, failing to investigate them after their occurrence. This went on for a significant period, in an attempt to redirect the popular uproar against the authorities into religious or national hatred and, thus, relieve the pressures the government faced. The presence of one Jewish girl, for example, in the group that assassinated Tsar Alexander II in 1881, was sufficient cause to launch pogroms against the Jewish population across Russia. They were held responsible for the assassination and accused of founding subversive revolutionary movements, although these had a very small number of Jewish members at the time. This situation changed, however, at the beginning of the 20th century, when the accusation against the Jews of joining the revolutionary parties was justified. By that time, large numbers of Jewish youth – including intellectuals, students and laborers – had joined the various parties. Jewish people played prominent roles in forming these parties and shaping their ideas, quantitatively and qualitatively, as the percentage of their membership in some organizations was ten times that of the Jewish percentage of the population, and they held several positions of leadership.[1] Some

---

1 For details, see Jacob Talmon, *Be-Idan ha-Alimut (The Age of Violence)*, pp. 209-226.

4. The Second Aliyah

of them also worked to "export" the revolution outside Russia, especially to eastern and western Europe.[2] Due to this, and with the mounting wave of popular resentment against tsarist rule, the Russian authorities periodically resumed planning pogroms against the Jews.

This new wave began with a pogrom in April 1903, in Kishinev. The massacre prompted Herzl to travel to Russia, where he met its minister of the interior, Plehve, and obtained – among other things – a promise to work on improving the conditions of the Russian Jews and alleviating their distress. Yet, only a few months later, in August, another pogrom took place in the town of Gomel. Its Jewish population had learned a lesson from what had happened in Kishinev, however, and had set up battalions ("Haganah") to defend themselves, which managed to inflict a number of casualties among the Russian attackers. This led the authorities to arrest and prosecute a number of Haganah members,[3] while the remainder fled to Palestine. There, they helped to lay the foundations of the Zionist Haganah organization in the country.

In the summer of 1904, a member of the Russian Socialist Revolutionary Party assassinated the minister of the interior, Plehve. His replacement was described as liberal but, barely a month after his appointment, two more pogroms took place in the towns of Smela and Rovno.[4] In the fall of 1904, the Russo-Japanese War broke out. Russian soldiers, on their way to the front, committed several pogroms against the Jewish population, holding the "Jewish press" in Britain and the United States responsible for inciting Japan to attack Russia. Pogroms against the Jews did not cease, even during the war. A pogrom took place in the town of Feodosia, in February 1905; another in Melitopol, in April of the same year; and a third in Zhytomyr, in the same month, where the Haganah battalions confronted the attackers

---

2   Ibid, pp. 226-234.

3   Yitzhak Mior, *Ha-Tnu'ah ha-Tzionit be-Rusia (Zionist Movement in Russia)*, pp. 273-275.

4   Ibid, p. 276.

and caused injuries among them.⁵ Prior to these attacks, some representatives of Jewish parties and groups had tried to hold a meeting in Odessa in December 1904 to discuss the option of establishing national defense battalions among the Jews in all parts of Russia. The police, however, arrested the representatives and stopped the meeting from taking place.⁶

The Russo-Japanese War of 1904-1905 ended with the defeat of Russia and the outbreak of a revolution in the country in the summer of 1905. Jewish people eagerly took part and were involved, in relatively large numbers, in all the parties that carried out revolutionary activity: Constitutional Democrats, Social Democrats and Socialist Revolutionaries.⁷ On October 17, 1905, the tsar was forced to issue a letter granting some democratic freedoms and promising to hold general elections for a parliament (duma) representing the people – the tsar's letter had not granted any exceptional rights to the Jews. The next day, however, a series of attacks and pogroms unfolded against the Jews all over the Russian Empire, in and outside the Pale of Settlement, which lasted for a week and caused severe damage to hundreds of Jewish communities.⁸

After this "constitutional" letter in 1905, Russia witnessed a period of relative freedom that it had not experienced before. Yet this did not last long. The tsar dissolved the first duma in July 1906, three months after the start of its term, because most of its elected members were from the opposition. A month earlier, a pogrom against the Jews had taken place in Bialystok. The second duma met the same fate, as it was dissolved in June 1907, four months after the start of its term. This measure confirmed the return of reactionary control over the country, especially after the authorities had taken various measures to suppress the revolution, including the establishment of field courts. In their short period of work, from August 1906 to April 1907, these

---

5 Ibid, pp. 280-286.

6 Ibid, p. 280.

7 Simon Dubnow, *Divrei Yemei Am Olam (History of the Jews)*, p. 713.

8 Ibid, p. 714.

4. The Second Aliyah

courts issued 683 death sentences that were all carried out. From 1905-1910, Russian military courts issued 5,735 death sentences, of which 3,015 were carried out, in addition to executions without trials.[9]

Amidst this reactionary sweep, elections were held for the third duma in the fall of 1907 and opposition members dropped to less than a quarter. An amendment to the law was then ratified, stripping the right to vote from Jewish people living outside the Pale of Settlement. Previous administrative procedures had also been ratified to limit the number of Jewish students allowed to enroll in Russian universities. This was then enacted in a special law, prompting greater numbers of these students to go to western Europe to study.[10] There, many of them participated in Zionist activity.

The reactionary sweep affected the authorities' attitude towards the Zionist movement as well. In 1906, the Zionists in Minsk had been able to obtain a license and register themselves as a legal organization but the attorney general repealed the decision. The state council, based on information provided by the minister of the interior, decided that "the Zionists show, in their activities, a tendency to strengthen the feeling of national separation among the Jewish masses, in an attempt to change the current conditions of the Jews, which will necessarily lead to the strengthening of the feeling of national hatred for the indigenous population." Thus, "Zionists are prohibited from organizing in the form of legal associations."[11] This remained in effect until the outbreak of the Russian Revolution in 1917, which then took a fiercer stance against Zionism – albeit with different motives.

In the wake of this decision, the Russian authorities tightened their grip on the Zionists and monitored them sharply, to the point where members of the Zionist Executive in Russia sent a letter in December 1907 to David Wolffsohn, Herzl's successor in the presidency of the Zionist Organization, informing him that

---

9   Mior, *Ha-Tnu'ah ha-Tzionit be-Rusia (Zionist Movement in Russia)*, p. 342.

10 Dubnow, *Divrei Yemei Am Olam (History of the Jews)*, p. 719.

11 Mior, *Ha-Tnu'ah ha-Tzionit be-Rusia (Zionist Movement in Russia)*, p. 343.

"no possibility remain[s] for [us] to carry out any Zionist activity, due to opposition by the authorities based on the emergency laws."[12] Wolffsohn could not tolerate this situation, for the Russian Zionists were then the largest group within the Zionist Organization. He resorted to the same method that Herzl had used before and asked to meet the Russian prime minister, Pyotr Stolypin, who agreed to his request. In the meeting that took place in July 1908, Wolffsohn heard the same statement from Stolypin that Herzl had heard from Plehve five years earlier: the Russian government did not oppose Zionist activity in the country as long as it was directed at the emigration of Jews, or the establishment of a state for them in Palestine, but it could not allow any activity related to Russia's internal affairs.[13] The Russian Zionists had, at the Helsingfors Congress (1906), decided to work on improving the conditions of the Jews in Russia as well. Organizations with a socialist character had appeared among them, opposing tsarist rule (see section 3 of this chapter). Thus Wolffsohn's visit to Russia did not yield any results, although the authorities allowed him to meet with his followers. He also met the Russian foreign minister and the Turkish ambassador to Russia in an attempt to induce them to work on facilitating Zionist settlement activity in Palestine.

After the suppression of the 1905 revolution and the tightening of reactionary rule in Russia, the attacks and pogroms against the Jews subsided and almost disappeared. However, in 1911, an event took place that reinstated terror in the hearts of Russian Jewish people. In the spring of that year, a young Jewish man, Mendel Beilis, was accused of killing a boy to use his blood in Jewish religious rituals (blood libel – see Introduction, section 7), and was brought to trial that lasted until the fall of 1913.[14] In that period, the Russian press launched an unprecedented campaign of incitement against the Jews, leading some writers – including Maxim Gorky – to protest against the government before Beilis

---

12   Ibid, pp. 343-344.

13   Ibid, pp. 345-346.

14   Dubnow, *Divrei Yemei Am Olam (History of the Jews)*, p. 719.

4. The Second Aliyah

was acquitted.[15] The crisis that prevailed for the country's Jewish population pushed more of them to emigrate.

During 1904-1914, the number of Jewish immigrants from Russia to Palestine increased when pressure intensified against the Jewish population in Russia, in 1905-1907, 1908-1909 and 1912-1913,[16] and then decreased when the pressure diminished.

This pressure was not the only reason, however, for Jewish immigration to Palestine. Russian Zionists also contributed to this, as most of them were proponents of the practical Zionist line calling for settlement in Palestine alone – a position that they held more strongly after the Uganda project was proposed at the Sixth Zionist Congress (1903). They saw it as their duty to push the largest number of Jews to Palestine as one of the means to thwart that project. Prominent in this regard was Menachem Ussishkin (see Chapter 3, section 6), a leading Russian Zionist, who had been visiting Palestine while the Sixth Congress was being held in Basel and had thus not attended the congress.

Ussishkin's visit to Palestine in the summer of 1903 was his second to the country, after his first in early 1891.[17] On this second visit, Ussishkin saw fit to work on organizing the Zionist settlers because "we now have a Hebrew Yishuv in the Land of Israel, living from labor," and "it is necessary to organize the permanent relationship between it and the authorities, public institutions and individuals outside the country," in order to serve "the public interest and organize the various needs and affairs of the public".[18] Ussishkin called for a meeting of representatives of all the Jewish settlements in Palestine. The meeting was held in Zichron Ya'acov, with 67 attendees, and Ussishkin founded the Yishuv representative organization. He also issued an appeal to Jewish teachers in Palestine, urging them to organize in a union of their own to facilitate their task of

---

15   Mior, *Ha-Tnu'ah ha-Tzionit be-Rusia (Zionist Movement in Russia)*, p. 368.

16   Ibid, p. 370.

17   See his diary of that visit in *Sefer Ussishkin (Book of Ussishkin)*, pp. 24-69.

18   Ibid, pp. 77-78.

educating and raising a generation full of strength and vitality, of healthy body and soul, that knows its people, country and language well and loves them, a generation that loves work and lives from its labor in its country, such that this labor is the source of its livelihood and meets the needs of its body and soul

then "creating one Hebrew public in the Land of Israel, and one Hebrew community of all the different sects that currently exist in the country ... each of which is [still] afraid to shed the character of the country of the diaspora from which it came".[19] Following this call, a meeting of Jewish teachers in Palestine was held and it was decided to establish their own organization. The first Yishuv organization that Ussishkin helped to establish did not succeed, and came to an end within a year of its founding,[20] but the second one, the Teachers' Association in Israel, is still in existence.

After the Sixth Congress had approved Herzl's proposal of sending a Zionist commission to Uganda to study the possibilities of Jewish settlement there, Ussishkin promptly returned to Russia to work on uniting its Zionists against that project and thwarting it, when most of them, at any rate, had declared their opposition to it at the Sixth Congress. As a prelude to this work, Ussishkin formulated his views on labor Zionism in a pamphlet titled *Our Program*,[21] which he published in 1904. In the pamphlet, Ussishkin departed from three basic assumptions: that "cultural Zionism, and the diplomatic Zionism of the congresses are nothing more than varying forms of the same basic idea – that of political Zionism"; that the elements necessary for the political revival of a nation are "the people, the territory, and outward conditions"; and that effort should focus on these three elements together, for "even if the people is entirely ready to take possession of the land, and the land also ready to receive the

---

19 Ibid, p. 91.

20 Hillel Yaffe, *Dor Ma'afilim (A Generation of Immigrants)*, p. 257.

21 In *Sefer Ussishkin (Book of Ussishkin)*, pp. 97-125.

4. The Second Aliyah

people, this possession does not always come about, if certain favorable outward conditions are not present."[22] In his analysis of the relatively little success of the Zionist movement in the first quarter-century of its activity – that is, from the beginning of the First Aliyah in 1881 until Herzl's death in 1904 – Ussishkin asserted that Lovers of Zion had been concerned with practical settlement activity in Palestine and had neglected political action, while Herzl had done the opposite. The correct way, in Ussishkin's view, was to combine the two.[23]

In presenting the foundations of his program, Ussishkin stated that the first function of the Zionist movement was to strengthen self-awareness among the Jews, and that all Zionist agencies – not just the Zionist Executive – had to work to this end. In this framework, "the regeneration of the Hebrew language must be just as intensively cultivated as the regeneration of the land and of the people. It must become the official language of our movement, of our leaders and workers." In addition, "political and diplomatic labor occupies one of the foremost places in our program." The motive for this was to influence Turkey, as well as European governments, to grant concessions to the Zionist movement for settlement in Palestine.

> In order to create a Jewish autonomous community, or rather, a Jewish state, in Palestine, it is above all necessary that the whole soil of Palestine, or at least the major portion of it, should be in the possession of Jews. Without property rights to the soil, Palestine will never be Jewish, no matter how many Jews there may be in the cities and even in the villages...

The best way to obtain these property rights, in Ussishkin's view, was to purchase land by ordinary means from its owners, and this was best done before Zionism acquired settlement concessions in Palestine, which would raise the price of land and make its owners more reluctant to sell. Thus, "the 'redemption of the

---

22   Ibid, pp. 97-98.

23   Ibid, pp. 99-102.

land' must be our watchword at the present moment."[24]

Ussishkin proposed that the land purchased by the Zionist agencies be allocated for the establishment of cooperative settlements, aiming to create a new generation of real Jewish farmers. However, there was a major obstacle, as he had observed on his visit to Palestine. The Jews in the agricultural settlements had not actually taken up farming, but had handed their land over to hired Arab laborers from the villages adjacent to the settlements to cultivate it. Thus,

> many thousand Arabs obtain work with the Jews, while many Jews are idle from lack of work... Among many thousand Arabs there are only a few Jewish laborers. That is in the broadest sense of the word a sore spot in our colonization. And, however difficult and unpleasant the solution of this problem may be, it must be obtained immediately and unconditionally... It is, then, once for all necessary to replace the Arab laborer by Jews.

Ussishkin recommended establishing a "Jewish Universal Society of Workmen", every member of which would "go to Palestine for three years, in order to perform there his military duty to the Jewish people, not with musket and sword, but with plow and sickle". Through this society, Ussishkin thought another goal would be achieved that was equally important as the first: "The bond between the Jews of Palestine and the Jews of the lands of the exile will cease to be a paper one (prayers, books, periodicals), and will become a living one."[25]

Ussishkin saw this living bond as necessary for "gaining economic control of Palestine". However, he maintained that "spiritual, cultural conquest" also had to take place, and "spiritual culture consists fundamentally in the education of the population." Thus,

> we Jews ... must have our schools in all colonies and cities...

---

24   Ibid, pp. 103-107.

25   Ibid, pp. 115-118.

4. The Second Aliyah

In these schools Hebrew must be the leading language of instruction... The lower schools must be followed by secondary, special technical and industrial schools, and these, finally, by higher institutions, such as a normal school and a polytechnic institute ... [and] a seminary for teachers.[26]

At the conclusion of *Our Program*, Ussishkin appealed to all Zionists "to return, not to the Chibbath Zion [Lovers of Zion], not to spiritual Zionism, not to diplomatic Zionism, but to a synthesis of all these tendencies, that is, to political Zionism, as it is formulated in the Basel program".[27] After this was done,

decades will pass by, our people will be strengthened spiritually, materially, and in organization; our land will gradually pass over into our actual possession. The peoples and rulers of the whole world will be penetrated with our ideas, and the fruit of our labor will ripen. The time will come to pluck this fruit. And the hero will arise, whose appearance our people has awaited for thousands of years. Neither the unemancipated nor the spiritual Ghetto of the lands of the exile will rear him, but the free spirit of the mountains of Judea and Galilee. He will open unto us the gates of our home not from without, but from within... Boldly and proudly will he plant in the sight of the whole world the ... banner ... upon Mount Zion.[28]

Based on this position, Ussishkin campaigned widely among the Zionists in Russia. He tried to dispel the despair that had overtaken them due to Herzl's death, on the one hand, and the crackdown on the supporters of the Uganda project, on the other.[29] In early January 1905, at Ussishkin's initiative, a meeting of the "Zionists of Zion" was held in Vilna, and a number of decisions were made in the spirit of *Our Program*. The 47

---

26 Ibid, p. 123.

27 Ibid.

28 Ibid, p. 125.

29 Mior, *Ha-Tnu'ah ha-Tzionit be-Rusia (Zionist Movement in Russia)*, p. 294.

participants, who represented Zionist associations in various parts of Russia, decided to reject the Uganda proposal because it "contradicts the historical goal of Zionism and the Basel Program", and to "move, without delay, towards carrying out actual activity in the Land of Israel, such as emancipation of the land; organization of the Yishuv; development of agriculture, crafts, trade and industry; establishment of schools; revival of the Hebrew language; and other [actions]".[30] They formed committees to follow up the implementation of these decisions. A result of this meeting was also to urge a number of Zionists to immigrate to Palestine.

To encourage this immigration, Ussishkin took advantage of an appeal sent to him by Yosef Vitkin (1876-1912),[31] a teacher in one of the Jewish schools in Palestine. In this appeal, which Vitkin signed in the name of "a group of youth in the Land of Israel", he urged Jewish youth outside Palestine to "come to the Land of Israel, to cultivate its land and settle in it ... without any assistance ... or with the least possible assistance,"[32] after organizing themselves in small groups of 50-100. Vitkin explained, in this appeal to Jewish youth, that the goal of their coming to Palestine was "to establish new settlements, to dispel the wrong notions among the people, in general, and the population of the country, in particular, regarding the present Yishuv and the potential for settlement in the country in the current circumstances".[33] These settlements, he stressed, had to be established not by Jewish individuals or groups from abroad, but by settlers in the country. Vitkin proposed that young immigrants

> should work, in the first stage, as laborers in the settlements and cities, wherever they find work. When they become accustomed to the conditions of the country and its region, and acquire some work experience – more than that which

---

30   Ibid, pp. 296-297.

31   In Yosef Vitkin, *Kitvei Yosef Vitkin (Works of Yosef Vitkin)*, pp. 23-31.

32   Ibid, p. 26.

33   Ibid.

their predecessors had – they should obtain their own plot of land by purchasing or leasing one for a good period of time from the JCA, the Jewish National Fund, or other companies, or from the Arabs or the government, if possible, and establish prosperous settlements on it – not with the help of millions, but with their limitless work, diligence and devotion.[34]

Ussishkin took advantage of this appeal very widely, printing and disseminating it in and outside Russia. During this period, a number of Zionist settlements were established in Palestine according to Vitkin's suggestions.

Over time, these views, which called for focusing efforts on encouraging practical settlement activity, took center stage among Russian Zionists, who saw one of their first duties as working to push more Jewish immigrants to Palestine. The Zionist Organization also officially adopted this policy, although this was after long battles fought by the Russian Zionists. Thus the motives of the Second Aliyah immigrants in coming to Palestine were not only to escape the persecution that they faced in Russia. Some of these motives lay in the activity of the Russian Zionists, who tried to exploit the wave of immigration resulting from that persecution (and other factors) to serve their aims, and were able to direct part of that immigration to Palestine.

2

As the vanguards of the Second Aliyah were arriving in Palestine, the Zionist movement was in a very critical situation due to Herzl's death, on the one hand, and the heightening dispute between the supporters and opponents of the Uganda project, on the other. Each group organized itself and closed ranks, in preparation for a final decision at the next Zionist congress. The dispute was mainly focused among the Russian Zionists. After the meeting held by the "Zionists of Zion" in Vilna, in January 1905, at which they decided to reject the Uganda project, their opponents in favor of the project held a counter-meeting in

---

34 Ibid, p. 30.

Warsaw, in April of the same year. This was attended by delegates from 15 cities. The attendees included Isaac Reines, leader of the Mizrahi movement (see Chapter 3, section 7). They decided to adopt the Uganda project and work, at the next Zionist congress, to amend the Basel Program and the regulations of the Jewish Colonial Trust, Jewish National Fund and other Zionist agencies on that basis.[35]

A month later, in May 1905, the Zionist Executive unanimously decided – after it had raised its members from 4 to 13, following Herzl's death – that it could not recommend the Zionist Congress to accept the Uganda project because of the discouraging report that studied the possibilities of settlement in that region, earlier that year.[36] In the wake of this announcement, the supporters and opponents of the project, each united and ready to settle the matter,[37] came to the Seventh Zionist Congress. This was held in Basel, from July 27 to August 2, 1905, with 497 delegates representing 137,071 Zionists. Before the congress convened, the Russian Zionist delegates held, as was their custom, a meeting to coordinate their positions, but they disagreed amongst themselves on the position regarding the Uganda project, and the meeting ended with no decision. The Zionist Congress itself, on its second day, held an extraordinary congress for two and a half days to discuss the question of Uganda. It was finally decided, by a large majority, to reject the project, while giving due thanks to the British government for presenting it to the Zionist movement. At this, the "Ugandans" left the congress hall in protest, announcing their split from the Zionist Organization.[38]

Nevertheless, with this matter closed, the congress turned to discussing Zionist policy in Palestine. It was decided, under the influence of proposals presented by the "Zionists of Zion",

---

35   Mior, *Ha-Tnu'ah ha-Tzionit be-Rusia (Zionist Movement in Russia)*, p. 297.

36   Ibid, p. 291.

37   Yitzhak Gruenbaum, *Ha-Tnu'ah ha-Tzionit (The Zionist Movement)*, Vol. 3, p. 24.

38   Mior, *Ha-Tnu'ah ha-Tzionit be-Rusia (Zionist Movement in Russia)*, p. 301.

"to undertake systematic work to support our positions in the Land of Israel, in parallel to the diplomatic, political activity, as a practical basis for this activity and in order to strengthen it". The congress defined this "systematic work" through these means:

> 1. Conduct multi-faceted research, 2. Develop agriculture, industry and the like [in Palestine], in democratic spirit, as much as possible, 3. Organize culturally and economically, and improve the status of the Jews in the Land of Israel through the immigration of new, intellectual forces, 4. Pursue administrative and legal reforms necessary to improve the conditions in the Land of Israel... The congress rejects prescribed settlement that lacks planning and methodology and is based on alms, and to which ... the first article of the Basel Program does not apply ["the expedient promotion of the settlement of Jewish agriculturists, artisans, and businessmen in Palestine"].[39]

The congress also decided to prevent the Jewish National Fund from purchasing land in Palestine "if this cannot be done on a guaranteed legal basis", but allowed the Zionist administration to discuss each land transaction individually.

After Nordau apologized for not abiding by the will of Herzl and nominating himself for the presidency of the Zionist Organization, the congress elected David Wolffsohn, another political Zionist who had been close to Herzl, to the post. Six other members were also elected to the Zionist Executive, half of them political and the other half practical Zionists, in order to satisfy both currents. The presidency of the organization was moved from Vienna to Cologne, where the new president was based.

The split of the "Ugandans" from the Zionist Organization at the Seventh Zionist Congress led to the emergence of a new class of Zionists: the "territorialists". The dissidents, numbering about 40, established the "Jewish Territorial Organization", which

---

39 In Gruenbaum, *Ha-Tnu'ah ha-Tzionit (The Zionist Movement)*, Vol. 3, pp. 36-37.

announced that its goal was to acquire any place in the world where Jews could be resettled on the basis of their autonomy. This organization, chaired by the British Zionist Israel Zangwill, set up branches in Britain, Russia and the United States, and made numerous efforts to obtain an area for the settlement of Jews in several countries, including Libya and Iraq.[40] All of its endeavors failed, however, and it dissolved itself in 1925.

Despite the preliminary decision taken by the Seventh Zionist Congress to strengthen practical settlement in Palestine, and the election of three practical Zionists to the Executive, the Zionist Organization did not make any advances in its cause. Its new president, David Wolffsohn, a close friend of the late Herzl, felt it his duty to follow in the footsteps of his mentor and, thus, tipped the balance, in the Executive, in favor of the politicians. The nature of Wolffsohn's work as a merchant also seemed to discourage him from conducting settlement "experiments" in Palestine with no guaranteed results. His only achievement between the seventh and eighth Zionist congresses was to issue a Hebrew weekly newspaper, *ha-Olam* (*The World*), to become the mouthpiece for the Zionist Organization. It was edited by the renowned Jewish writer Nahum Sokolow, editor-in-chief of *ha-Tsfira*, the leading Hebrew daily newspaper at the time. After Wolffsohn's election, he proposed to Sokolow that he be appointed his secretary when Sokolow insisted on launching the newspaper as a condition of his acceptance.[41] *Ha-Olam* then moved from one location to another, depending on the centers of Zionist activity, and was suspended for several periods before it was finally closed in 1949.

With the lack of settlement activity in Palestine by the Zionist administration, the practical Zionists prepared for another battle at the Eighth Zionist Congress. This was held in

---

[40] For details, see Michael Heymann, *Ha-Tnu'ah ha-Tzionit ve ha-Tochniot le-Yishuv Aram Naharayim be-Tkufa she le-Ahar Herzl (The Zionist Movement and the Schemes for Jewish Settlement in Mesopotamia after the Death of Herzl)*, pp. 7-53.

[41] Nahum Sokolow, *Ha-Tsofeh le-Beit Yisrael (Looking into the House of Israel)*, pp. 61-62.

4. The Second Aliyah 233

The Hague on August 19-21, 1907, with 329 delegates (almost half of them from Russia) representing 164,333 Zionists. The Russian Zionists had been able to close ranks, especially after the "territorialists" had split from them, and they held a meeting before the congress at which they resolved, unanimously, to push for a resolution from it to finally adopt the Zionist practical line.[42] At the congress, the attack was headed by Chaim Weizmann. In a speech, he stated that "our diplomatic work is important, but it will gain in importance by actual performance in Palestine. If we achieve a synthesis of the two schools of Zionism, we may get past the dead point."[43] Weizmann explained that even if the Zionists were to obtain a concession to settle in Palestine, this would have no real value "unless it rested, so to say, on the very soil of Palestine, on a Jewish population rooted in that soil, on institutions established by and for that population".[44] In this speech, Weizmann launched his famous slogan of "synthetic Zionism",[45] composed of all the Zionist currents: political, practical, cultural and spiritual. This synthetic Zionism became, at that point, the slogan of most Zionists.

At the end of the congress, and due to the diligence of the Russian Zionists and their practical friends from western Europe, the practical-synthetic Zionist line was approved by a large majority. The decisions of the congress included "the establishment of a special department for the affairs of the Land of Israel, in the Inner Actions Committee, chaired by a member of the committee", such that 25% of the Executive's income would be allocated to this department, in addition to the funds originally allocated for settlement. The congress decided to commission this department to conduct research on establishing a cooperative settlement in Palestine, according to Oppenheimer's theory, and to establish a trust fund in the branch

---

42   Mior, *Ha-Tnu'ah ha-Tzionit be-Rusia (Zionist Movement in Russia)*, pp. 320-322.

43   Chaim Weizmann, *Trial and Error*, p. 157.

44   Ibid.

45   Ibid, p. 158.

of the Jewish Colonial Trust that had been opened in Jaffa in 1903 to purchase or lease land in Palestine. The congress additionally requested that special attention be given to cultural institutions in the country.[46]

The decisions taken by the Eighth Zionist Congress included its recognition "in principle, of the Hebrew language as the official language of the Zionist movement and its administration, congresses and committees",[47] such that the decision would be implemented gradually (up until then, the protocols of the Zionist congresses had been recorded in German). The congress elected a new, tripartite Zionist administration headed by Wolffsohn. The Eighth Zionist Congress also saw the participation, for the first time, of four representatives of the Jews in Palestine: Yitzhak Ben-Zvi, Israel Shohat (also: Shochat), Yosef Aharonovich, and Eliezer Shohat.

Immediately after the end of the congress, the presidency of the Zionist Organization summoned Arthur Ruppin (1876-1943), who, despite being a law graduate, was mainly interested in Jewish sociology, and asked him to travel to Palestine and study the conditions of the Zionist settlements.[48] On his return, Ruppin gave an estimate – based on surveys he had conducted – that there were about 80,000 Jews in Palestine among 700,000 Arabs. The Jews owned about 400,000 dunums of the total land in the country (which, according to administrative divisions at the time, was about 29 million dunums). In his report, Ruppin noted that the Jews lived mainly in two areas. The first was in central Palestine, between the cities of Jerusalem, Jaffa, Gaza and Hebron. About 54,300 Jews lived in this area among 208,000 Arabs. Of the Jewish population, about 3,800 lived in agricultural settlements and cultivated about 72,300 dunums of land. The remaining Jews lived in the cities – especially Jerusalem, in which more than half of the Jewish population of Palestine lived at

---

46   Mior, *Ha-Tnu'ah ha-Tzionit be-Rusia (Zionist Movement in Russia)*, pp. 327-328.

47   Ibid, p. 328.

48   Arthur Ruppin, *Pirkei Hayai (Chapters of My Life)*, Vol. 2, p. 9.

4. The Second Aliyah

the time. The second area was in northeastern Palestine, in the upper Galilee, near the towns of Safad and Tiberias, where about 15,400 Jews lived (about 8,000 in Safad and 6,000 in Tiberias), while the remainder (1,350) lived in agricultural settlements and cultivated about 92,200 dunums.[49] The remaining lands that had been acquired by the Zionist agencies, and could not be made use of by Jewish settlers, were given to Arab farmers to cultivate. In his report, Ruppin stated that the Turkish government would not grant the Jewish population autonomy in Palestine unless they became a majority and owned most of its land and, since this was difficult to achieve in the foreseeable future, it was necessary to focus on specific areas in the country to ensure that the Jews were a majority, before unifying the areas, geographically, when the opportunity arose.[50] The Zionist Organization approved this plan and decided to launch an office in Palestine to implement it, and asked Ruppin to direct it. He stipulated his approval, however, on setting up a private company under his management, to purchase land in Palestine. The administration agreed and founded, in late 1907, the Palestine Land Development Company (also known as "Hachsharat ha-Yishuv", Preparation of the Yishuv, in Hebrew), with a capital of 50,000 pounds sterling. About three years later, this company became an agent of the Jewish National Fund to purchase land in Palestine, and continued to do so for the next 30 years. In April 1908, Ruppin arrived in Jaffa and opened the "Palestine Office" of the Zionist Organization.[51]

The Zionist administration also attempted, after the Eighth Zionist Congress, to establish relations with the new Turkish government that had come to power after the Young Turk Revolution in late July 1908. The Zionist administration contributed to the establishment of a bank in Istanbul, the Anglo-Levantine Banking Company, and appointed Victor Jacobson as its director, although his real mission was to make political

---

49   Alex Bein, *Toldot ha-Hityashvut ha-Tzionit (History of Zionist Settlement)*, pp. 35-36.

50   Ibid.

51   Ruppin, *Pirkei Hayai (Chapters of My Life)*, Vol. 2, pp. 38-43.

contacts with the Turkish authorities. Ze'ev Jabotinsky was assigned to work as his assistant. The Zionists also began to issue a French newspaper there, to influence public opinion. In June 1909, six months before the Ninth Zionist Congress, Wolffsohn traveled to Istanbul and met with Turkish officials but could not meet the sultan because of the revolution that had erupted against him. Wolffsohn attempted to induce the officials to change the previous position of the Turkish government – which Herzl had been notified of – and to encourage Zionist settlement in Palestine, but he failed.[52] In 1913, the Zionist Organization submitted a similar request to the Turkish authorities, but it was also denied.[53]

Thus, and despite these attempts by the Zionist Organization, after the Eighth Congress, to strengthen the foundations of settlement in Palestine, the Zionist leadership did not satisfy the practical Zionists. They tried to topple it at the Ninth Congress, which was held in Hamburg on December 26-30, 1909, with 364 delegates representing 182,808 Zionists. During the sessions, the practical Zionists launched a fierce attack on the president of the organization, Wolffsohn, and his administration, but the practical Zionists faced a fiercer counter-attack. The disputes escalated to such a degree that, especially after the opposition presented draft resolutions that ridiculed Wolffsohn, the congress could not elect a new administration and the previous one remained unchanged,[54] with a decision to move its headquarters to Cologne. After the Ninth Congress, the disputes intensified between the practical and political Zionists and almost threatened to split the movement, until a reconciliation took place at the annual meeting of the Zionist Organization that was usually held between the Zionist congresses. At this meeting, in Berlin, on June 27-29, 1910, the politicians pledged to agree to

---

[52] For details, see Gruenbaum, *Ha-Tnu'ah ha-Tzionit (The Zionist Movement)*, Vol. 3, pp. 127-141.

[53] Ibid, pp. 221-222.

[54] Mior, *Ha-Tnu'ah ha-Tzionit be-Rusia (Zionist Movement in Russia)*, pp. 351-357.

4. The Second Aliyah

all the demands of the practical Zionists at the upcoming Tenth Zionist Congress. This was held in Basel on August 9-15, 1911, with 387 delegates representing 175,893 Zionists. It elected Otto Warburg (1859-1938), professor of botany at the University of Strasbourg, as president of the organization. It also elected four other members to the Executive, all of them practical Zionists.[55] In this way, the practical Zionists managed – four years after the Eighth Zionist Congress (1907) had adopted their method of work – to assume control and the presidency of the Zionist Organization. Their victory was incomplete, however; the movement's financial agencies, the Jewish Colonial Trust and Jewish National Fund, remained out of their reach. Herzl had appointed his political friends to lead these agencies, which enjoyed relative independence in the administration of their affairs. At the 11th Zionist Congress, held in Vienna on September 2-9, 1913, with 539 delegates representing 217,231 Zionists (the last Zionist congress to be held before the First World War), the practical Zionists finally took control of the movement's financial agencies as well,[56] after the congress had re-elected the previous administration. The delegates also approved, with great enthusiasm, a proposal to establish a Hebrew university in Jerusalem.[57] Hermann Schapira, who had proposed the establishment of the Jewish National Fund to the First Zionist Congress, was also the author of this proposal, which Weizmann adopted and worked diligently to implement.[58]

Before the practical Zionists took over the Zionist Organization, however, Wolffsohn's political administration was able to make an important practical achievement in settling in Palestine. With a proposal by this administration, the Ninth Congress approved the Zionist movement's formal adoption of Oppenheimer's method to establish Jewish settlements in the

---

55   Ibid, pp. 357-363.

56   Max Nordau, *Kitvei Nordau (Works of Nordau)*, Vol. 4, pp. 185-186.

57   Mior, *Ha-Tnu'ah ha-Tzionit be-Rusia (Zionist Movement in Russia)*, pp. 387-391.

58   Weizmann, *Trial and Error*, pp. 152-155, 174-176, 180-182.

country. Oppenheimer had been invited, once again, to give a lecture to the congress on his theory of "cooperative settlement", which had three stages. The first involved the establishment of a large village, under the direction of an expert agricultural engineer. Its laborers were to receive, in addition to their wages (set according to their qualifications and productivity), part of the profits, which would rise each time their wages were increased. After this first stage, the workers would be expected to have saved a good amount of money, and they would unite in a "cooperative-productive agricultural labor association". This cooperative would, at its expense, assume management of the village and be responsible for its profit and loss. When this was achieved, the third and final stage would begin: the establishment of the "cooperative settlement", which non-agricultural workers, such as artisans, salesmen and self-employed individuals would also be allowed to settle. At this stage, the members of the cooperative would have the right to leave and cultivate their own piece of land that would be given to them, with the cooperative also able to accept new members in their place.[59] In the spring of 1910, Oppenheimer traveled to Palestine to oversee the establishment of the Merhavia settlement, near the town of Afula, south of Nazareth, per this method. However, his experiment did not meet with great success and, with time, fundamental changes were made to it. Yet, it was one of the bases that later sprouted communal settlements of the types "kvutzah", "kibbutz", and "moshav ovdim" (workers' settlement) in Israel. (The "kvutzah" and "moshavah" were smaller settlements, while the "kibbutz" and "moshav" were larger.)

In another sphere, and during the same period in which the secular Zionists, including the politicians, practical Zionists, spiritualists, and others, were waging a wide struggle that ultimately led to their union under the slogan of synthetic Zionism, the religious Zionists were engaged in a similar struggle that produced different results. The Mizrahi was affected by the dispute that arose between the political and practical Zionists,

---

59   For details, see Gezel Kressel, *Franz Oppenheimer*, pp. 49-58.

4. The Second Aliyah

leading to the rise of two currents within it as well: political and religious. Certain groups within the organization then began proclaiming, enthusiastically, the merits of Zionist unity and the need to cooperate with secular Zionists – and sometimes tolerate their "heresy" – in order to establish a Jewish state in Palestine. Although some Mizrahi followers considered this view to be harmful to traditional Jewish religious teachings,[60] they were reluctantly silent. Then, at the Tenth Zionist Congress (1911), the practical Zionists did not suffice with their victory in assuming leadership of the Zionist Organization – after electing all the members of the Executive from within their ranks – but they also compelled the congress to take a decision that "the Zionist Executive has a duty to organize and focus Hebrew cultural activity in the Land of Israel and the countries of the East."[61] This decision, which was taken despite strong Mizrahi opposition, rekindled the dispute between the secular and religious Zionists on the official position of the organization regarding cultural activity, after the dispute had abated following Herzl's death. The religious faction, on their part, had formulated a position on this issue, by which each class of secular or religious Zionists had the choice to engage in cultural activity as it saw fit, provided that the Zionist Organization did not officially intervene in favor of either party. The decision of the congress, however, violated this delicate balance. Such a decision meant, at the very least, obliging the religious Zionists to finance secular cultural projects, by means of the shekel membership fees that they paid to the Zionist Organization. These projects may have included – in the words of a religious individual – "covering the Land of Israel with a network of [secular] schools in a spirit of blasphemy and immorality, especially after the announcement of liberal principles abhorrent and alien to the sacred spirit of Israel, such as freedom of religion, granting women the right to vote, refusing to abide by the laws of the Torah, and the like",

---

60 For details, see Shlomo Eidelberg, "Crystallization of the Mizrahi idea by the First World War", in Simon Federbusch, ed., *Hazon Torah ve Tzion (The Vision of Torah and Zion)*, pp. 177-200.

61 Ibid, p. 192.

through "arrogant insolence, unparalleled in the Jewish world".[62]

The Mizrahi could not remain silent and, after the Tenth Congress, it held a meeting to study the new situation and consider the appropriate measures to take. Some of its members demanded a split from the Zionist Organization but the majority rejected this notion, calling for deliberation and restraint. The opponents, however, left the meeting hall, announcing their split from both the Zionist Organization and the Mizrahi.[63] These dissidents then contacted rabbis and groups of Orthodox Jews, notably in Frankfurt and Hungary, and decided to hold a congress of their own and establish a new religious organization.

This Orthodox congress was held in the town of Katowice, in the German Empire (today, Poland) in late May 1912. It was inaugurated by Jacob Rosenheim, a rabbi who declared that the goal of the meeting was not to establish an organization like the others, but "the reanimation of ... the entirety of Israel's body, filled and borne by its Torah". In his speech, Rosenheim asserted that "since the Jews were displaced from their country by the Romans, they carried with them, in their hands and hearts, [their] sacred Torah." Thus, he continued, they were able – through the teachings of the Torah and its cultural values, as well as their rejection by the societies that they lived amongst – to preserve their existence. This situation changed, however, at the outbreak of the French Revolution in 1789, due to the principles that it called for – such as universal liberation – such that "unfortunately, the Torah is no longer, in practice, the centerpiece of the whole Jewish existence... This is the cause of the calamity ... and a cure must be found." Rosenheim insisted that the relationship must be restored "between our children and all of the Jews, not just the spiritual relationship with the past, but with the Jewish masses, today".[64] Thus, "we must work for the benefit of all the Jews, in all areas of life," by devoting "our

---

62   Amram Blau, *Al Homotech, Yerushalayim (On Your Walls, Jerusalem)*, p. 139.

63   Meir Bar-Ilan (Berlin), *Me-Volozhin ad Yerushalayim (From Volozhin to Jerusalem)*, pp. 386-390.

64   Jacob Rosenheim, *Ktavim (Works)*, Vol. 1, pp. 98-100.

4. The Second Aliyah

forces to support and strengthen the teaching of the Torah and Jewish culture on a large scale", regulating the material aspect of Jewish existence "through popular organization based on the spirit of the Torah", and "standing ready to defend the sanctity of the Torah wherever needed, to insiders and outsiders".[65] Since this organization was "based on the authority of the Torah", a "council of Torah sages" had to be established as a "supreme spiritual body" to supervise it.[66] At the end of the congress, the formation of the international organization, "World Agudat Israel" (Union of Israel), was announced, based on the speech delivered by Rosenheim. In the "temporary regulations" issued by the organization, its main goal was "to solve the different issues facing all Jews in their daily lives, according to the spirit of the Torah and the [various religious] duties".[67]

Agudat Israel, as it was known, was hostile to all currents of the Zionist movement and expressed its reservations regarding Zionist activity on more than one occasion, sometimes at the international level.[68] The main reason for this was a fundamental difference in some of its basic concepts from those of Zionism. In the view of Agudat Israel, "the fake Zionist concept of [Jewish] unity strips the Jewish people of the testimony of its historical world uniqueness, as the bearer of the idea of absolute, divine monotheism, and renders it an illusory material unity."[69] The ideologists of Agudat Israel also opposed the religious Zionist concept of the "duty to settle the Land of Israel" which was used to compel Orthodox Jews to immigrate to Palestine and settle there (see Introduction, section 6).

> The duty to settle the Land of Israel is only one of 613 duties [that Judaism binds its followers to fulfill]... It cannot be abolished, at any rate, because of its misuse and lack of

---

65 Ibid, pp. 102-104.

66 Ibid, p. 105.

67 Hen-Melech Merchavia, *Am ou-Moledet (Nation and Homeland)*, p. 388.

68 For details, see Emile Marmorstein, *Heaven at Bay; the Jewish Kulturkampf in the Holy Land*, pp. 80-90.

69 Rosenheim, *Ktavim (Works)*, Vol. 1, p. 135.

understanding by Zionism... We allow ourselves to feel removed from the charge of imitating Zionism, and when history presents an occasion to perform this duty, accurately and in detail, [we would not hesitate to do so]... We are committed to fulfilling the 613 duties, while the Zionists commit to only one.[70]

Agudat Israel also opposed the concept of the "centrality of the Land of Israel in the life of the Jewish people", launched by the Zionist movement: "Agudat Israel does not condemn the diaspora, but it does not favor it, either... While redemption is yet remote, and the diaspora exists, Orthodox Judaism recognizes its existence and does not ignore it." Agudat Israel supported the settlement of Jews in Palestine, but "refrains from obliging the Yishuv with more than it can bear and making it ... the only basis of Judaism", even though it "considers it a preparation for redemption, and an easy condition to preserve the existence of the people ... and the Torah – but not an end in itself, nor the purpose of Jewish existence. The Land of Israel and the diaspora, for Agudat Israel, are two interconnected things that complement each other."[71]

In the early 1920s, a parallel organization to Agudat Israel was formed: "Po'alei Agudat Israel" (Agudat Israel Workers), which included labor groups committed to the teachings of the organization. During the British mandate over Palestine, Agudat Israel insisted on its recognition as an independent denomination, distinct from the main Jewish ones in the country – religious or secular – and it was granted this wish.

After the establishment of Israel, Agudat Israel and Po'alei Agudat Israel joined the United Religious Front, albeit feebly, as the two organizations would periodically unite and then split again.[72]

---

70   Ibid, pp. 191-192.

71   Blau, *Al Homotech, Yerushalayim (On Your Walls, Jerusalem)*, pp. 145-146.

72   Translator's note: Today, this front is part of the United Torah Judaism party, or Yahadut ha-Torah ha-Meuhedet, in Hebrew. Its members join the Israeli government, but only up to the capacity of deputy minister due to

3

In the second half of the 19th and early 20th century, economic changes came about in Russia that led to important social changes, reshuffled the natural and demographic map and produced new classes. Political organizations emerged that expressed this new reality. Most of the Jewish immigrants to Palestine during the Second Aliyah were from these new classes, which defined new political concepts for themselves and brought them to Palestine.

Since the mid-19th century, when Russia had embarked on the path of industrial development, its peasants had begun to be liberated from the control of feudal lords. By the early 20th century, a large working class had been formed in the country, which quickly became an important segment with a noticeable impact on domestic politics. Various revolutionary parties opposed to tsarist rule were formed, primarily with a socialist character. This development also affected the Jews in Russia. Tsarist rule, through its policies, persecuted the Jewish middle class that constituted the majority of the Jewish population, and turned most of them into laborers who found themselves enduring harsh living conditions. Most were concentrated in the Jewish Pale of Settlement, where living became difficult due to overcrowding after the tsarist authorities forbade the Jews to leave it.[73] These difficulties, in addition to the persecution that the Jews faced, were the main drivers that prompted them to immigrate to less densely populated areas within the Pale of Settlement, at the outset, and then outside Russia, especially to the United States.[74] It should be noted that developments almost identical to these took place in several European countries during this period, and led to the immigration of about 30 million people from Europe to the American continent in 1850-1925.

Emigration was not the only reaction among Russian Jews to their religious beliefs regarding the state.

73 Mior, *Ha-Tnu'ah ha-Tzionit be-Rusia (Zionist Movement in Russia)*, pp. 329-330.

74 Yehuda Slutsky, *Mevoa le-Toldot Tnu'at ha-Avoda ha-Yisraelit (Introduction to the History of the Israeli Labor Movement)*, pp. 56-62.

the conditions that they faced, however. Several million of them remained in the country despite the ongoing emigration from their ranks. The reactions of those who remained generally took three forms. Some joined the Zionist movement, others engaged in Russian revolutionary parties of various ideologies, while the remainder established Jewish socialist-labor organizations of their own.

The Jewish socialist movements that emerged in this period were not the pioneers of Jewish socialism. In the mid-1870s, for example, the "Hebrew Socialist Union"[75] had been formed in London, headed by Aaron Liebermann, a Jewish author. The experience of this organization did not extend beyond the theoretical,[76] however, unlike the socialist-labor organizations that appeared a quarter of a century later in Russia. These later organizations took hold among a large Jewish working class that faced deep-rooted problems, which were among the main reasons for the establishment of these organizations and prompted them to take very practical – sometimes daily – positions to confront these issues.

The motives for establishing Jewish socialist organizations, independent of other socialist organizations in Russia, were, in the view of Jewish socialists, two-fold. First, their sense of the unique problems facing the Jewish people led them to believe that they could only be solved by Jewish socialist organizations that cooperated with similar, non-Jewish ones in Russia to establish socialist rule. Second, more than one Russian socialist group had a negative attitude towards Judaism and Jews, as the capitalists among them were considered a part of the tsarist regime that was persecuting these socialist groups. This stance resulted, to a large extent, from the views of Karl Marx himself. In 1843, Marx wrote an article entitled *On the Jewish Question*,[77]

---

75 Tzvi Ben-Shoshan, *Toldot Tnu'at ha-Poalim be-Eretz Yisrael (History of the Labor Movement in the Land of Israel)*, Vol. 1, pp. 37-39.

76 See also the organization's regulations in Merchavia, *Am ou-Moledet (Nation and Homeland)*, pp. 349-350.

77 Article in Karl Marx, *Karl Marx, Friedrich Engels: Collected Works*, Vol. 3, pp. 145-174.

4. The Second Aliyah

in which he strongly criticized religions, especially Christianity and Judaism, and the social systems based on them. He called for the emancipation of man and state from these two religions and their spiritual and material influence. He used severe insults against Judaism:

> What is the worldly religion of the Jew? Huckstering [peddlers]. What is his worldly God? Money. Very well then! Emancipation from huckstering and money, consequently from practical, real Judaism, would be the self-emancipation of our time. An organization of society which would abolish the preconditions for huckstering, and therefore the possibility of huckstering, would make the Jew impossible. His religious consciousness would be dissipated like a thin haze in the real, vital air of society... We recognize in Judaism, therefore, a general antisocial element of the present time, an element which through historical development – to which in this harmful respect the Jews have zealously contributed – has been brought to its present high level, at which it must necessarily begin to disintegrate... Money has become a world power and the practical Jewish spirit has become the practical spirit of the Christian nations. The Jews have emancipated themselves insofar as the Christians have become Jews.[78]

Marx also stated that "Judaism continues to exist not in spite of history, but owing to history."[79] He added: "In the final analysis, the emancipation of the Jews is the emancipation of mankind from Judaism... The social emancipation of the Jew is the emancipation of society from Judaism."[80]

It would not have been necessary to present this article here, were it not for the positions and counter-positions that it evoked – which ultimately had the result, though odd, at first instance, of strengthening and refining Zionism. Many Marxists

---

78   Ibid, p. 170.

79   Ibid, p. 171.

80   Ibid, pp. 170, 174.

had reservations regarding these views and their generalized description of Jewish capitalists as applying to all the Jews, including their poor classes. Yet those views of Marx caused a large number of socialists to be reluctant to consider solutions to the Jewish question as socialist ideas began to spread. At best, the socialists ignored the question and sometimes attributed some of its manifestations to the "Jewish bourgeoisie", or overlooked those manifestations altogether. Even when the followers of Marx or those affected by his views decided to take a position on Zionism, they could not exit the framework of considering it a product of the Jewish bourgeoisie and then ignoring it – even though the idea had spread among the Jewish working class in particular. As mentioned above, the latter had grown significantly in tsarist Russia in the late 19th century, when the means of subsistence for Jewish craftsmen had diminished with the country's move towards industrial development. To a certain extent, those positions led to the "Zionist solution" appearing, at times, to be the only solution to the Jewish question. This helped to strengthen the Zionist movement and ideology.

The first Jewish labor organization to be formed in Russia was the Bund, or General Jewish Labor Bund in Russia and Poland (and, later, Lithuania). The Bund was founded at a meeting in Vilna, attended by 13 delegates of various Jewish socialist organizations, in mid-October 1897 – less than two months after the First Zionist Congress and the establishment of the Zionist Organization. Shortly after it was formed, the Bund joined the Russian Social Democratic Party (Vladimir Lenin's party), formed branches throughout Russia and became the largest organized Jewish group in the country, maintaining this position until the outbreak of the Russian Revolution, in 1917.[81]

The Bund's leadership, initially, was composed mainly of socialist Jews assimilated into Russian society. They did not bother with the Jewish "national question", even though the issue had been put forth by their opponents, the Zionists.

---

81   Slutsky, *Mevoa le-Toldot Tnu'at ha-Avoda ha-Yisraelit (Introduction to the History of the Israeli Labor Movement)*, pp. 76-79.

4. The Second Aliyah

With time, however, as various groups of Jewish socialists and laborers joined its ranks, the Bund slowly changed and began to demand the recognition of the right to Jewish autonomy in Russia and Poland, especially with regard to cultural affairs. This was based on the view that the Jews in Russia, like other national groups in the country, were a separate nation, with its own history, traditions and common interests, as well as its own language (Yiddish). This gradual change in the Bund's position took place, to a large extent, under the influence of the theory of Simon Dubnow (1860-1941) on "secular Jewish nationalism" in the diaspora (see Chapter 2, section 5). Dubnow was a professor of Jewish history at the Jewish People's University in St. Petersburg. He had been actively disseminating his views since the Bund's establishment, the rising Zionist activity in Russia with the establishment of the Zionist Organization in 1897, and the Zionists' enthusiastic promotion of their idea of solving the Jewish question by establishing a Jewish state in Palestine. Dubnow's views were an answer to the ideas of both the Zionists and the Bund, even though he supported neither of them.

Dubnow launched his campaign in a series of articles published in 1897-1902, in which he called on all Jews in the diaspora – regardless of their views – to adopt the theory of autonomy and to demand that they be granted this right in any country in which they lived in significant numbers, as the only means of preserving their existence. Dubnow based his theory on the fact that the Jewish diaspora had existed before the destruction of the Second Kingdom of Israel by the Romans in the 1st and 2nd centuries, and the Jews had maintained their presence in the diaspora since that time, that is for 2,000 years,

> through their own administration, the authority of their independent sects, and their public and cultural institutions... The recent development of the national movement has shown that the Jews are a living nation, divided among many countries, and religion is only one of its manifestations... Forefront in autonomy must be secular national organization,

not religious sect.[82]

In Dubnow's view, all Jewish segments had to make their primary goal the demand for their national rights – like those of other national minorities that lived in many countries – in addition to demanding civil rights for the Jews in the countries where they had not yet attained them.

The Bund was the first Jewish party to adopt Dubnow's theories, declaring in its fourth congress (1901) that "a country such as Russia, composed of many different nationalities, must, in future, become a federation of nationalities with complete national autonomy for each, regardless of the province it resides in." The Bund also decided that "the term 'nation' can also apply to the Jewish people," but since "it is premature, in the present circumstances, to demand national autonomy for the Jews," the party sufficed with "the struggle to abolish the special laws directed against the Jews, emphasizing the reality of persecution of the Jewish nation, and protesting it, by refraining from exaggerating national sentiment which may lead to obscuring the class consciousness of the proletariat and push it towards chauvinism".[83]

In its fifth congress (1903), the Bund made some aspects of this position clearer by declaring that it considered itself "the branch of the Social Democratic Party among the Jewish proletariat, unrestricted by narrow regional borders, and the Bund joins the party as the only representative of the Jewish proletariat". Thus, "the Bund's program is the general program of the [Social Democratic] Party, and the Bund has the right, with regard to issues arising from the special conditions of the Jews and their social relations, to supplement the party's program with special articles that do not contradict that program."[84] This position, however, did not meet with the approval of several factions of the Social Democratic Party, and was opposed, in particular, by

---

82   Dubnow, *Divrei Yemei Am Olam (History of the Jews)*, p. 706.

83   In Merchavia, *Am ou-Moledet (Nation and Homeland)*, pp. 353-354.

84   Ibid, p. 354.

4. The Second Aliyah

Lenin, who declared: "Absolutely untenable scientifically, the idea that the Jews form a separate nation is reactionary politically ... [and] runs counter to the interests of the Jewish proletariat."[85]

When this topic was raised for discussion at the second congress of the Social Democratic Party (1903), the majority (Bolsheviks) opposed the Bund's position, and the party declared that

> the establishment of organizational relations between the Jewish and Russian proletariat, on a federal basis, may become a major obstacle to the complete organizational convergence of classes with proletarian consciousness among the different peoples, and may cause great harm to the interests of the Russian proletariat, generally, and of the Jewish one, in particular.[86]

The Social Democratic Party presented this decision, opposing the Bund, by saying:

> A complete union of the Jewish proletariat and those of the other peoples amongst whom they live is an absolute necessity in our struggle for political and economic emancipation... Only such a complete union secures success for social democracy in its war against chauvinism and anti-Semitism... [T]he union does not compromise the independence of the Jewish labor movement with regard to details of its propaganda among the Jewish masses, arising from the special circumstances of reality and language.[87]

In the wake of this decision, the Bund split from the Social Democratic Party and was followed by most leaders and ideologues of the Jewish party. The Bund, however, rejoined the party in 1906, even though the bases of the disputes persisted between them. In the end, the Bund paid for its position – as Lenin dissolved it in the early 1920s after coming to power in

---

85 Dubnow, *Divrei Yemei Am Olam (History of the Jews)*, pp. 707-708.

86 Merchavia, *Am ou-Moledet (Nation and Homeland)*, p. 356.

87 Ibid, p. 355.

Russia. Not long after, however, the Soviet Union announced its recognition of its Jewish population as an independent nation, enjoying the same rights granted to other nationalities in the country (with this position, the Soviet Union was the first country to recognize the existence of a Jewish nation, long before the founding of Israel). The Soviet Union also recognized Yiddish as a national language of the Jews and allowed the publication of books and periodicals in it. This was the Bundist theory, without the Bund – for those were the demands for which the Bund had been accused of "chauvinist nationalist deviation" when it had raised the slogan of "cultural autonomy" of the Jews, which had led to its dissolution.

In another vein, it was clear that the Bund – despite this dispute – was at great odds with the Zionists, who were mutually hostile to it. The two currents did not stop fighting each other until their activity ended after the outbreak of the revolution in 1917. The Bund had decided, in its fourth congress (1901), that

> Zionism is a reaction by the bourgeois classes to anti-Semitism and the unnatural legal status of the Jewish people. The ultimate goal of political Zionism of acquiring a country for the Jewish people is not of great significance, nor does it put an end to the Jewish question when it is only possible to settle a small part of the Jewish people there... Further, Zionist propaganda raises national feeling among the people and may hinder the development of their class consciousness... The Zionists should never be granted a foothold in [the Bund's] economic and cultural agencies.[88]

The Bund also declared in its fifth congress (1903) that it was "necessary to fight Zionism in all its currents and trends", because it was nothing but "the movement of the small and medium bourgeois which suffers from a double burden, the burden of competition from great capital and the burden of discriminatory and inciting laws by the government and the Christian bourgeoisie". Moreover, Zionism, which "has taken

---

88 Ibid, p. 354.

4. The Second Aliyah

upon itself the task of establishing a multi-class state in the Land of Israel, by assuming that anti-Semitism is eternal, seeks to obscure the class conflict in the name of interests that it claims are generally Jewish". The Bund's congress decided that "the reactionary tactic of Zionism necessarily stems from its foundations," which leads it to take "an antagonistic position to the revolutionary movement of the Jewish proletariat; to support political indifference; to be subservient to the autocratic government; to impede the development of the feeling of citizenship among Jews; and to strengthen the ghetto psyche in their hearts".[89]

In return, the Zionists saw the Bund as "a group of assimilated Jews, denying their people's interests".

Several years after the Bund's adoption of Dubnow's theories on "secular Jewish nationalism", however, and the introduction of the slogan of "cultural autonomy" for Jews in the diaspora, the Russian Zionists took positions that were almost identical to those of the Bund after making changes to be in line with its ideology. The Zionists were forced to take these positions after their efforts failed in cooperating with other Jewish parties in Russia to defend the rights of the Jews, as well as the criticism directed at them of disregard for their conditions in the country, being excessively interested in future projects about the Jewish state and its agencies. The response of the Russian Zionists was – especially after they became convinced, following Herzl's death, that the road to establishing a Jewish state was very long[90] – a decision taken at their third general congress, held in Helsingfors in December 1906. They declared that they supported

> the Zionist masses naturally joining the liberation war waged by the peoples of … Russia, and … the necessity of unifying Judaism nationally, on the basis of making changes in the Russian political system in terms of recognizing Jewish nationality and its right to legal autonomy in all aspects of

---

89 Ibid, p. 355.

90 Mior, *Ha-Tnu'ah ha-Tzionit be-Rusia (Zionist Movement in Russia)*, p. 819.

Jewish national life.

Thus the Russian Zionists approved a political program in which they called for democratization of the Russian political system on a parliamentary basis, the granting of real political freedoms and autonomy for regions inhabited by independent nationalities and

> granting the Jews complete and absolute equality in rights ... recognizing the Jewish nation as an independent unit with the right to independent authority in everything related to its national affairs; holding a comprehensive Russian Jewish national meeting to shape the foundations of a national organization; recognizing the right to use the national language [which, for Zionism, was Hebrew, not Yiddish] in courts, schools and public life; and designating Saturday, instead of Sunday, as a holiday.[91]

This position of the Zionists was one reason for the tsarist authorities' tightening grip on them and the increased monitoring of their activity.

The dispute between the Bund and the Zionists, when their organizations were established in 1897, did not meet with the approval of many Russian Jews. They saw that their interest, theoretically, at least, did not lie in disagreement between the two currents but in attempting to reconcile them, by merging the foundations of socialism with Zionism. Among the first to emerge in this sphere was Nachman Syrkin (1868-1924), a Russian Jewish writer who had tried to promote his views at the Zionist congresses despite the opposition he had faced. In 1898, less than a year after the founding of the Bund and the Zionist Organization, Syrkin published a German pamphlet titled *The Jewish Question and the Jewish Socialist State*,[92] in which he explained the necessity of applying socialism to the Zionist solution of the Jewish question. This pamphlet was a prelude to

---

91 Merchavia, *Am ou-Moledet (Nation and Homeland)*, p. 398.

92 In Marie Syrkin, *Avi, Nachman Syrkin (My Father, Nachman Syrkin)*, pp. 155-198.

the formation of another current within the Zionist movement, "labor Zionism".

Syrkin began this pamphlet by stating that, from the time the Jews had lost their national and political independence in the Land of Israel, they had begun to live a strange life, with isolation, persecution and restrictions imposed on them by the Christians amongst whom they lived. This "added to their bitterness" and pushed them, in order to preserve their existence, to assume two personalities: one for the external world, and the other internal – seeking to break the restrictions of reality. Thus the Jews were not only a people of merchants and sellers, but also of intellectuals and sages. "Out of the sensitivity born of suffering," Syrkin wrote, a special atmosphere was created in the ghetto that could ensure the perseverance of the Jewish people despite all of life's troubles. "On the soil of hatred and persecution, oppression and contempt, there grew and flourished the hope of redemption – the hope for the speedy liberation of Israel and its national rebirth."[93]

This situation changed, however. "When the bourgeoisie gained supremacy over the nobility and the autocracy, it identified its own class interests with objective, general truth and proclaimed the inalienable rights of man," in order to secure those interests. Thus, it "emancipated the Jews, with striking suddenness, from their medieval servitude … with scarcely any exertion on their part". In order to accommodate this new situation of equal rights, the Jews gave up their "national foundation", such that "this encysted and conservative people, which in the course of its exile was nourished by its nationalism, suddenly became the exponent of national self-renunciation." Thus, "the synagogue began to draw toward the Frankfurt stockbrokers," creating a single entity which claimed that "the Jews are not a nation, but a religious sect created by God for the purpose of spreading the gospel of monotheism among the nations of the world." However, for Syrkin, the Jews' enthusiasm for their emancipation, as well as their solidarity and economic

---

93   Ibid, pp. 157-162.

activity, caused the emergence of anti-Semitism, which was spreading. "The classes fighting each other will unite in their common attack on the Jew."[94]

The protest of the Jewish population against the anti-Semitic tide only took on a civilized and moral character. This moral opposition was wrong, according to Syrkin, as it was not sufficiently strong to confront anti-Semitism, which would only disappear through

> social revolution and cessation of the class struggle... A classless society and national sovereignty are the only means of completely solving the Jewish problem... The Jew must, therefore, join the ranks of the proletariat, the only element which is striving to make an end of the class struggle and to redistribute power on the basis of justice. The Jew has been the torchbearer of liberalism which emancipated him as part of its war against the old society; today, after the liberal bourgeoisie has betrayed its principles ... the Jew must become the vanguard of socialism.

Syrkin attacked the assimilationist Jewish socialists, especially in western Europe, because, "though despoiled of all external national characteristics – being dispersed, speaking all languages and jargons, possessing no national property or creative national forces – they have been a distinct nation the fact of whose existence was sufficient reason for being." Thus, in his view, "the superior Jew must not deny his people ... rather he must ... endow this life with significant national content and ... remove all that obstructs the creative genius of the Jewish people... The socialism of the Jew must become a Jewish socialism." This would only happen when they "accept socialism as Jews, freeing it from assimilationist sham. The socialist proletariat is the only ally of the Jews; its victory will spell the end of Jewish suffering."[95]

In spite of this, according to Syrkin, socialism could only

---

94 Ibid, pp. 164-170.
95 Ibid, pp. 173-179.

solve part of the problems of the Jewish proletariat. The oppressed classes constituted the majority of this proletariat, on the one hand, and the socialist parties did not always side with the Jews, on the other. In Russia in particular, where most of them lived, the discriminatory laws against them could not be abolished until the final victory of socialism, which was likely to take a significant time. Even if the opposition attained victory in Russia, Syrkin maintained, those discriminatory laws would not be abolished, as there was not one class in the country with an interest in their abolition. The "unfortunate, strange result" of this was that Jewish people, at that time, had no tool to relieve their distress, and that is where Zionism, "the true expression of Jewish life", gained significance in its call for the establishment of a Jewish state that would solve part of their problems, regardless of its form. The class struggle also existed among themselves, however, who were split into different classes that opposed each other.[96] The Jewish proletariat and socialists could not, nor were they allowed to, contribute to the establishment of a republic born out of opposition to the principles of social cooperation. Thus, "Zionism must take into consideration the socialist bent of the middle class and intelligentsia. Zionism must of necessity fuse with socialism... The Jewish state can come about only if it is socialist."[97]

Syrkin ended his assessment of Zionism by saying: "Zionism is a creative work of the Jews, and it, therefore, stands not in contradiction to the class struggle but beyond it. Zionism can be accepted by each and every class of Jews."[98] It is clear that Syrkin's position, and the conclusions it drew, did not differ greatly from the positions of non-socialist Zionist groups. They both admitted that, in principle, Zionism was above ideological or factional disputes despite their different interpretations on the methods of its implementation. Thus, it did not take long for them to cooperate.

---

96 Ibid, pp. 180-187.

97 Ibid, p. 188.

98 Ibid.

When discussing how the Zionists would obtain Palestinian land and establish a state, Syrkin suggested, in contrast to the positions of most Zionist groups, that they "form an alliance with the oppressed peoples under Turkish rule ... [to] be liberated from the Turkish yoke". When this took place, "friendly population transfer and division of territory should ensue. The Jews should receive Palestine, which is very sparsely settled and where the Jews are already a part of the population," especially since the Western countries were interested in resettling their Jewish residents there in order to be rid of them. "Should, however, all efforts to obtain Palestine fail, then the Jews will have to acquire some other land which they can secure through purchase."[99]

Syrkin's views represented the early theoretical foundations of the ideology of the Zionist labor wing, which was destined to assume leadership of the Zionist movement, and eventually, of Israel (1930s-1970s).

However, Syrkin was not the only one in this period to try to merge Zionism with socialism; the same conditions that led to the founding of the Bund, the spread of Zionism in Russia, and the emergence of Syrkin and others, also led to the establishment of other national-socialist Jewish organizations in the country. Only a few years later, several Jewish parties and political groups emerged – especially before the outbreak of the Russian Revolution in 1905 and immediately after its failure. The groups included the Independent Jewish Workers Party (1901), which was opposed to the Bund; the Zionist Socialist Workers Party, which split into two currents, the first of which followed the territorialist Zionists, while the second advocated the principle of non-regional national parliaments as a legal solution to the Jewish "national problem"; and the People's Party, which was founded by Dubnow.[100] All those parties were in the anti-Zionist camp, in one way or another.

---

99   For the principles, regulations and positions of these parties, see Mer-chavia, *Am ou-Moledet (Nation and Homeland)*, pp. 365-377, 381-387.

100 Ibid.

4. The Second Aliyah

Of greater importance than the activity of those parties was the emergence of groups of Jewish workers in various parts of Russia, especially in the northern part of the Pale of Settlement, which called themselves "Po'alei Zion" (Workers of Zion). From their ranks came the first Jewish immigrants to Palestine during the Second Aliyah. One of the direct reasons for the emergence of Po'alei Zion in the form of independent associations was the anti-Zionist decision taken by the Bund at its fourth congress, held in late May 1901 (see earlier in this section), which led to the expulsion of Zionist workers from its ranks.

Po'alei Zion was initially made up of incoherent Zionist labor associations, with no organizational framework or common ideology other than their class affiliation and ideological Zionism that imposed general intellectual and political frameworks on them. With time, those associations grew and spread to several countries outside Russia, especially to Austria, Hungary, the United States and Palestine, with the immigration of Jewish people. They formed various institutions and organizational frameworks, which were communist, leftist, nationalist and even religious. Becoming another international Zionist organization that paralleled the first, sometimes coming into conflict with it as it repeated the same ideological, organizational and factional differences that governed the parent organization, there was one crucial distinction: the adherence of Po'alei Zion to their labor origins.

With the emergence of Po'alei Zion, two currents took shape. The first was known as the "Minsk current", after the Po'alei Zion association in Minsk that led it. Its followers were anti-Bund and anti-socialist, and declared at their first congress, held in late November 1901, that "our only goal is to improve the economic conditions of Jewish workers and raise their cultural level,"[101] in addition to their commitment to "the Zionist idea as expressed in the Basel Program ... and strengthening Jewish national sentiment among Jewish workers".[102] The second current in

---

101   Ibid, p. 495.

102   Ibid.

Po'alei Zion believed in socialist principles and Zionism at the same time, although it did not try to merge the two. One of the most prominent leaders of this group was Ber Borochov (1881-1917), who was a member of the Russian Social Democratic Party in 1900-1901, but was expelled from it "because of his harmful influence on Jewish workers".[103] In 1901, he founded what he called the "Zionist Socialist Workers Union".

The first noticeable development in the positions and ideology of Po'alei Zion in Russia took place in 1903-1905, due to the rising revolutionary tide in the country, the Kishinev pogrom and its aftermath and the dispute over the Uganda project.[104] The latter reason was the engine of change. The dispute at the Sixth Zionist Congress, and the resulting split in the movement, manifested most acutely among the Russian Zionists who were opponents of the project. They waged a fierce propaganda war on the territorialist minority, which ultimately led to the territorialists splitting from the Zionist Organization. To manage this conflict, Ussishkin recruited assistants, including Ber Borochov and Ze'ev Jabotinsky (1880-1940), a well-known journalist and speaker among Russian Zionists. The latter launched the campaign against the socialist Zionists: Syrkin's followers who supported the Uganda project.[105] (Syrkin announced his split, with his followers, from the Zionist Organization after the Seventh Zionist Congress finally rejected this project, but they rejoined the organization at the opening of the Ninth Congress, chastising themselves for the mistake they had made.) In his campaign, Borochov wrote a series of articles entitled *On the Question of Zion and Territory*,[106] in which he reached the conclusion – based on socialist principles – that the only solution to the Jewish question lay in the return of the Jews to Palestine and the establishment of a state for them in it. "Zion

---

103   Slutsky, *Mevoa le-Toldot Tnu'at ha-Avoda ha-Yisraelit (Introduction to the History of the Israeli Labor Movement)*, p. 100.

104   Ibid, pp. 101-103.

105   Mior, *Ha-Tnu'ah ha-Tzionit be-Rusia (Zionist Movement in Russia)*, p. 294.

106   In Ber Borochov, *Ktavim (The Works)*, Vol. 1, pp. 18-153.

4. The Second Aliyah

means the emancipation of the Jewish people ... the revival of Hebrew culture ... and a return to the ancient homeland." Borochov concluded his articles by stating: "The Land of Israel is the only region required ... available ... and allocated to us, and we will gradually occupy the Land of Israel by force of historical necessity."[107]

Ussishkin, however, had expressed his apprehension of Borochov's activity and the positions of the socialist Zionists, warning of the consequences of the anti-Semitic rhetoric in the writings of some of the fathers of socialism that was likely to push their followers to enmity towards Judaism. "Who can guarantee to us that the proletariat will also not forget that its first teachers were Karl Marx and Ferdinand Lassalle, just as the Christians did not forget who was Christ of Nazareth and Saint Paul?"[108] However, Jabotinsky, who later became the godfather and undisputed leader of the Zionist right in Palestine and, thus, the staunchest enemy of the labor wing, was more farsighted. He demanded, opposing Ussishkin, the support and strengthening of the right's activity, because

> Po'alei Zion's Zionism is clear, merely by their open acknowledgement of the need to establish a Jewish state, while the entire organized Jewish proletariat, before their [Po'alei Zion's] emergence, was against a Jewish state ... although they need ample time and freedom of development in order for their new theory ... to gain its proper place among the national and class viewpoints, and we must provide them with this freedom of development by recognizing them as an independent [Zionist] union, with the right to obtain adequate amounts from the fund of the Zionist Organization to cover its expenses.[109]

Jabotinsky was accurate in his predictions, as it was not long until Po'alei Zion was able to "harmonize the national and class

---

107 Ibid, p. 153.

108 Mior, *Ha-Tnu'ah ha-Tzionit be-Rusia (Zionist Movement in Russia)*, p. 310.

109 Ibid, p. 265.

viewpoints". In 1906, Borochov published four articles entitled *Our Platform*,[110] which were considered the foundations of Po'alei Zion's socialist Zionist ideology and complementary to Syrkin's pamphlet. Borochov based *Our Platform* on two main hypotheses that he had formulated in his previous articles, *On the Question of Zion and Territory*. The first hypothesis was that the national problem was a result of the conflict between the developing forces of production of one social group and its material circumstances, and the second was that land was the necessary basis for an independent national life. Applying these hypotheses, Borochov divided the Jewish population into five categories: the upper, middle and petty bourgeoisie; the masses who were being proletarianized; and those who were already the proletariat. All of these categories were city dwellers, as there was no peasantry among the Jews. Borochov did not place great importance on the first category, the upper bourgeoisie, especially since those in the other categories constituted the majority. The majority of the Jewish population suffered constantly from national competition with the peoples amongst whom they lived, such that they tended towards immigration and searched for new countries to live in. In Borochov's view, this immigration had been left to its own devices such that it spread across many countries, which affected the possibility of gathering Jewish people in one place and delayed the territorial solution to the Jewish question. Thus, the Jewish proletariat had to work to organize that immigration because they were the only ones who could do so.[111]

According to Borochov, "the middle bourgeoisie is only good at ceremonial declarations of Zionism and territorialism, creating an uproar about its Zionism, and manipulating politics in meetings and congresses." However, it was still possible to pin some hopes on it, because "its entrepreneurial spirit is very strong, despite the fact that its motives are equally weak." Hence, the role that the proletariat should play acquired a special significance, for the

---

110 In Borochov, *Ktavim (The Works)*, Vol. 1, pp. 193-310.

111 Ibid, pp. 193, 197, 201, 202, 209.

capitalistic economy has reached the stage where no revolutionary changes are possible without the participation of the working masses and especially of the organized sections of the proletariat... The liberation of the Jewish people will be brought about by the workers' movement, or it won't happen at all... Proletarian Zionism is possible only if Zionism can be implemented through class struggle; Zionism can be realized only if proletarian Zionism can be realized. However, if the Jewish proletariat has no special means of its own to implement Zionism, [then] Zionism is not viable.[112]

Borochov, however, realized that

proletarian Zionism is a very complex product, the result of the tortuous and prolonged course of development of Jewish proletarian ideology... [It] is the result of a prolonged conflict between the broad social need of the masses and the impossibility of providing it. The major forces that bring about the conflict work in two fundamental directions: a direct social conflict between the means of production of the Jewish proletariat and state of the relations of production of the Jewish proletariat and between the general conditions of production, within which it develops... The social conflict is always clearer and closer to the proletariat than the national conflict.[113]

The main limitation of this analysis was that the Jewish working class was still in a position in which it could only direct part of the immigration towards Palestine. Thus, Jewish workers had to be active in two spheres: the establishment of an independent Jewish entity, in cooperation with other classes, and the strengthening of their positions and power to carry out the socialist revolution when the opportunity arose.

Borochov did not expect that the Jewish immigrants, on their

---

112   Ibid, pp. 210-211.

113   Ibid, p. 211.

arrival in Palestine, would be met with resistance by its Arab inhabitants who, he determined,

> lack any independent economic and cultural character, and they are dissident and fragmented – not only because of the geographical character of the country... The children of the Land of Israel [Arabs of Palestine] are not one nation, and will not be so for a long time. They adapt themselves, very easily and quickly, to any civilization more advanced than their own, which may come from outside. They cannot unite to carry out an organized resistance to external influences, and are not prepared for a national competition... The inhabitants of the Land of Israel will adapt themselves to any civilized economic model that would economically control the country.

The result was that the Arabs of Palestine "will fuse economically and culturally with those who bring the system into the country, and will hand them the responsibility of developing its forces of production". Since "the Jewish immigrants are the ones who will develop the forces of production in the Land of Israel, the local population will fuse with them, in time, economically and culturally".[114]

In his attempts to apply Marxism to Zionism, Borochov wrote another article entitled "Nationalism and the Class Struggle". He explained that, in addition to the division of human society into classes according to the relations of production between them, there were also conditions of production, the bases of which were land and its geographical conditions, which affected relations between the different classes. "This feeling of kinship, created as a result of a perceived common historic past and rooted in the common conditions of production, is called nationalism." Thus, every nation was connected to a specific territory, and here lay the necessity of finding a territory for the Jews "to solve the national problem of the Jewish nation".[115]

---

114 Ibid, pp. 282-283.

115 For details, see also Slutsky, *Mevoa le-Toldot Tnu'at ha-Avoda ha-Yis-*

4. The Second Aliyah

Before Borochov's death, he delivered a speech to the Po'alei Zion congress held in Kiev in late 1917, in which he revised many of his positions.[116] By that time, however, his followers had spread and developed in other ways. Borochov's theories continued to be adopted by various Zionist factions, the last of which was the "Mapam" party that was founded in 1948 (and which was later assimilated into the Israeli Labor Party).

While Borochov was further developing his theories, Po'alei Zion were actively organizing themselves. They held their founding congress in Poltava, Russia, in March 1906, at which they announced the establishment of the Jewish Social Democratic Labor Party, Po'alei Zion. In its draft program, presented by its central committee to the congress, the party defined its goal as "transferring all means of production to society, as a whole, and establishing it on socialist foundations; the only way that the party recognizes to achieve this is class struggle by the Jewish proletariat among the ranks of world socialist democracy."

> [What] distinguishes Po'alei Zion from other social democratic parties, is the demand for territorial autonomy for the Jewish people, based on democratic foundations as a necessary condition for the free development of its forces of production... This territorial development may only be realized in the Land of Israel, and the Jewish proletariat is obliged to contribute to achieving it ... through class struggle. There is a direct relationship that cannot be severed between class struggle and the political education of the Jewish proletariat in the diaspora, on the one hand, and practical activity in the Land of Israel, on the other.[117]

About a year and a half after the founding of Po'alei Zion in Russia, its representatives – together with those of branches of the party operating in other countries – held a congress in The

---

raelit (Introduction to the History of the Israeli Labor Movement), pp. 111-120.

116 Speech in Moshe Shmueli, *Toldot ha-Tzionout ve Tnu'at ha-Avoda (History of Zionism and the Labor Movement)*, Vol. 2, pp. 83-84.

117 In Merchavia, *Am ou-Moledet (Nation and Homeland)*, pp. 502-503.

Hague, during the course of the Eighth Zionist Congress (1907). They decided to establish an international union, the "World Socialist Union of Jewish Workers – Po'alei Zion".

During the second congress of this union, which was held in Krakow in December 1909, it ratified its constitution as follows:

1. The World Socialist Union of Jewish Workers – Po'alei Zion, as part of the world proletariat, seeks on an equal footing with it to abolish the capitalist economic system and establish a socialist society, and, thus, (a) the Union organizes the working class in order to combat capitalism tactically and politically, (b) it joins Socialist International as an independent national bloc that seeks to achieve national equality of rights for the Jewish people in the socialist movement (or any other organization), in any country, 2. Po'alei Zion seeks, in cooperation with the Jewish people, to concentrate the majority of this people in the Land of Israel and create a Jewish community that enjoys autonomy there. Note: By "Land of Israel", we mean the Land of Israel and its neighboring countries, (a) Po'alei Zion joins the Zionist Organization as an independent body on a federal basis, demands proportional representation in all of its agencies, and participates in Zionist congresses. Note: We consider the Zionist Organization and its congresses a union of all classes, parties and currents of the Jewish people, that aims to find the territorial solution to the Jewish question in the Land of Israel, (b) the Union participates in the activities of Zionist agencies, such as the shekel and the Jewish National Fund, and demands the application of democratic principles in them, (c) the Union calls for all economic projects that are established with the funds of national agencies [in Palestine] to be done on cooperative bases, as far as possible, (d) the Union also seeks to create agencies that will help shape a Jewish labor camp in the Land of Israel, in towns and villages, and defend the interests of Jewish workers in their war with

4. The Second Aliyah

capitalism.[118]

Meanwhile, another type of Zionist labor associations emerged which called themselves "ha-T'hiyah" (Resurrection). They differed from Po'alei Zion in their reservation, and sometimes antagonism, towards socialism, and they denounced the concept of class struggle put forth by the social democrats. In 1906, at the only congress convened by the ha-T'hiyah associations, they declared that "Zionism can only be realized through the cooperation of all groups of the Jewish people, for the establishment of a national movement requires the unified and organized strength of all the people, not a single class that heads the [Zionist] Organization and runs the movement, alone." The congress also decided that "the settlement of Jews, which is managed by the Zionist Organization on a large scale in the Land of Israel, must be based on cooperative foundations..."[119] After this congress, most of the ha-T'hiyah associations merged with the "Tzeirei Zion" (Youth of Zion) movement.

The first Tzeirei Zion associations had been formed in Russia in 1898-1900 and were particularly active in 1903-1905. In their first congress, held in late 1906, Tzeirei Zion refrained from ratifying a binding political program and simply set general guidelines to explain their positions and political thought. The congress declared that the goal of the Tzeirei Zion associations was "to establish a federation of Zionist workers that unites Jewish workers, to defend their interests and improve their living and working conditions in the diaspora, as far as possible". The congress also declared that "Zionism is a historical need for the Jewish people," denounced Po'alei Zion's class positions because they "contravene the principles of general Zionist interest, for classism may lead to the denial of the Jewish people's special national interests and push them towards assimilation" and stated that the realization of socialism should be postponed "until the

---

118   Ibid, pp. 507-508.

119   Ibid, pp. 506-507.

establishment of our new society in the Land of Israel".[120]

Even when the Tzeirei Zion organization was established, in the course of the 11th Zionist Congress, in September 1913 in Vienna, it did not deviate much from these principles and did not develop a comprehensive political program, but found it sufficient to announce that it "considers its first duty, other than practical Zionist activity, to be cultural activity among the Hebrew masses; carrying out wide propaganda, especially among youth; collective self-education for young Zionists; and preparing pioneers [to send them] to the Land of Israel".[121] The organization also decided to strengthen its relations with the Hapoel Hatzair (Young Worker) party, which was ideologically close to it and had been formed in Palestine in 1905.[122]

From these two main parties, Po'alei Zion and Tzeirei Zion, came most of the Jewish immigrants, especially the enthusiastic youth, who entered Palestine during the Second Aliyah. They carried the principles of their parties to apply them, in practice, in the country.

4

When the pioneer immigrants of the Second Aliyah began to leave Russia in the last weeks of 1903, they did not encounter significant obstacles to their entry into Palestine. "Jewish settlement in the country had never had" – in the words of the chairman of the executive committee of Lovers of Zion in Palestine – "such a comfortable position with the [Ottoman] authorities as it did in those days."[123] It seems that Herzl's activity and contacts with the rulers of Turkey during that period,

---

120 Shmueli, *Toldot ha-Tzionout ve Tnu'at ha-Avoda (History of Zionism and the Labor Movement)*, Vol. 2, pp. 89-90.

121 Merchavia, *Am ou-Moledet (Nation and Homeland)*, p. 526.

122 See Ben-Shoshan, *Toldot Tnu'at ha-Poalim be-Eretz Yisrael (History of the Labor Movement in the Land of Israel)*, Vol. 1, pp. 58-59; Shmueli, *Toldot ha-Tzionout ve Tnu'at ha-Avoda (History of Zionism and the Labor Movement)*, Vol. 2, pp. 85-86.

123 Yaffe, H., *Dor Ma'afilim (A Generation of Immigrants)*, p. 250.

although they did not yield any political achievements for the Zionist Organization, helped to at least loosen the grip of the Ottoman authorities on Zionist settlement projects in Palestine and the entry of Jewish immigrants into it. The contacts made by Zionist leaders, after Herzl's death, also seemingly contributed to the Ottoman authorities maintaining this position until the outbreak of the First World War in 1914.

If the entry of Jewish immigrants to Palestine was not difficult, however, their adaptation to the country and assimilation among its Jewish residents were not equally easy, due to the characteristics of the immigrants themselves and the conditions of the settlements. Most of these immigrants had come to Palestine because of tsarist persecution in Russia, under influence of the new Zionist theories put forth by Po'alei Zion and Tzeirei Zion. The immigrants were middle-class Jewish people[124] who had no experience with agricultural or manual work that they were determined to do, with their fervent ideology, in order to establish a Zionist labor community in Palestine. At the same time, settlements in the country were not prepared to accommodate such immigrants.

At the start of the Second Aliyah, the Jewish residents of Palestine were divided – socially and economically – into two groups. The first were the old residents or "Yishuv", who had lived in the country before the beginning of the First Aliyah in 1881. They were mostly concentrated in the cities or towns and lived on the alms of the halukah system (see Introduction, section 7). Thus the new immigrants had no place among them. The second were the residents of the settlements that had been established during the First Aliyah, whose conditions were not much better than those of the old Yishuv. After Rothschild had abandoned the settlements that he had helped to establish in Palestine and had handed them over to the JCA in 1900, the company and the executive committee of Lovers of Zion in Palestine had become the spearheads of Zionist settlement in the

---

[124] Yehoshua Ofir, *Sefer ha-Oved ha-Leumi (Book of the National Worker)*, Vol. 1, pp. 13-14.

country. The JCA was more significant in its impact on settlement policy, given the greater financial means that were at its disposal.

When the JCA took over the administration of Rothschild's settlements in Palestine, the conditions of these settlements, and of their Jewish workers, were very poor.[125] The JCA, a non-Zionist Jewish company that was not concerned with establishing a Jewish state in Palestine as much as settling Jewish immigrants anywhere and then solving their problems, adopted a new policy in managing the settlements that were handed over to it – a different method from the guardianship employed by Rothschild. If his method was like "a mother who pampers her children" until she spoils them, the JCA company acted "like a wise stepmother, who only wants to fulfill her duties" towards her stepchildren.[126] The company worked to improve the settlers' conditions in various ways, in order to bring them to a stage of economic independence at which they could live through their own means, without administrative oversight or financial assistance. The company also purchased large areas of land to establish new settlements for those who did not have sufficient land, and established model farms to train Jewish farmers. Those for whom work could not be found, including a number of laborers, were paid the necessary expenses by the company to travel to any place they chose within Palestine, despite the opposition of the Zionist agencies to this policy.[127] Thus the immigrants of the Second Aliyah found no great welcome on their arrival in Palestine by any groups of Jewish people.

The Zionist settlements in Palestine were also in no need of additional workers when the new immigrants arrived, as Arab laborers were doing most of the work, whether in the settlers' fields, workshops or homes. The settlements had an estimated 5,000 Arab workers during that period, more than twice the number of the settlers themselves, compared with only about

---

125 Yaffe, H., *Dor Ma'afilim (A Generation of Immigrants)*, pp. 142-149.

126 Ben-Zion Dinur (Dinaburg), ed., *Sefer Toldot ha-Haganah (History of the Haganah)*, Vol. 1, Part 1, p. 39.

127 Yaffe, H., *Dor Ma'afilim (A Generation of Immigrants)*, pp. 218-228.

4. The Second Aliyah

350 Jewish workers.[128] Jewish settlers insisted on employing Arab workers and preferred them over Jewish ones for many reasons, key of which were their low wages and the quality of their work (see section 5 of this chapter). In addition, the early settlers – most of whom were religious conservatives – did not like the ideologies, principles and behavior of the new immigrants, which affected the relationship of the two groups. To add to this, the Zionist agencies did not care much for the workers or their problems and, for a brief period, even ceased any activity in Palestine.

In light of these discouraging circumstances, the new immigrants had to rely on themselves. They took whatever work was available in the towns or settlements[129] and began to adapt themselves to the new conditions. In seeking to secure their presence in Palestine, they established organizations and agencies that were destined to grow into the foundations of the Zionist system there at all levels: organizational, political, economic and even ideological. It is clear that these organizations were established, to a large extent, under influence of the political background that these immigrants had acquired in Russia, as well as the conditions that prevailed in Palestine. They were founded through a struggle with several parties: the official Zionist agencies; the early Jewish settlers in the country; the Palestinian Arabs, generally, and their workers, specifically – all of which marked these organizations with a unique character.

The first agencies established by the new immigrants in Palestine, shortly after their arrival, were their own political parties to bring them together and help them confront the new reality in light of their experience of political organization in Russia. The need for the new immigrants to earn a living was their primary motive. In July 1905, about 30-40 new immigrants who worked at the settlement of Petah Tikva held a meeting where they decided, due to the difficulties they faced in finding

---

128 Moshe Braslavski, *Tnu'at ha-Poalim ha-Eretz Yisraelit (Labor Movement in the Land of Israel)*, Vol. 1, pp. 59-60.

129 For details, see Bracha Habas, ed., *Sefer ha-Aliya ha-Shnia (Book of the Second Aliyah)*, pp. 161-297.

permanent work, to establish an association to "occupy work in the settlements" by Jewish workers.[130] A number of similar associations were established in other settlements as well, such as Rishon le-Zion, Rehovot and Ness Ziona. In October 1905, those associations held a congress in Jaffa attended by several dozen workers. They formed an organization to unite them, "Hapoel Hatzair" (Young Worker), the first Zionist party established by the new immigrants in Palestine. In April 1906, Hapoel Hatzair held a second congress to lay down its organizational and ideological foundations. The majority of its members, whose stance was close to Tzeirei Zion in Russia, opposed the formulation of a binding basic platform, especially in the ideological sense, and asked that general guidelines only be drawn up to define the party's work.

In August 1906, Hapoel Hatzair held another congress in Petah Tikva to study the political foundations that had been drafted, and ratified them as follows:

> General principles: 1. The occupation of economic and cultural positions in the Land of Israel plays a decisive role in the realization of Zionism, 2. The necessary condition for economic occupation is the concentration of property and labor in the hands of the Jews, 3. The mission of Hapoel Hatzair in the Land of Israel is to work towards the realization of Zionism, generally, and grant special attention to the occupation of labor by the Jews.

The party then proceeded to define its duties, which included:

> 1. Defending Jewish workers in the Land of Israel, increasing their number, and improving their economic and cultural conditions, 2. Occupying labor by the Jewish worker, organizing labor and studying its conditions, 3. Assisting Zionist settlement activity by providing key information and facts, 4. Giving due attention to the compatibility of institutions and

---

[130] Slutsky, *Mevoa le-Toldot Tnu'at ha-Avoda ha-Yisraelit (Introduction to the History of the Israeli Labor Movement)*, p. 175.

4. The Second Aliyah

their activities in the country with the goals and aspirations of the people, 5. Making efforts to improve the economic and cultural conditions of the Jews in the Land of Israel, 6. Focusing on the dominance of the Hebrew language in the Land of Israel.[131]

The party also defined in its founding declarations the various means that it would pursue to achieve its goals, including the establishment of housing, joint restaurants, popular markets, loan and aid funds, public baths and employment offices; encouraging small local industry and crafts; establishing libraries and organizing trips; facilitating the entry of Jews into Palestine; disseminating information about the situation in the country and its working conditions; carrying out public campaigns to encourage settlement; and establishing relations with all organizations that sought to settle Jewish people in Palestine.[132]

The Hapoel Hatzair party, unlike the other Zionist groups in Palestine, stressed the need to use the Hebrew language and began in 1907 to issue a Hebrew magazine bearing its name, which published literature, encouraged literary studies and dealt with political and ideological issues.[133] Yosef Aharonovich (1877-1937), one of the ideologues of the party, was the editor-in-chief of the magazine. Hapoel Hatzair also rejected the theory of class struggle adopted by Po'alei Zion, because "there is no place for class struggle, in its European concept, in the conditions in which the Jewish people live, or in the Land of Israel."[134] The most prominent leaders of Hapoel Hatzair, at its founding, also included Yosef Sprinzak (1885-1959) and Nachum Tversky.

In November 1905, a month after the founding of Hapoel Hatzair, about 90 members of Po'alei Zion who had arrived from Russia met in Jaffa. They decided to establish a branch of

---

131   Habas, ed., *Sefer ha-Aliya ha-Shnia (Book of the Second Aliyah)*, p. 616.

132   Ibid.

133   Ben-Shoshan, *Toldot Tnu'at ha-Poalim be-Eretz Yisrael (History of the Labor Movement in the Land of Israel)*, Vol. 1, pp. 89-91.

134   Slutsky, *Mevoa le-Toldot Tnu'at ha-Avoda ha-Yisraelit (Introduction to the History of the Israeli Labor Movement)*, p. 177.

their party in Palestine and elected a committee to formulate its platform. In October 1906, this committee met in Ramla and set up a "theoretical platform" (the "Ramla Program"), which the party ratified at its first congress in early January 1907 in Jaffa – adding a practical program to it. The branch established by Po'alei Zion in Palestine was a replica of its mother party in Russia, and even the name that the party took in Palestine, the Jewish Social Democratic Labor [also: Workers'] Party in the Land of Israel – Po'alei Zion, was identical to the party's name in Russia.

In its theoretical program in Palestine, Po'alei Zion followed Borochov's interpretation of Marxism and his attempts to apply it to Zionism. The first article of the party's program stated that "the history of humanity is a struggle between nations and classes. The way in which humans produce their essential consumer needs, and the historical and natural conditions surrounding that production process, are what divides humanity into societies and classes..." The program then addressed the situation in Palestine, declaring that

> a look at the economic-cultural life in the Land of Israel proves that the feudal system controls it. At the same time, there are signs of capitalism, which is growing through the forces of production that immigrate to the country, causing a revolution in the existing system. The forces of production among Jewish immigrants play an important role in this revolutionary development... The signs of developing capitalism appear, most clearly, in the agricultural sector, where medium capital is mainly active... The developing capitalism in the Land of Israel needs educated, energetic laborers. Since the native laborers are still at rock bottom, capitalist development in the Land of Israel is linked to the immigration of more developed laborers from outside the country.

The program maintained that capitalism, by "revolutionizing the feudal system, gradually transforms the peasants into a proletariat". The party did not expect any difficulties in the immigration of Jewish capital to Palestine, because the circumstances that this capital was experiencing outside Palestine would push it to do so.[135]

In the practical part of its program, Po'alei Zion in Palestine declared that it "seeks to unite the means of production and build a society on socialist foundations, and believes that the only means to that is class struggle, whose forms differ according to time and place". The party sought "political independence for the Jewish people" in Palestine. With this slogan, it was the first Zionist party to demand, in practice, the establishment of a Jewish state in the country, explaining that it would "fight all obstacles standing in the way of Jewish immigration to the Land of Israel, and [the party] requests from Jewish public institutions [the JCA and the Zionist Organization] to establish the necessary agencies in the Land of Israel to organize immigration to it". The party announced that it would participate in the Zionist congresses as an independent organization, strengthen its relations with Po'alei Zion outside Palestine, and join the Socialist International. Its "urgent requests are: the right to universal suffrage for the autonomous institutions in towns and settlements ... and democratic oversight of all the institutions that were established in the Land of Israel with the funds of the Jewish public". Also, "assuming that the chances of improving the economic conditions of the worker may be more likely to succeed if organizations are established with a large number of workers, the party acknowledges the need to organize Jewish workers in the Land of Israel in non-partisan trade unions," which the supporters of various parties may join (this principle was followed when the Histadrut, the General Union of Jewish Workers in Palestine, was established in 1920). Referring to the activity of the JCA and Lovers of Zion in Palestine, Po'alei Zion made it clear that it would "fight the alms system, to the extent that it leads to a deterioration in the moral level of the Jewish community of Palestine and hinders the growth of the forces of

---

135   Merchavia, *Am ou-Moledet (Nation and Homeland)*, pp. 513-514.

production".[136]

However, this "rigid" program, which was more suited to the theories of Po'alei Zion in Russia and elsewhere than to the conditions of the Jewish population in Palestine, did not gain the support of the party in the country, especially of the influential groups within it headed by David Grun (Ben-Gurion; 1886-1973) and Yitzhak Shimshelevich (Ben-Zvi; 1884-1963). (Ben-Gurion later became the first prime minister of Israel, from 1948-1953, and Ben-Zvi its second president, from 1952-1963.) They demanded that the program be changed and adapted to the reality in Palestine, by trying to draw near to Hapoel Hatzair, even if this led to a deterioration in relations with Po'alei Zion outside the country. These groups maintained their pressure and were able, with time, to induce the party to change its positions on three main points. The first was to replace Yiddish with Hebrew as a national language.[137] The second point was to shift from a position denouncing labor settlement to one supporting it, while the third stressed the need to move from the theory of class struggle to the struggle for "Hebrew labor".[138] At this stage, Po'alei Zion approached many of the positions of Hapoel Hatzair which, in turn, eased the latter's hostility to theories of class. The two parties began working together, even if each insisted on preserving its independent organizational structure.

At the start of their path, the Zionist parties in Palestine played a very important role in the lives of their members in an environment that was hostile to new immigrant workers, which showed no interest in them and sometimes boycotted them. The party became the main agency that guaranteed the

---

136 Ibid, pp. 514-515.

137 Po'alei Zion began, in 1910, to issue a Hebrew magazine, *Ahdut (Unity)*. (When the German Jewish association, Ezra, in 1913, at the inauguration of the Technion, the Institute of Applied Engineering in Haifa – which it had helped to establish – tried to use the German language for teaching, the settlers made an uproar and forced the administration to replace German with Hebrew.)

138 Slutsky, *Mevoa le-Toldot Tnu'at ha-Avoda ha-Yisraelit (Introduction to the History of the Israeli Labor Movement)*, p. 185.

livelihoods of the immigrants and paid due attention to their political education and vocational training, as it also became the social framework that united them. The parties were in intense competition to recruit the new immigrants to their ranks – a competition that distinguished Zionist partisan activity for some time. In order to implement the tasks that they had taken upon themselves, the parties established economic and social institutions to serve Jewish workers and, later, extended them to serve other settlers. In 1910, for example, Po'alei Zion established the "Land of Israel Workers' Fund" to provide loans to workers who wanted to establish production cooperatives.[139] The parties also set up workers' clubs, the first of which was in Petah Tikva in 1911. In 1913, the "Kupat Holim" (Sick Fund) was founded for health insurance,[140] and the first employment agency was launched in Petah Tikva.[141] Those institutions grew and branched out to provide many indispensable services to the Zionist settlers in Palestine.

The parties and immigrants carried out noticeable activity in the settlement-agriculture arena as well, organizing agricultural workers, contributing to the establishment of settlements and creating new methods of settlement. Jewish agricultural workers, who were the largest group among the new immigrants, were the first to feel the need to organize themselves in order to improve their working conditions due to the competition of Arab workers and the tendency of Jewish farmers to favor them. Jewish agricultural workers began organizing by establishing small, local associations, such as "ha-Horesh" (The Plowman) and "ha-Kollektiv" (The Collective), which were formed in al-

---

[139] Braslavski, *Tnu'at ha-Poalim ha-Eretz Yisraelit (Labor Movement in the Land of Israel)*, Vol. 1, p. 114; Ben-Shoshan, *Toldot Tnu'at ha-Poalim be-Eretz Yisrael (History of the Labor Movement in the Land of Israel)*, Vol. 1, pp. 187-188.

[140] Slutsky, *Mevoa le-Toldot Tnu'at ha-Avoda ha-Yisraelit (Introduction to the History of the Israeli Labor Movement)*, pp. 194, 223; Ben-Shoshan, *Toldot Tnu'at ha-Poalim be-Eretz Yisrael (History of the Labor Movement in the Land of Israel)*, Vol. 1, pp. 224-228.

[141] Slutsky, *Mevoa le-Toldot Tnu'at ha-Avoda ha-Yisraelit (Introduction to the History of the Israeli Labor Movement)*, pp. 194, 228.

Shajarah in 1907. However, these organizations soon disbanded after failing to perform their intended duties.

With the rising number of Jewish agricultural workers, after the establishment of new settlements and the arrival of additional waves of new immigrants, attempts were rekindled to form new labor organizations – this time with success. In mid-April 1911, a congress was held in the settlement of Degania (Um Juny), near Lake Tiberias (Sea of Galilee), with 17 representatives of agricultural workers throughout the Galilee. It was decided to establish the "Galilee Workers' Federation".[142] By the outbreak of the First World War, in 1914, the organization had held five congresses in which it discussed issues pertaining to agriculture, workers and settlement.[143] Less than two months after the founding of this organization, representatives of agricultural workers of the Jewish settlements in central Palestine also met in early June 1911, and decided to establish the "Judea Agricultural Workers' Federation".[144] By the outbreak of the war, this had held four congresses in which the same issues were discussed.[145] After the founding of the Histadrut, in 1920, the two organizations united within its framework and set up the Agricultural Workers' Union. In late May and early June 1914, the first congress of Jewish women workers was also held in the settlement of Merhavia.[146]

However, the more important activity of the Second Aliyah in this period was the establishment of new Zionist settlements in Palestine based on new principles, which later became the backbone of Zionist agricultural settlement in the country. This change was prompted by changing conditions that arose from multiple sources. With the onset of the Second Aliyah, the JCA was the main organization and, to a certain extent, the only one

---

142 Ben-Shoshan, *Toldot Tnu'at ha-Poalim be-Eretz Yisrael (History of the Labor Movement in the Land of Israel)*, Vol. 1, pp. 171-173.

143 Ibid, pp. 173-186.

144 Ibid, pp. 188-191.

145 Ibid, pp. 191-208.

146 Ibid, pp. 216-218.

4. The Second Aliyah

that worked in settling Jews in Palestine. At the start of its work, it refrained from launching many new settlements, preferring to instead complete the process of establishing the ones it had taken on from Rothschild. In 1904, for example, at the beginning of the Second Aliyah, the JCA only established one settlement (Atlit) and no other in the following two years, although it did not stop purchasing land in that period. This situation changed in 1907, however, when the Zionist Organization began to take the initial steps, based on the decisions of the Eighth Zionist Congress, to carry out settlement activity in Palestine. The organization sent Arthur Ruppin to the country to study the conditions of the Zionist settlements, then opened its "Palestine Office" in Jaffa in 1908 (see section 2 of this chapter). This change in policy stimulated the purchase of land in the country, with competition among the three main parties that worked in this arena: the Zionist Organization, through the Palestine Land Development Company and the Jewish National Fund; the JCA, in cooperation with Rothschild; and some independent individuals and groups that worked on their own account. This led to the purchase of large areas of Arab land in Palestine, so that Zionist ownership rose from 220,700 dunums in 1900 to 420,600 in 1914,[147] on the eve of the First World War. Of this land, about 242,440 dunums were bought by the JCA and Rothschild; 158,418 dunums, by individuals and private institutions; and 16,720 dunums by the Jewish National Fund.[148] A large part of these lands was in northeast Palestine, as the Zionists had been able to purchase about half of the land in the district of Tiberias during 1889-1902,[149] which had belonged to a feudal Arab family living in Damascus.

In 1907-1914, 15 new settlements were built on parts of these lands, concentrated in the northeast and center of Palestine,

---

147 *A Survey of Palestine, Prepared in December 1945 and January 1946 for the Information of the Anglo-American Committee of Inquiry*, Vol. 1, pp. 372, 376.

148 Moshe Smilansky, *Prakim be-Toldot ha-Yishuv (Chapters in the History of the Yishuv)*, Vol. 1, Book 4, p. 95.

149 Michael Assaf, *Ha-Yahasim bein Yehudim ve Aravim be-Eretz Yisrael, 1860-1948 (Jewish-Arab Relations in the Land of Israel, 1860-1948)*, p. 39.

near the two groups of settlements that had been established during the First Aliyah (see *Map 5 Jewish settlements in Palestine, 1882-1916*, in Chapter 2, section 7). Of the new settlements, three were established in 1907: Be'er Ya'akov, Ben Shemen, and Hulda; two in 1908: Kinneret (a kvutzah) and Mitzpeh; three in 1909: Degania (later, Degania Alef), Kinneret (a moshavah), and Ahuzat Bayit (later, Tel Aviv); one in 1910: Migdal; three in 1911: Kfar Milal, Merhavia, and Ruhama; and one in each of 1912, 1913 and 1914: Kfar Uria, Karkur (Pardes Hanna), and Nahalat Yehuda, respectively. The settlement experiment failed in five of them: Kfar Milal, Hulda, Kfar Uria, Karkur (Pardes Hanna), and Ben Shemen, and they were abandoned and then resettled in 1922, 1930, 1944, 1944 and 1952 respectively. Thus, by 1914, there were 40 Zionist settlements in Palestine with a population of about 12,000,[150] which were exploiting most of the land purchased by the Zionist agencies in the country. Most of the arable lands were used to cultivate grains, and there were small areas planted with various kinds of fruit trees, including about 20,000 dunums of vineyards, 10,000 dunums of olive groves and a similar area of eucalyptus.[151]

With the establishment of those settlements in Palestine, key agricultural and civil methods were introduced to the process of Zionist settlement in the country. Three settlements – Ben Shemen, Hulda and Kinneret – were model farms established by the Zionist agencies, whose representatives assumed direct oversight to train Jewish farmers in modern agricultural methods before relocating them to new settlements. Prior to the establishment of these farms, the agricultural school, founded by the Alliance in 1870 in Mikveh Israel, had been the only institution that trained agricultural workers. Four other settlements – Migdal, Ruhama, Kfar Uria and Karkur – were, at the outset, private farms owned by individuals or companies that became active in Palestine when the Zionist Organization

---

150   Dinur, ed., *Sefer Toldot ha-Haganah (History of the Haganah)*, Vol. 1, Part 1, p. 150.

151   Smilansky, *Prakim be-Toldot ha-Yishuv (Chapters in the History of the Yishuv)*, Vol. 1, Book 4, pp. 8-9.

4. The Second Aliyah

changed its settlement policy in the country. They paved the way for the establishment of private Jewish settlements belonging to individuals or companies, especially during the British Mandate. The remaining eight settlements were divided, in terms of their method of establishment, administration and organization of their settlers' living conditions, into two types. Five were established according to the traditional principles followed in other Zionist settlements in Palestine – that is, they were all "moshavot" (plural of "moshavah"). The moshavah is an ordinary village that is formed on the basis of private initiative. Its lands are the property of its settlers and are divided among them through private ownership. The settlers exploit their lands by working them or by hiring workers to help them. Most of the Jewish settlements established by Lovers of Zion or the JCA in Palestine were of this type. The three remaining settlements, Merhavia, Degania and Ahuzat Bayit, were new experiments.

Merhavia was established in 1911 on the basis of Oppenheimer's theory of cooperative settlement, which he had presented to the Sixth and the Ninth Zionist congresses (see Chapter 3, section 7; and section 2 of this chapter). However, this theory quickly proved to be unsuitable for application in Palestine.[152] That settlement failed in Merhavia. Fundamental modifications were then introduced to the theory and led to the founding of a new type of settlement, "moshav shitufi" (cooperative settlement), where only the production in the settlement – agricultural or otherwise – remained collective, while the rules of consumption and family life were established on private, personal bases. Only a very small number of settlements of this type were established in Palestine, however.

In Degania, a new, unique experiment was conducted that had a far-reaching impact on the future of Zionist settlement in Palestine. The lands of Degania (Um Juny), on the southern shore of Lake Tiberias, west of the Jordan River, were part of the Kinneret farm designated for training Jewish agricultural

---

[152] See Bein, *Toldot ha-Hityashvut ha-Tzionit (History of Zionist Settlement)*, p. 68.

workers. The Jewish National Fund had bought these lands and handed them over to the Palestine Land Development Company (PLDC) to manage, which appointed an agricultural engineer for this purpose. In the fall of 1909, a sharp dispute arose "between the bourgeois manager and the intellectual Jewish workers"[153] on the farm. They complained to Ruppin, demanding the manager's dismissal and the handing over of the entire (Kinneret) farm to them to manage it. Ruppin, however, declined their request and suggested giving them just the lands of Degania, a proposal that they agreed to. Ruppin made an agreement with that group ("kvutzah") of workers, six young men and a woman. They pledged to manage the farm for one year in return for a collective wage of 45 francs per month, as well as housing and half of the farm's profits for that year (if there were any) distributed equally among them. The management was handed over to two of these workers, who were given responsibility for the farm before the company and for the work of their colleagues.[154] After signing the agreement, Ruppin wrote to the leadership of the Jewish National Fund that was still based in Cologne, informing them of the measures he had taken and asking them not to announce this "communist" settlement experiment until it succeeded – which, in fact, it did. The agricultural season of that year was profitable, and the workers received their share. They declined to continue working on the farm, however, and moved elsewhere. A group of Jewish workers from Hadera, who were more experienced in the methods of collective work, were employed to manage the farm according to the same principles in their place. Through this act, Ruppin unknowingly laid the foundations for collective settlements of the "kibbutz" type, which subsequently played a major role in the history of Zionist settlement in Palestine.[155]

The goals of the PLDC included the establishment of

---

153   Ruppin, *Pirkei Hayai (Chapters of My Life)*, Vol. 2, p. 78.

154   Agreement in ibid, pp. 78-79.

155   To review the forms and types of Zionist settlement in Palestine, generally, see Yitzhak Lador (Leidermann), *Hityashvutenu ba-Aretz, 1870-1952, Toldoteha ve Tzoroteha (Our Settlement in the Country, 1870-1952, Its History and Forms)*, pp. 228-274.

4. The Second Aliyah

residential neighborhoods for Jews in Palestine, on a commercial basis.[156] To do this, the company was active in purchasing lands in the main cities of Jerusalem, Jaffa and Haifa. In Jaffa, the company joined efforts with a group of "60 Jewish families, most of them merchants, teachers and academics" who were fed up with living in the town "because its streets are very dirty, and the houses owned by the Arabs lack all amenities necessary to maintain health, by European standards".[157] Thus, those families formed a company, "Ahuzat Bayit", which purchased about 220 dunums of land north of Jaffa to establish homes on it. The PLDC helped to build them, then searched for other lands in the area and was able to purchase 793 dunums by 1918.[158] Other residential neighborhoods were built on these lands, which were planned to become an independent town called "Tel Aviv". This grew until it became the largest Jewish city in Palestine before finally absorbing its Arab neighbor, Jaffa.

In Jerusalem, the PLDC was able to purchase 192 dunums of land[159] on Mount Scopus, where the Hebrew University was later established, and in the area where Ben Yehuda Street and its adjacent streets in the new Jerusalem were developed. Those lands belonged to an English lord and to the Greek patriarch in Jerusalem.[160]

In Haifa, the company also purchased an area of 249 dunums on Mount Carmel by 1913. The Institute of Applied Engineering (Technion) was founded on part of this land. In 1918, the company purchased 2,536 additional dunums in various parts of the city, mostly owned by Germans who had lived there.[161]

---

156 Aminadav Eshbal, ed., *Shishim Shanot Hachsharat ha-Yishuv (Sixty Years of the Palestine Land Development Company)*, p. 13.

157 Ruppin, *Pirkei Hayai (Chapters of My Life)*, Vol. 2, p. 140.

158 Ibid, pp. 144-152; Eshbal, ed., *Shishim Shanot Hachsharat ha-Yishuv (Sixty Years of the Palestine Land Development Company)*, p. 39.

159 Eshbal, ed., *Shishim Shanot Hachsharat ha-Yishuv (Sixty Years of the Palestine Land Development Company)*, p. 39.

160 Ruppin, *Pirkei Hayai (Chapters of My Life)*, Vol. 2, pp. 162-167; Vol. 3, p. 86.

161 Ibid, Vol. 2, pp. 153, 160-162; Eshbal, ed., *Shishim Shanot Hachsharat*

5

The Second Aliyah also laid the foundations of the Zionist military in Palestine. This was done by pioneers from the Po'alei Zion party, who were members of the defense battalions operating among some Jewish communities in Russia. They had been forced to leave the country after being pursued by the tsar's police during the riots that erupted in the wake of the pogroms against the Jewish population. In addition to their quest to "occupy labor", these settlers brought to Palestine the idea of establishing similar defense battalions.[162] They noticed that the guarding of Jewish settlements was "occupied" by non-Jews, for each settlement had entrusted its security affairs to one of the Arab Bedouin tribes or the Circassians who lived close to it.[163] "The Circassian issue", in the words of a settler leader, Israel Shohat,

> gave me new ideas: a bunch of people in a sea of Arabs, but, nonetheless, they earned respect, spread their roots in the land and formed their own villages. Thus, we should not lose hope; we can persevere, settle the country, and spread our roots in it, and we can bring the Arab neighbor to respect us. For this, we need courage and persistence.[164]

In order to "bring the Arab neighbor to respect us", that group of immigrants (whose leaders, in addition to Israel Shohat, included Yitzhak Ben-Zvi, Alexander Zaid and Yehoshua Hankin, a major agent of the PLDC who purchased large areas of land for it) decided to focus on security. They contacted the leaders of Po'alei Zion to set up defense battalions for the settlements. Their request was denied, however. They then tried to gain the support of other settler leaders in Palestine, but the latter

---

ha-Yishuv (Sixty Years of the Palestine Land Development Company), p. 39.

162 Yitzhak Ben-Zvi, ed., *Sefer Hashomer (Book of Hashomer)*, p. 4; Mior, *Ha-Tnu'ah ha-Tzionit be-Rusia (Zionist Movement in Russia)*, pp. 278-281.

163 Ben-Zvi, ed., *Sefer Hashomer (Book of Hashomer)*, p. 5.

164 Ibid, p. 7.

4. The Second Aliyah

also expressed reservations. Thus the new immigrants turned to the establishment of paramilitary labor organizations, and were among the initiators of "ha-Horesh" and "ha-Kollektiv" associations in al-Shajarah settlement (see section 4 of this chapter), which did not achieve great success. The group then sought help from some Jewish leaders outside Palestine, but failed there as well.[165] Thus they decided to take matters into their own hands and work alone, under their own responsibility.

In late September 1907, the group took the first step in implementing its scheme. The third Po'alei Zion congress had convened in Jaffa. In attendance were the party's delegates to the Eighth Zionist Congress, Yitzhak Ben-Zvi and Israel Shohat. They had just returned from Europe after the end of the congress, where the practical Zionists had overcome the politicians and compelled the Zionist Organization to begin practical settlement activity in Palestine. During the Po'alei Zion congress, Ben-Zvi and Shohat explained to their colleagues the consequences that had arisen from this decision of the Zionist Organization – stressing that the time had come to implement their schemes without seeking approval or assistance. Subsequently, meetings were held in Ben-Zvi's room in Jaffa, attended by eight members of the party, who decided to establish a secret organization by the name of "Bar-Giora"[166] (commemorating a Jewish leader who had allegedly fought the Romans in Palestine, before the fall of the Second Kingdom of Israel). At the meeting, it was decided that the goal of the organization was to find adequate means to:

> (a) Reform the Yishuv: fight the halukah system and alms of all kinds, (b) Encourage work through free will, (c) Seek new ways of living and working based on raising the worker's responsibility, (d) Instill Hebrew labor and a Hebrew guard, (e) Instill a socialist Zionist culture, (f) Unify the working class, (g) Establish a defense/fighting force.[167]

---

165   Dinur, ed., *Sefer Toldot ha-Haganah (History of the Haganah)*, Vol. 1, Part 1, p. 202.

166   Ibid, pp. 202-203.

167   Ben-Zvi, ed., *Sefer Hashomer (Book of Hashomer)*, p. 15.

The group elected Israel Shohat as president and Yitzhak Ben-Zvi as the secret representative in the Po'alei Zion party.

It was not easy for the Bar-Giora group to implement its main goal – "establish a defense/fighting force" – due to its lack of means and the conditions in Palestine. Thus its members gathered in the settlement of al-Shajarah, with the goal of guarding it and training themselves on the use of weapons. They were entrusted with protecting the settlement after they tricked the Circassian watchman who was working there, stealing a mule from the livestock that he was assigned to guard such that the settlement manager dismissed him and handed them the job.[168] About a year and a half after the establishment of Bar-Giora, its members held a meeting in mid-April 1909 and decided to establish a public organization, which they called "Hashomer" (The Watchman). Its goal was "to develop the element of the Jewish watchmen in our country who deserve to do their work", by organizing the watchmen working in the settlements; purchasing sports equipment for them; teaching them horseback riding, sports and the use of weapons; improving their financial conditions; and establishing a loan fund for them.[169]

After its establishment, Hashomer actively worked to impose its control over the guarding of the Jewish settlements. By 1913-1914, it was able to assume this role in one way or another in most of the settlements that existed in Palestine, except for Petah Tikva, Zichron Ya'acov and Rosh Pina.[170] This success was short-lived, however, because of the nature of Hashomer and its methods. The organization acted as though it was the vanguard of the defense forces for the Jewish settlers in Palestine, but rejected any oversight or coordination by settler leaders or their parties. Hashomer also made a mistake in its stance towards the Arabs. On the one hand, its members tried to imitate the Arabs, get close to them and learn their language and customs,[171] which

---

168   Ibid, p. 17.
169   Ibid, p. 451.
170   Ibid, p. 32.
171   Ibid, pp. 26-27, 33.

4. The Second Aliyah

aroused the suspicions of the Zionist settlers and decreased their support for Hashomer. On the other hand, the organization's members resorted to the use of force with the Arabs while carrying out guard work – pushing them to use counter-force that led to the death of 10 members of Hashomer in the first five years of its establishment, even though it had no more than 30 members at the time.[172] The disputes that intermittently erupted between the Hashomer men and the Arab residents of the villages near the Jewish settlements forced the latter to gradually return the Arab guards alongside the Jewish ones, such that when the "Hebrew guard" failed it was replaced by a mixed one.[173]

When the Haganah was formed in 1920, a severe dispute arose between it and Hashomer that forced Hashomer to dissolve itself and hand over the task of defending the Jewish settlers in Palestine to the Haganah – although it did not hand over its weapons until 1929.

The emergence of Hashomer and its independent line also led to the establishment of local guard organizations in a number of Jewish settlements that had opposed this method and were committed to the decisions of the Zionist settler leaders. One of the most prominent was the "Jaffa Group", which was founded by Jewish youth in Tel Aviv at the end of the First World War.[174] This group did not make any significant achievements, but from its ranks came Eliyahu Golomb (1893-1945), the "godfather" of the Haganah and its chief architect from its founding in 1920 until his death. The group also included Moshe Shertok (Moshe Sharett; 1894-1965), who later became head of the political department of the Jewish Agency and the first foreign minister of Israel.[175]

---

172   Ibid, pp. 476-477.

173   Assaf, *Ha-Yahasim bein Yehudim ve Aravim be-Eretz Yisrael, 1860-1948 (Jewish-Arab Relations in the Land of Israel, 1860-1948)*, pp. 78-79, 82.

174   Dinur, ed., *Sefer Toldot ha-Haganah (History of the Haganah)*, Vol. 1, Part 1, pp. 387-389.

175   See also Uri Milstein, *Be-Dam ve Esh, Yehuda: Tsmihata shel ha-Otzma ha-Yisraelit (By Blood and Fire, Judea: Growth of Israeli Power)*, pp. 24-30.

6

The immigrants of the Second Aliyah were distinguished from previous Zionist organizations or leaders by taking an explicit, hostile political stance towards the Palestinian Arabs, which no other group had adopted until then (and which later affected, almost permanently, the entire Zionist Organization and Israel). This stance had taken shape before the pioneers of that wave of immigration had arrived in Palestine, as all of the Zionist leaders who had played prominent roles in formulating the ideology of those settlers, or who had actually urged them to immigrate, had taken clearly hostile stances against the Arabs. Ussishkin, for example, announced in *Our Program*, which was published a few months before the onset of the Second Aliyah and was a catalyst for some people to immigrate, that one of the main goals in Palestine was to "occupy" labor from the hands of the Arabs, especially in Jewish settlements. Borochov, in turn, predicted in *Our Platform* that the assimilation of the Arabs of Palestine with the immigrants would lead to the disappearance of the Arabs as a distinct, independent people. Since 1898, Syrkin had also demanded the displacement of the Arabs of Palestine from their country so that the Jewish immigrants would take their place (see sections 1 and 3 of this chapter).

With this position taken by the fathers of the Second Aliyah, the children, on their arrival in Palestine, had to take a practical stance no less severe, which was augmented by their difficulties in trying to assimilate in the country. These were caused by their inability to compete with Arab workers and replace them. The slogan of "occupation of labor" from Arab workers, launched by the Second Aliyah members as one of the main tenets of establishing a socialist Zionist society in Palestine, was not merely an embodiment of the theories that they had formulated prior to their arrival, but also an expression of their aim to meet their economic needs by securing the work for themselves.[176] In

---

176   Aharon Cohen, *Yisrael ve ha-Olam ha-Aravi (Israel and the Arab World)*, p. 70.

4. The Second Aliyah

their efforts to "occupy labor", the immigrants of the Second Aliyah faced grave difficulties, especially after Jewish employers, as mentioned earlier, generally preferred Arab workers. This was explained by a settler leader, Yosef Vitkin:

> The foreign [Arab] worker is convenient for them [Jewish employers], for several reasons: he is healthy and able to work, his wages are low and his requests few, and sometimes our farmers use him not only as a worker, but also as a guide in many jobs in which they are still beginners. In addition, he is always an obedient servant ... and can be exploited without any inconvenience on his part. The Jewish worker, conversely, is still inexperienced and sometimes lacks the physical strength needed for the difficult work, yet he does not lessen his usual requests: he insists on enjoying his holiday, preserves his dignity – at times, with some sick nervousness – and, most importantly, our farmers do not favor the growth of the element of Jewish workers.[177]

This description, which was applicable from the beginning of Zionist settlement in Palestine, detailed the main reason for the hostility of Jewish workers and Zionist agencies to Arab workers. Po'alei Zion and Hapoel Hatzair, the two main parties that led the Second Aliyah, did not agree on any point of their programs as much as they did on the "occupation of labor".

This slogan – which found a new formula in another expression, "Hebrew labor" – was not unique for long. Another slogan was soon devised to complement it: "occupation of land". This was also brought by Zionist immigrants from Russia, based on the views of some Russian intellectuals that land was the property of those who cultivated it.[178] Those two slogans

---

[177] Vitkin, *Kitvei Yosef Vitkin (Works of Yosef Vitkin)*, p. 42; for details, see also Jacob Rony, "Rehovot's Relationship with its Arab Neighbors", in Daniel Carpi, ed., *Ha-Tzionout, Me'asef le-Toldot ha-Tnu'ah ha-Tzionit ve ha-Yishuv ha-Yehudi be-Eretz Yisrael (Zionism: Studies in the History of the Zionist Movement and of the Jewish Community in the Land of Israel)*, Vol. 1, pp. 150-171.

[178] Slutsky, *Mevoa le-Toldot Tnu'at ha-Avoda ha-Yisraelit (Introduction to the History of the Israeli Labor Movement)*, p. 194.

became the chief preoccupation of the leaders of the Second Aliyah, who never stopped searching for the best ways to realize them. With the difficulties they encountered, whether due to the weakness of the settlers themselves or the objective conditions that prevailed in Palestine, the discussion intensified and new views were put forth. Vitkin of Hapoel Hatzair, for example, saw that Jewish workers had come to hate manual work as hired laborers and some of them were leaving the country. He felt that it was necessary to help them and establish special institutions for them, whose aim would be to create a large Jewish working class in Palestine, and then establish collective or cooperative settlements. "Occupation of labor is only accomplished by occupying land and settling it."[179] However, Yosef Aharonovich, editor of Hapoel Hatzair's magazine, was in opposition to this notion, stressing that it was private initiative that would establish a political entity for the Jewish settlers in Palestine. In his view, the owners of private businesses had to be convinced to hire settlers and to be told of the dangers of using Arab workers, which would impede the growth of an independent Jewish entity in the country. Aharonovich also felt it necessary to concentrate Jewish workers in branches of work that could be controlled and finally occupied by them – for only the settlements established by the official Zionist agencies could be obligated to follow the rules of "Hebrew labor".[180]

Those calls were joined by Yitzhak Ben-Zvi, of Po'alei Zion, who also noted that Jewish employers preferred Arab workers and that the economic situation in Palestine did not allow for the accommodation of new Jewish workers. The solution, in his view, lay in improving the economic conditions of Jewish workers and establishing settlements on cooperative bases, through the official Zionist settlement agencies.[181] Ben-Zvi was joined by his party colleague, Shlomo Kaplansky, who

---

179   Vitkin, *Kitvei Yosef Vitkin (Works of Yosef Vitkin)*, pp. 42-45.

180   Yosef Aharonovich, *Ha-Am ve ha-Aretz (People and Country)*, pp. 56-65.

181   In Yosef Gorny, *Prakim Nivharim be-Tkufat ha-Aliya ha-Shnia (Selected Chapters from the Second Aliyah Period)*, pp. 20-27.

4. The Second Aliyah

declared that the Jewish worker had proven to be unfit to carry out the task that was placed upon him, and that he was not a good worker to begin with. The solution he proposed was to find an independent settlement method with no relation to private capital.[182] Berl Katznelson, who was ostensibly non-partisan, described the reluctance of Jewish employers to hire Jewish workers as "economic anti-Semitism".[183] Presented by the leaders of the Second Aliyah, these proposals later formed part of the bases of Zionist agricultural settlement in Palestine, especially during the British Mandate.

The immigrant leaders did not cease their efforts to promote the methods of "occupation of labor" and "occupation of land" among the Jewish settlers. Some of the leaders made strenuous attempts to imbue these concepts with a positive character, claiming that

> the slogan of "occupation of labor" has a double concept: the occupation of workplaces for the Jewish worker, and the worker's occupation of himself, through work... We are the sons of a working people who were expelled from the camp and deprived of their right to work. We are not workers searching for a workplace here, but an entire people searching for their workplace in the world...

Further, "the workers are young, in overwhelming majority, and have not tried physical labor in the diaspora."[184] They were students, vendors, teachers and the like. Thus it was necessary to transfer them to work on the land, "to eliminate the Jewish diseases of the diaspora".

Among the most prominent theoreticians in this respect was Aaron David Gordon (1856-1922). He had emigrated from Russia to Palestine in 1904 at the age of 48, unlike most of the Second Aliyah immigrants who had come to Palestine before reaching

---

182 Ibid, pp. 27-29.

183 Ibid, p. 30.

184 Ben-Shoshan, *Toldot Tnu'at ha-Poalim be-Eretz Yisrael (History of the Labor Movement in the Land of Israel)*, Vol. 1, p. 75.

20 years of age. In Palestine, Gordon worked in agriculture, like most of the others, moving from one place to another in search of work. He was also a writer, and published dozens of articles on practical and theoretical issues faced by the settlers of the Second Aliyah. He reformulated their theories, deepened them, and infused them with a new character. Through this work, Gordon contributed, more than any other individual, to transmitting those concepts to later Jewish immigrants to Palestine.

In his theories, Gordon stressed the merits of work – which "strengthens the body and refines the soul" – and the need to direct the individual to engage in such a type of work, as well as to convert Jewish people, generally, to a life of productive employment.

> The Jewish people has been completely cut off from nature and imprisoned within city walls for two thousand years. We have been accustomed to every form of life, except a life of labor – of labor done at our behalf and for its own sake. It will require the greatest effort of will for such a people to become normal again. We lack the principal ingredient for national life. We lack the habit of labor … for it is labor which binds a people to its soil and to its national culture, which in its turn is an outgrowth of the people's toil and the people's labor.[185]

This new Jewish civilization, in Gordon's view, could only arise in Palestine, because

> the Land of Israel is the center of the whole people, and it, alone, should become a center for the unity of the people, its national aspirations and national work… There are those who say that the Land of Israel does not accommodate all Jews… I do not consider that a calamity … because the dispersed parts can become like branches that extend outside

---

185 Aaron David Gordon, *Ha-Uma ve ha-Avoda (The Nation and Labor)*, p. 134.

4. The Second Aliyah

the circle of their growth…[186]

> The revival of the people and renewal of its spirit in the form of a working, productive people can only take place through work in nature, and all the people of the nation must work… There is no country other than the Land of Israel where a Jew can taste the homeland, the natural, true homeland… The basis is to work in the Land of Israel … and live in it… The only safety for us is to work in and for the country.[187]

Like other leaders of the Second Aliyah, Gordon demanded the implementation of "Hebrew labor", but through his own concept:

> The method of labor, then the control of the Jewish worker over all branches of labor, is a wrong concept, and it is not for this, that is, for the sake of working on farms or factories of others that those with the idea of labor came here. This is not the philosophy of labor. This philosophy states, above all, that the worker must be autonomous in his work, in his own or collective farms or factories.

Thus, in Gordon's view, Hebrew labor had to completely prevail in these places and no Arab worker could be allowed to enter them – ignoring this requirement would have been nothing but "Jewish diaspora behavior". Gordon insisted that

> whoever settles land must cultivate it himself or with the help of his household, for the land belongs to the nation, and only those who cultivate it can eat its fruits… Our Mother, the Land of Israel, asks you for both body and soul, or else, nothing… You must realize that our Mother, the Land of Israel, can give you more than what you can give her.[188]

In view of Gordon's emphasis on the idea of labor as the

---

186 Ibid, pp. 226, 261.

187 Ibid, pp. 202, 261, 433.

188 Ibid, pp. 154, 201, 513, 521.

basis of Zionist presence in Palestine, his supporters called his teachings a "religion of labor".[189] Some considered them a summary of the "positive" principles produced by the Second Aliyah but, with his so-called "religion of labor", Gordon also founded what could be called the "religion of racism". His insistence on converting the Jews to a life of labor and his call to adhere to complete Hebrew labor had political consequences for the Arabs, who constituted most of the population of Palestine, and for their workers in particular. Gordon's calls became part of the ideology of the Zionist labor wing, which worked diligently to implement them – especially after taking control of the Zionist movement from the mid-1930s and remaining the main Zionist party to rule Israel until the mid-1970s. Gordon was very clear in his conclusions: "All our settlements, from their foundations to their roofs, their vineyards and groves, are founded by the Arabs, who work in them." In such a situation, "the country will not be ours more than it is now, and the people will not be livelier or less diasporic than they are now, even if we have the title deeds of the land that our practical Zionists strive for, or the settlement privileges that bring joy to the hearts of the politicians." Gordon stressed that the country would finally "belong to those who suffer for its sake and work in it more than others", for "if we do not cultivate the land with our hands, it will not belong to us in the social or national sense, nor in the political one."[190] Accordingly, he reiterated that it was not sufficient to purchase land from the Arabs but to also replace them with Jewish settlers to work on it.

Gordon, of course, realized the consequences of his calls for Hebrew labor. He knew that they would lead to confrontation with the Arabs, especially as he noticed the signs of the Arab nationalist awakening at the time. Thus, seemingly contradicting himself, he suggested finding "a path to a shared life with the Arabs, and shared labor, that would be a blessing for both

---

189   Eliezer Schweid, *Ha-Yahid: Olamo shel A. D. Gordon (The One and Only: The World of A. D. Gordon)*, p. 175.

190   Gordon, *Ha-Uma ve ha-Avoda (The Nation and Labor)*, pp. 96, 104, 150, 472.

4. The Second Aliyah 293

sides".[191] This had to happen, however, through "the historical right of the Jews in the country... This right to peaceful competition and expansion in the country is not only the right of the small [Jewish] group that lives here, but the right of all [Jewish people]." Gordon advised the settlers to purchase lands in Palestine through "extreme caution in our relations with the Arabs... It is advisable to placate the real owners of the land who live and work on it, when we are in dire need of their land." In the end, however, his conviction was that the land would belong to those who cultivated it, and the settlers were the ones who had to cultivate it and make it their own, for "our right to the Land of Israel exists as long as we exist, and as long as we intend to create a wonderful Land of Israel that was not created before, and which no one else can create."[192] Based on his position, Gordon strongly criticized the Po'alei Zion party for its adherence to the theory of class struggle and its call to establish a socialist society in Palestine. "We did not come to the Land of Israel for the sake of socialism, nor in its name ... nor for class struggle, class hatred and class stupidity... The struggle for labor here does not take on the character of class struggle, for its essence is purely nationalist."[193] He went on:

> What have the Arabs created, during their entire time in the country? ... The creation of the Torah, only, gives us an eternal right that cannot be revoked in the country in which [the Torah] was given, especially since the people who came after us did not create anything of this magnificence, indeed, nothing at all.[194]

With time, those views influenced more than one Zionist leader or intellectual. Gordon's stamp on the thinking of the Zionist labor wing[195] was no less than that of Nordau on the right-wing,

---

191 Ibid, p. 203.

192 Ibid, pp. 224-225, 553.

193 Ibid, pp. 155, 242, 546.

194 Ibid, p. 560.

195 For details, see Yehiel Halpern, *Ha-Mahpicha ha-Yehudit (The Jewish*

Revisionist Zionists.

Among the figures of the Second Aliyah who also promoted the Zionist idea of Hebrew labor was the writer Yosef Haim Brenner (1881-1921). Brenner had begun writing at a young age in his native Russia, and had continued to do so after immigrating to Palestine in 1909 where he published a number of literary works. In most of his writings, he described the Jewish existence in the diaspora in extremely negative terms and affirmed that the meaning of Zionism was to change the Jewish way of life and to return to a life of labor, to revive and purify the Jewish people.[196] Brenner was killed in the riots that broke out between the Palestinian Arabs and Jewish settlers in Jaffa and Tel Aviv in May 1921.

The immigrants of the Second Aliyah were not only verbally hostile towards the Arab workers. On more than one occasion, they took racist measures against them which were a harbinger of the policies they would enact on coming to power. In 1908, for example, the Palestine Land Development Company decided, at the outset of its work, to plant a forest of olive trees on the Ben Shemen farm, near Lod, in commemoration of Herzl. It employed a number of Arabs to do this work. In protest, Jewish workers held a meeting at Lod and a group of them uprooted the olive trees and replanted them,[197] for it was not permissible to "employ foreign workers in such a task relating to the honorable name of Herzl", and duty required "removing the shame from the name of the Yishuv and the people".[198] This behavior prompted the Zionist administration in Palestine, represented by the Palestine Office in Jaffa, to issue an order to the supervisors of its farms and settlements to refrain from employing Arabs – an order that became law.[199] In the fall of 1913, when the manager

---

Revolution), Vol. 2, pp. 427-447.

196 See also ibid, pp. 402-426.

197 Slutsky, *Mevoa le-Toldot Tnu'at ha-Avoda ha-Yisraelit (Introduction to the History of the Israeli Labor Movement)*, p. 197.

198 Gruenbaum, *Ha-Tnu'ah ha-Tzionit (The Zionist Movement)*, Vol. 3, p. 121.

199 Ibid; Slutsky, *Mevoa le-Toldot Tnu'at ha-Avoda ha-Yisraelit (Introduction*

4. The Second Aliyah

of the Kfar Uria farm hired Arab workers, the Jewish ones left their workplaces and refused to return. A year later, when the manager of al-Shajarah farm made the same "mistake", the workers declared a general strike that led to him being replaced.[200]

When Tel Aviv, the first and largest Jewish city in Palestine, was established, its founders also decided to refrain from hiring Arabs for the construction work.[201] They made this decision when building the first houses, but these collapsed due to the lack of experience of the Jewish workers. The founders were forced to turn to Arab workers, who were "famous for their skill and experience in the field of construction".[202] Palestinian Arab workers, at any rate – despite the Zionist claims of seeking to convert the Jews to a life of manual labor and production – continued building Tel Aviv and other Jewish cities from then onwards, during Ottoman rule in Palestine, the British mandate over the country and after the establishment of Israel.

The settlers of the Second Aliyah did not stop at this point in their war against the Arab workers – especially after it became clear that the latter were "agricultural worker[s] by birth",[203] with whom it was not easy to compete. The Zionist settlement agencies did not accept this reality, however, and kept searching for other means. They finally decided that if it was difficult for the western Jewish worker to compete with the Arab one, then perhaps the eastern Jewish worker could. Thus the settler leaders had no qualms about working to displace a number of Yemeni Jews to Palestine, hoping to exploit them, "due to their low standard of living",[204] to compete with and overcome Arab

---

to the History of the Israeli Labor Movement), p. 197.

200   Slutsky, *Mevoa le-Toldot Tnu'at ha-Avoda ha-Yisraelit (Introduction to the History of the Israeli Labor Movement)*, pp. 198-200.

201   Aryeh Yotvat, "Yahasei Yehudim ve-Aravim be-Rosheta shel Tel Aviv, 1909-1929 (Jewish-Arab Relations in Early Tel Aviv, 1909-1929)", in Carpi, ed., *Ha-Tzionout (Zionism)*, Vol. 3, pp. 521-522.

202   Ruppin, *Pirkei Hayai (Chapters of My Life)*, Vol. 2, p. 147.

203   Dinur, ed., *Sefer Toldot ha-Haganah (History of the Haganah)*, Vol. 1, Part 1, p. 135.

204   Ruppin, *Pirkei Hayai (Chapters of My Life)*, Vol. 2, p. 103.

workers in Jewish agricultural settlements. In 1911, the Palestine Office sent a leader of the Second Aliyah, Shmuel Yavnieli, as an emissary to Yemen to urge its Jewish population to immigrate to Palestine.[205] In order to persuade the religious Yemeni Jews, Yavnieli carried with him a letter addressed to them in ancient Hebrew, similar to that used by the rabbis and Jewish clerics.[206] He claimed that the rabbis of Palestine had found this ancient letter and asked him to deliver it to them. In reality, the letter was written by Abraham Isaac Kook (later the Ashkenazi chief rabbi of the Jews in Palestine). Through this trick, Yavnieli was able to induce about 2,000 Yemeni Jewish people to immigrate to Palestine before the First World War.

However, these Yemenis also failed to "occupy labor" in the Jewish settlements. When Yavnieli traveled to Yemen in 1911, Ahad Ha'am visited Palestine and wrote, as was his habit, an article after his visit. Based on the conditions of workers that he saw in the Jewish settlements, he expressed his doubts about the potential for achieving "Hebrew labor", due to the large number of Arab workers in those settlements and the impossibility of dispensing with their services. Ahad Ha'am wrote that, in the settlement of Zichron Ya'acov, "almost all of the workers are Arabs;" in Hadera, "most of the workers are Arabs, but there are a few dozen Jewish workers;" in Petah Tikva, "Arabs are in the thousands, and in some groves, there is not a single Jewish worker;" and, in Gedera, "there are no Jewish workers at all."[207] There was no significant change in this situation even three years after the arrival of the Yemenis to Palestine. According to Yitzhak Ben-Zvi, by the end of 1913 there were 1,200-1,300 Jewish workers, including 400 Yemenis, compared with 8,000-10,000 Arab workers in the Jewish settlements.[208] Yavnieli, himself, was

---

205 See Yavnieli's diary in Braslavski, *Tnu'at ha-Poalim ha-Eretz Yisraelit (Labor Movement in the Land of Israel)*, Vol. 1, pp. 344-347.

206 Letter in Ruppin, *Pirkei Hayai (Chapters of My Life)*, Vol. 2, pp. 104-105.

207 Ahad Ha'am, *Kol Kitvei Ahad Ha'am – Al Parshat Drachim (Complete Works of Ahad Ha'am – At the Crossroads)*, pp. 474-475.

208 In Gorny, *Prakim Nivharim be-Tkufat ha-Aliya ha-Shnia (Selected Chapters from the Second Aliyah Period)*, p. 28.

4. The Second Aliyah

forced to admit that "the immigration of Yemenis ... has not solved the question of Hebrew labor, for they did not penetrate the most important branches of agricultural work."[209]

Despite this failure to realize the slogans of "occupation of labor", "occupation of land", and "Hebrew labor",[210] most immigrants of the Second Aliyah, including their leaders and intellectuals, remained committed to them and strived to realize them, without trying to find any other policy towards the Arabs. When a few individuals criticized this policy, the response of the majority was to insist on adhering to it. The first (and possibly the only one) to condemn this policy and warn of its dangers was Yitzhak Epstein, who called for an alliance with the Arab Peasants' Party and to stop persecuting the Arabs and seizing their land (see Chapter 2, section 7). However, Epstein found no support. Those who responded to him, including the farmer-writer Moshe Smilansky (1874-1953), provided justifications that deepened the racism in the ideology of the Second Aliyah:

> If it is forbidden for us to rob the peasants and treat them cruelly, so that the looted do not turn into looters, we should not help them, either, so that they do not gain strength! ... We must do our work in the fields and workshops by means of Jews, only, so that the Arabs do not gain wealth and power from this work, and so that the number of Jews will rise... We must not get too close to the Arab peasants, so that our young children do not follow in their paths and learn their ugly habits... There is no need for them to learn our methods in working the field and preserving the trees. If they are distinguished by their numerical majority and physical strength, let us keep in our hands the attribute of civilized life and work, and there will come a day when they turn to us, asking us to teach them, and then we will teach them! When they are convinced that there is a blessing in civilized life and work, then we will not expose ourselves to danger when we

---

209 Ibid, p. 22.

210 See also Smilansky, *Prakim be-Toldot ha-Yishuv (Chapters in the History of the Yishuv)*, Vol. 1, Book 3, pp. 120-121.

teach them our methods, because we will be the majority, by then![211]

(Smilansky, however, changed his position after he became president of the Jewish Farmers' Federation during the British Mandate. Instead of pure "Hebrew labor", he began calling for "mixed work" of Jews and Arabs, and supported the establishment of a bi-national state of both in Palestine.)

Yitzhak Ben-Zvi, on behalf of his party, Po'alei Zion, also addressed this issue. The party had faced criticism due to its call for the establishment of a socialist society, and its principles of class struggle and proletarian solidarity – while, at the same time, hounding Arab workers. Ben-Zvi addressed this by saying that "when there is a clash between a national principle and a socialist one, the socialist principle must be abandoned in favor of national work." To him, the Jewish workers who demanded fulfillment of the "Hebrew labor" slogan were defending a national principle; thus, they had to be supported. Further,

> the emancipation of land through its purchase has begun to be realized, to some extent, but the emancipation of labor is still remote... The development of the Jewish Yishuv should proceed at a faster pace than the Arab. It is true that, from our point of view, we must help the Arab worker ... and improve his conditions ... but as long as we have not become a force that others are obliged to recognize and to take into consideration – whether they like it or not – we cannot, and should not, work to help others.[212]

As for Hillel Yaffe, chairman of the executive committee of Lovers of Zion in Palestine, whose settlements were full of Arab workers, he declared: "We are obliged to strongly oppose any proximity to Arab society."[213]

---

211   In Gorny, *Prakim Nivharim be-Tkufat ha-Aliya ha-Shnia (Selected Chapters from the Second Aliyah Period)*, p. 34.

212   Ibid, pp. 35-43.

213   Yaffe, H., *Dor Ma'afilim (A Generation of Immigrants)*, p. 169.

4. The Second Aliyah

It is clear that these ideas held by the immigrants of the Second Aliyah affected their political stance towards the Arabs and pushed them, at best, to ignore their presence and distance themselves from them (a position that later dominated the mentality of many Zionist factions). Based on this stance, or perhaps to complement it, the leaders of the Second Aliyah placed great hopes on the revolution that broke out in Turkey in 1908 and expected it to be the beginning of a new era for them. The Po'alei Zion party in Palestine issued a special, secret memorandum praising the revolution[214] and flattering its leaders. After their disappointment with the revolution, however, the settlers did not change their position nor try to take a clearer stance towards the Arabs. Some settler leaders, headed by David Ben-Gurion and Yitzhak Ben-Zvi, instead traveled to Turkey in 1911 to study the Turkish language and learn, up close, the situation in the country in order to better understand the Turks and deal with them when necessary.[215] Yet it did not occur to those settlers to study the language of their Arab neighbors. Also, the two main parties of the Second Aliyah, Po'alei Zion and Hapoel Hatzair, held about 25 congresses and general meetings from their establishment in 1905 until the outbreak of the First World War in 1914, but none of them seriously reconsidered their position towards the Arabs.[216] One of the rare cases in which a leader of the Second Aliyah took a stance on the matter was the demand made by Shlomo Kaplansky, the delegate of Po'alei Zion to the Tenth Zionist Congress (1911), that the Zionist administration take measures to clarify the "benefits of Zionism" to the Arabs.[217]

The leaders of the Second Aliyah insisted on their position, despite the fact that the period in which they came to

---

214 In Gorny, *Prakim Nivharim be-Tkufat ha-Aliya ha-Shnia (Selected Chapters from the Second Aliyah Period)*, pp. 55-56.

215 David Ben-Gurion, *Zichronot (Memoirs)*, Vol. 1, pp. 52-57.

216 Peretz Merchav, *Toldot Tnu'at ha-Poalim be-Eretz Yisrael 1905-1965 (History of the Labor Movement in the Land of Israel, 1905-1965)*, pp. 356-357.

217 Cohen, A., *Yisrael ve ha-Olam ha-Aravi (Israel and the Arab World)*, p. 88.

Palestine (1904-1914) also witnessed the beginning of serious opposition by the Arab national movement to both them and to the Ottoman authorities. Several Arabic newspapers were published in Palestine, including *al-Carmel* (*The Carmel*), *Filistin* (*Palestine*) and *al-Muntada* (*The Forum*), which attacked the settlers vehemently.[218] In early 1912, the Zionist Palestine Office in Jaffa had established a special unit to monitor the Arab press and provide the Zionist agencies with a summary of its statements.[219] Arab opposition intensified, in particular in 1909-1911, after a rise in the purchase of Arab lands and the insistence of Zionist settlers on implementing "Hebrew labor", dismissing Arab workers from their jobs in Jewish settlements. News of this opposition reached the central Ottoman authorities in Istanbul, where Arab representatives in the Turkish parliament warned of the consequences of Jewish immigration to Palestine and Zionist purchase of lands there. About 150 notables from the district of Nazareth sent a telegram of protest to the Ottoman authorities in March 1911.[220] Despite this, the settler leaders made no change and only declared that "the Christian Arabs, educated by the Jesuit monks, are the ones inciting against the Jews."[221] This view on the hostile position of Christian Arabs was prevalent in many Zionist circles,[222] which used it to conclude that Arab opposition was limited to very few groups – although some Zionists warned of the danger of believing that Arab Muslims were any less

---

218 See also Yotvat's documents in Carpi, ed., *Ha-Tzionout (Zionism)*, Vol. 3, pp. 523-526.

219 Yacov Ro'i, "The Zionist Attitude to the Arabs, 1908-1914", *Middle Eastern Studies*, Vol. 4, No. 3, pp. 207, 216, 228.

220 For details, see Paul Abraham Ellsberg, "The Arab Question in the Policy of the Zionist Administration Before the First World War", in Ben-Zion Dinur (Dinaburg), ed., *Shivat Tzion (Return to Zion)*, Vol. 4, pp. 165-170.

221 Dinur, ed., *Sefer Toldot ha-Haganah (History of the Haganah)*, Vol. 1, Part 1, p. 187.

222 Ro'i, "The Zionist Attitude to the Arabs, 1908-1914", pp. 203, 206, 224-227; see also Ellsberg in Dinur, ed., *Shivat Tzion (Return to Zion)*, Vol. 4, pp. 165, 168.

hostile to them than the Christians.²²³

The position of the leaders of the Second Aliyah in ignoring the Arabs was also consistent with the policy followed by the Zionist Organization. After the death of Herzl, who had ignored the presence of the Arabs in Palestine, the conflict between the political and practical Zionists to take control of the organization left them with no time to formulate, or implement, any alternative Arab policy. No Zionist leadership was elected that was capable of this until the conflict was resolved between the two factions, the political and practical, in favor of the latter, at the Tenth Zionist Congress (1911). By then, the Zionist movement had established two offices, in Istanbul and Jaffa, in which the officials found themselves having to deal with the Arabs. Victor Jacobson in Istanbul and Arthur Ruppin in Jaffa, the officials in these offices, both called for reaching an understanding with the Arabs. This common position resulted from the objective circumstances that the officials faced in their work. Jacobson was concerned with lessening the opposition of Arab representatives in the Turkish parliament to Zionism, so that he could encourage the authorities to reduce the restrictions they had imposed on Jewish immigration to Palestine,²²⁴ while Ruppin was interested in easing Arab opposition to the Zionist settlement process in the country itself.²²⁵ In order to achieve this goal, Ruppin also declared his reservations on the policy of "Hebrew labor" and demanded the reorganization of the settlers in Palestine – a call that Weizmann supported.²²⁶

Jacobson and Ruppin began sending reports to the Zionist Organization in Berlin based on these positions, demanding that a clear stance be taken on the Arabs and a Zionist policy be defined towards them. The Zionist administration met more

---

223 Ro'i, "The Zionist Attitude to the Arabs, 1908-1914", p. 228

224 Neville Mandel, "Attempts at an Arab-Zionist Entente, 1913-1914", *Middle Eastern Studies*, Vol. 1, No. 3, p. 250; Ro'i, "The Zionist Attitude to the Arabs, 1908-1914", p. 212.

225 Ro'i, "The Zionist Attitude to the Arabs, 1908-1914", p. 222.

226 Ibid, pp. 204-205.

than once to discuss the issue, but it did not make any clear, binding decision. The pressure from Jacobson and Ruppin increased, however, as did the rise in opposition to the Zionists. Anti-Zionist associations were established in cities in Palestine and its vicinity, including Jerusalem, Haifa, and Nablus as well as Beirut and Istanbul.[227] The Zionist leadership was forced to respond. In early 1914, it sent Nahum Sokolow, the writer and member of the Zionist Executive, to the Levant to assess the situation.[228] Since his election at the Tenth Zionist Congress (1911), the Executive had assigned Sokolow to manage the political affairs of the organization, and he had clearly oriented the Zionist policy towards the West. After his appointment, Sokolow had extensive contacts with most western European countries and his emissaries were active even to the United States. He focused all his efforts in winning the support of these countries for Zionism and their assistance in achieving its goals,[229] while he settled on only establishing close relations with the Turkish authorities.

Prior to Sokolow's arrival in Palestine in March 1914, the Zionist officials had managed to make contact with a number of Arab leaders. Sokolow met with some of them to try to find ways of understanding between them and the Zionists and to unite the efforts of the Levant. It was agreed to hold an Arab-Zionist meeting in Broummana, near Beirut, in the summer of 1914. Some Arab leaders, especially those of the Decentralization Party in Egypt and some intellectuals from Beirut, had attempted to draw near the Zionists and persuade them to stand with them against the Turks.[230] As a result, the Arab Congress in Paris in June 1913 refrained from taking a public stance against Zionist immigration to Palestine.[231] However, at the implementation

---

227 Mandel, "Attempts at an Arab-Zionist Entente, 1913-1914", p. 257.

228 Ibid, p. 253.

229 Cohen, A., *Yisrael ve ha-Olam ha-Aravi (Israel and the Arab World)*, p. 101.

230 For details, see Mandel, "Attempts at an Arab-Zionist Entente, 1913-1914", pp. 240-264.

231 Ellsberg in Dinur, ed., *Shivat Tzion (Return to Zion)*, Vol. 4, p. 174.

4. The Second Aliyah

phase, it became clear that reaching any agreement was very difficult, for neither the Arabs nor the Zionists had anything to offer each other. The Arab leaders had hoped to obtain the necessary funds to develop their countries after expelling the Turks from them, while the Zionist movement was, in practice, very poor, and did not have even a tiny part of these funds. The Arab leaders also asked the Zionists to pledge not to expel the Arab peasants from their lands, which the Zionists could not explicitly commit to. In addition, those leaders feared dealing openly with the Zionists due to the hostility towards the latter in various Arab circles.[232] As for the Zionists, it became clear to them, when they were confronted with the problems arising from the "Arab question", that they had no clear policy or position towards the Arabs, and nothing worth offering to them, including money. The Zionists even lacked the necessary manpower to pursue Arab affairs.[233]

With the end of the Second Aliyah, on the eve of the First World War in 1914, the Jewish population in Palestine had returned to an isolationist way of life, socially and economically, that it had been accustomed to in Europe. This was due to the insistence of the Second Aliyah settlers on the "occupation of land", "occupation of labor", and "Hebrew labor", with their racist policy towards the Arabs, and the establishment of "military" organizations to resist them. With this stance, together with the push of the Zionists to gain Western support for their schemes in Palestine by ignoring its Arab population, the only option left to the Palestinians was to struggle against Zionism.

7

During the Second Aliyah, from 1904-1914, about 35,000-40,000 Jewish immigrants entered Palestine – most of whom left the

---

[232] Ibid, p. 177, Mandel, "Attempts at an Arab-Zionist Entente, 1913-1914", pp. 258, 264.

[233] Ro'i, "The Zionist Attitude to the Arabs, 1908-1914", pp. 205, 214, 218-219, 221, 223; see also Cohen, A., *Yisrael ve ha-Olam ha-Aravi (Israel and the Arab World)*, pp. 103-108.

country again. On the eve of the First World War, about 11,000 remained. Many of those, in turn, also emigrated during the war, leaving only about 2,000 settlers of this wave of immigration in the country.[234] Despite their small number, however, they played a key role in the history of the Zionist presence in Palestine during Ottoman rule and the British Mandate. Their influence extended until after the establishment of Israel, in a manner greater than that of any other wave of Zionist immigrants.

The same conditions that forced most immigrants who came during the Second Aliyah to leave, however, bolstered those who remained and pushed them – by adhering to their expansionist, anti-Arab ideology and their declared goals of controlling the country – to establish their own partisan/political, cultural, social, settlement, and even military institutions.[235] In doing so, those immigrants were the first to work on moving the Zionist center that still existed outside Palestine to the country,[236] at a time when most other Zionist leaders found no time to even visit despite their work to establish a Jewish state there. The immigrants of the Second Aliyah prepared the ideological and organizational principles that later immigrants only had to accept and develop. With time, the institutions established by the Second Aliyah grew and expanded, and in certain cases were replaced by more advanced institutions founded on the same principles. They played a major role in shaping the Zionist entity in Palestine, then in establishing Israel. Most of them are still carrying out their functions today.

Po'alei Zion in Palestine, for example, which was the largest party of the Second Aliyah, came together in 1919 with a group of non-partisans to form Ahdut HaAvoda, which in 1903 united with Hapoel Hatzair to establish Mapai. This, in turn, merged with two groups that had split from it in 1944 and 1965 (Ahdut

---

[234] See Yosef Gorny, "Changes in the Social and Political Structure of the Second Aliyah, 1904-1940" in Carpi, ed., *Ha-Tzionout (Zionism)*, Vol. 1, pp. 204-205; Ofir, *Sefer ha-Oved ha-Leumi (Book of the National Worker)*, Vol. 1, p. 14.

[235] Dinur, ed., *Shivat Tzion (Return to Zion)*, Vol. 1, pp. 36-37.

[236] Ibid, p. 39.

4. The Second Aliyah

HaAvoda and Rafi) to form the Israeli Labor Party in 1968. From the founding of the Po'alei Zion party in 1905, regardless of its subsequent names, it was the largest Zionist party among the Jewish settlers in Palestine, and the ruling party in Israel from the state's establishment until the mid-1970s. When the Mapai party was founded in 1930, 16 out of 20 members of its central committee were immigrants of the Second Aliyah[237] and, when elections were held for the Knesset (Israeli parliament) for the first time in 1949, 11 members out of 120 were elected from Mapai, also from among those immigrants.[238] The party establishment in Israel still plays a significant role in the lives of its members,[239] as it did when it first took shape at the turn of the last century.[240] The Zionist parties, generally, have turned into large economic institutions.

The organizations of agricultural workers established by immigrants of the Second Aliyah in northern and central Palestine were the nucleus from which the Histadrut, the General Union of Jewish Workers in Palestine, emerged in 1920. This transformed into a huge organization that comprised the majority of Jewish workers. Besides being a trade union, the Histadrut played very important political and economic roles in the history of the Zionist entity in Palestine.

The Hashomer organization was dissolved in 1920, and the Haganah was established in its place. This spawned two other organizations during the British mandate over Palestine. From these, the Israeli army emerged in 1948.

The kibbutz, whose foundations were laid in Degania, in 1908, grew and crystallized, and became the spearhead in the implementation of Zionist settlement projects in Palestine. Kibbutz workers established most of the Jewish settlements, and their children were among the most enthusiastic Zionist youth. They were the main manpower that implemented most of the

---

237   Gorny in Carpi, ed., *Ha-Tzionout (Zionism)*, Vol. 1, p. 245.

238   Asher Tsidon, *Beit ha-Nivharim (House of Representatives)*, pp. 382-391.

239   For details, see Uri Avnery, *Israel Without Zionists*, pp. 166-179.

240   Dinur, ed., *Sefer Toldot ha-Haganah (History of the Haganah)*, Vol. 1, Part 1, pp. 142-143.

critical Zionist functions, during the British Mandate and even after the establishment of Israel.

The healthcare and social security institutions, newspapers and publishing houses, and cooperatives have all been in existence since their establishment during the Second Aliyah. Since then, of course, their number has risen and their functions have grown.

In addition, the Second Aliyah produced a number of leaders who played important roles in the history of Zionism, both in and outside Palestine, helping to support and strengthen the institutions established by their colleagues. Among them, for example, was David Ben-Gurion, general secretary of the Histadrut (1921-1935), head of the Jewish Agency (1935-1948), and the first prime minister and a defense minister of Israel (1948-1953 and 1955-1963, respectively); Yitzhak Ben-Zvi, head of the National Council ("Va'ad Leumi"), the executive arm of the Jewish community in Palestine ("Knesset Yisrael"; 1931-1948), and the second president of Israel (1952-1963); Levi Eshkol, a major figure in Zionist settlement in Palestine during the British Mandate, and the third prime minister of Israel (1963-1969); Yosef Sprinzak, general secretary of the Histadrut (1945-1948), and speaker of the Knesset (1949-1959); Berl Katznelson, founder of *Davar (Word;* 1925), the semi-official Histadrut newspaper, and of the "Am Oved" publishing house, and "cultural commissioner" of the worker settlers in Palestine; Yitzhak Tabenkin, ideologist of the kibbutz movement and leader of the Ahdut HaAvoda party (1954-1968); Abraham Hartsfield, chief implementer of the Zionist settlement program in Palestine from the mid-1920s; Shmuel Dayan, one of the founders of the "moshav" type of settlement (and father of Moshe Dayan, an Israeli military leader who assumed several ministerial posts); Ada Maimon (Fishman), one of the founders of the women's labor organization, and others.

It is true to say, therefore, that the Second Aliyah laid the foundations of the Zionist entity in Palestine, on which Israel was subsequently built.

5. The First World War and the Balfour Declaration: The Alliance of Colonialism and Zionism (1914-1917)

1

The First World War and its aftermath were a turning point for Zionism. At its outbreak, the war took the Zionist Organization by surprise. It confused its leaders and created critical problems for them. The presidency of the organization was in Berlin, which made it easier for the organization to endeavor to maintain the Jewish presence in Palestine, as well as send financial assistance to the settlers by exploiting Germany's influence with the Ottoman Empire. But, on the other hand, Germany was at war with Russia, where most Jews and Zionists lived, whose contact with their leadership was severed with the outbreak of the war. The Zionist leadership had to act cautiously, especially in its dealings with Germany, for fear that any position on its part might be considered antagonistic by Russia, which would lead to an aggravation of the tsarist persecution against its Jewish population. The leadership also had to deliberate and refrain from allying, at least publicly, with any of the warring parties, in order not to harm any of the Zionist groups that were spread throughout eastern and western Europe – especially as it was unclear at the outbreak of the war who would be the victor.[1]

The administration of the Zionist Organization comprised six individuals at the time, with two of them as the heads of the organization: Otto Warburg and Arthur Hantke, who were German Zionists, while the other four were Victor Jacobson,

---
1   Yitzhak Gruenbaum, *Ha-Tnu'ah ha-Tzionit (The Zionist Movement)*, Vol. 4, pp. 13-17.

Nahum Sokolow, Yechiel Chlenov and Shmaryahu Levin, who were Russians. The latter four could not go to Berlin after the outbreak of the war to participate in the sessions of the Zionist Executive. In December 1914 it was decided to move the presidency of the Zionist Organization to Copenhagen, in neutral Denmark, to make it easier for Zionist contacts around the world. Warburg and Hantke, meanwhile, remained in Berlin. In Copenhagen, meetings were periodically held between Zionist leaders. The Jewish National Fund headquarters were also moved from Cologne to The Hague, and the fund's administration was handed over to the leader of the Dutch Zionists, Nehemia De Lieme.[2]

At the outset of the war, some Jewish organizations in Germany, together with German Zionists, set up the "German Committee for the Freeing of Russian Jews (Committee for the East)". It was headed by Franz Oppenheimer, author of the Zionist cooperative settlement theory. Max Bodenheimer, who had formulated the regulations of the Zionist Organization, was also a member. The goal of this committee was to work on liberating the Jewish populations of Poland and eastern Russia with the help of the German army.[3] However, when the Greater Actions Committee of the Zionist Executive met in Copenhagen in December 1914, for the first time after the outbreak of the war, it denounced the formation of this committee and declared its opposition to the participation of Zionist leaders in "any political activity, to the extent that it may harm the security of the Jews in one of the warring countries".[4] The executive declared an official Zionist position of neutrality towards all of these countries, but the presidency of the organization was also tasked with working to secure the "national and political rights" of Jewish people in the countries in which they had not gained them. The presidency was also to implement the Basel Program to achieve

---

2   Yitzhak Mior, *Ha-Tnu'ah ha-Tzionit be-Rusia (Zionist Movement in Russia)*, p. 407.

3   Ibid, pp. 407-408.

4   Gruenbaum, *Ha-Tnu'ah ha-Tzionit (The Zionist Movement)*, Vol. 4, p. 16.

5. WWI and the Balfour Declaration 309

rights for the settlers in Palestine, making the necessary contacts with the concerned countries to bring this about even if they were participants in the war. The Zionist committee appealed to Jewish populations around the world to donate funds and equipment to assist the Jewish settlers in Palestine.[5]

In order to implement its decisions, the Zionist Executive decided to dispatch one of its members, Yechiel Chlenov, to Britain to campaign there. He requested that Sokolow accompany him. In Britain, the two joined Weizmann and Ahad Ha'am who together formed the nucleus of a Zionist group that worked to encourage the British government to adopt Zionist demands.[6] The executive also sent Shmaryahu Levin to the United States to perform a similar task. Once there, he was able to earn the confidence of a prominent Jewish leader, Louis Brandeis, and they formed the "Provisional Executive Committee for General Zionist Affairs".[7] Brandeis was a friend and advisor to the American president, Woodrow Wilson, who had appointed him a judge in the US Supreme Court, making him the first Jewish person to hold this position. By that time, some Zionist organizations had been formed in the United States with the membership of Russian Jewish immigrants.

In spite of the war, the Zionist Executive kept working and held two more meetings in Copenhagen in June 1915 and March 1916. The center of Zionist activity, however, was shifting to Britain, notably to Chaim Weizmann and his companions. Weizmann was a lecturer of chemistry at the University of Manchester and, in September 1914, he met Charles Prestwich Scott, editor of the *Manchester Guardian* newspaper, and convinced him of the validity of Zionist efforts to establish a Jewish state in Palestine, and of the need for Britain to adopt this project in order to secure its interests in the region. Scott enjoyed close relations with many British political figures, and

---

5 Ibid, pp. 16-17.

6 Moshe Shmueli, *Toldot ha-Tzionout ve Tnu'at ha-Avoda (History of Zionism and the Labor Movement)*, Vol. 2, pp. 384-388.

7 Ibid, pp. 380-384.

he introduced Weizmann to a number of them so that he could present his views. Weizmann had decided not to abide by the decision of the Zionist Executive, which had appealed to Zionist leaders to take neutral positions in their relations with the warring countries. When the Copenhagen office was opened, he boycotted it – instead strengthening his relations with Brandeis and Levin in the United States.[8] Weizmann believed that Britain was the only country that could assist Zionism to achieve its goals[9] and so, as soon as he had an opportunity to meet with British officials, he took it. In December 1914, he and Scott met with two British ministers, Lloyd George and Herbert Samuel (who was the first practicing Jew to serve as a cabinet minister), to discuss the schemes of the Zionist movement and the future of Palestine.[10] A month later, Samuel presented a memorandum to the British prime minister, Herbert Henry Asquith, and followed it up with a similar memorandum to the remaining cabinet ministers in March 1915. He proposed the establishment of a British protectorate in Palestine that would allow Jewish immigrants to settle there and establish a spiritual and cultural center, which would positively affect the stance of Jewish people around the world towards Britain. Samuel also suggested that the Jewish settlers be granted autonomy that could develop, over time, into a state loyal to Britain. The idea was supported by Edward Grey, the foreign secretary, and Lloyd George, who "does not care a damn for the Jews or their past or their future, but thinks it will be an outrage to let the Holy Places pass into the possession or under the protectorate of 'agnostic and atheistic' France".[11] Opposition from Asquith, however, eventually led to the project being dropped. The Zionists had to wait for the moment when their schemes in Palestine would align with those

---

8   Chaim Weizmann, *Trial and Error*, pp. 210-211.

9   Ibid, pp. 123-124.

10 Ibid, pp. 190-192; see also Herbert Louis (Viscount) Samuel, *Memoirs*, pp. 139-145.

11 Weizmann, *Trial and Error*, pp. 193-194; Leonard Stein, *The Balfour Declaration*, pp. 103-116.

5. WWI and the Balfour Declaration 311

of the Western countries. This began to come about, but only after important changes took place in the Allied position towards the Ottoman Empire.

The Ottomans joining the First World War against the Allies provided a unique opportunity for the latter to pursue their ambitions in seizing large, strategically and economically significant regions from under Ottoman rule. Several Western countries had sought, long before the war, to annex or control various areas of the Ottoman Empire, and had succeeded in some of their endeavors but most of their attempts had failed due to competition with each other. This led a few of the Allies, on more than one occasion, to intervene in favor of the Ottomans, in order to prevent other Western countries from seizing control of certain regions of their territory.

By the end of the 19th century, Britain had come to control Egypt, which was formally under Ottoman rule, while France was trying to do the same in Greater Syria. Until the outbreak of the war, British policy was aimed at keeping its foothold in Egypt in order to secure the route to India through the Suez Canal, and to preserve Ottoman rule in the Levant and prevent France and other European countries from infiltrating the Ottoman Empire. This situation changed, however, when Britain entered an alliance with France and Russia in the war against the Ottomans, and Italy joined them. The Allies then moved to adopt a unified policy towards the Ottoman Empire and the regions under its control.

Negotiations between Britain, France and Russia over the fate of the areas under Ottoman rule, especially the Levant, began in mid-March 1916. One British and one French representative, Mark Sykes and François Georges-Picot respectively, went to Russia for talks.[12] Prior to this, Britain had concluded a round of negotiations with Sharif Hussein of Mecca as a representative of the Arabs in an attempt to lure him to the side of the Allies. In those negotiations, Britain had taken a clear stance on the fate of the Levant regions after the end of the war. The negotiations took

---

12   George Antonius, *The Arab Awakening*, p. 245.

the form of 10 letters, exchanged between Sharif Hussein and Henry McMahon, the British high commissioner in Egypt, from July 14, 1915 until March 10, 1916. The two agreed that Sharif Hussein would revolt against the Turks, and the Arabs would wage war on them on the side of the Allies – which actually took place – on the condition that Britain would provide assistance to the Arabs and pledge to recognize the independence of the Levant after its liberation from the Ottoman yoke. It was also agreed that Britain would enjoy economic and political influence in the region after its independence. When, in November 1917, Britain issued the Balfour Declaration and announced its intention to establish a national home for Jewish people in Palestine, a wide discussion arose – the echoes of which can still sometimes be heard – on whether Palestine was among the regions included in Britain's promise of Arab independence after the war, or whether it was excluded from those pledges. (The British government did not officially publish the McMahon-Hussein Correspondence until early 1939,[13] at the convening of the London Conference. The Arabs and Jews were invited to this conference in an attempt to find a solution to the Palestine issue, as the Great Arab Revolt of 1936-1939 was nearing its end. The British government then appointed a special committee of British and Arab members to examine this correspondence, but the committee declared[14] that it was unable to reach a consensus on the interpretation of the correspondence, or to determine the obligations that Britain had undertaken towards Palestine.)[15]

In any case, and regardless of the clarity of the pledges that Britain had made, it was clear that when Sykes and Picot went

---

13 Great Britain, Parliamentary Papers, 1939, *Command 5957: Correspondence between Sir Henry McMahon, His Majesty's High Commissioner at Cairo, and the Sherif Hussein of Mecca, July 1915 - March 1916.*

14 Great Britain, Parliamentary Papers, 1939, *Command 5974: Report of a Committee Set Up to Consider Certain Correspondence Between Sir Henry McMahon [His Majesty's High Commissioner in Egypt] and The Sharif of Mecca in 1915 and 1916, March 16, 1939.*

15 *A Survey of Palestine, Prepared in December 1945 and January 1946 for the Information of the Anglo-American Committee of Inquiry*, Vol. 1, p. 50.

5. WWI and the Balfour Declaration

to Russia to negotiate the fate of the territories under Ottoman rule (including the Levant), Britain had already pledged – in its correspondence with Sharif Hussein, and in a manner that left no doubt – to recognize the independence of the Arabs in the Levant after the war. Yet this did not deter it from entering into negotiations with France and Russia on the fate of the region, at the end of which the three countries reached a totally contradictory agreement to what Britain had pledged in the McMahon-Hussein Correspondence. This was the first episode in a series of imperialist conspiracies to strengthen the power of Western colonial states over the Levant and other regions in Asia and Africa.

The negotiations between Britain, France and Russia continued for about two months and ended on May 9, 1916, with the signing of the Sykes-Picot Agreement. The territories under Ottoman rule were divided into regions of control for the three countries, either individually or collectively[16] (see *Map 6 Division of the Levant among Britain, France, Russia and Italy per the Sykes-Picot Agreement, 1916* below).

According to this agreement, Istanbul, the Bosphorus Strait and surrounding lands, as well as the Armenian regions of Trebizond, Erzurum and Bitlis to the south of the Black Sea, along with other lands northeast of these regions and uninhabited by Arabs, were designated as a zone of control for Russia. In return, it granted Britain and France the freedom of action in the other regions, on the condition that the religious rights of the Christian Russian Orthodox sect in the Levant were protected. Those regions were then divided into five areas, each with its own status. The agreement stipulated that in areas "A" and "B", an Arab independent state or federation of states would be formed, bound by subordinate relations to France and Britain, respectively, who would have priority to grant loans to that Arab country or countries and to provide them with foreign experts and workers. The blue and red areas would be subjected, respectively, to direct rule by France and Britain. The

---
16 Antonius, *The Arab Awakening*, pp. 428-430.

Map 6 Division of the Levant among Britain, France, Russia and Italy per the Sykes-Picot Agreement, 1916

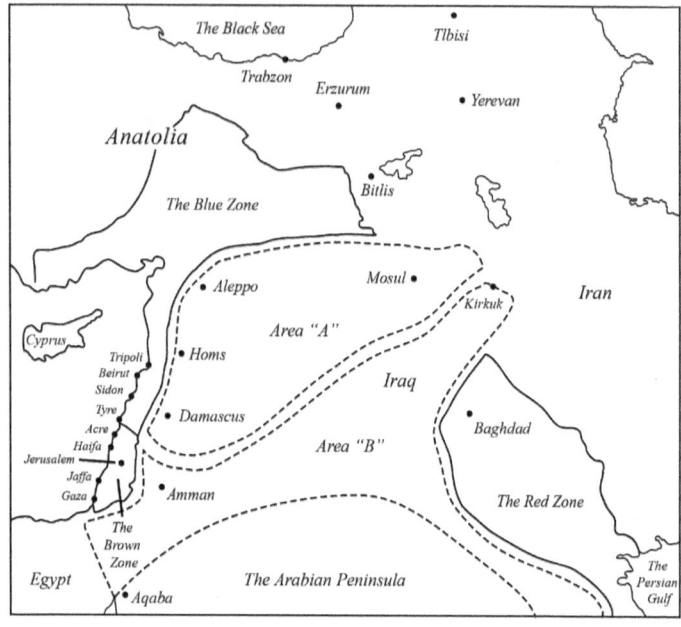

brown area, which included the northern part of Palestine with its borders of the British Mandate – the Jordan River, in the east; the Mediterranean, in the west; the Galilee region, in the north; and the Jerusalem-Gaza line, in the south, would be subjected to international administration formed after consultation with Russia, the other Allied countries, and representatives of Sharif Hussein. This agreement was a compromise between Britain and France, where Britain had demanded exclusive power over the region in order to control the Suez Canal while France wanted to annex Palestine to the areas it controlled. The agreement also stipulated placing the ports of Haifa and Acre, in Palestine, under British control.[17] In April 1917, when Italy joined the war on the side of the Allies, the agreement was amended to place

17 Ibid, pp. 244-248.

the region of Anatolia under Italian control. The intention behind this agreement was simply to divide the countries of the Levant between British and French colonialism in order to control the fate of the region and exploit its resources. With the end of the war, those ambitions found expression in the establishment of several distinct Arab states in the Levant: Iraq, Syria, Lebanon, Palestine and Transjordan (later, Jordan). In late 1917, the Bolsheviks, after the success of their revolution in Russia, published this secret agreement and disavowed it.

The contradictory promises that the British had made in the McMahon-Hussein Correspondence and the Sykes-Picot Agreement significantly complicated the position of the major Western powers towards the fate of the Levant in general and of Palestine in particular. This initially affected the Zionists, as both the correspondence and the agreement contravened the Zionist demands regarding Palestine. The British government broke off negotiations with the Zionists for a whole year, but this situation changed in December 1916, when the Asquith government resigned and the succeeding one was headed by Lloyd George, with Arthur James Balfour as foreign secretary. This change was significant to the Zionists, as Lloyd George was more receptive to them than Asquith. As noted above, Lloyd George had supported the two memoranda presented by Herbert Samuel to the British government in the first half of 1915, suggesting that Britain keep control of Palestine after the war and allow Jewish immigration to it. After the signing of the Sykes-Picot Agreement, Lloyd George hoped to use the Zionist demands to enable Britain to evade its obligations to its allies. By supporting the Zionists and encouraging them to request British protection, Britain could, at the end of the war, assume sole control over Palestine.[18]

In addition to this, before his appointment as prime minister, Lloyd George had become closely acquainted with Weizmann. In early 1916,[19] Britain experienced a shortage of explosives

---

18 See also David Lloyd George, *The Truth about the Peace Treaties*, Vol. 2, pp. 1115-1116.

19 David Lloyd George, *War Memoirs*, Vol. 1, p. 348.

necessary for its war effort. Lloyd George, who was in charge of armaments, summoned Weizmann – at the recommendation of Scott, editor of the *Manchester Guardian* – and commissioned him to find a way to produce explosives based on a method that Weizmann had devised.[20] Lloyd George recounted, in his memoirs of the war, that he felt a deep appreciation for Weizmann after the success of his mission, and informed him that he would ask the competent authorities to reward him. Weizmann, however, replied that he did not want a reward "for himself, but for his people". It can be deduced from the memoirs of Lloyd George, and his words about Weizmann, that the Balfour Declaration came, to some extent, as this reward.[21] Thus, upon the formation of the new British government in December 1916, headed by Lloyd George, conditions were very favorable for Weizmann and his companions to resume contact regarding their requests to Britain. This was also expedited by British military action in the Levant. As the new government was being formed, British forces stationed in Egypt had launched an attack on the Ottoman forces in the Sinai Peninsula and occupied some of their frontline positions in its northwest, in preparation for a complete offensive against and occupation of Palestine. In March 1917, the British forces attacked Gaza City but they were repelled.[22] With this struggle to seize Palestine, it was necessary to expedite contact with the Zionists and agree that they would demand Britain's sole control of the country after the war to establish their national home there. The British authorities promptly changed their policy towards Zionism, which had varied between indifference and lukewarm support, and replaced it with an open alliance – in an attempt to also gain the support of Jewish populations worldwide, especially in Russia and the United States, and exploit them to serve Britain's interests. Barely two months after the new government was formed, it resumed contact with the Zionists.

---

20 Weizmann, *Trial and Error*, pp. 220-222.

21 Lloyd George, *War Memoirs*, Vol. 1, pp. 348-349.

22 See also Stein, *The Balfour Declaration*, pp. 386-393.

5. WWI and the Balfour Declaration 317

Before then, the Zionists had submitted another memorandum to the British government in October 1916, explaining their schemes for Palestine and asking that the country be declared a national home for the Jewish people, such that they would be entitled to immigrate there from anywhere in the world and enjoy full political, national and civil rights. This would be achieved by granting settlement concessions in Palestine to a Jewish company, allowing the settlers autonomy, and recognizing Hebrew as an official language.[23] In late January 1917, in response to this memorandum, Sykes sent for the two Zionist leaders, Weizmann and Sokolow, and informed them that Britain looked with sympathy upon their endeavors and was searching for a way to help them achieve their aims, and that negotiations should be held between the two parties to that end.

Formal negotiations between the Zionists and the British government began on February 7, 1917, at the home of Moses Gaster, chief rabbi of the British Sephardic community. Eight Zionist representatives attended, including James de Rothschild (son of the French Baron Rothschild), Herbert Samuel, Nahum Sokolow and Chaim Weizmann, while Mark Sykes (who was also a member of the British War Cabinet) represented Britain in his "private capacity".[24] In this meeting, most of the Zionists expressed their opposition to the establishment of international rule in Palestine and their desire for Britain to rule the country alone. In the words of Weizmann: "Jews all over the world trusted England. They knew that law and order would be established by British rule, and that under it Jewish colonizing activities and cultural development would not be interfered with"[25] – unlike France, which was trying to impose the "French spirit" on the countries under its rule.[26] Weizmann also stressed that Jewish

---

23 Ibid, p. 369.

24 Gruenbaum, *Ha-Tnu'ah ha-Tzionit (The Zionist Movement)*, Vol. 4, pp. 178-179.

25 Weizmann, *Trial and Error*, p. 242.

26 Gruenbaum, *Ha-Tnu'ah ha-Tzionit (The Zionist Movement)*, Vol. 4, pp. 197-198.

people would immigrate to Palestine "to constitute a Jewish nation, not to become Arabs or Druses or Englishmen", and that no rule should be established in the country that would impose restrictions on Jewish immigration to it.[27] It is clear that the Zionists, in their insistence on exclusive British rule in Palestine, without the involvement of any of the Allies, gained the confidence of Sykes in their first round of talks with him. Sykes, in turn, explained that "the idea of a Jewish Palestine had his full sympathy." He did not expect difficulties to arise from the Zionist insistence on using the term "nationality". Rather, the problem in his view lay with the major powers, especially France, which insisted on appropriating Greater Syria including Palestine – a position he could not understand. (The Zionist leaders were not aware of the Sykes-Picot Agreement, and did not hear about it until mid-April 1917.)[28] Finally, Sykes suggested that the Zionist leaders discuss this issue with the French government. He also did not fail to warn them of the Arab nationalist movement in Palestine and its neighboring countries, which may resist their plans. To this end, he advised them to try to reach an agreement with the Arabs in order to facilitate Zionist work in Palestine.[29]

Weizmann and Sokolow were not enthusiastic about discussing the future of Palestine with the French government, and declared that they would prefer the British government to do so – especially as it was also interested in creating a Jewish Palestine that would help it to contain French influence in Syria. Sykes, however, told them that his government had barely managed to keep the question of Palestine pending in its contacts with France. He repeated his request for the Zionists to meet Picot, the representative of the French foreign ministry, and explain their demands. Sykes then introduced Sokolow to Picot, who was on a visit to London. The French, for their part, were not ignorant of the nature of the Zionist movement and

---

27   Ibid, p. 180.

28   Weizmann, *Trial and Error*, p. 241.

29   Gruenbaum, *Ha-Tnu'ah ha-Tzionit (The Zionist Movement)*, Vol. 4, pp. 182-183.

5. WWI and the Balfour Declaration

its goals. (Nordau recounted, in one of his articles, that in 1913 he had met with the French foreign minister, Stephen Pichon, and discussed the conditions of the Zionist movement with him. Nordau asserted that it was Pichon who proposed to Sykes to make contact with the Zionists and try to exploit them to serve the aims of the Allies.[30]) Sokolow met with Picot twice, on February 8 and 9, 1917, and tried to get a sense of the French government's stance on the Zionist project after informing Picot that the Zionist movement preferred Palestine to be under British rule. Picot replied that the issue did not concern Britain and France alone, for there were also their allies, Russia and Italy. Sokolow told him that Russia was not much concerned with what was happening in Palestine, and "the Zionists have friends in Italy" who could manage the issue; thus, only Britain and France remained. Picot promised to do everything he could to explain the Zionist viewpoint to the French government, but advised Jewish people, especially those in the neutral countries, to show their sympathy for the Allies – prompting Sokolow to comment that if the Allies were to agree to the Zionist requests, the matter would be easier. Picot went on to say that Italy's viewpoint should also be sought, and that the Zionists should do that.[31] Weizmann and Sokolow, however, after consulting Sykes, decided to wait until the American position became clear, for Brandeis and Levin were working to induce President Wilson to declare his support for Zionism.

After the meeting between Sokolow and Picot in London, the French response did not take long. Ten days later, Sokolow was heading to Paris to see Picot and complete their negotiations. In this meeting, Picot announced that the French government had no objection to the Zionist project in Palestine other than the issue of the concession to settle the country being granted to a Jewish company, a request that France could not approve. Picot also made it clear that France was demanding the right

---

30 Max Nordau, *Kitvei Nordau (Works of Nordau)*, Vol. 4, pp. 122-124, 193.

31 Gruenbaum, *Ha-Tnu'ah ha-Tzionit (The Zionist Movement)*, Vol. 4, pp. 184-188.

to rule Palestine alone, and that it would not agree to Britain's participation, nor even that of the United States. However, he told Sokolow that the Zionists could rely on France[32] if they had a good relationship. Again, he suggested that Sokolow go to Italy and seek its government's position. In this way, Picot believed that if Sokolow was able to induce the Italians to support the Zionist demands, France would be rid of competition from Italy and be left with only Britain to compete with for power in Palestine – and this it would find a way to resolve. As for Russia, the fourth partner in the Sykes-Picot Agreement, it seemed clear that, after the anti-tsarist revolution had begun, it was gradually losing interest in the affairs of the Levant.

Sokolow, for his part, did not relish Picot's request to meet with the Italian officials, and expressed his displeasure to Weizmann. After consulting Sykes, however, who insisted that Sokolow carry out the task requested by Picot, Sokolow traveled to Rome in early April 1917. There, he found another surprise as the Italian officials insisted that he meet the pope first to gather his position. On May 4, Sokolow met with Pope Benedict XV in the Vatican and presented the Zionist project. The pope stressed, in a manner that "brought a shiver down Sokolow's spine", the necessity of preserving the Christian holy sites in Palestine and the need to conclude an international treaty to guarantee this. When Sokolow insisted on obtaining moral support from the Vatican for his schemes, the pope replied: "I hope that we will be good neighbors" in Palestine.[33] Four days after this meeting, Sokolow met with the Italian secretary general of foreign affairs, Francesco De Martini, informed him of the results of his talks with the pope and requested support. De Martini replied that he could announce on behalf of the foreign minister that "Italy will not be an initiator in this matter, but will give moral support to the historical demands of the Jews."[34] Four days later, Sokolow

---

32 Stein, *The Balfour Declaration*, p. 399.

33 Florian Sokolow, *Avi, Nahum Sokolow (My Father, Nahum Sokolow)*, pp. 148-151.

34 Gruenbaum, *Ha-Tnu'ah ha-Tzionit (The Zionist Movement)*, Vol. 4, p. 193.

5. WWI and the Balfour Declaration 321

also met with the Italian prime minister, Paolo Boselli, who told him that he had seen his requests and was pleased to approve them, adding that his government would "try to be of use to the Zionists".[35] At the end of his address, the Italian prime minister also stressed the need to preserve the Christian holy sites in Palestine through an international agreement. He added that "Italy will participate in negotiations with the other countries and will support the proposals presented by Sokolow,"[36] and would inform the French government of this position.

Sokolow returned from Rome to Paris to resume negotiations with the French. Before he had gone to Italy, he had been able to persuade Baron Rothschild and other Jewish leaders in France – after he had ensured the acquiescence of the Alliance Israélite Universelle – to seek from the French government a clearly positive stance towards the Zionist demands. Rothschild had succeeded in this endeavor, and when Sokolow returned to Paris and informed the French government of the results of his talks with the pope and the Italian officials, the French decided to announce their position in the form of a letter sent by Jules Cambon, the secretary general of foreign affairs, to Sokolow on June 4, 1917. This letter, which was the first official pledge obtained by the Zionists from one of the Allied countries, stated that

> circumstances permitting, and the independence of the Holy Places being safeguarded on the other hand, it would be a deed of justice and of reparation to assist, by the protection of the Allied Powers, in the renaissance of the Jewish nationality in that Land from which the people of Israel were exiled so many centuries ago. The French Government, which entered this present war to defend a people wrongfully attacked, and which continues the struggle to assure the victory of right over might, can but feel sympathy for your cause, the triumph of which is bound up with that of the Allies. I am

---

35 Ibid.

36 Ibid.

happy to give you herewith such assurance.[37]

Sykes was happier, though, as a copy of this letter was soon leaked to the British foreign office, and could be used as a means of pressure when necessary. It was also to be brandished in the face of French officials if they should declare opposition to Zionist demands or Britain's adoption of them in the future.[38]

After these developments, the Zionists focused all their pressure on the British government to induce it to announce a clear position in support of Zionism. While Sokolow was negotiating in Paris and Rome, Weizmann was active in Britain to gain its support. On March 22, 1917, he met with the foreign secretary, Balfour. Weizmann had first met Balfour in 1906, while the latter was on an election campaign in Manchester, then again in 1914. In this second meeting, Balfour was "moved to the point of tears" in his sympathy to the Zionist cause, as presented by Weizmann[39] – even though Balfour had been prime minister of the government that had issued the Aliens Act of 1905, limiting Jewish immigration from Russia and eastern Europe to Britain, and had later made the Uganda proposal to the Zionist Organization. In April 1917, a month after his meeting with Balfour, Weizmann also saw the British Prime Minister Lloyd George and urged him to swiftly take a public stance in favor of Zionism.[40]

Balfour, in another vein, traveled to the United States that month to discuss the strengthening of its government's relations with Britain. During his visit, the Zionists prompted their leader, Brandeis, to meet him. The two men met twice, first when Balfour arrived in late April and again on May 10. Brandeis was able to gain Balfour's trust and to influence him,[41]

---

37   Ibid, p. 195; Stein, *The Balfour Declaration*, pp. 416-417.

38   For details on these negotiations, see Stein, *The Balfour Declaration*, pp. 394-421.

39   Stein, *The Balfour Declaration*, p. 157.

40   Gruenbaum, *Ha-Tnu'ah ha-Tzionit (The Zionist Movement)*, Vol. 4, pp. 196-198.

41   Shmueli, *Toldot ha-Tzionout ve Tnu'at ha-Avoda (History of Zionism and*

5. WWI and the Balfour Declaration

suggesting that Britain's consent to Zionist demands would earn the appreciation of Jewish Americans who would, in turn, make efforts to convince their government to strengthen its relations with Britain and provide it with economic assistance – which it was in dire need of, on the threshold of the final stage of the First World War. Brandeis was also able to influence President Wilson[42] to express his support of the Zionist requests to Balfour and his wish for the British government to consent to them. Wilson, however, was also seeking to end the war by making peace with the Central powers, Germany and the Ottoman Empire. He decided to dispatch an American mission to Gibraltar in June 1917 to make contact with them. The mission was headed by Henry Morgenthau Sr., former US ambassador to the Ottoman Empire, who was of Jewish origin. Its members included the Zionist representatives Felix Frankfurter, judge in the US Supreme Court, and Lewis Epstein. In Gibraltar, they were joined by a French representative, Colonel E. Weyl, who was also of Jewish origin. Britain, France and the Zionists were dissatisfied with these moves, as peace without military settlement – with the Ottoman Empire at least – would mean continued Ottoman control over the Levant and the remaining regions that those parties were coveting. They could not, however, openly oppose Wilson's scheme, and felt it better to work on indirectly thwarting it. Britain delegated Weizmann to travel to Gibraltar to see the members of the mission, where he held a meeting "which was intended to decide on the unilateral peace with Turkey".[43] Weizmann was able to persuade the members to abandon their mission and go home but, unlike his habit, he mentioned nothing in his memoirs about the justifications he gave to convince them.[44]

With the failed attempts to conclude a unilateral peace with the Ottomans, and Balfour's return from the United States,

---

the Labor Movement), Vol. 2, p. 398.

42 Ibid, p. 402.

43 Gruenbaum, *Ha-Tnu'ah ha-Tzionit (The Zionist Movement)*, Vol. 4, p. 201.

44 Weizmann, *Trial and Error*, pp. 246-251.

negotiations intensified between the Zionists and the British government regarding its statement to adopt Zionist demands. On July 18, 1917, Lord Rothschild, on behalf of the Zionist group, submitted to Balfour, at his request, a draft declaration to present to the government requesting that Britain "accept the principle of recognizing Palestine as the National Home of the Jewish people and the right of the Jewish people to build up its national life in Palestine", as well as "the grant of internal autonomy to the Jewish nationality in Palestine, freedom of immigration for Jews, and the establishment of a Jewish National Colonizing Corporation for the re-establishment and economic development of the country", such that the details of implementation would be "determined with the representatives of the Zionist Organization".[45] Before the British government could consider this proposal, however, new difficulties arose due to the opposition of non-Zionist Jews in Britain to any pledge regarding a "Jewish national home" in Palestine, explaining that they viewed Judaism as a religion, not a people. They had a "representative" in the British War Cabinet, Edwin Montagu, secretary of state for India, who vehemently opposed the Zionist demands, declaring that "I have spent my life trying to escape the ghetto,"[46] and that he had no wish to return to it. Before Montagu presented his objections, David Alexander, president of the Board of Deputies of British Jews (see Introduction, section 3), and Claude Montefiore, president of the Anglo-Jewish Association, also issued a statement in May 1917 expressing reservation about the Zionist program. The two leaders explained that they had cooperated with the Zionist organizations in the cultural field but could not continue this cooperation because of the political goals of Zionism. In their statement, Alexander and Montefiore opposed the Zionist program on two basic points: first, it was not permissible to impose a national-political character on the Jewish people in Palestine and create a secular Jewish nationality, because Jews were only a religious sect and, second, it was not

---

45   Ibid, p. 256.

46   Lloyd George, *The Truth about the Peace Treaties*, Vol. 2, pp. 1133-1134.

5. WWI and the Balfour Declaration

permissible to grant the settlement company that the Zionists were seeking to establish any political and economic privileges, because this would harm the principle of equality and may affect the civil and political rights of the Jewish populations in the countries that had emancipated them.[47]

These objections, however, did not affect the policies that the British government decided to follow regarding the Zionists, especially after Alexander and Montefiore were forced to resign their posts due to the uproar that the Zionists created against them. The objections were sufficient, however, to reduce the obligations that the government took upon itself. On September 3, 1917, the British government examined the Zionist requests and decided to consent to the demands in principle. It planned to issue a declaration to that effect, but introduced fundamental changes to the draft that the Zionists had submitted – taking into account several amendments presented by various individuals.[48] It proposed a commitment to facilitate the establishment of a Jewish national home in Palestine, rather than considering the whole country a national home for the Jewish people, provided that this did not prejudice the rights of non-Jewish communities there nor the rights of Jewish people acquired elsewhere.[49] Due to the circumstances of the war, however, the announcement of the declaration was postponed.[50]

The Zionists were uncomfortable with this delay and resumed their pressure. On October 3, 1917, Weizmann and Rothschild submitted another memorandum to the British government.[51] Six days later, Weizmann sent a telegram to Brandeis to inform him that "it is essential to have not only President's approval of text, but his recommendation to grant this declaration without

---

47 Gruenbaum, *Ha-Tnu'ah ha-Tzionit (The Zionist Movement)*, Vol. 4, p. 205.

48 See drafts in Stein, *The Balfour Declaration*, p. 664.

49 In Weizmann, *Trial and Error*, p. 260; see also Lloyd George, *The Truth about the Peace Treaties*, Vol. 2, p. 1136.

50 Lloyd George, *The Truth about the Peace Treaties*, Vol. 2, p. 1117.

51 Tosco. R. (T. R.) Fyvel, "Weizmann and the Balfour Declaration", in Meyer W. Weisgal and Joel Carmichael, eds., *Chaim Weizmann, A Biography by Several Hands*, p. 160.

delay," and that Brandeis as well as other Zionists and some prominent non-Zionists in the United States must also declare their support.[52] This was the second time that Weizmann had contacted Brandeis for this purpose, as he had first sent him a telegram on September 19 with the text of the proposed declarations submitted by each of the Zionists and the British. For their part, the British had contacted the American president to seek his opinion on September 4, a day after their government session that approved the initial policy on the Zionist demands. Wilson, however, forgot the memo, which one of his assistants had given him, and only found it on October 13. He then declared that he supported the text proposed by the British government and asked that it be informed of his support.[53] The news reached the government after three days. (One and a half years later, on March 3, 1919, Wilson would announce in a statement to the American people that "in Palestine shall be laid the foundation of a Jewish Commonwealth.")[54]

On October 31, 1917, the British government met and decided its final position on the Zionist demands. On November 2, Balfour, in his capacity as foreign secretary, issued the following statement (since known as the "Balfour Declaration") in the form of a letter addressed, on the advice of Weizmann, to Lord Rothschild:

> His Majesty's Government view with favour the establishment in Palestine of a national home for the Jewish people, and will use their best endeavours to facilitate the achievement of this object, it being clearly understood that nothing shall be done which may prejudice the civil and religious rights of existing non-Jewish communities in Palestine, or the rights and political status enjoyed by Jews in any other country.[55]

---

[52] Weizmann, *Trial and Error*, p. 260.

[53] Gruenbaum, *Ha-Tnu'ah ha-Tzionit (The Zionist Movement)*, Vol. 4, pp. 209-210.

[54] Lloyd George, *The Truth about the Peace Treaties*, Vol. 2, p. 1139.

[55] Letter from the United Kingdom's Foreign Secretary Arthur Balfour to Lord Lionel Walter Rothschild, issued by the British Foreign Office, No-

5. WWI and the Balfour Declaration 327

After the British government approved this decision, Sykes left the session and rushed out to Weizmann who was waiting nearby, exclaiming: "Dr. Weizmann, it's a boy!" Weizmann later wrote of his reaction to this good news: "Well – I did not like the boy at first. He was not the one I had expected."[56] The fact is that the declaration was not issued in the form expected by the Zionists. They had demanded that all of Palestine be recognized as a Jewish national home, while the declaration spoke of "the establishment in Palestine of a national home for the Jewish people". The Zionist movement had also called on the British government to make every effort to facilitate the establishment of this home after discussing the necessary means and consulting with the Zionist Organization, but Balfour had instead spoken of "the civil and religious rights of existing non-Jewish communities in Palestine". The Balfour Declaration, in this final form, was the result of multiple considerations that the British government had taken. On the one hand, the government sought to gain the support of the Zionists in order to remove the French influence from Palestine. Britain also wanted to exploit Jewish influence among the Allied countries, mainly in the United States and among the Bolsheviks in Russia, during the last, decisive period of the First World War. Finally, it sought to prevent Germany from issuing a similar statement.[57] However, Britain was also obliged to take into account the positions of its non-Zionist Jewish population, as well as the conditions that prevailed in Palestine.[58] Thus the Balfour Declaration, in the words of Vera, Weizmann's wife, "like most diplomatic documents ... tried to please too many people – and succeeded in pleasing too few!"[59] Despite this, the declaration was the first international recognition of political Zionism and its project as per Herzl's concept, while also being compatible with Weizmann's synthetic Zionism. Weizmann, on

---

vember 2, 1917.

56 Weizmann, *Trial and Error*, p. 262.

57 Lloyd George, *The Truth about the Peace Treaties*, Vol. 2, pp. 1120-1122.

58 See also Christopher Sykes, *Crossroads to Israel*, pp. 27-28.

59 Vera Weizmann, *The Impossible Takes Longer*, p. 77.

his part, had made great efforts to convince British officials, with their varying views, of the benefits that their country would gain if they adopted the Zionist movement and its demands. He had spoken with each of them – as Herzl had done, previously – in his own language.[60]

It is noted that the Balfour Declaration only referred to the Arabs of Palestine as "non-Jewish communities", which, according to Lloyd George, fought "for the Turks".[61] Those "non-Jewish communities" were about 90% of the population of Palestine and owned most of its land. Thus the talk about "not prejudicing" their "civil and religious" rights, with no mention of their political ones, was only a harbinger of the fate devised for the Arabs of Palestine with the establishment of the Jewish national home. It must also be noted that the Balfour Declaration was issued at a time when Britain had no authority, practically or legally, over Palestine, and thus did not have the right to speak on behalf of its Arab population nor to take any decision regarding their fate. One truthful description of this declaration, by the Hungarian-born Jewish writer Arthur Koestler, was that "one nation solemnly promised to a second nation the country of a third."[62] Perhaps this was the reason that kept Britain from officially publicizing the Balfour Declaration in Palestine after it was issued. It only did so about two and a half years later.[63]

2

On the eve of the First World War in 1914, the Jewish population in Palestine had reached about 85,000. With the outbreak of the war, many found themselves in a critical situation because

---

60 T. R. Fyvel in Meyer W. Weisgal and Joel Carmichael, eds., *Chaim Weizmann, A Biography by Several Hands*, p. 167.

61 Lloyd George, *The Truth about the Peace Treaties*, Vol. 2, p. 1119.

62 Arthur Koestler, *Promise and Fulfilment – Palestine 1917-1949*, p. 4. Editor's note: Koestler was a Zionist and his honesty here stands in marked contrast to the picture offered in his well-known novel *Thieves in the Night*, analysed in detail by Ghassan Kanafani in *On Zionist Literature* for its pro-Zionist agenda and framing.

63 Sykes, *Crossroads to Israel*, p. 34.

5. WWI and the Balfour Declaration 329

large numbers of them, especially those who had come from Russia, were the citizens of an enemy country that was at war with the Ottoman Empire. The latter had, on September 11, 1914, about two weeks after it entered the war against the Allies, canceled the privileges of the protection system[64] enjoyed by its foreign citizens, including the Jewish immigrants. As mentioned previously (see Chapter 2, section 2), this system was like a fortress behind which the Zionist settlers enjoyed exceptional rights that they exploited to bolster their power in Palestine at the expense of its Arab inhabitants. The loss of those privileges led to demonstrations of support in Jaffa and Jerusalem by Arabs supporting their cancellation, such that one of the crowds chanted "protection is [as lowly as] a shoe!"[65] The war between Russia and the Ottomans also led to the closure of the Dardanelles and Bosphorus straits, such that the Russian ships – which had carried money and letters to the settlers from their families and organizations in Russia – were now unable to make that journey. Thus the settlers, in addition to their critical political situation in the country, found themselves in difficult economic conditions as well.[66]

The leadership of the Zionist Organization, which was then based in Berlin, did not lack the means to overcome these problems, however. It was able to influence German officials to request from their Ottoman allies that they treat settlers in Palestine favorably. Arthur Ruppin, director of the Palestine Office in Jaffa, also persuaded the United States ambassador to Istanbul, Henry Morgenthau, to mediate with the Ottoman government. Ruppin's suggestion to solve the problem of settlers in Palestine, who were citizens of enemy countries of the Ottomans, was to give them two options: to obtain Ottoman citizenship, with all its rights and duties (including volunteering

---

64 Ben-Zion Dinur (Dinaburg), ed., *Sefer Toldot ha-Haganah (History of the Haganah)*, Vol. 1, Part 1, p. 322.

65 Moshe Smilansky, *Prakim be-Toldot ha-Yishuv (Chapters in the History of the Yishuv)*, Vol. 1, Book 4, p. 12.

66 Dinur, ed., *Sefer Toldot ha-Haganah (History of the Haganah)*, Vol. 1, Part 1, p. 315.

for the Turkish army), or to leave the country.[67] At the same time, Ruppin sent, via Morgenthau, an urgent appeal to Jewish American organizations to help the Jewish population in Palestine.[68] Accordingly, a special committee headed by Brandeis was set up[69] to collect donations in the United States. The first batch of financial aid was sent with one of the American warships, North Carolina, which arrived in Palestine in late 1914.[70] The ship then worked to relocate the settlers who had refused to apply for Ottoman citizenship and who preferred to leave the country. In 1915, about 11,000 settlers left Palestine by this ship – most of them to Alexandria. The ship continued this task until late 1916, when it stopped coming to Palestine due to the concentration of submarines.[71] Thus, economic aid from American Jews also stopped. Ruppin, who had been exiled from Palestine to Turkey in September 1916, was nevertheless able to establish solid relations with the presidency of the Zionist Organization in Berlin, which secured the continued sending of financial aid to the Jews in Palestine.[72] While in Istanbul, Ruppin also worked through the German embassy in the city to reduce the severity of the anti-Jewish measures that Cemal Pasha, the Ottoman leader, had taken in Palestine.[73] The Germans were pressuring the Ottoman authorities to take a friendly stance towards the settlers in order to limit the activities of the Allies. Thus the Ottomans had to make vague pledges to a Jewish mission, of which Ruppin was a member,[74] similar to those that the British government had made to the Zionists prior to the

---

67 Ibid, p. 325; Shmueli, *Toldot ha-Tzionout ve Tnu'at ha-Avoda (History of Zionism and the Labor Movement)*, Vol. 2, p. 335.

68 Arthur Ruppin, *Pirkei Hayai (Chapters of My Life)*, Vol. 2, p. 228.

69 Dinur, ed., *Sefer Toldot ha-Haganah (History of the Haganah)*, Vol. 1, Part 1, p. 320.

70 Ruppin, *Pirkei Hayai (Chapters of My Life)*, Vol. 2, pp. 228-229.

71 Dinur, ed., *Sefer Toldot ha-Haganah (History of the Haganah)*, Vol. 1, Part 1, p. 321.

72 Ruppin, *Pirkei Hayai (Chapters of My Life)*, Vol. 2, pp. 257-258, 263, 271.

73 Ibid, p. 272.

74 Ibid, p. 275.

5. WWI and the Balfour Declaration

Balfour Declaration.

As a result of this political activity and continued economic assistance, the conditions of the settlers in Palestine during the First World War were generally better than those of the remaining population. The Zionist settlers had taken a number of measures during the war to alleviate their distress, such as the redistribution of the available work among them according to the needs of each of their groups and the establishment of consumer cooperatives. One of the most famous of these was "Hamashbir", which was originally set up to buy food grains from their producers and sell them to individuals at cost.[75] This association grew and became one of the largest consumer cooperatives among the Jewish population in Palestine. The period of the war was also not without settlement activity. In 1916, Hashomer members established a new settlement in the far north of the country near Metula and called it "Kfar Giladi". Thus, there were 41 Zionist settlements in Palestine on the eve of the Balfour Declaration.[76] Despite this, Jewish emigration continued during the war and led to about 30,000 Zionist settlers leaving the country, bringing its Jewish population down from about 85,000, at the start of the war, to about 56,000 by its end.[77] Settlers in Palestine also had their share of the policy of persecution of Cemal Pasha, who hounded Arab nationalists in the areas under his rule in Greater Syria. On May 6, 1916, he executed 21 Arab leaders in Beirut and Damascus by hanging, including three Palestinians, and took numerous repressive measures to maintain Ottoman control over the Levant. Within this policy, the Ottoman authorities banned Zionist activity in Palestine and ordered the dissolution of all Jewish organizations, Zionist or otherwise.[78] Cemal Pasha exiled a number of prominent Zionist leaders, especially those

---

75 Shmueli, *Toldot ha-Tzionout ve Tnu'at ha-Avoda (History of Zionism and the Labor Movement)*, Vol. 2, pp. 362-363.

76 Yitzhak Ben-Zvi, ed., *Sefer Hashomer (Book of Hashomer)*, pp. 344-345.

77 Dinur, ed., *Sefer Toldot ha-Haganah (History of the Haganah)*, Vol. 1, Part 1, p. 315.

78 Ibid, p. 328.

who had attended the Zionist congresses, including David Ben-Gurion; Yitzhak Ben-Zvi, leader of the Po'alei Zion party; Judah Leib Maimon (Fishman), rabbi and leader in the Mizrahi party; Yosef Aharonovich, editor of the magazine, *Hapoel Hatzair*; Israel Shohat, founder of the Hashomer organization; and Yehoshua Hankin, a major land buyer. At a later stage, Ruppin was also exiled, as noted above, as well as Albert Antebi, even though the latter had been a friend of Cemal Pasha.[79]

Ottoman measures against Jews in Palestine had intensified in late 1917, when the authorities uncovered a Jewish espionage network that worked for the British and called itself "Nili".[80] The network was led by Aaron Aaronsohn, an agronomist and head of an agricultural research station in Atlit on the Mediterranean coast. He had been close to Cemal Pasha, who had earlier appointed him as a consultant to fight a crop-destroying, desert locust invasion in and around Palestine during the war.[81] Aaronsohn, however, left Palestine in the summer of 1916 and contacted the British, who moved him to their headquarters in Egypt to coordinate between them and his network – with which contact was resumed in early 1917. The network had about 40 members and was tasked with collecting military, political and any other information that might benefit the British war effort. In late 1917, the Ottomans arrested a few of its members whose confessions exposed their work. The Ottoman forces then imposed a siege on some Jewish settlements, harassed their residents, arrested large numbers of them and executed a number of Nili's leaders.[82] These measures against the Jewish population increased in severity with the rising turmoil among the Ottoman forces at the start of the British attack from Sinai

---

79   Ibid, p. 329.

80   "Nili" are the first letters of the Hebrew translation of "He who is the Glory of Israel does not lie…" (*Torah*, 1 Samuel 15:29)

81   Dinur, ed., *Sefer Toldot ha-Haganah (History of the Haganah)*, Vol. 1, Part 1, p. 354.

82   For details, see ibid, pp. 353-386; for the complete account of Nili, see also Eliezer Livneh, *Nili: Toldoteha shel He'azah Medinit (Nili, A History of Political Daring)*, p. 408.

5. WWI and the Balfour Declaration

on southern Palestine.

Nili, however, revealed a deep dispute among the Zionist settlers in Palestine on the political line that they should follow in anticipation of either the victory of the Allies or of the Ottomans, which would put the Jewish presence in Palestine in the balance. The dispute intensified between Hashomer, which was calling for cooperation with the Turks, and Nili, which stood with the British. Hashomer's members had attempted to assassinate Yosef Lishansky, the leader of Nili in Palestine,[83] after the network of spies was exposed – fearing that he would fall into the hands of the Ottomans who would, in turn, harass the settlers – though the Ottomans later arrested and executed him. Most of the settler leaders in Palestine expressed their reservations regarding Nili and its activity. Nili had been able to uncover the Ottoman fortification and defense plan in southern Palestine and transmit information on it to the British, which caused panic among the Jewish settler leaders, fearing that the Turks would commit the same massacres against the Yishuv that they had perpetrated against the Armenians. The dispute had another, ideological aspect, as well, for

> the Nili group was from the "moshavot" [settlements], while Hashomer was from the Second Aliyah, and those immigrants considered the residents of the moshavot to be exploitative Jews, property owners who hired Arabs and were strangers to the Jewish masses in the diaspora. Moshavot residents, in turn, considered the Second Aliyah immigrants to be conscription runaways [from Russia] who had barely arrived in the country and wanted to teach the older, experienced settlers what to do.[84]

The echoes of this dispute would continue for about 60 years, in which Nili would be infamously remembered as a "curse" among the Zionist settlers in Palestine. The organization's contribution

---

83 Uri Milstein, *Be-Dam ve Esh, Yehuda: Tsmihata shel ha-Otzma ha-Yisraelit (By Blood and Fire, Judea: Growth of Israeli Power)*, p. 25.

84 Ibid, p. 34.

was only acknowledged in late 1967, when the president of Israel awarded a posthumous medal to Sarah Aaronsohn, one of the Nili leaders who had committed suicide in prison after her arrest. Nili's experience, and the willingness of the Yishuv leaders in Palestine to hand the members of the network over to the Ottoman authorities, revealed the extent that those leaders would go to due to their organizational fanaticism, on the one hand, and their endeavor to maintain their power within the Yishuv, on the other. This was an indication of the relations that would prevail between the various Zionist parties or military organizations in Palestine during the Mandate (as the tense disputes between the Haganah and the Irgun later showed).

The difference in viewpoints among the various Zionist groups on the position towards the countries participating in the world war did not stop at this point. At a time when the official Zionist leadership in Copenhagen decided to maintain neutrality towards the two camps, Weizmann and his companions in Britain worked to obtain the Balfour Declaration, while some Jews in Palestine took the opposite stance to both the above and joined the Ottoman army, convinced that their duty was to defend the Ottoman Empire. Some groups of Jewish settlers were enthusiastic about the decision of the Ottoman authorities, after the outbreak of the war, to grant Ottoman citizenship to every settler who applied for it. Those groups launched a wide campaign to urge the largest possible number of settlers, who held foreign citizenships, to apply. Then their enthusiasm grew and they sought to establish Jewish battalions in the Ottoman army. This alignment with the Ottomans did not succeed, but it was sufficient to push a few dozen Jews in Palestine – most of them high school students – to volunteer in the army.[85] From those volunteers, two senior Haganah leaders later emerged in Palestine during the Mandate: Eliyahu Golomb and Dov Hoz.[86]

The attempts to establish Jewish military forces, though

---

[85] For details, see Dinur, ed., *Sefer Toldot ha-Haganah (History of the Haganah)*, Vol. 1, Part 1, pp. 333-344.

[86] Milstein, *Be-Dam ve Esh, Yehuda (By Blood and Fire, Judea)*, pp. 26-27.

5. WWI and the Balfour Declaration

unsuccessful in Palestine, did succeed elsewhere. After the outbreak of the First World War, thousands of settlers left Palestine and went to Egypt, where the British authorities sent most of them to Alexandria. A number of them demanded to join the British Army. This movement was led by Joseph Trumpeldor, a Jewish former officer in the Russian Army who had immigrated to Palestine in 1912, then left for Egypt with the first batches of settlers who left the country in late 1914. Trumpeldor was joined by Ze'ev Jabotinsky, who had originally gone to Egypt as a journalist. The two tried to persuade the British Army to recruit a number of settlers, but their request was denied. It was instead proposed to them that Jewish battalions work in transportation. Jabotinsky refused and left Egypt to try and implement his scheme elsewhere, but Trumpeldor agreed and, in early 1915, the British Army in Egypt formed what it called the "Zion Mule Corps", which had about 650 Jewish volunteers. In mid-April 1915, this battalion was moved to Gallipoli, where it transported ammunition and supplies to the British forces. When the attack failed, the battalion was returned to Alexandria, where it was demobilized in mid-1916.[87] About 120 of its volunteers, however, joined the British Army and became the nucleus of the Jewish Legion that was formed in 1917.

The establishment of the Jewish Legion in the British Army came, to some extent, as a result of Jabotinsky's activity.[88] After leaving Egypt, he went to Britain via Europe and campaigned for the establishment of Jewish battalions along the way. Trumpeldor joined Jabotinsky in Britain before Colonel John Henry Patterson, commander of the Zion Mule Corps, assisted him in his campaign. The three had the support of Weizmann and Joseph Cowen (1868-1932), president of the British Zionist Federation. The British government refused to agree to their request. It only changed its stance in August 1917, after it had drawn up the final plans to attack and occupy Palestine. It then

---

87 Shmueli, *Toldot ha-Tzionout ve Tnu'at ha-Avoda (History of Zionism and the Labor Movement)*, Vol. 2, pp. 405-410.

88 For details, see Joseph B. Schechtman, *Rebel and Statesman, The Vladimir Jabotinsky Story*, pp. 201-257.

issued an order to establish the first battalion of the Jewish Legion,[89] which was supposed to participate, at least according to Zionist settlers, with the British Army in occupying Palestine. This battalion, however, carried out no such activity. On October 20, 1917, only two months after the battalion was formed, the British Army launched an artillery attack on Gaza City on the southern border of Palestine. The attack was a cover for the main operation that it launched on November 6 on the area between Gaza and Beersheba. This offensive ended on December 9 with the advance of the British Army into Jerusalem. On December 11, 1917, 40 days after the Balfour Declaration, General Edmund Allenby, commander of the British forces, entered Jerusalem – starting a new phase in the history of Palestine and of Zionism.

---

89   Ibid, pp. 411-414.

6. British Mandate over Palestine, Part I: The Mandate System and its Frameworks (1918-1923)

1

The Allied victory in the First World War and the subsequent peace agreements redrew the map of the world and led to the emergence of several states, some of which achieved independence while others fell under some form of imperial control. The global balance of power was in favor of the Allies, some of whom managed to extend their control over large territories of Asia and Africa, including the countries of the Levant that had been under Ottoman rule. Within the framework of achieving the ambitions of the Allied powers, the foundations were also laid for the "Jewish national home" in Palestine. This process took about six years, starting on November 2, 1917, when Britain issued the Balfour Declaration. On September 29, 1923, the British mandate over Palestine officially took effect, and was drafted in a manner that clearly showed its main objective: to facilitate the establishment of that "home".

The Peace Conference was the international framework that approved the mandate system and its foundational principles. The conference was held in Paris on January 18, 1919, two months after the end of the First World War. The war had ended with a truce on November 11, 1918, a day after Germany's surrender; its ally, the Ottoman Empire, had surrendered ten days earlier on October 31. The Peace Conference sought to solve the problems caused by the war and find new methods of dealing between peoples and countries in light of the new global balance of power. The victorious Allies had the final say in that conference, as the "Council of Ten", its main body, was made up of two delegates from each of the five major Allied powers: Britain, France, Italy, the United States and Japan. Regarding the Levant, Britain and France had decided on its fate as Britain and its Arab allies were in control of most of its territories.

As mentioned in the previous chapter, the Allied countries, particularly Britain, had sought to lure the Arabs to their side during the First World War and encourage them to join their fight against the Ottoman Empire – which then ruled most of the Levant. This was agreed on in the McMahon-Hussein Correspondence, by which Britain pledged to recognize the independence of the Arab territories after the war. At the same time, however, Britain and France made the Sykes-Picot Agreement to divide the countries of the Levant into zones of control between them after the war. Simultaneously, Britain issued the Balfour Declaration to the Zionists – pledging to facilitate the establishment of a Jewish national home in Palestine.

These contradictory agreements and pledges did not greatly concern the British leaders, or their French allies, while their efforts were focused on winning the war. In late 1917, however, as the war came to its final year, Arab doubts about the intentions of the British and French began to surface. One of the main reasons was the revelation by the Bolsheviks, after the victory of the October Revolution in Russia, of the content of the Sykes-Picot Agreement that the tsarist government had also been party to. The revelation of the Balfour Declaration strengthened these doubts. Britain and France, which were then preparing to fight the final and decisive battle of the First World War, were in no position to incur the wrath and enmity of the Arabs, and so the two countries proceeded to make a series of statements and promises to alleviate the doubts of the Arabs and placate them, at least until the end of the war.

On January 4, 1918, Commander David George Hogarth of the British "Arab Bureau" in Cairo visited Sharif Hussein, who had declared himself king of the Hejaz, in Jeddah. Hogarth relayed a message from the British authorities that "the Entente Powers are determined that the Arab race shall be given full opportunity of once again forming a nation in the world. This can only be achieved by the Arabs themselves uniting, and Great Britain and her Allies will pursue a policy with this ultimate unity in view."[1] With respect to Palestine, the letter affirmed the determination of the British government that "no people shall be subject to another."[2] Yet the letter limited the Palestinian issue to the religious sphere, for

> in view of the fact that there are in Palestine shrines, Wakfs and Holy places ... of interest to vast masses of people outside Palestine and Arabia, there must be a special regime to deal with these places approved of by the world. As regards the Mosque of Omar, it shall be considered as a Moslem concern alone, and shall not be subjected ... to any non-Moslem authority.[3]

The letter did not renege on the promises made by Britain to the Zionists but, on the contrary, made clear that

> since the Jewish opinion of the world is in favour of a return of Jews to Palestine ... and, further, as His Majesty's Government view with favour the realisation of this aspiration, His Majesty's Government are determined that in so far as is compatible with the freedom of the existing population, both economic and political, no obstacle should be put in the way of the realisation of this ideal.[4]

---

[1] *Statements made on behalf of His Majesty's Government during the Year 1918, in Regard to the Future Status of Certain Parts of the Ottoman Empire, Miscellaneous No. 4, 1939 (Cmd. 5964)*, p. 3; see also translation in *Palestine Documents File*, Vol. 1, p. 229.

[2] *Statements made on behalf of His Majesty's Government during the Year 1918, in Regard to the Future Status of Certain Parts of the Ottoman Empire, Miscellaneous No. 4, 1939 (Cmd. 5964)*, p. 3.

[3] Ibid.

[4] Ibid.

The letter's authors did not neglect to advise Sharif Hussein, at its end, that

> the friendship of world Jewry to the Arab cause is equivalent to support in all States where Jews have a political influence. The leaders of the movement are determined to bring about the success of Zionism by friendship and co-operation with the Arabs, and such an offer is not one to be lightly thrown aside.[5]

Colonel J. R. Bassett, the acting British agent in Jeddah, also visited Sharif Hussein a month later and gave him a second letter from the British foreign secretary, Balfour, affirming the previous pledges regarding the liberation of the Arab peoples. However, Balfour refrained from commenting on the Sykes-Picot Agreement in his letter, or the promise that he had made to the Zionists and what this could mean for the Arabs.[6] This letter came to dispel the fears raised by a second letter which Cemal Pasha, commander of the Turkish forces in Syria, had sent to Emir Faisal on November 26, 1917, with a copy to Ja'far al-Askari, commander of the Arab forces. Cemal Pasha had sent this letter after the Sykes-Picot Agreement had come to light, warning that the Allies had deceived the Arabs when they had incited them to revolt against the Ottoman Empire, and that the Allies intended to control the Levant and divide it into zones of power between them at the end of the war.[7] In the face of this, Sharif Hussein sufficed with the reassurance in the Balfour letter that Bassett relayed, but then he formally protested to the British government against the Sykes-Picot Agreement on June 5, 1918. The British authorities responded by attempting to evade the agreement and its consequences, pointing out that the outbreak of the Bolshevik Revolution and Russia's withdrawal from the war, after its change of governance, had created "a completely

---

5 Ibid.

6 Robert John and Sami Hadawi, *The Palestine Diary*, Vol. 1, pp. 100-101.

7 Ibid, p. 95.

6. British Mandate over Palestine, Part I 341

different situation"[8] than was previously the case.

In the same month, on June 16, 1918, the British authorities issued a statement known as the "Declaration to the Seven", in response to a memorandum submitted by seven leaders of the Syrian Unity Party which was formed in Cairo in 1918 after a dispute between its leaders and Sharif Hussein. In their memorandum, the leaders had called on Britain to clarify the truth of its intentions regarding the political future of the Arab regions. The Declaration to the Seven was clearer than previous statements, for the British authorities confirmed that

> in regard to ... areas in Arabia which were free and independent before the outbreak of war; [and] areas emancipated from Turkish control by the action of the Arabs themselves during the present war ... His Majesty's Government recognise the complete and sovereign independence of the Arabs inhabiting these areas and support them in their struggle for freedom. In regard to the areas occupied by Allied forces ... it is the wish and desire of His Majesty's Government that the future government of these regions should be based upon the principle of the consent of the governed, and this policy has and will continue to have the support of His Majesty's Government. In regard to the areas ... still under Turkish control ... it is the wish and desire of His Majesty's Government that the oppressed peoples of these areas should obtain their freedom and independence, and towards the achievement of this object His Majesty's Government continue to labour.[9]

This statement had been drafted with the help of the French government and was widely publicized in the Arab press, per British instructions.

Despite those statements, however, the suspicions of various

---

8 *Palestine Documents File*, Vol. 1, p. 233.

9 *Statements made on behalf of His Majesty's Government during the Year 1918, in Regard to the Future Status of Certain Parts of the Ottoman Empire, Miscellaneous No. 4, 1939 (Cmd. 5964)*, pp. 5-6.

Arab circles were not completely dispelled. Britain and France then issued the joint "Anglo-French Declaration", also known as the "Anglo-French Joint Statement of Aims in Syria and Mesopotamia", on November 7, 1918. This statement exceeded all the previous ones in clarity, stating that

> the object aimed at by France and Great Britain in prosecuting in the East the War let loose by the ambition of Germany is the complete and definite emancipation of the [Arab] peoples and the establishment of national governments and administrations deriving their authority from the initiative and free choice of the indigenous populations. In order to carry out these intentions France and Great Britain are at one in encouraging and assisting the establishment of indigenous Governments and administrations in Syria and Mesopotamia, now liberated by the Allies, and in the territories the liberation of which they are engaged in securing, and recognising these as soon as they are actually established.[10]

The two countries did not intend "to impose on the populations of these regions any particular institutions". Their only concern was

> to ensure by their support and by adequate assistance the regular working of Governments and administrations freely chosen by the populations themselves. To secure impartial and equal justice for all, to facilitate the economic development of the country by inspiring and encouraging local initiative, to favour the diffusion of education, to put an end to dissensions that have too long been taken advantage of by Turkish policy, such is the policy which the two Allied Governments uphold in the liberated territories.[11]

Only four days after this declaration, however, the First World War ended, making those promises subject to the new balance of power that prevailed. The victorious Allies began preparing

---

10 *Palestine Documents File*, Vol. 1, p. 238.

11 Ibid.

to share the spoils and compensate their losses through various means that included spreading their control over new regions of the world – among them the Levant. The Sykes-Picot Agreement was the basis on which Britain and France shaped their policies in the region, competing and trying to gain power over larger territories at the expense of each other and the peoples of these countries. While France was the more ferocious in pursuing its demands and insisting on their fulfilment, Britain was the more confident due to its two allies who were bound to it – the Arabs, led by Sharif Hussein and his sons, and the Zionists – and thus concerned with the success of its policy in the region. British policy had scored a victory in the first duel with France over the fate of the region less than two weeks after the end of the war. The French prime minister, Georges Clemenceau, visited London in late November 1918 and agreed to the requests of his British counterpart, Lloyd George, to annex the Mosul area to Iraq and to recognize British control over Palestine from "Dan to Beersheba". In return, France was to receive 25 percent of profits from the oil that could be discovered in Mosul. Clemenceau ratified this consent in a letter to the British government, dated February 5, 1919, which also contained a record of French interests in Syria.[12] In so doing, he approved the first amendment to the Sykes-Picot Agreement in favor of the British – the original agreement had stipulated that Mosul was supposed to belong to the French zone of power in Syria while Palestine was to be subject to international administration, with France as one of the parties.

This preliminary agreement did not settle the issue of exclusive British control over Palestine, however, which the upcoming Peace Conference had to recognize. Thus, the Eastern Committee of the British War Cabinet met in December 1918 to discuss the position that Britain should take regarding Palestine at the conference. The British foreign office presented a report to the committee, stressing that

---

12 David Lloyd George, *The Truth about the Peace Treaties*, Vol. 2, p. 1151.

the problem of Palestine cannot be exclusively solved on the principle of self-determination, because there is one element in the population – the Jews – which, for historical and religious reasons, is entitled to a greater influence than would be given to it if numbers were the sole test. It is necessary, therefore, to devise some scheme of Government which will at once protect Arab interests, and give effect to the national aspirations of the Jewish race.[13]

Prime Minister Lloyd George expressed his opinion before the committee that "the Arabs and Zionists in Palestine want us,"[14] and that British control of Palestine was strategically necessary to defend the Suez Canal.[15] A general in the committee also declared that if the Jewish settlers did not get control of Palestine, "we should have the whole of Jewry turning Bolsheviks and supporting Bolshevism in all the other countries as they have done in Russia."[16] At the end of its deliberations, the committee adopted a series of recommendations for the British delegation to the Peace Conference, declaring that it opposed any form of international administration in Palestine and instead preferred the choice of a single major power by the League of Nations to administer it. This power, however, "should not be France or Italy, but should be either the United States of America or Great Britain. While we would not object to the selection of the United States of America, yet if the offer were made to Great Britain we ought not to decline."[17]

2

While Britain was laying out its plans to secure its rule over Palestine, its military forces were practically in control of the country and most of its surrounding areas. In late 1917, the

---

13   David Lloyd George, *War Memoirs*, Vol. 2, p. 673.
14   Ibid, p. 1147.
15   Ibid, p. 1148.
16   Ibid, p. 1150.
17   Ibid, pp. 1154-1155.

6. British Mandate over Palestine, Part I 345

British forces occupied the southern part of Palestine (up to a line connecting Jerusalem and Jaffa) from their bases in Sinai. On December 11, General Allenby, commander of these forces, entered Jerusalem.[18] From these positions, the British forces occupied Jericho on February 21, 1918. By the end of March, they had penetrated east of the Jordan River. The fighting on this front then ceased for about six months. On September 18, the British forces stationed in southern Palestine, together with the Arab ones east of the Jordan River, launched a comprehensive attack on the Turkish forces in the north and occupied Haifa and Acre on September 23. They continued pushing north and occupied Damascus on October 1, and Tripoli, Homs, Hama and Aleppo between October 13-26.[19] On October 31, 1918, an armistice was announced with the Ottoman Empire after its surrender.

On entering Palestine, the British imposed military rule on the areas that they occupied. With the end of the fighting and the occupation of Greater Syria, the region was divided into three military administrations (see *Map 7 Areas of British and French military administration in and around Palestine after the First World War, 1918-1920*, below), each of which was known as an OETA – Occupied Enemy Territory Administration. The southern administration (OETA South) included almost all of Palestine and was subject to a British officer based in Jerusalem. The northern administration, which included coastal Lebanon and Syria, was handed over to a French officer based in Beirut, while the eastern administration, comprising the remaining areas of Syria and Transjordan, was placed under the command of an Arab officer based in Damascus.

Yet, despite this division, the British were trying to evade their commitments to France under the Sykes-Picot Agreement, striving to ensure their sole control over the largest possible area of the Levant.[20] As explained earlier (see Chapter 5, section 1),

---

18 *A Brief Record of the Advance of the [British] Egyptian Expeditionary Force, July 1917 to October 1918*, p. 10.

19 Ibid, pp. 15, 19, 31-34.

20 See Evyatar Friesel, *Ha-Mediniout ha-Tzionit le-ahar Hatzharat Balfour, 1917-1922 (Zionist Policy after the Balfour Declaration, 1917-1922)*, p. 58 and sources mentioned.

Map 7 Areas of British and French military administration in and around Palestine after the First World War, 1918-1920[21]

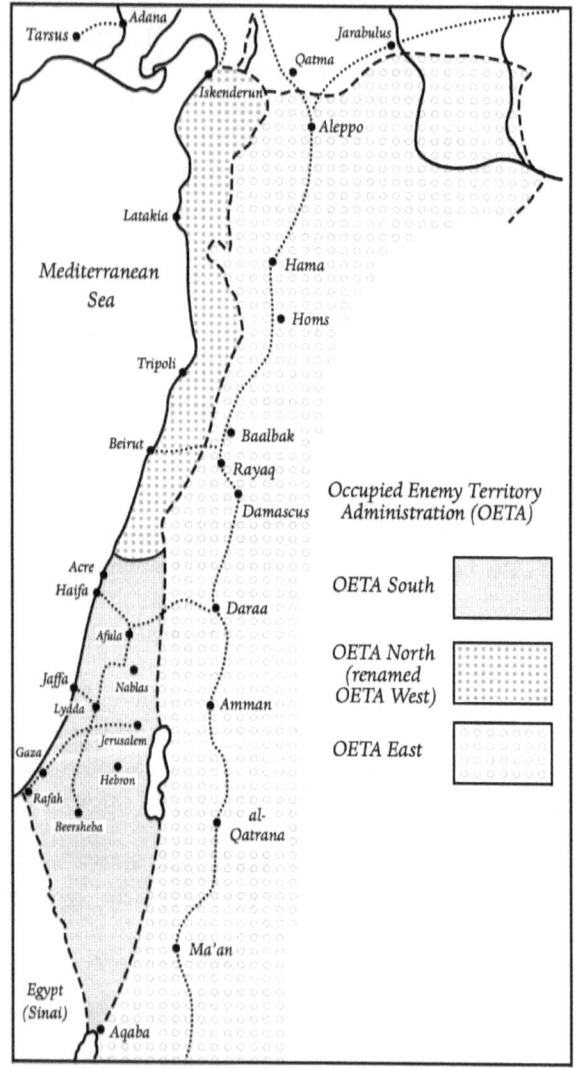

21 Map was drawn in accordance with that in Yehuda Wallach, *Atlas Carta le-Toldot Eretz Yisrael mi-Rashit ha-Hityashvut ve ad Koum ha-Medina (Carta's Atlas of History of the Land of Israel from the Start of Settlement until the Establishment of the State)*, Map 46, p. 38.

6. British Mandate over Palestine, Part I 347

British Prime Minister Lloyd George had set his mind on exploiting the Zionists in order to ensure Britain's control over Palestine and prevent the establishment of any international administration in it, as should have occurred per the agreement[22] (this goal was one of the key reasons that had prompted the British government to issue the Balfour Declaration). Thus, the British encouraged the Zionists to raise their demands and request that the establishment of the national home in Palestine be under British mandate alone.

The two parties began implementing these plans before the end of the war. On February 14, 1918, the Zionists, with the support and guidance of the British, managed to secure a letter from the French foreign ministry in which France pledged to support the establishment of the Jewish national home in Palestine.[23] On May 19, they obtained a similar letter from the Italian ambassador to London.[24] At the same time, and only a few weeks after Britain had occupied southern Palestine, the British foreign office decided to send a Zionist commission ("Va'ad ha-Tsirim", or Delegates' Committee in Hebrew) to Palestine "to survey the situation and to prepare plans in the spirit of the Balfour Declaration".[25] In order to add an international character to their project, the British authorities included representatives of the Jewish populations from the countries allied with Britain (most of which had agreed, in one way or another, to the issuance of the Balfour Declaration). The commission was chaired by Weizmann and included Joseph Cowen, director of the Jewish Colonial Trust and its banking arm, the Anglo-Palestine Company[26] (later known as Bank Leumi le-Israel); David Eder (1865-1936), agent of the non-Zionist Jewish Territorial Organization; Leon Simon (1881-1965), representing British Jews; and Sylvain Lévi (1863-

---

22   Ibid, p. 52.

23   See letter in *Report[s] of the Executive of the Zionist Organization to the XIIth Zionist Congress (1921), I. Political Report*, p. 72.

24   See letter in ibid, p. 73.

25   Chaim Weizmann, *Trial and Error*, p. 266.

26   See also Chapter 3, section 5.

1935) and Angelo Levi-Bianchini (1887-1920) as representatives of French and Italian Jews, respectively. Representatives of Jewish people in the United States and Russia were also scheduled to join. However, the United States, which was then not at war with the Ottoman Empire, did not see fit to send a representative of its Jewish population (one American Zionist did, however, join the commission in 1919), while a Jewish representative from Russia could not join due to the conditions in the country after the outbreak of the Bolshevik Revolution. In addition, William Ormsby-Gore (1885-1964) joined the commission as a liaison officer between it and the British authorities. James de Rothschild, the well-known benefactor of Zionist projects, was appointed Ormsby-Gore's assistant.[27] The British authorities worked to raise the profile of the commission and organized a visit by Weizmann, on the eve of its travels, to British King George V,[28] to highlight the importance of the commission and its work.

The formation of the Zionist Commission came as part of Britain's preparations for the upcoming Peace Conference, to exploit the Zionists' influence and encourage the conference to issue resolutions consistent with British interests. Before proceeding, however, it was necessary to try to reconcile the Zionists and the Arabs, to prevent contradictory demands at the conference, and to bolster the front opposing French influence in the Levant and curtail this influence as far as possible.

British attempts to reconcile the Zionists and Arabs began at an early stage. In late March 1918, Weizmann arrived in Egypt as the head of the Zionist Commission that was en route to Palestine. The British high commissioner in Egypt suggested to the members of the commission to meet a few Arab leaders who were involved in Syrian affairs, to dispel any doubts that they had regarding the Zionist plans. Weizmann agreed[29] and met

---

27   See also *Report[s] of the Executive of the Zionist Organization to the XIIth Zionist Congress (1921), I. Political Report*, pp. 15-16.

28   Weizmann, *Trial and Error*, pp. 267-269.

29   For details, see Yosef Luntz, "Diplomatic Contacts between the Zion-

with a few of the exiled Syrian leaders in Cairo, including Faris Nimr, Said Shqeir, Abd al-Rahman Shahbandar, Rafiq al-Azm and others.[30] A few of these leaders tried to reach an agreement with Weizmann and his companions, but the latter refused to accept the proposals presented to them.[31] When the Zionist Commission arrived in Palestine, Weizmann, with the support of Ormsby-Gore, met with a number of well-known Arab figures in the country for the same purpose – though political issues were not discussed at those meetings.[32] The attempts resumed a few months later. On the advice of General Allenby, Weizmann met with Emir Faisal on June 4, 1918, at his headquarters north of Aqaba, and answered his questions about the Zionist program.[33] Faisal expressed his wish "to see the Jews and Arabs working in harmony during the Peace Conference which was to come".[34] The two men did not reach any full agreement, however.

With the help of the British, the Zionists renewed their attempts to meet Faisal and reach an agreement with him after his arrival in Paris in late 1918 to attend the Peace Conference. Faisal was in a difficult position. He had arrived at the French port of Marseille, then gone to London and returned to France to attend the conference. Upon his entry, the French government had welcomed him but made it clear that it was doing so in his capacity as a mere visitor, with no official status and not representing anyone.[35] The government also opposed granting the Hejaz mission a seat at the Peace Conference, and only backtracked under intense pressure from Britain. France's behavior was a harbinger of the position that

---

ist Movement and the Arab National Movement at the Close of the First World War", *Ha-Mizrah ha-Hadash*, Vol. 12, Issue 2, pp. 216-217.

30   Neil Caplan, *Futile Diplomacy*, Vol. 1: *Early Arab-Zionist Negotiation Attempts, 1913-1931*, pp. 32-34.

31   Ibid; also see proposals on pp. 135-138.

32   Luntz, "Diplomatic Contacts between the Zionist Movement and the Arab National Movement at the Close of the First World War", p. 218.

33   Weizmann, *Trial and Error*, p. 293.

34   Ibid.

35   John and Hadawi, *The Palestine Diary*, Vol. 1, p. 113.

it would take towards Arab demands for independence, and of the difficulties that it would create – especially since the French had brought two Arab delegations, from Syria and Lebanon, to the conference to demand that France be granted the right of mandate over these countries. With Faisal's weak position, the Zionists and the British tried to coerce him. They implied that the Zionists, with their influence in several countries, could help him to obtain Arab independence if he agreed to "sacrifice" and "relinquish" Palestine for the sake of the other Arab regions. It seems that Faisal was somehow given to understand that the British would be willing to reject French demands to control parts of the Levant, as per the Sykes-Picot Agreement, if the Balfour Declaration was accepted. At the same time, Faisal was not in a position to ignore the requests of the British, who were financing his activity. The Zionists raised their pursuit of him during the conference, trying to draw near him in various ways,[36] and succeeded in arranging a meeting between him and the American president, Wilson. Those efforts finally bore fruit, as Faisal signed an agreement with Weizmann on January 3, 1919. This agreement was formulated in English by Faisal's British companion and advisor, T. E. Lawrence, who was described by Weizmann as a "remarkable personality" worth a "tribute to the services which [he] rendered our cause".[37]

The Faisal-Weizmann Agreement[38] stipulated (after the introduction that hailed the "racial kinship and ancient bonds" between the Arabs and Jews) that two states would be established in the Levant: Palestine, and a neighboring Arab state. Per the agreement, "immediately following the completion of the deliberations of the Peace Conference, the definite boundaries between the Arab State and Palestine shall be determined by a Commission to be agreed upon by the parties hereto."[39] Further, the agreement specified that

---

36 For details, see also ibid, pp. 114-115.

37 Weizmann, *Trial and Error*, p. 294.

38 See agreement in *Palestine Documents File*, Vol. 1, pp. 251-252.

39 Ibid.

6. British Mandate over Palestine, Part I   351

in the establishment of the Constitution and Administration of Palestine all such measures shall be adopted as will afford the fullest guarantees for carrying into effect the British Government's Declaration of the 2nd of November, 1917 [the Balfour Declaration]. All necessary measures shall be taken to encourage and stimulate immigration of Jews into Palestine on a large scale, and as quickly as possible to settle Jewish immigrants upon the land through closer settlement and intensive cultivation of the soil. In taking such measures the Arab peasant and tenant farmers shall be protected in their rights, and shall be assisted in forwarding their economic development.[40]

One of the articles also stated that "the parties hereto agree to act in complete accord and harmony in all matters embraced herein before the Peace Congress,"[41] which was the bottom line. Faisal, however, added his handwritten reservations to this agreement, explaining that

provided the Arabs obtain their independence as demanded in my Memorandum dated the 4th of January, 1919, to the Foreign Office of the Government of Great Britain, I shall concur in the above articles. But if the slightest modification or departure were to be made [in relation to the demands in the Memorandum] I shall not be bound by a single word of the present Agreement which shall be deemed void and of no account or validity, and I shall not be answerable in any way whatsoever.[42]

Faisal's reservations, however, had practically no value for the British, as the main goal behind this agreement was to convince the Peace Conference that the Arabs did not oppose the Zionist schemes in Palestine. The agreement played this role, especially after Faisal acted in accordance with it in his speech to the

---

40   Ibid.

41   Ibid.

42   Ibid, p. 252.

conference. At the end of the month in which the agreement was signed, the Peace Conference decided that the occupied Arab territories in the Levant would not be returned to Ottoman rule. On February 3, 1919, four days after this decision, the Zionists presented their demands to the conference in a memorandum[43] that Herbert Samuel helped to draft with the approval of the British foreign office. In this document, the Zionists focused on the need for recognition of the so-called "historical relationship" between the Jews and Palestine, the declaration of the country as a national home for Jewish people, and granting Britain the mandate over it.[44] They attached a map specifying the area where they demanded the establishment of the Jewish national home, which included all of Palestine (with its borders that would be drawn during the British Mandate), southern Lebanon to the north of the Litani River, the Golan region in southern Syria and all the inhabited part of Transjordan up to the Hejaz Railway.[45] Three days after these demands, on February 6, 1919, Faisal spoke before the Peace Conference and demanded that all the countries of the Levant be granted independence except Palestine, whose fate should be decided by all the parties concerned due to its "universal character".[46] He then requested that a commission of inquiry be sent by the Peace Conference to the Levant to consult its population before deciding on their fate. He was supported in this by Howard Bliss, president of the Syrian Protestant College (after 1920, the American University of Beirut), in the latter's testimony before the conference.

On February 27, 1919, the Peace Conference heard the testimonies of the Zionist delegation, headed by Sokolow and Weizmann. Sokolow repeated the content of the Zionist memorandum submitted earlier, while Weizmann spoke in detail

---

43 See memorandum in *Report[s] of the Executive of the Zionist Organization to the XIIth Zionist Congress (1921), I. Political Report*, pp. 74-83.

44 Ibid.

45 See *Map 3 Region of the "Jewish national home" demanded by the Zionist Organization at the Paris Peace Conference*, in Introduction, section 6.

46 John and Hadawi, *The Palestine Diary*, Vol. 1, p. 128; Caplan, *Futile Diplomacy*, p. 37.

of the steps that should be taken to create a "Jewish National Home".[47] When Robert Lansing, the American secretary of state, asked him what he meant by this phrase, Weizmann replied that he meant creating conditions under which, by means of Jewish immigration, Palestine would become "as Jewish as England is English",[48] citing as an example the alleged success achieved by French colonialists in Tunisia.[49]

The Zionists' revelation of their intentions regarding Palestine raised Faisal's doubts and anger. A Parisian newspaper published a subsequent interview with him in which he used phrases hostile to Zionism. The Zionists and their allies resumed their pressure on him, so he wrote a letter[50] on March 3, 1919, to Felix Frankfurter, member of the American Zionist delegation, to mitigate the negative impression left by the interview. At the beginning of this letter, Faisal repeated the familiar phrases of kinship between the "cousins": the Arabs and the Jews, and declared:

> The Arabs, especially the educated among us, look with the deepest sympathy on the Zionist movement. Our deputation here in Paris is fully acquainted with the proposals submitted yesterday by the Zionist Organization to the Peace Conference, and we regard them as moderate and proper. We will do our best, in so far as we are concerned, to help them through: we will wish the Jews a most hearty welcome home.[51]

Although the fate of Palestine was finally decided by the Peace Conference based on imperial interests and the balance of

---

47   Weizmann, *Trial and Error*, p. 305.

48   Ibid.

49   See also Weizmann's report of his testimony before the Peace Conference in *Ha-Protocolim shel ha-Va'ad ha-Poel ha-Tzioni (Records of Sessions of the Zionist Executive)*, pp. 52-56.

50   Weizmann, *Trial and Error*, pp. 307-308; *Report[s] of the Executive of the Zionist Organization to the XIIth Zionist Congress (1921), I. Political Report*, pp. 23-24.

51   Ibid; see also Harlan B. Phillips, *Felix Frankfurter Reminisces*, pp. 155-156.

power – which made the Weizmann agreement with Faisal, and the latter's correspondence with Frankfurter, of marginal significance – in his autobiography, Weizmann twice asserted that these two documents were of great importance and "had much to do with the positive attitude toward Zionist aspirations of the Big Four".[52]

After hearing the demands and testimonies regarding the Levant, the Peace Conference refrained from taking any decision on its fate for the first three months of 1919. This was due to the deepening disputes between the major Allies regarding their ambitions in the region, which the conference was unable to resolve. Further, the Ottoman Empire had not, until that time, "waived its rights" to the countries that it had ruled before the Allied states occupied them, which delayed the decision. The conference instead decided, due to the conflicting proposals submitted to it, to accept another suggestion – this time by American President Wilson – to send a commission of inquiry on its behalf to the Levant, in order to determine the attitudes of its population towards their self-determination and mode of governance. The commission was to include representatives from Britain, France, Italy and the United States. The first three countries, however, refrained from sending delegates in one way or another. Thus the commission had to finally head to the Levant, on May 29, 1919, with two American delegates only: Henry King and Charles Crane, who arrived in Palestine on June 10.[53] (This commission was the first of many that were destined to review the Palestine issue until the end of the British mandate over the country, in 1948.)

The King-Crane Commission spent several weeks in the region visiting various places and meeting with delegations, including representatives of the settlers in Palestine, who pledged that the Arabs would obtain the rights of a national minority

---

52 Weizmann, *Trial and Error*, pp. 294, 308.

53 *Chronologiah le-Toldot ha-Yishuv ha-Yehudi be-Eretz Yisrael (Chronology of the Jewish Yishuv in the Land of Israel)*, Vol. 1: 1917-1935, p. 28.

6. British Mandate over Palestine, Part I

in the country when its rule would pass over to the British.[54] Hundreds of petitions were presented to the commission by various sections of the population. The commission then returned to Europe and submitted its report on August 28, 1919, which stated that

> the feeling against the Zionist programme is not confined to Palestine, but shared very generally by the people throughout Syria, as our conferences clearly showed. More than seventy-two per cent – 1,350 in all – of all the petitions in the whole of Syria were directed against the Zionist programme. Only two requests – those for a united Syria and for independence – had a larger support.[55]

The commission also stated that the majority of the population supported granting the mandate – if it had to be imposed – to the United States as a first choice, followed by Britain, while a French mandate was rejected by the majority. The reason for preferring an American mandate was that President Wilson had announced, on January 8, 1918, what he called the "Fourteen Points" to settle the problems arising after the war. The fifth point stated the necessity of settling any colonial problem in line with the interests of the colonized peoples, not only the will of the colonizing powers. The 12th point suggested the possibility of granting autonomy to non-Turkish peoples in the Ottoman Empire, including the Arabs – positions that the other Allied countries, particularly Britain and France, did not share.

However, after the King-Crane report, President Wilson did nothing despite the commission's statements on Arab demands for independence and their right to self-determination, a slogan that the United States had raised aloft. Wilson refrained even from publishing the report (it was only published after the approval of the British mandate over Palestine). It seems that he did this in order to not embarrass the French with the feelings of

---

54 Neil Caplan, *Palestine Jewry and the Arab Question, 1917-1925*, p. 37.

55 *Palestine Documents File*, Vol. 1, p. 259; see also full commission's report in George Antonius, *The Arab Awakening*, pp. 443-458.

hostility that were reported towards them, on the one hand, and, on the other, as a result of Zionist pressure – especially by his friend, Brandeis – because of the hostility towards the Zionists that the report had also made clear. At any rate, there was room for doubt as to the effectiveness of any step that President Wilson could have taken on the basis of the report. The isolationist political current had gained strength in the United States – calling for refraining from immersing the country in non-American problems in general and European ones in particular – to the extent that the US Congress rejected the Treaty of Versailles when it was presented to it on November 19, 1919 and rejected it again on March 19, 1920. The United States then lost all effective influence on the Peace Conference, as it also abstained from joining the League of Nations that was established in early 1920. Instead, the US concluded separate peace agreements, in 1921 and 1922, with the countries that it had been at war with, including the Ottoman Empire, and then secluded itself for a good period of time. Japan was also induced to take a similar position. Thus, the road was paved for Britain, France and Italy to control the Peace Conference and its deliberations to secure their colonial interests to the fullest.

In any case, even before these developments, the Allied Powers had taken their decisions regarding the fate of the countries that had been subject to Ottoman rule, including those of the Levant. On June 28, 1919, two months before the King-Crane Commission submitted its report, the Treaty of Versailles and the Covenant of the League of Nations were signed. On July 9, Germany ratified the treaty, which came into effect on January 10, 1920. In its covenant, the League of Nations created a new system of governance to apply to the peoples of the formerly colonized countries and called it a "mandate", after it became clear that it was not advisable to subject these countries to direct colonial rule. This system, according to the Covenant of the League of Nations (Article 22), applied to "those colonies and territories which as a consequence of the late war have ceased to be under the sovereignty of the States which formerly governed them and which are inhabited by peoples not yet able to stand by themselves under the strenuous conditions of the modern world", and "there should be applied the principle that the well-being and development of such peoples form a sacred trust of civilization and that securities for the performance of this trust should be embodied in this Covenant." The Allied countries decided that

> the best method of giving practical effect to this principle is that the tutelage of such peoples should be entrusted to advanced nations who by reason of their resources, their experience or their geographical position can best undertake this responsibility, and who are willing to accept it, and that this tutelage should be exercised by them as Mandatories on behalf of the League.

Various types of mandate were approved, the "highest" of which was that imposed on

> certain communities [including the Arab peoples] formerly belonging to the Turkish Empire [who] have reached a stage of development where their existence as independent nations can be provisionally recognized subject to the rendering of administrative advice and assistance by a Mandatory until such time as they are able to stand alone. The wishes of these communities must be a principal consideration in the selection of the Mandatory.[56]

In other words, the purpose of imposing the mandate of one of the "advanced" nations on a certain country and assigning it to govern and organize its affairs for a period of time – which differed according to the state of development reached by that country – was to help it to advance and improve its conditions until it reached a stage where it could achieve independence and establish its own national rule. This is what finally transpired, in one way or another, in many countries of the Levant, including Syria, Lebanon and Iraq, and in several African countries. This

---
56 Article 22(4) of the Covenant of the League of Nations.

was not the case in Palestine, however, for which the mandate was drafted in a manner aimed primarily at facilitating the establishment of the Jewish national home in it.

3

While the Allied Powers were implementing their designs for the Levant and other regions, trying to agree on how to share the spoils after the First World War, the Arabs were expressing their opposition to the imposition of the foreign powers' authority over them and the granting of exceptional rights to Zionists in Palestine. The resistance by the Palestinian Arabs to the settlers was renewed shortly after the British occupation of the country. In mid-1918, Muslim-Christian associations were formed in several places in Palestine to oppose Zionism (some of these associations were allegedly formed at the suggestion of British officers sympathetic to the Arabs). Several other political and cultural associations were also formed[57] with the aim of preserving the Arab character of Palestine. On November 2, 1918, the first anniversary of the Balfour Declaration, a protest march took place in Jerusalem and clashed with the police, after which two Arabs were sentenced to prison. This led to the first Arab demonstration, led by Musa Kazim al-Husseini, mayor of Jerusalem, who submitted a written protest to the British and the United States' governments.[58] A delegation of Arab figures in Jerusalem and Jaffa also submitted a formal protest to the British military authorities against the establishment of a Jewish national home in Palestine.[59] In early 1919, Ze'ev Jabotinsky informed the Zionist Commission – after he had established an affiliated "information unit" – about the formation of armed Palestinian organizations, including "al-Ikha wal Afaf" (Brotherhood and

---

57 Abdel Wahhab Kayyali, *Palestine: A Modern History*, p. 116; see also Yosef Olitsky, *Mi-Pzura le-Medinah (From Dispersal to State)*, Vol. 1, p. 172.

58 Kayyali, *Palestine: A Modern History*, p. 119.

59 Olitsky, *Mi-Pzura le-Medinah (From Dispersal to State)*, Vol. 1, p. 175; also see *Chronologiah le-Toldot ha-Yishuv ha-Yehudi be-Eretz Yisrael (Chronology of the Jewish Yishuv in the Land of Israel)*, Vol. 1, p. 21.

6. British Mandate over Palestine, Part I 359

Chastity, in Arabic) and "Fida'iyya" (Freedom Fighters), which were preparing to fight the Jewish settlers.

> They are working to amass weapons and train on their use, preparing lists of names of Jewish notables and their places of residence, carrying out incitement among the Bedouins in the Naqab (Negev) and Transjordan, organizing policemen and officers, and spying on the Jews. There are similar organizations in Jerusalem, Jaffa, Gaza, Nablus, Tulkarm, Haifa, and other cities and places.[60]

In the first three months of 1919, while the Peace Conference was deliberating the fate of Palestine, the Palestinians who had been exiled by the Turks from the country sent more than one protest to the conference against severing Palestine from Syria, making it a Jewish national home and allowing the immigration of settlers.[61] Delegates to the first Palestine Arab Congress also sent a telegram to the Peace Conference on February 3, 1919, in which they expressed

> strong protest because of what we have heard that the Zionists have won a promise of making our country a national home for them, and that they intend to immigrate to this country and colonize it. We, Muslims and Christians gathered as delegates of a living Arab nation among the weak nations ... have come with a total rejection of every decision taken in this regard before seeking our opinion ... and our wishes and aspirations that we shall present.[62]

The first Palestine Arab Congress was held in Jerusalem from January 27-February 10, 1919, with representatives of Muslim and Christian associations in various parts of Palestine, to discuss presenting the demands of the Palestinians to the

---

60 Ben-Zion Dinur (Dinaburg), ed., *Sefer Toldot ha-Haganah (History of the Haganah)*, Vol. 1, Part 2, p. 557.

61 See protests in Abdel Wahhab Kayyali, ed., *Documents of Arab Palestinian Resistance to British Occupation and Zionism: 1918-1939*, pp. 1-3, 5-9.

62 Ibid, p. 4.

Peace Conference. In addition to the telegram that it sent to the conference, the congress took a series of resolutions in which it stated that

> we consider Palestine nothing but part of Arab Syria and it has never been separated from it at any stage. We are tied to it by national, religious, linguistic, moral, economic, and geographic bounds... Our district Southern Syria or Palestine should be not separated from the Independent Arab Syrian Government and be free from all foreign influence and protection.[63]

The delegates pledged to "maintain friendly relations with Britain and the Allied powers, accepting help if it did not affect the country's independence and Arab unity".[64]

To affirm its desire that "Southern Syria or Palestine should be not separated from the Independent Arab Syrian Government", the first Palestine Arab Congress sent delegates to attend the General Syrian Congress held in early July 1919 in Damascus. This congress demanded that "the Government of this Syrian country should be a democratic civil constitutional Monarchy ... and ... the King be the Emir Faisal." It also demanded "independence for emancipated Mesopotamia [Iraq]".[65] The congress called for the revocation of the Sykes-Picot Agreement, the Balfour Declaration and any scheme to divide Syria or to establish a Jewish state in Palestine. It rejected the political tutelage incorporated in the proposed mandate systems and agreed to accept foreign assistance for a limited period, "provided that such assistance does not infringe the complete independence and unity of our country". To this end, the congress stated it would "seek the technical and economic assistance from the United States of America", and, "in the event of America not finding herself in a position to accept our desire

---

63 Kayyali, *Palestine: A Modern History*, pp. 127-128.

64 Ibid; see also Muhammad Azza Darwaza, *On the Modern Arab Movement*, Vol. 3, pp. 35-36.

65 *Palestine Documents File*, Vol. 1, p. 255.

6. British Mandate over Palestine, Part I 361

for assistance, we will seek this assistance from Great Britain."[66] The congress refused that France "should assist us or have a hand in our country under any circumstances and in any place".[67]

After these two congresses and the arrival of the King-Crane Commission in the country, the Arabs of Palestine persisted in sending memoranda of protest to the British military authorities and to other international bodies, declaring their rejection of the idea of a Jewish national home in their country and the permission for Jewish people to immigrate to it, as well as its separation from Syria.[68]

Those congresses, resolutions and protests bore no fruit, however, as Britain and France had other designs. When the Peace Conference failed to reach an agreement between Britain and France to secure their colonial interests in the Levant during its sessions in Paris in early 1919, the two countries resumed their bilateral negotiations. These negotiations, which lasted for some time, ended with the signing of the Deauville Agreement on September 15, 1919, in Paris, under which Britain pledged to withdraw its forces from Syria before November 1 of the same year in preparation for placing the country under French rule. The two countries also agreed to replace, in the same period, the Arab garrisons in the cities of Damascus, Homs, Hama and Aleppo with French soldiers.[69]

A few days after the agreement was signed, Faisal was informed of its contents and he lodged his protest. The British government then convinced him of the need to go to Paris to negotiate with the French government and try to reach an agreement. Faisal had no choice but to act on this advice after Britain had abandoned him. He arrived in Paris in late November 1919 and held talks with Clemenceau that led to a temporary agreement, stipulating the right of the French to control the

---

66 Ibid.

67 Ibid.

68 See some of these memoranda in Kayyali, ed., *Documents of Arab Palestinian Resistance to British Occupation and Zionism: 1918-1939*, pp. 10-14.

69 John and Hadawi, *The Palestine Diary*, Vol. 1, p. 154.

coastal areas of Syria and Lebanon. In mid-January 1920, Faisal returned to Syria and tried to encourage its leaders to understand the dynamics of the situation that had arisen as a result of the British-French agreement. He called for the formation of a delegation to accompany him to Paris and resume negotiations with the French government. His suggestions were unwelcome, however, and he did not succeed in forming any delegation. Demonstrations broke out in several Syrian cities calling for unity and independence, and the leaders of the Arab nationalist movement did not hesitate to draw their conclusions based on their rejection of foreign control over Syria. On March 8, 1920, the General Syrian Congress met in Damascus and declared the independence of Syria (including Lebanon and Palestine) as a constitutional monarchy, and installed Faisal as its king. A similar congress was held in Iraq, and Emir Abdullah, Faisal's brother, was chosen as king there. Britain and France announced that they did not recognize these measures, and Faisal was invited to Europe to resume negotiations.[70] The two countries were working to legitimize the division of the Levant into spheres of power between them, as per the Sykes-Picot Agreement, through the Peace Conference. (The Peace Conference reconvened in San Remo, in early 1920, as the Council of the League of Nations, which the Allies had established.)

The attempts of Britain and France to impose their control over the countries of the Levant provoked a period of turmoil and armed clashes against them. These began in southern Syria and spread to northern Palestine and elsewhere in the country, in the first half of 1920, before spreading to Iraq in the second half of the year. Similar events had erupted in Egypt throughout 1919 and early 1920, in protest of Britain's refusal to recognize the country's independence.

In Syria, armed clashes were launched in late 1919 and early 1920 in an attempt to prevent the French from entering and controlling the country following the withdrawal of the British forces after the Deauville Agreement in September 1919.

---

70   Ibid, pp. 154-157.

6. British Mandate over Palestine, Part I   363

Arab militants launched offensives at different locations against the French garrisons, which retaliated with counterattacks on various villages – usually burning or destroying them.

In early 1920, with increasing talk of the imminent reconvening of the Peace Conference, the possibility of imposing a British mandate over Palestine and the official announcement of the establishment of a national home for the Jewish people, those clashes were directed against the settlers as well. On February 27, 1920, Arab demonstrations – with a license from the military authorities – broke out in Jerusalem and other places in Palestine. The protests were in response to a press interview given by General Louis Bols, head of the British military administration in the country, regarding the approval of the Allied Powers to establish a national home for the Jews – despite his assertion that this approval did not mean the establishment of a Jewish state in Palestine.[71] Three days later, on March 1, 1920, Palestinian militants launched an attack on Jewish settlements in northern Palestine, destroying Tel Hai, a small settlement that had been established in 1918 south of Metula, and forcing residents of the neighboring Kfar Giladi settlement to flee. During the attack on Tel Hai, six settlers were killed, including Joseph Trumpeldor[72] – one of the founders of the Jewish Legion who had gone to Tel Hai to help in its defense just after returning from Russia. The residents of those settlements were not surprised at the attack and had informed their leadership in Tel Aviv as much, as they had anticipated it for some time due to the unrest in the region. A wide discussion had ensued among the settler leaders on how to confront this situation, and opinions were divided. Some called for the defense of those settlements at any cost, while others suggested their temporary evacuation and a return when the situation stabilized. Eventually, the first opinion prevailed –

---

71   Dinur, ed., *Sefer Toldot ha-Haganah (History of the Haganah)*, Vol. 1, Part 2, pp. 603-604; Olitsky, *Mi-Pzura le-Medinah (From Dispersal to State)*, Vol. 1, p. 146; *Chronologiah le-Toldot ha-Yishuv ha-Yehudi be-Eretz Yisrael (Chronology of the Jewish Yishuv in the Land of Israel)*, Vol. 1, p. 41.

72   For details, see Dinur, ed., *Sefer Toldot ha-Haganah (History of the Haganah)*, Vol. 1, Part 2, pp. 567-585.

calling for the defense of the settlements, because

> if we fall there, in the north, we will continue falling all the way to the desert. We need courage to leave Tel Hai and Kfar Giladi, because this is the first withdrawal... And if we flee in fear of thieves, we shall, by extension, have to leave not only the Upper Galilee, but the Land of Israel in its entirety... We shall not leave ... a place that we have occupied. Those who leave are traitors![73]

The settler leaders also decided to send forces from other areas to defend those settlements. The forces were unable to reach the area before the attack took place, however.

The settlements of Tel Hai and Kfar Giladi remained deserted for about half a year after the attack, until they were resettled in late 1920. This attack, the first of its kind, had long-term benefits for the Zionists. They took advantage of the presence of Jewish settlements in the area, which drew the attention of the British and the French after the fighting that took place, to demand the expansion of the borders of Palestine to include these settlements and their adjacent lands, which contained part of the sources of the Jordan River. They succeeded, despite earlier opposition from the French. From this experience, the Zionists learned a lesson that many of them clung to for a long time: that any area they settled was likely to remain under their permanent control. Legends were woven of the "heroism of the defenders of the settlements", who had sacrificed their lives "in defense of the homeland", especially Trumpeldor, whose account was presented as an example for young people to emulate (the right-wing Revisionist Zionists later formed a youth organization in his name). The outcome of this attack also influenced the ongoing debate on the method of organizing the Haganah defense brigades, which were beginning to be established. It was decided to follow the method of popular field defense on a national level by establishing Haganah cells in every settlement,

---

[73] Olitsky, *Mi-Pzura le-Medinah (From Dispersal to State)*, Vol. 1, pp. 202-203.

and to reject the other method that Jabotinsky had called for, namely establishing professional defense brigades through central agencies.[74]

A week after the attack on Tel Hai and Kfar Giladi, Arab demonstrations were revitalised in Palestine on the occasion of Syria's declaration of independence and the inauguration of Faisal as its king. Three weeks later, the demonstrations were again renewed on a large scale. In the first week of April 1920, at the Nebi Musa Islamic festival[75], which coincided with the Jewish Passover and the Christian Easter, marches headed to Jerusalem from its neighboring villages to participate in the celebrations as was custom.[76] On its arrival in Jerusalem on April 4, the Hebron delegation stopped several times to listen to speeches delivered by the mayor of Jerusalem, Musa Kazim al-Husseini, and by Aref al-Aref and Hajj Amin al-Husseini. These speakers urged the crowds to demand the independence and unity of Syria (including Palestine) and to defend the independence of their country and oppose turning it into a national home for the Jews. When the march reached Jaffa Gate, a clash unfolded. The Arabs began throwing stones at nearby Jewish shops and fighting with the settlers who, in turn, began attacking the Arabs, under supervision of the Jerusalem Haganah that Jabotinsky had organized.[77] The clashes persisted for about a week, despite the declaration of martial law, killing five Jews and four Arabs, injuring 211 Jews and 21 Arabs[78] and damaging property.

The April events in Jerusalem had significant results, on

---

74 For details, see Dinur, ed., *Sefer Toldot ha-Haganah (History of the Haganah)*, Vol. 1, Part 2, pp. 584-585.

75 An annual, seven-day religious festival that was celebrated by Palestinian Muslims. The festival began on the Friday before Good Friday and included a procession to the Nebi Musa shrine (tomb of Moses) near Jericho.

76 For the nature and origins of the Nebi Musa festivities, see also Emile Al-Ghouri, *Palestine through Sixty Years*, Vol. 1, pp. 45-46.

77 See Dinur, ed., *Sefer Toldot ha-Haganah (History of the Haganah)*, Vol. 1, Part 2, pp. 626-638.

78 *A Survey of Palestine, Prepared in December 1945 and January 1946 for the Information of the Anglo-American Committee of Inquiry*, Vol. 1, p. 17.

several levels. The British authorities removed Musa Kazim al-Husseini from his post as mayor, accusing him of inciting the Arabs against the Jewish population, and appointed Raghib al-Nashashibi, of the opposing clan to the Husseinis, in his place after obtaining his prior written pledge to accept the position if offered to him.[79] In so doing, the British authorities deepened the clan-political divide that existed between the Husseinis and Nashashibis, and repeatedly exploited it afterwards, which generally affected the political positions of the Arabs of Palestine and fostered their division. Musa Kazim al-Husseini, upon his removal from his post, moved to the ranks of the public opposition and assumed leadership of the Palestinian national movement until his death in 1934.

Following the April events, the British authorities also arrested a number of Arabs and settlers and brought them to trial on the charge of inciting riots. Prison sentences were meted out to Jabotinsky and his group from the leaders of the Jerusalem Haganah, and to a number of Arabs including Hajj Amin al-Husseini and Aref al-Aref. The latter two disappeared, however, and the authorities were unable to arrest them.

Those sentences also had long-term consequences. Jabotinsky (who found himself leader of the Haganah in Jerusalem somewhat against his will, as he was demanding the establishment of a legitimate military force in place of the Haganah to defend the Jewish settlers) accused the Zionist leadership of abandoning him after his imprisonment. This was the beginning of a rift between them that deepened with time and eventually led to Jabotinsky assuming leadership of the right-wing Zionist opposition. This began to strongly contest the alliance of Weizmann and his group with the Zionist labor wing – an opposition the echoes of which long persisted within the Zionist entity. The April events also spurred panic among the settlers, who gradually began to leave the mixed Arab-Jewish neighborhoods and move to separate ones of their own.[80] (This

---

79   Ronald Storrs, *Orientations*, pp. 390-391.

80   Olitsky, *Mi-Pzura le-Medinah (From Dispersal to State)*, Vol. 1, p. 225.

process continued, intensifying after the occurrence of clashes around the country, until most of the Jewish population in Palestine were living in Jewish cities, settlements, or separate neighborhoods in Arab towns by the end of the British Mandate. This helped to fortify the areas inhabited by the settlers and facilitated their administration, which had consequences in the 1948 war.)

On the other hand, the prison sentence against Hajj Amin al-Husseini contributed to the popularity of his name and was a first step on a relatively short path that brought him to the leadership of the Palestinian national movement.

The events of April 1920 also had an impact at the international level, as detailed below. The Zionists exploited them to pressure the Council of the League of Nations to approve a British mandate over Palestine, and to persuade the British government to replace the military administration in Palestine with civil authorities.

The British military administration in Palestine had been met with hostility from the Zionists from its early days, after it had refused to agree to the various exceptional privileges that they had demanded. The administration had instead insisted on a policy of preserving the status quo in the country until its political fate was decided. This conflict even led to the replacement of some officers in the administration, especially after Brandeis' visit to Palestine in the summer of 1919, when he exerted pressure on Balfour to appoint officers who it was easy for the Zionists to deal with, and to give them clear instructions.[81]

After the clashes in Jerusalem, the British administration conducted a military investigation through the "Palin Commission" to investigate their causes. The commission's report stated that the reasons included "[Arab] disappointment at the non-fulfilment of promises [of independence] made to them ... inability to reconcile the Allies' declared policy of self-determination with the Balfour Declaration ... extensive Jewish immigration fill[ing] [them] with a panic fear ... fear of

---

81 John and Hadawi, *The Palestine Diary*, Vol. 1, pp. 149-154.

Jewish competition and domination".[82] The report also stated that those fears were exacerbated by the activities of the Zionist Commission in Palestine.

The Zionists, however, despite the report, used the April events as proof of the failure of the military administration in Palestine and its inability to rule the country and impose law and order. They repeated their previous requests of the necessity to replace the military administration with a civil one. The Zionists also intensified their pressure on the Council of the League of Nations, which was meeting in San Remo at the time that the Jerusalem clashes took place, and recruited the help of Balfour and Samuel who were made to come to the meeting venue[83] to help in the campaign and speed up the decision regarding Palestine.

Finally, on April 24, 1920, a day before its adjournment, the Council of the League of Nations decided to impose a British mandate over Palestine (with Transjordan) and Iraq, and a French mandate over Syria and Lebanon, thus implementing most of the provisions of the Sykes-Picot Agreement. On the same day, Palestinian militants launched an attack on an Indian battalion affiliated with the British forces that was stationed in the town of Samakh, near the Jordan River. Three days later, on April 27, another attack took place on Ayelet ha-Shahar, a settlement in the Upper Galilee.[84]

Those attacks did not, of course, change the nature of the decisions that were taken. On the day of the attack on Ayelet ha-Shahar, the British military administration in Palestine informed the Arab leaders of the decisions of the San Remo Conference[85] and published, officially and for the first time, the text of the

---

82 *A Survey of Palestine, Prepared in December 1945 and January 1946 for the Information of the Anglo-American Committee of Inquiry*, Vol. 1, p. 17.

83 Olitsky, *Mi-Pzura le-Medinah (From Dispersal to State)*, Vol. 1, pp. 228-230.

84 For details, see Dinur, ed., *Sefer Toldot ha-Haganah (History of the Haganah)*, Vol. 1, Part 2, pp. 589-594.

85 See also *Chronologiah le-Toldot ha-Yishuv ha-Yehudi be-Eretz Yisrael (Chronology of the Jewish Yishuv in the Land of Israel)*, Vol. 1, p. 44.

Balfour Declaration. The British government also announced its intention to abolish military rule in Palestine and replace it with a civil administration as of July 1, 1920. (As for France, it issued an ultimatum to Faisal on July 14, 1920, which ended with his expulsion from Damascus and the control of the French over it.)

4

Prior to its decision to impose the British and French mandates over the countries of the Levant, the Council of the League of Nations in San Remo had discussed the draft mandate instrument for Palestine that Britain had submitted, but had not ratified it. The ratification was postponed for a good period of time for several reasons, including Italy suspending its approval until its demands were met regarding the Asiatic region of the Ottoman Empire.[86] Likewise, the Ottoman Empire refused to "waive its rights" in the Levant. This was only achieved after signing the Treaty of Sèvres between it and the Allies on August 10, 1920. However, the treaty did not receive final ratification by the Ottoman authorities when Kemal Ataturk came to power, signalling the end of the Ottoman Empire. Thus negotiations resumed until a new peace agreement was signed in Lausanne on July 24, 1923, and was considered effective as of August 6, 1924. Under Article 16 of the Treaty of Lausanne, the newly formed Republic of Turkey waived its rights in all areas outside its new borders that were drawn after its defeat in the war, recognizing the new reality and leaving the fate of those areas – including Palestine – to the Allied powers.

Another delay resulted from the intervention of the American government to secure its interests in Palestine, which led to new obstacles that prevented the speedy ratification of the mandate instrument – especially since the United States had refrained from joining the League of Nations. The Zionists and the British had to exert their efforts to secure American support for the Jewish national home in Palestine. This did not happen until May

---

86 Lloyd George, *The Truth about the Peace Treaties*, p. 1175.

3, 1922, when the US Congress, as a result of Zionist and British efforts, adopted a resolution declaring that the United States "favors the establishment in Palestine of a national home for the Jewish people".[87] The US House of Representatives followed suit with a similar resolution on June 30. A few weeks before, a joint British-American statement had been issued announcing that a treaty would be concluded between the two parties regarding Palestine.[88] Negotiations on this treaty continued for a significant time, however, and it was signed on December 3, 1924.[89] The treaty established American recognition of the British mandate over Palestine, with all its bases and premises, in return for recognizing the rights of US citizens and granting them trade facilities in the country, as well as allowing an American company to explore for oil in the Naqab (Negev) region in southern Palestine[90] (this exploration ceased in the same year, however, after geological research indicated the absence of oil in the area[91]). Through its agreement with the United States, Britain secured the approval of all the major concerned powers for the establishment of the Jewish national home in Palestine after France and Italy had declared their approval in the first half of 1918.[92]

Parallel to the American intervention, the Vatican also demanded guarantees for the status of the holy sites in Palestine in a manner that obliged Britain to redraft Articles 13 and 14

---

87 *A Survey of Palestine, Prepared in December 1945 and January 1946 for the Information of the Anglo-American Committee of Inquiry*, Vol. 1, p. 21.

88 *Report[s] of the Executive of the Zionist Organization to the XIIth Zionist Congress (1921)*, I. Political Report, p. 8.

89 See treaty in *Report by His Britannic Majesty's Government to the Council of the League of Nations on the Administration of Palestine and Trans-Jordan for the year 1925 (Colonial No. 20)*, pp. 163-166.

90 Leonard Stein, *The Balfour Declaration*, pp. 598-599; *Palestine Royal Commission Report, July 1937 (Cmd. 5479)*, p. 31.

91 See details in Michael Aran, "The Concessions for Oil and Potash Exploration in the Land of Israel", *Catedra*, No. 31, pp. 154-158.

92 World Zionist Organization, *The Mandate for Palestine, Memorandum Submitted to the Council of the League of Nations by the Zionist Organization*, pp. 3-5.

6. British Mandate over Palestine, Part I 371

of the mandate instrument to ensure that the Catholic Church would not oppose it.[93] The opposition of the Palestinian Arabs, which was adopted in some influential circles in Britain, as well as the reconsideration of the fate of Transjordan by the British, also contributed to the delay in the final ratification of the mandate by the League of Nations. This final ratification did not transpire until July 24, 1922, when the mandate instrument was signed in London. However, despite this ratification, the mandate coming into force was again delayed as it was planned that the French mandate over Syria and the British one over Palestine would begin simultaneously. This finally took place on September 29, 1923, after the French-Italian disputes over Syria were settled.

Regardless of the delay, the mandate instrument was the legal basis of British civil rule in Palestine that began on July 1, 1920. It was not surprising, therefore, that the Zionists made great efforts to draft this instrument in a manner that served their interests. Negotiations between the British government and the Zionist movement, as well as among the various Zionist groups, regarding the final version of the mandate instrument, lasted about two years, starting in early 1919 and ending in the final months of 1920.[94] During this period, several drafts were presented by the Zionist movement and about 10 versions and counter-versions were exchanged between it and the British government[95] before agreeing on and ratifying the final text of the mandate instrument.[96]

Attempts to compile this mandate instrument began in

---

93 See also *Mandate for Palestine; Letter from the Secretary to the Cabinet to the Secretary-General of the League of Nations of July 1, 1922, Enclosing a Note in Reply to Cardinal Gasparri's Letter of May 15, 1922, Addressed to the Secretary General of the League of Nations*, Miscellaneous No. 4, 1922 (Cmd. 1708).

94 For details, see *Report[s] of the Executive of the Zionist Organization to the XIIth Zionist Congress (1921), I. Political Report*, pp. 27-32.

95 Friesel, *Ha-Mediniout ha-Tzionit le-ahar Hatzharat Balfour, 1917-1922 (Zionist Policy after the Balfour Declaration, 1917-1922)*, p. 121; see also *Palestine Royal Commission Report, July 1937 (Cmd. 5479)*, pp. 31-32.

96 Esco Foundation for Palestine, Inc., *Palestine: A Study of Jewish, Arab, and British Policies*, Vol. 1, pp. 164-177; Weizmann, *Trial and Error*, pp. 347-348.

March 1919 when the American Zionist leader, Felix Frankfurter, submitted his own draft in an effort to reconcile the different Zionist views. The first phase of talks on the text began between the Zionists and the British authorities in the same month and continued until mid-July, when the first draft instrument was drawn up.[97] A new round of talks began in relation to this draft in September, based on notes that Balfour had made on the Zionist proposals to the Peace Conference. This stage ended in mid-December with the adoption of an "agreed provisional text"[98] between the Zionists and the British. With the approval of the British mandate over Palestine in April 1920, however, the British authorities began to reconsider the instrument in order to submit it to the Council of the League of Nations for ratification. This process ended in June of that year.[99] The French and the Italians, though, were surprised by the text because of its "Jewish tone",[100] such that the British had to reconsider it once more to try and diminish that tone. This came to the knowledge of the Zionists, who did everything in their power to prevent it. They succeeded in their endeavors, as their interests were secured in the final version that was approved by the Council of the League of Nations in mid-December 1920, at the expense of the rights and interests of the Palestinian Arabs.[101] The main objective of approving the text of the mandate instrument was to work on the establishment of the Jewish national home in Palestine – not to help the country's population to attain its independence, like those of other countries, as was the ostensible aim of adopting the mandate system in general. Because of these shortcomings and its conflict with the provisions and spirit of Article 22 of the

---

97 *Report[s] of the Executive of the Zionist Organization to the XIIth Zionist Congress (1921), I. Political Report*, p. 27.

98 Friesel, *Ha-Mediniout ha-Tzionit le-ahar Hatzharat Balfour, 1917-1922 (Zionist Policy after the Balfour Declaration, 1917-1922)*, p. 123.

99 For British-Zionist negotiations on drafting the mandate instrument, see also *Report[s] of the Executive of the Zionist Organization to the XIIth Zionist Congress (1921), I. Political Report*, pp. 27-32.

100 Ibid, p. 189.

101 For details, see ibid, pp. 120-125, 186-191.

6. British Mandate over Palestine, Part I 373

Covenant of the League of Nations – the article that formed the legal basis for the entire mandate system – there are claims that the imposition of the British mandate over Palestine was an illegal act,[102] yet this did not prevent Britain from ruling the country.

The eagerness of the authors of the mandate instrument to turn it into a tool for actualizing the Jewish national home in Palestine is evident in several of its articles, including the introduction that contained the text of the Balfour Declaration. In their draft of the instrument, the Zionists had taken out even the paragraph that stipulated preserving the civil and religious rights of non-Jewish communities in Palestine, but the paragraph was added back at the insistence of the French delegate at the San Remo Conference after he had waived his reservations on other articles in the instrument.[103] The Zionists did, however, succeed in adding another paragraph to the introduction, which they had not managed to include in the text of the Balfour Declaration when it was issued, which stated that the imposition of the British mandate over Palestine and the implementation of the Balfour Declaration constituted a recognition of the "historical connection of the Jewish people with Palestine" and the "grounds for reconstituting their national home in that country".

This introduction to the mandate instrument found expression in a number of its articles, which expounded it and set the conditions and tools for its implementation. Article 2 of the instrument stipulated that

> the Mandatory shall be responsible for placing the country under such political, administrative and economic conditions as will secure the establishment of the Jewish national home ... and the development of self-governing institutions, and also for safeguarding the civil and religious [not the political] rights of all the inhabitants of Palestine, irrespective of race

---

102 As an example, see W. F. Boustany, *The Palestine Mandate, Invalid and Impracticable*.

103 Lloyd George, *The Truth about the Peace Treaties*, pp. 1163-1175, 1182-1190.

and religion.

In Article 4, the mandate government was stipulated to recognize a

> Jewish agency ... as a public body for the purpose of advising and co-operating with the Administration of Palestine in such economic, social and other matters as may affect the establishment of the Jewish national home and the interests of the Jewish population in Palestine, and, subject always to the control of the Administration to assist and take part in the development of the country. The Zionist organization, so long as its organization and constitution are in the opinion of the Mandatory appropriate, shall be recognized as such agency.

(The British authorities legally recognized the Zionist Organization as the Jewish Agency, and dealt with it as such, until the latter was established, in practice, in 1929.)

The mandate instrument also advised the Zionist Organization to "take steps in consultation with His Britannic Majesty's Government to secure the cooperation of all [non-Zionist] Jews who are willing to assist in the establishment of the Jewish national home". Article 6 of the instrument obliged the mandate government to "facilitate Jewish immigration [to Palestine] under suitable conditions and [to] encourage, in co-operation with the Jewish agency ... close settlement by Jews on the land, including State lands and waste lands not required for public purposes". In Article 7, the government was "responsible for enacting a nationality law ... [with] provisions framed so as to facilitate the acquisition of Palestinian citizenship by Jews who take up their permanent residence in Palestine". Article 11 allowed the government of Palestine to "arrange with the Jewish agency ... to construct or operate, upon fair and equitable terms, any public works, services and utilities, and to develop any of the natural resources of the country, in so far as these matters are not directly undertaken by the Administration [government]". Finally, Article 22 recognized Hebrew as an official language, stating that "English, Arabic and Hebrew shall be the official languages of Palestine."[104] The British military administration in Palestine had refrained from taking such a step.

The second issue discussed by the Council of the League of Nations in San Remo, with regard to Palestine, was the question of the country's borders, although the council did not make a final decision on them. The border issue was a matter of dispute between Britain and France, which negotiated it for a considerable time. The dispute was focused on the northern and northeastern borders of Palestine – for the western border is the Mediterranean Sea; the southern border between Palestine and Egypt was the one imposed by Britain on Turkey in 1906[105] and was unchanged after ratification of the British mandate over Palestine; and the designation of the eastern border was subject to the will of Britain alone, which controlled Palestine and Transjordan (as well as Iraq, to the east).

According to the Sykes-Picot Agreement, the northern border of Palestine was along a straight line extending from the north of the town of Acre to the north of Lake Tiberias (the Sea of Galilee). This border, however, did not satisfy the British and the Zionists, who wanted to expand it to include – in the words of Lloyd George – "Scriptural Palestine, extending from Dan [in the north] to Beersheba [in the south]", so that the northern water sources such as the Litani River, Baniyas River, Lake Hula and others would lie within it.[106] The Eastern Committee of the British War Cabinet, which met in December 1918 to discuss Britain's demands regarding Palestine at the Peace Conference, had also recommended that "every effort should be made ... to secure an equitable readjustment of the boundaries of Palestine,

---

104 See the official mandate instrument for Palestine in *Mandate for Palestine, Together with a Note by the Secretary-General Relating to its Application to the Territory known as Transjordan, Under the Provisions of Article 25, December 1922 (Cmd. 1785)*.

105 For details, see *Correspondence respecting the Turco-Egyptian Frontier in the Sinai Peninsula (With a Map), Egypt No. 2, 1906 (Cmd. 306)*.

106 Lloyd George, *The Truth about the Peace Treaties*, p. 1144.

both on the north and east and south."[107]

During the Peace Conference in early 1919, the question of the northern border was raised and a lengthy discussion took place. Britain demanded the extension of this border to the north to include the water sources in the region or, in the event that this request was not met, for France to commit not to divert the courses of the Jordan River if they fell in the area under its mandate, so as not to deprive Palestine of its water. To support those requests, Lloyd George declared before the conference that "Britain would only accept a Mandate for a real Palestine, the Palestine of ancient history; which should not merely include the barren rocks of Judea, that might at any moment be rendered a desert through the cutting off of the waters flowing through the same."[108] The French delegate refused to agree to the British demands, pointing out that the water in the north was also necessary to irrigate the lands that it passed through. The Zionists attempted to put pressure on the conference while it was in session. Brandeis, at the Zionists' behest, sent a telegram to Lloyd George on February 16, 1919, asking him to work on expanding the northern border of Palestine to include the Litani River as well as water estuaries in Mount Hermon, the Golan Plain and Hawran. The French delegate refused this request as well, and commented on the telegram by saying that it showed Brandeis had an exaggerated sense of self-importance.[109] The Peace Conference adjourned without taking a decision on the borders.

Yet the British did not cease their efforts to modify the northern border of Palestine, and continued their pressure on the French government until they succeeded. During negotiations on the Deauville Agreement that was signed on September 15, 1919, by which Britain recognized French power over Syria, the British were able to persuade the French to agree to the expansion of the border of Palestine. The northern border line,

---

107 Ibid, p. 1155.

108 Ibid, p. 1177.

109 Ibid; see also pp. 1179-1180.

6. British Mandate over Palestine, Part I

which had been drawn under the Sykes-Picot Agreement, was replaced by another, semi-straight line extending from Naqoura until the north of Lake Hula (see *Map 8, Drawing of Palestine's northern border, 1916-1923,* below). Yet even this new border did not satisfy the British and the Zionists, as the main water sources in the north remained beyond it and so the two parties renewed their pressure on France.

From mid-1920, a new round of negotiations began between the British and the French to settle the border issues and other matters that had arisen after the imposition of the mandates on the countries of the Levant. A new agreement was signed on December 23, 1920.[110] This agreement included the expansion of the northern border of Palestine to encompass that narrow rectangle of land (the "finger") to the north of Tiberias, which included the Jewish settlements of Metula, Tel Hai, Kfar Giladi and others that had been attacked by the Arabs in March 1920.[111] France agreed that this area would be annexed to Palestine after the British insisted, claiming it was necessary to enable Pinhas Rutenberg (1879-1942), a Russian Zionist engineer and leader, to build reservoirs and water dams for electricity generation.[112] It was also agreed to allow the British mandate authorities to exploit the surplus waters of the Yarmouk and Jordan rivers to irrigate the lands of Palestine.[113] Within the agreement, the two countries appointed a commission to draw the borders by actual land survey.[114] This commission drew the borders from

---

110 *Franco-British Convention of December 23, 1920 on Certain Points connected with the Mandates for Syria and the Lebanon, Palestine and Mesopotamia (Cmd. 1195).*

111 Olitsky, *Mi-Pzura le-Medinah (From Dispersal to State),* Vol. 1, p. 206.

112 Gideon Biger, "Geographic and Political Considerations in the Process of Drawing the Northern Borders of the Land of Israel during the Mandate Period", in Avshalom Shmueli, Arnon Sofer and Nurit Kliot, ed., *Artzot ha-Galil (Lands of the Galilee),* Vol. 1, p. 437.

113 *Franco-British Convention of December 23, 1920 on Certain Points connected with the Mandates for Syria and the Lebanon, Palestine and Mesopotamia (Cmd. 1195),* p. 3.

114 On negotiations regarding the northern border of Palestine, see Friesel, *Ha-Mediniout ha-Tzionit le-ahar Hatzharat Balfour, 1917-1922 (Zionist*

the Mediterranean Sea to al-Hamma in a way that annexed the Tiberias and Hula lakes, as well as part of the Jordan River water sources, to Palestine. A report/agreement on this was signed between the British and French representatives on February 3, 1922. The implementation of this agreement was delayed for about a year,[115] however, until a new treaty regarding the border was signed on March 10, 1923,[116] which adopted the findings of the report of the border commission (that was also presented to the League of Nations). Finally, the issue of the border between Baniyas and Metula remained unresolved until the following year[117] when Metula and its vicinity were annexed to Palestine from April 1, 1924.[118]

With this drawing of the border in its almost final form, it became clear that it had led to the split of about 20 villages on the Palestinian-Lebanese border between the two countries, as well as 18 villages on the Palestinian-Syrian border whose lands were similarly divided.[119]

Policy after the Balfour Declaration, 1917-1922), pp. 196-203; *Report[s] of the Executive of the Zionist Organization to the XIIth Zionist Congress (1921), I. Political Report*, pp. 33-39.

115 Biger in Shmueli, A., et al. ed., *Artzot ha-Galil (Lands of the Galilee)*, Vol. 1, p. 438.

116 *Agreement between His Majesty's Government and the French Government respecting the Boundary Line between Syria and Palestine from the Mediterranean to El Hamme (With Three Maps), Treaty Series No. 13, 1923 (Cmd. 1910).*

117 Ibid; see also *Report of the High Commissioner on the Administration of Palestine, 1920-1925 (Colonial No. 15)*, p. 55.

118 *Chronologiah le-Toldot ha-Yishuv ha-Yehudi be-Eretz Yisrael (Chronology of the Jewish Yishuv in the Land of Israel)*, Vol. 1, p. 102; see also *Report by His Britannic Majesty's Government to the Council of the League of Nations on the Administration of Palestine and Trans-Jordan for the year 1925 (Colonial No. 20)*, p. 5.

119 Biger in Shmueli, A., et al. ed., *Artzot ha-Galil (Lands of the Galilee)*, Vol. 1, p. 439.

6. British Mandate over Palestine, Part I

Map 8 Drawing of Palestine's northern border, 1916-1923[120]

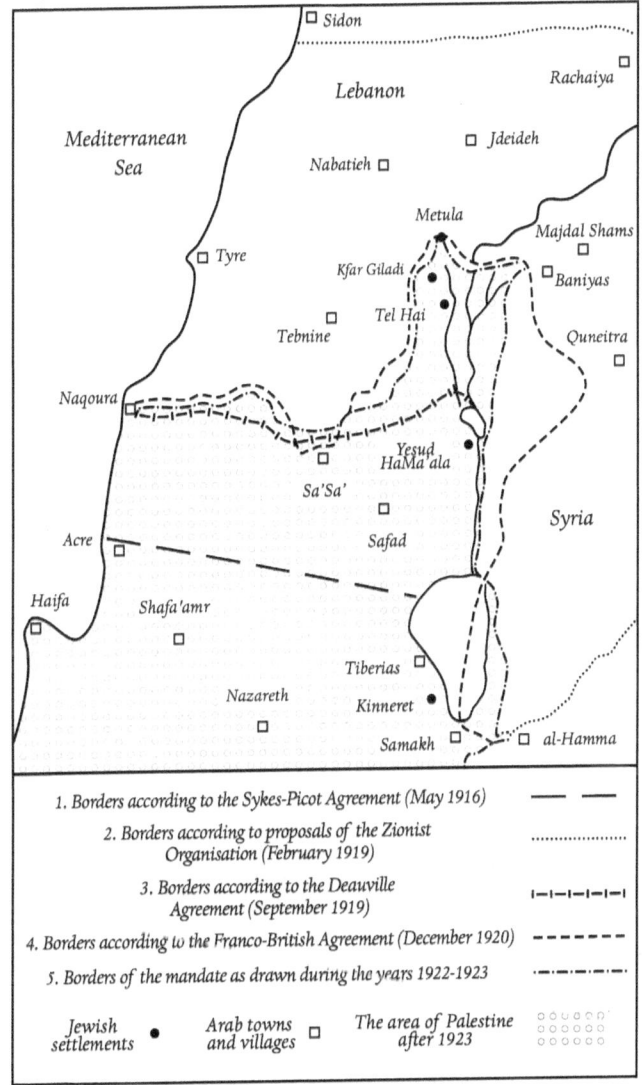

120 Map was drawn in accordance with that in Wallach, *Atlas Carta le-Toldot Eretz Yisrael mi-Rashit ha-Hityashvut ve ad Koum ha-Medina (Carta's Atlas of History of the Land of Israel from the Start of Settlement until the Establishment of the State)*, Map 51, p. 40.

As a result, and to control the border administration process and facilitate matters for the residents of those villages, the British and French mandate authorities signed an agreement of good neighborly relations between Palestine, Syria and Lebanon on February 2, 1926.[121] The residents of those villages were generally permitted to cross the border with their identification cards, without the need for passports, and to work their lands on the other side. They were also permitted to transfer their agricultural produce across the border without paying customs fees. This agreement was later amended on November 3, 1938.[122]

Minor modifications were made to the northern border even after 1924, between Palestine, Lebanon and Syria, mainly due to the construction of transportation routes between the three countries.[123] Similar modifications were made to the border between Palestine and Transjordan, which led to a reduction in the area of the Bisan district after Britain and France signed a protocol to define the borders between Syria and Transjordan in 1931.[124]

The process of drawing the eastern border of Palestine took place in 1922, after a political decision was made on the fate of the lands east of the Jordan River (see section 5 of this chapter). With these borders and their various modifications, the area of Palestine was 10,434 square miles: 10,162 of land and 272 of lakes and rivers (or 27,024 square kilometers: 26,320 of land and

---

121 *Agreement between Palestine and Syria and the Lebanon to Facilitate Good Neighbourly Relations in connection with Frontier Questions (Signed at Jerusalem, February 2, 1926), Treaty Series No. 19, 1927 (Cmd. 2919).*

122 *Agreement between Palestine and Syria and the Lebanon, Amending the Agreement of February 2, 1926, Regarding Frontier Questions, November 3, 1938, Treaty Series No. 34, 1939 (Cmd. 6065).*

123 Biger in Shmueli, A., et al. ed., *Artzot ha-Galil (Lands of the Galilee)*, Vol. 1, p. 439.

124 See protocol in *Report by His Majesty's Government in the United Kingdom of Great Britain and Northern Ireland to the Council of the League of Nations on the Administration of Palestine and Trans-Jordan for the year 1931 (Colonial No. 75)*, pp. 207-210.

704 of lakes and rivers).[125]

5

After being chosen as the mandatory authority over Palestine on April 24, 1920 by the Council of the League of Nations at San Remo, Britain announced its intention to abolish military rule in the country and replace it with a civil administration. This was to take effect on July 1 of the same year, and over the next three years the British mandate system took shape in Palestine. The final form of this system was influenced by each of the different parties' conflicting interests: the Allies, Britain, the Zionists and the Palestinian Arabs.

With Britain's announcement of its intention to establish civil rule in Palestine, its representatives at the San Remo conference also announced the selection of Herbert Samuel as the first high commissioner in the country. There was no better choice to implement the national home project. The first Jewish minister in the British government, Samuel was one of the pillars of the group of British leaders who had been active in encouraging the government to adopt the Zionist project and then to issue the Balfour Declaration.[126] Samuel, who had visited Palestine in early 1920[127] to review its conditions firsthand, accepted the post after consulting and gaining the approval of Weizmann and Sokolow. The three had attended the meetings of the League of Nations held in San Remo at the invitation of British prime minister Lloyd George.[128] The Zionists also appointed a number of their supporters to critical administrative posts in Palestine.

---

125 *A Survey of Palestine, Prepared in December 1945 and January 1946 for the Information of the Anglo-American Committee of Inquiry*, Vol. 1, pp. 103-104; *Statistical Abstract of Palestine, 1939*, pp. 2, 11.

126 For details, see Chapter 5, section 1.

127 *Chronologiah le-Toldot ha-Yishuv ha-Yehudi be-Eretz Yisrael (Chronology of the Jewish Yishuv in the Land of Israel)*, Vol. 1, p. 40.

128 Friesel, *Ha-Mediniout ha-Tzionit le-ahar Hatzharat Balfour, 1917-1922 (Zionist Policy after the Balfour Declaration, 1917-1922)*, pp. 130, 134.

Among the most prominent ones were Norman Bentwich, as judicial officer to the administration – in this capacity, he was also responsible for drafting the laws issued by the mandate government; Albert Hyamson, chief immigration officer; and Max Nurock, who was moved from his work in the Zionist Organization and appointed assistant secretary to the mandate government.[129]

Samuel immediately proceeded to establish the civil administration and prepare the country to strengthen the Jewish national home. At his inauguration ceremony on July 9, 1920, he announced the reopening of the land registry office (Tabu), which had been closed since the outbreak of the First World War. In October, the office was opened, removing a major obstacle facing the Zionist land-purchase institutions. Its closure had almost paralyzed their activity, as the transfer of land ownership only officially took place at the Tabu. After this, courts were established to settle land ownership disputes and a survey department was set up.[130] Samuel had also announced the expansion of the field of public works, such as constructing roads, facilities and the like, which would be financed by the government. A significant number of new Jewish immigrants were employed on these works. Samuel also intended to form a body to supervise the railways and pledged to make efforts to establish electricity generation stations and telegraphic communication agencies, as well as to dry up marshes, improve health and cultural conditions and work on other matters.[131] In August 1920, Jewish immigration to Palestine resumed[132] after a special law was issued to allow 16,500 Jewish immigrants to enter the country within a year. On October 1, Samuel issued an order making Hebrew an official language in Palestine (in

---

129 For details, see John and Hadawi, *The Palestine Diary*, Vol. 1, p. 167.

130 *An Interim Report on the Civil Administration of Palestine During the Period 1st July 1920-30th June 1921, August 1921 (Cmd. 1499)*, p. 16.

131 Olitsky, *Mi-Pzura le-Medinah (From Dispersal to State)*, Vol. 1, p. 242.

132 *An Interim Report on the Civil Administration of Palestine During the Period 1st July 1920-30th June 1921, August 1921 (Cmd. 1499)*, p. 18.

6. British Mandate over Palestine, Part I 383

addition to Arabic and English), before this was ratified by the mandate instrument – although Hebrew was not used in districts where the Jewish population was less than a fifth of the total population.[133]

At the same time, pardons to both Arabs and Jews were given to those convicted in the events of April 1920, including Amin al-Husseini, Aref al-Aref and Ze'ev Jabotinsky, in what seemed to be the first step in a policy of keeping the balance between the two communities. As for the system of governance, Samuel announced his intention to form an advisory council that he would preside over, with 20 members: 10 British officials, seven Arabs (four Muslims and three Christians) and three Jews.[134] The council held its first session on November 6, 1920.[135] Various administrative departments were gradually established at the same time, where the majority of senior officials (including the judiciary and public prosecution) were British.[136]

Before and during these measures, the Arabs of Palestine continued to express their opposition to them and to the policy of their country becoming the Jewish national home. After the decisions of the San Remo conference to impose the British mandate over Palestine, the second Palestine Arab Congress was called to convene in May 1920 to discuss the policy following the new developments. The British military authorities, however, prevented the holding of the congress and also imposed – under the pretext of maintaining the policy of balance – a ban on a session of the Jewish Assembly ("Knesset Yisrael") that was scheduled during the same month.[137]

---

133 *Report of the High Commissioner on the Administration of Palestine, 1920-1925 (Colonial No. 15)*, p. 38.

134 *An Interim Report on the Civil Administration of Palestine During the Period 1st July 1920-30th June 1921, August 1921 (Cmd. 1499)*, p. 10.

135 *Chronologiah le-Toldot ha-Yishuv ha-Yehudi be-Eretz Yisrael (Chronology of the Jewish Yishuv in the Land of Israel)*, Vol. 1, p. 50; *Report on Palestine Administration, 1923 (Colonial No. 5)*, p. 3.

136 *An Interim Report on the Civil Administration of Palestine During the Period 1st July 1920-30th June 1921, August 1921 (Cmd. 1499)*, p. 9.

137 Olitsky, *Mi-Pzura le-Medinah (From Dispersal to State)*, Vol. 1, p. 234.

The Arab leaders began to closely follow Samuel's activities on his arrival in Palestine in order to understand his policy. At the same time, they experienced disappointment at the fall of Faisal's rule in Damascus in July 1920 and the effect that would have on the future of Palestine. Thus, the third Palestine Arab Congress was not convened until the end of that year.

Held in Haifa during December 13-18, 1920, the third congress faced grave problems. It found itself obliged to define the bases of a new Palestinian strategy in light of the imposition of the British mandate over Palestine, on the one hand, and the French control of Syria, on the other (especially since Palestinian leaders insisted on regarding Palestine as part of Syria and demanded the formation of one government for the area as a whole). After five days of deliberations, however, decisions were taken that indicated an acquiescence to the new reality. The congress called on Britain to establish "a national government responsible to a representative assembly, whose members would be chosen from the Arabic-speaking people who inhabited Palestine until the outbreak of the War",[138] without any challenges to the legitimacy of the British Mandate or any hint of unity with Syria. It is clear that the silence on the demand for this unity was due to the French control of Syria, although some historians claimed that it was also to "spite" Faisal who had "forsaken" Palestine at the Peace Conference. Whatever the motives that prompted the congress to take this position, its decisions were the beginning of a new era in which the Palestinian national movement was active on its own, generally without recognising events in the neighboring Arab countries. The Arab national movements in these countries, in turn, paid little heed to what was happening in Palestine. This lasted for about 16 years. The outbreak of the Great Arab Revolt in 1936-1939 then drew the attention of the Arab countries back to Palestine, but only after the Jewish national home had significantly grown in it.

Other decisions taken by the third Palestine Arab Congress

---

138 *Palestine Documents File*, Vol. 1, p. 277.

were also moderate. The congress sufficed with declaring that "the people are dissatisfied with the form of the current administration, because it is contrary to their wishes and rights,"[139] for several reasons, including:

> 1. The [British administration] taking the power to enact laws by itself, that is, without an elected, representative legislative assembly, and before the final decision of the League of Nations, 2. Its recognition of the Zionist Organization as an official body, 3. Its implementation of Zionist schemes through the entry of Jewish immigrants, use of Hebrew as an official language, and silence on the banner of Zionism, 4. Its establishment of an advisory council appointed by it, to give the illusion of a legislative council in Palestine that is representative of the population, 5. The presence of Zionist leaders in its highest positions, even though Palestine is the Holy Land of the Christian and Muslim worlds, and [therefore] must not be allowed to fall into non-Muslim or non-Christian hands.[140]

Despite this, however,

> this congress extends its thanks to Great Britain [because] it is sure that its request [forming a national government] would be well-accepted and met with the quickest response, and that hesitation in responding to it would perpetuate the unnecessary and avoidable discontent of the Arab people, and burden the British people with heavy expenses for the sake of internal and external comfort.[141]

Despite these conservative decisions, and the election of an executive committee of moderate Palestinian figures headed by Musa Kazim al-Husseini, the high commissioner announced his refusal to recognize the congress, claiming that it did

---

139 Ibid.
140 Ibid.
141 Ibid.

not represent the Palestinian people. A campaign was then launched, issuing statements and leaflets and holding public meetings across the country in support of the congress, such that Samuel had to reconsider his decision. He began a dialogue with those leaders and told them that he was ready to recognize any Arab body that represented an important segment of the people, on the condition that it would not make any decisions or proposals that contradicted the terms of the Mandate. The Palestinian leaders declined to agree, but they consented to the possibility of establishing personal, friendly relations with the high commissioner.[142] The Jewish Assembly, for its part, agreed to these proposals, and Samuel recognized it.

Samuel maintained his policy of offering minor concessions to the Palestinian leaders and seeking to win the favor of some of them, in an attempt to maintain calm in the country, as long as this did not contradict the principles of the Mandate or provoke opposition from the Zionists.

Two months after the third Palestine Arab Congress, Samuel had the opportunity to again ensure British interests. The mufti of Jerusalem, Kamel al-Husseini, passed away in March 1921, and attention turned to the election of his successor. At the time, the position of mufti was as significant as that of mayor. As the latter position was with the Nashashibis, after Raghib al-Nashashibi had been appointed mayor of Jerusalem in the wake of Musa Kazim al-Husseini's dismissal, it was necessary to preserve the pretence of balance and to give the mufti position to the Husseinis. Hajj Amin al-Husseini was chosen, and the authorities maneuvered to secure his election after Samuel had met and agreed with him.[143] Hajj Amin al-Husseini came fourth in the first round of elections, especially as the Nashashibis nominated a strong competitor, Sheikh Husam al-Din Jarallah. The candidate for the mufti's position was elected from among the top three contenders, and so the authorities rushed to

---

142 Kayyali, *Palestine: A Modern History*, pp. 165-167.

143 Elie Kedourie, "Sir Herbert Samuel and the Government of Palestine", *Middle Eastern Studies*, Vol. 5, No. 1, p. 51.

present Sheikh Jarallah with temptations for him to withdraw his candidacy, so that only three candidates remained. Hajj Amin was then appointed mufti, although his appointment was not confirmed in any official document.[144]

There are various interpretations of the motives that led Samuel to choose Hajj Amin al-Husseini for the position of mufti, other than the desire to maintain a balance between the Husseini and Nashashibi clans and thus exploit the traditional rivalry between them to split the ranks of the Palestinian national movement. The Husseini family had inherited this position but, at the same time, led by Musa Kazim al-Husseini, it played an important role in the leadership of the national movement. Thus, the British were eager to appease and win it over. Hajj Amin al-Husseini had also played a prominent role in the Jerusalem events of 1920, and his appointment to a prestigious position was grounds to push him to ally with the authorities – or to at least constrain him.

As Samuel was taking his first steps in Palestine, however, the British government had decided to reconsider its policy regarding the Levant, especially those areas that were brought under its mandate. A conference of British officials in the region, including politicians, military personnel and administrators, was held in Cairo in early March 1921. The conference was headed by Winston Churchill, the British colonial secretary, and aimed to establish the details of this new policy. It decided to install Faisal, whom the French had expelled from Syria, as king of Iraq under the British Mandate. While the conference was in session, Emir Abdullah, Faisal's brother, came from the Hejaz to Amman in Transjordan with a force of his followers to attack the French in Syria. This prompted the British to intervene. When Churchill came to Jerusalem at the end of that month, he met with Emir Abdullah and agreed with him that he would "carry on the administration of Trans-Jordania, under the general direction of the high commissioner of

---

144   Ibid, p. 55.

Palestine".[145] Abdullah then began to strengthen his relations with the British, who agreed to provide him with advisors and economic assistance. In 1922, the emir visited London and concluded an agreement with the British government that recognized the existence of an "independent government"[146] under his leadership in Transjordan. It was decided that the provisions of the mandate instrument over Palestine and the establishment of the Jewish national home would not apply to Transjordan. The Council of the League of Nations was informed of this on September 16, 1922.[147] At a later stage, the British authorities added a special article to this effect to the mandate instrument (Article 25), and obtained the approval of the Council of the League of Nations.[148]

Before the text of the British mandate instrument over Palestine was approved by the League of Nations on September 24, 1922, the British authorities issued a decree on the 1st of that month defining the borders of the country. Transjordan was severed from Palestine, and the borders between them were drawn by "a line extending from a point two miles west of the city of Aqaba, located on the Gulf of Aqaba, to the middle of Wadi Araba, the Dead Sea and the Jordan River at its confluence with the Yarmouk River, extending to the middle of the Yarmouk River and then the Syrian border"[149] (see *Map 9 Division of the Levant after the First World War*, below). Thus, the way was paved for the establishment of the Emirate of Transjordan and the appointment of Abdullah as its emir. (On February 20, 1928, another agreement was made between

---

[145] *An Interim Report on the Civil Administration of Palestine During the Period 1st July 1920-30th June 1921, August 1921 (Cmd. 1499)*, p. 21.

[146] *Report of the High Commissioner on the Administration of Palestine, 1920-1925 (Colonial No. 15)*, p. 53.

[147] *Mandate for Palestine, Together with a Note by the Secretary-General Relating to its Application to the Territory known as Transjordan, Under the Provisions of Article 25, December 1922 (Cmd. 1785)*, p. 10.

[148] Ibid, pp. 10-11.

[149] Robert Drayton, *The Laws of Palestine*, Vol. 4, p. 3360.

6. British Mandate over Palestine, Part I 389

Britain and Emir Abdullah, reinforcing British recognition of his rule in Transjordan. This agreement was later amended by a treaty on June 2, 1934.[150]) The Zionists tried to protest these measures, claiming that Transjordan was only "the eastern Land of Israel" and that it had to be included in the region allocated for the establishment of the Jewish national home – even though neither the Balfour Declaration nor the mandate instrument had referred to any borders. Their objections were stifled.[151] Some historians claim that the British goal of establishing the Emirate of Transjordan in this manner, separating it from the area designated for the establishment of the national home, was to find a shelter for the Palestinian Arabs who would be forced to leave their homes because of the realization of the Zionist project. Whatever the validity of these claims, it is clear that the British authorities insisted – with an almost categorical firmness – on preventing any Zionist infiltration east of the Jordan River[152] during the entire period of the mandate,[153] even though a number of sheikhs in Transjordan expressed their willingness to cooperate with the Zionists and even to allow them to establish settlements on lands that the sheikhs controlled.[154]

---

150 See treaty in *Report by His Majesty's Government in the United Kingdom of Great Britain and Northern Ireland to the Council of the League of Nations on the Administration of Palestine and Trans-Jordan for the year 1934 (Colonial No. 104)*, pp. 297-298.

151 See also Abraham Ellsberg, "Drawing the Eastern Borders of the Land of Israel", in Daniel Carpi, ed., *Ha-Tzionout, Me'asef le-Toldot ha-Tnu'ah ha-Tzionit ve ha-Yishuv ha-Yehudi be-Eretz Yisrael (Zionism: Studies in the History of the Zionist Movement and of the Jewish Community in the Land of Israel)*, Vol. 3. pp. 229-246.

152 For details, see Olitsky, *Mi-Pzura le-Medinah (From Dispersal to State)*, Vol. 1, pp. 427-435.

153 Ibid.

154 For details, see, for example, Anita Shapira, "Issue of Priority Rights over the Lands of Emir Abdullah in Ghor el-Kabed: Start of Contacts between the Zionist Administration and Emir Abdullah" in Carpi, ed. *Ha-Tzionout (Zionism)*, pp. 259-345; also "Mithqal Pasha ... and the Project to Purchase Lands in Moab", in Eliyahu Eilat, *Shivat Tzion ve Arav (Return to Zion and the Arabs)*, pp. 125-137.

390   The Foundations of Zionism

Map 9 Division of the Levant after the First World War

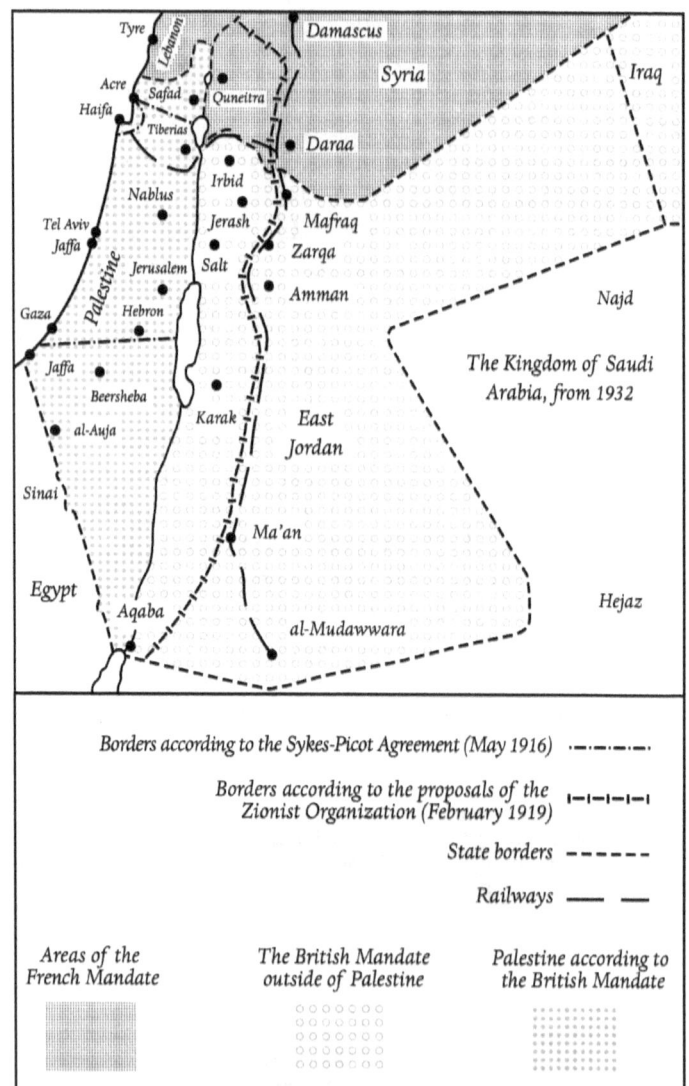

To complete the implementation of the policy approved by the conference of British officials held in Cairo under Churchill, the British government issued a White Paper outlining its position on Iraq in June 1921. Emir Faisal arrived in Baghdad as a candidate to the throne, and a referendum was held after which he was crowned king of Iraq on August 23, 1921.

While Churchill was in Cairo in March 1921, the executive committee elected by the third Palestine Arab Congress decided to form a delegation to travel to him and present Palestinian demands. Churchill reluctantly met the delegation and refrained from discussing political issues, explaining that he would receive the members of the congress in Jerusalem later that month. At the meeting in Jerusalem, the Palestinian leaders asked him to work on revoking the Balfour Declaration, stopping Jewish immigration to Palestine and facilitating the establishment of an elected national government in the country. Churchill responded that the fulfillment of the first two requests was "not in [his] power" and "not [his] wish".[155] He added, however, that Arab interests would be safeguarded and that the establishment of the national home did not mean "a Jewish government to dominate the Arabs".[156]

Churchill's position did not appease the Palestinians, who soon found an occasion to express their anger. A month later in late April 1921, the Jewish Socialist Workers Party ("MOPS", in Hebrew), which had communist leanings, distributed leaflets in Hebrew, Yiddish and Arabic in Tel Aviv and Jaffa. The party called on Jewish and Arab workers to abstain from work and demonstrate on the occasion of Labor Day, and urged them to establish a Palestinian soviet.[157] On May 1, the party organized an unauthorized procession which headed from Tel Aviv to Jaffa and clashed with another demonstration led by the Ahdut HaAvoda party. When the police tried to disperse the MOPS

---

155 John and Hadawi, *The Palestine Diary*, Vol. 1, p. 169.

156 Ibid.

157 *Disturbances in May 1921. Report of the Commission of Inquiry with Correspondence Relating Thereto, October 1921 (Cmd. 1540)*, pp. 19-22.

demonstration, its members sought refuge in the Manshiyya Arab neighborhood in Jaffa. Rumors spread of settlers attacking Arabs, and the Arabs attacked a hotel designated to receive new Jewish immigrants and killed a number of its guests.[158] Riots then erupted in other areas of Palestine and lasted several days, during which the Arabs attacked a number of Jewish settlements, including Petah Tikva, Rehovot and Hadera.[159] The riots, in addition to property damage, led to the death of 47 settlers and the injury of 146, most of whom were injured by the Arabs, and the death of 48 Arabs and injury of 72,[160] most of whom were injured by the police and the army. The Arab leaders declared a boycott of the settlers,[161] but this measure did not last long.

The British authorities appointed a commission of inquiry into the cause of the riots. The commission was led by the chief justice in Palestine, Thomas Haycraft. In its report published in October 1921, the Haycraft Commission stated that the causes of the riots lay in "a feeling among the Arabs of discontent with, and hostility to, the Jews, due to political and economic causes, and connected with Jewish immigration, and with their conception of Zionist policy".[162] The commission stressed the Arab "fear that through extensive Jewish immigration Palestine will become a Jewish dominion".[163]

The events of May 1921 left their mark. Samuel, himself, was among those affected, prompting him to reconsider his Palestine

---

[158] For details, see ibid, pp. 22-26; Dinur, ed., *Sefer Toldot ha-Haganah (History of the Haganah)*, Vol. 2, Part 1, pp. 77-91.

[159] *Disturbances in May 1921. Report of the Commission of Inquiry with Correspondence Relating Thereto, October 1921 (Cmd. 1540)*, pp. 4-16, 36-43.

[160] Ibid, p. 60.

[161] Dinur, ed., *Sefer Toldot ha-Haganah (History of the Haganah)*, Vol. 2, Part 1, pp. 91-92.

[162] *Disturbances in May 1921. Report of the Commission of Inquiry with Correspondence Relating Thereto, October 1921 (Cmd. 1540)*, p. 59.

[163] *A Survey of Palestine, Prepared in December 1945 and January 1946 for the Information of the Anglo-American Committee of Inquiry*, Vol. 1, pp. 18-19; see also *Palestine Documents File*, Vol. 1, pp. 303-305.

policy[164] and attempt to convince London of his point of view. Through his work as high commissioner, Samuel had reached the conviction that it was impossible to implement the Zionist program to its fullest extent or to meet all of the Zionists' demands due to Arab opposition, on the one hand, and the weakness of the Zionist movement and its lack of financial resources, on the other. The Zionist agencies in Palestine were unable to absorb even the small number of Jewish immigrants who had arrived by that time, which contributed to exacerbating the economic problems that plagued the country during 1921-1922. It also strengthened Samuel's feeling that the Zionists, especially Weizmann, had deceived him into accepting the position of British high commissioner in Palestine, deluding him that they were a reliable force in the country and abroad.[165] The May events created new problems and deepened those convictions for Samuel, pushing him to formulate a policy (which he pursued until the end of his term in 1925) of primarily securing British interests in Palestine[166] while assigning Britain the least possible economic and political burdens, especially since its economic conditions were not favorable in the early 1920s together with the political turmoil in its colonies. As for the Arabs, Samuel's policy was again one of leniency[167] and making concessions to them, as long as these did not affect the basis of the mandate system. He implemented this policy by encouraging the moderate leaders while trying to contain those he perceived as hardliners through positions and titles as well as personal, friendly relations – pitting those two sides against each other by attempting to distract them with fringe issues. The Zionists were to obtain facilities commensurate with their size only, without concern for their ambitions, even if this angered them and pushed them towards a

---

164 Friesel, *Ha-Mediniout ha-Tzionit le-ahar Hatzharat Balfour, 1917-1922 (Zionist Policy after the Balfour Declaration, 1917-1922)*, p. 256.

165 Ibid, p. 262; see also Olitsky, *Mi-Pzura le-Medinah (From Dispersal to State)*, Vol. 1, p. 253.

166 Friesel, *Ha-Mediniout ha-Tzionit le-ahar Hatzharat Balfour, 1917-1922 (Zionist Policy after the Balfour Declaration, 1917-1922)*, p. 264.

167 Ibid, p. 259.

policy of patient perseverance.[168]

The first evidence of Samuel's changed policy was a speech he delivered on June 3, 1921, on the occasion of the British king's birthday, in which he presented a new interpretation of the Balfour Declaration. He denied that Britain's goal was to enable outsiders to control the Arabs of Palestine, their lands and holy sites, but to instead allow a number of Jewish immigrants, which would be determined according to the interests of the population, to come to the country and contribute to its development to the advantage of all its inhabitants.[169] At the end of his speech, Samuel said:

> If we see ourselves in the need to take any measures to convince the Muslim and Christian inhabitants that the government will take into account, in practice, and in its application, these principles and preserve their rights fully, we will not hesitate to take them. It is unreasonable for the British government, which has become the guardian of the happiness of the people of Palestine by virtue of its mandate over it, to impose any policy that they are justified in thinking is in conflict with their religions and with their political and economic interests.[170]

This speech helped placate some moderate Palestinian leaders while Weizmann, at the first opportunity, lodged a protest with Lloyd George. Churchill, however, announced while speaking on the Palestinian issue on June 14, 1921 in the British parliament that he was "following with very great confidence [Samuel's] action and giving him every possible measure of confidence and support".[171]

Samuel's measures also included a temporary stop to Jewish

---

[168]   For details on Samuel's policy and motives in Palestine, see Kedourie, "Sir Herbert Samuel and the Government of Palestine", pp. 44-68.

[169]   John and Hadawi, *The Palestine Diary*, Vol. 1, p. 172.

[170]   *Palestine Documents File*, Vol. 1, p. 307.

[171]   Kayyali, ed., *Documents of Arab Palestinian Resistance to British Occupation and Zionism: 1918-1939*, p. 35.

6. British Mandate over Palestine, Part I 395

immigration to Palestine. When calm had returned after the 1921 riots, immigration would be resumed – though under another law.[172] The basic immigration law was replaced by a new one in which immigrants were split into four categories. Category (A) included "any person who is in bona fide possession and freely disposes of a capital of not less than one thousand pounds", or 500 pounds if he was "a member of a liberal profession", 250 pounds if he was "skilled in certain trades or crafts" or "has a secured income of not less than four pounds a month, exclusive of earned income".[173] Category (B) included "persons whose maintenance is assured", such as orphans in public institutions, people with religious occupations, and students. Category (C) included "persons who have a definite prospect of employment in Palestine", and, finally, category (D) included "dependents of permanent residents or immigrants belonging to Categories A, B (ii) [religious occupations] and C".[174] No restrictions were imposed on the entry of immigrants of categories A, B, and D, while the entry of immigrants of category C, the workers, was regulated by granting the Zionists the right to control their entry into Palestine. This was a matter of significance, as immigrants in the workers' category were among the largest in number. Under this arrangement, the immigration regulations granted the executive of the Jewish Agency in Palestine the right to notify the director of immigration that

> there is a reasonable prospect of employing a number of persons either named or unnamed in Palestine and to make an application for permission for their entry into Palestine, but every such application shall be accompanied by a guarantee to maintain the person or persons in respect of whom it is made for a period of not less than one year.[175]

---

172 *An Interim Report on the Civil Administration of Palestine During the Period 1st July 1920-30th June 1921, August 1921 (Cmd. 1499)*, pp. 18-19, 23.

173 Drayton, *The Laws of Palestine*, Vol. 4, pp. 861-862.

174 Ibid.

175 Ibid, p. 864.

The director of immigration would then prepare "Labour Schedules [of immigrant workers] … after considering any proposals made in that regard by the Executive of the Jewish Agency".[176]

It was customary to prepare two schedules per year, at the end of September and March, with the "maximum number of persons belonging to the various sexes or trades, industries and callings"[177] who were permitted to enter as immigrants to Palestine during a specified period. After approval of these schedules by the high commissioner, immigration certificates were issued and "transmitted to the Executive of the Jewish Agency for distribution by them".[178] The Jewish Agency took advantage of the powers granted to it to admit Jewish immigrants who met its political or economic agendas, and withheld the certificates from the Zionist groups opposed to it, which deepened the disputes within the Zionist camp. With time, amendments were made to the immigration law, but its fundamental principles remained until the late 1930s, when British policy changed towards Jewish immigration to Palestine (with the end of the Great Arab Revolt, on the eve of the Second World War, in 1939).

With growing conviction after the events of May 1921, Samuel tried to further adjust British policy in Palestine. First, he entered into a dialogue with Weizmann to convince him of his point of view but failed. He also tried to encourage the British government to reconsider its policy, but failed there after Weizmann's intervention.[179] In mid-1921, the British government held a session to discuss its policy in Palestine but only transferred the responsibility of governing the country from the foreign office to the colonial office, while stressing the need to adhere to the Balfour Declaration. It seemed, in a memorandum

---

176 Ibid.

177 Ibid.

178 Ibid.

179 Friesel, *Ha-Mediniout ha-Tzionit le-ahar Hatzharat Balfour, 1917-1922 (Zionist Policy after the Balfour Declaration, 1917-1922)*, p. 270.

submitted by Churchill, that he was reconsidering his position,[180] but Samuel had to work for a whole year to convince the British government of his point of view.

The Palestinian leaders held the fourth Palestine Arab Congress on May 29, 1921 in the wake of the riots. The congress adopted the same resolutions as the third, but it also decided to send a delegation to Britain to explain the Palestinian demands to its government. The delegation remained in Britain for about a year,[181] meeting multiple leaders. On August 12, 1921, it submitted a memorandum to the British government, "the ally of the Arabs", in which it demanded a solution to the Palestine problem on the basis of

> establishing a national government that would be responsible before a parliament elected by the population who inhabited Palestine before the war, including Muslims, Christians and Jews; revoking the idea of establishing a national home for the Jews in Palestine; stopping Jewish immigration to Palestine while a national government is formed; governing the country by the Ottoman law that was in effect before the war, revoking all laws and regulations enacted after the British occupation, and enacting no laws until after a national government is formed,[182]

and, finally – an old demand – "not severing Palestine from its neighboring Arab provinces".[183] On October 24, 1921, the delegation submitted a second memorandum to the British colonial secretary, requesting that it be communicated to the British government and that the view of the colonial office on it be sought, and stressing that

> 93 percent of the population of Palestine supports the cause

---

180   Ibid, p. 271.

181   Darwaza, *On the Modern Arab Movement*, Vol. 3, p. 39.

182   Kayyali, ed., *Documents of Arab Palestinian Resistance to British Occupation and Zionism: 1918-1939*, p. 26-33.

183   Ibid.

we present to you... The significant and growing resentment of the people of Palestine emerges from their firm belief that the policy of the current British government is directed at expelling them from their country or rendering them nothing in it, in order to make it a national kingdom for the Jewish immigrants.[184]

The delegation's demands were positively received among some British circles, as the House of Lords recommended that the government reconsider its policy in Palestine[185] and revoke the Balfour Declaration,[186] but the House of Commons refused to adopt this resolution.[187] Those meetings were in vain, and Samuel invited a number of figures in Palestine, during the delegation's stay in London – in an attempt to undermine its position – to consult with him on the draft constitution. Those invited refused to discuss this matter, however, stating that it was premature to do so before a decision was made on the fate of the mandate.

With the fourth anniversary of the Balfour Declaration, on November 2, 1921, clashes were renewed in Palestine. Although smaller in scale, they killed five settlers and three Arabs. The Haganah had learned a lesson from the May events and taken the measures it deemed necessary to defend the settlers[188] (in the summer of 1921, the British authorities had supplied the Jewish settlements with sealed boxes of ammunition that they were permitted to use if they were attacked.)[189] Some Muslim figures helped to placate spirits and limit the spread of the clashes, but the tension remained.

Despite this, Samuel found the situation in Palestine at the end of 1921 calm enough to allow him to conduct new maneuvers – this time to equalize the Muslims with the Jews in terms of their

---

[184] Ibid, p. 34.

[185] Darwaza, *On the Modern Arab Movement*, Vol. 3, p. 39.

[186] See also Weizmann, *Trial and Error*, p. 360.

[187] Darwaza, *On the Modern Arab Movement*, Vol. 3, p. 39.

[188] See Dinur, ed., *Sefer Toldot ha-Haganah (History of the Haganah)*, Vol. 2, Part 1, pp. 133-140.

[189] Ibid, p. 208.

6. British Mandate over Palestine, Part I

religious administration. The settlers had held elections on April 19, 1920 at the first Jewish Assembly, whose powers included the supervision of their religious affairs. The assembly launched its first session on October 7, 1920. On the 24th of that month, Samuel recognized its newly formed (executive) National Council ("Va'ad Leumi") on the condition that it recognized the mandate and its provisions.[190] With this, it was necessary to take similar steps for the other communities. Most of these, however, especially the Christian ones, were already organized according to the Ottoman Millet (confessional community) law, and each had its own sectarian institutions and courts that supervised its religious affairs – except for the Muslims, who found their religious affairs being managed by the non-Muslim British after Ottoman rule. It was thus necessary to organize Muslim affairs as well.

The British mandate authorities began working on this a few months after the establishment of civil rule in Palestine. On November 9, 1920, the high commissioner formed a committee, headed by him and with the membership of eight British officials and 10 notable Muslim figures to study issues related to Islamic affairs. The committee issued "resolutions"[191] in which it called for the establishment of a supreme Islamic Shari'a council with almost comprehensive authority to supervise Muslim religious affairs. This included nominating the judges and inspectors of Shari'a courts, as well as the judges and the head of the Shari'a court of appeal, then appointing them after approval from the government. If this approval was withheld, the government was obliged to inform the council of its reasons. The council was also entrusted with appointing muftis, the head and officials of the waqf (endowments institutions) and all employees of the Shari'a courts, as well as supervising all waqf committees. In addition, the committee in session demanded that the council be given the

---

190 Moshe Attias, ed., *Sefer ha-Te'udot shel ha-Va'ad ha-Leumi le-Knesset Yisrael be-Eretz Yisrael (Book of Documents of the National Council of Knesset Israel)*, pp. 34-35.

191 See minutes of committee's meeting in *The Committee for Moslem Religious Affairs*.

power to dismiss employees of the waqf, Shari'a courts or any other institution funded by waqf monies, as well as to manage its own budget, while simply communicating its decisions to the government.[192] The authorities could not, at any rate, implement these "resolutions",[193] and merely issued an order in March 1921 to form a committee to oversee the administration of Islamic waqf institutions and Shari'a courts.[194] This decision sparked opposition from the sheikhs and scholars, prompting the authorities to reconsider, and the high commissioner to appoint a new committee[195] to make recommendations in August 1921. These were not very different from those made by the previous committee, but the high commissioner accepted them without serious objection. On December 9, 1921,[196] he issued a law establishing the Supreme Islamic Shari'a Council[197] (also the Supreme Muslim Council) and cancelled the previous order issued in March.[198] In the first week of 1922, elections were held for the council[199] and the mufti, Hajj Amin al-Husseini, was elected as its president.

The mandate authorities' announcement of the formation of the Supreme Muslim Council had the effect, perhaps unknown to them, of further deepening the divide among the Muslims of Palestine, who were then more than three-quarters of the population. This had a clear impact on the ability of the Palestinian Arabs to pursue their national cause, especially after this division spread in their ranks. The elections for the council, in which all adult male Muslims were allowed to participate,

192 *A Survey of Palestine, Prepared in December 1945 and January 1946 for the Information of the Anglo-American Committee of Inquiry*, Vol. 2, pp. 901-902.

193 *Report on Palestine Administration, July 1920-December 1921*, p. 92.

194 Olitsky, *Mi-Pzura le-Medinah (From Dispersal to State)*, Vol. 1, p. 262; see also *An Interim Report on the Civil Administration of Palestine During the Period 1st July 1920-30th June 1921, August 1921 (Cmd. 1499)*, p. 12.

195 *Report on Palestine Administration, July 1920-December 1921*, pp. 92-93.

196 Ibid, p. 50.

197 See law in *The Palestine Gazette*, Issue 58, 1/1/1922.

198 Ibid, Supplement.

199 *Report on Palestine Administration, July 1920-December 1921*, p. 93.

increased the competition between the Husseini and Nashashibi clans and their supporters so that, according to one witness,

> it was not long until Husseinism and Nashashibism became a partisan flag for the supporters of each of the two clans, a manifestation of the competition between them, and a preoccupation... The Arabs' deprivation of governance was a motive for them to turn towards the council and find distraction in it, placing the highest hopes on it in a subliminal response to that desire [for governance], so that it became a cause for jealousy, envy, competition, resentment, complacency, deprivation, attainment, and bestowal that were most highly exploited by both the authorities and the opponents, until a time came when the Muslims almost forgot the government and its millions, departments, thousands of employees, laws, and schools ... to focus only on the council, scrutinizing its work, practices and projects, peering into every small and large aspect, and gazing at its petty tens of thousands of pounds, the few tens of its staff, and the narrow arena of its construction and material work – for which they held trips and meetings and formed fronts, finding in this a placation of the desire to govern and an outlet for the appetite to criticize, both of which they were deprived of.[200]

The area of land subject to the waqf administration – of the "proper" waqf category ("waqf sahih", in Arabic), that is, pertaining to privately owned land – had been estimated in 1930 to be about 100,000 dunums, whose annual returns were 10,000-20,000 Palestinian pounds. There were also 75-100 Arab villages whose land area was 750,000-1 million dunums, which were mostly in the "amiriyya" category – pertaining to originally royal or sultanic land – and the returns from their tithes that were paid to the waqf were about 30,000 pounds a year.[201] Those two incomes constituted about three-quarters of the waqf's

---

200 Darwaza, *On the Modern Arab Movement*, Vol. 3, pp. 51-53.

201 *Report on Immigration, Land Settlement and Development, By Sir John Hope Simpson, October 1930 (Cmd. 3686)*, p. 30.

annual income.²⁰² The accountant of the waqf department had submitted a report to the high commissioner stating that the average annual waqf income for 1926-1931 was about 51,000 Palestinian pounds.²⁰³

Among the outcomes of the dispute over the Supreme Muslim Council and its activities was "increased rhetoric and maneuvers and the split of Muslims [followed by Christians, as well] into two, hostile camps":²⁰⁴ the "council" group ["majlisiyoon", in Arabic], that is, supporters of the council [majlis], together with the Husseinis; and the "opposition", that is, supporters of the Nashashibis. People joined these two currents "under the influence of the everlasting custom in Palestine: the ['traditional'] Qays-Yaman rivalry, and they forgot, or almost forgot, the national cause".²⁰⁵

It is clear from the actions of the mandate authorities that they were very happy with this conflict, as they did everything in their power to prolong and entrench it. In 1926, the council's first term ended and elections were held. The opposition challenged their integrity and the Supreme Court ruled them invalid. The authorities then quickly enacted a special law, by which they formed a new council²⁰⁶ of the mufti and his supporters, and appointed a committee to study the amendments that should be made to the original council law.²⁰⁷ The committee submitted its report in 1928,²⁰⁸ and it was published the following year in

---

202 Yaacov Shimoni, *Aravei Eretz Yisrael (The Arabs in the Land of Israel)*, p. 90.

203 See Yuval Arnon-Ohana, *Herev mi-Bayit: Ha-Ma'avak ha-Pnimi ba-Tnu'ah ha-Leumit ha-Falastinit, 1929-1939 (Sword from Within: The Internal Struggle in the Palestinian National Movement, 1929-1939)*, p. 45 and sources mentioned.

204 Darwaza, *On the Modern Arab Movement*, Vol. 3, pp. 51-53.

205 Ibid, p. 53.

206 *Report by His Britannic Majesty's Government to the Council of the League of Nations on the Administration of Palestine and Trans-Jordan for the year 1926 (Colonial No. 26)*, p. 100.

207 Ibid, p. 4.

208 *Report by His Majesty's Government in the United Kingdom of Great Britain and Northern Ireland to the Council of the League of Nations on the Admin-*

the form of a new draft law.[209] However, the Buraq Uprising that erupted in Palestine that year prevented its approval.[210] The original law was amended and the high commissioner was given the power to appoint members to the council in place of those who passed away.[211] The mufti remained the appointed head of the council, with the blessing of the mandate authorities, until 1937[212] when he was dismissed because of the role he played in the Great Arab Revolt (1936-1939). By that time, however, the mufti had used the influence and power of his two positions to rally supporters around him in a way that made him the most powerful man among the Arabs in Palestine. This deepened the conflict with the opposition and diminished any hope of reconciliation, with negative repercussions for the Palestinian cause.

6

Despite the Palestinian preoccupation with the conflict over the elections for the Supreme Muslim Council in early 1922, the Arab leadership found time to send another delegation to Britain for discussions with its government. The delegation arrived at a time when the colonial office was working to define British policy in Palestine. In London, the delegation entered into negotiations with the colonial office in the form of exchanged memoranda, but the colonial office pressured the delegation to accept the proposed British policy. This correspondence lasted nearly

---

istration of Palestine and Trans-Jordan for the year 1929 (Colonial No. 47), pp. 15-16; see also law in *The Palestine Gazette*, Issues 160, 1/4/1926 and 166, 16/7/1926.

209 *A Survey of Palestine, Prepared in December 1945 and January 1946 for the Information of the Anglo-American Committee of Inquiry*, Vol. 2, pp. 902-903.

210 For details, also see *Report by His Majesty's Government in the United Kingdom of Great Britain and Northern Ireland to the Council of the League of Nations on the Administration of Palestine and Trans-Jordan for the year 1929 (Colonial No. 47)*, pp. 39-41.

211 *The Palestine Gazette*, Issues 232, 1/4/1929 and 234, 1/5/1929.

212 *A Survey of Palestine, Prepared in December 1945 and January 1946 for the Information of the Anglo-American Committee of Inquiry*, Vol. 2, pp. 902-903.

three months,[213] at the end of which the delegation refused to accept the proposals submitted by the government which were, essentially, a diluted Balfour Declaration. Instead, the delegation called on Britain to work on securing the civil, political and economic interests of the inhabitants of Palestine by forming an independent Palestinian national government committed to preserving the legitimate rights of foreigners, minorities and the mandatory power.[214] After attempting to challenge the legitimacy of the delegation's representation of the Palestinian Arabs, the British government rejected this request and explained in its correspondence that it had no intention "of repudiating the obligations into which [it had] entered towards the Jewish people",[215] and that the establishment of a national government in Palestine "would preclude the fulfilment of the pledge"[216] stipulated in the Balfour Declaration. The British government also stressed that "there can be no question of rescinding the Balfour Declaration," and that "no useful purpose would be served by farther discussion of the policy underlying these pledges."[217] It advised the delegation to take a constructive stance and focus on discussing the "safeguards"[218] that the Palestinian Arabs might need, in light of the implementation of the Jewish national home in Palestine.

As these negotiations were nearing their end, Samuel returned to London in May 1922 with the intention of inducing his government to issue a clear statement regarding its policy in Palestine, as he felt it necessary "after two years of experience" in the country.[219] Samuel wasted no time in achieving his goal.

---

213 For details, see *Correspondence with the Palestine Arab Delegation and the Zionist Organization, June 1922 (Cmd. 1700)*, pp. 2, 17.

214 Ibid, p. 4; see also *The Holy Land. The Moslem-Christian Case against Zionist Aggression*; Official Statement of the Palestine Arab Delegation, p. 10.

215 *Correspondence with the Palestine Arab Delegation and the Zionist Organization, June 1922 (Cmd. 1700)*, p. 5.

216 Ibid, p. 6.

217 Ibid, p. 16.

218 Ibid.

219 *Report of the High Commissioner on the Administration of Palestine, 1920-*

By the 24th of that month, he had drafted a statement that he presented to Churchill who approved it three days later without modification[220] (this statement was subsequently issued as the "White Paper"). On June 3, the British government sent the text of the proposed statement to the Zionist Organization, requesting an explicit commitment to accept and act on it.[221] A similar copy was sent to the Palestinian delegation with the same request.

In its response, the Palestinian delegation adhered to its previous position of rejecting the British proposals[222] and sent a memorandum to the colonial secretary on June 17, 1922, explaining that it viewed the goal of the White Paper as finally enabling the Jewish settlers to control Palestine. The delegation expressed its fears that Britain's insistence on establishing the Jewish national home would lead to the "disappearance or subordination of the Arabic population, language, and culture in Palestine".[223] As for the Zionists, they attempted to further amend the White Paper to their advantage but failed.[224] Thus the Zionist Executive soon declared its approval of the British requests, explaining in a letter sent by Weizmann to the colonial office on June 18, 1922 – a day after the Palestinian delegation had sent its reply – that they "assure His Majesty's Government that the activities of the Zionist Organization will be conducted in conformity with the policy therein set forth".[225] This took place after it was "made clear" to the Zionists – according to Weizmann – that "confirmation of the Mandate would be

---

1925 (Colonial No. 15), p. 27.

220 Friesel, *Ha-Mediniout ha-Tzionit le-ahar Hatzharat Balfour, 1917-1922 (Zionist Policy after the Balfour Declaration, 1917-1922)*, p. 302.

221 *Correspondence with the Palestine Arab Delegation and the Zionist Organization, June 1922 (Cmd. 1700)*, p. 17.

222 See response in ibid, pp. 21-28.

223 Ibid, p. 28.

224 Friesel, *Ha-Mediniout ha-Tzionit le-ahar Hatzharat Balfour, 1917-1922 (Zionist Policy after the Balfour Declaration, 1917-1922)*, p. 305.

225 *Correspondence with the Palestine Arab Delegation and the Zionist Organization, June 1922 (Cmd. 1700)*, p. 29.

conditional on [their] acceptance of the policy as interpreted in the White Paper," and thus they "had to accept it".[226] Even Jabotinsky, a member of the Zionist Executive, who later took an uncompromising stance towards British policy in Palestine and carried the banner of opposition to the leadership of Weizmann and his circle, agreed with the White Paper at the time and "raised no serious objection",[227] because he "felt it [his] moral duty to share with [his] colleagues even the shame of a defeat".[228]

Churchill's White Paper of 1922 was the first document to clearly lay out the proposed British policy in Palestine. The document, however, was drafted in the spirit of what the British government did not intend to do in the country,[229] and determined the rights of the Arabs only by imposing restrictions on the Zionists.[230] The White Paper stated that it was drawn up with a view to the "settlement of the outstanding questions which have given rise to uncertainty and unrest", and that "the tension which has prevailed from time to time in Palestine is mainly due to apprehensions, which are entertained both by sections of the Arab and by sections of the Jewish population."[231] Thus it was necessary to remove these fears by clarifying the rights of both Arabs and Jews, as Britain saw them, together with the details of the mandate instrument.[232] The paper first provided a new interpretation of the Balfour Declaration, stating that the British government never contemplated "the disappearance or the subordination of the Arabic population, language or culture

---

226 Weizmann, *Trial and Error*, p. 361.

227 Ibid.

228 Joseph B. Schechtman, *Rebel and Statesman, The Vladimir Jabotinsky Story*, Vol. 1, p. 422.

229 *Report of the High Commissioner on the Administration of Palestine, 1920-1925 (Colonial No. 15)*, p. 27.

230 Friesel, *Ha-Mediniout ha-Tzionit le-ahar Hatzharat Balfour, 1917-1922 (Zionist Policy after the Balfour Declaration, 1917-1922)*, p. 303.

231 See *Correspondence with the Palestine Arab Delegation and the Zionist Organization, June 1922 (Cmd. 1700)*, pp. 17-21.

232 Ibid, pp. 17-18.

in Palestine". It drew "attention to the fact that the terms of the Declaration referred to do not contemplate that Palestine as a whole should be converted into a Jewish National Home, but that such a Home should be founded in Palestine".[233] Secondly, as for the Jewish settlers,

> when it is asked what is meant by the development of the Jewish National Home in Palestine, it may be answered that it is not the imposition of a Jewish nationality upon the inhabitants of Palestine as a whole, but the further development of the existing Jewish community, with the assistance of Jews in other parts of the world, in order that it may become a center in which the Jewish people as a whole may take, on grounds of religion and race, an interest and a pride. But in order that this community should have the best prospect of free development and provide full opportunity for the Jewish people to display its capacities, it is essential that it should know that it is in Palestine as of right and not on sufferance. That is the reason why it is necessary that the existence of a Jewish National Home in Palestine should be internationally guaranteed, and that it should be formally recognized to rest upon ancient historic connection.[234]

This was, therefore, "the interpretation which His Majesty's Government place upon the Declaration of 1917, and, so understood, the Secretary of State is of opinion that it does not contain or imply anything which need cause either alarm to the Arab population of Palestine or disappointment to the Jews".[235]

The White Paper laid out the means by which the British government would implement this policy, stating that "it is necessary that the Jewish community in Palestine should be able to increase its numbers by immigration,"[236] subject to "the

---

233   Ibid.

234   Ibid, p. 18.

235   Ibid, p. 19.

236   Ibid.

economic capacity of the country".²³⁷ As for the system of governance, "it is the intention of His Majesty's Government to foster the establishment of a full measure of self-government in Palestine. But they are of the opinion that, in the special circumstances of that country, this should be accomplished by gradual stages and not suddenly."²³⁸ The British government considered that the first step on this path had been taken with the establishment of the Advisory Council, and "it is now proposed to take a second step by the establishment of a Legislative Council containing a large proportion of members elected on a wide franchise."²³⁹ However,

> the Secretary of State is of the opinion that before a further measure of self-government is extended to Palestine and the Assembly placed in control over the Executive, it would be wise to allow some time to elapse... After a few years the situation will be again reviewed, and if the experience of the working of the constitution now to be established so warranted, a larger share of authority would then be extended to the elected representatives of the people.²⁴⁰

The policies announced in the White Paper remained generally in effect until 1939, when another paper was issued.

With the issuance of Churchill's White Paper, the measures to lay the constitutional basis of the mandate system in Palestine proceeded at a steady pace. On July 24, 1922, the Council of the League of Nations approved the text of the mandate instrument presented to it by the British government in light of the interpretations in the White Paper. Two weeks later, the British authorities issued the Constitution of Mandatory Palestine, formally known as the "10 August 1922 Palestine Order-in-Council". This order granted the high commissioner the power

---

237   Ibid.

238   Ibid, p. 20.

239   Ibid.

240   Ibid, pp. 20-21.

6. British Mandate over Palestine, Part I

to govern the country as the head of its executive authority,

> according to the tenour of any Orders in Council ... as may be issued to him under His Majesty's Sign Manual and Signet, and according to such instructions as may from time to time be given to him, for the purpose of executing the provisions of the Mandate ... or by His Majesty through one of His Principal Secretaries of State, and to such laws and ordinances as are now or shall hereafter be in force in Palestine...[241]

The high commissioner was to be assisted by an "Executive Council",[242] whose members would be appointed by the British government. The high commissioner was also granted all rights to "public lands or mines or minerals ... in, under or on any land or water".[243] He was permitted to "make grants or leases of any such public lands or mines or minerals" and "permit such lands to be temporarily occupied on such terms or conditions as he may think fit".[244] His authority included the appointment and dismissal of public officers, as well as granting pardons for crimes.

The order also stipulated the formation of a legislature in the form of a council, composed of the high commissioner and 22 members, "of whom 10 shall be official members and 12 shall be unofficial members",[245] including eight Muslims, two Christians and two Jews, elected by all male Palestinians over 25 years of age. The Palestine Legislative Council Election Order, 1922,[246] which set out the procedures for the elections, was issued on August 10, 1922, the same day as the Palestine Constitution. The authorities granted the Legislative Council

---

241 Palestine constitution decree of 1922, in Drayton, *The Laws of Palestine*, Vol. 4, pp. 3307-3310.

242 Ibid, p. 3309.

243 Ibid.

244 Ibid, p. 3310.

245 Ibid, p. 3311.

246 See decree in ibid, pp. 3386-3394.

full power and authority, without prejudice to the powers inherent in, or reserved by this Order to, His Majesty, and subject always to any conditions and limitations prescribed by any Instructions under the Sign Manual and Signet, to establish such Ordinances as may be necessary for the peace, order and good government of Palestine... No Ordinance shall be passed which shall be in any way repugnant to or inconsistent with the provisions of the Mandate.[247]

The powers of the council were, in fact, very limited, for "no Ordinance shall take effect until ... the High Commissioner shall have assented thereto,"[248] and he could, "according to his discretion ... declare that he assents to any Ordinance, or refuse his assent to the same".[249]

In addition, the order stipulated the establishment of a judiciary consisting of various courts, and ordered that "all Ordinances, official notices and official forms of the Government ... shall be published in English, Arabic and Hebrew."[250]

Under this order, a proclamation was issued on June 1, 1924, dividing Palestine into three administrative districts, with 18 sub-districts, and revoking a previous order issued on August 15, 1920, by which Palestine had been divided into seven districts.[251] The new administrative divisions were: the Jerusalem district, whose center was Jerusalem, and which comprised the sub-districts of Bethlehem, Hebron, Jericho, Jerusalem and Ramallah; the Northern district, whose center was Haifa, and which comprised the sub-districts of Acre, Bisan, Haifa,

---

247   Ibid, p. 3311.

248   Ibid, p. 3313.

249   Ibid.

250   Ibid, p. 3328.

251   These districts were: Jerusalem, Jaffa, Gaza, Beersheba, Samaria (centered in Nablus), Phoenicia (centered in Haifa), and the Galilee (centered in Nazareth). *Chronologiah le-Toldot ha-Yishuv ha-Yehudi be-Eretz Yisrael (Chronology of the Jewish Yishuv in the Land of Israel)*, Vol. 1, p. 48; see also *An Interim Report on the Civil Administration of Palestine During the Period 1st July 1920-30th June 1921, August 1921 (Cmd. 1499)*, p. 25.

Jenin, Nablus, Nazareth, Safad, Tiberias, and Tulkarm; and the Southern district, whose center was Jaffa, and which comprised the sub-districts of Beersheba, Gaza, Jaffa and Ramla.[252] Later modifications were made to these divisions to distribute the administrative burden after the spread of the Zionist settlements in Palestine. In October 1937, the Northern district was divided into two: the Galilee-Acre district, whose center was Nazareth, and which comprised the sub-districts of Acre, Bisan, Nazareth, Safad and Tiberias; and the Haifa-Samaria district, whose center was Haifa, and which comprised the sub-districts of Haifa, Jenin, Nablus and Tulkarm.[253] These divisions were again modified in July and December 1939, changing the Galilee-Acre district to the Galilee district. The Haifa district was divided into two: the Haifa district, whose center was Haifa and which only comprised the Haifa sub-district; and the Samaria district, whose center was Nablus, and which comprised the sub-districts of Jenin, Nablus and Tulkarm. The Southern district was also divided into two: the Lydda district, whose center was Jaffa, and which comprised the sub-districts of Jaffa and Ramla; and the Gaza district, whose center was Gaza, and which comprised the sub-districts of Gaza and Beersheba.[254] Thus, Palestine was re-divided into six districts – a division that remained in effect until the end of the British Mandate, with the exception of a slight change in June 1945 when the sub-districts of Bethlehem and Jericho were abolished and merged into the sub-district of Jerusalem[255] (see *Map 10 Administrative divisions in Palestine, 1924-1939*, below).

---

252 Administrative divisions decree, Drayton, *The Laws of Palestine*, Vol. 4, p. 3337.

253 *The Palestine Gazette*, Supplement No. 2 to Issue 733, 28/10/1939.

254 Ibid, Supplement No. 2 to Issue 900, 1/7/1939, and Issue 974, 30/12/1939.

255 Ibid, Supplement No. 2 to Issue 1415, 7/6/1945, and Issue 1552, 1/1/1947.

412   The Foundations of Zionism

Map 10 Administrative divisions in Palestine, 1924-1939[256]

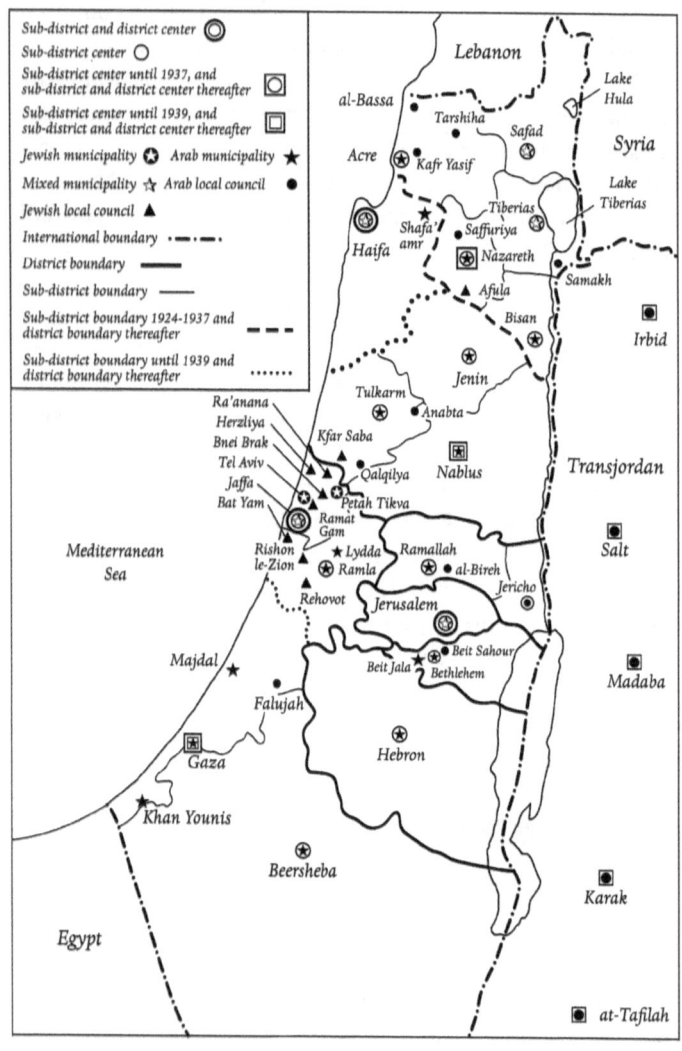

256 Borders of districts and sub-districts of Palestine in this map were drawn in accordance with those in *Palestine Royal Commission Report, July 1937 (Cmd. 5479)*, Appendix, Map No. 9; data was added regarding the conditions of cities, villages and various settlements based on the administrative divisions decree, Drayton, *The Laws of Palestine*, Vol. 4, p. 3337, and its amendments noted in *The Palestine Gazette*, Supplement No. 2 to Issue 733, 28/10/1937, Issue 900, 1/7/1939, and Issue 974, 30/12/1939.

After announcing this policy, the British government tried to gain the approval of the Arabs and settlers. The two parties had seen the details of the constitutional documents, the Constitution order and the Legislative Council elections order, when the White Paper was presented to them. The Zionists considered this policy "a serious whittling down of the Balfour Declaration",[257] because it "detached trans-Jordan [the 'eastern Land of Israel'] from the area of Zionist operation, and it raised the subject of a legislative council", which the Zionists feared would become a tool in the hands of the Arab majority that could use it to hinder Zionist development. The Zionists also expressed reservation on the issue of linking Jewish immigration with the country's economic absorptive capacity. A strong opposition appeared among the settlers in Palestine in particular, but the Zionist leadership forced them to change their stance in order that Samuel should not fail.[258]

As for the Arabs, the Palestine Executive Committee announced in a statement on July 8, 1922 that, by essentially rejecting the mandate, it could not agree to any constitutional measures based on it. The committee called for the holding of a new Palestine Arab congress "to lay down new plans perceived by the nation as the safest and closest to attain the main goal".[259] The fifth congress was held on August 22-24 in Nablus, after the return of the Palestinian delegation from London, "which arrived from its trip directly to the congress".[260]

At the fifth Palestine Arab Congress, the delegation that had returned from London presented the assembly with statements on its efforts, saying it had exerted "such a strong influence that the House of Lords had decided the Zionist policy should be

---

257 Weizmann, *Trial and Error*, p. 361.

258 For details, see Caplan, *Palestine Jewry and the Arab Question, 1917-1925*, pp. 151-157.

259 Kayyali, ed., *Documents of Arab Palestinian Resistance to British Occupation and Zionism: 1918-1939*, p. 47.

260 Darwaza, *On the Modern Arab Movement*, Vol. 3, p. 43.

repealed".[261] The delegation also expressed its opinion that, if the Arabs were to boycott the proposed legislative council, "a new horizon and hope would be opened to them."[262] The congress adopted a series of resolutions, key of which were "support for rejecting the mandate system in the name of Palestine... Rejection of the new constitution of Palestine and boycotting the Legislative Council elections... Boycotting the Jews in the purchase and sale of immovable property, with the Executive Committee entrusted with setting a date and method of implementation" of these resolutions.[263] The Fifth Congress also approved a "Palestine National Charter", in which it declared commitment to achieving "Palestine's independence, Arab unity, and rejection of the Jewish national home and Zionist immigration".[264]

The mandate authorities did not attach great importance to this Arab opposition, however, and moved forward in implementing their plans. On October 22-23, 1922, the authorities conducted a general census in Palestine[265] as a prelude to the Legislative Council elections. The census showed the population to be 752,048, of whom 660,641 (87.9 percent) were Arabs (of which 589,177, or 78.3 percent, were Muslims and 71,464, or 9.6 percent, were Christians) and 83,790 (11.1 percent) were Jews. The remainder, 7,617 (1 percent) belonged to minorities of different nationalities and religions.[266]

In late February and early March 1923, elections were held for the Legislative Council, but the Arabs announced that they would boycott them.[267] Thus, despite the extension of the

261 Darwaza, *On the Modern Arab Movement*, Vol. 3, p. 43.

262 Ibid.

263 Kayyali, ed., *Documents of Arab Palestinian Resistance to British Occupation and Zionism: 1918-1939*, pp. 55-56.

264 Ibid, pp. 53, 55.

265 Barron, J. B., *Report and General Abstracts of the Census of 1922: Taken on the 23rd of October, 1922*, p. 1.

266 *A Survey of Palestine, Prepared in December 1945 and January 1946 for the Information of the Anglo-American Committee of Inquiry*, Vol. 2, p. 142.

267 See statements in Kayyali, ed., *Documents of Arab Palestinian Resis-*

election period (from February 28 to March 7, then to March 31), only 134 candidates were elected out of 800 intended representatives in Arab electoral districts.[268] In Jewish electoral districts, all the representatives were elected, numbering 79 people.[269] The Arab community then exerted intense pressure on its elected representatives such that they all had to submit their resignations, one after the other.

In view of the failure of the Legislative Council elections, the British government issued a new order on May 4, 1923 stating that "the elections held in Palestine ... are hereby declared null and void."[270] For this reason, "the High Commissioner [alone] shall have full power and authority ... to promulgate such Ordinances as may be necessary for the peace, order, and good government of Palestine,"[271] until the election of a new legislative council[272] – which did not take place until the end of the British Mandate in 1948. At the same time, the authorities revived the Advisory Council and raised the number of its members from 10 to 15 – all of them government employees[273] – to avoid facing the boycott or rejection of any opponents of British policy.

The Arabs were very happy that they had thwarted the constitutional projects of the government, especially the formation of the Legislative Council, but the settlers were happier. They had participated in the elections reluctantly and feared that the council would succeed, gradually gaining broader powers and becoming a real parliament whose policy would be decided by the Arab majority in the country, thereby freezing the hopes of establishing the Jewish national home. This Zionist

---

tance to British Occupation and Zionism: 1918-1939, pp. 57-65.

268 *Papers relating to the Elections for the Palestine Legislative Council, 1923 (Cmd. 1889)*, pp. 7-8.

269 Ibid.

270 Ibid, p. 11; see also Drayton, *The Laws of Palestine*, Vol. 4, pp. 3332-3333.

271 Ibid.

272 *Papers relating to the Elections for the Palestine Legislative Council, 1923 (Cmd. 1889)*, p. 12.

273 Drayton, *The Laws of Palestine*, Vol. 4, pp. 3360-3361.

position became clear in the early 1930s, when the idea of establishing the Legislative Council was again proposed and a number of Arab leaders agreed. The Jewish settlers, who had then become a significant force in Palestine, rejected it and got their wish.

After thwarting the Legislative Council, the Arabs returned to their previous policy of holding congresses, issuing statements and sending delegations. The sixth Palestine Arab Congress was held in Jaffa on June 16-20, 1923, where it adopted 27 resolutions,[274] most of which were repeated from the previous congresses and not implemented. The congress also decided to send a delegation to London, but its government refused to receive the delegation or negotiate with it. The delegation's leader then issued a new statement calling for "the establishment of a national representative government in Palestine".[275]

For its part, the British government was not ready to receive the delegation because its presence in London coincided with the conclusion of the peace treaty with Turkey, in Lausanne, on July 24, 1923, which replaced the Treaty of Sèvres that Ataturk had refused to ratify. The last legal obstacles to the approval of the mandate over Palestine were thus removed, and it came into effect – conclusively and definitively – on September 29, 1923. The British government was thus not inclined to hear protests, rejections or challenges to its mandate over Palestine – by Palestinian Arabs or anyone else.

Despite this, however, in late 1923 the British government presented a new proposal to the Palestinians to establish an Arab agency that would participate in governing Palestine, like the Jewish Agency. It seems that this was an attempt to put an end to the turbulent security situation in Palestine and to improve its economic conditions, saving Britain significant expenses[276] that

---

[274] For details, see Kayyali, ed., *Documents of Arab Palestinian Resistance to British Occupation and Zionism: 1918-1939*, pp. 73-75.

[275] Ibid, p. 76.

[276] *Proposed Formation of an Arab Agency; Correspondence with the High Commissioner for Palestine (Cmd. 1989)*, p. 6.

its economic capacity could not bear.

On October 11, 1923, the high commissioner summoned a number of notable Arab figures from various parts of Palestine to a meeting held at Government House in Jerusalem. He informed them of the new instructions that he had received from the colonial secretary, namely that the British government had made its political decisions on Palestine based on the Balfour Declaration and its dual commitment to the Arabs and Jews, and that it did not intend to backtrack on that policy.[277] However, the government saw that the situation in Palestine was unsatisfactory – as was evident from the many grievances of the Arabs, especially those related to the Jewish Agency and the perception that its existence may cause the authorities to grant privileges to the settlers.[278] To rectify this situation, the high commissioner continued, the government proposed the establishment of an Arab agency that would occupy the same position as the Jewish one. The members of this Arab agency would be appointed by the high commissioner and it would have the right to express an opinion on immigration, like the Jewish Agency,[279] with the consent of all the parties involved. The high commissioner was thus authorized to make contact with the Arabs, while the colonial secretary would communicate with the leadership of the Zionist Organization in London, and this arrangement would persist until the election of a new legislative council if it came into effect.[280] At the end of the meeting, the attendees were given time to consult on their response.

The head of the Palestine Executive Committee, Musa Kazim al-Husseini, rejected the proposal. Afterwards, al-Husseini issued a statement explaining that

> the suggestion that the Arabs participate in the administration of their country through an Arab agency, whose forma-

---

277 Ibid, pp. 3-4.

278 Ibid, p. 5.

279 Ibid.

280 Ibid, p. 6.

tion depends on negotiations with the League of Nations for approval, and which would have an official status like the Jewish Agency, and the consideration ... of this proposal as a major step towards fulfilling the wishes of the Arab people, were met with great surprise by the nation. For how could they accept this project, after they had rejected the Legislative Council and the Advisory Council, both with greater powers than those of the agency? How could they accept it when it puts the Arabs, the indigenous inhabitants of the country, on the same level as the Jews – other than the fact that the name of the agency, itself, makes them feel as though they are strangers in their own land?[281]

In the face of this, the British government expressed its weariness with the Palestinian Arabs. On November 9, 1923, the colonial secretary announced that his government was "driven to [the] conclusion that further efforts on similar lines would be useless and accordingly decided not to repeat the attempt".[282] (The Zionist Executive and Jewish Assembly had also opposed the efforts to establish the Arab agency.[283]) With these positions, negotiations ceased between the British government and Palestinian leaders, with Palestine experiencing a period of stagnation for several years.

With this path coming to an end, the first phase of the British Mandate also ended in 1923, during which the positions of the three parties (the British, Palestinian Arabs, and settlers) solidified. Each of the parties remained generally committed to the basic premises that were formulated during this stage, at least until the outbreak of the Second World War in 1939.

The British, the most powerful side of the conflict, considered it their right to rule Palestine like other areas allocated to

---

281 Kayyali, ed., *Documents of Arab Palestinian Resistance to British Occupation and Zionism: 1918-1939*, p. 81.

282 *Proposed Formation of an Arab Agency; Correspondence with the High Commissioner for Palestine (Cmd. 1989)*, p. 12.

283 *Chronologiah le-Toldot ha-Yishuv ha-Yehudi be-Eretz Yisrael (Chronology of the Jewish Yishuv in the Land of Israel)*, Vol. 1, p. 96.

them and their allies after their victory in the First World War. They were therefore unwilling to agree to the demands of the Palestinians for independence and autonomy. The Palestinians, for their part, did not realize that the balance of world powers at the time did not allow or help them to achieve any of these demands. On this basis, the British insisted on implementing the policy of the Balfour Declaration – aiming to secure their interests through gaining favor with the Zionists and prompting them to stick with Britain to maintain its control of Palestine, so that the national home could be established under British tutelage. The most that Britain did in the face of Arab opposition was agree to reduce the privileges granted to the settlers under the declaration, compared with the privileges it offered when it was issued.

The Palestinian leaders, including those from notable families, merchants and some intellectuals, did not sufficiently appreciate the magnitude of the international changes that had arisen at the end of the world war. Those leaders began talking about the right to self-determination, independence and Arab unity at a time when no one was willing to hear them, and when they did not have even a modicum of the necessary power to fulfill any of these demands.

The Palestinian people were also not able to form an alternative leadership, especially after four centuries of repressive Ottoman rule, during which they had been weighed down by poverty, disease and ignorance. The matter did not stop there, as competition and rivalry soon dominated the Palestinian leadership and split it in two. The national current, the Husseinis and their supporters, was careful not to assume any public position that implied approval of the Balfour Declaration or the Jewish national home, but at the same time its leaders cooperated with the British who implemented this policy. As for the opposition, the Nashashibis and their supporters, it sometimes showed flexibility in its positions that could be understood as its willingness, under certain circumstances, to reach an understanding with the British, and perhaps with the settlers. As a result, it was exposed to intense campaigns of vilification and skepticism. Due to this situation, a Palestinian public opinion began to form that insisted on the Palestinians getting all or nothing – and their share, ultimately, was close to nothing.

The Zionists were the most practical political force. They appraised their strength and capabilities accurately and pursued a policy of "take, and ask for more", implementing it with great flexibility. They were quick to bend, sometimes to hide, in the face of storms – only to return, after their passing, to resume their work in building the national home gradually, one brick after another, another dunum and another goat. This was largely achieved thanks to the dynamic, pragmatic Zionist leadership that emerged in light of the changes that occurred in the conditions of the world Zionist movement after the First World War.

7. British Mandate over Palestine, Part II: Foundations of the "Jewish National Home" (1918-1923)

1

The five years (1918-1923) after the First World War were the period of establishment of the "Jewish national home" in Palestine, parallel to the British mandate taking shape in the country. This process was affected by the changing position of Jewish people around the world after the war, and the changing Zionist activity. The war led to significant political changes in Russia and eastern Europe, with new systems of governance or states being formed that had a considerable effect on the conditions of about seven million Jews, who comprised more than half of the global Jewish population. When the maps were redrawn after the war had been settled, the Jewish populations of Russia and eastern Europe, the center of Zionist activity, found themselves in markedly different political, economic and social conditions.

The key changes took place during the first phase of fighting in Poland and eastern Russia. About five million Jewish people lived in these regions, who were the locus and main incubator of Zionism. A few months into the war, in March 1915, the Germans launched a comprehensive attack on the eastern part of tsarist Russia. By October, Germany had occupied most of Poland and the areas north of it, up to the Baltic Sea. About three million Jews who lived in this region fell under German rule, while about two million remained under tsarist rule in Russia.

The German authorities pursued a liberal occupation policy

in the areas they came to control. They aimed to ensure calm and stability for Germany and help it when the war with Russia resumed, and then to work on creating independent states in those regions to form a future barrier between Germany and Russia. The Jews in these regions also benefited from this liberal policy, especially since Germany had emancipated its Jewish population and abolished the last remaining restrictions with its unification at the end of the 1870s. The German authorities began implementing this policy as soon as the situation in Poland stabilized. Shortly after their occupation of Warsaw, they announced the establishment of civil rule and an autonomous administration, with no mention of any of the exceptional measures that had been in force against the Jews.[1] Thus the Germans abolished, implicitly and without much ado, all the restrictions that tsarist Russian rule had imposed on Jewish people in Poland for decades.[2]

This act was not only initiated by the German authorities. The Zionist Committee for the East in Germany[3] had played a part in urging the government to apply these measures. Since Germany's occupation of Poland and its neighboring regions, the committee encouraged the authorities to establish a unified state there and recognize the national minority rights of the various inhabitants, including Jews. The latter had become one of the largest minorities in that region, and wanted to draw nearer to Germany.[4] However, when the German authorities approved their final policy towards these occupied areas, they rejected this proposal and took measures to establish an independent Polish state and three small states to its north: Lithuania, Latvia and Estonia. They also rejected the proposal of the Committee for the East to recognize the Jewish people as a nation in these countries.

---

1   Yitzhak Gruenbaum, *Ha-Tnu'ah ha-Tzionit (The Zionist Movement)*, Vol. 4, p. 75.

2   Introduction, section 4.

3   Chapter 5, section 1.

4   Gruenbaum, *Ha-Tnu'ah ha-Tzionit (The Zionist Movement)*, Vol. 4, pp. 133, 160-161.

They instead took the opinion of Agudat Israel[5] – as expressed by the Orthodox rabbis in Frankfurt, which had a prominent Talmudic rabbinical center – that Judaism is a religion, not a nationality. When Germany announced its intention to establish an independent Polish kingdom in November 1916, it issued, at the same time, a law recognizing the equality between Jewish people and other citizens. It allowed the Jewish community to organize on a religious basis and granted the rabbis extensive powers to administer its affairs.[6] A few months later, in April 1917, the German occupation authorities recognized the Zionist Organization in Poland[7] and allowed it to work publicly, after it had been banned under tsarist rule.

While the conditions of the Jewish population and the Zionists among them were changing in Poland, similar changes took place in Russia. With the February Revolution in 1917 and the tsar's abdication on March 2, a new government was formed that differed in its stance from its predecessor. Only 18 days later, it signed a new law that was drafted in consultation with Jewish jurists and published on March 22. The law stipulated equal rights for Jewish people as those of other citizens and abolished approximately 150 laws that had been issued by the tsarist government with various restrictions on the Jews.[8] Public Zionist activity immediately resumed in Russia, and Russian Zionists began preparing for their seventh congress that was held in Petrograd during May 24-30, 1917. The congress took a number of decisions, key of which was the call to work on granting Jewish people national minority rights and autonomy in Russia, as well as boosting Zionist settlement in Palestine and establishing an independent Jewish national center there.[9]

---

5   Chapter 4, section 2.

6   For details, see Gruenbaum, *Ha-Tnu'ah ha-Tzionit (The Zionist Movement)*, Vol. 4, pp. 78-84.

7   Ibid, pp. 144-145.

8   Yitzhak Mior, *Ha-Tnu'ah ha-Tzionit be-Rusia (Zionist Movement in Russia)*, pp. 429-431.

9   For details, see ibid, pp. 446-449.

To implement these decisions, the Zionists sought to hold a general Jewish congress in Russia and – after agreeing with even the parties that opposed them, especially the Bund – elections were held to choose the representatives (see section 3 of this chapter). The outbreak of the Bolshevik Revolution in November 1917, however, prevented the congress from being held.[10]

Jewish delegations from several countries attended the Peace Conference in Versailles in 1919, after the war, to urge the world powers to recognize the national minority rights of the Jews and to find the means to guarantee those rights, especially in eastern Europe. Some Zionist groups had been actively campaigning since the start of the war. In early 1915, Ruppin, director of the Palestine Office in Jaffa, had asked Brandeis, the American Zionist leader, to work on unifying the Jewish population of the United States to influence the Peace Conference and encourage it to approve Jewish and Zionist demands. By late 1916, the American Zionists had formed a committee for this purpose that also included non-Zionist Jewish leaders.[11] In 1918-1919, "national councils" were formed by a number of minorities in Austria, Hungary, Germany and Russia, aiming for the recognition of their minority rights by the Peace Conference before their countries achieved independence and new borders were drawn up. Jewish people across the continent also established a number of their own councils.[12] In late 1918, the Zionist office in Copenhagen, which was the headquarters of the official, neutral Zionist leadership during the war, made three requests to the upcoming Peace Conference: declaring Palestine a national home for the Jewish people, creating the necessary conditions for the establishment of that home; recognizing the equal rights of Jews in all the

---

10   For details, see Gruenbaum, *Ha-Tnu'ah ha-Tzionit (The Zionist Movement)*, Vol. 4, pp. 121-129.

11   Ibid, pp. 59-68.

12   Shmuel Ettinger, *Toldot Am Yisrael ba'Et ha-Hadasha (History of the Jews in Modern Times)*, Vol. 3 (Haim Hillel Ben-Sasson, ed.), p. 223.

countries that they inhabited; and granting national autonomy to the Jews in the cultural, social and political spheres in the countries with a large Jewish minority, or to any Jewish minority in any country that claimed those rights.[13] Jewish community leaders in Britain, France and the United States had also called on their governments to place the Jewish question on the agenda of the Peace Conference when it convened.

Despite this activity, however, no Jewish groups were invited to attend the Peace Conference. Yet Jewish delegations from several countries came to the venue at Versailles. During the conference, a difference of opinion emerged between these delegations; the British and French delegations insisted on asking the conference to recognize the equality of Jews in civil rights with other peoples, while the delegations from the United States, Russia and eastern Europe (which set up a joint body with the Zionists, the "Committee of Jewish Delegations", to represent them at the conference) wanted to also demand granting Jews the right of national autonomy in any countries or regions with a Jewish minority.[14] Negotiations on these demands continued at length, until the Jewish delegations achieved their first victory with the signing of the peace treaty between Germany and Poland. Germany insisted on introducing two "minorities' clauses" to this treaty, by which Poland pledged to recognize the rights of its ethnic or religious minorities, including Jews, and their right to autonomy in their social and cultural institutions.[15] Poland also pledged to include similar clauses in its agreements with the other countries participating in the conference. These clauses became the model by which guarantees were given to minorities in several European countries. By 1923, when this process was finalized, four countries that had gained their independence after the war – namely, Czechoslovakia, Romania,

---

13   Shimshon Leib Kirschenbaum, *Toldot Am Yisrael be-Doreinu (The History of the Jews in Our Generation)*, Vol. 1, p. 40.

14   Ibid, pp. 37-41.

15   See "Minorities' Clause" in Horace Meyer Kallen, *Zionism and World Politics: A Study in History and Social Psychology*, pp. 185-187.

Yugoslavia and Greece – had signed similar treaties. Four of the countries that were defeated in the war – Austria, Hungary, Bulgaria and Turkey – were also forced to sign these clauses, while Lithuania, Latvia, Estonia, Albania and the authorities of some other regions pledged to recognize the rights stipulated in the "minorities' clauses". These clauses applied to about 5.75 million Jewish people (about 3 million in Poland, 350,000 in Czechoslovakia, 1 million in Romania, 70,000 in Yugoslavia, 75,000 in Greece, 150,000 in Austria, 450,000 in Hungary, 50,000 in Bulgaria, 150,000 in Turkey, 90,000 in Lithuania, 150,000 in Latvia, 4,000 in Estonia and 150,000 in Albania).[16]

The Council of the League of Nations, established in 1920, was entrusted with monitoring the implementation of these agreements. The minorities concerned were permitted to submit complaints to it against the states that denied them their rights. It soon became apparent that this procedure was irrelevant, however, as the League of Nations lacked the powers or agencies to enforce compliance.[17] In spite of this a number of Jewish minorities in several European countries were granted the rights stipulated in the agreements, which in turn facilitated Zionist activity in these countries.

The worldwide situation settled down after the conclusion of the peace treaties, the drawing up of final borders of various countries and the formation of new systems of governance after the war, until the outbreak of the Second World War in 1939. The global Jewish population had risen from about 10 million in 1900 to 13 million on the eve of the First World War in 1914, then to 16.1 million on the eve of the Second in 1939. The majority of Jews lived in five regions: eastern, western and central Europe, the Soviet Union and the United States[18] (see *Table 2 World Jewish population, 1900-1939*, below). In the

---

16   Simon Dubnow, *Divrei Yemei Am Olam (History of the Jews)*, pp. 732-734; see also Ettinger, *Toldot Am Yisrael ba'Et ha-Hadasha (History of the Jews in Modern Times)*, Vol. 3, p. 234.

17   See also Ettinger, *Toldot Am Yisrael ba'Et ha-Hadasha (History of the Jews in Modern Times)*, Vol. 3, pp. 233-235.

18   For details, see *Encyclopaedia Judaica*, Vol. 13, pp. 889-892.

period between the two world wars, Zionist activity expanded in an unprecedented manner among Jewish communities in dozens of countries. It was spurred on by the enthusiasm that was felt after the Balfour Declaration was published, the imposition of the British mandate over Palestine and Britain's pledge to work on the establishment of a Jewish national home.

Despite this expansion of Zionist activity, however, its effectiveness was limited to very few countries. The majority of Jews, worldwide, failed to respond to Zionist calls to immigrate to Palestine or to provide effective economic assistance to establish the Zionist entity there. Even Jewish people in America, whose number rose from about 3.9 million in 1918 to 4.5 million in 1939, making them the largest Jewish community in the world, took a similar stance. During the First World War, an active Zionist movement arose in the United States and played a significant role in Zionist activity in the last years of the war and immediately afterwards, but its leaders quickly disagreed with Weizmann and his faction (see section 4 of this chapter) which dampened cooperation between them. This situation was not remedied until the late 1920s but, even after that, the majority of American Jews tended to assimilate into their society while only supporting Zionism "theoretically" and providing occasional economic assistance to the settlers in Palestine.[19] Zionist activity remained focused among the Jews who had originally embraced Zionism – that is, those in Russia and Poland.

Of the estimated 300,000 immigrants to Palestine during 1919-1939, the majority were from Russia, Poland and then Germany, as the rise of Nazism in Germany and the persecution of Jewish people played a similar role to the repression in those two former countries in driving its Jewish population to emigrate – rather than a belief in Zionism alone.[20]

---

19   For details, see Kirschenbaum, *Toldot Am Yisrael be-Doreinu (The History of the Jews in Our Generation)*, Vol. 1, pp. 133-152.

20   Introduction, section 4.

Table 2 World Jewish population, 1900-1939 (thousands)[21]

Country/region	Jewish population in 1900		Jewish population in 1939	
	Number	%	Number	%
Western Europe	1,074	10.4	1,300	8.1
Austro-Hungarian Empire*	1,951	18.8	-	-
Eastern Europe	372	3.6	2,020	12.5
Poland	5,111	49.4	3,250	20.1
USSR (Europe)			2,800	17.3
USSR (Asia)	105	1.0	220	1.4
Remaining Asian countries	277	2.7	350	2.2
Australia & New Zealand	17	0.2	35	0.2
North Africa	280	2.7	540	3.3
South Africa	60	0.6	95	0.6
United States	1,016	9.8	4,500	27.9
Canada			165	1.0
South America	35	0.3	150	0.9
Argentina			270	1.7
Palestine	50	0.5	450	2.8
Total	**10,348**	**100**	**16,145**	**100**

* For 1939 estimates, the Jewish population of Austria is included in the figures of western Europe, and the Jews of Hungary in eastern Europe.

21 Extracted from Evyatar Friesel, *Atlas Carta le-Toldot Am Yisrael be-Zman ha-Hadash (Carta's Atlas of Modern Jewish History)*, pp. 12, 13, 85; see also Yehuda Wallach, *Atlas Carta le-Toldot Eretz Yisrael mi-Rashit ha-Hityashvut ve ad Koum ha-Medina (Carta's Atlas of History of the Land of Israel from the Start of Settlement until the Establishment of the State)*, pp. 67-69; *Encyclopaedia Judaica*, Vol. 8, p. 754.

Table 3 World Jewish immigration by destination, 1900-1939 (thousands)[22]

Country/region	1901-14		1915-31		1932-39	
	Number	%	Number	%	Number	%
South Africa	20	1.2	15	2.0	10	1.8
United States	1,365	83.8	415	54.2	110	20
Canada	95	5.8	50	6.5	15	2.7
South America	12	0.7	65	8.5	60	10.9
Argentina	88	5.4	80	10.5	25	4.6
Palestine	40	2.5	115	15	225	40.9
Other countries*	10	0.6	25	3.3	105	19.1
Total	**1,630**	**100**	**765**	**100**	**550**	**100**

While most of these earlier immigrants had gone to the United States, the American authorities changed their attitude towards immigration during and after the First World War. In 1917, the United States imposed restrictions on immigrants to it from certain countries, including many in eastern Europe. In 1921 and again in 1924, it reduced the number of immigrants allowed to enter altogether. Canada and South Africa imposed similar restrictions.[23] This affected Jewish immigration from Europe, forcing a greater number of those immigrants to head to Palestine, as it was open to them. The number of worldwide Jewish immigrants in 1915-1939 was estimated at 1.315 million, of whom 625,000 (47.5 percent) went to the United States and

---

*   This includes countries to which Jewish people immigrated at the start of their emigration waves, and from which they later re-emigrated.

22   Extracted from Evyatar Friesel, *Atlas Carta le Toldot Am Yisrael be-Zman ha-Hadash (Carta's Atlas of Modern Jewish History)*, pp. 12, 13, 85; see also Yehuda Wallach, *Atlas Carta le-Toldot Eretz Yisrael mi-Rashit ha-Hityashvut ve ad Koum ha-Medina (Carta's Atlas of History of the Land of Israel from the Start of Settlement until the Establishment of the State)*, pp. 67-69; *Encyclopaedia Judaica*, Vol. 8, p. 754.

23   *Encyclopaedia Judaica*, Vol. 8, p. 754.

340,000 (25.9 percent) went to Palestine, while the rest went to South America, South Africa, Canada and other countries (see *Table 3 World Jewish immigration by destination, 1900-1939*, above).

As can be seen in the table, the rate of Jewish immigration to Palestine was low in the first part of that period (1915-1931) and high in the second (1932-1939), in contrast to the United States where the rate dropped after the restrictions on immigration went into force. The proportion of Jewish immigrants to the United States dropped from 54.2 percent of all Jewish immigrants in 1915-1931 to 20 percent in 1932-1939, while the proportion of those who entered Palestine rose from 15 percent in the first period to 40.9 percent in the second. Those immigrants were the main force for the establishment of the Jewish national home in Palestine until the outbreak of the Second World War in 1939. The Zionist leadership did everything in its power to provide the appropriate conditions for their entry and settlement in the country.

2

The Zionists resumed their organized activity in Palestine at the first opportunity they had before the end of the First World War. In early April 1918, only a few months after the British forces occupied southern Palestine, the Zionist Commission (see Chapter 6, section 2) arrived in Tel Aviv.[24] The commission assumed supervision of the Palestine Office that the Zionist Organization had established in 1908 in Jaffa.[25] In November 1918, the office was merged into the commission,[26] which exercised its functions as a representative of the Zionist Organization in Palestine until November 1921. As per the decision of the 12th Zionist Congress, it then became the Palestine Zionist Executive, composed of members of the executive who resided

---

24   Chaim Weizmann, *Trial and Error*, pp. 270-272.

25   Chapter 4, section 2.

26   *Report[s] of the Executive of the Zionist Organization to the XIIth Zionist Congress (1921), I. Political Report*, p. 48.

7. British Mandate over Palestine, Part II 431

in Palestine, with its headquarters in Jerusalem.[27] Its leadership was successively held by individuals of different political leanings. Among the most prominent was Ze'ev Jabotinsky, who served as a political liaison with the British military authorities in Palestine, and Menachem Ussishkin, who headed the Palestine Zionist Executive from October 1919. Both men were known for their intransigent stance towards the Arabs.

At the suggestion of its Eastern Committee, the British government had granted the Zionist Commission wide powers upon sending it to Palestine on January 19, 1918. The commission was authorized to act as "a link between the British authorities and the Jewish population in Palestine, [and contribute to] relief work ... the development of Jewish settlements and the organization of the Jewish population, in general ... the collection of information and presentation of reports on ... the future of Jewish development in Palestine",[28] in light of the Balfour Declaration. The commission was also asked "to help in establishing friendly relations between Jews ... and Arabs".[29] The Zionists attempted to induce the British government to further expand these powers of the commission, but failed.[30]

In fact, on its arrival, the Zionist Commission found a cool reception by the British military authorities in Palestine, despite the letters of recommendation that Weizmann carried with him from Lloyd George and Balfour to General Allenby.[31] This was

---

27 *Report[s] of the Executive of the Zionist Organization to the XIIIth Zionist Congress (1923)*, p. 33.

28 Evyatar Friesel, *Ha-Mediniout ha-Tzionit le-ahar Hatzharat Balfour, 1917-1922 (Zionist Policy after the Balfour Declaration, 1917-1922)*, pp. 419-420; for comparison, see also Yosef Olitsky, *Mi-Pzura le-Medinah (From Dispersal to State)*, Vol. 1, p. 161.

29 Friesel, *Ha-Mediniout ha-Tzionit le-ahar Hatzharat Balfour, 1917-1922 (Zionist Policy after the Balfour Declaration, 1917-1922)*, p. 419; see also *Report[s] of the Executive of the Zionist Organization to the XIIth Zionist Congress (1921), I. Political Report*, pp. 14-15.

30 See documents in Friesel, *Ha-Mediniout ha-Tzionit le-ahar Hatzharat Balfour, 1917-1922 (Zionist Policy after the Balfour Declaration, 1917-1922)*, pp. 420-423.

31 Olitsky, *Mi-Pzura le-Medinah (From Dispersal to State)*, Vol. 1, p. 162.

due to several reasons. When the commission arrived in Palestine, the war in Europe was at its height, forcing Britain to withdraw a good number of its forces from under Allenby's command and move them there. This made the security situation in Palestine, to some extent, subject to the appeasement of its Arab inhabitants. Weizmann also discovered that "Arab agitators lost no time in proclaiming that 'the British had sent for the Jews to take over the country.'"[32] He noticed that senior officers in Allenby's command had not even heard of the Balfour Declaration. The positions taken by the commission were another reason for the cool relations between it and the British authorities, as its members insisted on

> immediate involvement in the military administration, the establishment of a land committee with the participation of experts from Jewish organizations ... and being granted the right to select Jewish candidates for the police and to adjust their salaries. They also demanded, and even began, the training of military defense battalions of their own, and insisted on the recognition of Hebrew as an official language.[33]

The British military authorities, in response, refused to recognize the commission, and pursued a policy of preserving the status quo in the country while it was subject to military occupation – according to international law and custom – until its political fate was decided. The authorities maintained this stance until the end of their military rule in mid-1920, despite the disputes that broke out between them and the Zionist Commission and leadership.[34]

Just as it failed to establish favorable relations with the British military authorities in Palestine, and faced several obstacles as a result, the Zionist Commission made no significant achievements among the Jewish settlers in the country, at least during its initial

---

32 Weizmann, *Trial and Error*, p. 272.

33 Olitsky, *Mi-Pzura le-Medinah (From Dispersal to State)*, Vol. 1, p. 166.

34 See also Zionist criticism of the British military administration in Palestine in *Report[s] of the Executive of the Zionist Organization to the XIIth Zionist Congress (1921), I. Political Report*, pp. 43-55.

work. After its arrival in Palestine, the commission made visits to Jewish settlements and communities in the areas that Britain had occupied to review the situation of the settlers, distribute assistance to them and work on uniting them. These unification attempts failed, however, due to the principled differences and mutual suspicions that prevailed between the Jews of the old Yishuv, who lived off the halukah alms, and the new settlers of the Second Aliyah and its various parties.[35] The commission could not, in the end, even unite the funeral associations.[36] While in Palestine, Weizmann attempted to purchase the Wailing Wall (al-Buraq) in Jerusalem but failed.[37] He succeeded, instead, in laying the cornerstone of the Hebrew University on Mount Scopus on July 24, 1918.[38] Weizmann was finally convinced that he would not be able to achieve the Zionist aims in Palestine unless a clear British policy took shape.[39] He returned to London in October 1918.

Despite the failure of the Zionist Commission to unite the settlers, however, attempts persisted until the settlers succeeded in unifying themselves. The first attempt to organize Jews in Palestine had been made in 1903, with Ussishkin's visit to the country, but it had failed and the organization established for that purpose had disintegrated shortly afterwards.[40] The attempts then ceased, before being resumed with great fervor after the British occupied the southern part of Palestine. On November 18, 1917, only three days after the British forces entered Jaffa, a group of settler leaders met in the "mother of the settlements", Petah Tikva, at the invitation of Bezalel Yaffe (1868-1925), president of the Tel Aviv Jewish Council and ex-member of the

---

35 Introduction, section 7; Chapter 4, section 4; Chapter 5, section 2.

36 Olitsky, *Mi-Pzura le-Medinah (From Dispersal to State)*, Vol. 1, p. 164.

37 Ibid, pp. 176-178.

38 Weizmann, *Trial and Error*, p. 295.

39 Friesel, *Ha-Mediniout ha-Tzionit le-ahar Hatzharat Balfour, 1917-1922 (Zionist Policy after the Balfour Declaration, 1917-1922)*, p. 56.

40 Moshe Attias, ed., *Sefer ha-Te'udot shel ha-Va'ad ha-Leumi le-Knesset Yisrael be-Eretz Yisrael (Book of Documents of the National Council of Knesset Israel)*, p. 1.

Zionist Executive. They formed a provisional committee to work on establishing a unified organization for the Jews in Palestine. The committee issued a call to the various Jewish settlements, urging them to send their delegates to a meeting to be held at the earliest opportunity,

> for we stand, at this hour, on the threshold of a new system of rule ... which should not find, here, a Jewish scattering of nations, nor assimilated Jews among a mixture of [Arab] city dwellers and peasants in the country, but a united, national, organized Hebrew Yishuv with an independent culture, institutions and representatives of its own, envoys of its organization who express its needs and demands before the new system of rule, so that the government negotiates with us through them.[41]

Less than two months after this call, representatives of most of the Jewish settlements and communities in the southern part of Palestine met in Jaffa during January 2-3, 1918. They decided to establish a "Provisional Committee for the Jews of the Land of Israel", which was charged with holding elections for a "constituent assembly".[42] This committee met a few months later, during June 17-19, with the participation of Weizmann and representatives of the Jews of Jerusalem who had been able to organize themselves. The committee did not achieve much progress because of the opposition of religious Jews to granting women the right to vote, however. A third meeting took place during December 18-22, with 114 delegates representing the settlers throughout Palestine after Britain had also occupied the northern part of the country. The delegates decided to form a new committee, composed of 32 members, and assigned it a single task: to hold elections for a constituent assembly, after the

---

41 Attias, ed., *Sefer ha-Te'udot shel ha-Va'ad ha-Leumi le-Knesset Yisrael be-Eretz Yisrael (Book of Documents of the National Council of Knesset Israel)*, Introduction, pp. j-j a (10-11), 3.

42 Ibid, p. j a (11).

7. British Mandate over Palestine, Part II 435

majority supported granting women the right to vote.[43] Despite being unelected, the new committee represented the settlers before the British occupation authorities until elections were held on April 19, 1920 for the first Jewish constituent assembly, "Asefat ha-Nivharim" (Assembly of Representatives).[44] This became the core body of the Jewish Assembly ("Knesset Yisrael") – the Jewish community organization in Palestine. About 22,200 Jews, or 77 percent of those entitled to vote, participated in the elections for the first Assembly of Representatives and elected 314 representatives from 20 partisan, local, professional, sectarian (Sephardic and Ashkenazi), and other electoral lists.[45] The religious voters (about 2,040) solved the problem of their opposition to granting women the right to vote – this time – by setting up their own ballot boxes which women were forbidden from using. This point of contention was one of the main reasons that split the organized Jewish community in Palestine into two parts, when it was later recognized by the mandate authorities.

The Assembly of Representatives met for the first time on October 7, 1920, after the British mandate was imposed over Palestine and the authorities lifted their ban on the assembly's meetings (see Chapter 6, section 5).[46] The assembly elected an executive council: the Jewish National Council ("Va'ad Leumi"), composed of 38 members. They in turn elected, from amongst themselves, an executive of 11 members. (In 1927, the British authorities formally recognized this organization.)

Under the guise of participating with Britain in the First World War, the Zionist settlers in Palestine had formed a Jewish

---

43 Ibid.

44 *Chronologiah le-Toldot ha-Yishuv ha-Yehudi be-Eretz Yisrael (Chronology of the Jewish Yishuv in the Land of Israel)*, Vol. 1: 1917-1935, p. 32.

45 Attias, ed., *Sefer ha-Te'udot shel ha-Va'ad ha-Leumi le-Knesset Yisrael be-Eretz Yisrael (Book of Documents of the National Council of Knesset Israel)*, pp. j c-j d (13-14), 430-433.

46 *Chronologiah le-Toldot ha-Yishuv ha-Yehudi be-Eretz Yisrael (Chronology of the Jewish Yishuv in the Land of Israel)*, Vol. 1, pp. 43-44; *Report[s] of the Executive of the Zionist Organization to the XIIth Zionist Congress (1921), I. Political Report*, p. 50.

armed force in cooperation with the Zionists abroad – in the hope that this force would remain at their disposal afterwards and bolster their position. This led to the establishment of the Zion Mule Corps (see Chapter 5, section 2),[47] from among the Jewish settlers who had left Palestine after the outbreak of the war and gone to Egypt. The battalion was demobilized in mid-1916, after participating in the failed British campaign in Gallipoli and returning to Egypt. However, about 120 of the battalion's soldiers joined the British army at the end of the year and were moved to London to later form the nucleus of the Jewish Legion.

As noted in Chapter 5, Ze'ev Jabotinsky and Joseph Trumpeldor were among the key initiators of the establishment of the Zion Mule Corps. Jabotinsky, however, refused to join the battalion when it was formed, because the British authorities did not entrust it with combat missions – which Trumpeldor acquiesced to. Jabotinsky then left Egypt for Europe, stopping in Rome and Paris to promote his idea for the establishment of Jewish battalions, to fight alongside the British army for the occupation of Palestine. He finally arrived in London, where most British Zionist leaders opposed his plan, fearing that its implementation would lead to reprisals by the Ottomans against the Jewish settlers in Palestine. He won Weizmann's support for his project, however, and cooperated, in particular, with the engineer Pinhas Rutenberg (later, the concessionaire of electricity generation in Palestine).[48]

Despite the obstacles Jabotinsky faced, he persisted in promoting his idea. He volunteered in the British army, and, together with Trumpeldor, who had followed him to Britain,

---

[47] See Chapter 5, section 2.

[48] Born in Ukraine, Rutenberg had been a member of the Russian Social Democratic Party in his youth, and had then joined the Socialist Revolutionary Party and participated in the 1905 revolution in Russia. After its failure, he was forced to leave the country, especially when he organized his party's assassination of Gapon, one of the Tsar's leading secret agents. Rutenberg finally moved to Italy, where he drew near the Zionists and then joined them. When Jabotinsky met him while passing through Rome in 1916, he discovered that they shared the same conviction regarding the formation of Jewish battalions.

submitted a request to the authorities to establish the Jewish battalions.[49] In the end, the authorities responded to these attempts, after drawing up the final plans to attack and occupy Palestine by the British forces present in Egypt. In late August 1917, a Jewish battalion was formed in the British army: the 38th Battalion, Royal Fusiliers. It was led by Colonel Patterson, who had commanded the Zion Mule Corps, and Jabotinsky was appointed a lieutenant.[50]

This battalion was moved to Palestine in June 1918. In September, it was joined by the 39th Battalion that was composed of Jewish volunteers in the United States and Canada.[51] They included David Ben-Gurion and Yitzhak Ben-Zvi, whom Cemal Pasha had expelled from Palestine during the war.[52] The Zionist leaders in the United States, including those of the Po'alei Zion party, had initially rejected the idea of establishing the Jewish battalions but changed their position after the Balfour Declaration, declaring that it was their duty to contribute to the expulsion of the Ottomans from Palestine. The 39th Battalion, however, undertook no such activity, as most of its soldiers arrived in the country after the war had ended. The 38th Battalion took part in the fighting to occupy the northern part of Palestine in late 1917 and seized Ottoman positions east of the Jordan River.

In parallel with the efforts to form Jewish battalions in Britain and the United States, attempts were made among the Jews already in Palestine after the occupation of its southern region. In mid-February 1918, a two-day "volunteers' congress" was held in Jaffa and attended by 42 delegates, to formulate terms for volunteering in the British Army. This move sparked intense debate among the Jewish settlers. While the Po'alei Zion party

---

49   See also Joseph B. Schechtman, *Rebel and Statesman, The Vladimir Jabotinsky Story*, Vol. 1, pp. 442-491.

50   Ben-Zion Dinur (Dinaburg), ed., *Sefer Toldot ha-Haganah (History of the Haganah)*, Vol. 1, Part 2, pp. 449-468.

51   For details, see ibid, pp. 489-496.

52   Chapter 5, section 2.

supported it, its opposing party, Hapoel Hatzair, voiced its strong rejection, declaring that such an act could jeopardize the Jewish settlements in the Galilee that were still under Ottoman rule. The debate was settled when the British military authorities announced their agreement to accept Jewish volunteers in Palestine on June 10, 1918. The authorities began to transfer those volunteers to Egypt for training and formed a battalion for them, the 40th, which had approximately 1,100 soldiers by the autumn of 1918.[53] Like the 39th Battalion, however, it could not take part in the fighting to occupy the northern part of Palestine, as the war had ended before the battalion's training was complete.

The 40th Battalion was moved from Egypt to Palestine after the war, where it joined the other two battalions to form a Jewish force of about 5,000 soldiers in early 1919. This number soon dwindled when the volunteers from the United States and Britain went home, prompting a number of volunteers from within Palestine to leave the battalions and return to their homes as well.

Nevertheless, the Zionist leadership insisted on retaining the soldiers who remained in these battalions and encouraged the British military authorities to reorganize them. The leadership hoped to recruit new volunteers from the settlers in Palestine such that, together with the remaining soldiers, they would form part of the garrisons charged with maintaining security in the country. As a result of these efforts, the volunteers were reorganized in a single battalion. In late 1919, this battalion was given a new name: "First Judeans", who chose a Jewish emblem: a menorah with seven branches, with the word "Kadimah" ("forward", in Hebrew) underneath.

The battalion's days were numbered, however. Its presence sparked significant tension among the Arabs, as some of its soldiers participated in more than one riot in Palestine in early 1920. In late March, the British authorities issued an order

---

53 Dinur, ed., *Sefer Toldot ha-Haganah (History of the Haganah)*, Vol. 2, Part 1, pp. 499-511.

to demobilize the battalion. The execution of this order was postponed, by Weizmann's efforts, until late July,[54] then a final request was sent by the high commissioner at the end of March 1921.[55] In May of that year, the soldiers of the battalion were finally discharged.[56]

Yet, despite this end of the Jewish battalions, the experience was useful in the long term for the Zionists in Palestine. The idea arose, among these battalions, of unifying the labor groups, and some of these soldiers helped to implement it. Later, a significant number of Zionist leaders, both political and military, emerged from their ranks.

3

In the early 1920s, as the British were coordinating with the Zionist leadership to establish the Jewish national home in Palestine, the Zionist labor forces were doing their own work in the country and abroad. Differences of opinion prevailed among the Zionist laborers after the British mandate was imposed and Britain announced its intention to establish the Jewish national home there. The victory of the revolution in Russia also prompted the labor camp to re-evaluate its positions. In the early 1920s, several conferences were held that led to splits in most of the Zionist labor organizations and an almost complete reshuffling of their forces in terms of both organizational frameworks and ideological stances. Disagreements on adhering to socialism and whether it could solve the "Jewish question", or whether Zionism could be merged with socialism, were the main axes around which the revisions, splits and new organizational processes developed. At the same time, Zionist activity began to center around Poland.

These processes, in Palestine and abroad, began in the final stage of the First World War. In Palestine, the Zionist

---

54 For details, see ibid, pp. 516-532.

55 *Chronologiah le-Toldot ha-Yishuv ha-Yehudi be-Eretz Yisrael (Chronology of the Jewish Yishuv in the Land of Israel)*, Vol. 1, p. 47.

56 Ibid, p. 60.

laborers stepped up their efforts to unify their ranks and prepare themselves for their perceived role in establishing the national home. During February 25-27, 1918, about three months after the British had occupied the southern part of the country, the Judea Agricultural Workers' Federation[57] held its seventh convention in Rehovot. The convention aimed to clarify the position of agricultural workers on the future of Zionist activity in Palestine, but it did not address this issue due to the ongoing war. Instead, it discussed agricultural matters and adopted a series of resolutions in which it declared that "the focus of Zionist activity in the near future is broad, effective work to emancipate and nationalize the land, and to create political, settlement, economic and cultural conditions that allow for wide popular immigration."[58] It also declared that the lands acquired in Palestine by the Zionists should be placed at the disposal of the Jewish National Fund[59] in order to become "the perpetual property of the Hebrew nation", and that they should be allocated "to build a free, labor Yishuv".[60] The convention called on the Zionist Organization to establish "a private financial institution, with the objective of land reclamation and granting agricultural loans"[61] to Jewish settlers.

A number of delegates, however, led by Levi Eshkol (born Levi Yitzhak Shkolnik, 1895-1969, prime minister of Israel from 1963-1969), complained of the partisan competition that dominated the federation, with each group working for its own interests without any concern for the whole.[62] The partisan strife between Po'alei Zion and Hapoel Hatzair had reached its peak at the time. It alienated the non-partisans and pushed them to form

---

57 See also Chapter 4, section 4.

58 Moshe Braslavski, *Tnu'at ha-Poalim ha-Eretz Yisraelit (Labor Movement in the Land of Israel)*, Vol. 1, p. 149.

59 See also Chapter 3, section 5.

60 Braslavski, *Tnu'at ha-Poalim ha-Eretz Yisraelit (Labor Movement in the Land of Israel)*, Vol. 1, p. 194.

61 Tzvi Ben-Shoshan, *Toldot Tnu'at ha-Poalim be-Eretz Yisrael (History of the Labor Movement in the Land of Israel)*, Vol. 1, p. 292.

62 Ibid.

a bloc, the "non-partisan party", and the convention was unable to take any measure to reduce the intensity of competition between these groups.

Despite the adjournment of the convention without a position on the future of Zionist activity in Palestine, the debate continued among the various labor groups. Some of the events of 1918 contributed to this, especially the arrival of the Zionist Commission in Palestine in April, the decision to volunteer for the Jewish battalions in the summer and Britain's occupation of the northern part of the country in the fall. After the convening of the Peace Conference in early 1919, which revived Zionist hopes in the near imposition of a British mandate over Palestine and the establishment of a Jewish national home, the debate intensified and it seemed necessary to resolve this disagreement before any further work could be done. The discussion was focused on three issues: the role of the workers in building the Zionist entity in Palestine; "the core of relations between the Land of Israel and the diaspora, in general, and between the labor movement in the country and the diaspora, in particular";[63] and "the method of organizing the workers; should this be done on a political-partisan or a comprehensive, non-partisan class basis?"[64]

With the raging partisan disputes, it was not easy to resolve these issues. A group of non-partisans, from the soldiers of the Jewish battalions who had returned to Palestine, thus raised the slogan of abolishing the political parties and replacing them with a comprehensive organization to unite the workers on a class basis. This group included Berl Katznelson (1887-1944), Yitzhak Tabenkin (1888-1971), David Remez (1886-1951), Shmuel Yavnieli (1884–1961) and others, who later became major leaders of the Zionist labor wing in Palestine.

This non-partisan group found a response to its calls among many segments of Po'alei Zion. Since its formation in 1905, the members of this party's branch had gradually moved away from the "intransigent" theoretical positions of its

---

63 Ibid, p. 293.

64 Ibid.

mother party in Russia and begun to fit their ideology to the new reality in Palestine.[65] By 1913, they had almost completely abandoned the ideological bases of Po'alei Zion in Russia, which were based on Marxism, in its Borochovian (see Chapter 4, section 3) interpretation, and replaced them with what they termed "constructive socialism". They had reservations on the conventional theory of class struggle, but did not abandon it completely. Instead, they emphasized the effective, constructive role of the Zionist workers in establishing the Jewish national home in Palestine – not in engaging in application of the theory of class struggle to a non-existent society. "Socialism is not only a theory of destruction. If there is nothing in the Land of Israel to destroy, there is ample room to create… We have created, in the country" – in the words of Ben-Gurion – "a project that had not occurred to our comrade, Borochov, who lives abroad… It became clear to us that it is not enough to seize power in order to overthrow the social system, nor is it sufficient to destroy the system, but we must strive to build a new national economy."[66] Thus, Po'alei Zion was quick to respond to the non-partisan calls to unify the Zionist labor parties in Palestine. Hapoel Hatzair, however, took an opposing stance. It refused the call for unity and instead suggested the establishment of a "federal union"[67] of parties – a proposal that was rejected.

In light of these positions, the advocates of unity formed a six-party committee composed of Ben-Gurion and Ben-Zvi, on behalf of Po'alei Zion, and Tabenkin, Katznelson, Remez and Yavnieli, on behalf of the non-partisans. The committee called for a general convention of agricultural workers, which was held in Petah Tikva on March 26, 1919. After discussing the unity proposals, the delegates, numbering about 1,500, elected 58 representatives to make a decision. Since most of the

---

65 For details, see Chapter 4, section 5.

66 Yosef Gorny, *Ahdut HaAvoda, 1919-1930: Ha-Yesodot ha-Ri'iyonim ve ha-Shita ha-Mdinit (Ahdut HaAvoda, 1919-1930: Ideological Principles and Political System)*, p. 23.

67 Ibid, pp. 23, 26.

representatives were supporters of unity (28 non-partisans and 19 from Po'alei Zion, versus 11 from Hapoel Hatzair), it was decided, contrary to the view of Hapoel Hatzair, to establish the united party. On the third day, a general convention of worker representatives was held, including non-agricultural ones in addition to members of trade unions and some intellectuals. It had 81 delegates (47 for agricultural workers, 15 for urban workers, and 19 for volunteers in the Jewish battalions) representing 1871 workers. The convention decided to establish the "Zionist Socialist Federation of the Workers of the Land of Israel, Ahdut ha-Avoda [Labor Unity, in Hebrew]", which replaced Po'alei Zion in Palestine. This party soon came to comprise most of the Jewish workers in the country, despite the reluctance of Hapoel Hatzair and a small, left-wing minority from Po'alei Zion to join it.[68]

Ahdut ha-Avoda viewed itself as more than just a new party. It sought to be a comprehensive, pioneering organization to unify the Zionist forces and establish a Jewish labor society in all its components. In its constitution, the party considered "the [Zionist] labor movement in the Land of Israel a branch of the worldwide socialist labor movement, which seeks the complete emancipation of humanity from the yoke of the existing system in which private capital controls the destiny of a nation, its economic and cultural output, and relations of peoples and countries".[69] In order to bring about this emancipation, the party asserted, it was necessary to establish a society that lived on labor, after "the transfer of primary resources and property, amassed over generations, from individual ownership to the authority of the collective, and the organization of all matters of labor and ownership through the labor society".[70] The party also considered

---

68   Ben-Shoshan, *Toldot Tnu'at ha-Poalim be-Eretz Yisrael (History of the Labor Movement in the Land of Israel)*, Vol. 1, p. 315.

69   In the constitution of Ahdut Ha-Avoda, in Hen-Melech Merchavia, *Am ou-Moledet (Nation and Homeland)*, pp. 517-518.

70   In Braslavski, *Tnu'at ha-Poalim ha-Eretz Yisraelit (Labor Movement in the Land of Israel)*, Vol. 1, pp. 359-360.

the labor movement in the Land of Israel as a branch of the Zionist movement among the Jews, seeking to rescue them from the diaspora. Its goal is to revive the Jews, whose masses are returning to their country to settle it ... and become a free people that governs its country and speaks its Hebrew language, organizes its life as it pleases, and creates and develops its material and spiritual values.[71]

The party augmented these general principles in its constitution with specific declarations that it understood Zionism as an "organized, widespread, popular immigration movement"[72] whose goal was to "rebuild the life of the Hebrew people in the Land of Israel, as a labor society, free and equal in rights, that lives by its toil, controls its possessions, and organizes its labor, economy, and culture as it pleases".[73] To implement these objectives, it was necessary to:

a. Transfer land in the Land of Israel, and its waters and natural resources, to the Jews to be in perpetual possession of the whole people; b. Establish a national capital ... for land reclamation and the creation of permanent facilities to serve the nation (railways, ports, forests, ships, dams, lighting and electricity), and a national fund [for the development of] agriculture and industry...; c. Bring pioneers to the country to live a life of labor, in order to pave the way and create the conditions for a widespread popular immigration, and participate in creating a vital working class that establishes the future labor society; d. Disseminate the Hebrew language and cultural values among all segments of the people, create a cultural life and involve the working public in it.[74]

Based on this position, Ahdut ha-Avoda declared its acceptance of all those who earned a living through their labor into its

---

71 Ibid.

72 Ibid, p. 360.

73 Ibid.

74 Ibid.

ranks, even if they were not in the class of wage workers, as long as they did not exploit the labor of others. The party based its organizational structure on independent professional unions, such that those who belonged to the unions would also be members of the party. At the conclusion of its program, the party announced that it would join the Zionist Organization and the Socialist International as an independent national organization.[75]

With time, Ahdut ha-Avoda became the largest Zionist party in Palestine. Through its various names and formations, it came to lead Zionist activity in the country and to govern Israel for a long time after its establishment. (In 1930, Ahdut ha-Avoda united with Hapoel Hatzair to form Mapai which, after 1968, united with other labor groups to form the Israeli Labor Party. This remained in power until 1977.)

In another vein, the Russian Zionists, who were then the largest and most significant Zionist group worldwide, resumed their activity publicly after the 1917 February Revolution in Russia, when the various tsarist restrictions on the country's Jewish population were abolished. After the outbreak of the revolution, the central committee of the Russian Zionists issued a statement of commitment to the Helsingfors Program, which their third congress had approved in 1906.[76] As mentioned earlier (see section 1 of this chapter), the Russian Zionists then held their seventh congress – the only one held legally by the Zionist Organization in Russia – in Petrograd, during May 24-30, 1917. There were 552 delegates representing about 140,000 organized, dues-paying Zionists.[77] At its conclusion, the congress took a series of resolutions in the spirit of statements made by Ussishkin and Chlenov. Most important was the call to work on granting the Jewish population in Russia national minority rights and autonomy, as well as invigorating Zionist settlement in Palestine and demanding the establishment of a Jewish national

---

75   Ibid, p. 361.

76   For details, see Chapter 4, section 3.

77   Gruenbaum, *Ha-Tnu'ah ha-Tzionit (The Zionist Movement)*, Vol. 4, p. 98.

center there.[78] To implement these resolutions, the Russian Zionists sought to convene a general Jewish congress in Russia after they had reached an agreement with their opposing parties, led by the Bund. Per this agreement, the Russian Zionists were to include the question of Palestine as a secondary issue on the agenda of the congress and to focus on the problems and demands of the Jews in Russia and the neighboring regions that had been under its rule.[79] On November 25, 1917, elections were held among the Jewish population in Russia for representatives at this congress, and 1,285 delegates were elected: 568 Zionists, 199 from the Bund, 152 religious, 134 socialists, 70 from Po'alei Zion, 31 from the Jewish People's Party and 131 non-partisans[80] (results that reflected the extent of partisan division among Russian Jews at the time). It was decided to hold the congress in early 1918.

In addition to these moves by the Zionist Organization in Russia, other Zionist parties were active. In preparation for the seventh Russian Zionist congress in 1917, Tzeirei Zion hastened to hold its second congress a week before in Petrograd (the first had been held in 1913). By that time, the contradictions between the ideologies of the various groups within Tzeirei Zion had further sharpened,[81] such that three currents manifested in its congress: "socialist", "proletarian" and "democratic", each with incompatible views. In order to prevent a split, the congress adopted a middle program. It announced the formation of an independent bloc, not a party,[82] within the Zionist Organization: the "Popular Bloc of Tzeirei Zion", with a motto of "Land and Labor".[83] The congress considered Zionism to be "a

---

78 See resolutions in Mior, *Ha-Tnu'ah ha-Tzionit be-Rusia (Zionist Movement in Russia)*, pp. 446-450.

79 For details, see Gruenbaum, *Ha-Tnu'ah ha-Tzionit (The Zionist Movement)*, Vol. 4, pp. 121-126.

80 Ibid, p. 126.

81 For details, see Chapter 4, sections 3, 4.

82 Ben-Shoshan, *Toldot Tnu'at ha-Poalim be-Eretz Yisrael (History of the Labor Movement in the Land of Israel)*, Vol. 1, p. 371.

83 Mior, *Ha-Tnu'ah ha-Tzionit be-Rusia (Zionist Movement in Russia)*, pp. 454-456.

comprehensive, non-class national movement ... whose ultimate goal is to revive the Jewish people in the Land of Israel".[84] Thus, "Tzeirei Zion seeks to establish an independent political center in the Land of Israel, on sound socialist grounds, and to organize national-political entities (on a personal basis) for the Jews of the diaspora, converging around this center."[85] Tzeirei Zion maintained its previous conservative position towards Marxism. It also stressed that "the national language ... the language of the people in the Land of Israel, must – and can – be Hebrew, only," even though the party did not mind "the allocation of a suitable place for Yiddish, as well".[86] Tzeirei Zion defined the focus of Zionist activity as "the creation of a Jewish majority in the Land of Israel, based on agriculture and Hebrew labor".[87] (This program, however, did not prevent a later split in the organization.)

At the same time, a similar development took place within Po'alei Zion in Russia. Many groups within the organization had gradually moved from the Zionist line towards socialist positions. This transformation was complete by 1909, and the Russian Po'alei Zion congress held in Vienna decided to withdraw from the Zionist Congress and sever relations with the Zionist Organization, "because socialists cannot participate in one organization with representatives of the bourgeoisie".[88] This trend intensified after the outbreak of the 1917 February Revolution in Russia, when Po'alei Zion focused most of its efforts in laying out projects for "rebuilding the Jewish existence on a national basis in democratic Russia".[89] This position did not win the approval of the pro-Zionist minority, however, which announced its split from the party and the formation of a new one, the "Socialist-Radical Party, Po'alei Zion". They declared

---

84 Ibid, p. 454.

85 Ibid, p. 455.

86 Ibid.

87 Ibid.

88 Ibid, p. 457.

89 Gruenbaum, *Ha-Tnu'ah ha-Tzionit (The Zionist Movement)*, Vol. 4, p. 97.

that, despite their approval of the "program of national revival of the Jewish people", which had been formulated before the split, their main goal was to "seek to establish a Jewish state in the Land of Israel, under socialist principles, and by recognizing the unity of the nation".[90] The new party was supported by Po'alei Zion in Austria, Britain and the United States, and rallied under the slogan, "Jewish workers of the world, unite!"[91]

Yet the Zionist "honeymoon" in Russia did not last long. Only a few months later, the 1917 October Revolution broke out and the situation changed again. The new regime was not in favor of Zionism, but it was compelled to overlook Zionist activity while it was establishing its rule. With the spread of the revolution, the revolutionaries began to escalate its stance and take various containment measures against the movement while working to abolish any discrimination against Jewish people and grant them full rights like other peoples of the Soviet Union. The implementation of these measures took a significant period of time, which ended in the early 1930s when Zionist activity was completely banned in the country. By that time, however, the Zionists had made progress in more than one arena, which had an impact on the establishment of the Jewish national home in Palestine.

The Soviet authorities approved the measures – announced by the leaders of the February Revolution – to abolish the restrictions that had been imposed on the Jews during tsarist rule, and made anti-Semitism and racial discrimination crimes punishable by law. The constitution of the Soviet Union also recognized the country's Jewish population as an independent nation, contrary to the theories of Marx, Lenin and Joseph Stalin. It granted them the same rights as other nationalities, including the right to use Yiddish, which was considered the national Jewish language, in their cultural institutions, schools and courts.[92] The Soviet Union was the first country to recognize

---

90 Mior, *Ha-Tnu'ah ha-Tzionit be-Rusia (Zionist Movement in Russia)*, p. 457.

91 For details, see ibid, pp. 458-459.

92 Kirschenbaum, *Toldot Am Yisrael be-Doreinu (The History of the Jews in*

7. British Mandate over Palestine, Part II 449

Jewish people as a nation. Five provinces – three in Ukraine and two in Crimea – were considered "Jewish national areas" whose residents had the right to establish schools that taught in Yiddish. The majority of Jewish students, however, preferred schools that taught in Russian, in order to facilitate their assimilation into Soviet society.[93]

As for its position towards the Zionists, the first measure taken by the new government was to ban the general Russian Jewish congress in early 1918. Despite this, however, the presidency of the Zionist Organization in Petrograd and its branches in the provinces continued to operate until mid-1919. After the Soviets took control of Ukraine, the Jewish section of the Council of People's Commissars of the Soviet Union issued a resolution in which it considered Hebrew a "reactionary, counter-revolutionary language".[94] In late August of the same year, its teaching was banned. The Zionists protested this decision, and the Supreme Soviet issued a statement calling on official institutions not to interfere with Zionist cultural activity as long as it could not be considered counter-revolutionary. The police, however, did not heed this announcement. In September 1919, they searched the presidency offices of the Zionist Organization, arrested a few of its members and tightened the monitoring of others.[95] The Zionist Organization then called for a meeting in Moscow in late April 1920 to discuss the position that should be taken. Two days into the meeting, the police surrounded its venue, arrested all the participants and only released those who signed a pledge to refrain from any Zionist activity.[96] A phase of clandestine activity thus began and the Zionists established a special office in Moscow to supervise it.

The Zionist Organization tried to mediate with the Soviet authorities, sending David Eder, head of the political department

---

Our Generation), Vol. 1, pp. 108-109.

93   Ibid, pp. 118-121.

94   Mior, *Ha-Tnu'ah ha-Tzionit be-Rusia (Zionist Movement in Russia)*, p. 505.

95   Ibid, p. 506.

96   Ibid.

of the Zionist Commission, to Russia in 1921 in an attempt to reach an understanding and allow Zionist activity. This attempt failed, however, like two others before – the first by Herzl in 1903 and the second by Wolffsohn in 1908.[97] The Soviet authorities persisted in their policy, occasionally arresting a number of Zionists and sentencing them to prison or forcing them into exile.[98] The last of these arrest campaigns took place during 1929-1930 and led to the arrest of more than 1,000 Zionists from all over the Soviet Union, who were all exiled to Siberia.[99] Thus, Zionist activity was almost completely halted in Russia.

Zionists in other countries also increased their efforts to reorganize themselves. Tzeirei Zion, which was allied with the Hapoel Hatzair party in Palestine, was the first to conduct an internal review. In Poland, the majority of Tzeirei Zion declared in late 1919 that it considered itself an independent, socialist party. It severed its relations with the Zionist Organization and decided to participate in its meetings in Poland for propaganda purposes only. This decision did not win the approval of the minority "proletariat" faction of the party, however, who considered themselves socialist revolutionaries and had reservations towards pure Marxism. They split from the party and founded a new one that they called "Popular Zionist Bloc, Hapoel Hatzair",[100] to confirm their ties to the Hapoel Hatzair party in Palestine.

In Russia, Tzeirei Zion held its third congress secretly in Kharkov in May 1920, about a month after the arrest of the members of the Zionist Organization in Moscow. Tzeirei Zion declared that, from that point on, it did not consider itself a "popular bloc" but a party, the "Socialist Zionist Party, Tzeirei Zion".[101] The new party refrained from taking any position on

---

97   For details, see Chapter 3, section 6; Chapter 4, section 1.

98   For details, see Mior, *Ha-Tnu'ah ha-Tzionit be-Rusia (Zionist Movement in Russia)*, pp. 508-510, 533-537.

99   Kirschenbaum, *Toldot Am Yisrael be-Doreinu (The History of the Jews in Our Generation)*, Vol. 1, p. 123.

100 Ben-Shoshan, *Toldot Tnu'at ha-Poalim be-Eretz Yisrael (History of the Labor Movement in the Land of Israel)*, Vol. 1, pp. 373-374.

101 Ibid, p. 373.

Marxism and simply announced that it accepted any socialist Zionist who called for focusing on Zionist activity in Palestine into its ranks. The party also declared its "recognition of the theory of class struggle but with a constructive interpretation [similar to the 'constructive socialism' advocated by Ahdut ha-Avoda in Palestine], in a manner aimed at integrating ... the constructive settlement functions in the Land of Israel into the functions of the class struggle".[102] Again, however, this transformation did not have the consent of the "proletariat" faction, which insisted on retaining the former name: "Popular Bloc, Tzeirei Zion".

The Hapoel Hatzair party, meanwhile, which was originally established in Palestine and was ideologically close to Tzeirei Zion, had expanded and formed branches in more than one European country, most notably in Germany. This branch followed what it termed "popular socialism", with reservations towards materialist Marxism, and emphasized the uniqueness of Jewish existence. The branch of Hapoel Hatzair in Germany was headed by Chaim Arlozorov (1899-1933; head of the political department of the Jewish Agency in the early 1930s) and Martin Buber (1878-1965; a renowned Jewish Zionist philosopher). In early 1920, the two parties merged. They called for a congress that was held in Prague in late March, and attended by a number of senior leaders of Hapoel Hatzair in Palestine, including Yosef Sprinzak (later, speaker of the Knesset in Israel), Aaron David Gordon, Eliezer Yaffe, Zvi Yehuda and others. It was decided to establish an organization called the "World Union [ha-Hit'ahdut, in Hebrew] of Hapoel Hatzair and Tzeirei Zion", comprising the branches of both parties in eastern and western Europe as well as in Palestine.[103] In its constitution, the union called for merging all labor and socialist groups within the Zionist Organization,

> because a common goal unites them all, the establishment of a free Hebrew society in the Land of Israel, on the basis of self-labor, without exploiting or being exploited ... and they

---

102   Ibid.

103   Ibid, pp. 374-376.

all aim, as well, to revive the life of the people in the diaspora on the basis of a labor society that neither exploits nor is exploited.[104]

This program was clearly based on Gordon's theories of the "religion of labor".[105] The union endorsed the positions of Hapoel Hatzair which, since its founding, had maintained its reservations towards Marxism. This program did not win the approval of the party's adherents to Marxism, however. In 1921, they established a separate body called the "World Union of Socialist Zionists, Tzeirei Zion". Among its most prominent leaders were Israel Bar-Yehuda (1895-1965) and Zalman Aran (1899-1970) – who would later become ministers of the interior and of education and culture, respectively, in Israel. Thus, Tzeirei Zion split into two (and in 1925 the Socialist Zionists merged with the Ahdut ha-Avoda party in Palestine).

Similar developments took place within the World Union of Po'alei Zion, which was then the largest Zionist labor organization. Its members had risen from 4,000-5,000, on the eve of the First World War, to about 60,000 in the early 1920s. This led the party to act as if it were the head of all Jewish labor organizations. Despite its growth, however, its members were far from harmonious ideologically, with several contradictory currents among them. The outbreak of the revolution in Russia exacerbated these contradictions, especially since Po'alei Zion had initially declared its commitment to Marxism – even if that was Borokhov's interpretation of Marxism.[106] Again, the disputes were focused mainly in two spheres: the position on the socialist revolution, and the relationship with the Zionist entity in Palestine.

With the end of the First World War, the central committee of the Po'alei Zion union held a meeting in Stockholm in 1919,

---

104 Braslavski, *Tnu'at ha-Poalim ha-Eretz Yisraelit (Labor Movement in the Land of Israel)*, Vol. 1, p. 244.

105 For details, see Chapter 4, section 3.

106 Braslavski, *Tnu'at ha-Poalim ha-Eretz Yisraelit (Labor Movement in the Land of Israel)*, Vol. 1, p. 238.

in which it declared that it "supports building a socialist Land of Israel, the nationalization of lands and natural resources, and the adoption of the social-cooperative principle with respect to all branches of settlement, labor, industry, commerce, and crafts".[107] The committee also decided to send a mission to Palestine to study its situation. Upon its return, the mission stated the necessity of settling Jewish people there "on socialist bases" but warned against the illusion of "belief that the Zionist Congress, with its current [bourgeois] social structure, can oversee the creation of a cooperative Land of Israel".[108] Thus, it called for a general Jewish labor congress under the auspices of Po'alei Zion, to work on securing the necessary financial resources to achieve this, in the belief that the Jewish laborer, "at a time when capitalist society is being undermined, is the only one who can build a socialist Land of Israel, and is compelled and obligated to do so".[109]

This decision was met with the opposition of the Po'alei Zion currents that favored cooperation with non-labor groups to establish the national home in Palestine. The differences deepened within the international union to a level that almost paralyzed it. Thus the union held a general congress in Vienna, during July 27-August 8, 1920, to discuss two main issues: the relationship with the Socialist International, and the position on Zionist activity in Palestine. On the first issue, 178 members voted for a motion calling for secession from the Socialist International and joining the Communist International (Comintern), while 179 members abstained from voting, and one member voted against the motion. In view of this, there was no point in putting the second issue to the vote, as the world union split into two: a "right-wing" part that included Po'alei Zion in the United States, Britain and Argentina, and was also joined by the Ahdut ha-Avoda party in Palestine; and a "left-wing" part that was joined by the branches of the union in most eastern European countries,

---

107 Ibid.

108 Ibid.

109 Ibid.

which comprised the majority of Po'alei Zion. Each union also included a number of ideologically disparate groups.[110]

The split of Po'alei Zion significantly affected its activities in Palestine. The right-wing union was a minority, most of which refused to immigrate to the country, while the left-wing union abandoned the Zionists and engaged in negotiations with the Comintern to be accepted as a member. During these talks, three currents also took shape within the left-wing union. The first demanded the joining of the Comintern at any cost and severing any relationship with the Zionists to facilitate this, the second announced a stance in favor of Zionism and the third took a middle position that sought to maintain a relationship with both sides. With the failure of these negotiations, which lasted for about two years, the union disintegrated. Several groups and parties with different ideological leanings split from it, including Zionist, Zionist-left and communist groups. Similar developments had taken place within that minority of Po'alei Zion in Palestine that had refused to join Ahdut ha-Avoda upon its establishment in 1919. This minority founded a new party, the "Socialist Workers Party" ("Mifleget ha-Po'alim ha-Socioalistit" – MOPSI – in Hebrew) which then changed its name to become the "Jewish Socialist Workers Party". Soon, two currents emerged within this party, as well: socialist-Zionist and communist. In 1922 and 1923, the ideologically close groups in Palestine and abroad united to establish two new parties: Po'alei Zion Smol (Left Workers of Zion), and the (Jewish) Palestine Communist Party.[111]

The Left Workers of Zion had declared in their second congress, held during April 2-4, 1920, that their political program was based on "socialism as a final goal, revolutionary class

---

110 Ben-Shoshan, *Toldot Tnu'at ha-Poalim be-Eretz Yisrael (History of the Labor Movement in the Land of Israel)*, Vol. 1, pp. 382-384; Braslavski, *Tnu'at ha-Poalim ha-Eretz Yisraelit (Labor Movement in the Land of Israel)*, Vol. 1, pp. 239-242.

111 For details, see Peretz Merchav, *Toldot Tnu'at ha-Poalim be-Eretz Yisrael 1905-1965 (History of the Labor Movement in the Land of Israel, 1905-1965)*, pp. 68, 72-75, 83.

7. British Mandate over Palestine, Part II 455

struggle as a method, and the dictatorship of the working class ... as a means".[112] The party also announced its opposition to joining the Zionist institutions, because of the "class character of the Zionist movement".[113] With regard to the "Arab problem", the party believed that

> the settlement of Jewish masses in the Land of Israel, on socialist bases, does not conflict with the interests of the Arab workers and peasants ... who are the only ones able to create a peaceful revolutionary movement among the Arab labor and semi-labor masses ... but it is the Party's duty to help create the nucleus of this movement.[114]

The Left Workers of Zion later abandoned this endeavor, however. They also demanded the establishment of a "national revolutionary party, based on national units",[115] both Arab and Jewish – and, until that was done, they stated that the Jewish unit would carry out the functions of this united party.[116] In practice, the Left Workers of Zion was a marginal organization during the mandate, periodically splitting and uniting again[117] until it later merged in 1946 with the Ahdut ha-Avoda party, which was then in process of splitting from Mapai.

In addition to the above, a new Zionist organization was formed during this period: Hehalutz (Vanguards, in Hebrew). This was composed of youth groups whose aim was to train their members on all kinds of manual labor, especially agricultural, in preparation for their immigration to Palestine. The first Hehalutz groups appeared in mid-1916 among the Jewish population of

---

112   From the party's program, in Baruch Ben-Efram, *Miflagot ou Zramim Politim be-Tkufat ha-Bayit ha-Leumi, 1918-1948 (Parties and Political Currents during the Period of the National Home, 1918-1948)*, p. 63.

113   Ibid, p. 64.

114   Ibid.

115   Ibid.

116   Ibid.

117   See also some of the party's statements and resolutions in Adam Doron, ed., *Mekorot la-Toldot Tnu'at ha-Avoda ha-Yisraelit (Sources for the History of the Israeli Labor Movement)*, pp. 130-133.

Crimea and then spread throughout Russia, although without having a solid inter-organizational relationship. With the rise in number of these associations, the second congress of Tzeirei Zion held in May 1917 in Petrograd decided to help them. After the Balfour Declaration, Tzeirei Zion issued a statement urging its members to join Hehalutz and prepare to immigrate to Palestine, because "the country will not be ours unless the labor in it is under our control."[118] This led to a significant rise in the number of Hehalutz members and associations. In mid-January 1918, Tzeirei Zion initiated a meeting of the heads of Hehalutz associations in Kharkov, in which it considered "Hehalutz as the proletarian vanguard who immigrate to the Land of Israel to solve the settlement problem. The goal of Hehalutz is to prepare the country for the people, by uniting and focusing all the forces that are ready to work towards this goal."[119]

Hehalutz, however, did not limit itself as such. Its membership quickly grew, with large numbers of non-partisans joining it, such that it was freed from the control of Tzeirei Zion and began to operate as an independent organization. Joseph Trumpeldor, who devoted most of his time to Hehalutz, especially in 1918, helped shape this trend.[120] Hehalutz spread among Jewish youth in all eastern European countries. Each branch had its own character, but they were all united by one goal: to train their members on all kinds of manual labor in preparation for their immigration to Palestine.[121]

The Russian branch of Hehalutz, however, had the highest membership and activity. It held its first congress in Petrograd in January 1919 and amended its objectives to state that it considered itself "a proletarian supra-partisan organization of members who have decided to immigrate to the Land of Israel,

---

118 Mior, *Ha-Tnu'ah ha-Tzionit be-Rusia (Zionist Movement in Russia)*, p. 484.

119 Ibid, p. 486.

120 Ibid, pp. 486-487.

121 Yehuda Erez, ed., *Sefer ha-Aliyah ha-Shlishit (The Third Aliyah Book)*, Vol. 1, pp. 13-17.

7. British Mandate over Palestine, Part II 457

to live an independent life of labor without exploiting others", and that Hehalutz "unites, trains, transports and settles them in the country",[122] with the aim of "establishing a [Jewish] regional national center in the Land of Israel, consistent with the absolute, general, national and social interests of the proletariat".[123] The organization also declared its commitment to the decisions and instructions of the Zionist congresses and its recognition of Hebrew as a national language in Palestine, and called for the "nationalization" of its lands for the Jews.[124] Hehalutz began to close its ranks and expand its activities in Russia after the congress, creating dozens of new branches, especially in Crimea and Ukraine, in 1921 and 1922. In 1926, Hehalutz held an international congress at Danzig, in which it redefined its objectives, stressing its association with the Histadrut and the kibbutz system.[125]

Hehalutz did not make these achievements alone, but thanks to the position of the Soviet authorities that recognized and cooperated with it, in contrast to their position on other Zionist organizations. During the first period of Soviet rule and the New Economic Policy, the regime was in dire need of revitalizing agriculture and expanding production, such that it had to cooperate with any group working in this area. For its part, Hehalutz had been able to encourage a number of Jewish bodies, especially the ORT vocational training organization, the Joint social aid organization and the JCA company,[126] to provide it with agricultural and other machinery that the Soviet Union desperately needed. Thus the Central Committee of the Soviet Communist Party announced in 1920 that it did not oppose

---

122 Ibid, p. 12.

123 Ibid.

124 Mior, *Ha-Tnu'ah ha-Tzionit be-Rusia (Zionist Movement in Russia)*, p. 487.

125 See objectives in Chaim Gvati, *Meah Shanot Hityashvut (A Hundred Years of Settlement)*, Vol. 1, p. 269.

126 Kirschenbaum, *Toldot Am Yisrael be-Doreinu (The History of the Jews in Our Generation)*, Vol. 1, p. 117; see also Mior, *Ha-Tnu'ah ha-Tzionit be-Rusia (Zionist Movement in Russia)*, p. 528.

the activity of Hehalutz as long as it did not contradict the law, despite the fact that the organization was working to "attract the proletariat, whom the Soviet Union needs, to Palestine".[127] In 1923, the authorities officially recognized Hehalutz despite the opposition of the Jewish section of the Council of People's Commissars of the Soviet Union.[128] The following year, the organization was granted permission to issue its own newspaper in Hebrew, *Hehalutz*, which remained in publication until 1928. Recognition by the Soviet authorities was also a cause of the organization's split in two in September 1923 – following an internal dispute on the settlement method that should be adopted (kvutzah or moshav) in Palestine – along the lines of the "leftist-class" and "rightist-proletarian" factions. Many attempts to resolve the dispute were unsuccessful.[129]

Hehalutz worked publicly in the Soviet Union until the late 1920s, when it was dissolved with other Zionist organizations during 1929-1930. By that time, however, Hehalutz had rendered great services to the Zionist entity in Palestine, exceeding those of Po'alei Zion and Tzeirei Zion combined. In 1919-1925, about 20,000 Jews emigrated from the Soviet Union to Palestine and in 1926-1936 a further 12,500[130] did. After the dissolution of Hehalutz in the Soviet Union, its branches continued working in eastern Europe – especially in Poland. (The British mandate authorities estimated the number of Soviet Jews immigrating to Palestine in 1922-1929 at about 20 percent of Jewish immigrants who entered the country during that period, compared with 46 percent from Poland.[131]) Large numbers of those immigrants were members of Hehalutz. They made an effective contribution

---

[127] Kirschenbaum, *Toldot Am Yisrael be-Doreinu (The History of the Jews in Our Generation)*, Vol. 1, p. 122.

[128] Ibid, p. 123; Mior, *Ha-Tnu'ah ha-Tzionit be-Rusia (Zionist Movement in Russia)*, p. 529.

[129] For details, see Mior, *Ha-Tnu'ah ha-Tzionit be-Rusia (Zionist Movement in Russia)*, pp. 529-531.

[130] Ibid, p. 538.

[131] *A Survey of Palestine, Prepared in December 1945 and January 1946 for the Information of the Anglo-American Committee of Inquiry*, Vol. 1, p. 186.

7. British Mandate over Palestine, Part II 459

to laying the foundations of the Jewish national home in Palestine, and Hehalutz remained in existence until after the Second World War.

The period of the First World War and the years that followed also witnessed the birth of another Zionist organization, "Hashomer Hatzair" (The Young Guard, in Hebrew). This organisation emerged in 1911-1913 in the form of Jewish scout and youth associations under the influence of the Free German Youth. Most of the associations' members were from affluent Jewish families in the province of Galicia, which was then under German rule.[132] In mid-1916, a number of these associations united under the name of "Hashomer" (The Guard), influenced by an organization of that name in Palestine. In 1919, they changed their name to Hashomer Hatzair.[133] These groups then moved away from their original character and were influenced by Hehalutz such that they began to demand the establishment of their own settlements in Palestine after their pioneer immigrants arrived in the country in 1919-1920.[134] They announced their commitment to the Zionist program but had reservations on partisan control as a means of implementing it.[135] In Palestine, Hashomer Hatzair acquired a unique character as its members secluded themselves from society to establish their own. Significant changes gradually took place, however, in their ideology, and they moved from "Sufi" (mystical) thought to a kibbutz-settlement movement, largely influenced by the "radical socialism"[136] within Zionist intellectual frameworks. Finally, Hashomer Hatzair adopted what it called revolutionary Marxism

---

132   Erez, ed., *Sefer ha-Aliyah ha-Shlishit (The Third Aliyah Book)*, Vol. 1, p. 34.

133   Details in Yitzhak Ben-Zvi, ed., *Sefer Hashomer (Book of Hashomer)*, Vol. 1, pp. 19-60.

134   See also ibid, pp. 63-64, 73-75, 81-83.

135   For details, see Elkana Margalit, *Hashomer Hatzair: Me-Idat No'arim le-Marxism Mahpichani, 1913-1936 (Hashomer Hatzair: From Youth Community to Revolutionary Marxism, 1913-1936)*, pp. 17-52.

136   Shmuel Noah Eisenstadt, *Ha-Hevrah ha-Yisraelit (Israeli Society)*, pp. 22-23.

and began to demand the establishment of a bi-national state of Arabs and Jews in Palestine. (In 1948, the United Workers Party, Mapam, emerged from this movement.)

In addition to these labor organizations, non-labor Jewish or Zionist organizations were active in Palestine during this period. The religious Mizrahi organization, which had been established in 1902 (see Chapter 3, section 7),[137] launched a branch in Palestine in late 1917. During September 2-3, 1918, this branch held its first congress in Jaffa[138] and in late August 1920 the Mizrahi moved its headquarters from London to Jerusalem.[139] The Agudat Israel[140] organization was also active among Orthodox Jews in Jerusalem and Jaffa in particular.

The differences remained between the Mizrahi and Agudat Israel during the British mandate. These differences, which were essentially a reason for the formation of each of them and their distinction from each other, resulted from their differing viewpoints on the relationship of Zionism to Judaism.[141] This led to occasional disputes between them, or between each of them and the secularists. The Mizrahi considered "Zionism as the gate of a historic station ... and the beginning of the bells of salvation... This is what distinguishes it from its opponents among the Orthodox, especially Agudat Israel."[142] The Mizrahi also believed that "religion and nationality [for the Jews] are the same thing."[143] It was a "religious-national organization, with

---

[137] Chapter 3, section 7.

[138] Moshe Ostrovsky, *Toldot ha-Mizrahi be-Eretz Yisrael (History of the Mizrahi in the Land of Israel)*, pp. 18-20.

[139] *Chronologiah le-Toldot ha-Yishuv ha-Yehudi be-Eretz Yisrael (Chronology of the Jewish Yishuv in the Land of Israel)*, Vol. 1, pp. 40, 48; see also Simon Federbusch, ed., *Hazon Torah ve Tzion (The Vision of Torah and Zion)*, p. 203.

[140] See Chapter 4, section 2.

[141] For comparison, see Chapter 3, section 7; Chapter 4, section 2.

[142] From an article by Yeshayahu Aviad (Wolfsberg), a Mizrahi leader, in Ben-Efram, *Miflagot ou Zramim Politim be-Tkufat ha-Bayit ha-Leumi, 1918-1948 (Parties and Political Currents during the Period of the National Home, 1918-1948)*, p. 246.

[143] From an article by Rabbi Fishman (Maimon), in ibid, p. 247.

7. British Mandate over Palestine, Part II 461

known aspirations and special obligations ... that values Hebrew as the religious and national language of the Jewish people ... and believes that work to revive the country and the language is part of Judaism".[144] The Mizrahi cooperated "with various [secular] Zionist groups in order to build and settle the country".[145] With regard to Zionism's stance on religion, the Mizrahi denounced the view that religion is a private matter left to individual choice. It called for religious teachings and tradition to dominate public and private Jewish life in Palestine. Adherence to those teachings was the main factor that had preserved the Jewish existence over generations, in its view,[146] and Jewish law had to be the basis of order in the Jewish state to ensure its survival. "The adherence of the Jews to the Sabbath preserved them, more than they preserved it."[147] Based on these principles, the Mizrahi constantly sought to impose the dominance of religion over Jewish life in Palestine. It was ready, in most cases, to ally with any Zionist group that was willing to make concessions to it in the religious sphere, and it often provoked crises due to disagreements over religious affairs. (In 1956, the Mizrahi united with ha-Po'el ha-Mizrahi to form the National Religious Party – Mafdal, which became, about half a century later, the Religious Zionist Party.)

Agudat Israel, on the other hand, did not hold such a belief in Zionism and favored Zionist activity in Palestine, only to the extent that it could create conditions to allow the Jewish settlers to live there according to the teachings of the Torah.[148] The organization saw Jewish life in the diaspora as equally important as that in Palestine. Thus, "it [put] itself in the work of building the Land of Israel ... but [did] not see that as the end of the

---

144   Ibid.

145   Ibid.

146   Ibid, p. 248.

147   From a speech of Rabbi Meir Berlin (Bar-Ilan) to the 12th Zionist Congress, in Haaretz, 19/9/1921, p. 2.

148   Amram Blau, *Al Homotech, Yerushalayim (On Your Walls, Jerusalem)*, p. 146.

road."[149] The world congress of Agudat Israel (which did not recognize the Zionist Basel Program) was held in Zurich in late February 1919, where it announced its demands:

> The Jewish people, for which the settlement of the Land of Israel was an obligation during the period of its exile, claims for itself the right to establish a Jewish society in the country, on a very broad base, under the protection of the League of Nations or its mandatory, through immigration and organized settlement, and under conditions that secure the independent development of its religious culture on strong economic and social foundations, through a friendly agreement with the non-Jewish population of the country.[150]

On a practical level, the dispute between the two organizations manifested in how the Mizrahi conceived of itself and its work, operating within the framework of the Zionist movement like other secular parties, while Agudat Israel tended to fight Zionism or – at best – cooperate with it reservedly and in limited cases.

At the same time, the non-partisan entity, the Women's International Zionist Organization (WIZO), was established in July 1920 in London, and declared its commitment to the Basel Program and to "Jewish heritage".[151] The aim of this organization, per its constitution, was "to develop national awareness among Jewish women all over the world ... [to] contribute, effectively, to the revival of the Land of Israel through cultural and professional preparation ... [and] social activity ... and to secure the interests of women and children in the Land of Israel".[152] (In the United States, WIZO worked through Hadassah, the Women's Zionist Organization of America).

Despite the existence of these numerous organizations,

---

149   Ibid.

150   In Merchavia, *Am ou-Moledet (Nation and Homeland)*, p. 389.

151   From the organization's amended constitution of 1931, in Merchav, *Toldot Tnu'at ha-Poalim be-Eretz Yisrael 1905-1965 (History of the Labor Movement in the Land of Israel, 1905-1965)*, p. 129.

152   Ibid.

however, they had little effect in terms of Zionist activity in Palestine in the early 1920s, due to their limited membership or weak financial resources. The main Zionist activity remained with the labor wing and its two organizations, Po'alei Zion - Ahdut ha-Avoda and Tzeirei Zion - Hapoel Hatzair.

4

After the First World War, notable changes also took place within the Zionist Organization that led to a change in its leadership in accordance with the shifting centers of power. The German Zionist group had controlled the organization since Herzl's time, but fell after Germany's defeat in the war. The group's leader, Otto Warburg, head of the Zionist Organization until then, relinquished his position. After the Balfour Declaration, the leadership of the Zionist movement passed to Chaim Weizmann and his group of British Zionists, because of the role that they had played in securing that declaration.

At the same time, similar changes occurred for the Zionists in Soviet Russia and the United States. The Russian Zionist leadership began to lose its influence on the movement after the ban imposed by Soviet Russia in the country. The American Zionists moved to occupy a significant sphere within the organization – especially after their leader, Louis Brandeis, was involved in securing the imposition of the British mandate over Palestine.

Weizmann did not assume leadership of the Zionist movement easily or by himself, as the British authorities were essential to his election. As much as he needed them to accept him, they were also "ready to fall under his charm"[153] and support him in taking the reins of the Zionist leadership. This was, perhaps, due to their feeling that he was almost completely subservient to them. The British revealed their preference for Weizmann early on, as they appointed him head of the Zionist Commission to Palestine without consultation or approval

---
153 Friesel, *Ha-Mediniout ha-Tzionit le-ahar Hatzharat Balfour, 1917-1922 (Zionist Policy after the Balfour Declaration, 1917-1922)*, p. 32.

of any Zionist body.[154] Upon his return to Britain in late 1918, Weizmann was the most powerful leader in the movement and could implement his theory of synthetic Zionism[155] to build the Zionist entity in Palestine – espousing a moderate policy and gathering together all forces, Zionist or otherwise, that were ready to work in building the national home, nurturing it to "grow like a plant",[156] in Weizmann's words, if given proper care (see Chapter 3, section 7).

The first step taken by Weizmann and his group was to call for a Zionist conference, which was held in London during February 24-March 12, 1919, three months after the end of the First World War and attended by delegates from several countries. This was the first almost comprehensive Zionist meeting since the 11th Zionist Congress in 1913. New provisional bodies of the Zionist Organization were created, including a new Zionist executive, to which Weizmann was added,[157] and a central office for the organization in London, while the official headquarters of the Zionist leadership in Copenhagen was turned into the central immigration office.[158] An office for the organization was also established in Palestine, as well as departments for settlement and finance. During the conference, two currents emerged regarding the position on settlement in Palestine. The first called for focusing on systematic research and purchasing the largest possible area of land before actual settlement began, while the second called for an immediate start to settlement activity. The conference did not take any decision, however.[159]

After the conference, the newly established bodies began to draw up the necessary plans to build the Zionist entity in

---

154 Ibid, p. 29.

155 See Chapter 3, section 7; Chapter 4, section 2.

156 Weizmann, *Trial and Error*, p. 63.

157 *Ha-Protocolim shel ha-Va'ad ha-Poel ha-Tzioni (Records of Sessions of the Zionist Executive)*, Vol. 1, p. 43.

158 Ibid, pp. 43-44.

159 Yehuda Slutsky, "Ha-Tnu'ah ha-Tzionit be-Shnot ha-Aliya ha-Shlishit (The Zionist Movement in the Years of the Third Aliyah)", in Erez, ed., *Sefer ha-Aliyah ha-Shlishit (The Third Aliyah Book)*, Vol. 1, p. 50.

7. British Mandate over Palestine, Part II 465

Palestine – focusing primarily on the problems of settlement and financing.[160] The Executive decided not to rush in starting any activity in Palestine until it had completed its plans and raised the necessary funds for their implementation. The Zionist Organization issued a call to the Zionist organizations in all European countries in July 1919, urging them to refrain from sending immigrants to Palestine before preparations were complete for their absorption.[161]

Within a few months, however, the Zionist leadership discovered that the projects and plans it had made needed significant funds to implement, only a small part of which could be raised. It called for a second conference, which was held in London during February 11-24, 1920. The leadership ensured that the American Zionists, led by Brandeis, would be properly represented at this conference. It hoped that they would take the place of the Russians in fundraising, as contact with them had been severed. These hopes were soon dashed, however, when sharp disagreements arose between Weizmann and Brandeis during the conference over the functions of the Zionist Organization. Brandeis and his followers declared that the political function of the organization would end with the ratification of the British mandate,[162] and thereafter its focus had to shift to building the national home economically, without resorting to financial assistance from various sources, by encouraging the employment of Jewish and other capital in Palestine on the basis of individual initiative. Brandeis also opposed granting the settlers in Palestine any assistance from the funds of the Zionist Organization, insisting that they had to manage their own affairs as immigrants to the United States did.

This strategy was not supported by Weizmann and his group,

---

160   For more details on the conference resolutions, see *Chronologiah le-Toldot ha-Yishuv ha-Yehudi be-Eretz Yisrael (Chronology of the Jewish Yishuv in the Land of Israel)*, Vol. 1, pp. 25-26.

161   *Ha-Protocolim shel ha-Va'ad ha-Poel ha-Tzioni (Records of Sessions of the Zionist Executive)*, Vol. 1, pp. 106, 127, 133, 226-227.

162   Slutsky in Erez, ed., *Sefer ha-Aliyah ha-Shlishit (The Third Aliyah Book)*, Vol. 1, p. 51.

who believed that the Zionist entity could only be built by means of "national funds" to finance any project which needed support, without concern for any profits and losses. Their goal was to build a national home, in all its aspects, and in their view this could not be achieved through individual initiative or private capital.[163] Weizmann was supported by Ahdut ha-Avoda and Hapoel Hatzair, the main Zionist parties working in Palestine, as well as the World Union of Po'alei Zion. The labor groups had become more fixed on this position after the failure of two funds, the "Keren ha-Hakhanah" (Preparation Fund) and "Ķeren ha-Ge'ulah" (Restoration Fund), which had been set up in 1918 and 1919.[164] The groups thus called for the establishment of a public fund, overseen by the Zionist Organization. The Zionist labor wing also determined its position, and decided that this would be done through "pioneering [immigration], and labor settlement on national land [with the help of] national capital".[165]

Thus, the February 1920 Zionist conference in London had no significant results due to the differences between Weizmann and Brandeis. Afterwards, Weizmann and his group made great efforts to settle the conflict as they were in dire need of the funds from the American Zionists to contribute to building the national home. The American Zionists, however, left no room for reconciliation. Their followers resigned from the Zionist Executive in March 1920, and Weizmann appointed replacements from among his circle. Brandeis and his group then decided to stop transferring the funds that were collected by the Zionist Organization of America, which was under their control, to the institutions of the Zionist Organization. They instead sent the funds to the American Zionist Medical Unit, which

---

163 For details, see Yonatan Shapira, "The Dispute between Chaim Weizmann and Louis Brandeis, 1919-1921", in Daniel Carpi, ed., *Ha-Tzionout, Me'asef le-Toldot ha-Tnu'ah ha-Tzionit ve ha-Yishuv ha-Yehudi be-Eretz Yisrael (Zionism: Studies in the History of the Zionist Movement and of the Jewish Community in the Land of Israel)*, Vol. 3, pp. 258-272.

164 Ben-Shoshan, *Toldot Tnu'at ha-Poalim be-Eretz Yisrael (History of the Labor Movement in the Land of Israel)*, Vol. 1, p. 353.

165 Ibid, p. 351.

7. British Mandate over Palestine, Part II   467

had been working in Palestine since 1918. (This unit was later merged with the American Hadassah Organization for medical and social services, which insisted on keeping its independence within the Zionist Organization.) In July 1920, at another Zionist conference held in London, some tried to reconcile Weizmann and Brandeis to no avail, and relations between them worsened. This led to a bitter struggle between the two camps, which Weizmann exacerbated as he traveled to the United States in April 1921 to explain his point of view, ignoring the "official" Zionist leadership in the country. Weizmann led the Zionist Organization of America, which convened in Cleveland shortly after his arrival, to elect a leadership whose majority supported him, and in response Brandeis and his followers resigned. The congress then elected Louis Lipsky, a supporter of Weizmann, as president of the Zionist Organization of America.[166] This led to the exclusion of a number of influential American Zionists, which weakened the Zionist Organization – especially financially. As mentioned earlier, the American Zionists generally refrained from active Zionist activity, especially during the 1920s and 1930s, content with the moral support of the movement. Only a very small number of them immigrated to Palestine, and despite their large number they did not contribute significantly to financing Zionist projects.[167] Most of these Zionists, like other Jews in the United States at the time, were second- or third-generation immigrants from tsarist Russia and eastern European countries, who were busy assimilating into American society. (This position did not change until after the Biltmore Conference in 1942, although the number of their immigrants to Palestine remained relatively small.)

In contrast to the American Zionists, the Zionist community in Poland was highly active and zealous. The Zionist idea had first spread among Jewish people in Poland, tsarist Russia and

---

166   For details, see Evyatar Friesel, "Night of Crisis between Weizmann and Brandeis", in Carpi, ed., *Ha-Tzionout (Zionism)*, Vol. 4, pp. 146-164; Weizmann, *Trial and Error*, pp. 330-339.

167   See also Olitsky, *Mi-Pzura le-Medinah (From Dispersal to State)*, Vol. 1, p. 336.

some eastern European countries (see Introduction, section 1). Then, after Germany's occupation of Poland in late 1915, Polish Zionists came to enjoy very comfortable conditions compared with those that had existed under tsarist rule. The German authorities abolished the tsarist discriminatory laws against the Jewish population, considered them an independent religious sect and, finally, recognized the Zionist Organization. These conditions generally persisted after Poland's independence, based on the Polish Minority Treaty that was signed as part of the peace agreement (see section 1 of this chapter).

The Jews of Poland thrived in these conditions and went on to become a world center for Judaism. They established their own schools and cultural institutions – both rabbinic and secular – issued their independent newspapers in Hebrew and Yiddish and founded Jewish theaters. Jewish people also played an important role in the political life of the country. They founded their own parties, labor unions and youth organizations. They were nevertheless divided by the religious and political currents that had manifested among them in the tsarist era, which coalesced into three main wings: the traditional religious rabbinate or the Hasidic, the Bund and its followers among the non-Zionist labor groups and finally the Zionists of different political leanings. A fierce rivalry raged between them, forcing the Zionists to intensify their activity in an unprecedented manner in order to meet the challenges of their religious and Bundist opponents.[168] The ranks of the Zionists swelled and their number grew, such that it was hoped and expected to contribute effectively to the establishment of the national home in Palestine, particularly financially. After Poland's independence, however, its government followed an economic policy that aimed to curtail the Jewish middle class and break its purported monopoly on several sectors, which led to its destabilization and forced large numbers of it to emigrate. The Zionist institutions thus found themselves in need of greater funds to absorb those Polish immigrants instead

---

168 For details, see Kirschenbaum, *Toldot Am Yisrael be-Doreinu (The History of the Jews in Our Generation)*, Vol. 1, pp. 89-107.

of relying on them to finance Zionist projects. As a result, the Polish Zionists became one of the most fervent Zionist groups and were the most involved in Palestine. Between the two world wars, they decisively influenced the Zionist movement. With their large numbers relative to other groups, their representatives held about a third of the seats in all the Zionist congresses during that period (see *Table 6 World distribution of Zionist forces, 1922-1939*, below).

From the Polish Jews, too, came the largest proportion of immigrants who entered Palestine during this phase. This immigration had begun in mid-1919 and rose during the following years, forcing the Zionist leadership to do everything in its power to raise the necessary funds to absorb the Polish settlers. In order to find the means to do so, and then agree on the policies to be adopted for the establishment of the Jewish national home in Palestine, the Zionists held a third, extensive conference in London during July 7-24, 1920. At the time, Herbert Samuel was taking his first steps in laying the foundations of the British mandate system in Palestine. Weizmann called for the conference, which was attended by about 280 delegates. Following the disappointment with Brandeis and the American Zionists, most of the invitees were supporters of Weizmann's politics.[169] Although chaos dominated the conference,[170] harmony prevailed among most of its participants, and important decisions were taken that would mark Zionist activity during the entire course of the mandate.

The first important topic of discussion was the issue of land acquisition, and it was decided that "the main basis of Zionist land policy is to make the land on which Jewish settlement is established the property of the Jewish people."[171] Further, "the entity authorized to implement the policy of Hebrew land, in

---

169 See also Max Nordau, *Kitvei Nordau (Works of Nordau)*, Vol. 4, pp. 196-198.

170 Friesel, *Ha-Mediniout ha-Tzionit le-ahar Hatzharat Balfour, 1917-1922 (Zionist Policy after the Balfour Declaration, 1917-1922)*, p. 138.

171 Merchavia, *Am ou-Moledet (Nation and Homeland)*, p. 189.

towns and villages, is the Jewish National Fund."[172] The functions of the fund, as decided by the participants, were

> the acquisition of lands in the Land of Israel through the funds donated by the people, such that these lands would belong to [the people] and be granted for purposes of agriculture or construction, by lease [without sale] subject to the laws of inheritance. The worker who lacks capital is allowed to settle in [these lands], provided that [the Jewish National Fund] secures Hebrew labor, monitors the means of investment of the lands, and prevents speculations on them.[173]

Through these terms, the settlers who adhered to the principles of the Jewish National Fund were more entitled than others to obtain loans from the Zionist institutions. The conference also demanded the establishment of an official agency by the Zionist Organization to supervise the land sale market[174] (which the organization failed to implement).

These decisions matched the views of the Zionist labor groups – although they did not meet all their demands – which considered the land owned by the Jewish National Fund to be "national land". This criterion was met through the restrictions imposed by the Zionist institutions on the transfer of land ownership or the means of its exploitation, to ensure it remained in Zionist hands. However, the conference also included a number of non-socialist Zionists who demanded that private capital and individual initiative be allowed to take part in building the national home (Weizmann, himself, adopted a similar position). Thus the conference took other decisions to accommodate these views and recommended "finding ways by which private capital can participate with the Jewish National Fund in the purchase of lands ... such that the land acquired in

---

172 Ibid.

173 Ibid.

174 Ibid.

this manner ultimately becomes the property of the people".[175] Despite this decision, however, private capital did not play a major role in land acquisition in Palestine, leaving the arena to the Jewish National Fund and other Zionist agencies.

The second important topic at the London conference was the issue of securing funds to build the Jewish national home in Palestine. It was decided to establish a financial institution for immigration and absorption, which the Zionists called "Keren Hayesod" (Palestine Foundation Fund; later, the United Israel Appeal). On March 23, 1921, this was registered in Britain as a limited company, the purpose of which was "to carry out all acts which are necessary, or which may be useful, in order to implement the declaration of His Majesty's Government [known as the Balfour Declaration], dated November 2, 1917, concerning the establishment of a Jewish national home in the Land of Israel".[176] Following its creation, Keren Hayesod issued a manifesto "to the Jews of the world"[177] declaring that its purpose was "to bring about the settlement of Palestine by Jews ... in steadily increasing numbers ... and to provide for the economic development of the country to the advantage of its Jewish and its non-Jewish inhabitants alike".[178] Keren Hayesod stated that

> there is land to be bought and prepared, there are roads and railways, harbours and bridges to be built, there are hills to be forested, there are marshes to be drained, there is fertile soil to be irrigated, there is latent waterpower to be utilized, there are towns to be laid out, there are crafts and industries to be developed ... [as well as] provision for the social welfare of the population, for public health, and ... education.[179]

---

175 Ibid, p. 190.

176 Ibid, p. 199.

177 See manifesto of Keren Hayesod in *Report(s) of the Head Office of the Palestine Foundation Fund to the XIIth-XXIst Zionist Congresses, 1921-1939*, London: Zionist Organization, 1921-1925, pp. 5-6.

178 Ibid, p. 6.

179 Ibid.

The organization described its program as "flexible, and ... readily adapted to every variety of undertaking... For twenty centuries it has been patiently awaited. It will not recur in our lifetime, nor in that of our children's children."[180] Thus, it was imperative that all the Jews would contribute to support this program. However, "no casual charity will suffice. The exceptional effort which is called for today must take the form of self-taxation – steady, persistent, systematic, inspired by the noble Jewish tradition of the Tithe."[181]

The Zionists pinned great hopes on Keren Hayesod as a complement to the Jewish National Fund (Keren Kayemet), with which it would supervise all aspects of Zionist settlement in Palestine. The former was planned to purchase lands for settlement, while the latter would work to settle immigrants on these lands and secure their livelihoods. The urgency of these hopes increased due to the critical financial situation of the Zionist Organization and the difficulties it faced in funding its projects. It did not take long, however, for it to be clear that these hopes were misplaced. Keren Hayesod made extensive efforts among Jewish and Zionist groups worldwide, yet it was only able to raise about 300,000 pounds sterling in the first year of its founding, out of a needed sum of 25 million pounds during that year.[182] In fact, the organization was not able to raise this amount even after a quarter century as the total of its contributions raised until mid-1947 was about 21.5 million pounds. (Keren Hayesod was active in the United States from the second year of its founding. In 1926, it changed its name to the "United Palestine Appeal", then again, in 1939, to the "United Jewish Appeal". Today, it is the "United Israel Appeal".)

The scarcity of financial resources of the Zionist Organization directly affected its policy and led many Zionists

---

180 Ibid; see also Merchavia, *Am ou-Moledet (Nation and Homeland)*, pp. 197-198.

181 Ibid; see also economic resolutions in Jacob Metzer, *Hon Leumi le-Bait Leumi (National Capital for a National Home)*, pp. 141-145, 152-154.

182 See also Haaretz, 20/8/1920.

7. British Mandate over Palestine, Part II 473

to abandon the dreams that they had entertained since the Balfour Declaration. The lack of financial means, which led to the curtailment of Zionist projects, was also one of the main reasons that prompted the Zionist leadership to agree to the British shrinking of the pledges they had made to them. First, Transjordan was severed from the designated area of the Jewish national home. Second, the Churchill White Paper of 1922 officially interpreted the Balfour Declaration to mean the establishment of a national home for the Jewish people in Palestine, not the conversion of all of Palestine into a Jewish national home (see Chapter 6, section 6). Finally, the entry of Jewish immigrants into Palestine was to take place according to the country's economic capacity to absorb them.

In addition to the two aspects discussed by the third Zionist conference in London in July 1920, an old, controversial issue was raised for discussion: the official Zionist position on education and cultural affairs. The reason for this dispute, which had raged during Herzl's time, was the deep differences between secular and religious Zionists in their basic views towards education and culture, with each of them attempting to push the Zionist Organization and its agencies to officially adopt their viewpoint.[183]

After Herzl's death, the two sides had reached an agreement stating that either current – secular or religious – was free to engage in cultural activity as it saw fit, provided that the Zionist Organization did not officially interfere in favor of either party. In spite of this, however, disputes and tumultuous discussions occasionally erupted between the secular and religious currents on these issues. This controversy stopped during the First World War but resumed, with great fervor, at its end.[184]

---

183 For details, see Chapter 4, section 2.

184 See Moshe Renault, "The Debate on Shaping the Hebrew Education System in the Land of Israel, 1918-1920", in Carpi, ed., *Ha-Tzionout (Zionism)*, Vol. 5, pp. 78-108; Menachem Friedman, "The Conflict over the Nature of Religious and Rabbinical Schools in Jerusalem during the First Year of the British Occupation", in Carpi, ed., *Ha-Tzionout (Zionism)*, Vol. 2, pp. 105-118.

With the convening of the third London Zionist conference, the religious current, represented by the Mizrahi organization, demanded recognition of its own independent education department. The conference rejected the proposal and instead approved another compromise between the religious and secular views. It passed resolutions to endorse pluralism in the Jewish education system in Palestine and recognize different types of schools, including public ones demanded by the secular current and religious ones for the religious current, such that each would have their own educational programs. The only common ground between these schools was their focus on the "Hebrew language and Jewish national identity"[185] – although the latter was not defined in the resolutions. Religious schools were granted complete autonomy with respect to cultural affairs, and significant autonomy in their administration and finances. By agreeing to this compromise, the secularists hoped that the Mizrahi would win the religious Jewish groups over for the benefit of the Zionist movement. The Mizrahi achieved this, to some extent, but also worked to expand the religious camp, which repeatedly tried to impose its views on all Zionist factions. (This solution, with different schools, currents, educational curricula and cultures, is still in effect in Israel, which officially maintains more than one school system.)

In addition, the London Zionist conference in July 1920 discussed the issue of whether to organize, track and supervise Zionist activity around the world. (The head of the organizational department in the Zionist Organization had announced, at the conference, that the number of registered Zionists at the time amounted to about one million.[186]) The conference made no decision, however, and referred the matter to the Zionist Congress, which was to take place the following year.

---

185 Renault in Carpi, ed., *Ha-Tzionout (Zionism)*, Vol. 5, p. 108.

186 See Hantke's lecture at the conference in Haaretz, 22/8/1920.

7. British Mandate over Palestine, Part II 475

Table 4 Composition of 12th-16th Zionist congresses, 1921-1929 (number and proportion of delegates by party factions)[187]

	Congress	12th	13th	14th	15th	16th
	Location	Carlsbad	Carlsbad	Vienna	Basel	Zurich
	Date	Sep. 1-13 1921	Aug. 6-18 1923	Aug. 18-31 1925	Aug. 30 -Sep 11, 1927	Jul. 28-Aug 14, 1929
Parties/ Factions						
General Zionists	No.	376	165	177	151	145
	%	73.4	49.9	56.9	53.7	46.8
Radicals (Democrats)	No.	-	21	15	11	12
	%	-	6.3	4.8	3.9	3.9
Mizrahi	No.	95	76	55	46	51
	%	18.6	23	17.7	16.4	16.4
Po'ale Zion (Labor Faction)	No.	41	69	59	63	81
	%	8.0	20.8	19	22.4	26.1
Revisionists	No.	-	-	5.0	10	21
	%	-	-	1.6	3.6	6.8
Total	**No.**	512	331	311	281	310

---

187 Extracted from *Ha-Congress ha-Tzioni ha-22 ve ha-Moshav shel Moa'tzit ha-Sokhnout ha-Yehudit be-1946 (Records [of Sessions] of the 22nd Zionist Congress and the 1946 Council Session of the Jewish Agency)*, Introduction, p. k e (25); *Ha-Congress ha-Tzioni ha-21 ve ha-Moshav shel Moa'tzit ha-Sokhnout ha-Yehudit be-1939 (Records [of Sessions] of the 21st Zionist Congress and the 1939 Council Session of the Jewish Agency)*, Introduction, p. k f (26).

Table 5 Composition of 17th-21st Zionist congresses, 1931-1939 (number and proportion of delegates by party factions)

	Congress	17th	18th	19th	20th	21st
	Location	Basel	Prague	Lucerne	Zurich	Geneva
	Date	Jun. 30-Jul 17, 1931	Aug. 21-Sep. 14, 1933	Aug. 20-Sep. 6, 1935	Aug. 3-21 1937	Aug. 16-25 1939
Parties/ Factions						
General Zionists*	No.	-	74	-	-	-
	%	-	23.3	-	-	-
Union of General Zionists - A*	No.	25	-	99	128	159
	%	9.8	-	21.4	26.4	30.2
League of General Zionists - B*	No.	59	-	50	43	33
	%	23.2	-	10.8	8.9	6.2
Radicals (Democrats)♦	No.	8	15	-	-	-
	%	3.2	4.7	-	-	-
Mizrahi	No.	35	39	74	80	75
	%	13.8	12.3	16	16.5	14.2
Po'ale Zion (Labor Faction)	No.	75	138	226	224	234
	%	29.5	43.4	48.8	46.3	44.4
Leftist Zionist Workers	No.	-	-	-	-	13
	%	-	-	-	-	2.5
Revisionists†	No.	52	45	-	-	-
	%	20.5	14.1	-	-	-
Jewish State Party✦	No.	-	7	13	9	10
	%	-	2.2	2.8	1.9	1.9
Independents (Unaffiliated)	No.	-	-	1	-	3
	%	-	-	0.2	-	0.6
Total	**No.**	**254**	**318**	**463**	**484**	**527**

*   In 1931, the General Zionists split into two factions: Union of General Zionists - A, and League of General Zionists - B. The two factions reunited at the 18th congress, but then split, again.

♦   In 1933, the Radicals (Democrats) joined the Union of General Zionists - A.

†   The Revisionist Zionists left the Zionist Organization and founded the New Zionist Organization in 1935.

✦   The Jewish State Party split from the Revisionist Zionists after the latter left the Zionist Organization.

7. British Mandate over Palestine, Part II 477

Table 6 World distribution of Zionist forces, 1922-1939[188] (by country, per shekel units[189])

Country	Number†	%	Country	Number†	%
Poland	2973.3	32.2	Yugoslavia	127.2	1.4
USA	1646.7	17.8	Serbia	122.7	1.3
Palestine	814.2	8.8	Latvia	117.1	1.3
Germany	480.4	5.2	Bulgaria	95.5	1.0
Britain	296.4	3.2	Bukovina	88.7	1.0
Czechoslovakia	263.6	2.9	Argentina	73.6	0.8
South Africa	251.3	2.7	Hungary	72.4	0.8
Lithuania	222.7	2.4	Greece	52.4	0.6
Austria	213.1	2.3	Holland	49.8	0.5
Romania	181.2	2.0	France	45.8	0.5
Canada	175.3	1.9	Other countries★	707.7	7.6
Transylvania	164.8	1.8	**Total**	**9235.9**	**100**

---

188 Extracted from *Ha-Congress ha-Tzioni ha-19 ve ha-Moshav shel Moa'tzit ha-Sokhnout ha-Yehudit be-1935 (Records [of Sessions] of the 19th Zionist Congress and the 4th Session, 1935 of the Council Session of the Jewish Agency)*, pp. XVII-XVIII; *Ha-Congress ha-Tzioni ha-20 ve ha-Moshav shel Moa'tzit ha-Sokhnout ha-Yehudit be-1937 (Records [of Sessions] of the 20th Zionist Congress and the 5th Session, 1937 Council Session of the Jewish Agency)*, pp. XIV-XV; *Ha-Congress ha-Tzioni ha-21 ve ha-Moshav shel Moa'tzit ha-Sokhnout ha-Yehudit be-1939 (Records [of Sessions] of the 21st Zionist Congress and the 1939 Council Session of the Jewish Agency)*, Introduction, p. k - k a (20-21).

189 The shekel was the unit of the subscription fee to the Zionist Organization. Delegates to the Zionist congresses were chosen from different countries according to the percentage of shekel units paid by the Zionists in these countries to the Zionist Organization, from one congress to another.

The composition of the Zionist congresses, however, in terms of the countries from which the Zionist delegates came, does not exactly match the percentages cited in this table. This is because members of the Zionist Executive and some delegates of regional Zionist unions were sometimes considered delegates to the Zionist congresses, without the rules of the shekel fees applying to them.

† Numbers are approximated to the nearest 1,000 shekels.

★ This includes about 20 countries where the average fees collected during this period were less than 0.5% of the total shekel fees.

After a long period of preparation, and in a state of weakness that dominated the Zionist Organization, the 12th Zionist Congress (the first to be held after the First World War) convened in Carlsbad, Czechoslovakia, during September 1-14, 1921. It was attended by 512 delegates, representing 855,590 registered dues-paying Zionists (see *Table 4 Composition of 12th-16th Zionist congresses, 1921-1929*, above). It is noted that the number of registered Zionists increased significantly during the war years and afterwards. By 1921, they were about four times the number on the eve of the previous Zionist Congress in 1913 (with 217,231 dues-paying members). It is clear that the Balfour Declaration and then the imposition of the British mandate over Palestine, with the revived hopes of establishing a Zionist entity, were the main reasons behind this rise. Prior to the 12th Congress, the various Zionist organizations could not hold elections to choose delegates due to the organizational disarray as a result of the war. Thus it was agreed to appoint 376 delegates representing national Zionist organizations in various countries, as well as 95 from the Mizrahi and 41 from labor parties. The congress adopted resolutions that approved most of the measures taken by the Zionist leadership since the end of the war. Weizmann was elected president of the Zionist Organization and Sokolow as chairman of the Zionist Executive (also known as the "Zionist Administration"), whose members were divided into two groups, one residing in London and the other in Jerusalem.

In addition, the 12th Zionist Congress approved new regulations of the Zionist Organization that defined its various bodies and specified the rights, duties and powers of each.[190] Regulations were put in place for elections at the Zionist congresses, to supervise the establishment of regional Zionist federations and to monitor their activities. A "court of honor" was also formed to consider ideological, and sometimes organizational, violations. These regulations were later amended

---

190 See Arabic translation of regulations in *Palestine Documents File*, Vol. 1, pp. 311-322.

7. British Mandate over Palestine, Part II 479

by more than one Zionist congress.[191] The measures were taken in an attempt by the Zionist Organization to align itself with the instructions of Article 4 of the mandate deed, in order to be recognized as the Jewish Agency sought by the mandate, "so long as its organization and constitution are in the opinion of the Mandatory appropriate", as per the deed. In this capacity, the instrument assigned the Zionist Organization the task of "advising and co-operating with the Administration of Palestine in such economic, social and other matters as may affect the establishment of the Jewish national home and the interests of the Jewish population in Palestine" (see Chapter 6, section 4). This was to be until the formation of such a Jewish agency, which the Zionist Organization was unable to implement until 1929. Otherwise, the 12th Zionist Congress had no noteworthy results and Weizmann described it as doing well "to bring the movement down to earth, to some appreciation of the hard facts, and to set our feet on the only path that could lead to success – the path of slow, laborious and methodical work in Palestine".[192]

Two years later, the 13th Zionist congress was also held in Carlsbad, on August 6-18, 1923, with 331 delegates representing 957,982 dues-paying Zionists (see *Table 4 Composition of 12th-16th Zionist congresses, 1921-1929*, above). Among the chief discussions was a proposal to formally establish the Jewish Agency that the mandate deed stipulated. The proposal called for the participation of non-Zionist Jews as well in order to benefit from their financial capacities in establishing the agency and helping oversee its management. This idea was supported by Weizmann but aroused the opposition of a minority of delegates.[193] Ussishkin and Jabotinsky withdrew from the Zionist Executive, and the congress elected a new one that followed Weizmann's position.

The results of elections for the 13th Zionist Congress had

---

191 See regulations and amendments in Merchavia, *Am ou-Moledet (Nation and Homeland)*, pp. 113-122.

192 Weizmann, *Trial and Error*, p. 344.

193 For details, see Haaretz, 9/8/1923.

shown that the Zionist movement in the early 1920s was under the control of a moderate right-wing Zionist current, known as the General Zionists (with 169 out of 331 seats, or 51 percent, in the congress). This was despite the great commotion of the Zionist labor wing, in all its manifestations, and the religious Zionists of the Mizrahi and other organizations. The name "General Zionists" was given to those groups only committed to the Basel Program, who had no fixed position on the economic or social aspects of the Jewish national home in Palestine or, more specifically, were not members of labor associations or religious organizations. Their activity was limited to spreading the Zionist idea in the diaspora, supporting Zionist activity and demands and securing the necessary funds to build the Zionist entity in Palestine – without concern, for example, for the establishment of economic institutions or projects for their members in Palestine, as the workers or religious wing did. This was a major reason for the decline of the General Zionists in the long term. The General Zionists considered themselves to be part of the centrist liberal democratic parties and could be regarded as a new edition of the democratic Zionist bloc,[194] which had been active in Herzl's time.

In 1923, a number of General Zionist associations had issued, on a rare occasion when the group had voiced its political positions, a program in which they declared that

> the political objectives of Zionism can be implemented, in practice, only through the efforts and powers of the whole nation, not those of individuals or groups, or the forces of one class or another. To achieve its goals, the Zionist movement unites all categories and classes of the people, prioritizing national issues over internal problems of social growth. Thus, the style of the movement's work should not be based on class struggle or separate partisan activity, but on the activity of a comprehensive popular organization, which unites all the social foundations of the movement and its intellectu-

---

194 Chapter 3, section 7.

al currents.[195]

For this reason, "the movement should set its sights only on creating conditions that would help exploit the popular energy in the project of Jewish revival, without [interfering] in the work resulting from revived national activity."[196] The Zionists considered Weizmann to be the leader of the General Zionist current and the best representative of its political positions.[197]

The end of this period also saw the emergence of a fourth Zionist party/current – in addition to the General Zionists, the Mizrahi and the labor wing – which was the Radical Zionists (the Democrats, from 1929), whose 21 delegates participated in the 13th Zionist Congress. Most of the Radical Zionists were Polish. They were led by Yitzhak Gruenbaum (1879-1970; interior minister of Israel in 1948-1949) and Nahum Goldmann (1895-1982; president of the World Jewish Congress in 1951-1978 and of the World Zionist Organization in 1956-1968). The Radicals did not differ much from the General Zionists in their basic positions. They were distinct, however, in opposing Weizmann's "flexible" policy based on concessions to the British, and did not agree on including non-Zionists in the Jewish Agency. They also supported socialist or cooperative labor settlement as a basis for building the Zionist entity in Palestine.[198] Thus the Radical Zionists found themselves, despite their "right-wing" nature, siding with the labor wing, while stressing secularization and opposing the Mizrahi. The General Zionists, however, remained the dominant force in the Zionist Organization until the early 1930s (see *Table 5 Composition of 17th-21st Zionist congresses, 1931-1939*, above).

---

195 Merchavia, *Am ou-Moledet (Nation and Homeland)*, p. 462.

196 Ibid.

197 See also Arieh Tartakower, *Am ve Olamo (A People and its World)*, p. 166.

198 See also Radical Zionists' program in Merchavia, *Am ou-Moledet (Nation and Homeland)*, p. 463.

5

In Palestine, the supporters of Ahdut ha-Avoda, Hapoel Hatzair and other labor parties were the main Zionist forces on the eve of the British occupation and the imposition of the mandate, even though the moderate Zionist right, represented by the General Zionists of various leanings, was then the dominant force in the Zionist Organization.

The splits within the Jewish and Zionist labor camp outside Palestine had the opposite effect on the Zionist workers in the country, fueling their tendency to rely on themselves and close their ranks. They saw themselves as fighting the battle to actually realize Zionism in Palestine and, thus, could not allow themselves the luxury of theoretical disputes. The Zionist workers played an important role in this stage of establishment of the Jewish national home, for they were the only ones that assumed the implementation of the Zionist project in Palestine. This was mostly achieved without paying great heed to the grand decisions of the Zionist congresses abroad, when those decisions conflicted with the workers' objectives.

During this period, the Zionist workers were generally dissatisfied with the policy of the Zionist Organization – especially on the question of settlements. (Their position did not change until the mid-1930s, when they took control of the organization.) This dissatisfaction was due to two reasons: first, the organization did not provide them with sufficient financial support for their settlements and other projects and, second, the "bourgeois" leadership of the organization – represented by the Zionist Executive that was mostly composed of General Zionists (until the early 1930s) – interfered in the workers' affairs, opposing the socialist settlement experiments and seeking to strengthen the "bourgeois" element among the settlers in Palestine at the expense of the socialists. The workers were also dissatisfied with the policy of the British mandate government in Palestine, after the authorities refused to grant them settlement rights in extensive areas of land that they were demanding be handed to them for free. Their disappointment with both the Zionist leadership and the British authorities, however, did not last long or affect them much. They soon adapted to the new reality and decided to pursue a policy of self-reliance, gradually developing their financial and labor capacities (a continuation of the method adopted by the Zionist workers of the Second Aliyah since 1904). Thus they began to establish various economic, settlement, union and other institutions to strengthen their positions, as well as absorbing new immigrants, particularly workers. This policy was implemented with remarkable determination and achieved great success. The workers were able to control most of the facilities of the Zionist entity in Palestine by the mid-1930s, before proceeding to control the Zionist Organization as a whole.

The Zionist labor wing could not achieve these successes alone, however. It quickly emerged from its isolation and found supporters outside its camp who rendered it great services. One of the most prominent was Weizmann himself, as president of the Zionist Organization and undisputed Zionist leader at the time. Through his supervision of general Zionist activity, Weizmann had reached the conviction that the workers were the only group capable of implementing his synthetic Zionism. He decided to help them, because,

> between the abyss and the actual work in Palestine stood the phalanx of the workers, to whom – though I never identified myself with them – I considered myself attached. Gradually an unwritten covenant was created between the small group of my friends in the so-called general Zionist movement and the great mass of workers in the settlements and factories of Palestine which formed the core of the Zionist movement. This was the guarantee of our political sanity, of our sense of realism and our freedom alike from Revisionist delusions and methods of violence.[199]

The historian of the labor movement that opposed "Weizmann's workers" (the national trade union, "Histadrut ha-Ovdim ha-

---

199   Weizmann, *Trial and Error*, p. 448.

Li'umit", which was founded in the mid-1930s under the auspices of the right-wing Revisionist Zionists) described the results of this "unwritten covenant": "The leaders of the labor parties were very close to Weizmann in their concept of Zionism... When they made an alliance [with him], they supported his leadership, of course, while he ensured the transfer of money from Zionist funds for their projects."[200]

Despite the support from Weizmann and his group, the Zionist workers did not give up their independent policy aimed at securing their interests. In late 1918, immediately after the end of the war, small numbers of Jewish immigrants continued to arrive in Palestine. Their number grew during the first half of 1919, prompting the presidency of the Zionist Organization to issue appeals to its branches in various European countries to stop sending immigrants to Palestine until preparations were complete to accommodate them.[201] These calls displeased the workers, who were eager to increase their number in Palestine at any cost. In their first challenge to the presidency of the Zionist Organization, they sent envoys abroad to urge immigrants to come to the country. The envoys helped organize the process, such that several thousand new Jewish immigrants arrived in Palestine in 1919 and the first half of 1920, before the British mandate authorities issued the first law regulating immigration. Those immigrants were the pioneers of a new wave of immigration, known as the "Third Aliyah", which lasted until 1923 and brought about 35,000 Jewish immigrants to Palestine (of whom about 1,800 arrived in 1919, and more than 8,000 during each of the years 1920-1923). About 13,000 of those immigrants came from the Soviet Union, 9,000 from Poland and the remainder from various European and Asian countries (see *Table 7 Jewish immigrants to Palestine, 1919-1939 (by wave of immigration)* and *Table 8 Jewish immigrants to Palestine, 1919-1939 (by country of origin)*, below).

---

200   Yehoshua Ofir, *Sefer ha-Oved ha-Leumi (Book of the National Worker)*, Vol. 1, p. 23.

201   *Ha-Protocolim shel ha-Va'ad ha-Poel ha-Tzioni (Records of Sessions of the Zionist Executive)*, Vol. 1, pp. 106, 127, 133, 226-227.

Table 7 Jewish immigrants to Palestine, 1919-1939[202] (by wave of immigration)

Year	Number	%	Year	Number	%
Third Aliyah			Fifth Aliyah		
1919	1,800[*]	0.53	1929	5,200	1.53
1920	8,200	2.42	1930	4,900	1.45
1921	8,300	2.45	1931	4,100	1.21
1922	8,700	2.57	1932	9,600	2.83
1923	8,100	2.39	1933	30,300	8.94
Total	35,100	10.36	1934	42,400	12.51
Fourth Aliyah			1935	61,900	18.26
1924	12,900	3.81	1936	29,700	8.76
1925	33,800	9.97	1937	10,500	11.30
1926	13,100	3.86	1938	21,900	3.81
1927	2,700	0.80	1939	27,600	8.14
1928	2,200	0.65	Total	239,100[†]	70.55
Total	64,700	19.09	Overall Total	338,900	100

---

[202] *A Survey of Palestine, Prepared in December 1945 and January 1946 for the Information of the Anglo-American Committee of Inquiry*, Vol. 1, pp. 185, 193-194; *Encyclopaedia of Zionism and Israel*, Vol. 1, pp. 536-538; *Encyclopaedia Judaica*, Vol. 9, p. 533.

[*] Numbers are approximated to the nearest 100 immigrants.

[†] Includes 25,400 individuals as illegal immigrants or tourists who entered Palestine during this period and did not exit (1933: about 2,500 people; 1934: 4,000; 1935: 3,800; 1936: 1,800; 1937: 700; 1938: 1,400; 1939: about 11,200 people).

Table 8 Jewish immigrants to Palestine, 1919-1939[203] (by country of origin)

Country	Jewish population in 1939	Immigrated to Palestine*			Total	
		1919-23	1924-31	1932-39	Number	%
Poland	3,250,000	9,200	38,600	90,800	138,600	40.9
Germany	504,000	500	1,000	43,800	45,300	13.4
Soviet Union	3,020,000	13,400	14,900	5,500	33,800	10.0
Romania	800,000	1,400	4,100	10,900	16,400	4.8
Yemen (and Aden)	47,000	200	2,500	7,200	9,900	2.9
United States	4,500,000	900	800	6,700	8,400	2.5
Greece	75,000	200	700	5,800	6,700	2.0
Czechoslovakia	400,000	100	400	6,100	6,600	1.9
Austria	80,000	500	300	5,600	6,400	1.9
Lithuania	155,000	900	300	5,200	6,400	1.9
Latvia	95,000	400	900	3,200	4,500	1.3
Turkey	5,000	500	1,300	2,200	4,000	1.2
Iraq	115,000	200	2,600	100	2,900	0.9
Bulgaria	50,000	300	1,200	1,200	2,700	0.8
Hungary	400,000	300	300	1,600	2,200	0.6
Iran	85,000	200	900	500	1,600	0.5
Britain	350,000	200	200	800	1,200	0.4
Others[†]	2,169,000	5,700	7,900	27,700	41,300	12.1
Total	16,145,000	35,100	78,900	224,900	338,900	100

---

203 Ibid; see also Dan Horowitz and Moshe Lissak, *Me-Yishuv le-Medina (From Yishuv to State)*, p. 344; Friesel, *Atlas Carta le-Toldot Am Yisrael be-Zman ha-Hadash (Carta's Atlas of Modern Jewish History)*, p. 84.

* Numbers are approximated to the nearest 100 immigrants.

† Includes about 40 countries where the proportion of Jewish immigrants from each was less than 0.4% of the total number of immigrants who entered Palestine during this period.

Most of the new immigrants, especially those from the Soviet Union and Poland, were members of the Hehalutz organization. They were trained in manual professions, such as agriculture, and close in their sociopolitical views to the immigrants of the Second Aliyah (who had come to Palestine during 1904-1914 and established various labor institutions). Thus they found no difficulty in integrating with them and quickly formed a cohesive force that sought to establish the Zionist "labor society" in Palestine. The pioneers of these immigrants were unable to establish their own settlements on their arrival, due to the lack of sufficient agricultural land in the possession of the Zionist agencies, as well as the immigrants' lack of financial capacities. Thus they took up any jobs that were available. The British authorities were actively seeking to establish modern administrations in Palestine, which provided many fields of work that accommodated most of these immigrants. They worked in construction, road development, railway and telephone facilities, ports, transport and various government jobs. More than half of the Third Aliyah immigrants were single or young couples, which helped them adapt to the new conditions with relative ease.[204]

Only a few months after the arrival of these immigrants in Palestine, they assumed a distinguished role that resonated among the labor settlers. Their first step was their goal of organizing themselves independently. On August 25, 1920, during a memorial ceremony six months after Trumpeldor's death, a group of them decided to establish what they called the "Yosef Trumpeldor Labor and Defense Battalion", or "Labor Battalion" ("Gdud ha-Avoda", in Hebrew).[205] Most of the founders were former Hehalutz members in Russia who had been affected by the Bolshevik Revolution. Their goal was to establish a comprehensive labor organization, which would accept every worker or immigrant involved in pioneering

---

204 Slutsky in Erez, ed., *Sefer ha-Aliyah ha-Shlishit (The Third Aliyah Book)*, Vol. 1, pp. 6, 25, 38.

205 See also Gvati, *Meah Shanot Hityashvut (A Hundred Years of Settlement)*, Vol. 1, pp. 195-196.

work to establish the Zionist labor society in Palestine. This contradicted the notion of establishing that society through agricultural settlement alone, within the streams of the kvutzah or the moshav (the last products of organizational thought of the Second Aliyah immigrants).

The Labor Battalion only had a few dozen members at the start, but gradually acquired more than 2,000 workers within about five years. The battalion held its first congress in June 1921 and declared that its goal was "to build the country through the establishment of a general commune of Jewish workers in the Land of Israel", by "organizing members in disciplined groups", creating a "public fund" to provide their needs, securing "private production" to support that fund and "expanding the economic base and improving work conditions by exploiting surplus profits".[206] The Labor Battalion formed groups that carried out various works throughout Palestine and cooperated with other labor groups, such as supporters of the large kvutzah and members of Hashomer Hatzair.

In addition, the Third Aliyah immigrants called for the establishment of a Jewish labor union in Palestine. A main motive was the tense relations between labor groups with different political leanings. After the establishment of the Ahdut ha-Avoda party in late 1919, and the refusal of Hapoel Hatzair to join it, the tension rose between the two parties as their competition intensified. Each party began to establish its own institutions, such that it did not take long before there were two employment offices, two immigrant absorption offices, two health insurance institutions, two construction contracting companies and so on.[207] New immigrants found themselves compelled to go to one of these institutions to manage their affairs and, thus, to determine their political affiliation and be considered members

---

[206] Braslavski, *Tnu'at ha-Poalim ha-Eretz Yisraelit (Labor Movement in the Land of Israel)*, Vol. 1, pp. 188-189, 191.

[207] Ben-Shoshan, *Toldot Tnu'at ha-Poalim be-Eretz Yisrael (History of the Labor Movement in the Land of Israel)*, Vol. 1, p. 421.

of either party,[208] which most of them were not ready for. This led to calls for the establishment of a general, non-partisan labor union that would accept any worker regardless of their partisan leanings, overseeing all union affairs. The new immigrants were the most supportive of this idea. The parties were reluctant to announce their agreement, however, and negotiations continued between them for several months until they succeeded under pressure from the non-partisans. In July 1920, Ahdut ha-Avoda and Hapoel Hatzair agreed to call for a "general congress of the workers of the Land of Israel to discuss the means of joint work, and to establish the necessary institutions to do so ... [provided] that the abolition of parties is not on the agenda".[209]

After this agreement, the first step was to hold general elections among the workers to choose their representatives at the congress. A total of 4,433 workers (of both genders) participated, with votes distributed among four lists. Ahdut ha-Avoda won 1,864 votes; Hapoel Hatzair, 1,324; the new immigrants list (which included Hehalutz and Hashomer Hatzair), 842; and the Jewish Socialist Workers party, with communist leanings, won 303 votes. The delegates to the congress were named from the candidates of those lists and numbered 87, split among the four aforementioned parties at 38, 27, 16 and 6, respectively.

The General Congress of Jewish Workers in Palestine was held during December 5-9, 1920, at the Institute of Applied Engineering (Technion) in Haifa. In addition to the delegates, a gathering of workers and Zionist officials took part. The participants discussed labor affairs and all aspects of Zionist activity in Palestine as well as their aspirations for the future, as they saw that the function of the congress was broader than union affairs and extended to include most aspects of the national home that they had hoped to contribute to. This position was evident in the decisions taken by the congress, which announced the formation of a general labor union, "ha-Histadrut ha-

---

208   Braslavski, *Tnu'at ha-Poalim ha-Eretz Yisraelit (Labor Movement in the Land of Israel)*, Vol. 1, p. 198.

209   Ben-Shoshan, *Toldot Tnu'at ha-Poalim be-Eretz Yisrael (History of the Labor Movement in the Land of Israel)*, Vol. 1, p. 198.

Klalit shel ha-Ovdim ha-Ivriyyim be-Erez Yisrael", the General Federation of Jewish Labor in the Land of Israel, known simply as the "Histadrut". (The union refrained from accepting Arab members throughout the British Mandate and for 22 years after Israel's establishment. Only in its 10th congress, held in Tel Aviv in January 1966, did the Histadrut take a decision to accept Arab workers as members and to remove the word "Jewish" from the name of the organization. The congress, however, rejected a proposal to replace the phrase "Land of Israel" with the word "Israel".)

The first article of the Histadrut constitution stated that

> the General Federation [Histadrut] unites and organizes all workers [and those of independent professions] ... who live on the fruits of their labor without exploiting the labor of others, for the purpose of arranging all the communal, economic, and, also, cultural affairs of the workers in the country,[210] to build a labor society in the Land of Israel.[211]

It was decided that the Histadrut would be formed from professional unions, so that individuals could only join it through membership in the labor unions of their professional sectors.

To build a "labor society in the Land of Israel", the Histadrut sought to organize union affairs and also touched on other matters that it deemed necessary. It announced that its sphere of activity included, for example, "organization and development of agricultural villages and other branches of work in towns and villages, and organization of labor battalions and groups for agriculture and industry"; implementation of construction works; "organization of workers in comprehensive professional unions, uniting all workers professionally on a non-partisan basis"; improvement of working conditions and productivity; vocational training; cooperatives; social security;

---

210 A dispute had arisen in the congress on the relationship of the Histadrut to cultural affairs and so the article was approved in this manner.

211 In Ben-Shoshan, *Toldot Tnu'at ha-Poalim be-Eretz Yisrael (History of the Labor Movement in the Land of Israel)*, Vol. 1, p. 446.

"organization of security and defense affairs"; accommodation of immigrants and providing work for them; organization of workers' immigration from outside Palestine; dissemination of Hebrew among workers; establishment of cultural, general, agricultural or professional institutions; and publication of professional newspapers.[212] The Histadrut also declared that it would strengthen its relations with all Jewish labor organizations outside Palestine that believed in the necessity of "building a working Land of Israel", and that it would send its delegates to the Zionist settlement agencies.[213]

The General Congress of Jewish Workers also took a number of organizational decisions, announcing the formation of a Histadrut council, comprising 27 members. Four of its seats were left vacant: two for delegates of immigrant workers from Yemen and two for delegates of women workers. The council was charged with electing the Histadrut executive committee and managing its central institutions. The congress also entrusted the Histadrut with managing the non-partisan institutions that the parties had established, and recommended the establishment of a general union for agricultural workers, a unified public works office and a workers' bank to finance Histadrut projects. In another challenge by the workers to the Zionist leadership, the congress announced its adoption and support of four small settlement outposts that the Zionist settlement agencies had decided, for economic reasons, should be removed.[214]

During the first year of its establishment, the Histadrut was engaged in forming its agencies. First were the labor councils, which were considered its regional branches in the cities and other regions. It was decided that the workers would choose their representatives in these bodies by vote for parties or individuals, not on the basis of profession as in the Histadrut congress. This was done to expand the base of proportional representation and

---

212 Ibid.

213 Ibid, pp. 446-447.

214 Ibid.

ensure that minorities were represented in these councils.[215]

In early 1921, the "Construction and Public Works" company was also founded, whose name was changed to "Solel Boneh" (Paving and Building, in Hebrew) in 1924, after the merger of two construction companies belonging to Ahdut ha-Avoda and Hapoel Hatzair. This company played a prominent role in securing work for large numbers of Jewish workers during the first years of the Histadrut, especially as the size of the public works undertaken by the mandate authorities dwindled.[216] Immediately after its formation, the Histadrut executive committee, in cooperation with the presidency of the Zionist Organization, began taking the necessary measures to establish "Bank Hapoalim" (The Workers' Bank), which obtained a license on May 1, 1921 to carry out its activities. The bank, whose founding shares were deposited with the Histadrut executive committee, aimed to finance Histadrut projects rather than grant loans to individual workers. Another financial institution was established for this purpose, the "Kupat Milve" (Loan Fund).[217]

At the same time, the Histadrut made great efforts to convince the largest number of workers to join it – making significant progress within a short time. On September 10, 1922, less than two years after its establishment, its executive committee conducted a general census of Jewish workers in Palestine. This revealed that 8,394 workers out of 16,608, or just over half (50.54 percent), had joined the Histadrut. (14,424 workers answered the question on the date of their arrival in Palestine, showing that 2,390 workers, or 16.6 percent, were born in the country; 476, or 3.3 percent, had come with the Lovers of Zion immigration – First Aliyah; 2,572, or 17.8 percent, had come during the Second Aliyah; and 8,986, or 62.3 percent, during the Third Aliyah.[218]) The number of Histadrut members continued to rise until it included about two-thirds of all Jewish workers in Palestine, and

---

215   Ibid, Vol. 2, pp. 15-17.

216   Ibid, pp. 20-23.

217   Ibid, pp. 49-52.

218   Ibid, pp. 18-19.

turned into a significant power center for the Zionist workers.

This result did not come about by chance. It was due to the perseverance of the labor wing in pursuing a policy of self-reliance and strengthening its own institutions, at the forefront of which was the Histadrut, to face what it termed the "right-wing" control of the Zionist Organization and its agencies. Two years after its founding, the Histadrut held a second congress in Tel Aviv, during January 7-20, 1923. The election of delegates to this congress led to the Ahdut ha-Avoda party winning a majority of seats (69 of 130), while Hapoel Hatzair won 36. The remainder were split among seven small lists, three of which were leftist or had communist leanings. All together, these lists won 10 seats. This proportion remained unchanged in subsequent Histadrut congresses, in one way or another, until the end of the British Mandate. All the elections to those congresses led to Ahdut ha-Avoda (and the Mapai Party, from 1930) winning more than half the seats, with the remainder split among a group of small lists[219] (this situation did not change significantly after the establishment of Israel, either). This enabled Ahdut ha-Avoda (and then Mapai) to control the Histadrut since its establishment and turn it into a tool in the hands of the party, which used it to implement its policy – although it did not oppose the involvement of any group with which it could reach an understanding in administering the Histadrut. As a result, the Histadrut had a stable, self-confident leadership, enabling it to fulfill its functions to the best.

The second Histadrut congress was held at an uncomfortable time for the Zionist workers. Signs of an economic downturn began to manifest in Palestine in 1923, in a number of sectors in which large numbers of workers were concentrated – threatening them with unemployment. As a result, about 3,500 veteran immigrants left Palestine in 1923, compared with 8,100 immigrants who arrived in the same year. This crisis forced the Histadrut to respond and assume new responsibilities. Thus the second congress was arguably more important than the first, in

---

219 Merchav, *Toldot Tnu'at ha-Poalim be-Eretz Yisrael 1905-1965 (History of the Labor Movement in the Land of Israel, 1905-1965)*, p. 353.

terms of clarifying the objectives of the Histadrut, defining its functions and establishing its permanent agencies.

The second congress sought to amend the constitution of the Histadrut, including the basic (first) article, removing the word "also" before "cultural affairs" (see earlier in this section) so as to remove any restrictions on the union's work in the cultural field. The second instance of the term "workers" was also replaced by "the working class", such that the article read as follows:

> The General Federation of Jewish Labor in the Land of Israel [Histadrut] unites and organizes all workers who live on the fruits of their labor without exploiting the labor of others, for the purpose of arranging all the communal, economic, and cultural affairs of the working class in the country, to build a labor society in the Land of Israel.[220]

The congress recognized the right of every male or female worker who had reached 17 years of age to join the Histadrut, as long as they agreed with its principles, regardless of their political position.

Another article was added to the constitution of the Histadrut to include the establishment of fellowship relations with Arab workers in Palestine and the development of relations with the Jewish and labor movement worldwide.[221]

The congress decided to issue a daily newspaper of the Histadrut in Hebrew, *Davar* (*Word*).[222] This was done two years later, in 1925.[223] Another decision was to establish a publishing house, "Am Oved" (Working Nation). This would only be founded in 1942. The powers were expanded for each of the executive committee and the Histadrut council, the two bodies charged with supervision of the union and administration of its daily affairs. (The constitution of the Histadrut was again

---

220   Ibid, pp. 354-355.

221   Merchavia, *Am ou-Moledet (Nation and Homeland)*, p. 272.

222   *Davar*, in Hebrew, also means "something".

223   The independent, liberal-leaning newspaper, *Haaretz (The Country)*, had been issued in Palestine since 1919.

amended in its third congress, in 1928.)[224]

However, the most important achievement of the second Histadrut congress was to lay the organizational and legal foundations for the economic activity of the union. This aspect was very important to the Histadrut founders and raised a number of questions to the congress. The members were, first and foremost, groups of immigrants to Palestine who were concerned with attracting more immigrants to help them establish the "Jewish labor society". It had to be clear to what extent the Histadrut and its agencies could be used to facilitate the expansion of immigration through the establishment of various economic projects. Secondly, a guarantee was needed that the Histadrut projects, if successful, would not turn into capitalist institutions and exploit the remaining workers. "How will we preserve its class, social and Zionist character? ... [Finally,] how will we acquire the necessary means to expand and develop our economic activity?"[225] The congress discussed these questions at length and decided to "establish a higher economic body for the working masses, with legislative powers, which monitors and directs the Histadrut's economic activity in all its aspects".[226] This body was called "Hevrat ha-Ovdim" (Society/Community of Workers, also the "General Cooperative Association of Labor in Israel"), a "Jewish cooperative for settlement, industry, contracting and supply works", with the mission to "organize, develop and strengthen economic activity ... of the working masses, in all branches of settlement and work in towns and villages, on the basis of mutual aid and responsibility".[227] In other words, the Histadrut considered itself an economic institution in addition to being a labor union so that whoever joined it would be considered a member of a labor union and a shareholder in

---

224 See original texts and amendments in Merchavia, *Am ou-Moledet (Nation and Homeland)*, pp. 272-282.

225 Ben-Shoshan, *Toldot Tnu'at ha-Poalim be-Eretz Yisrael (History of the Labor Movement in the Land of Israel)*, Vol. 2, p. 91.

226 Ibid, p. 92.

227 Ibid.

a company.

The Histadrut congress defined the powers of Hevrat ha-Ovdim as

> the owner of all Histadrut financial and cooperative institutions, with the right to establish institutions, projects and funds. The founding shares of The Workers' Bank ("Bank Hapoalim") ... and other subsidiary companies are deposited in it. It also has the right to impose taxes and determine work wages in its institutions and farms ... and the right to estimate product prices. Hevrat ha-Ovdim coordinates the work of the various institutions, monitors their management, approves their projects, supervises their implementation, and directs their activities for the benefit of the working masses.[228]

Hevrat ha-Ovdim declared in its founding constitution, when it was registered by the mandate authorities on March 12, 1924, that its goal was "to unite Jewish workers in the Land of Israel, on cooperative bases, in all branches of work, whether manual or office".[229] To implement this goal, the association granted itself the authority to work in several fields, including the settlement of its members in towns and villages; working in hunting or fishing; establishing factories and workshops; engaging in construction works; opening shops and warehouses; possession of land, sea and air transport; establishment of banks and other financial institutions; assisting its members in bringing their relatives from abroad; provision of life insurance; establishment of subsidiary companies to publish books and newspapers; establishment of libraries, theaters, and labor educational and cultural institutions; establishment of medical organizations and carrying out "everything that would help achieve the goals of the association".[230]

---

228 Ibid.

229 See constitution of Hevrat ha-Ovdim in Merchavia, *Am ou-Moledet (Nation and Homeland)*, pp. 282-286.

230 Ibid.

7. British Mandate over Palestine, Part II 497

Hevrat ha-Ovdim adhered to its goals and worked in the aforementioned fields and in others as well, spreading its activities to all aspects of the Zionist economy in Palestine. Only a short while later, it became evident that the Zionist labor wing, when it had established the Histadrut and its union and economic components, had founded one of the most important institutions that would grow rapidly and have a decisive influence on the Zionist presence in Palestine. It appeared, at times, especially in the late 1920s and early 1930s, that the Jewish national home in Palestine had found expression in the Histadrut and its agencies. The Histadrut joined the International Federation of Trade Unions in Amsterdam in 1924 and, the following year, Hevrat ha-Ovdim joined the International Cooperative Alliance.[231] By the mid-1930s, the Histadrut had turned into a power center within the Zionist entity in Palestine and abroad, which was not easy to compete with. The labor wing exploited this influence and proceeded to take control of the Zionist Organization.

The Histadrut did not make these achievements merely through the clarity of its goals or the scope of its work, despite the importance of these, however. This was also due to a dynamic, pragmatic labor leadership that seized the reins of the union and oversaw it for a significant period of time. In November 1921, less than a year after the founding of the Histadrut, David Ben-Gurion, the man of Ahdut ha-Avoda, was elected a member of its executive committee. Within a short time, he began to act as though he was the union's secretary general, although he was never elected to this post that was only created in 1947.[232] During the First World War, Ben-Gurion had been expelled from Palestine, with his colleague, Yitzhak Ben-Zvi, and they had made their way to the United States. There, they worked in organizing Po'alei Zion and Hehalutz, then volunteered in the Jewish battalions and returned with them to Palestine (see section

---

[231] Ben-Shoshan, *Toldot Tnu'at ha-Poalim be-Eretz Yisrael (History of the Labor Movement in the Land of Israel)*, Vol. 2, p. 187.

[232] David Ben-Gurion, *Zichronot (Memoirs)*, Vol. 1: until 1934, pp. 181-182; see also Shabtai Teveth, *Kinat David (The Jealousy of David)*, pp. 5, 149, 167.

2 of this chapter). After the battalions were demobilized, Ben-Gurion was sent to London to run the political office of Po'alei Zion, a function he undertook until late 1921. He then returned to Palestine and was elected to his new position. The "comrade secretary general", upon his appointment – as a firm believer in the "message of socialist Zionism" – held very specific concepts on the substance of the Histadrut and its functions. In its second congress, he declared that

> our organization, the labor union of the Land of Israel, is the heart of the movement to revive the Jewish people, and the center of blood flow in the arteries of our national and social revival – the center to which, through covert, implicit channels, all streams of activity and life in the rising body of the nation flow, and from which they are distributed and absorbed in the new tissue to build our future in the country. Our movement – the Jewish labor movement in the Land of Israel – is the condensed essence of the great national and social upheaval that has awakened the Jewish people of our time, the echoes of which have reverberated in the Zionist movement and the Jewish labor movement.[233]

At the third congress of his party, Ahdut ha-Avoda, which had been held shortly before the second Histadrut congress, Ben-Gurion had declared that he "[did] not stand with the Zionist shekel-payers' organization,[234] but with the organization of those who realize[d] Zionism in their lives and work – the Histadrut".[235] Ben-Gurion maintained this idea of the Histadrut and worked hard to strengthen the organization and raise its status as the body that should, in the end, replace the Zionist Organization in establishing the Jewish national home in Palestine and overseeing its growth. He expressed his theory in

---

[233] Ben-Gurion, *Memoirs*, Vol. 1, pp. 211-212; see also Ben-Shoshan, *Toldot Tnu'at ha-Poalim be-Eretz Yisrael (History of the Labor Movement in the Land of Israel)*, Vol. 2, pp. 85-86.

[234] That is, the Zionist Organization.

[235] Ofir, *Sefer ha-Oved ha-Leumi (Book of the National Worker)*, Vol. 1, p. 21.

the slogan "From Class to Nation" that he put forth in the late 1920s and early 1930s, declaring that it was the Jewish workers who would establish the Zionist entity in Palestine, not the "capitalists" (or the "homeowners", as he put it).

David Ben-Gurion's control of the Histadrut, as its secretary general, was the first step on a long road that he walked in the service of Zionism. He remained in this position for 14 years, during which he was able to transform the Histadrut, with its various agencies, into the largest power center within the Zionist entity in Palestine. Ben-Gurion was always "where the power was",[236] as was his party, Ahdut ha-Avoda. In 1935, after resigning from the Histadrut, Ben-Gurion was elected chairman of the Jewish Agency at a time when it was leading the Zionist struggle for control of Palestine. He held this position for 13 years. When Israel was founded in 1948, Ben-Gurion became its prime minister and defense minister, and continued to perform these functions for 15 years (except for a brief period, during 1953-1955, in which he "retired" from politics, although his influence on Israeli politics had reached its peak at the time). He resigned in 1963. It is clear, from this record, that Ben-Gurion played a decisive role in establishing the Zionist entity in Palestine, a role that was possibly not matched by any other Zionist figure.

6

The First World War severely affected Zionist settlement activity in Palestine and almost froze it. During the four years of the war, only one settlement was established, Kfar Giladi, by members of Hashomer in 1916. At the end of the war, in late 1918, the representative of the JCA[237] company in Palestine, Haim Margalit-Kalvarisky (1868-1947), established four small settlements, including Tel Hai, in the far north of the country

---

236 Uri Avnery, *Israel Without Zionists*, p. 87.

237 On the JCA, see Introduction, section 4; Chapter 4, section 4.

without consulting the JCA.[238] The company refused to approve the project and three of these settlements were removed, leaving Ayelet ha-Shahar. After the war, the various labor groups and new immigrants expected that the agencies of the Zionist Organization would be quick to revitalize settlement operations. The organization was only able to return to settling immigrants about two years later, however, when its policy was shaped in building the national home. This was affected by Weizmann's view that had prevailed, on the one hand, and the ratification of the British mandate over Palestine, on the other. The Zionist settlement agencies were also forced to wait due to the weak financial capabilities of the Zionist Organization, as well as the closure of the land registry offices (Tabu) in Palestine, which stopped the sale and purchase transactions of land.

The new body that assumed supervision of settlement operations, the settlement department of the Zionist Organization, could not establish its first new settlement (Degania Bet) until late 1920. This was despite the department's administration being handed to two pillars of the labor wing, the engineers Yitzhak Elazari-Volcani (1880-1955) and Akiva Ettinger (1872-1945), who were very enthusiastic about the establishment of new settlements. In the same few months, another new settlement, Kiryat Anavim, was established near Jerusalem.

Despite this meagre activity, this period was rich with novel settlement ideas that had a significant effect on the nature and trends of Zionist settlement in Palestine. Moshavah-type settlements,[239] based on private ownership (most of the settlements established by Lovers of Zion or Rothschild in Palestine, during the First Aliyah, were of this type), did not win the favor of the new officials of settlement operations nor the approval of the settler candidates themselves. The reason was that Arab workers dominated the labor in these settlements,

---

238 Moshe Smilansky, *Prakim be-Toldot ha-Yishuv (Chapters in the History of the Yishuv)*, Vol. 1, Book 4, p. 62.

239 The moshavah is a smaller moshav.

making them unfit for the establishment of a "Jewish labor society". Thus, there was no interest in establishing similar ones. The Zionist Organization had basically worked to counter this type of settlement since it had decided to begin actual settlement in Palestine after Herzl's death. It adopted a new experiment to establish what was called a "cooperative settlement" in Merhavia, which was founded in 1911 (see Chapter 4, section 2).[240] Ten years later, however, it became evident that the experiment had failed, for various reasons.[241] As a result, the only type of settlement that was left was known as the "kvutzah", similar to that which was established in Degania Alef in 1909.[242] However, the experience of the kvutzah – which was limited to small groups of settlers – aroused opposition among others. They began to demand new methods of settlement.

The hopes held by the Zionists that they would soon be settling in the country, with a more systematic and thought-out plan than the previous immigrants, prompted them to publicly express their opinions. One of the most prominent critics of the kvutzah experiment was Shlomo Lavi (Levkovich, 1882-1963), who explained, in a series of articles published in *Conters*, a magazine of Ahdut ha-Avoda, that the kvutzah was unsuccessful because its founders could not continue their "first revolutionary step" by increasing their number. Thus the fate of the small kvutzah, closed in on itself and narrow-minded, was "permanent poverty, making do with the least possible, stagnation, petty quarrels, ongoing replacement of members, and endless problems".[243] The alternative was the large kvutzah, which could accommodate new immigrants with work in agriculture, industry and crafts, seeking self-sufficiency and "ridding itself of poverty, distress and permanent budget

---

240 See Chapter 3, section 8; Chapter 4, section 2.

241 See Ben-Shoshan, *Toldot Tnu'at ha-Poalim be-Eretz Yisrael (History of the Labor Movement in the Land of Israel)*, Vol. 1, pp. 408-409.

242 See Chapter 4, section 4.

243 Ben-Shoshan, *Toldot Tnu'at ha-Poalim be-Eretz Yisrael (History of the Labor Movement in the Land of Israel)*, Vol. 1, p. 413.

deficit".[244] Production on a large farm was also less costly than on a small one. The small kvutzah, with its limited number of members, inevitably needed to hire Arab workers during the harvest, which affected its ideological-social foundations. The large kvutzah had no need for that, as it could recruit workers from among its skilled members, such as carpenters, tailors or masons, to work in agriculture when needed and return to their original work after completing the necessary tasks. The goal was "for the farm to produce most of its goods by itself, in order to be the least market-dependent. The market exploits the product; thus, it is necessary to strive for as much self-sufficiency as possible."[245] This program had been presented to the 13th Zionist Congress (1923), which had approved it. It was the basis for establishing a form of settlement known as the kibbutz, which is a large kvutzah.

In addition to the kibbutz, another form of settlement that was devised during this period was the "moshav ovdim" (workers' settlement). This proceeded from the same Zionist base as the kibbutz movement, but differed in demanding that the family – not the individual – be considered the principal settlement unit. The leader of the moshav current, Eliezer Yaffe (1882-1942), believed that "the family is a natural and essential element in the life of the people,"[246] and its living conditions within the kvutzah were uncomfortable and had to be changed. Yaffe called for the establishment of the moshav on "national land" owned by Zionist settlement agencies,[247] particularly the Jewish National Fund, such that each family would be given a specific area to be exploited by its members alone and its crops would be sufficient to meet their needs. Families would

---

244 Ibid.

245 Ibid, p. 414.

246 Ibid, p. 416.

247 See Eliezer Yaffe's article on "Moshav Ovdim" in Braslavski, *Tnu'at ha-Poalim ha-Eretz Yisraelit (Labor Movement in the Land of Israel)*, Vol. 1, p. 371; Yosef Rubin, ed., *Moshavei Ovdim, Antologia (Workers' Settlements, Collection of Essays)*, pp. 17-33.

7. British Mandate over Palestine, Part II 503

cooperate and assist each other in carrying out seasonal chores, as well as setting up joint marketing or procurement bodies. Each family would keep the profits from its farm and use them as it pleased, as long as it did not conflict with the general interest of the moshav. In practice, the moshav was only a revision of Oppenheimer's theory of cooperative settlement.[248] The Hapoel Hatzair party enthusiastically supported this proposal. The idea of establishing moshavim[249] had been approved by the Zionist conference held in London in February 1920,[250] then presented to the 12th Zionist Congress (1921) which had also approved it.[251]

These new settlement ideas remained theoretical, however, until the imposition of the British mandate over Palestine and the establishment of civil rule in it. The land registry offices (Tabu) then reopened, enabling the Zionists to conclude new land purchase deals (such transactions had stopped with the outbreak of the First World War in 1914.) The Zionists renewed their activity to purchase lands in various parts of Palestine and were able, by late 1922, to own or seize about 173,400 dunums (of which about 131,200 dunums were officially registered as sold in the land registry offices, while the remainder were purchased through temporary or unregistered contracts or leased from the government).[252] Thus the area of land that the Jews came to control in Palestine, by the end of 1922, amounted to about 594,000 dunums, up from an estimated 420,600 dunums in 1914[253] (see *Table 9 Distribution of Jewish land ownership and appropriation in Palestine, 1882-1939*, below).

---

248 For details, see Alex Bein, *Toldot ha-Hityashvut ha-Tzionit (History of Zionist Settlement)*, pp. 172-180.

249 Plural of "moshav".

250 *Chronologiah le-Toldot ha-Yishuv ha-Yehudi be-Eretz Yisrael (Chronology of the Jewish Yishuv in the Land of Israel)*, Vol. 1, p. 41.

251 Bein, *Toldot ha-Hityashvut ha-Tzionit (History of Zionist Settlement)*, p. 232.

252 *A Survey of Palestine, Prepared in December 1945 and January 1946 for the Information of the Anglo-American Committee of Inquiry*, Vol. 1, pp. 244, 376.

253 Ibid.

Table 9 Distribution of Jewish land ownership and appropriation in Palestine, 1882-1939[254] (approximate areas in dunums)

	1882-1914	1920-1922	1923-1927	1928-1932	1933-1936	1937-1939
Jewish National Fund	16,000	72,400	196,700	296,900	369,800	463,500
Palestine Jewish Colonization Association (PICA)	369,000		323,000		435,000	419,100
Palestine Land Development Company (PLDC), private institutions, and individuals	35,600	484,600	345,000	709,800	426,000	473,000
Public property	-	37,000	38,300	51,800	161,800	177,800
Total	420,600	594,000	903,000	1,058,500	1,392,600	1,533,400
Percentage of land area of Palestine (10,162 square miles or 26,320 square kilometers)	1.59	2.25	3.43	4.02	5.29	5.83

The lands that the Jews acquired during these years lay in different areas of Palestine. There were, for example, about 2,200 dunums of the lands of Abu Ghosh village, west of

---

254 This table was prepared according to data in *A Survey of Palestine, Prepared in December 1945 and January 1946 for the Information of the Anglo-American Committee of Inquiry*, Vol. 1, pp. 244, 267-268, 372, 376; *Report by His Majesty's Government in the United Kingdom of Great Britain and Northern Ireland to the Council of the League of Nations on the Administration of Palestine and Trans-Jordan for the year 1930 (Colonial No. 59)*, pp. 249-250; *Report by His Majesty's Government in the United Kingdom of Great Britain and Northern Ireland to the Council of the League of Nations on the Administration of Palestine and Trans-Jordan for the year 1937 (Colonial No. 146)*, pp. 69-70; *Report by His Majesty's Government in the United Kingdom of Great Britain and Northern Ireland to the Council of the League of Nations on the Administration of Palestine and Trans-Jordan for the year 1938 (Colonial No. 166)*, pp. 76-77; Abraham Granott, *Agrarian Reform and the Record of Israel*, pp. 28, 166; Yosef Weitz, *Ha-Ma'avak al ha-Adamah (The Struggle for the Land)*, pp. 110-114; Yosef Weitz, *Hitnahlutenu be-Tkufat ha-Sa'ara (Our Settlement Activities in a Stormy Period)*, p. 11; Aharon Cohen, *Yisrael ve ha-Olam ha-Aravi (Israel and the Arab World)*, p. 191; Avnery, *Israel Without Zionists*, pp. 256, 258; Kenneth W. Stein, *The Land Question in Palestine, 1917-1939*, pp. 226-227.

7. British Mandate over Palestine, Part II 505

Jerusalem, which were handed over to the settlement of Kiryat Anavim;[255] 5,000 dunums near Kfar Saba, on which the town of Ra'anana was later built;[256] 19,000 dunums east of Haifa, where kibbutz Yagur and the Nesher cement factory were set up;[257] and 16,000 dunums in the coastal plain, north of Jaffa, where the town of Herzliya was founded.[258] However, the largest land sale during this period took place, again, through the Sursock family in Beirut, from which the Zionists purchased 70,000 dunums of the most fertile agricultural land in Marj ibn Amir, south of Nazareth.[259] The Zionists had purchased, from this family, about 53,000 dunums of land in the same region, before the First World War[260] (the Merhavia settlement had been built on part of these lands). Thus, the area of land that they acquired in that region rose to about 120,000 dunums, divided into three parts, close to one another. Over time, a number of prosperous Zionist settlements were built on these lands. However, it also became evident that the acquisition of these lands was of unique strategic value, for the settlements established on them became a link between the two sets of Zionist settlements that existed in Palestine before the First World War: the first, north of Tiberias, and the second, along the coastal plain between Haifa and Jaffa. This created a vital territorial extension of Jewish settlement between the settlements located in the far north of Palestine and those in the far south (see *Map 11 Jewish settlements in Palestine, 1918-1923*, below). (These settlements also formed, with their expansion and increase in population, a Jewish human barrier separating the Galilee region, in the north of Palestine, from the remainder of the country, creating a reality that had its impact when the division of Palestine was proposed, at a later stage. This also enabled the Zionists to control these areas with relative ease, after improving their strategic position in them, during the 1948 war.)

---

255 Aminadav Eshbal, ed., *Shishim Shanot Hachsharat ha-Yishuv (Sixty Years of the Palestine Land Development Company)*, p. 50.

256 Ibid.

257 Ibid.

258 Ibid, pp. 55-57.

259 Arthur Ruppin, *Shloshim Shanot Binyan be-Eretz Yisrael (Thirty Years of Building in the Land of Israel)*, pp. 164-167.

260 Saadiyah Baz, *Zichronot (Memoirs)*, pp. 160-161.

Map 11 Jewish settlements in Palestine, 1918-1923

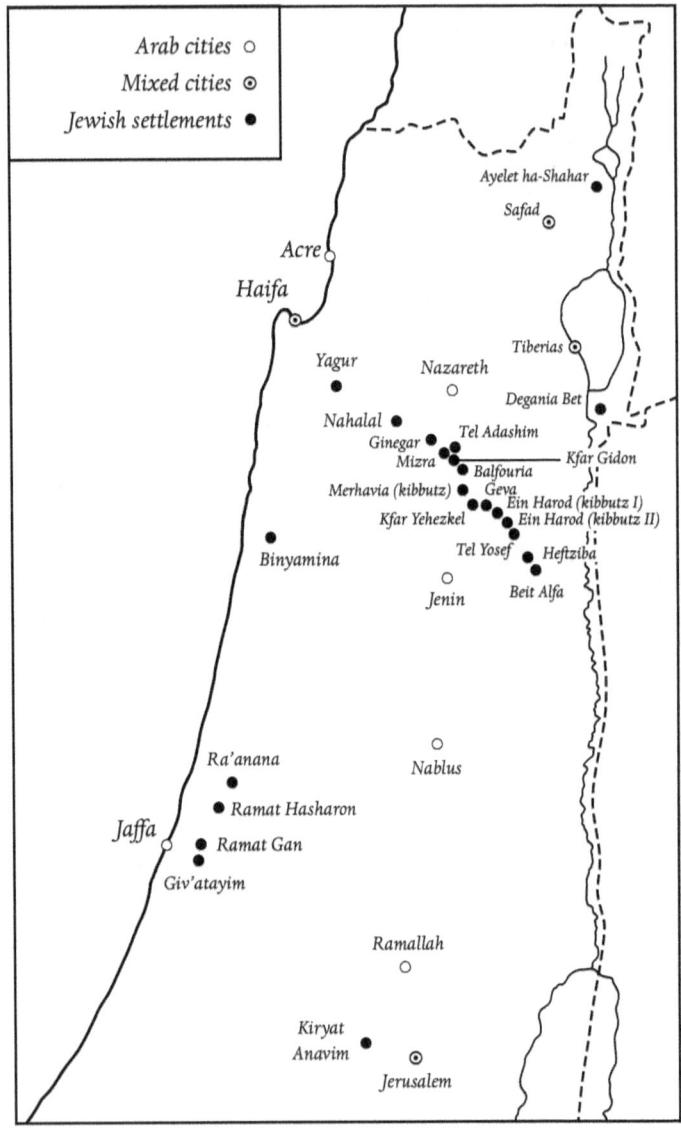

It is worth noting that most of the land acquired by the Zionists in Palestine during or after this period, like all the land that they had purchased before the British Mandate, was sold to them by major feudal lords or landowners residing outside the country. Moshe Smilansky, head of the Jewish farmers' association, stated in a memorandum to the Peel Commission (1936-37) that, by March 1936, the Jews had purchased 1.2319 million dunums of land in Palestine, of which 1.125 million (91.3 percent) were sold to them by major feudal lords. (Of this area, about 443,000 dunums, or 36 percent, had owners residing in Syria and Egypt.) The Jews only purchased about 106,900 dunums, or 7.8 percent, from small farmers,[261] and about 115,400 dunums from notable Palestinian families.[262] According to the memorandum, the Jews were also exploiting, by that date, about 161,800 dunums of "state lands", that is, public properties that the British authorities had handed over to them through various concessions for long periods. (This area rose, by 1943, to 175,088 dunums, while the Arabs were handed an area of 1,222 dunums, only.)[263] Article 6 of the mandate instrument had stated the need to facilitate the settlement of Jews on "lands not required for public purposes" in Palestine (see Chapter 6, section 4).

The Zionists were able to purchase the Arab lands that they did in Palestine due to several factors. First they exploited the many loopholes in the Ottoman land laws in this regard. They also took advantage of the power of their allies in government departments, on the grounds of the special status granted to the Zionists in the mandate instrument, to amend these land laws or influence the enactment of new ones in a manner that served Zionist interests and facilitated their land acquisitions. From the early 1920s until the late 1930s, the Zionists, unlike the Arabs, were constantly in the know regarding all the deliberations on

---

261 Cohen, A., *Yisrael ve ha-Olam ha-Aravi (Israel and the Arab World)*, p. 191.

262 For details, see Stein, K. W., *The Land Question in Palestine, 1917-1939*, pp. 228-239; Avnery, *Israel Without Zionists*, pp. 197-201.

263 *A Survey of Palestine, Prepared in December 1945 and January 1946 for the Information of the Anglo-American Committee of Inquiry*, Vol. 1, p. 267.

land legislation and the resultant procedures that the mandate authorities sought to approve. The Zionists were thus able to amend all this legislation, in one way or another, before its adoption and publication, in a way that served their interests or ensured, at least, that they were not seriously harmed.[264] There was no change in this situation except during 1928-1931, when relations were strained between the British authorities and the Zionists, but all the proposals relating to the modification of the system of lands and their use, which were made during these three years and were mostly uncomfortable for the Zionists, were not implemented in the end.[265] The Zionists also exploited, in this regard, the many weaknesses in Palestinian Arab society, which was politically and socially divided, in addition to the weakness of the Arab rural economy and the poor economic conditions of the peasants. Further, the mandate authorities, in practice, refrained from seriously intervening to protect the Arab peasants and help them retain their lands.[266] Despite much talk of the need to enact legislation or take measures towards this, no effective action was taken, even partially, until 1940.

As soon as they began to purchase lands, after the First World War, the Zionist settlement agencies resumed their activity in establishing new settlements on them. In late 1920, they established the Kiryat Anavim settlement near Jerusalem. During this period, the foundations were also laid for new types of settlements. A dispute arose among the settlers in Degania, near Lake Tiberias, due to a demand by some of them to convert it from a small kvutzah, with a few dozen settlers, to a large kibbutz, with a few hundred. The kibbutz supporters split from the mother settlement and established Degania Bet.[267] (At a later stage, Degania Alef, the original settlement, also turned into a

---

[264] Stein, K. W., *The Land Question in Palestine, 1917-1939*, pp. 30, 33, 43, 94, 142, 154, 212.

[265] Ibid, pp. 80-81.

[266] Ibid, p. 212.

[267] See also Bein, *Toldot ha-Hityashvut ha-Tzionit (History of Zionist Settlement)*, pp. 163-168.

kibbutz.)

During the same period too, another dispute arose in Degania Alef. The idea of establishing a moshav gained momentum in the settlement, leading to sharp squabbles that outweighed those between the supporters of the kvutzah and those of the kibbutz. The supporters of the kvutzah, in the end, had acquiesced to the idea of the kibbutz and even agreed to share their lands with its supporters. The idea of the moshav, however, was no more than intolerable "heresy"[268] to them. They forced its advocates to leave the settlement, and then the entire area. The settlement department handed the defectors an area of land in Marj ibn Amir, on the main Haifa-Nazareth road, where in late 1921 they established the first settlement of the moshav type, Nahalal.[269] Among its founders were Eliezer Yaffe, the originator of the moshav idea, and Shmuel Dayan, the later secretary of the moshav movement (and father of Moshe Dayan, an Israeli general and politician).

In 1921, seven other settlements were established: the moshav of Kfar Yehezkel; three kibbutzim (plural of "kibbutz"): Geva, Tel Yosef and Ein Harod[270] (members of the Labor Battalion, or Gdud ha-Avoda, established the kibbutz of Ein Harod, which later split into two kibbutzim, both with the same name); the town of Ra'anana; and the town of Ramat Gan.

In 1922, eight new settlements were established: the kibbutzim of Beit Alfa (established by a group from Hashomer Hatzair), Heftziba, Yagur and Ginegar; two moshavim: Balfouria, established in memory of Balfour, and Merhavia (the first Merhavia settlement turned into a kibbutz); the town of Binyamina, established by Baron Edmond Benjamin James de Rothschild, in his name;[271] and the town of Giv'atayim.

---

268 See also Shabtai Teveth, *Moshe Dayan*, p. 33.

269 See Bein, *Toldot ha-Hityashvut ha-Tzionit (History of Zionist Settlement)*, pp. 232-234; Smilansky, *Prakim be-Toldot ha-Yishuv (Chapters in the History of the Yishuv)*, Vol. 1, Book 4, pp. 106-116.

270 See Smilansky, *Prakim be-Toldot ha-Yishuv (Chapters in the History of the Yishuv)*, Vol. 1, Book 4, pp. 117-146.

271 Ibid, pp. 151-156.

In 1923, four new settlements were established: Mizra, a kibbutz; Kfar Gidon, a moshavah; Tel Adashim, a moshav; and the town of Ramat Hasharon.

The town of Ra'anana and moshav Balfouria were established by a group of American Zionists who founded a company, "Kehilat Zion Amricayit" (American Zion Commonwealth), to settle individual immigrants in Palestine. This worked on the same bases as the Palestine Land Development Company. The two later cooperated to establish a number of Zionist settlements in the country.[272]

Between 1918 and the end of the Third Aliyah, in 1923, a further 23 Jewish settlements (of the kibbutz or moshav type, as well as towns and cities) were established in Palestine. With the 41 settlements[273] that had been established until the issuance of the Balfour Declaration, in 1917, the total number of Jewish settlements rose, by late 1923, to 64 (see *Map 11 Jewish settlements in Palestine, 1918-1923*, above).

7

The attitude towards the Arabs in Palestine and relations with them was one of the main problems faced by the Zionists after the British occupation of the country, as had been the case for their predecessors during Ottoman rule. Despite the centrality of this point, most Zionists did not give it considerable attention – especially when interest in the "Arab question" was only theoretical after Britain's mandate. Zionists responded in three ways. The first view was that relations with the Arabs were an important issue that required great concessions to resolve, the second saw the Arab presence in Palestine as a problem that had to be eliminated, while the third asserted that relations with the Arabs would only be resolved through a new reality of Jewish domination in the country.[274] At the outset of his

---

272 Smilansky, *Prakim be-Toldot ha-Yishuv (Chapters in the History of the Yishuv)*, Vol. 2, Book 5, p. 15.

273 See Chapter 5, section 2.

274 Neil Caplan, *Palestine Jewry and the Arab Question, 1917-1925*, pp. 3-5.

activity, Weizmann considered the Palestinian issue as part of the entire Arab question. He believed that this issue would be solved economically, when the standard of living of Palestine's Arab population improved as a result of the Zionist projects, and politically, outside the country, in the "triangle formed by Damascus, Mecca and Baghdad" – the center of the Arab movement.[275] The position of other Zionist leaders was not very different, for "the individuals who headed the political department of the Zionist Commission considered their primary function to be the establishment of stable relations between the Commission and the British staff."[276] Ussishkin, one of the heads of that department, once said: "There is a Jewish question in the whole world; has the world done anything about it? So what if an Arab question arises [in Palestine]?"[277]

There were, at any rate, a number of factors that prompted the Zionists to take these positions. Their leadership was engaged in negotiations with Britain and other countries to impose the British mandate over Palestine, and then to formulate its instrument in a manner that would ensure the establishment of the Jewish national home in the best and easiest way possible. Meanwhile, the new immigrants of the Third Aliyah quickly found themselves emulating their predecessors of the second, who had openly hostile positions towards the Arabs.[278] The new immigrants preferred, at best, to ignore the "Arab question", and were preoccupied with solving the problems of their own position in Palestine, together with establishing various labor organizations. All the settlers pinned their hopes on Britain to maintain law and order in Palestine and enable them to establish the national home based on what they considered their "rights" under the Balfour Declaration and the extended interpretations that they gave it, as well as the mandate instrument and its articles.

---

275   Ibid; see also Simha Flapan, *Zionism and the Palestinians*, pp. 55-57.
276   Olitsky, *Mi-Pzura le-Medinah (From Dispersal to State)*, Vol. 1, p. 260.
277   Ibid.
278   For details, see Chapter 4, section 6.

Only a short time later, however, it became evident to most Zionist leaders and individuals that their great hopes and optimistic expectations were misplaced. Britain remained committed to its pledge regarding the establishment of the national home, but it reduced the scope of this pledge, announced a policy of "double commitment" towards the Arabs and the Jews and rejected a number of exceptional requests made by the Zionists – especially the suggestions that the country's security forces, whether the garrisons or the police, be comprised of settlers who would be appointed after consultation with the Zionist institutions.[279] The Zionists soon suspected that Britain had "abandoned" them,[280] and that its main concern was to ensure its own position in Palestine by appeasing the Arabs and winning their favor or, at least, their calm. As for the Arabs of Palestine, they declared their strong opposition to the Zionists as soon as the British entered the country. The Arabs began launching periodic armed attacks on the settlers, causing deaths among them, as happened in March and April 1920 in Tel Hai and Jerusalem, and in May and November 1921 in Jaffa, Jerusalem and some Jewish settlements.

In the face of these new conditions, the Zionists gradually began to reconsider their position towards the Arabs. After the events of March 1920, the Jewish Assembly issued an appeal to the Arabs in which it refuted the plans attributed to the settlers of expelling Arabs from their lands, explaining that "the Jews did not come to the country to fight the Arabs, but to work with them"[281] for the benefit of everyone. After the clashes of May 1920 in northern Palestine, the Zionists were forced to broach the issue of their relations with the Arabs – these discussions resulted in blaming the British authorities, however, which had not taken due care to maintain security. The Zionists then

---

279 Caplan, *Palestine Jewry and the Arab Question, 1917-1925*, p. 20.

280 For details, see Dinur, ed., *Sefer Toldot ha-Haganah (History of the Haganah)*, Vol. 1, Part 2, pp. 641-652.

281 *Chronologiah le-Toldot ha-Yishuv ha-Yehudi be-Eretz Yisrael (Chronology of the Jewish Yishuv in the Land of Israel)*, Vol. 1, p. 42.

decided to strengthen the Haganah, their defense battalions,[282] while the Jewish Assembly issued another appeal to the Arabs: "The Land of Israel is our only homeland ... [But] there is space in the country for us and for you, as well."[283] The statement claimed that the settlers intended to come to Palestine "to make its deserts bloom and develop its natural resources ... [through] our energy, knowledge, and material and spiritual forces ... We do not seek war or disputes that only result in harm ... to both parties."[284] This call became a model for others issued by the Zionists after every period of tension in Palestine. The Zionist leadership decided to form a committee to deal with Arab relations,[285] but the decision was not implemented.

The Zionists followed this pacification approach after the May 1920 clashes, moving to implement some of the decisions they had made as they attempted to improve their relations with the Arabs. This amounted to the Zionist Executive deciding to set up a special fund to grant loans and bribes to Arab supporters[286] and create a pro-Zionist Arab party, however. Kalvarisky, who believed that the Arabs were materialistic and could be dealt with on this basis,[287] was quickly able to establish and fund this party, which was called the "Muslim National Associations". It was intended as a counterweight to the anti-Zionist, Muslim-Christian associations that were active at the time. The new party did not last long, however.[288] Attempts were made to establish other such organizations or parties, but most of them

---

282 Caplan, *Palestine Jewry and the Arab Question, 1917-1925*, pp. 61-62.

283 Attias, ed., *Sefer ha-Te'udot shel ha-Va'ad ha-Leumi le-Knesset Yisrael be-Eretz Yisrael (Book of Documents of the National Council of Knesset Israel)*, p. 15.

284 Ibid.

285 Caplan, *Palestine Jewry and the Arab Question, 1917-1925*, pp. 63-64.

286 For details, see ibid, pp. 98-104.

287 Neil Caplan, "Arab-Jewish Contacts in the Land of Israel after the First World War", *Ha-Mizrah ha-Hadash*, Vol. 27, Issues 1-2 (105-106), p. 19.

288 Caplan, *Palestine Jewry and the Arab Question, 1917-1925*, pp. 127-144; see also Eliyahu Eilat, *Shivat Tzion ve Arav (Return to Zion and the Arabs)*, pp. 259-265.

were eventually dissolved or turned against the Zionists.[289]

With the convening of the 12th Zionist Congress in September 1921, the Zionists were still in a spiral of disagreements over their position towards the Arabs. This found clear expression in the speeches of a number of delegates. While some criticized the Zionist leadership for its neglect of the Arab question,[290] Ussishkin declared that the Arabs would not recognize the new reality in Palestine until the number of settlers had risen and they had gained strength.[291] Jabotinsky called for indifference to the Arab opposition, "because America did not obtain the consent of the Red Indians when it settled the whites there, nor did Australia seek the consent of the blacks".[292] A few Zionist leaders were more pragmatic, however. The labor leader, Berl Katznelson, demanded broad autonomy for the Arabs and Jews in Palestine,[293] while Sokolow, chairman of the Zionist Executive, advised the Arabs to seek an agreement with the settlers and live together with them, rather than pinning hopes on the revocation of the Balfour Declaration.[294] Weizmann was clearer in declaring that the Zionists were ready to reach an agreement with the Arabs, but only on the basis of the Balfour Declaration.[295]

At its conclusion, the 12th Zionist Congress took a decision calling for action to reach an agreement with the Arabs, as "a spirit of peace motivates [the Jewish people], and ... it is [their] desire to live together with the Arab people in fraternal peace on this land," in an effort towards the "revival and uplifting" of Palestine – for "our good, for yours, and for the good of the

---

289 Details in Caplan, "Arab-Jewish Contacts in the Land of Israel after the First World War", pp. 24-30.

290 See, for example, the speech of Isaac Leib Goldberg, in Haaretz, 27/9/1921, and of David Yellin, in ibid, 6/10/1921.

291 In Menachem Ussishkin's speech, ibid, 28/9/1921.

292 In Ze'ev Jabotinsky's speech, ibid, 26/9/1921.

293 In Berl Katznelson's speech, ibid, 25/9/1921.

294 In Nahum Sokolow's speech, ibid, 19/9/1921.

295 In Chaim Weizmann's speech, ibid, 16/9/1921.

whole country".²⁹⁶ Some Zionists attempted to interpret this decision as a recognition of the national rights of the Palestinian people, but it soon became evident that it was only intended to present a moderate Zionist stance to Britain so that it would remain committed to accepting its mandate over Palestine.²⁹⁷ The high commissioner, Samuel, had urged the Zionists to take such a decision,²⁹⁸ which ultimately had no impact on the Zionist position towards the Palestinians.

The issue of establishing relations with the Palestinian Arabs was also not subject to the will of the Zionists alone – notwithstanding that they had nothing to offer the Arabs to encourage them to establish relations with them. The Zionist movement was not in a position of strength to take political stances independently of the British. The latter, as their actions showed, were not interested in any Arab-Jewish concord but were instead content to exploit the conflict to their advantage (Weizmann, himself, was well aware of this fact).²⁹⁹ The British worked, on more than one occasion, to thwart any Jewish-Arab contacts. During 1919 and 1920, for example, the Zionists did everything in their power to strengthen their relationship with Faisal and made various proposals to him, including the formation of an alliance and mutual "diplomatic representation" between the two sides. Weizmann even assigned a representative to Faisal's court in Damascus, who remained there from September 1919 until July 1920.³⁰⁰ The British, however, who knew of these attempts, were reluctant to give their consent and

---

296 Olitsky, *Mi-Pzura le-Medinah (From Dispersal to State)*, Vol. 1, p. 310; see also Caplan, *Palestine Jewry and the Arab Question, 1917-1925*, p. 15.

297 Caplan, *Palestine Jewry and the Arab Question, 1917-1925*, pp. 115-116; Ben Halpern, *The Idea of the Jewish State*, p. 337.

298 Neil Caplan, *Futile Diplomacy*, Vol. 1: *Early Arab-Zionist Negotiation Attempts, 1913-1931*, p. 114; Martin Buber, *A Land of Two Peoples, Martin Buber on Jews and Arabs* (Paul Mendes-Flohr, ed.), p. 62.

299 Friesel, *Ha-Mediniout ha-Tzionit le-ahar Hatzharat Balfour, 1917-1922 (Zionist Policy after the Balfour Declaration, 1917-1922)*, p. 296.

300 For details, see Nakdimon Rogel, "Weizmann's Man in Damascus: Dr. Shlomo Felman's Mission to Faisal's Court, September 1919 – July 1920", in Carpi, ed., *Ha-Tzionout (Zionism)*, Vol. 8, pp. 279-353.

finally instructed the Zionists to desist from them.[301]

In early 1922, contacts and negotiations took place between representatives of the Zionist Organization and some Arab leaders, including Riad al-Solh and Fares al-Khoury, in Cairo and Geneva. Again, these contacts ceased when the British found out about them.[302] In late 1922, Abdullah, the emir of Transjordan, visited London to hold talks with the British government. While there, he met with Weizmann five times. During those meetings, Abdullah tried to get a sense of the Zionist Organization's position on a proposal he had submitted, that was for the organization to recognize him as the emir of Palestine in addition to Transjordan in return for his pledge to facilitate the establishment of the national home in both these regions. This proposal was met with enthusiasm by most of the Zionist administration, and even the intransigent Jabotinsky agreed to it. The British, however, opposed it.[303] (Abdullah kept his aspiration to become the emir of Palestine and subsequently tried[304] to escape the grip of the British and work to achieve his dream. All his attempts failed, however, until the Arab-Israeli war broke out in 1948 and new opportunities arose for him.)

In the face of this British opposition, as well as the difficulty or unwillingness to reach an agreement with the Arabs for fear of the restrictions that may be imposed on Zionist activity in Palestine, the Zionists stopped making any new attempts to reconcile with the Arabs. By late 1923, after calm had been restored to the country, the Zionists almost forgot about the Arabs and were busy organizing their own affairs.

One of the main lessons that the settlers learned from the

---

301 For details, see Meir Werte, "Zionist-Arab Negotiations in Spring 1919 and British Policy", *Tzion*, Vol. 32, pp. 75-115.

302 See Cohen, A., *Yisrael ve ha-Olam ha-Aravi (Israel and the Arab World)*, pp. 177-183; Olitsky, *Mi-Pzura le-Medinah (From Dispersal to State)*, Vol. 1, pp. 310-314.

303 Cohen, A., *Yisrael ve ha-Olam ha-Aravi (Israel and the Arab World)*, p. 184.

304 Olitsky, *Mi-Pzura le-Medinah (From Dispersal to State)*, Vol. 1, pp. 429-435; Caplan, *Palestine Jewry and the Arab Question, 1917-1925*, pp. 62-64, 104-120; Frederich Hermann Kisch, *Palestine Diary*, p. 36.

clashes between them and the Arabs in Palestine in the early 1920s, and the British authorities' inability to prevent them, was the necessity of self-reliance and the establishment of a Jewish military organization that would handle defense affairs (haganah) for all the Zionist settlers.[305] The Hashomer men began to set up "defense committees" for the Jews across Palestine, and sought to enlarge their ranks by accepting new volunteers. Hashomer decided to hold an extensive congress to discuss the means of organizing defense affairs. Sharp disagreements arose at the congress, however, which was held in the settlement of Tel Adashim on May 18, 1920. Eventually, a decision was made to dissolve Hashomer and establish a "national, non-partisan and secret organization" in its place, "to assume defense affairs of the entire Yishuv, in towns and villages",[306] such that the members of Hashomer would implement this, in agreement with the Ahdut ha-Avoda party.

Shortly after Hashomer's decision, the first congress of Ahdut ha-Avoda was held during June 13-15, 1920, a few months after its founding. The party thanked Hashomer for the trust it had given it, and decided "through its sense of the historical importance and responsibility, to respond to the initiative imposed on it by the Hashomer organization regarding the arrangement of defense affairs, organizing workers' contributions to the defense system, and securing the national and social content of a popular Haganah in the country".[307] The congress also decided to oblige party members to comply with the instructions of the Haganah committees when they were established in their areas. Hashomer was charged with establishing the "Haganah Organization", provided that it was "established in such a way as to be under the monitoring of its participants, and seeks to accept among its ranks every person suitable for carrying out defense work, who agrees to carry this burden".[308] With this

---

305 See Chapter 4, section 5; Chapter 5, section 2.

306 Ben-Zvi, ed., *Sefer Hashomer (Book of Hashomer)*, p. 57.

307 Ibid.

308 Ibid.

decision, Ahdut ha-Avoda formed a five-member committee to implement it, including three former Hashomer members: Israel Shochat (1886-1961), Yosef Nachmani (1891-1965), and Issachar Sitkov, and two demobilized Jewish battalion soldiers, Eliyahu Golomb (1893-1945) and Dov Hoz (1894-1940). A dispute broke out among the committee members over the manner of organization and method of work of the Haganah, and prevented any progress. Hashomer's men, as "experts" in security matters, insisted on being given the freedom to establish the organization as they saw fit, without "interference in their affairs", such that an independent organization would finally be formed. Golomb and Hoz fiercely opposed this, declaring that a military force such as the Haganah had to be subject to the control of approved, democratically elected institutions. Thus, "it is the right and duty of the organized Yishuv to oversee each step taken by the Haganah, which should be the force defending [public] safety and security."[309] The position of Golomb and Hoz gained the support of Ahdut ha-Avoda, which demanded, as the largest Zionist party, the supervision of any military organization to be established by the Jewish settlers.[310] At the founding of the Histadrut, Ahdut ha-Avoda was eager to urge the adoption of a resolution to this effect for the "organization of security and defense affairs" (see section 5 of this chapter), despite the opposition of Hapoel Hatzair. The decision was in the Histadrut's capacity as the institution that represented the Jewish workers in Palestine and included most of them in its ranks, and therefore also had to supervise their security affairs and those of all the settlers. The Histadrut remained, at least officially, responsible for the affairs of the Haganah until 1929.

Despite these decisions, however, it was not easy for the Histadrut to implement the "organization of security and defense affairs", even with the support of Ahdut ha-Avoda. This was due to the disagreements among Zionist circles in Palestine over the

---

309 Dinur, ed., *Sefer Toldot ha-Haganah (History of the Haganah)*, Vol. 2, Part 1, p. 65.

310 Dinur, ed., *Sefer Toldot ha-Haganah (History of the Haganah)*, Vol. 1, Part 2, pp. 654-656.

essence and function of the Haganah, or even the feasibility of its establishment. In addition to the disagreements that erupted between the Hashomer group, led by Shochat, and the men of the "organized Yishuv", led by Golomb, on the concept of each regarding the Haganah, other Zionist groups announced their reservation or opposition to the establishment of any military force. The Hapoel Hatzair party, which was influenced by the teachings of Gordon and his "religion of labor",[311] had peaceful leanings that preferred the workers not to approach the question of security and the establishment of military forces, because such acts were essentially within the competence of the mandate authorities. This faction within Hapoel Hatzair retained this position for a long time and formed – even after the union of its party with Ahdut ha-Avoda and the establishment of Mapai in 1930 – what came to be known as the "doves" wing within the new party.[312] The agricultural workers in the old settlements, the "moshavot"[313], also declared their dissatisfaction with the attempts of the left wing to establish a military force, fearing that such a force would be used in future to control them[314] and force them to apply the rules of "Hebrew labor". A third current also appeared, led by Jabotinsky, which opposed the engagement of "amateur" workers in the establishment of secret military organizations. It demanded, instead, the formation of a public Jewish military force to assume the functions of maintaining law and order in Palestine with the consent of the mandate authorities.

These opposition circles were also joined, in time, by the presidency of the Zionist Organization, which feared that the labor wing would put pressure on it after creating a military force. In mid-1920, David Eder, head of the political department

---

311 See Chapter 4, section 6.

312 Uri Milstein, *Be-Dam ve Esh, Yehuda: Tsmihata shel ha-Otzma ha-Yisraelit (By Blood and Fire, Judea: Growth of Israeli Power)*, pp. 47-48.

313 Plural of "moshavah".

314 Dinur, ed., *Sefer Toldot ha-Haganah (History of the Haganah)*, Vol. 2, Part 1, p. 18.

of the Zionist Commission, was quick to warn Weizmann that

> all these organizations [the Haganah committees] are ready to be used as political tools, to impose certain partisan programs... I, as you know, sympathize with the labor movement, but I do not like leaders to impose their demands through a force, which they claim to be military, standing behind them. Samuel will take the necessary measures to maintain the security of the Jewish settlements in Palestine. And with more confidence in the new government, we can count on its permanent forces, then gradually dissolve the Haganah committees.[315]

However, the presidency of the Zionist Organization was unable to dissolve these committees. This made the disagreements between it and the Haganah more complex, especially after the latter refused to respond to the request of the British authorities to end its activity – a request that the Zionist Organization supported. Thus, in late 1922, the Zionist administration decided to stop the financial and political assistance that it was granting the Haganah.[316]

Due to this opposition, and the differing positions on the Haganah, its activity ebbed and flowed, rising when tension rose between the Arabs and the Jews, then returning to its internal and external disputes when the situation calmed down. The first organizational steps it took during this period were to elect Haganah committees in most Jewish areas, especially after the May 1921 clashes, then to appoint leaders in the major cities in 1922. The Haganah also launched some training courses during this period, purchased quantities of weapons from Vienna, including machine guns, and transported them to Palestine via the port of Beirut. With security and calm prevailing in Palestine, however, the disputes returned and the Haganah split up into

---

315 Dinur, ed., *Sefer Toldot ha-Haganah (History of the Haganah)*, Vol. 2, Part 2, p. 640.

316 Dinur, ed., *Sefer Toldot ha-Haganah (History of the Haganah)*, Vol. 2, Part 1, p. 163.

two parts in late 1922, before it had completed establishing its organizational structure: the Shochat group and the Golomb group. It then fell into inactivity for seven years, until the Al-Buraq Uprising in 1929.[317]

Until then, a situation of calm prevailed in Palestine while the Zionists were busy building their national home and strengthening its foundations.

---

317 Details in ibid, pp. 119, 129-130, 144-150, 164.

Conclusion: Zionism in the Service of Colonialism

1

Only a quarter century after the founding of its organization in 1897, the Zionist movement was able, at least in theory, to achieve its main goal: obtaining the recognition of the major European powers – the victors in the First World War – of its right to establish a "national home" for the Jews in Palestine. This was realized in the Balfour Declaration (1917), followed by the imposition of a British mandate over Palestine, in which Britain made a commitment for the establishment of this home, with the approval of all the Allied countries.

In an attempt to justify this policy, it was alleged that it was based on recognition of the "historic relationship" between the Jewish people and Palestine. This was, however, only a form of European colonial deceit, as Christian Europe had never recognized the rights of the Jewish people either in Palestine or elsewhere. Rather, it had persecuted them over many centuries and in various ways – considering them responsible for the crucifixion of Christ and for not accepting his message. Moreover, talk of this relationship was no more than a myth with no historical backing. For 18 consecutive centuries – from the defeat of the Jews in their war with the Romans, which ended after the fall of Jerusalem and the destruction of the Temple in 73 A.D., until the emergence of the first buds of the Zionist movement during the second half of the 19th century – no Jewish group in the world had made any attempt to revive a Jewish political entity in Palestine. For thousands of years, the Jewish presence in Palestine was limited to two specific periods, neither of which exceeded 80 years. More than a dozen nations and peoples passed through, lived in or ruled the country, including the ancient Egyptians, Canaanites, Israelites, Assyrians, Babylonians, Achaemenids, ancient Greeks, Romans, Parthians, Sasanians, Byzantines and Arabs. The Jewish people were not the only ones among them to claim exclusive rights for themselves and no one else.

In truth, the events that transpired during the five years after the First World War, with the issuance of the Balfour Declaration and the subsequent imposition of the British mandate over Palestine, essentially stemmed from a convergence of interests between colonialism and Zionism. Great Britain, the largest colonial power in the world, found in the Zionists a pliable tool that could be exploited to enhance British colonial control over the countries, people and natural resources of the Levant during and after the First World War. The Zionist settlers were very cooperative due to their weakness and need for protection in a hostile environment, which left them with limited options to pursue independent policies or to rebel against their British benefactors. The Zionists, and then Israel, fully realized their urgent, permanent need for a superpower that would adopt their positions and protect them when necessary, in exchange for services that they would provide to guarantee Britain's interests and influence in the Levant. The Zionists never forgot this. When it became clear to them, at the end of the Second World War, for example, that Britain's role in supporting and protecting them was nearing its end, they were quick to turn their backs on the imperialist power. Before announcing the establishment of Israel in 1948, they had equally leaned towards the United States and the Soviet Union. By the mid-1950s, however, with the tripartite British-French-Israeli attack on Egypt, the Zionists again moved to align themselves with Britain and France. In the 1967 war, their relationship was with France alone. Finally, in the 1973 war, the Zionists shifted their alignment to the United States – where their loyalty remains to this day.

It must also be noted that these colonial-Zionist measures

and schemes were approved, in one way or another, by all the European colonial countries, though the implementation was with Britain. Those plans were carried out without moral qualms or a prick of conscience (on the assumption that colonialism had morals or a conscience). The mandate system, which was devised by the victorious colonial powers in the First World War and adopted by the League of Nations, was an odd, hybrid invention aimed, primarily, to secure the interests of the superpowers at the expense of the vulnerable peoples of the colonies, and even to put a humanitarian face on colonialism. In Palestine, the mandate was a blatant assault on the country and its Arab population and an open attempt to control them and rob them of their homeland. Egyptian president Gamal Abdel Nasser gave a fitting description of Britain's promises to the Zionists: "He who does not own has made a promise to him who does not deserve."[1]

As well as having no moral justification, the national home had no practical basis. When it was decided to implement it, the Jewish settlers constituted a tiny minority and owned an equally small area of land in Palestine. Britain facilitated the entry of Jewish immigrants and turned a blind eye to their purchase of land, especially from Arab feudal lords, and the establishment of Jewish settlements. All forms of Palestinian resistance failed in dissuading the British from this policy. The mandate authorities also sought to grant a form of autonomy to the Jewish settlers by enacting special laws for local authorities – whether municipalities or local/village councils – and granting them a fair range of powers to manage the affairs of their residents. This facilitated the establishment of a separate, independent Jewish entity and turned it into a state within a state, against the interests of the Arab majority that inhabited Palestine.

Despite these appropriate conditions for the establishment

---

1   Gamal Abdel Nasser, letter to John F. Kennedy, Office of the President, The United Arab Republic, Alexandria, Egypt, August 22, 1961. English translation: John F. Kennedy Presidential Library and Museum.

of the national home, however, the Zionist entity did not grow significantly in Palestine during the first decade of the mandate (1922-1932). The number of Jewish residents rose from about 84,000 (11 percent) of the population in 1922 to 192,000 (18 percent) in 1932, an annual growth rate of less than 1 percent. The reason was the reluctance of the Jewish masses, in general, to accept the escapade of the national home, on the one hand, and the weak economic resources of the Zionist agencies to settle them, on the other. Fate, however, conspired to help the Zionists in a way that had never occurred to them or to anyone else.

In 1933, the Nazis, led by Adolf Hitler, came to power in Germany. This event sparked strong reactions in many countries due to the racist and deadly policies that the Nazis espoused, especially towards Jewish people. Many forces in Europe and the United States, including various Jewish organizations, declared a political war on Germany and demanded its boycott, isolation and restriction. However, not all the Jews or Zionists believed in immediately pursuing such a policy towards Nazi Germany. There were those who wished to exploit the new conditions for the benefit of the Zionist entity in Palestine. In their view, if the Nazis wanted to rid Germany of its Jewish population, then it was prudent to reach an understanding with them to achieve this, taking the necessary measures to direct those Jewish people in exile to Palestine – as Herzl had tried to do with the authorities of tsarist Russia in his day.

Attempts to implement this scheme began by private Jewish agencies in Palestine with no direct relationship to the official Zionist ones. The first to implement it was Hanotea, an agricultural company, whose owners proposed to the German officials, through the German consulate in Jerusalem, to allow Jewish people to immigrate to Palestine after selling their properties in Germany and depositing the proceeds in a German bank. The company would then use those funds to purchase machinery and agricultural products from Germany, and pay those immigrants the equivalent of their deposits in local currency upon their arrival in Palestine. The authors of this scheme suggested that Germany would have its Jewish population exiled, on the one hand, while also acquiring hard currency, which it desperately needed due to the boycott imposed on the country, on the other. In turn, the Jewish company would contribute to the displacement of the Jews to Palestine and reap profits from the sale of the goods that it imported and the commissions it made. This model caught the attention of the official Zionist agencies, which decided to adopt it and conducted direct negotiations with the German authorities in 1933. The scope of cooperation was expanded to include all types of German goods, as well as any Jewish person who wanted to emigrate from Germany, while the German Zionist organization undertook the follow-up of implementation. This agreement was known as the Haavara (transfer, in Hebrew), and a company with that name (Haavara Ltd.) was established in Palestine in August 1933 to oversee the process.

This Zionist-Nazi agreement did not pass quietly, but sparked strong disputes across the Jewish and Zionist communities. The agreement was one of the main reasons that led to the split of the Zionist Organization in the mid-1930s and the establishment of the New Zionist Organization led by the right-wing Revisionists. It is also alleged that the 1933 assassination of Haim Arlosoroff, head of the political department of the Jewish Agency, was because he signed this agreement. The agreement was the subject of discussion in the Zionist congresses held in 1933 and 1935, where the opposition demanded its cancellation, but both congresses rejected the request. This agreement then remained in effect and was actively pursued until the outbreak of the Second World War in 1939.

The Haavara Agreement was of great benefit to the Zionists, in a manner unforeseen to them. It also paved the way for important political events that changed the course of the conflict in Palestine. At the internal Zionist level, the agreement bolstered the Jewish national home, which grew significantly. During 1933-1939, an average of 40,000 immigrants entered

Palestine annually (compared with 15,000 in previous years), raising the Jewish population from 192,000 to 445,000 (a 130 percent increase). By the end of that period, they came to form about a third of the total population, up from 5 percent during the First World War. Those immigrants brought huge sums of capital, amounting, annually, to about half of the budget of the mandate government. This money entered Palestine in the form of various German goods and industrial tools, with which the Zionists were able to establish many economic and industrial projects, such as cement and iron factories, bakeries, wineries, printing presses, irrigation equipment, medical laboratories, construction material suppliers and others. Furthermore, and no less important, dozens of new settlements were built in various parts of Palestine. Using this money, the Zionists also established various public companies, such as the Mekorot water company, which is still in operation. The Haavara model was so successful that it prompted the Zionists to establish a similar company in Poland, which they called Halifin (exchange, in Hebrew). Six other companies of this type were also established among the Jews in various European countries, including Czechoslovakia, Romania, Hungary and Italy.

The arrangements with Nazi Germany formed a very important, even unique, pillar in the development of the Jewish national home in Palestine, and its transformation from a primarily agricultural society into the nucleus of an industrial one capable, with development, of establishing a modern state. In this regard, if Britain was the party that laid the political and legal foundations for the national home, then Nazi Germany was the one that laid its economic and industrial foundations – as both countries played equally important roles in creating the Zionist entity in Palestine for their own ends.[2]

[2] It can also be said that Germany did not serve the Zionists only during the life of Nazism, but after its demise as well. In 1952, an Israeli-German Reparations Agreement was signed, according to which Germany pledged to compensate Israel, as the "heir" of the Jewish people, for the losses that they suffered during the Nazi era. This agreement was important for supporting Israel's economy, just as the Haavara had been for the national home. Germany's multifaceted support for Israel has persisted to this day,

The Nazi-Zionist cooperation in transporting Jewish immigrants and their money from Europe was fateful for the Palestinian Arabs, as the benefits that it provided to the Zionist regime ultimately wreaked disaster on Palestine's indigenous Arab population. The growth of the Jewish national home raised serious fears among the Palestinians, who were certain that if the situation persisted it would not be long before the Jews became the major force in the country and worked to expel its indigenous inhabitants.

The first countermeasure by the Palestinians was to call for a general strike all over Palestine, which began in the spring of 1936 and lasted for about 6 months. This did not achieve any change in Britain's policy, however, and gradually turned into an armed rebellion from 1936-1939, known as the Great Arab Revolt in Palestine. The mandate authorities suppressed this by force, in cooperation with the Zionists, and heavily persecuted and harmed the Palestinians with the habitual measures of colonial suppression. Among the worst results of this campaign was the dismantling of the political leadership of the Palestinians, imprisoning their leaders or forcing them to flee the country, and then eliminating their organizational frameworks. The Palestinians turned into a flock without a shepherd, which impacted their future course of action.

As had repeatedly happened in the history of Palestine, new, objective circumstances – beyond the control of the conflicting parties – played a role in ending this revolt. By the end of the 1930s, conditions had worsened in Europe as the tension with the Nazi regime increased, and it seemed that a new global conflict was imminent. Faced with such existential challenges and expecting a fierce war to break out at any moment, "Perfidious Albion"[3] could no longer continue to antagonize the

---

driven by the guilt complex of Nazism.

3 "Perfidious Albion" is a pejorative phrase used within the context of international relations diplomacy to refer to acts of diplomatic slights, duplicity, treachery and hence infidelity (with respect to perceived promises made to or alliances formed with other nation states) by monarchs or governments of the United Kingdom (or Great Britain prior to 1801, or England

Arabs of Palestine and the neighboring countries sympathetic to them. Britain had to appease them and gain their silence and calm, as well as prevent them from joining the hostile camp, in order to devote itself to its war effort. Thus, after all attempts to reach a Jewish-Arab agreement in Palestine had failed, including a proposal to divide the country that no one accepted, the British decided to adopt their own, independent policy to preserve what they considered their vital interests. In 1939, they published a white paper in which they announced that they would impose severe restrictions on Jewish immigration to Palestine, allowing no more than 5,000 new immigrants to enter the country every year for the next 10 years. They also imposed restrictions on the purchase of land by settlers and the establishment of settlements. The Zionists protested these restrictions vehemently, but did not take any significant actions against them. In the war on Nazi Germany and its anti-Jewish policies, the Zionists had no choice but to cooperate with Britain in order to preserve their existence and wait for relief at the end of the war. During the war years, the Zionist leadership was particularly active in organizing campaigns for Jewish youth to volunteer for military service alongside the British. Hundreds of them received training, so that they became, with their demobilization after the end of the war in 1945, the nucleus of the Jewish, then the Israeli, forces that fought the 1948 war against the Arabs.

With the end of the Second World War, it was apparent to the Zionists and to others that the Balfour Declaration had become history, especially after the war had "reduced" the status of Britain and France to second-class powers. The Americans and Soviets began to dominate the global scene and to emerge as the new power centers. At this juncture, the Zionists resumed their old policy, originally laid by Herzl himself, in searching for a new superpower to ally with – and take orders from, when necessary – so that it would adopt their project and help them

---

prior to 1707) in their pursuit of self-interest.

"Perfidious" means not keeping one's faith or word (from the Latin word, "perfidia"), while "Albion" is an ancient and now poetic name for Great Britain.

to finish implementing it. This time they found two powers, not one.

As the war was nearing its end, and it became clear that victory over Nazi Germany was only a matter of time, discussion began between the Allies as a prelude to rearranging the global situation after the war. As had happened at the end of the First World War, this stage witnessed the tension and pull of alliances with overlapping and contradicting interests and, again, the Zionists had their say. This time, they publicly called for the liberation of Palestine from the British and the establishment of a Jewish state.

The two superpowers that emerged after the war, the United States and the Soviet Union, were not very sympathetic to Britain or concerned with allowing it to continue its control of its colonies. Thus, the Zionist calls found reception among those powers. Neither of them objected, at least in principle, to establishing a Jewish state in the heart of the Levant, which could help them, in exchange for their adoption of it, to expand their power and influence in the region. Their initial acceptance of the Zionist proposals grew, after further contact with the Zionists, into clear support for the Jewish state project. During the United Nations' deliberations that led to the decision to partition Palestine into two states in 1947, one Arab and one Jewish, the Americans and Soviets were competing to mobilize the greatest support for the plan. The Soviet delegate, Andrei Gromyko (later the foreign minister of the Soviet Union and chairman of the presidium of the Supreme Soviet), gave a resonant speech during those deliberations in support of Zionist demands that would put the most hardline Zionists to shame.

With this overconfidence, the Zionists stoked the competition between the Americans and the Soviets over which of them would be the first to recognize the Jewish state. The Americans were the first, as US president Truman announced his country's recognition of Israel seven minutes after the announcement of its establishment on the evening of May 14, 1948, while the Soviets did not make their announcement until the next day.

Against this background, the newly established Israel practically enjoyed two new Balfour Declarations, one American and the other Soviet. The Soviets had supplied it with arms in the final stage of the 1948 war, through Czechoslovakia (as they later did with Egypt, under Nasser, in the mid-1950s).[4] This support, together with the internal Zionist strength, contributed to Israel's establishment. The Zionists had finalized their plans for war in Palestine, to seize the territory that might be allocated to them in the event of a decision to partition it, by approving what they called "Plan Dalet" (D, in Hebrew), set down in 1946. This plan stipulated controlling the Arab villages and towns located in the area designated for the Jewish state, and expelling the Arabs before demolishing their villages so that no one could return. In the territory that Israel came to control after the war – roughly three-quarters of Mandatory Palestine – about 350 Palestinian towns and villages were destroyed in this way. The sites that were suitable for Zionist settlement were taken over, and those that were not were planted with forests or turned into public parks to completely eradicate them from history. The Palestinians of those areas, who were estimated at 700,000 and constituted about half of the population of Palestine, were turned into refugees in neighboring Arab countries, in a gross humanitarian disaster.

Through this act, Israel imitated the white colonialists of Europe who destroyed, for example, the indigenous peoples of North and South America, Australia, New Zealand and other countries that they came to occupy. The Israelis were short of luck, however, as conditions were not favorable and, as the last colonial movement in the world, they had missed the boat. Today, decades after the Nakba, and after more than 150 years of Zionist activity, the indigenous Palestinian Arabs still constitute about half of the population between the river and the sea. Indeed, in a decade, the number of Palestinians worldwide is likely to surpass the number of Jewish people. The Palestinians' adherence to

---

4   This reflected a change in stance of the Soviet Union towards Israel by that time (see Section 2 of this chapter).

their rights has never diminished. Their young generations recall history, are hostile to Israel and demand justice. It is not known when this chapter will come to an end – but the indigenous people have not forgotten their rights and will not give them up.

2

The 1948 war, and the Nakba that afflicted the Palestinians, ended with the imposition of armistice agreements on the Arab countries neighboring Israel and made it an almost clearly defined state. The seven Arab countries that participated in the war had no alternative, as most of them had entered the war in an uncoordinated and improvised manner. The total number of fighters sent by all those countries to Palestine was less than the Jewish soldiers they faced. In addition, all of those countries, except for Jordan, went into war without a specific goal. Jordan had other designs. It aimed to annex that part of Palestine allocated to the Arabs to its own lands, an idea that had been proposed by the British in the late 1930s. With the United Nations' Partition Plan for Palestine in 1947, those ambitions resurfaced, leading to secret Zionist-Jordanian negotiations. The Jewish Agency agreed to hand the part of Palestine allocated to the Arabs to Jordan, in return for its refraining from attacking settlers in the areas allocated to them. In 1950, Jordan annexed the eastern part of Palestine (known since as the "West Bank") and considered it part of its kingdom (in 1951, a group of Palestinian activists plotted the assassination of King Abdullah of Jordan in response to these policies). This relationship with the West Bank persisted until 1988, a year after the outbreak of the First Intifada, when Jordan decided to disengage from the territory – transferring responsibility for it to the Palestine Liberation Organization (PLO).

In its early years, Israel was the spoiled child of the Americans and the Soviets, while it made sure to keep its distance from both. This situation changed, however, in the early 1950s, after the escalation of the Cold War between the two camps, which had led, among other things, to the outbreak of the Korean War

Conclusion 533

in 1950. Israel could no longer remain neutral towards the two countries, and had to take a stance in support of either camp. Ben Gurion, the Israeli prime minister, chose to side with the United States and declare his support for it. This led to strained relations with the Soviet Union and its followers, which persisted until its overthrow in the early 1990s.

It seemed that Israel, though, even after becoming a state recognized by the United Nations and many peoples of the world, was unable to abandon the international support that marked its Balfour Declaration mindset, which called for an alliance with at least one superpower whose support could be counted on. In fact, the Israeli state almost lost its senses and behaved erratically each time it felt that it stood alone. In the first half of the 1950s, for example, the United States sought to establish an alliance of Arab and Islamic countries (later, the Baghdad Pact) in the Middle East to contain the communist threat. The Arab countries nominated to join this alliance, led by Iraq, did not agree to accept Israel as a member. The US administration, under Eisenhower and his secretary of state, John Foster Dulles, did not give Israel much weight and, in the face of the Arab opposition, decided to keep it out of the proposed alliance. Israel then sought to reaffirm its place in global politics. In preparation for the establishment of this alliance of Arab countries, Britain's withdrawal from the Suez Canal was raised – a development that was not favored by Israel as it would give the Egyptians complete freedom of movement in their country. To thwart these plans, the Israelis instructed their spies in Egypt to set off explosives in some public places in the country, to show that the Egyptian regime under Nasser was weak and lacked control and that, therefore, the British should not conclude any agreements with it. The result was that the Egyptian authorities arrested those that had conducted the sabotage and executed two of them. This escapade was later revealed in Israel and came to be known as the "shameful case", with repercussions that nearly shook the foundations of the Israeli system.

However, fate would not shun Israel for long. During the

mid-1950s, when those efforts were being made to establish pro-Western military alliances in the Levant, a revolution erupted in Algeria against the French colonization of the country. Nasser immediately assisted the revolution with money and arms, openly and without reservation. This angered the French who, at the time, did not consider Algeria a colony but rather a part of France. In addition, Nasser had pursued a policy of positive neutrality in an attempt to maintain the same distance from the two world camps. As a result, the West turned hostile to him and he was subjected to a blockade of money and arms. Western countries stopped selling arms to Egypt, and the World Bank retracted a pledge to contribute to the construction of the High Dam in Aswan. Nasser responded by nationalizing the Suez Canal Company in the summer of 1956.

The West saw this as a dangerous challenge that necessitated a response. A plan was then put together between Israel and France, quickly joined by Britain, to launch a war against Egypt and overthrow Nasser. Israel was to attack Egyptian territory in the Sinai, giving Britain and France a pretext to send their forces to break up the warring parties and safeguard the proper functioning of the Suez Canal. This plan was carried out in late October 1956, and became known as the Tripartite Aggression on Egypt. Israel attacked the Sinai and occupied large parts of it, in addition to the Gaza Strip, while French and British air forces bombed Port Said as their fleets tried to storm the Suez Canal. Things did not go as they wished, however. This aggression drew the ire of the Soviet Union, which had good relations with Egypt. It came strongly to its defense, issuing a public warning for the aggressors to cease, or it would militarily intervene – possibly targeting London and Paris with ballistic missiles. There were also reports of preparations to land Soviet forces in Egypt to fight alongside its army. This decisive intervention repelled the aggressors, especially after the United States also expressed its opposition to the escapade. The military campaign against Egypt stopped, and all of the invading forces – including the Israelis – withdrew after a period of time.

Despite the failure of the Tripartite Aggression, it had far-reaching effects both regionally and globally. Britain finally realized that it had become a second-class power, and later announced that it would shut down all of its bases east of the Suez (which ultimately paved the way for the Americans to take its place). Britain also distanced itself from Israel. France, conversely, strengthened its relations with Israel and entered into multiple agreements with it. It supported it militarily and began to sell it all the modern arms that it needed, on the basis of the two countries' hostility to the Arabs and their endeavor to break the thorn of Egypt, on the one hand, and to preserve French colonial control over Algeria, on the other.

The French-Israeli areas of cooperation expanded during the second half of the 1950s and became almost comprehensive, to the point where it seemed as if the old Balfour had changed his nationality and become French. The alliance only faded and signs of divergence began to appear in the early 1960s, when the French decided to recognize the independence of Algeria and withdraw from the country. French-Israeli relations then gradually waned, as France turned its back on its previous colonial policy and withdrew from many of its areas of influence in Africa, recognizing their independence. With the outbreak of the 1967 war (known as the Naksa, or Setback), those relations turned into clear estrangement when France imposed an embargo on arms exports to Israel – considering it to be the aggressor in the war.

Despite the end of the French role of Israel's "Balfour", the French cooperation with Israel had by then majorly supported its military force, notably in the 1967 war. Israel triumphed over three Arab armies and occupied large territories of Egypt and Syria, along with what was left of Palestine (the West Bank and Gaza Strip), creating a new situation in the Arab world that has persisted for almost 60 years.

With the end of the 1967 war, Israel entered a state of narcissism, arrogance and belittling of others to the point where it almost seemed as if it no longer needed any new Balfour and could manage its affairs alone, without protection or coordination with any superpower. In its mania, however, Israel paid no heed to the irony of its victory. In its occupation of the remaining Palestinian territory that had been outside its rule, Israel had unified all of Palestine into a single entity – even if this was under a system of occupation. Before long, the Palestinian cause re-united all of its elements, which it had had before the founding of Israel, and gradually imposed itself as an independent factor with its own weight in regional and international politics. Thus Zionism returned to square one, after all its efforts to obliterate the Palestinians had failed. At some point, sooner or later, and whether it wishes to or not, Zionism will have to accept its responsibility in solving the Palestinian problem.

After the 1967 war, with the intransigence that overtook Israel, it continued to despise the Arabs and to belittle any opinion or proposal from the United Nations or any individual state to solve the problems caused by that war or seek peace between the countries of the region. In particular, Israel rejected any proposals related to the Palestinian problem, which it did not acknowledge as existing in the first place.

Israel remained in this state until the outbreak of the next war in October 1973, which took it by surprise and nearly toppled its balance. On the eve of that war, Israel had reached a degree of arrogance through which it had convinced itself that no Arab country would dare to attack it and, even if it did, it would face destruction. This war and its results shook Israel to the core. The Egyptian army managed to destroy the fortifications of the Bar Lev Line on the eastern bank of the Suez Canal, and Egyptian armored forces crossed into the Sinai within six hours of the outbreak of the fighting (which is why some dubbed this the "Six-Hour War", as opposed to the "Six-Day War" in 1967). About 2,700 Israelis were killed.

The war lasted for about two weeks but, well before its end, it had turned into a political one. While the fighting was ongoing, Egyptian president Anwar Sadat called for a peace conference in Geneva to solve the problems between Israel and the Arabs and lay the foundations for peace in the region. At this juncture, Israel again felt the need for a new Balfour – this time, it was American. The United States had mobilized to help it during the war and had set up an air bridge to supply it with large quantities of new ammunition when the Israeli army's arsenal was about to run out. This act demonstrated a strong and renewed American presence in the region, as evidenced in the negotiations after the war.

The United States was dominant in these negotiations, which ended in 1979 with a separate Egypt-Israel peace treaty. Egypt overlooked the interests of the larger Arab world and abandoned the Palestinian cause. Sadat also broke with the policy of neutrality followed by Nasser and aligned Egypt with the United States, submitting to its policy – a position that has persisted for about half a century.

Since then, Israel has been protected in the shadow of the American Balfour – doing everything in its power to coordinate with the Americans and not inconvenience or disagree with them in any substantial way. Israel markets itself as one of their greatest, strongest allies in the Middle East and the most committed to their interests. It is also assisted by the Israel lobby in the United States, which wields powerful influence. Israel has remarkably succeeded in this endeavor, with the United States pouring unprecedented amounts of military and other aid into the country. Some American circles have even called for Israel to be made as strong as all of the Arab states combined.

Despite this commitment and assistance, however, Israel does not seem willing to put all its eggs in the American basket, for fear that the United States would abandon it as France once did. Thus, in addition to preserving its relations with the Americans, Israel is trying to build bridges with other powers, including Russia, China and India. It has established a fair level of cooperation and joint interests with each of them.

Balfour died long ago, and his declaration became history. Yet, the Balfour psyche still dominates Zionist thought and activity, in terms of building alliances and working within the framework of mutual interests, to the benefit of the Zionists.

3

The goal of Zionism, which originated mainly among the Jews of Russia and eastern Europe, was to establish a Jewish state in Palestine and use the Jewish population of those areas to settle and populate it. With the establishment of Israel in 1948, however, three years after the end of the Second World War, there were not enough Jewish masses left in Europe who could form the nucleus of a new state as millions of them had been killed in the Holocaust. This situation constituted a real crisis for the leadership of the emerging Jewish state; the lands of Palestine, which Israel had seized after expelling their Arab inhabitants, needed masses of people to settle, control and exploit them, and to prevent Palestinian refugees from returning to their homes and properties.

In the face of this challenge, the Israeli leadership, which was overwhelmingly made up of Western Ashkenazi Jews, found no choice but to turn to the countries of the East, especially the Arab ones, and work to displace their Jewish populations to Israel – even though it felt no great respect or love for them. The necessity of the Zionist cause, however, forced them to undertake this plan.

At the same time, most Arab Jews were not fans of Ashkenazi Zionism and did not believe in its doctrine, complexes and myths. From the emergence of Zionism until the establishment of Israel, only a very small minority of them had immigrated to Palestine. The Jewish population in the Arab world, and in the Islamic countries in Asia and Africa, was never subjected to the kinds of pogroms and attacks that their brethren endured in Europe, as the Western Christian concept of anti-Semitism was not widespread among the Arabs or Muslims. Thus, most of the Arab Jews felt no great need to immigrate to the Jewish Ashkenazi state and live under a system of government that was not necessarily friendly to them.

In the face of these uncomfortable, and even hostile,

conditions for the Zionist project, the Israeli leadership did not hesitate to use devious means to ensure the displacement of those Jewish populations to Palestine. During the first years of Israel's establishment, its envoys paid bribes or bestowed benefits on the relevant authorities in various Arab countries to push their Jewish populations to immigrate to Israel. In Iraq, for example, when its Jews did not respond to these calls, the Israeli immigration agencies organized an operation to throw a bomb at a synagogue in Baghdad, to intimidate them and force them to leave. The agencies then concluded an agreement with the Iraqi authorities that suddenly led to revoking the Iraqi citizenship of Jewish people in the country, in exchange for a sum of money paid for each head. In the end, direct flights were organized from Baghdad airport to Israel to transport those immigrants. This activity, which was mainly concentrated in Iraq, Yemen, Morocco and other Arab countries, led to the displacement of about 600,000 Jews from these countries to Israel by the mid-1950s.

On their arrival, the new immigrants were not received with flowers, however. The Ashkenazi Zionist institution that had imported them was not much interested in improving the conditions of its Eastern Jewish brethren but, rather, in exploiting them to strengthen Zionist colonization in the areas that it had occupied in Palestine. Thus it distributed those Arab Jewish people throughout Israel without concern for their wishes or ambitions. It forced them to live in areas that it specified and worked hard to civilize them in its eyes, imposing certain cultural and social norms to "cleanse" them of their previous Arab lifestyle and give them what the settlers saw as the civilization of eastern European Jews. Those efforts destroyed the collective identity of the new immigrants and pushed them to abandon the values and concepts that they knew, while failing to give them the bases of this Ashkenazi Zionist "civilization". In so doing, this created a human mass out of them with no specific civilizational or cultural character.

This distorted education, which was imposed on the Arab Jews, had harmful long-term effects on the political and social conditions in Israel, especially after the number of those Jews grew to about two-thirds of its population. Firstly, they developed deep feelings of hatred towards the Ashkenazi establishment that was essentially affiliated with the Zionist left-wing labor movement, and they began to turn to the right-wing forces and parties until they became the majority and brought them, in the end, to power in Israel. Secondly, they came to hate the Arabs as well, on the grounds that one could not be an Israeli Zionist patriot without doing so – a great irony for this bloc of Jews that had an Arab history and lifestyle, even if they were influenced by new Ashkenazi traditions.

It is notable that the settlers from the East, despite their numerical majority, did not produce a single prime minister or significant leader in Israel. The same applies to the small groups of races, ethnicities, religions, colors and sects that the Zionist regime imported into the country, aiming to fuse them into a single entity and create a natural or normal people out of them. This experiment did not achieve great success. In a 2015 speech, Reuven Rivlin, the former president of Israel, described its society as consisting of four main "tribes": the secularists, the national religious (who are the most racist), the ultra-Orthodox haredim, and the Palestinian Arabs.

The foolish policies and persecution measures against the settlers from the East were not much different from those followed towards this last sector: the Palestinian Arabs, who had remained in Israel and become its citizens, at least officially, and eventually came to form about a fifth of its population. Since the establishment of the state, it had subjected its remaining Palestinian inhabitants to a systematic policy of repression, by imposing military rule over them, restricting their movement, seizing large areas of their land and harming their livelihood – similarly to what Jewish people had endured in tsarist Russia. With time, the harsh persecution measures faded, to be replaced by a policy of soft discrimination across various spheres. This policy, in turn, eventually began to wane, and at times it seemed that it would end – until it finally became evident that Zionist racism never disappears, it simply changes form. The most recent

Conclusion 541

form of this racism was to enact the Israeli Nation-State Law of 2018 (by a majority of 62 against 55 votes in parliament). This law, in some of its provisions, was almost shamelessly similar to the Nazi Nuremberg Laws (1935) that were enacted against the Jewish population of Germany. The law, for example, prohibited the establishment of new villages or towns for the Palestinian citizens of Israel, regardless of their increasing population. It also attacked the status of the Arabic language and attempted to downgrade it.

In truth, those racist attitudes towards the Palestinians in Israel are only an extension of the Zionist position towards the Palestinian people as a whole, as the settlers attempt to fragment it and replace it with themselves. The Palestinian-Zionist conflict has raged for more than a century, during which many proposals were made to resolve it, to no avail. One suggestion was to divide Palestine into two states, Jewish and Arab. This idea was first proposed by Britain, in its search for solutions during the Great Arab Revolt in Palestine (1936-1939). The idea was again raised about 10 years later, when the United Nations adopted it and issued its Partition Plan in 1947. The Palestinian Arabs rejected this plan that aimed to take half their country and hand it over to settlers, while the Jews accepted it and proceeded to take control of the portion of the country that was allocated to them – as well as about 40% of the portion that was allocated to the Palestinian state.

About half a century after the establishment of Israel, the idea of division returned and was put into effect with the signing of the Oslo Accords in 1993 between the PLO and Israel, after the two parties recognized one another. The Palestinian Authority was then established. This was intended to continue negotiations with Israel until a final agreement was reached on all of the outstanding issues and a permanent peace was achieved within the framework of what was known as the "two-state solution".

The Oslo Accords were seen by many Palestinians as unjust and a major capitulation. The PLO had recognized Israel without the latter recognizing a Palestinian state; the accords proposed the establishment of this future state on only 22% of historic

Palestine; and the terms of the accords made the Palestinians politically and economically subservient to Israel, with almost no elements of true sovereignty. Nevertheless, the "two-state solution" received almost universal approval after dozens of countries around the world adopted it as a policy or, at least, did not oppose it. This was not the position of the hardline Zionists, however – the right-wing, religious elements. They expressed savage opposition to those agreements and launched a raging wave of incitement against the Israeli Prime Minister Yitzhak Rabin, ultimately leading to his assassination in 1995 – a year after the Oslo Accords had gone into effect. With this act, those forces dealt a painful blow to any peace endeavor between the two parties. Zionist opposition did not cease to any peaceful solution that might lead to a recognition of Palestinian rights, even in part. Obstacles continued to be placed in the way of developing or expanding the Oslo Accords, until the five-year period had ended, the Palestinians had lost their confidence in the feasibility of any political path with Israel, and the Second Intifada erupted in 2000. Israel suppressed this uprising violently, through destruction and assassinations. Finally, in 2004, it assassinated the Palestinian partner in Oslo, Yasser Arafat, by inserting polonium radioactive dust into his food.[5] There is no doubt that this act was the height of villainy and ingratitude, other than the fact that it entailed a grave historical and political mistake. By signing the Oslo Accords, Arafat had broken a deep, decades-long cycle of hostility between the Israelis and Palestinians and had effectively signed a capitulation. From an Israeli perspective, he should have been thanked and rewarded, not killed.

This Zionist arrogance reflects a narrow-mindedness that leads to disaster after disaster, and is the result of not just the colonial Zionist mentality and the support that Zionism enjoys from its Western benefactors but of zealous interpretations of Judaism itself. Fundamentalist Judaism considers its followers

---

[5] In late 2012, as part of the investigation into Arafat's mysterious death, his body was exhumed, in the presence of Swiss experts, and it was found that his bones had turned into black masses as a result of atomic poisoning. (Angelique Chrisafis and Harriet Sherwood, "Yasser Arafat may have been poisoned with polonium, tests show", *The Guardian*, November 6, 2013.)

"God's chosen people", distinct from all the other peoples and nations of the world, and discriminates, openly and blatantly, against the gentiles – that is, everyone who is not Jewish – but also against the women of the world, including Jewish ones. This ideology recognizes the humanity of the Jewish man alone, and no one else, among all the beings on the planet. (There is even a daily blessing that a Jewish man should recite, thanking God for not making him a gentile, a woman or a slave.[6]) The zealousness of this once marginal and small, religious faction of Judaism has spread to all currents within Israeli society to become one of the leading ideologies of Judaism today, thanks to the successes of Zionism.[7]

Polls conducted in Israel show, time and again, that the majority of settlers consider themselves a chosen people.[8] In fact, as an extension of this exclusive mentality, Israel rarely accepts asylum seekers, and it is very difficult for non-Jews to acquire Israeli citizenship by naturalization. This view of being the "chosen people" gives Jewish Israelis a mental justification to demand what they do not grant to others. In so doing, they provoke others into a retaliatory stance; their insistence on their right to a "Jewish state", for example, may have prompted some Muslim currents to demand the establishment of a "Muslim state". Similarly, if Israel insists on defining itself as a "Jewish" ethnostate, rather than as a state that is secular and democratic, it cannot accuse other states when they define themselves as "Muslim" and subscribe to religious values in the same way.

Many Jewish Israelis, and many Jews and Christians worldwide, particularly in the United States and Western Europe, are quick to label any party that criticizes Israel and Zionism as anti-Semitic, without realizing that the hostility

---

6   Max DuBoff, "The Three Blessings: Past and Future".

7   Editor's note: For more on this, see the work of Israel Shahak, including *Jewish Fundamentalism in Israel*.

8   Gideon Levy, "79 Percent of Right-wingers Believe Jews Are the Chosen People. Are You for Real?", *Haaretz*, September 15, 2018; Ami Kaufman, "Poll: 70% of Israeli Jews believe Jews are 'Chosen People'", *+972 Magazine*, January 27, 2012.

towards the Israeli state is only a reaction to its crimes, including its transformation of the Jewish concept of being the "chosen people" into a racist, supremacist base for persecuting others. Likewise, they do not realize or appear to care that the harm they suffered in the Holocaust was caused by Germany and contributed to by many European peoples, while the Arabs of Palestine had nothing to do with it.

These factors combined, although they served the Zionist project in the past, will not necessarily continue to do so in the future. The events of more than a century have proven that the Palestinians, and the increasing number of peoples around the world who support and sympathize with them, are not willing to accept Zionist colonial bullying, the forfeiting of Arab rights in Palestine or the continued submission to Western neo-colonial arrogance.

Several centuries ago, Palestine was subjected to invasions by the Crusaders, who gained the support of the largest power in Europe in the Middle Ages – the papacy – and relied primarily on Christian religious components, similar to the Zionists' reliance on Jewish ones. The Crusaders remained in the Levant for a considerable period, establishing kingdoms, alliances and other entities. In the end, due to their inability to come to an understanding with their Arab neighbors and live in peace with them, the peoples of the Arab Islamic region eliminated them, and all that remained of them were ruins and remains of castles.

Centuries later, in the face of Zionism, it was not surprising that the Palestinian Arabs, due to their feelings of injustice and aggression against them, and their fear of a policy that might ultimately lead to uprooting them from their homeland (which is what ultimately transpired), adopted positions of hostility and open resistance to the Zionist project through armed clashes and wars. This resistance has never ceased, although it changed forms in different periods. In 2023, a century after the mandate was imposed on Palestine, and 75 years after the establishment of Israel, the Palestinian resistance organizations in Gaza launched a fierce armed attack on Israel that threatened to ignite the entire Middle East region in the war that followed.

Conclusion

This war has persisted, unexpectedly, for almost two years, at the time of writing, during which Zionist Israel has committed the most horrific, despicable atrocities, with the support or acquiescence of those Western countries that have not rid themselves of their colonial mentality – this time headed by the United States.

The attack launched by the Palestinian resistance in the Gaza Strip on October 7, 2023 was a shocking, extensive operation. Even by Israeli admission, it was a heavy blow to Israel's security apparatus and its heretofore uncontested military and intelligence, and killed about 1,200 Israelis – the largest number to be killed in one day since Israel's establishment. Of this number, 373 were Israeli soldiers and security forces who were on duty in the army bases and militarized settlements that have besieged Gaza's inhabitants for decades.[9] Later reporting, however, showed hundreds of Israelis were killed by the Israeli security forces themselves. In Gaza City, three escaped Israeli captives were shot dead by Israeli ground troops in December 2023.[10] In addition, about 250 Israeli hostages were taken to Gaza – a third of them soldiers. The severity of this attack can be attributed to the fact that all of its perpetrators had been subjected to a stifling Israeli blockade on Gaza for about 17 years, which controlled all aspects of its people's daily lives. Further, there is no doubt that most of the attackers, if not all of them, were descendants of refugees who had been expelled during the 1948 war from the very lands that those attackers now targeted. Whatever the nature of the attack, it did not pose – for a single moment – an immediate existential threat to Israel. However, it was another opportunity to expose the hypocrisy and complicity of the American and European colonialists as it revealed, once again, their designs.

---

9 "Israel social security data reveals true picture of Oct 7 deaths", France 24 (AFP), December 15, 2023.

10 Eric Tlozek, Orly Halpern and Allyson Horn, "Israeli forces accused of killing their own citizens under the 'Hannibal Directive' during October 7 chaos", *ABC News*, September 6, 2024; Asa Winstanley, "How Israel killed hundreds of its own people on 7 October", *The Electronic Intifada*, October 7, 2024.

The Palestinian resistance attack from Gaza marked a new wave of pilgrimage to Israel for the leaders of the United States and major European powers, in order to support the Zionist entity and give it assurances. The first of those pilgrims was the "Zionist" (as he defines himself) American President Joe Biden who, as soon as he heard of the attack, rushed to mobilize American fleets and send them to the Middle East to protect Israel. He hastened to visit the country and, in an unprecedented move, participated in the meeting of the Israeli war cabinet. Then he began sending shipments of arms and ammunition to Israel to continue its destructive war, continuing to support and defend its actions within the international community, as usual. Biden was joined, with great fervor, by the German chancellor Olaf Scholz. The German state is nearly maniacal in supporting the Zionists and has expanded the definition of anti-Semitism to include any criticism of Israel. In the recent war, Germany's arms exports to Israel increased ten-fold. The French president, Emmanuel Macron, and the prime ministers of Britain and Italy, Rishi Sunak and Giorgia Meloni, also participated in this wave of pilgrimages. Since October 7, intense contacts and consultations have continued between the various intelligence and military agencies in those countries and their Israeli counterparts.

With this moral and material colonial support, Israel called in its reserve forces and began waging a war on Gaza – one of the most densely populated areas of the world – in order to "crush" and "eliminate" the Hamas movement, in the words often used by Israeli leaders and the military. Even before the war began, it was clear that this goal was unattainable due to the different methods of fighting on each side. The Palestinian resistance, which knew that it faced a much stronger enemy, planned to resist it in its own way. It entrenched itself in tunnels tens of meters below ground, which had been dug and prepared over long periods. On the few occasions when Israeli forces tried to storm these tunnels, they were hit back with force by the Hamas fighters. In practice, the Israelis only entered a small number of tunnels from which the resistance fighters had withdrawn for tactical reasons.

Conclusion 547

Israel knew, even from its previous attacks on Gaza, that its war with the tunnel fighters was futile and would not achieve any gains. Thus, in parallel, it launched another criminal war of genocide on the people of Gaza, and even on the nature of the entire strip. The world watched, via live broadcast on TV channels and social media platforms, the war of extermination waged by Israel on the small, blockaded and densely populated area. Israel systematically and disgustingly destroyed homes, families, hospitals, mosques, churches and schools overcrowded with children, women and the elderly in areas where the displaced took shelter. It cut off supplies of food, water, medicine, electricity and fuel from 2.3 million Palestinians, starving them and giving them a choice between death or a new Nakba, to finish what the Zionists were unable to achieve in the first Nakba of 1948.

Now 20 months into the war, the Gaza Ministry of Health has confirmed that more than 61,944 people have been killed, while independent estimates of the true death toll are significantly higher than that. About 10,000 victims are buried under the rubble of destroyed buildings, with rescue teams unable to retrieve or identify them. The number of the wounded or maimed is estimated at 151,000, many with life-altering injuries such as loss of limbs.[11] About 17,000-19,000 children are orphaned, according to UNICEF, but the International Rescue Committee reported that actual numbers may be much higher.[12] Most of the casualties are civilians. Many were killed in their homes, with their families, targeted by precision missiles through tracking their phones. This technology was supplied to Israel by the United States and Germany.

In March 2025, Israel intensified its blockade of food, water, medicine and fuel into Gaza to near-total levels. Since then, the strip degenerated into an even more catastrophic situation of famine, with the UN and other organizations unable to get aid to its bombarded, besieged population. More than 200 Palestinians

---

11 "Briefing to the Security Council on Gaza" (Report), United Nations Office for the Coordination of Humanitarian Affairs (OCHA), August 11, 2025.

12 "Unaccompanied and separated children in Gaza" (Report), International Rescue Committee, August 31, 2024.

have starved to death, at the time of writing, almost half of them babies and children.[13] Israel and the United States stopped the UN from aid delivery in Gaza and set up their own "Gaza Humanitarian Foundation (GHF)", which has been described by witnesses as a "human slaughterhouse". At the GHF's aid sites, to which thousands of hungry, desperate Palestinians rush to try to find any food for themselves and their families, Israeli and American forces have been shooting at the crowds on a daily basis. Nearly 2,000 people have been killed so far, unarmed, hungry and desperate.[14] The Israeli government has stated its aim of occupying Gaza City and launched a severe attack on it to force Palestinians out.

As the Gaza genocide rages on, Israeli settler attacks against Palestinians and their properties in the West Bank have also risen to unprecedented levels, with the aim of driving people off their land. Since October 7, 2023, more than 1,000 Palestinians have been killed by Israeli forces and settlers in the occupied West Bank.[15]

This Israeli immorality would not have persisted, with all its audacity and horrific human and material losses, without the Western support and assistance led by the United States. This is not out of sympathy for the Jewish people in Israel, but to protect the investment of the West and to safeguard its interests in the region. The United States, in particular, rushed to send its fleets, soldiers, leaders and experts after the Hamas attack, provided huge financial and arms support to Israel, and was ever ready to use its veto power in the United Nations Security Council to thwart any attempt to hold Israel accountable for its war crimes or to enforce a ceasefire.

In the face of this, the Palestinian cause shot onto the world's radar with unprecedented urgency. Masses of people

---

13 "Famine kills nearly 200 in Gaza amid 'apocalyptic' battle for survival", Al Jazeera, August 7, 2025.

14 "Gaza doctor describes 'daily patterns' in Israeli maiming at GHF sites", Al Jazeera, August 13, 2025.

15 Mat Nashed, "Israel has killed 1,000 Palestinians in the West Bank since October 7, 2023", Al Jazeera, July 1, 2025.

around the globe came out in demonstrations in support of the Palestinians and to demand a ceasefire, and this wave spread to the most prestigious universities in the United States itself. The October 7 attack had other effects as well. It disrupted the process of normalization between Israel and its Arab and Islamic surroundings. This was intended to link those countries to a network of economic and security interests to consolidate Israel's so-called qualitative superiority, guarantee its sole ownership of nuclear armaments, and qualify it to lead a re-engineered Middle East in order to perpetuate Western hegemony over this key geostrategic region. Ultimately, the Middle East was to be employed in the raging Western conflict to confront the rise of Russia and China and to entrench the unipolar international order.

Coincidentally, this sinful relationship between colonialism and Zionism was further exposed – as if further evidence is required – in April 2024. Israel had long been accustomed to bombing various targets in its neighboring countries, with impunity. On April 1, it bombed the Iranian consulate in Damascus, killing a number of people, including members of Iran's Islamic Revolutionary Guard. Iran officially announced that it would respond. On April 13, it launched more than 300 drones and missiles at Israel. The American forces deployed in the region – this time with the help of British and French ones, in addition to Jordan and Saudi Arabia – helped repel the attack in defense of Israel and its Zionist regime.

In June 2025, Israel launched an attack on Iran – killing a number of senior commanders and nuclear scientists, as well as hundreds of civilians. In response, Iran fired hundreds of missiles at Israel. Nine days later, the United States also launched an attack on Iran's nuclear sites. The "12-day war" ended with a US-brokered truce between Israel and Iran, but tensions remained high. In 2023-2024, Israel had carried out attacks against Hezbollah in Lebanon, an ally of Iran that had supported the Gaza resistance with the firing of rockets into Israel. The Israeli attacks led to the weakening of Hezbollah and apparent dismantling of its network of operations, as well as causing wanton destruction in Lebanon and killing and displacing thousands of people.

The Israeli state persists in its belligerence against the entire region, confident in its Western support. Many analysts predict that the region will be at war for years to come.

The bottom line, in this story of Zionism, is the West's colonial quest to control the Arab Levant. This quest began in the mid-19th century, with the decline of the Ottoman Empire, and has continued to this day. Britain led this activity, only to be replaced by the United States in the 1960s. The Palestinian people paid a heavy price for those policies, and lost their homeland to the Zionist state. Those colonial plans have not been exhausted. Rather, they have a more dangerous sequel, as noted above: to impose Israel on the Levant, as a deterrent force and agent of the American colonists along with their European partners, and normalize the settler colony as part of the Middle East, on the road to liquidating the Palestinian cause.

Given this reality, there seems to be no solution except to eliminate this Western influence in the region, by strengthening and unifying the national forces that resist colonialism and Zionism and working to restrict or replace the regimes cooperating with them or, at least, to change their policies. In addition, strong alliances must be created with the emerging global powers that are hostile to the West and its colonialism. The vile genocidal war against Gaza and its people is nothing but a flash in this direction. Hamas has placed its finger on the wound. With its attack, it has thwarted the plot to liquidate the Palestinian cause and has revealed what Israel always has been – a tool of Western colonialism in the region. Israel's military onslaught on Syria, launched after the fall of Bashar al-Assad and the overthrow of the country's government in December 2024, is further testimony to these expansionist designs.

It seems that the Zionists are making the same mistakes today as the Crusaders had historically, in appealing to the religious bases of their movement for legitimacy and thus provoking the feelings of the Muslims and Christians surrounding them. The Zionists should take the historical lessons of the Crusaders to heart, for God has many soldiers.

Bibliography

Hebrew

Books

Aescoly, Aaron Zeev, *Ha-Tnu'ot ha-Mashiachot be-Yisrael (Jewish Messianic Movements in Israel)*, 2 vols., Jerusalem: Bialik Institute, 1956.

Ahad Ha'am, *Kol Kitvei Ahad Ha'am – Al Parshat Drachim (Complete Works of Ahad Ha'am – At the Crossroads)*, Tel Aviv: Dvir, 1965.

Aharonovich, Yosef, *Ha-Am ve ha-Aretz (People and Country)*, Tel Aviv: Tarbut ve-Hinuch, 1970.

Ahimeir, Abba, *Brit ha-Birionim (The Strongmen Alliance)*, Vol. 3, Tel Aviv: Committee for Ahimeir Publications, 1972.

Akavia, Avraham (ed.), *Ha-Yedid, Orde Wingate (The Friend, Orde Wingate)*, Tel Aviv: Maarachot, 1968.

Amikam, Bezalel, *Nirim Rishonim (First Tillings)*, Jerusalem: Yad Yitzhak Ben-Zvi Institute, 1980.

Arnon-Ohana, Yuval, *Herev mi-Bayit: Ha-Ma'avak ha-Pnimi ba-Tnu'ah ha-Leumit ha-Falastinit, 1929-1939 (Sword from Within: The Internal Struggle in the Palestinian National Movement, 1929-1939)*, Tel Aviv: Yariv-Hadar and Shiloah Institute, 1981.

Assaf, Michael, *Ha-Yahasim bein Yehudim ve Aravim be-Eretz Yisrael, 1860-1948 (Jewish-Arab Relations in the Land of Israel, 1860-1948)*, Tel Aviv: Tarbut ve-Hinuch, 1970.

Attias, Moshe (ed.), *Sefer ha-Te'udot shel ha-Va'ad ha-Leumi le-Knesset Yisrael be-Eretz Yisrael (Book of Documents of the National Council of Knesset Israel)*, Jerusalem: Raphael Haim ha-Cohen Press, 1963.

Avidar, Yosef, *Ba-Derech le-Tsahal (On the Eve of Forming the Israeli Defense Forces)*, Tel Aviv: Maarachot, 1970.

Avigur, Shaul, *Im Dor ha-Haganah (With the Haganah Generation)*, Vol. 1, 4th ed., Tel Aviv: Maarachot, 1970; 2nd ed., 1977.

Avneri, Arieh L., *Ha-Hityashvut ha-Yehudit ve Ta'anat ha-Nishul, 1878-1948 (Jewish Land Settlement and the Claim of Dispossession [of the Palestinian Peasants], 1878-1948)*, Tel Aviv: Ha-Kibbutz ha-Meuchad, 1980.

Avriel, Ehud, *Pithu Sha'arayim! (Open the Gates!)*, Tel Aviv: Sifriat Maariv, 1976.

Bar-Ilan (Berlin), Meir, *Me-Volozhin ad Yerushalayim (From Volozhin to Jerusalem)*, 2 vols., Tel Aviv: Meir Bar-Ilan Publication Committee, 1971.

Bar-Zohar, Michael, *Ben-Gurion*, 3 vols., Tel Aviv: Am Oved, 1975-1977.

Baz, Saadiyah, *Zichronot (Memoirs)*, Haifa: Author's family edition, 1963.

Bein, Alex, *Theodor Herzl, Biographia (Theodor Herzl, A Biography)*, Tenth (last) volume of *Kitvei Herzl (Works of Herzl)*, Jerusalem: The Zionist Library and M. Newman, 1961.

Bein, Alex, *Toldot ha-Hityashvut ha-Tzionit (History of Zionist Settlement)*, Ramat Gan: Masada, 1970.

Bela, Moshe, *Olamo shel Jabotinsky (The World of Jabotinsky)*, Tel Aviv: Dfusim, 1972.

Ben-David, Yehuda, *Plugot ha-Esh Naot ba-Layla (The Brigades of Fire Move at Night)*, Tel Aviv: Ha-Kibbutz ha-Meuchad, 1984.

Ben-Efram, Baruch, *Hever ha-Kvutsot (League of the Kvutsot [Communal Workers' Settlements])*, Tel Aviv: Am Oved, 1976.

Ben-Efram, Baruch, *Miflagot ou Zramim Politim be-Tkufat ha-Bayit ha-Leumi, 1918-1948 (Parties and Political Currents during the Period of the National Home, 1918-1948)*, Jerusalem: Zalman Shazar Center, 1978.

Bibliography

Ben-Gurion, David, *Michtavim el Paula ve el ha-Yeladim (Letters to Paula and the Children)*, Tel Aviv: Am Oved, 1968.

Ben-Gurion, David, *Mi-Ma'amad le-Am (From Class to Nation)*, Tel Aviv: Am Oved, 1974.

Ben-Gurion, David, *Pgishot im Manhigim Araviim (Meetings with Arab Leaders)*, Tel Aviv: Am Oved, 1967.

Ben-Gurion, David, *Zichronot (Memoirs)*, 5 vols., Vol. 1: until 1934; Vol. 2: 1934-1935; Vol. 3: 1936; Vol. 4: 1937; Vol. 5: 1938, Tel Aviv: Am Oved, 1917-1938.

Ben Nachman, Moses (Ramban), *Kitvei Ramban (Works of Ramban)*, 2 vols., Jerusalem: Rabbi Kook Institute, 1963.

Ben-Sasson, Haim Hillel, *Prakim be-Toldot Am Yisrael be-Yemei ha-Binayim (Chapters of the History of the Jews in the Middle Ages)*, Tel Aviv: Am Oved, 1969.

Ben-Sasson, Haim Hillel, *Toldot Am Yisrael be-Yemei ha-Binayim (History of the Jews in the Middle Ages)*, Tel Aviv: Dvir, 1969.

Ben-Sasson, Haim Hillel, ed., *Toldot Am Yisrael be-Yemei Kedem (History of the Jews in the Old Ages)*, Tel Aviv: Dvir, 1969.

Ben-Shoshan, Tzvi, *Toldot Tnu'at ha-Poalim be-Eretz Yisrael (History of the Labor Movement in the Land of Israel)*, 3 vols., Tel Aviv: Am Oved, 1963.

Ben-Yerucham, Ch. (ed.), *Sefer Beitar (Beitar Book)*, 2 vols., Jerusalem-Tel Aviv: Committee for Publishing Beitar Books, 1969.

Benziman, Uzi, *Yerushalayim: Ir Lelo Homa (Jerusalem: A City Without Walls)*, Tel-Aviv: Schocken, 1973.

Ben-Zvi, Yitzhak, *Eretz Yisrael ve-Yishuvah be-Yemei ha-Shilton ha-Otomani (Land of Israel and its Settlers Under Ottoman Rule)*, Jerusalem: Bialik Institute, 1963.

Ben-Zvi, Yitzhak, ed., *Sefer Hashomer (Book of Hashomer)*, Tel Aviv: Dvir, 1957.

Biger, Gideon, *Moshavat Keter o Bayit Leumi (Crown Colony or National*

Homeland), Jerusalem: Yad Yitzhak Ben-Zvi Institute, 1983.

Blau, Amram, *Al Homotech, Yerushalayim (On Your Walls, Jerusalem)*, Bnei Brak: Netzach, 1967.

Bodenheimer, Henrietta, *Toldot Tochnit Basel (History of the Basel Program)*, Jerusalem: Rubin Mass, 1947.

Borochov, Ber, *Ktavim (The Works)*, 3 vols., Tel Aviv: Ha-Kibbutz ha-Meuchad and Sifriat Poalim, 1955.

Braslavski, Moshe, *Tnu'at ha-Poalim ha-Eretz Yisraelit (Labor Movement in the Land of Israel)*, 4 vols., Tel Aviv: Ha-Kibbutz ha-Meuchad, 1966.

Brit Shalom Association, *Shi'ifutenu (Our Aspirations)* monthly journal, 6 collections and 2 vols., Jerusalem: Brit Shalom, 1927-1933.

Carpi, Daniel, ed., *Ha-Tzionout, Me'asef le-Toldot ha-Tnu'ah ha-Tzionit ve ha-Yishuv ha-Yehudi be-Eretz Yisrael (Zionism: Studies in the History of the Zionist Movement and of the Jewish Community in the Land of Israel)*, 9 vols., Tel Aviv: Tel Aviv University and Ha-Kibbutz ha-Meuchad, 1970-84.

Chronologiah le-Toldot ha-Yishuv ha-Yehudi be-Eretz Yisrael (Chronology of the Jewish Yishuv in the Land of Israel), Vol. 1: 1917-1935; Vol. 2: 1936-1947, Jerusalem: Yad Yitzhak Ben-Zvi Institute, 1974, 1979.

Cohen, Aharon, *Yisrael ve ha-Olam ha-Aravi (Israel and the Arab World)*, Merhavia: Sifriat Poalim, 1964.

Cohen, Yitzhak (ed.), *Ha-Tzionout ve ha-She'elah ha'Aravit (Zionism and the Arab Question)*, Jerusalem: Zalman Shazar Center, 1979.

Cohen, Yonah, *Prakim be-Toldot ha-Tnu'ah ha-Datit ha-Leumit (Chapters in the History of the National Religious Movement)*, Tel Aviv: National Religious Party, 1973.

Dayan, Shmuel, *Ke-Holmim (Like Dreamers)*, Tel Aviv: Masada, 1956.

Dinur (Dinaburg), Ben-Zion, *Binyamin Ze'ev Herzl (Benjamin Ze'ev Herzl)*, Ramat Gan: Masada, 1968.

Dinur (Dinaburg), Ben-Zion, ed., *Sefer Toldot ha-Haganah (History of*

Bibliography 555

the Haganah), Vol. 1: 2 parts, 1954; Vol. 2: 3 parts, 1964, Tel Aviv: Maarachot; Vol. 3: 3 parts (Yehuda Slutsky, ed.), Tel Aviv: Am Oved, 1972.

Dinur (Dinaburg), Ben-Zion, ed., *Shivat Tzion (Return to Zion)*, 4 vols., Jerusalem: The Zionist Library, 1950-56.

Doron, Adam (ed.) *Mekorot la-Toldot Tnu'at ha-Avoda ha-Yisraelit (Sources for the History of the Israeli Labor Movement)*, Tel Aviv: Beit Berl, 1981.

Dothan, Shmuel, *Pulmus ha-Halukah bi-Tkufat ha-Mandat (The Partition Controversy during the British Mandate)*, Jerusalem: Yad Yitzhak Ben-Zvi Institute, 1979.

Dror, Levi, and Rosenzweig, Yisrael, *Sefer Hashomer Hatzair (Hashomer Hatzair Book)*, Vol. 1, Merhavia: Sifriat Poalim, 1956.

Duhring, Eugen, *Die Judenfrage als Frage der Rassenschadlichkeit fur Existenz, Sitte und Kultur der Volker, mit einer weltgeschichtlichen Antwort (The Jewish Question as a Question of Racial Harm to the Existence, Customs and Culture of the People, with a World-Historical Answer)*, Karlsruhe and Leipzig: Verlag von H. Reuther, 1886.

Dubnow, Simon, *Divrei Yemei Am Olam (History of the Jews)*, Tel Aviv: Dvir, 1969.

Eilat, Eliyahu, *Shivat Tzion ve Arav (Return to Zion and the Arabs)*, Tel Aviv: Dvir, 1974.

Eisenstadt, Shmuel Noah, *Ha-Hevrah ha-Yisraelit (Israeli Society)*, Jerusalem: Magnes, 1967.

Elam, Yigal, *Ha-Haganah: Ha-Derekh ha-Tzionit el ha-Koah (The Haganah: The Zionist Way to Power)*, Tel Aviv: Zamorah, Bitan and Modan, 1979.

Erez, Yehuda (ed.), *Sefer ha-Aliyah ha-Shlishit (The Third Aliyah Book)*, 2 vols., Tel Aviv: Am Oved, 1964.

Eshbal, Aminadav, ed., *Shishim Shanot Hachsharat ha-Yishuv (Sixty Years of the Palestine Land Development Company)*, Jerusalem: Palestine Land Development Company, 1970.

Ettinger, Shmuel, *Toldot Am Yisrael ba'Et ha-Hadasha (History of the Jews in Modern Times)*, Vol. 3 (Haim Hillel Ben-Sasson, ed.), Tel Aviv: Dvir, 1969.

Federbusch, Simon, ed., *Ha-Hasidut ve Tzion (Hasidism and Zion)*, Jerusalem and New York: Rabbi Kook Institute and Moria, 1963.

Federbusch, Simon, ed., *Hazon Torah ve Tzion (The Vision of Torah and Zion)*, New York: Moria, 1960.

Friedlander, Yehuda, ed., *Uri Zvi Greenberg, Mivhar Ma'marim al Yetzirato (Uri Zvi Greenberg, Selected Studies on his Works)*, Tel Aviv: Am Oved, 1974.

Friedman, Menachem, *Hevrah ve Dat: Ha-Ortodoxiah ha-Lo Tsionit be-Eretz Yisrael, 1918-1936 (Society and Religion: The Non-Zionist [Jewish] Orthodoxy in the Land of Israel, 1918-1936)*, Jerusalem: Yad Yitzhak Ben-Zvi Institute, 1977.

Friesel, Evyatar, *Atlas Carta le-Toldot Am Yisrael be-Zman ha-Hadash (Carta's Atlas of Modern Jewish History)*, Jerusalem: Carta, 1983.

Friesel, Evyatar, *Ha-Mediniout ha-Tzionit le-ahar Hatzharat Balfour, 1917-1922 (Zionist Policy after the Balfour Declaration, 1917-1922)*, Tel Aviv: Tel Aviv University and Ha-Kibbutz ha-Meuchad, 1977.

Frumkin, Gad, *Derekh Shofet Bi-Yerushalayim (The Path of a Judge in Jerusalem)*, Tel Aviv: Dvir, 1957.

Frumkin, Heschel, *Aliyah ou Pituah ba-Derekh la-Medinah (Immigration and Development on the Road to State)*, Tel Aviv: Tarbut ve-Hinuch, 1971.

Gat, Ben-Zion, *Ha-Yishuv ha-Yehudi be-Eretz Yisrael 1840-1881 (The Jewish Community in the Land of Israel in 1840-1881)*, Jerusalem: Board of Trustees of the Hebrew College, 1963.

Getter, Miriam, *Chaim Arlosoroff: Biographia Politit (Chaim Arlosoroff, Political Biography)*, Tel Aviv: Tel Aviv University, 1977.

Giladi, Dan, *Ha-Yishuv be-Tkofat ha-Aliyah ha-Reve'it (The Yishuv during the Fourth Aliyah)*, Tel Aviv: Am Oved, 1973.

Bibliography

Goldenberg, Musa, *Ve ha-Keren Odeinah Kayemet (And the [Jewish National] Fund Still Exists)*, Merhavia: Sifriat Poalim, 1965.

Goldstein, Yaakov, *Ba-Derech la-Hegemonia: Mapai - Hitgabshut Mediniyutah, 1930-1936 (Towards Hegemony: Mapai - The Crystallization of its Policy, 1930-1936)*, Tel Aviv: Am Oved, 1980.

Goldstein, Yaakov and Shavit, Yaakov, *Lelo Psharot (Without Compromise)*, Tel Aviv: Yariv-Hadar, 1979.

Gordon, Aaron David, *Ha-Uma ve ha-Avoda (The Nation and Labor)*, Jerusalem: The Zionist Library, 1952.

Gorny, Yosef, *Ahdut HaAvoda, 1919-1930: Ha-Yesodot ha-Ri'iyonim ve ha-Shita ha-Mdinit (Ahdut HaAvoda, 1919-1930: Ideological Principles and Political System)*, Tel Aviv: Tel Aviv University and Ha-Kibbutz ha-Meuchad, 1973.

Gorny, Yosef (Ed.), *Medinaei be-Itot Mashber, Derko shel Chaim Weizmann be-Tnu'ah ha-Tzionit (A Statesman in Times of Crisis: Chaim Weizmann and the Zionist Movement)*, Tel Aviv: University of Tel Aviv and Ha-Kibbutz ha-Meuchad, 1977.

Gorny, Yosef, *Prakim Nivharim be-Tkufat ha-Aliyah ha-Shnia (Selected Chapters from the Second Aliyah Period)*, Tel Aviv: University of Tel Aviv, 1967.

Gorny, Yosef, *Shutafout ou Ma'avak: Chaim Weizmann ve Tnu'at ha-Poalim be Eretz Yisrael (Partnership and Conflict: Chaim Weizmann and the Jewish Labor Movement in the Land of Israel)*, Tel Aviv: Tel Aviv University and Ha-Kibbutz ha-Meuchad, 1976.

Granot, Avraham, *Be-Hitnahel Am (When a People Settles)*, Tel Aviv: Dvir, 1951.

Gruenbaum, Yitzhak, *Ha-Tnu'ah ha-Tzionit (The Zionist Movement)*, 4 vols., Jerusalem: Zionist Organization and Rubin Mass, 1956.

Gvati, Chaim, *Meah Shanot Hityashvut (A Hundred Years of Settlement)*, 2 vols., Tel Aviv: Ha-Kibbutz ha-Meuchad, 1981.

Habas, Bracha, ed., *Sefer ha-Aliyah ha-Shnia (Book of the Second Aliyah)*, Tel Aviv: Am Oved, 1947.

Ha-Congress ha-Tzioni ... ve ha-Moshav ... shel Moa'tzit ha-Sokhnout ha-Yehudit (Records [of Sessions] of the ... Zionist Congress and the ... Council Session of the Jewish Agency): 19th Congress and 4th Session, 1935; 20th Congress and 5th Session, 1937; 21st Congress, 1939; 22nd Congress, 1946, Jerusalem: Administration of the Zionist Organization, 1936 (?), 1938 (?), 1940 (?), 1947 (?).

Ha-Encyclopaedia ha-Ivrit (Encyclopaedia Hebraica), Vol. 6, Jerusalem and Tel Aviv: Encyclopaedia Publishing Company, 1957.

Halpern, Yehiel, *Ha-Mahpicha ha-Yehudit (The Jewish Revolution)*, 2 vols., Tel Aviv: Am Oved, 1961.

Ha-Protocol shel ha-Congress ha-Tzioni ha-Rishon (Protocols of First Zionist Congress), Jerusalem: Rubin Mass, 1946.

Ha-Protocol shel ha-Congress ha-Tzioni ha-Yud Tet (Protocols of 19th Zionist Congress), Jerusalem: Jewish Agency, 1937.

Ha-Protocolim shel ha-Va'ad ha-Poel ha-Tzioni (Records of Sessions of the Zionist Executive), Vol. 1, Feb. 1919 – Jan. 1920, Tel Aviv: University of Tel Aviv and Ha-Kibbutz ha-Meuchad, 1975.

Heller, Joseph, *Be-Ma'avak la-Medinah: Ha-Mediniout ha-Tzionit be-Shanim 1936-1948 (The Struggle for the Jewish State: Zionist Politics, 1936-1948)*, Jerusalem: Zalman Shazar Center, 1984.

Herzl, Theodor (Benjamin Ze'ev), *Kitvei Herzl (Works of Herzl)*, Vol. 1: *Medinat ha-Yehudim, Altneuland (The Jewish State, the Old New Land)*, Vols. 2, 3, 4: *Ha-Yoman (Diaries)*, Vols. 7, 8: *Bifnei Am ve-Olam (Before the Nation and the World)*, Vol. 10: Bein, Alex, *Theodor Herzl, Biographia (Theodor Herzl, A Biography)*, Jerusalem: The Zionist Library, 1960-61.

Heymann, Michael, *Ha-Tnu'ah ha-Tzionit ve ha-Tochniot le-Yishuv Aram Naharayim be-Tkufa she le-Ahar Herzl (The Zionist Movement and the Schemes for Jewish Settlement in Mesopotamia after the Death of Herzl)*, Tel Aviv: University of Tel Aviv, 1965.

Horowitz, Dan and Lissak, Moshe, *Me-Yishuv le-Medina (From Yishuv to State)*, Tel Aviv: Am Oved, 1977.

Bibliography 559

Ideologia ve Mdiniout Tzionit (Zionist Doctrine and Policy), a collection of articles, Jerusalem: Zalman Shazar Center, 1978.

Ilan, Amitzur, *America, Britania ve Eretz Yisrael, 1937-1948 (America, Britain and the Land of Israel, 1937-1948)*, Jerusalem, Yad Yitzhak Ben-Zvi Institute, 1979.

Jabotinsky, Ze'ev (Vladimir), *Hazit ha-Milhamah shel Am Yisrael (The Jewish War Front)*, Jerusalem: Kopp, 1940.

Jabotinsky, Ze'ev (Vladimir), *Kitvei Jabotinsky (Works of Jabotinsky)*, Vols. 4, 5, 8, 9, 11, 12, Jerusalem: Eri Jabotinsky (Publisher) Ltd., 1958.

Kalischer, Zvi Hirsch, *Drishat Zion (Seeking Zion)*, Jerusalem: Rabbi Kook Institute, 1964.

Katz, Ben-Zion, *Rabanut, Hasidut, Haskalah (Rabbinate, Hasidism, and Haskalah)*, 2 vols., Tel Aviv: Union of Jewish Writers and Dvir, 1956.

Katzburg, Nathaniel, *Mi-Halukah la-Sefer ha-Lavan (From Partition to White Paper)*, Jerusalem: Yad Yitzhak Ben-Zvi Institute, 1974.

Kaufmann, Yehezkel, *Toldot ha-Imuna ha-Yisraelit (History of the Israelite Faith)*, 4 vols., Tel Aviv: Bialik Institute and Dvir, 1972.

Kirschenbaum, Shimshon Leib, *Toldot Am Yisrael be-Doreinu (The History of the Jews in Our Generation)*, 2 vols., Tel Aviv: Amnot, 1965.

Klausner, Israel, *Ha-Tnu'ah le-Tzion be-Rusia (Zionist Movement in Russia)*, Vol. 1: *Be-Hit'orer Am (When a People Awakens)*, Vols. 2, 3: *Me-Katowice ad Basel (From Katowice to Basel)*, Jerusalem: The Zionist Library, 1962.

Klausner, Israel, *Hibbat Tzion be-Romania (Lovers of Zion in Romania)*, Jerusalem: The Zionist Library, 1958.

Klausner, Joseph, *Menehei ha-Yesod shel Medinat Yisrael (Founders of the State of Israel)*, Jerusalem: Ahiasaf, 1955.

Kleiman, Aharon, *Hafred ou Mshol: Mediniyout Britania ve Halukat Eretz Yisrael, 1936-1939 (Divide and Rule: British Policy and the Partition of Palestine, 1936-1939)*, Jerusalem: Yad Yitzhak Ben-Zvi Institute, 1983.

Kollek, Teddy, *Yerushalayim Ehat (One Jerusalem)*, Tel Aviv: Sifriat Maariv, 1979.

Kressel, Gezel, *Franz Oppenheimer*, Tel-Aviv: Yavneh, 1972.

Lador (Leidermann), Yitzhak, *Hityashvutenu ba-Aretz, 1870-1952, Toldoteha ve Tzoroteha (Our Settlement in the Country, 1870-1952, Its History and Forms)*, Tel Aviv: Ofek, 1952.

Lestschinsky, Jacob, *Ha-Tfutsa ha-Yehudit (Jewish Scattering)*, Jerusalem: Bialik Institute, 1960.

Livneh, Eliezer, *Nili: Toldoteha shel He'azah Medinit (Nili, A History of Political Daring)*, Tel Aviv: Schocken, 1961.

Loker, Berl, *Me-Kitov ad Yerushalayim (From Kitov to Jerusalem)*, Jerusalem: Zionist Library, 1970.

Maimon, Ada, *Hamishim Shanot Tnu'at ha-Poa'lot (Fifty Years of the Women Workers' Movement)*, Tel Aviv: Ayanot, 1956.

Malachi, Eliezer Raphael, *Prakim be-Toldot ha-Yishuv ha-Yashan (Chapters in the History of the Old Yishuv)*, Tel Aviv: Tel Aviv University and Ha-Kibbutz ha-Meuchad, 1971.

Margalit, Elkana, *Hashomer Hatzair: Me-Idat No'arim le-Marxism Mahpichani, 1913-1936 (Hashomer Hatzair: From Youth Community to Revolutionary Marxism, 1913-1936)*, Tel Aviv: Tel Aviv University and Ha-Kibbutz ha-Meuchad, 1971.

Medzini, Moshe, *Ha-Mediniut ha-Tzionit (Zionist Policy)*, Jerusalem: Schechter, 1934.

Merchav, Peretz, *Toldot Tnu'at ha-Poalim be-Eretz Yisrael 1905-1965 (History of the Labor Movement in the Land of Israel, 1905-1965)*, Merhavia: Sifriat Poalim, 1967.

Merchavia, Hen-Melech, *Am ou-Moledet (Nation and Homeland)*, Jerusalem: Halevi, 1948.

Meridor, Monia, *Shlihout Alumah (Secret Mission)*, 6th ed., Tel Aviv:

Maarachot, 1965.

Metzer, Jacob, *Hon Leumi le-Bait Leumi (National Capital for a National Home)*, Jerusalem: Yad Yitzhak Ben-Zvi Institute, 1979.

Milstein, Uri, *Be-Dam ve Esh, Yehuda: Tsmihata shel ha-Otzma ha-Yisraelit (By Blood and Fire, Judea: Growth of Israeli Power)*, Tel Aviv: Levin-Epstein, 1973.

Mior, Yitzhak, *Ha-Tnu'ah ha-Tzionit be-Rusia (Zionist Movement in Russia)*, Jerusalem: The Zionist Library, 1974.

Nahon, Shlomo Umberto, *Moshe Montefiori (Moses Montefiori)*, Tel Aviv: Dvir, 1969.

Nedava, Joseph (ed.), *Sugiot be-Tzionout, 1918-1948 (Chapters of Zionism, 1918-1948)*, Haifa: University of Haifa, 1979.

Nedava, Joseph, *Ze'ev Jabotinsky (Ze'ev Jabotinsky)*, Tel Aviv: International Administration of the Herut Union – Revisionist Zionists, 1964.

Neumann, Emanuel, *Be-Zirat ha-Ma'avak ha-Tzioni (In the Arena of the Zionist Struggle)*, Jerusalem: The Zionist Library, 1976.

Niv, David, *Ma'arachot ha-Irgun ha-Tzvai ha-Leumi (Battles of the National Military Organization [Etzel])*, Vol. 1, 1931-1937; Vol 2, 1937-1939, Tel Aviv: Klausner Institute, 1965.

Nordau, Max, *Kitvei Nordau (Works of Nordau)*, 4 vols., Jerusalem: The Zionist Library, 1954.

Nurock, Mordechai, *Ve'idat Tzioni Rusia be-Minsk (Russian Zionist Congress in Minsk)*, Jerusalem: The Zionist Library, 1963.

Ofir, Yehoshua, *Sefer ha-Oved ha-Leumi (Book of the National Worker)*, Vol. 1, Tel Aviv: National Committee of General Union of Jewish Workers, 1959.

Olitsky, Yosef, *Mi-Pzura le-Medinah (From Dispersal to State)*, Vol. 1, 1917-1939, Jerusalem: Ahiasaf, 1959.

Oren, Elhanan, *Hityashvut be-Shnot Ma'avak, 1936-1947 (Settlement Amidst Struggles, 1936-1947)*, Jerusalem: Yad Yitzhak Ben-Zvi Institute, 1978.

Ostrovsky, Moshe, *Toldot ha-Mizrahi be-Eretz Yisrael (History of the Mizrahi in the Land of Israel)*, Jerusalem: Rubin Mass, 1943.

Peleg, Rachel, and Benjamin, Avraham, *Ha-Haskalah ha-Gvuhah ve ha-Aravim be-Yisrael (Higher Education and the Arabs in Israel)*, Tel Aviv: Am Oved, 1977.

Pinsker, Leon, *Auto-emancipatsia (Auto-Emancipation)*, translated to Hebrew by Ahad Ha'am, as quoted in Shmuel Yavnieli in *Tkufat Hibbat Zion (Period of Lovers of Zion)*, Vol. 2, pp. 3-21, Jerusalem: Bialik Institute, 1961.

Reshimat ha-Yeshuvim, Okhlusiatam ve-Semelihem, 31/12/1971 (List of Settlements, their Population and Symbols, 31/12/1971), Jerusalem: Central Bureau of Statistics, Technical Publications Series No. 37, 1972.

Rishomot (Israeli Gazette), Bulletin Collection 354, 10/6/1954; *Book of Laws* 138, 3/12/1953.

Rivlin, Gershon (ed.), *La-Esh ou la-Magen, Toldot ha'Notrut ha'Ivrit (Fire and Defense: History of the Jewish Guard Brigade)*, Tel Aviv: Maarachot, 1962.

Rivlin, Haim, *Ma'alat ha-Aretz Eretz Yisrael be-Pirush ha-Ramban le-Torah (Greatness of the Country, the Land of Israel, in Ramban's Interpretation of the Torah)*, Jerusalem: World Zionist Organization, 1969.

Rosenheim, Jacob, *Ktavim (Works)*, 2 vols., Jerusalem: World Agudat Israel, 1970.

Rothschild, Meir Menachem, *Ha-Halukah (The Charity Division)*, Jerusalem: Rubin Mass, 1969.

Rubin, Yosef (ed.), *Moshavei Ovdim, Antologia (Workers' Settlements, Collection of Essays)*, Vol. 2, Tel Aviv: Workers' Settlements Movement in Israel, 1970.

Ruppin, Arthur, *Pirkei Hayai (Chapters of My Life)*, 3 vols., Tel Aviv: Am Oved, 1968.

Ruppin, Arthur, *Shloshim Shanot Binyan be-Eretz Yisrael (Thirty Years of Building in the Land of Israel)*, Jerusalem: Schocken, 1936.

Sasson, Eliyahu, *Be-Derekh el ha-Shalom (On the Road to Peace)*, Tel Aviv: Am Oved, 1978.

Schereschewsky, Ben-Zion, *Dinei Mishpaha (Family Law)*, Jerusalem: Rubin Mass, 1971.

Schweid, Eliezer, *Ha-Yahid: Olamo shel A. D. Gordon (The One and Only: The World of A. D. Gordon)*, Tel Aviv: Am Oved, 1970.

Sefer Ussishkin (Book of Ussishkin), Jerusalem: Book of Ussishkin Committee, 1934.

Shapira, Anita, *Berl [Katznelson] (Berl Katznelson)*, 2 vols., Tel Aviv: Am Oved, 1980.

Shapira, Anita, *Ha-Ma'avak ha-Nikhzav, Avoda Ivrit, 1929-1939 (The Futile Struggle: Hebrew Labor, 1929-1939)*, Tel Aviv: Tel Aviv University and Ha-Kibbutz ha-Meuchad, 1977.

Shapira, Yosef, *Meah Shana Mikveh Yisrael (Mikveh Israel: 100 Years)*, Tel Aviv: Tarbut ve-Hinuch, 1970.

Sharett, Moshe, *Yoman Medini (Political Diaries)*, 4 vols., Vol. 1, 1936; Vol. 2, 1937; Vol. 3, 1938; Vol. 4, 1939, Tel Aviv: Am Oved, 1967-1974.

Shavit, Yaakov, *Me-Rov le-Medina (From Majority to State)*, Tel Aviv: Yariv-Hadar, 1978.

Shimoni, Yaacov, *Aravei Eretz Yisrael (The Arabs in the Land of Israel)*, Tel Aviv: Am Oved, 1946.

Shmueli, Moshe, *Toldot ha-Tzionout ve Tnu'at ha-Avoda (History of Zionism and the Labor Movement)*, Vols. 1, 2, Tel Aviv: Tarbut ve-Hinuch, 1961.

Slutsky, Yehuda, *Ha-Itonout ha-Yehudit-Rusit ba-Meah ha-Tsha'esrei (Russian Jewish Press in the 19th Century)*, Jerusalem: Bialik Institute, 1970.

Slutsky, Yehuda, *Mevoa le-Toldot Tnu'at ha-Avoda ha-Yisraelit (Introduction to the History of the Israeli Labor Movement)*, Tel Aviv: Am

Oved, 1973.

Smilansky, Moshe, *Prakim be-Toldot ha-Yishuv (Chapters in the History of the Yishuv)*, 7 books in 2 vols., Tel Aviv: Dvir, 1959.

Smolenskin, Peretz, *Peretz Smolenskin – Mivhar Ma'amarav (Peretz Smolenskin, Selected Articles)*, Tel Aviv: Shravrak, undated.

Sokolow, Florian, *Avi, Nahum Sokolow (My Father, Nahum Sokolow)*, Jerusalem: The Zionist Library, 1970.

Sokolow, Nahum, *Ha-Tsofeh le-Beit Yisrael (Looking into the House of Israel)*, Jerusalem: The Zionist Library, 1961.

Syrkin, Marie, *Avi, Nachman Syrkin (My Father, Nachman Syrkin)*, Jerusalem: The Zionist Library, 1970.

Talmon, Jacob, *Be-Idan ha-Alimut (The Age of Violence)*, Tel Aviv: Am Oved, 1975.

Tartakower, Arieh, *Am ve Olamo (A People and its World)*, Jerusalem: M. Newman, 1963.

Teveth, Shabtai, *Kinat David (The Jealousy of David)*, Vol. 2: *Ben-Gurion: Ish Mrout (Ben-Gurion: A Man of Authority)*, Tel Aviv: Schocken, 1980.

Teveth, Shabtai, *Moshe Dayan*, Tel Aviv: Schocken, 1972.

Torah (Old Testament).

Tsidon, Asher, *Beit ha-Nivharim (House of Representatives)*, 6th ed., Jerusalem: Ahiasaf, 1971.

Tucazinsky, Nissan Aharon, *Ha-Aretz le-Gvuluteiha, Yerushalayim be-Tmounot (The Borders of the Country – Jerusalem in Pictures)*, Jerusalem: Solomon Printing Press, 1970.

Tzur, Ze'ev, *Ha-Kibbutz ha-Meuchad be-Yishuvah shel Haaretz (The Unified Kibbutz and the Settlement of the Country)*, Vol. 1, 1927-1939, Tel Aviv: Ha-Kibbutz ha-Meuchad, 1979.

Vitkin, Yosef, *Kitvei Yosef Vitkin (Works of Yosef Vitkin)*, Tel Aviv: Am Oved, 1961.

Wallach, Yehuda, *Atlas Carta le-Toldot Eretz Yisrael (Carta's Atlas of History of the Land of Israel)*, Jerusalem: Carta, 1972.

Wallach, Yehuda, *Atlas Carta le-Toldot Eretz Yisrael mi-Rashit ha-Hityashvut ve ad Koum ha-Medina (Carta's Atlas of History of the Land of Israel from the Start of Settlement until the Establishment of the State)*, Jerusalem: Carta, 1974.

Weitz, Yosef, *Ha-Ma'avak al ha-Adamah (The Struggle for the Land)*, Tel Aviv: Tversky, 1950.

Weitz, Yosef, *Hitnahlutenu be-Tkufat ha-Sa'ara (Our Settlement Activities in a Stormy Period)*, Merhavia: Sifriat Poalim, 1947.

Weitz, Yosef, *Yomani ve-Agrotai la-Banim (My Diary and Letters to the Children)*, Vol. 1: 1927-1938, Vol. 2: 1939-1944, Ramat Gan: Masada, 1965.

Yaffe, Hillel, *Dor Ma'afilim (A Generation of Immigrants)*, Jerusalem: The Zionist Library, 1971.

Yaffe, Leib, ed., *Sefer ha-Congress (Book of the [First Zionist] Congress)*, Jerusalem: Jewish Agency, 1950.

Yardeni, Galia, *Ha-Itonout ha-Ivrit be-Eretz Yisrael (Hebrew Press in the Land of Israel)*, Tel Aviv: Tel Aviv University and Ha-Kibbutz ha-Meuchad, 1969.

Yavnieli, Shmuel, *Tkufat Hibbat Zion (Period of Lovers of Zion)*, 2 vols., Jerusalem and Tel Aviv: Bialik Institute and Dvir, 1961.

Yisraeli, David, *Ha-Reich ha-Germani ve Eretz Yisrael (The German Reich and the Land of Israel)*, Jerusalem: Bar-Ilan University in Tel Aviv, 1974.

Zahavi, Zvi, *Mi ha-Hatam Sofer ad Herzl (From the Hatam Sofer to Herzl)*, Jerusalem: The Zionist Library, 1967.

Studies and articles

Aran, Michael, "The Concessions for Oil and Potash Exploration in the Land of Israel", *Catedra*, No. 31, April 1984, pp. 135-158.

Baer, Gabriel, "Orientalism in Israel during the Last Thirty Years", *Ha-Mizrah ha-Hadash*, Vol. 28, Issues 3-4 (111-112), 1980, pp. 175-181.

Biger, Gideon, "Geographic and Political Considerations in the Process of Drawing the Northern Borders of the Land of Israel during the Mandate Period", *Artzot ha-Galil (Lands of the Galilee)*, Avshalom Shmueli, Arnon Sofer and Nurit Kliot (ed.), Haifa: University of Haifa and the Ministry of Defense, 1983, Vol. 1, pp. 427-443.

Caplan, Neil, "Arab-Jewish Contacts in the Land of Israel after the First World War", *Ha-Mizrah ha-Hadash*, Vol. 27, Issues 1-2 (105-106), 1977, pp. 17-45.

Carpi, Daniel, "Weizmann's Political Activities in Italy from 1923 to 1934", in Daniel Carpi, ed., *Ha-Tzionout, Me'asef le-Toldot ha-Tnu'ah ha-Tzionit ve ha-Yishuv ha-Yehudi be-Eretz Yisrael (Zionism: Studies in the History of the Zionist Movement and of the Jewish Community in the Land of Israel)*, Vol. 2, pp. 169-207.

Ellsberg, Abraham, "Drawing the Eastern Borders of the Land of Israel", in Daniel Carpi, ed., *Ha-Tzionout, Me'asef le-Toldot ha-Tnu'ah ha-Tzionit ve ha-Yishuv ha-Yehudi be-Eretz Yisrael (Zionism: Studies in the History of the Zionist Movement and of the Jewish Community in the Land of Israel)*, Vol. 3, pp. 229-246.

Friedman, Menachem, "The Conflict over the Nature of Religious and Rabbinical Schools in Jerusalem during the First Year of the British Occupation", in Daniel Carpi, ed., *Ha-Tzionout, Me'asef le-Toldot ha-Tnu'ah ha-Tzionit ve ha-Yishuv ha-Yehudi be-Eretz Yisrael (Zionism: Studies in the History of the Zionist Movement and of the Jewish Community in the Land of Israel)*, Vol. 2, pp. 105-118.

Friesel, Evyatar, "Night of Crisis between Weizmann and Brandeis", in Daniel Carpi, ed., *Ha-Tzionout, Me'asef le-Toldot ha-Tnu'ah ha-Tzionit ve ha-Yishuv ha-Yehudi be-Eretz Yisrael (Zionism: Studies in the History of the Zionist Movement and of the Jewish Community in the Land of Israel)*, Vol. 4, pp. 146-164.

Giladi, Dan, "The Economic Crisis during the Fourth Aliyah", in Daniel Carpi, ed., *Ha-Tzionout, Me'asef le-Toldot ha-Tnu'ah ha-Tzionit* ve ha-Yishuv ha-Yehudi be-Eretz Yisrael *(Zionism: Studies in the History of the Zionist Movement and of the Jewish Community in the Land of Israel)*, Vol. 2, pp. 119-147.

Goldstein, Jacob, "Zionism and its Position on the Palestinian Question, 1920-1947", *Gesher*, Vol. 26, Issues 1-3, Spring-Summer 1980, pp. 66-81.

Luntz, Yosef, "Diplomatic Contacts between the Zionist Movement and the Arab National Movement at the Close of the First World War", *Ha-Mizrah ha-Hadash*, Vol. 12, Issue 2, 1962, pp. 211-229.

Nimrod, Yoram, "The Husseini Party and the Non-Zionists", in Daniel Carpi, ed., *Ha-Tzionout, Me'asef le-Toldot ha-Tnu'ah ha-Tzionit ve ha-Yishuv ha-Yehudi be-Eretz Yisrael (Zionism: Studies in the History of the Zionist Movement and of the Jewish Community in the Land of Israel)*, Vol. 6, pp. 161-240.

Oren, Elhanan, "Tel Amal: The First in the 'Wall and Tower' [settlements]", in Daniel Carpi, ed., *Ha-Tzionout, Me'asef le-Toldot ha-Tnu'ah ha-Tzionit ve ha-Yishuv ha-Yehudi be-Eretz Yisrael (Zionism: Studies in the History of the Zionist Movement and of the Jewish Community in the Land of Israel)*, Vol. 3, pp. 165-182.

Renault, Moshe, "The Debate on Shaping the Hebrew Education System in the Land of Israel, 1918-1920", in Daniel Carpi, ed., *Ha-Tzionout, Me'asef le-Toldot ha-Tnu'ah ha-Tzionit ve ha-Yishuv ha-Yehudi be-Eretz Yisrael (Zionism: Studies in the History of the Zionist Movement and of the Jewish Community in the Land of Israel)*, Vol. 5, pp. 78-114.

Rogel, Nakdimon, "Weizmann's Man in Damascus: Dr. Shlomo Felman's Mission to Faisal's Court, September 1919 – July 1920", in Daniel Carpi, ed., *Ha-Tzionout, Me'asef le-Toldot ha-Tnu'ah ha-Tzionit ve ha-Yishuv ha-Yehudi be-Eretz Yisrael (Zionism: Studies in the History of the Zionist Movement and of the Jewish Community in the Land of Israel)*, Vol. 8, pp. 279-353.

Sela, Abraham, "Conversations and Contacts between Zionist Leaders and Palestinian Arab Leaders, 1933-1939", Part 1: 1933-1936,

Ha-Mizrah ha-Hadash, Vol. 22, Issue 4 (88), 1972, pp. 401-424; Part 2: 1937-1939, Vol. 23, Issue 1 (89), 1972, pp. 1-21.

Shapira, Anita, "Between Self-Restraint and Terrorism: The Yishuv Meeting in July 1937", in Daniel Carpi, ed., *Ha-Tzionout, Me'asef le-Toldot ha-Tnu'ah ha-Tzionit ve ha-Yishuv ha-Yehudi be-Eretz Yisrael (Zionism: Studies in the History of the Zionist Movement and of the Jewish Community in the Land of Israel)*, Vol. 6, pp. 365-425.

Shapira, Anita, "Issue of Priority Rights over the Lands of Emir Abdullah in Ghor el-Kabed: Start of Contacts between the Zionist Administration and Emir Abdullah", in Daniel Carpi, ed., *Ha-Tzionout, Me'asef le-Toldot ha-Tnu'ah ha-Tzionit ve ha-Yishuv ha-Yehudi be-Eretz Yisrael (Zionism: Studies in the History of the Zionist Movement and of the Jewish Community in the Land of Israel)*, Vol. 3, pp. 295-345.

Shapira, Anita, "The Debate in Mapai on the Use of Violence, 1932-1935", in Daniel Carpi, ed., *Ha-Tzionout, Me'asef le-Toldot ha-Tnu'ah ha-Tzionit ve ha-Yishuv ha-Yehudi be-Eretz Yisrael (Zionism: Studies in the History of the Zionist Movement and of the Jewish Community in the Land of Israel)*, Vol. 5, pp. 141-181.

Shapira, Anita, "'The Left' in the Gdud ha-Avoda (Labor Brigade) and the Palestine Communist Party until 1928", in Daniel Carpi, ed., *Ha-Tzionout, Me'asef le-Toldot ha-Tnu'ah ha-Tzionit ve ha-Yishuv ha-Yehudi be-Eretz Yisrael (Zionism: Studies in the History of the Zionist Movement and of the Jewish Community in the Land of Israel)*, Vol. 2, pp. 148-164.

Shapira, Yonatan, "The Dispute between Chaim Weizmann and Louis Brandeis, 1919-1921", in Daniel Carpi, ed., *Ha-Tzionout, Me'asef le-Toldot ha-Tnu'ah ha-Tzionit ve ha-Yishuv ha-Yehudi be-Eretz Yisrael (Zionism: Studies in the History of the Zionist Movement and of the Jewish Community in the Land of Israel)*, Vol. 3, pp. 141-181.

Sheffer, Gabriel, "Mechanism for Maintaining the Political Capacity of a Charismatic Leader: Weizmann after his Dismissal from the Leadership of the Zionist Movement", *Medina, Mimshal ve Yahasim Benleumim*, No. 10, Spring 1977, pp. 36-55.

Sheffer, Gabriel, "Political Considerations in British Policy-Making on Jewish Immigration to the Land of Israel, 1929-1939", in Daniel Carpi, ed., *Ha-Tzionout, Me'asef le-Toldot ha-Tnu'ah ha-Tzionit ve ha-Yishuv ha-Yehudi be-Eretz Yisrael (Zionism: Studies in the History of the Zionist Movement and of the Jewish Community in the Land of Israel)*, Vol. 5, pp. 198-226.

Werte, Meir, "Zionist-Arab Negotiations in Spring 1919 and British Policy", *Tzion*, Vol. 32, 1967, pp. 75-115.

Newspapers

Davar (Tel Aviv), daily newspaper, issue of 12/6/1973.

Haaretz (Tel Aviv), daily newspaper, issues of 20-23/8/1920; 16/9/1921; 19/9/1921; 25-28/9/1921; 6/10/1921; 9/8/1923; 3/7/1931, 5/7/1931, 14/7/1931, 16-17/7/1931.

English

Books and pamphlets

Antonius, George, *The Arab Awakening*, London: Hamish Hamilton, 1961.

Avnery, Uri, *Israel Without Zionists*, New York: Macmillan, 1968.

Barbour, Nevill, *Nisi Dominus*, Beirut: The Institute for Palestine Studies, 1969 (Reprint).

Barron, J. B., *Report and General Abstracts of the Census of 1922: Taken on the 23rd of October, 1922*, Jerusalem: Greek Convent Press, 1922.

Bethell, Nicholas, *The Palestine Triangle: The Struggle for the Holy Land, 1935-48*, New York: G. P. Putnam's Sons, 1979.

Black, Edwin, *The Transfer Agreement: The Dramatic Story of the Pact Between the Third Reich and Jewish Palestine*, New York and London: Macmillan Publishing Company, Collier Macmillan Publishers, 1984.

Boustany, W. F., *The Palestine Mandate, Invalid and Impracticable*, Beirut: American University Press, 1936.

Brenner, Lenni, *Zionism in the Age of the Dictators*, London and Canberra: Croom Helm; Westport (Connecticut): Lawrence Hill, 1983.

Buber, Martin, *A Land of Two Peoples, Martin Buber on Jews and Arabs*, (Paul Mendes-Flohr, ed.), New York: Oxford University Press, 1983.

Caplan, Neil, *Futile Diplomacy*, Vol. 1: *Early Arab-Zionist Negotiation Attempts, 1913-1931*, London: Frank Cass, 1983.

Caplan, Neil, *Palestine Jewry and the Arab Question, 1917-1925*, London: Frank Cass, 1978.

Documents on German Foreign Policy, 1918-1945, Series C, Vol. I, Washington: Department of State, 1960.

Documents on German Foreign Policy, 1915-1945, Series D, Vol. V, Washington: United States Government Printing Office, 1953.

Drayton, Robert, *The Laws of Palestine*, 4 vols., Jerusalem: Government of Palestine, 1934.

El Kodsy, Ahmad, and Lobel, Eli, *The Arab World and Israel*, New York: Monthly Review Press, 1970.

Enardu, Maria Grazia, *Palestine in Anglo-Vatican Relations, 1936-1939*, Firenze: Clusf, 1980.

Encyclopaedia Britannica, London: Encyclopaedia Britannica Inc., 1964.

Encyclopaedia Judaica, Vols. 5, 8, 9, 13, New York: Macmillan, 1971; Jerusalem: Keter, 1972.

Encyclopaedia of Zionism and Israel, Vol. 1, New York: Merzl Press/McGraw Hill, 1971.

Esco Foundation for Palestine, Inc., *Palestine: A Study of Jewish, Arab, and British Policies*, 2 vols., New Haven: Yale University Press, 1947.

Flapan, Simha, *Zionism and the Palestinians*, London: Croom Helm, 1979.

Furlonge, Geoffrey, *Palestine Is My Country: The Story of Musa Alami*, London: John Murray, 1969.

Gilbert, Martin, *The Arab Israeli Conflict: Its History in Maps*, London: Weidenfeld and Nicolson, 1974.

Granott, Abraham, *Agrarian Reform and the Record of Israel*, London: Eyre and Spottiswoode, 1956.

Great Britain and Palestine, 1915-1945, published in 1946 by the Royal Institute of International Affairs, London, Reprinted; Westport, Connecticut: Hyperion Press, Inc., 1976.

Haim, Yehoyada, *Abandonment Of Illusions: Zionist Political Attitudes Toward Palestinian Arab Nationalism, 1936-1939*, Boulder, Colorado: Westview Press, 1983.

Halpern, Ben, *The Idea of the Jewish State*, Cambridge: Harvard University Press, 1969.

Hattis, Susan Lee, *The Bi-National Idea in Palestine During Mandatory Times*, Haifa: Shikmona Publishing Company, 1970.

Herzl, Theodor, *The Jewish State, Proposal of a Modern Solution for the Jewish Question*, translated by Sylvie D'Avigdor, London: Central Office of the Zionist Organization, 1934.

Herzl, Theodor, *The Old New Land (Altneuland)*, Translated by Lotta Levinshon, New York: Bloch Publishing Company and Herzl Press, 1960.

Hess, Moses, *Rome and Jerusalem*, New York: Bloch Publishing Company, 1945.

Hurewitz, J. C., *The Struggle for Palestine*, New York: W. W. Norton and Company, 1950.

Hyamson, Albert M., *The British Consulate in Jerusalem, 1838-1914*, 2 vols., London: The Jewish Historical Society of England, 1939.

John, Robert and Hadawi, Sami, *The Palestine Diary*, 2 vols., Beirut: Palestine Research Centre, Palestine Liberation Organization, 1970.

Kallen, Horace Meyer, *Zionism and World Politics: A Study in History and Social Psychology*, Garden City, New York, and Toronto: Doubleday, Page and Company, 1921.

Kedourie, Elie and Haim, Sylvia G. (eds.), *Zionism and Arabism in Palestine and Israel*, London: Frank Cass, 1982.

Khalidi, Walid, ed., *From Haven to Conquest*, Beirut: Institute for Palestine Studies, 1971.

Kisch, Frederick Hermann, *Letter from Col. F. H. Kisch: To the Chairman Political Commission, XVII*[th] *Zionist Congress and the Chairman Political Commission II*[nd] *Assembly of the Council of the Jewish Agency for Palestine; Accompanied by a Report on the Work of the Joint Bureau for Arab Relations, and a Memorandum on Intellectual, Social and Economic Cooperation Between Jews and Arabs*, London: Azriel Press, 1931.

Kisch, Frederich Hermann, *Palestine Diary*, London: Victor Collancz, 1938.

Koestler, Arthur, *Promise and Fulfilment – Palestine 1917-1949*, New York: The MacMillan Company, 1949.

Laqueur, Walter, *A History of Zionism*, London: Weidenfeld and Nicolson, 1972.

Leon, Abram, *The Jewish Question: A Marxist Interpretation*, New York: Pathfinder Press, 1970.

Lloyd George, David, *Memoirs of the Peace Conference*, 2 vols., New Haven: Yale University Press, 1939.

Lloyd George, David, *The Truth about the Peace Treaties*, 2 vols., London: Victor Gollancz Ltd., 1938.

Lloyd George, David, *War Memoirs*, 2 vols., London: Odhams Press, 1938.

Magness, Judah L., *Like All The Nations?* Jerusalem: Weiss Press, 1930.

Marmorstein, Emile, *Heaven at Bay; the Jewish Kulturkampf in the Holy Land*, London: Oxford University Press, 1969.

Marx, Karl, *Karl Marx, Friedrich Engels: Collected Works*, Vol. 3 (1843-

Bibliography 573

1844), Moscow: Progress Publishers, 1975.

Memorandum on the Jewish Agency with Appendix of Documents, London: The Board of Deputies of British Jews, April 1929.

Mendelsohn, Ezra, *Class Struggle in the Pale: The Formative Years of the Jewish Workers' Movement in Tsarist Russia*, London: Cambridge University Press, 1970.

Meyer W. Weisgal and Joel Carmichael, eds., *Chaim Weizmann, A Biography by Several Hands*, London: Weidenfeld and Nicolson, 1962.

Patai, Raphael, ed., *The Complete Diaries of Theodor Herzl*, translated by Harry Zohn, 5 vols., New York and London: The Herzl Press and Thomas Yoseloff, 1960.

Phillips, Harlan B., *Felix Frankfurter Reminisces*, London: Socker and Warburg, 1960.

Report on the Legal Structure, Activities, Assets, Income and Liabilities of Keren Kayemet le-Yisrael, Jerusalem: Keren Kayemet le-Yisrael, 1963.

Reports of the Experts, Submitted to the Joint Palestine Survey Commission, Boston, Massachusetts: Daniels Printing Press, 1928.

Samuel, Herbert Louis (Viscount), *Memoirs*, London: Cresset Press, 1945.

Schechtman, Joseph B., *Rebel and Statesman, The Vladimir Jabotinsky Story*, 2 vols., New York: Thomas Yoseloff, 1956.

Schechtman, Joseph B. and Benari, Yehuda, *History of the Revisionist Movement*, Vol.1, 1925-1930, Tel Aviv: Hadar, 1970.

Shahak, Israel and Mezvinsky, Norton, *Jewish Fundamentalism in Israel*, London: Pluto Press, 2004.

Smith, Gary V., ed., *Zionism: The Dream and the Reality; a Jewish Critique*, New York: Barnes and Noble, 1974.

Sokolow, Nahum, *History of Zionism, 1600-1918*, 2 vols., London: Longmans, Green and Co., 1919.

Stein, Kenneth W., *The Land Question in Palestine, 1917-1939*, Chapel Hill and London: The University of North Carolina Press, 1984.

Stein, Leonard, *The Balfour Declaration*, London: Vallentine Mitchell, 1961.

Stein, Leonard, *The Palestine White Paper of October 1930 (Memorandum)*, London: Jewish Agency for Palestine, 1930.

Storrs, Ronald, *Orientations*, London: Ivor Nicholson and Watson, 1937.

Sykes, Christopher, *Crossroads to Israel*, London: Collins, 1965.

Talmon, Jacob Leib, *Israel Among the Nations*, London: Weidenfeld and Nicolson, 1970.

Weizmann, Chaim, *The Zionist movement 1916-1931: Statement of policy submitted to the XVIIth Zionist Congress, Basle, July 1st, 1931*, London: The Zionist Federation of Great Britain and Northern Ireland, 1931.

Weizmann, Chaim, *Trial and Error*, London: East and West Library, 1950.

Weizmann, Vera, *The Impossible Takes Longer*, London: Hamish Hamilton, 1967.

Studies, articles and letters

Abdel Nasser, Gamal, letter to John F. Kennedy, Office of the President, The United Arab Republic, Alexandria, Egypt, August 22, 1961. English translation: John F. Kennedy Presidential Library and Museum, https://www.jfklibrary.org/asset-viewer/archives/jfknsf-169-005#?image_identifier=JFKNSF-169-005-p0013, accessed December 29, 2024.

Bowden, Tom, "The Politics of Arab Rebellion in Palestine: 1936-1939", *Middle Eastern Studies*, Vol. 2, No. 2, May 1975, pp. 147-174.

DuBoff, Max, "The Three Blessings: Past and Future", Cairo Genizah T-S NS 229:2 and Cambridge Add. 3160:1 (Kahn, 12), Sefaria, https://www.sefaria.org.il/sheets/119367?lang=he (accessed January 9, 2025).

Gorni (Gorny), Yosef, "Zionist Socialism and the Arab Question, 1918-1930", *Middle Eastern Studies*, Vol. 13, No. 1, January 1977, pp. 50-70.

Haim, Yehoyada, "Zionist Policies and Attitudes towards the Arabs on the Eve of the Arab Revolt, 1936", *Middle Eastern Studies*, Vol. 14, No. 2, May 1978, pp. 211-231.

Khatib, Rasha, McKee, Martin, and Yusuf, Salim, "Counting the dead in Gaza: difficult but essential", *The Lancet*, Vol, 404, No. 10449, July 20, 2014, pp. 237-238, https://www.thelancet.com/journals/lancet/article/PIIS0140-6736(24)01169-3/fulltext. Accessed on January 11, 2025.

Kedourie, Elie, "Sir Herbert Samuel and the Government of Palestine", *Middle Eastern Studies*, Vol. 5, No. 1, January 1969, pp. 44-68.

Mandel, Neville, "Attempts at an Arab-Zionist Entente, 1913-1914", *Middle Eastern Studies*, Vol. 1, No. 3, April 1965, pp. 238-267.

Mandel, Neville, "Ottoman Policy and Restrictions on Jewish Settlement in Palestine, 1881-1908", *Middle Eastern Studies*, Vol. 10, No. 3, October 1974, pp. 312-332.

Mandel, Neville, "Ottoman Practice as Regards Jewish Settlement in Palestine, 1881-1908", *Middle Eastern Studies*, Vol. 11, No. 1, January 1975, pp. 33-46.

Ro'i, Yacov, "The Zionist Attitude to the Arabs, 1908-1914", *Middle Eastern Studies*, Vol. 4, No. 3, April 1968, pp. 198-242.

Rose, Norman, "The Debate on Partition, 1937-1938: The Anglo Zionist Aspect, I. The Proposal", *Middle Eastern Studies*, Vol. 6, No. 3, October 1970, pp. 297-318; "... II. The Withdrawal", ibid., Vol. 7, No. 1, January 1971, pp. 3-24.

Ussishkin, Anne, "The Jewish Colonisation Association and a Rothschild in Palestine", *Middle Eastern Studies*, Vol. 9, No. 3, October 1973, pp. 347-357.

News articles

Chrisafis, Angelique and Sherwood, Harriet, "Yasser Arafat may have been poisoned with polonium, tests show", *The Guardian*, November 6, 2013, https://www.theguardian.com/world/2013/nov/06/yasser-arafat-poisoned-polonium-tests-scientists. Accessed January 4, 2025.

"Israel social security data reveals true picture of Oct 7 deaths", France 24 (AFP), December 15, 2023, https://www.france24.com/en/live-news/20231215-israel-social-security-data-reveals-true-picture-of-oct-7-deaths. Accessed January 5, 2025.

Kaufman, Ami, "Poll: 70% of Israeli Jews believe Jews are 'Chosen People'", *+972 Magazine*, January 27, 2012, https://www.972mag.com/poll-shows-israel-slowly-but-surely-turning-into-a-theocracy/. Accessed January 5, 2025.

Levy, Gideon, "79 Percent of Right-wingers Believe Jews Are the Chosen People. Are You for Real?", *Haaretz*, September 15, 2018. https://www.haaretz.com/opinion/2018-09-15/ty-article/.premium/79-percent-of-right-wingers-believe-jews-are-the-chosen-people-are-you-for-real/0000017f-f000-d487-abff-f3fef8be0000. Accessed January 5, 2025.

Tlozek, Eric, Halpern, Orly and Horn, Allyson, "Israeli forces accused of killing their own citizens under the 'Hannibal Directive' during October 7 chaos", *ABC News*, September 6, 2024, https://www.abc.net.au/news/2024-09-07/israel-hannibal-directive-kidnap-hamas-gaza-hostages-idf/104224430. Accessed January 5, 2025.

Winstanley, Asa, "How Israel killed hundreds of its own people on 7 October", *The Electronic Intifada*, October 7, 2024, https://electronicintifada.net/content/how-israel-killed-hundreds-its-own-people-7-october/49216. Accessed January 5, 2025.

Jamaluddine, Zeina, Abukmail, Hanan, Aly, Sarah, Campbell, Oona M R, and Checchi, Francesco, "Traumatic injury mortality in the Gaza Strip from Oct 7, 2023, to June 30, 2024: a capture–recapture analysis", *The Lancet*, January 9, 2025, https://www.thelancet.com/

journals/lancet/article/PIIS0140-6736(24)02678-3/fulltext. Accessed January 11, 2025.

Publications of Palestinian bodies

Arab Higher Committee:

Memorandum Submitted by the Arab Higher Committee to the Permanent Mandates Commission and the Secretary of State for the Colonies, dated July 23rd, 1937.

Palestine Arab Congress:

Report on the State of Palestine during Four Years of Civil Administration submitted to the Mandates Commission of the League of Nations through H. E. The High Commissioner for Palestine by the Executive Committee of the Palestine Arab Congress, Jerusalem, 1924.

Report on the State of Palestine submitted to His Excellency the High Commissioner for Palestine by the Executive Committee, Palestine Arab Congress on 13 October 1925, Jerusalem, 1925.

Two Memoranda submitted to the Council and Permanent Mandates Commission of the League of Nations through H. E. the High Commissioner for Palestine by the Executive Committee, Jerusalem, 1925.

Palestine Arab Delegation:

The Holy Land. The Moslem-Christian Case against Zionist Aggression; Official Statement of the Palestine Arab Delegation, London: February 1922.

British government publications

I. Great Britain, Parliamentary Papers:

Agreement between His Majesty's Government and the French Government respecting the Boundary Line between Syria and Palestine from the Mediterranean to El Hamme (With Three Maps), Treaty Series No. 13, 1923 (Cmd. 1910), London: His Majesty's Stationary Office, 1923.

Agreement between Palestine and Syria and the Lebanon to Facilitate Good

Neighbourly Relations in connection with Frontier Questions (Signed at Jerusalem, February 2, 1926), Treaty Series No. 19, 1927 (Cmd. 2919), London: H.M.S.O., 1927.

Agreement between Palestine and Syria and the Lebanon, Amending the Agreement of February 2, 1926, Regarding Frontier Questions, November 3, 1938, Treaty Series No. 34, 1939 (Cmd. 6065), London: H.M.S.O., 1939.

An Interim Report on the Civil Administration of Palestine During the Period 1st July 1920-30th June 1921, August 1921 (Cmd. 1499), London: H.M.S.O., 1921.

Correspondence respecting the Turco-Egyptian Frontier in the Sinai Peninsula (With a Map), Egypt No. 2, 1906 (Cmd. 306), London: H.M.S.O., 1906.

Correspondence with the Palestine Arab Delegation and the Zionist Organization, June 1922 (Cmd. 1700), London: H.M.S.O., 1922.

Disturbances in May 1921. Report of the Commission of Inquiry with Correspondence Relating Thereto, October 1921 (Cmd. 1540), London: H.M.S.O., 1921.

Franco-British Convention of December 23, 1920 on Certain Points connected with the Mandates for Syria and the Lebanon, Palestine and Mesopotamia (Cmd. 1195), London: H.M.S.O., 1921.

Great Britain, Parliamentary Papers, 1939, *Command 5957: Correspondence between Sir Henry McMahon, His Majesty's High Commissioner at Cairo, and the Sherif Hussein of Mecca, July 1915-March 1916.*

Great Britain, Parliamentary Papers, 1939, *Command 5974: Report of a Committee Set Up to Consider Certain Correspondence Between Sir Henry McMahon [His Majesty's High Commissioner in Egypt] and The Sharif of Mecca in 1915 and 1916, March 16, 1939.*

Mandate for Palestine; Letter from the Secretary to the Cabinet to the Secretary-General of the League of Nations of July 1, 1922, Enclosing a Note in Reply to Cardinal Gasparri's Letter of May 15, 1922, Addressed to the Secretary General of the League of Nations, Miscellaneous No. 4, 1922 (Cmd. 1708), London: H.M.S.O., 1922.

League of Nations:

Mandate for Palestine, Together with a Note by the Secretary-General Relating to its Application to the Territory known as Transjordan, Under the Provisions of Article 25, December 1922 (Cmd. 1785), London: H.M.S.O., 1922.

Palestine Land Transfers Regulations, Letter to the Secretary General of the League of Nations, London, February 28, 1940, Miscellaneous No. 2, 1940 (Cmd. 6180), London: H.M.S.O., 1940.

Palestine Partition Commission Report, October 1938 (Cmd. 5854), London: H.M.S.O., 1938.

Palestine Royal Commission Report, July 1937 (Cmd. 5479), London: H.M.S.O., 1937.

Papers relating to the Elections for the Palestine Legislative Council, 1923 (Cmd. 1889), London: H.M.S.O., 1923.

Policy in Palestine. Dispatch Dated 23rd December 1937, from the Secretary of State for the Colonies to the High Commissioner for Palestine (Cmd. 5634), London: H.M.S.O., 1938.

Proposed Formation of an Arab Agency; Correspondence with the High Commissioner for Palestine (Cmd. 1989), London: H.M.S.O., 1923.

Proposed New Constitution for Palestine, March 1936 (Cmd. 5119), London: H.M.S.O., 1936.

Report of the Commission on the Palestine Disturbances of August 1929, March 1930 (Cmd. 3530), London: H.M.S.O., 1930.

Report on Immigration, Land Settlement and Development, By Sir John Hope Simpson, October 1930 (Cmd. 3686, 3687), London: H.M.S.O., 1930. 2 vols.

Statement of Policy by His Majesty's Government in the United Kingdom, October 1930 (The Passfield White Paper; Cmd. 3692), London: H.M.S.O., 1930.

Statement of Policy by His Majesty's Government in the United Kingdom, July 1937 (Cmd. 5513), London: H.M.S.O., 1937.

Statement by His Majesty's Government in the United Kingdom, November 1938 (Cmd. 5893), London: H.M.S.O., 1938.

Statements made on behalf of His Majesty's Government during the Year 1918, in Regard to the Future Status of Certain Parts of the Ottoman Empire, Miscellaneous No. 4, 1939 (Cmd. 5964), London: H.M.S.O., 1939.

Statement of Policy, May 1939 (Cmd. 6019), London: H.M.S.O., 1939.

Statement with Regard to British Policy, May 1930 (Cmd. 3582), London: H.M.S.O., 1930.

The Western or Wailing Wall in Jerusalem. Memorandum by the Secretary of State for the Colonies, November 1928 (Cmd. 3229), London: H.M.S.O., 1928.

II. Great Britain, Non-Parliamentary Publications:

A Brief Record of the Advance of the [British] Egyptian Expeditionary Force, July 1917 to October 1918, Compiled from Official Sources, London: H.M.S.O., 1919.

Palestine Royal Commission:

Minutes of Evidence Heard at Public Sessions (Colonial No. 134), London: H.M.S.O., 1937.

Palestine Royal Commission, Summary of Report, Official Communique No. 9/37, July 7th, 1937.

Report of the Commission Appointed by His Majesty's Government in the United Kingdom of Great Britain and Northern Ireland, with the Approval of the Council of the League of Nations to Determine the Rights and Claims of Moslems and Jews in Connection with the Western or Wailing Wall at Jerusalem, December 1930, London: H.M.S.O., 1931.

Statement by His Majesty's Government in the United Kingdom, Official Communique No. 8/38, November 9th, 1938.

III. Great Britain, Colonial Office:

Report by His Britannic Majesty's Government on the Administration under Mandate of Palestine and Trans-Jordan for the year 1924 (Colonial No. 12), London: H.M.S.O., 1925.

Report by His Britannic Majesty's Government to the Council of the League of Nations on the Administration of Palestine and Trans-Jordan for the year 1925 (Colonial No. 20), London: H.M.S.O., 1926; ... *year 1926 (Colonial No. 26)*, 1927; and ... *year 1927 (Colonial No. 31)*, 1928.

Report by His Majesty's Government in the United Kingdom of Great Britain and Northern Ireland to the Council of the League of Nations on the Administration of Palestine and Trans-Jordan for the year 1928 (Colonial No. 40), London: H.M.S.O., 1929; ... *year 1929 (Colonial No. 47)*, 1930; ... *year 1930 (Colonial No. 59)*, 1931; ... *year 1933 (Colonial No. 94)*, 1934; ... *year 1934 (Colonial No. 104)*, 1935; ... *year 1931 (Colonial No. 75)*, 1932; ... *year 1932 (Colonial No. 82)*, 1933; ... *year 1935 (Colonial No. 112)*, 1936; ... *year 1936 (Colonial No. 129)*, 1937; ... *year 1937 (Colonial No. 146)*, 1938; and ... *year 1938 (Colonial No. 166)*, 1939.

Report of the High Commissioner on the Administration of Palestine, 1920-1925 (Colonial No. 15), London: H.M.S.O., 1925.

Report on Palestine Administration, 1923 (Colonial No. 5), London: H.M.S.O., 1924.

Government of Palestine publications:

A Survey of Palestine, Prepared in December 1945 and January 1946 for the Information of the Anglo-American Committee of Inquiry, 3 vols., Jerusalem: Government Printer, 1946.

Census of Palestine 1931, Vol. 1: Report; Vol. 2: Tables, by E. Mills, Alexandria (Egypt): Whitehead Morris Ltd., 1933.

The Committee for Moslem Religious Affairs, Jerusalem: Government Printer (?), 1921.

Memoranda, Prepared by the Government of Palestine for the use of the Palestine Royal Commission, 3 vols., Jerusalem: Government Printing Press, 1936 (?).

Government of Palestine reports:

Daily Report on the Effects of the Israeli Aggression in Palestine, From October 7th until June 28th, 2025, Minister's Office, Ministry of Health, State of Palestine, 28 June 2025, https://site.moh.ps/Content/File/

t8S7FCtVUpmfKadFvldmz1zQ_MYfJIzqozBzQFoLyzgAkw4vH. pdf. Accessed June 28, 2025.

First Report on Agricultural Development and Land Settlement in Palestine, by Lewis French (Director of Development), Jerusalem: Government Printer (?), December 1931.

Report on Palestine Administration, July 1920-December 1921, London: H.M.S.O., 1922.

Statistical Abstract of Palestine 1936; …1939; …1940, Jerusalem: Government Printer, 1936, 1939 and 1940.

Supplementary Report on Agricultural Development and Land Settlement in Palestine, by Lewis French, Jerusalem: Government Printer (?), 1932.

International Rescue Committee:

"Unaccompanied and separated children in Gaza" (Report), International Rescue Committee, August 31, 2024, https://www.rescue.org/report/unaccompanied-and-separated-children-gaza-executive-summary. Accessed January 9, 2025.

Publications of the World Zionist Organization, the Jewish Agency and their agencies

World Zionist Organization:

The Mandate for Palestine, Memorandum Submitted to the Council of the League of Nations by the Zionist Organization, 7 July 1922, London: Zionist Organization, 1922.

World Zionist Organization, Zionist Congress:

Report[s] of the Executive of the Zionist Organization to the XIIth Zionist Congress (1921), I. Political Report, II. Palestine Report, III. Organization Report, IV. Financial Report, London: National Labour Press, Ltd., 1921; *Report … to the XIIIth … Congress (1923)*, London, 1923; *… to the XIVth … Congress, at Vienna, August 18th-28th, 1925, … to the XVth … Congress, at Basle, August 30th-September 9th, 1927; … to the XVIth … Congress, at Zu-*

rich, July 28th-August 7th, 1929, London: Central Office of the Zionist Organization, 1925, 1927 and 1929.

World Zionist Organization, the Jewish Agency for Palestine:

Report of the Executive of the Zionist Organization Submitted to the XVIIth Zionist Congress, at Basle, June 30th-July 10th, 1931 and Report of the Executive of the Jewish Agency to the Council of the Agency, ... to the XVIIIth ... Congress, at Prague, August 21st-29th, 1933; ... to the XIXth Congress, at Lucerne, August 20th-30th, 1935, London: Central Office of the Zionist Organization, 1931, 1933 and 1935.

Report of the Executives of the Zionist Organization and the Jewish Agency for Palestine submitted to the XXth Zionist Congress and the Vth Session of the Council of the Jewish Agency at Zurich, August 1937; ... to the XXIst ... Congress and ... VI Session ... at Geneva, August 1939, Jerusalem: Executives of the Zionist Organization and of the Jewish Agency for Palestine, 1937 and 1939.

The Jewish Agency for Palestine:

Constitution of the Jewish Agency for Palestine, London: The Jewish Agency for Palestine, 1929.

The Jewish Case against the Palestine White Paper, London: Jewish Agency for Palestine, 1939.

Memorandum submitted to the Palestine Royal Commission on Behalf of the Jewish Agency for Palestine, London: Jewish Agency for Palestine, November 1936.

Political Report of the Executive of the Jewish Agency submitted to the XXth Zionist Congress and the Vth Session of the Council of the Jewish Agency at Zurich, August 1937; ... to the XXIst ... Congress and ... VIth Session of ... Agency at Geneva, August 1939, Jerusalem: Executive of the Jewish Agency, 1937 and 1939.

Report on the Political Work of the Executive of the Jewish Agency in Palestine submitted to the 19th Zionist Congress and the 4th Meeting of the Council of the Jewish Agency at Lucerne, August 20th-September 5th, 1935, Jerusalem: Jewish Agency, 1935.

The Jewish Agency for Palestine, Central Bureau for the Settlement of German Jews:

Report to the XIXth Zionist Congress and to the IVth Council of the Jewish Agency in Lucerne (1935), ... to the XXth ... Congress ... and ... Agency in Zurich (1937), ... to the XXIst ... Congress ... and ... Agency in Geneva (1939), Jerusalem: Central Bureau for the Settlement of German Jews in Palestine, 1935, 1937 and 1939.

Jewish National Fund (Keren Kayemet le-Yisrael Ltd.):

Report of the Head Office of the Jewish National Fund to the XIIth Zionist Congress, 1921, London: National Labour Press Ltd., 1921.

Report[s] of the Head Office to the XVIth-XXIst Zionist Congresses, 1929-1939, Jerusalem: Head Office of the Keren Kayemet le-Yisrael Ltd. Palestine National Fund, 1929-1939.

Palestine Foundation Fund (Keren Hayesod):

Report(s) of the Head Office of the Palestine Foundation Fund to the XIIth-XXIst Zionist Congresses, 1921-1939, London: Zionist Organization, 1921-1925, Jerusalem: Head Office of the Keren Hayesod, 1927-1939.

Arabic

Books

Al-Ghouri, Emile, *Palestine through Sixty Years*, 2 vols., Beirut: Dar al-Nahar, 1972-1973.

Al-Hussein, Abdullah bin (King), *The Complete Works of King Abdullah bin al-Hussein*, Beirut: United Publishing House, 1979.

Darwaza, Muhammad Azza, *On the Modern Arab Movement*, Vol. 3, Sidon and Beirut: Modern Library Publications, 1959.

Kayyali, Abdel Wahhab, ed., *Documents of Arab Palestinian Resistance to British Occupation and Zionism: 1918-1939*, Beirut and Baghdad: Institute for Palestine Studies and the Palestine Fund Society, 1968.

Bibliography 585

Kayyali, Abdel Wahhab, *Palestine: A Modern History*, Beirut: Arab Foundation for Studies and Publishing, 1970.

Khilleh, Kamel Mahmoud, *Palestine and the British Mandate 1922-1939*, Beirut: Palestine Research Center, Palestine Liberation Organization, 1974.

Palestine Documents File, 2 vols., Cairo: Ministry of Guidance, State Information Service, 1969.

Sakhnini, Essam, *Palestine the State; the Roots of the Issue in Palestinian History*, Nicosia: Palestine Research Center, Palestine Liberation Organization, 1985.

Tannous, Izzat, *The Palestinians: A Glorious Past and a Brilliant Future*, Vol. 1, Beirut: Palestine Research Center, Palestine Liberation Organization, 1982.

The Palestine Gazette (official gazette of the British mandate government), issues of 1/1/1922, 1/4/1926, 16/7/1926, 1/4/1929, 1/5/1929, 28/10/1937, 1/7/1939, 28/10/1939, 30/12/1939, 7/6/1945, 1/1/1947.

Zu'aytir, Akram, *Documents of the Palestinian National Movement 1918-1939: from the Akram Zu'aytir Papers*, prepared by Bayan Nuwayhid al-Hout, Beirut: Institute for Palestine Studies, 1979.

Zu'aytir, Akram, *The Palestine National Movement 1935-1939: Diaries of Akram Zu'aytir*, Beirut: Institute for Palestine Studies, 1980.

Index

Abraham 41-42, 44-45, 48-49, 69, 296, 300, 306, 389, 504,

Acre 52-53, 107, 116-117, 314, 345, 375, 410-411

Advisory Council 408, 415, 418

Agudat Israel 241-242, 423, 460-462, 562

Ahad Ha'am (Ginsberg, Asher Zvi) 92-93, 97, 133-138, 140-141, 143, 145, 147-148, 150, 161, 192, 202, 208, 296, 309

Aharonovich, Yosef 234, 271, 288, 332

Ahdut (Unity) 274, 304, 306, 391, 442-445, 451-455, 463, 466, 482, 488-489, 492-493, 497-499, 501, 517-519

Ahdut ha-Avoda 443-445, 451-455, 463, 466, 482, 488-489, 492-493, 497-499, 501, 517, 518-519

Ahuzat Bayit – see Tel Aviv 278-279, 281

al-Aref, Aref 365-366, 383

Aleppo 43, 345, 361

Alexander II 23, 76, 87, 218

Alexandria 106, 111, 330, 335, 524

Algeria 34, 142, 166, 534-535

al-Husseini, (Hajj) Amin 365-367, 386-387, 400

al-Husseini, Musa Kazim 358, 365-366, 385-387, 417

al-Kalai, Judah 67-69, 72-73, 76, 98, 168

al-Khadeira – see Hadera

Allenby, Edmund 336, 345, 349, 431-432

Alliance (Alliance Israélite Universelle) 18, 61, 70, 121, 321

al-Shajarah – see also Ilania 144, 275, 283-284, 295

Altneuland 161-162, 212, 558, 571

America – see United States

Anti-Semitism 33, 35, 37-40, 51, 73, 84, 90, 135, 154-158, 185, 190-191, 198, 210, 249, 250-251, 254, 259, 289, 448, 538, 546

Aqaba 42, 45, 349, 388

Arab Agency 416, 418

Arab Executive Committee
– see Palestine Executive Committee, Palestine Arab Congress

Index

Argentina 19, 36, 126, 142, 158, 428-429, 453, 477

Ashkenazi – see Jewish sects

Austria 2, 16, 20, 32-33, 38, 54-55, 106, 114, 166, 168, 178, 196, 257, 424, 426, 428, 448, 477, 486

Auto-Emancipation – see also Pinsker, Judah Leib (Leon) 92-93, 95, 126, 154

Baal Shem Tov – see ben Eliezer, Israel

Baghdad 391, 511, 533, 539

Balfour, Arthur James 315, 322-324, 327, 340, 367-368, 372, 509, 535, 537

Balfour Declaration 187, 213-214, 307, 312, 316, 326-328, 331, 334, 336-338, 347, 350-351, 358, 360, 367, 369, 373, 381, 389, 391, 394, 398, 404, 406, 413, 417, 419, 427, 431-432, 437, 456, 463, 471, 473, 478, 510-511, 514, 522-523, 529, 531, 533

Basel – see also Zionism: congresses: First, Second, Third, Fifth, Sixth, Seventh, Tenth 69, 79, 112, 153, 165, 167-168, 170-171, 186, 188, 195-197, 201, 223, 227-228, 230-231, 237, 257, 308, 462, 475-476, 480

Bat Shlomo 125, 131, 142

Beersheba (Bir al-Sabe) 43, 336, 343, 375, 410-411

Be'er Tuvia 131, 142, 144, 150

Beirut i, v, 52, 111, 113, 116, 302, 331, 345, 352, 505, 520

Ben-Gurion, David 274, 299, 306, 332, 437, 442, 497-499

ben Maimon, Moses – see Maimonides

Ben-Yehuda, Eliezer 64, 83, 95-98, 109, 212

Berlin 11, 24, 29, 33, 38-39, 70, 82, 92, 99, 206, 209, 236, 240, 301, 307-308, 329-330, 461

Bethlehem 410-411

Bilu'im 108, 119-120, 125, 127

Bir al-Sabe – see Beersheba

Bismarck, Otto von 38, 63

Bnei Moshe 136-139

Bnei Moshe society 137, 139

Bodenheimer, Max 167-168, 176-177, 308

Borochov, Ber 258-263, 272, 286, 442

Brandeis, Louis 309-310, 319, 322-323, 325-326, 330, 356, 367, 376, 424, 463, 465-467, 469

Britain 4, 15-16, 18-19, 34, 54, 59-60, 64, 68, 81, 82, 121, 140, 165, 166, 168, 176, 179, 181-182, 187-188, 213-214, 219, 232, 309, 310-317, 319-320, 322-324, 327-328, 334-335, 337-339, 341-343, 344, 347-349, 351-352, 354-356, 360-362, 369, 370-371, 373, 375-376, 380-381, 384-385, 389, 393-

394, 397, 402-406, 416, 419, 425, 427, 432-439, 441, 448, 453, 464, 471, 477, 486, 504, 510-512, 515, 522, 523, 524, 527-530, 533-535, 541, 546, 549

Bulgaria 82, 85, 111, 166, 168, 426, 477, 486

Bund 25, 135, 203, 246-252, 256-257, 424, 446, 468

Cairo 182-183, 312, 338, 341, 349, 387, 391, 516

Canada 428-430, 437, 477

Carlsbad 475, 478-479

Catholic Church 4, 371

Cemal Pasha 330-332, 340, 437

Chamberlain, Houston Stewart 38, 182-183

Chibbat Zion (also: Hibbat Zion) – see Lovers of Zion

Chlenov, Yechiel 308-309, 445

Churchill, Winston 387, 391, 394, 397, 405-406, 408, 473

Cologne 156, 231, 236, 280, 308

Colonization 34, 172-173, 194, 226, 534, 539

Communist International 453-454

Congress of Berlin, 1878 24, 82

Congress of Vienna, 1815 15, 22

Cooperative settlement 233, 238, 279, 308, 501, 503

Copenhagen 308-310, 334, 424, 464

Crane, Charles 354-356, 361

Crimea 449, 456-457

Cromer, Lord (Baring, Evelyn) 182, 184

Cyprus – see also Zionist settle projects

Czechoslovakia 425-426, 477-478, 486, 527, 531

Damascus 43, 59, 277, 331, 345, 360-362, 369, 384, 511, 515, 549

Democratic Faction 197-200, 202, 207, 212, 214

Dreyfus, Alfred 39-40, 154, 207

Drishat Zion (Seeking Zion) – see Kalischer, Zvi Hirsch

Dubnow, Simon 2-5, 8, 9-12, 14, 16-17, 19-20, 23-25, 29-30, 38-40, 53-54, 77-78, 134-135, 220-222, 247, 248-249, 251, 256, 426

Duhring, Eugen 38, 154

Eastern Committee (British War Cabinet) 343, 375, 431

Eastern Europe 1, 10, 17, 20, 24, 31, 36-37, 69, 104, 108, 166, 181, 211, 322, 421, 424-425, 428-429, 458, 538

Index 589

Eastern Jews 190, 211

Egypt 7, 34, 41-42, 44, 48, 149, 178, 182, 302, 311-312, 316, 332, 335, 348, 362, 375, 436-438, 507, 523-524, 531, 533-535, 537

Ekron 108, 123, 131, 142

el-Arish – see Zionist settlement projects

Epstein, Yitzhak 141, 147-150, 297, 323

Eretz Yisrael 119

Eshkol (Shkolnik), Levi 306, 440

Estonia 422, 426

Europe 1-2, 4-5, 9-10, 12-15, 17-20, 24, 26, 31, 33-37, 53, 59-60, 68-69, 75, 78, 90, 92, 96, 104, 108, 119-121, 123, 135, 149, 155, 158, 162, 164, 166, 181, 195, 207-208, 210-211, 219, 221, 233, 243, 254, 283, 303, 307, 322, 335, 355, 362, 421, 424- 426, 428-429, 432, 436, 451, 458, 522, 525, 528, 531, 538, 544

Faisal (Emir) 340, 349-354, 360-362, 365, 369, 384, 387, 391, 515

First Aliyah 79, 101, 108, 144, 147, 150, 225, 267, 278, 492, 500

First World War 1, 5, 14, 20, 31, 39, 110, 217, 237, 239, 267, 276-277, 285, 296, 299, 300, 303-304, 307, 311, 323, 327-328, 331, 335, 337-338, 342, 345-346, 349, 358, 382, 388, 390, 419-421, 426-427, 429-430, 435, 439, 452, 459, 463-464, 473, 478, 497, 499, 503, 505, 508, 513-514, 522-524, 527, 530

France 2, 4, 14-15, 18, 26, 33-34, 39-40, 54-55, 73, 75, 81, 114, 121, 124, 130, 156, 190, 196, 310-311, 313-314, 317-321, 323, 338, 342-345, 347, 349-350, 354-356, 361-362, 369-370, 375-377, 380, 425, 477, 523, 529, 534-535, 537, 545

Frankfurt 3, 70, 206, 240, 253, 423

Frankfurter, Felix 323, 353-354, 372

Galilee ii-iv, vi, 53, 67, 112, 141, 227, 235, 276, 314, 364, 368, 375, 377-378, 380, 410-411, 438, 505

Gan Shmuel 141-142, 144

Gaza i, vi, 52, 116, 131, 234, 314, 316, 336, 359, 410-411, 534-535, 545-548, 550

Gedera 108, 125, 127, 131, 142, 150, 296

General Federation of Jewish Labor in the Land of Israel – see Histadrut

Germany 2, 13, 16-20, 26, 29, 33-34, 37-39, 54, 73, 89, 100, 106, 123, 163, 165-166, 168, 177-179, 196, 307-308, 323, 327, 337, 342, 356, 421-425, 427, 451, 463,

468, 477, 486, 525-527, 529, 530, 541, 544, 546, 548

Ghetto 3, 21, 153, 157, 251, 253, 324

Ginsberg, Asher Zvi – see Ahad Ha'am

Golan, the 352, 376

Golomb, Eliyahu 285, 334, 518-519, 521

Grand Duke of Baden (Frederick I) 163, 178-179

Greece 33, 85, 89, 426, 477, 486

Hadera (al-Khadeira) 140-142, 150, 280, 296, 392

Haganah (Defense) 109, 112, 114, 116, 143-145, 150, 219, 268, 278, 283, 285, 295, 300, 305, 329-332, 334, 359, 363-366, 368, 392, 398, 437-438, 512-513, 517-520

ha-Horesh (The Plowman) 275, 283

Haifa iv-v, 19, 52-53, 105, 116, 140, 205, 274, 281, 302, 314, 345, 359, 384, 410-411, 489, 505, 509

Halukah 57-58, 62, 133, 267, 283, 433

Hapoel Hatzair (Young Worker) 266, 270-271, 274, 287-288, 299, 304, 332, 438, 440, 442-443, 445, 450-452, 463, 466, 482, 488-489, 492-493, 503, 518-519

ha-Shahar (The Dawn) 29, 83, 368, 500

Hashomer (The Guard) 282-285, 305, 331-333, 459, 488-499, 509, 517-519

Hashomer Hatzair (The Young Guard) – see also Mapam 459, 488-489, 509

Hasidic – see Jewish Sects

Haskalah – see also Maskilim 10-14, 17-18, 24-25, 27, 29, 83, 87, 91, 133, 135, 208

Hebrew labor 64, 274, 283, 287-288, 291-292, 294, 296-298, 300-301, 303, 447, 470, 519

Hebron 52-53, 205, 234, 365, 410

Hehalutz (Vanguards) 455-459, 487, 489, 497

Hejaz 339, 349, 352, 387

Helsingfors 222, 251, 445

Hermon (Jabal el-Sheikh) 43, 45, 376

Herzl, Theodor 1, 34, 40, 67-70, 76, 91-93, 142, 144, 152-166, 170-199, 202, 204, 205, 206, 207, 208, 209, 212-214, 216-217, 219, 221-222, 224-225, 227, 229-232, 236-237, 239, 251, 266-267, 294, 301, 327-328, 450, 463, 473, 480, 501, 525, 529

Hess, Moses 69, 73-76, 81, 154, 161, 571

Hevrat ha-Ovdim (Society/

Community of Workers, also: the General Cooperative Association of Labor in Israel) – see also Histadrut 495-497

Hibbat Zion (also: Chibbat Zion) – see Lovers of Zion

Hirsch, Maurice de – see also Jewish Colonization Association (JCA or ICA) 19, 36, 69, 70, 72, 122, 142-143, 155-156, 160, 559

Histadrut (General Federation of Jewish Labor in the Land of Israel) 273, 276, 305-306, 457, 483, 489-499, 518

Holland 2, 4, 15-16, 54, 477

Homs 43, 345, 361

House of Lords 16, 181, 398, 413

Hovevei Zion – see Lovers of Zion

Hula 107, 117, 140, 375, 377-378

Hungary 32-33, 38, 69-70, 89, 166, 201, 240, 257, 424, 426, 428, 477, 486, 527

Hussein, Sharif 311-314, 338, 340-341, 343

Iraq 6, 149, 180, 232, 315, 343, 357, 360, 362, 368, 375, 387, 391, 486, 533, 539, 550

Isaac (Prophet) 25, 42, 44, 45, 48-49, 193, 200-201, 230, 296, 514

Israeli Labor Party – see also Ahdut ha-Avoda, Mapai 263, 305, 445

Istanbul 9, 52, 60, 119, 163, 179-181, 235, 236, 300-302, 313, 329, 330

Italy 2-3, 12, 15, 33-34, 70, 73, 89, 114, 189, 311, 313-314, 319-321, 338, 344, 354, 356, 369-370, 436, 527, 546

Jabal el-Sheikh – see Hermon

Jabotinsky, (Vladimir) Ze'ev 215, 236, 258-259, 335, 358, 365-366, 383, 406, 431, 436-437, 479, 514, 516, 519

Jacob (Prophet) 44-45, 48-49

Jacobson, Victor 235, 301-302, 307

Jaffa 19, 52-53, 61, 63, 70, 103, 106, 108, 112, 116, 139-141, 162, 175, 205, 234-235, 270-272, 277, 281, 283, 285, 294, 300-301, 329, 345, 358-359, 365, 391-392, 410-411, 416, 424, 430, 433-434, 437, 460, 505, 512

Japan 34, 219, 338, 356

Jericho 44, 345, 365, 410-411

Jerusalem iii, 6 7, 10, 43, 49-50, 52-55, 60-64, 67, 69, 73, 75-76, 94, 97, 102-103, 106, 109, 111-113, 141, 154, 164, 167, 179, 200, 205, 216, 234, 237, 240, 242, 281,

302, 314, 329, 336, 345, 358-359, 363, 365-368, 380, 386-387, 391, 410-411, 417, 431, 433-434, 460-461, 473, 478, 500, 505, 508, 512, 522, 525

Jewish Agency 285, 306, 374, 395-396, 416-418, 451, 475, 477, 479, 481, 499, 526, 532

Jewish Assembly (Knesset Yisrael) 383, 386, 399, 418, 435, 512-513

Jewish Colonization Association 19, 28, 113, 142-145, 154-155, 174, 205, 229, 267-268, 273, 276-277, 279, 457, 499-500

Jewish National Fund (Keren Kayemet) 174, 176-177, 188, 214, 229-231, 235, 237, 264, 277, 280, 308, 440, 470-472, 502, 504

"Jewish question", The vi, 1, 26, 30, 34, 50, 70, 74, 80, 82-84, 88-89, 92-96, 135, 154-155, 157-158, 161, 164, 172-173, 202, 246-247, 250, 252, 258, 260, 264, 425, 439, 511

Jewish sects

    Ashkenazi 2, 5, 10, 13, 52, 59, 296, 435, 538-540

    Hasidic 10-12, 14, 24-25, 29, 52

    Orthodox 3, 8-9, 17, 23, 50, 69, 71-72, 74, 75, 80, 83, 85, 89, 92, 153, 188, 192-195, 199, 200-201, 211, 240-242, 313, 423, 460, 540

    Sephardic 2, 4, 7, 52-54, 58-59, 67, 317, 435

Jewish Socialist Workers Party (MOPSI) 391, 454

Jewish state 35, 67, 71-72, 74, 81-82, 88, 90, 124, 126, 142, 155, 159-163, 171-172, 174, 177, 183, 188, 190-191, 202, 204, 225, 239, 247, 251, 255, 259, 268, 273, 304, 309, 360, 363, 448, 461, 530-531, 538, 543

Jordan 41, 43, 45, 75, 82, 94, 140, 148, 279, 314-315, 345, 364, 368, 370, 376-378, 380, 388-389, 402-403, 413, 437, 504, 532, 549

Jordan River 43, 45, 82, 140, 279, 314, 345, 364, 368, 376, 378, 380, 388-389, 437

Judea Agricultural Workers' Federation 276, 440

Kabbalah – see also Messianism 7, 9, 10, 67

Kalischer, Zvi Hirsch 69-73, 75-76, 81, 98, 161

Katowice 79, 112, 123-127, 165, 240

Katznelson, Berl 289, 306, 441-442, 514

Keren Hayesod (Palestine Foundation Fund; later, the United Israel Appeal) 471-472

Keren Kayemet – see Jewish National Fund

Kfar Giladi 331, 363-365, 377, 499

Kharkov 102, 119, 189, 450, 456

Kibbutz 238, 280, 305-306, 457, 459, 502, 505, 508-510

Kinneret 278- 280

Kiryat Anavim 500, 505, 508

Kishinev 183-184, 219, 258

Knesset Yisrael – see Jewish Assembly

Kvutzah 238, 278, 280, 458, 488, 501-502, 508-509

Labor Battalion (Gdud ha-Avoda) 487-488, 509

Lake Tiberias 276, 279, 375, 508

Land of Israel (Eretz Yisrael) vi, 20, 32, 40-41, 45-46, 49-58, 60-64, 66, 70-72, 79, 82, 86-87, 89-91, 96, 99, 115, 119-120, 126, 137, 141, 147, 151, 173, 188, 205, 210-211, 223-224, 228, 231, 233, 239, 241-242, 244, 251, 253, 259, 262-266, 269-273, 275-277, 285, 287, 289-291, 293, 296, 299, 346, 354, 358, 363-364, 368, 370, 377-378, 379, 381, 383, 389, 402, 410, 413, 418, 428-429, 434-435, 439, 440-444, 446-448, 450-457, 460-462, 465-466, 470-471, 473, 488-491, 493-498, 501-503, 505, 512-514

Latvia 422, 426, 477, 486

League of Nations 344, 356-357, 362, 367-373, 375, 378, 380-381, 385, 388-389, 402-403, 408, 418, 426, 462, 504, 524

Lebanon iii, v, 41-43, 315, 345, 350, 352, 357, 362, 368, 377, 380, 549-550

Legislative Council 408-409, 413-416, 418

Lenin, Vladimir 246, 249, 448

Levin, Shmaryahu 308-310, 319

Lilienblum, , Moshe Leib 30, 83, 87-91, 97, 124, 134-135

Lithuania 25, 29, 203, 246, 422, 426, 477, 486

Lloyd George, David 187, 310, 315-316, 322, 324-328, 343-344, 347, 369, 373, 375-376, 381, 394, 431

London 163, 171, 175, 181, 187, 206, 244, 312, 318-319, 343, 347, 349, 371, 388, 393, 398, 403-404, 413, 416-417, 433, 436, 460, 462, 464-467, 469, 471, 473-474, 478, 498, 503, 516, 534

Lovers of Zion 19, 25, 30, 63-64, 77-78, 83-84, 86-88, 91-93, 95-99, 101-106, 108, 111-112, 114, 117-118, 121-128, 131-134, 136-141, 143, 145, 153, 165, 172-173, 192-193, 205, 207-209, 225, 227, 266-267, 273, 279, 298,

492, 500

Mafdal 215, 461

Maimonides (ben Maimon, Moses; also, Rambam) 7-8, 153

Mapai (The Workers Party of the Land of Israel) – see also Ahdut ha-Avoda, Po'alei Zion 304-305, 445, 455, 493, 519

Mapam (United Workers Party) 263, 460

Marx, Karl 26, 73, 244-246, 259, 448

Marxism 26, 262, 272, 442, 447, 450-452, 459

Maskilim – see also see also Haskalah 17, 29, 69, 74, 80, 83, 88-89, 91, 94-95, 98, 126, 195

McMahon, Henry 312-313, 315, 338

Meir Shaveh 131, 142, 144

Mendelssohn, Moses 10-13, 74

Merhavia 206, 238, 276, 278-279, 501, 505, 509

Messianism (Mashichiot) 8, 67, 208

Metula 141-142, 150, 331, 363, 377-378

Mikveh Israel 19, 61-62, 70, 121-122, 129, 278

Mishmar ha-Yarden 140, 142, 144

Mizrahi – see also Orthodox Jews 99, 188, 200-202, 209, 215, 230, 238-240, 332, 460-462, 474-476, 478, 480-481

Mlabes – see Petah Tikva

Mohilever, Samuel 98-99, 107, 121, 123, 126-128, 141, 193

Montefiore, Claude 59-61, 64, 70, 81-82, 102, 324-325

Moreh Nevukhim (The Guide for the Perplexed) – see Maimonides

Moscow 6, 79, 119, 449-450

Moses 44-45, 48

Moses Montefiore Testimonial Fund 61, 64, 81, 102

Mozambique – see also Zionist settlement projects

Nablus 52-53, 302, 359, 410-411, 413

Napoleon 14-15, 22

National (executive) Council (Va'ad Leumi) 306, 399, 433-435, 513

Nazareth iii, 116, 206, 238, 259, 300, 410-411, 505, 509

Nazism 13, 39, 427, 527-528

Negev 44, 359, 370

Nili 332-334, 560

Nordau, Max 156, 166, 172-173, 175, 187, 207-213, 215-216, 231,

237, 293, 319, 469

North Africa 2, 19, 428

Odessa 22, 29, 83, 91, 107, 119, 124, 133, 137-138, 220

Old Yishuv 58, 62, 65, 109, 112, 133, 267, 433

On the Revival of the Jewish People in the Land of Our Fathers – see Lilienblum, Moshe Leib

Oppenheimer, Franz 206, 233, 237-238, 279, 308, 503

Oral Torah (Torah She-be'al-Peh) – see Torah

Orthodox Jews – see Jewish sects

Ottoman Empire 31, 53-54, 59, 110, 115, 180, 307, 311, 323, 329, 334, 337-341, 345, 348, 354-356, 369, 549

Palestine i, iii-vi, 2, 5, 7, 9-10, 13, 15, 19, 23-24, 31-33, 35-36, 40-41, 43, 49-55, 57-70, 72-73, 77-83, 86-88, 91, 94, 96, 97-102, 104-128, 130-150, 154, 158, 161-164, 167-168, 170-172, 174-180, 183-184, 186, 188-189, 191, 193, 196, 198, 204-206, 208, 212-214, 217, 219, 222-226, 228-239, 241-243, 247, 256-259, 261-262, 264, 266-290, 292-296, 298-310, 312, 314-321, 324-355, 358-389, 391-400, 402-419, 421, 423-424, 427-443, 445-446, 448, 450-461, 463-469, 471-474, 477-489, 491-495, 497-501, 503-508, 510-532, 535-536, 538-539, 541-542, 544-545, 547

Palestine Arab Congress

    First (1919) 359, 360, 361

    Second (1920 – cancelled) 383, 384, 386

    Third (1920) 384, 385, 386, 391

    Fourth (1921) 397

    Fifth (1922) 413, 414

    Sixth (1923) 416

Palestine Executive Committee 413, 417

Palestine Foundation Fund – see Keren Hayesod

Palestine Land Development Company 235, 277, 280-282, 294, 504-505, 510

Palestine Office (Jaffa) 235, 277, 294, 296, 300, 329, 424, 430

Paris 45, 47, 69, 96-97, 120-122, 132, 143, 152, 154, 156, 187, 190, 207, 302, 319, 321-322, 337, 349, 352-353, 361-362, 436, 534

Paris Peace Conference, 1919 45, 47, 352

Petah Tikva 63-64, 106, 112, 125, 127, 130-131, 142, 150, 269-

270, 275, 284, 296, 392, 433, 442

Petrograd 423, 445-446, 449, 456

Picot, François Georges 311-312, 318-320, 345

Pines, Yechiel Michel 61, 64, 81, 102, 108, 132

Pinsker, Judah Leib (Leon) 83, 91-95, 97, 123-124, 126-127, 139-140, 154, 161

Plehve, Vyacheslav Konstantinovich von 183-186, 189, 219, 222

Po'alei Zion (Workers of Zion) 257-260, 263-267, 271-275, 282-284, 287-288, 293, 298-299, 304-305, 332, 437, 440-443, 446-448, 452-454, 458, 463, 466, 497-498

Poland 1, 2, 5, 12, 14, 20-21, 23-25, 28-32, 50, 52-53, 63, 66, 70, 77, 101, 108, 124-125, 203, 240, 246-247, 308, 421-423, 425-428, 439, 450, 458, 467-468, 477, 484, 486-487, 527

Portugal 4, 17, 34, 184

Protocols of the Elders of Zion, The 39

Psalms 11, 92, 105

Ra'anana 505, 509, 510

Rabbis 5-12, 25, 70-72, 74, 80, 100, 127, 133, 139, 153, 165, 192-193, 200, 211, 240, 296, 423

Rauf Pasha 109, 111, 113

Rehovot 98, 139-140, 142, 150, 270, 287, 392, 440

Reines, Isaac 193, 200-201, 230

Rishon le-Zion 54, 103, 105, 107, 118, 122, 125, 130, 142, 270

Romania 19, 23-24, 52, 59, 66, 79, 82, 84-85, 87, 91-92, 97-98, 100-101, 104-106, 111, 118, 122, 124, 165-166, 168, 211, 425-426, 477, 486, 527

Rome 69, 73, 76, 154, 320-322, 436

Rosh Pina 24, 105, 122, 140, 142, 148, 150, 284

Rothschild, Lionel de 16, 19, 36, 69, 106, 107, 121, 122, 123, 125, 127, 128, 129, 130, 131, 132, 133, 139, 140, 141, 142, 143, 144, 145, 156, 160, 163, 164, 205, 267, 268, 277, 321, 324, 325, 326, 500

Rothschild, Edmond James de 120

Rothschild, James de 317, 348, 509

Rothschild, Mayer 181

Ruppin, Arthur 234-235, 277, 280-281, 295, 296, 301-302, 329, 330, 332, 424, 505

Russia 1, 5-6, 16-17, 20-33, 35-36, 38, 40, 50-54, 59, 63, 66, 72, 76-84, 86-88, 91-92, 95-96, 100-104, 106-108, 110-115, 118-127, 129-132, 135, 137-141, 143, 145,

150, 165, 168, 181, 183-186, 188-189, 191, 193, 197-201, 203-204, 206, 209, 211, 217-224, 227-230, 232-234, 236-237, 243-244, 246-248, 250-251, 255-259, 263, 265-267, 269-272, 274, 282, 287, 289, 294, 307-308, 311, 313-316, 319, 320, 322, 327, 329, 333, 338, 340, 344, 348, 363, 421-425, 427, 436, 439, 442, 445-450, 452, 456-458, 463, 467-487, 525, 537-538, 540, 548

Russian Social Democratic Party 246, 258, 436

Safad iv, 2, 7, 9, 52-53, 64, 104-105, 107, 116, 140, 205, 235, 411

Samuel, Herbert 98, 107, 121, 123, 141, 193, 310, 315, 317, 332, 352, 368, 381-384, 386-387, 392-394, 396-399, 404, 413, 469, 515, 520

San Remo 362, 368-369, 373, 375, 381, 383

Schapira, Hermann 168, 176, 237

Scott, Charles Prestwich 309-310, 316

Second World War 13, 216, 396, 418, 426, 430, 459, 523, 526, 529, 538

Seeking Zion, (Drishat Zion) – see also Kalischer, Zvi Hirsch 69-71

Sephardic Jews – see Jewish sects

Shohat (also: Shochat), Israel 234, 282-284, 332

Sinai 42, 48, 177, 181-182, 316, 332, 345, 375, 534, 536

Smilansky, Moshe 103, 105-107, 129-132, 139, 143, 150, 277-278, 297-298, 329, 500, 507, 509-510

Smolenskin, Peretz 30, 83-87, 95, 97

Sokolow, Nahum 30, 66, 162, 232, 302, 308-309, 317-322, 352, 381, 478, 514

Solomon, Yoel Moshe 62-64

Spain 1-2, 4, 7-9, 17, 34, 49, 52, 110, 114

Sprinzak, Yosef 271, 306, 451

St. Petersburg – see Petrograd

Supreme Muslim Council 400, 402-403

Sursock 113, 116, 505

Switzerland 15, 19, 165, 196

Sykes, Mark 311-315, 317-320, 322, 327-328n, 338, 350

Sykes-Picot Agreement 313-315, 318, 320, 338, 340, 343, 345, 350, 360, 362, 368, 375, 377

Syria 41, 43, 91, 138, 140, 149, 174, 177, 211, 311, 315, 318, 331, 340, 342-343, 345, 350, 352, 355, 357, 359-362, 365, 368, 371, 376-378, 380, 384, 387, 507, 535, 550

Syrkin, Nachman 203, 252-256, 258, 260, 286

Tabenkin, Yitzhak 306, 441-442
Talmud 6-7, 71, 98
Technion (Institute of Applied Engineering) 19, 274, 281, 489
Tel Aviv 127, 162, 278, 281, 285, 294-295, 363, 391, 430, 433, 490, 493
Tel Hai 363-365, 377, 499, 512
The Hague 233, 263, 308
Tiberias 43, 52, 53, 113, 140, 205, 235, 276-277, 279, 375, 377-378, 411, 505, 508
Torah 6-7, 11-12, 41-44, 48-51, 57-58, 61, 63, 70, 92, 98-99, 102-103, 105, 107, 119, 192, 200-201, 239-242, 293, 332, 460-461
Transjordan 315, 345, 352, 359, 368, 371, 375, 380, 387-389, 473, 516
Trumpeldor, Joseph 335, 363-364, 436, 456, 487
Tzeirei Zion (Youth of Zion) 265-267, 270, 446-447, 450-452, 456, 458, 463

Uganda – see Zionism settle projects
Ukraine 22, 436, 449, 457
United Israel Appeal – see Keren Hayesod
United Jewish Appeal – see Keren Hayesod
United Nations Partition Plan for Palestine, 1947 170
United Palestine Appeal – see Keren Hayesod
United States 14-15, 23, 31-32, 36, 54-55, 77-79, 81, 86-87, 90, 101, 104, 140, 162, 165-166, 168, 217, 219, 232, 243, 257, 302, 309-310, 316, 320, 322-323, 326-327, 329-330, 338, 344, 348, 354-356, 358, 360, 369-370, 424-430, 437-438, 448, 453, 462-463, 465, 467, 472, 486, 497, 523, 525, 530, 533-534, 537, 544-546, 548-549
United Workers Party, Mapam – see Mapam
Ussishkin, Menachem 127, 142-144, 174, 188, 198, 223-229, 258-259, 286, 431, 433, 445, 479, 511, 514

Va'ad Leumi – see National (executive) Council
Versailles 356, 424-425
Vienna 3, 15, 22, 29, 39, 82-83, 152, 157, 162-164, 169-170, 184, 195, 214, 216, 231, 237, 266, 447, 453, 475, 520
Vilna 29, 128, 137, 200, 203, 227, 229, 246
Vitkin, Yosef 228-229, 287-288

Warburg, Otto 237, 307-308, 463

Warsaw 26, 29, 124, 137-138, 192, 230, 422

Weizmann, Chaim 193, 195-196, 198-199, 203, 207, 209, 233, 237, 301, 309-310, 315-320, 322-323, 325-328, 334-335, 347-350, 352-354, 366, 371, 381, 393-394, 396, 398, 405-406, 413, 427, 430-434, 436, 439, 463-467, 469-470, 478-479, 481, 483-484, 500, 511, 514-516, 520

Western Europe 12-13, 15, 17-20, 24, 26, 31, 33-34, 36, 92, 120-121, 164, 195, 210-211, 219, 221, 233, 254, 307, 428, 451

Western Jews – see Ashkenazi Jews

Wilson, Woodrow 309, 319, 323, 326, 350, 354-356

Wolffsohn, David 156, 174, 221-222, 231-234, 236-237, 450

Yavnieli, Shmuel 63-64, 77, 86-88, 92-93, 96, 98, 101-103, 105-106, 108, 111-112, 118, 121-122, 296, 441-442

Yaffe, Eliezer 451, 502, 509

Yesud ha-Ma'ala 102, 107, 117, 125, 131, 142

Yiddish 13, 92, 247, 250, 252, 274, 391, 447-449, 468

Yugoslavia 426, 477

Zichron Ya'acov 24, 118, 122, 130-131, 142, 223, 284, 296

Zionism i, iii-v, 1, 3, 5-6, 8-9, 13-14, 17, 19, 21-22, 26-27, 30, 33-35, 37, 39-41, 49, 51, 55, 61, 63, 66, 67, 69-70, 72, 77, 81-83, 91, 98, 100-101, 103, 120, 123-126, 129, 131, 133, 135-136, 140, 143, 145, 152, 154, 162, 164, 166-167, 171-173, 176, 178-181, 183, 186, 190-192, 194, 196-200, 203-205, 207-213, 215, 221, 224-225, 227-228, 233, 238, 241-242, 245-246, 250-253, 255-263, 265-266, 270, 272, 287, 294-295, 299-307, 309-310, 316, 319, 322, 324, 327, 330-331, 335-336, 340, 353, 358-359, 361, 385, 389, 394, 397, 413-416, 418, 421, 425, 427, 439, 444, 446, 448, 454, 460-462, 464, 466-467, 473-474, 480, 482-485, 498-499, 511, 515, 522-523, 536, 538, 543-544, 549-550

Congresses

First (Basel, 1897) 35, 98, 138, 141-142, 153, 165- 172, 176, 178, 188, 191-192, 194, 195, 203, 205, 237, 246

Second (Basel, 1898) 168, 171, 175, 191-192, 203, 205, 215

Third (Basel, 1899) 153, 171, 174, 179, 191, 203, 207

Fourth (London, 1900) 171,

176, 181, 191, 193

Fifth (Basel, 1901) 171-172, 176, 191, 196, 198, 204, 206

Sixth (Basel, 1903) 171, 176, 186, 188-189, 191, 202, 206, 208, 214, 223-224, 258, 279

Seventh (Basel, 1905) 148, 213, 230-232, 258

Eighth (The Hague, 1907) 232, 234, 236-237, 264, 277, 283

Ninth (Hamburg, 1909) 236-237, 258, 279

Tenth (Basel, 1911) 209, 237, 239-240, 299, 301-302

11th (Vienna, 1913) 209, 237, 266, 464

12th (Carlsbad, 1921) 430, 474-475, 478-479, 503, 514

13th (Carlsbad, 1923) 475, 478-479, 481, 502

14th (Vienna, 1925) 475, 478

   currents

Democratic 198-199, 202, 207, 212, 214, 446

Political 172-173, 192, 224, 227, 236, 250, 236-327

Practical 172-174, 176, 192, 198, 203, 205-206, 208-209, 231-232, 236-238, 239, 283, 292, 301

Religious 72, 94, 200, 208, 238, 239, 473, 480

Socialist 202-204, 208, 258-259, 470, 498

Spiritual 192, 200, 208, 226-227, 233, 238, 245

Synthetic 196, 203, 209, 233, 238, 327, 464, 483

   settlement projects

Uganda 183-184, 187-189, 208, 223-224, 227-230, 258, 322

el-Arish 42, 45, 178, 181-184, 187, 206

Cyprus v, 181-182

Mozambique 184

Zionist Commission (Va'ad ha-Tsirim) 348-349, 358, 368, 430-433, 441, 450, 463, 511, 520

Zionist Executive 169-171, 176, 187, 195, 209, 221, 225, 230-231, 239, 302, 308-310, 353, 405-406, 418, 430-431, 434, 464-466, 477-479, 482, 484, 513-514

Zionist Socialist Federation of the Workers of the Land of Israel, Ahdut ha-Avoda – see Ahdut ha-Avoda

Zurich 462, 475-476

www.ingramcontent.com/pod-product-compliance
Lightning Source LLC
Chambersburg PA
CBHW020512080526
44583CB00013B/567